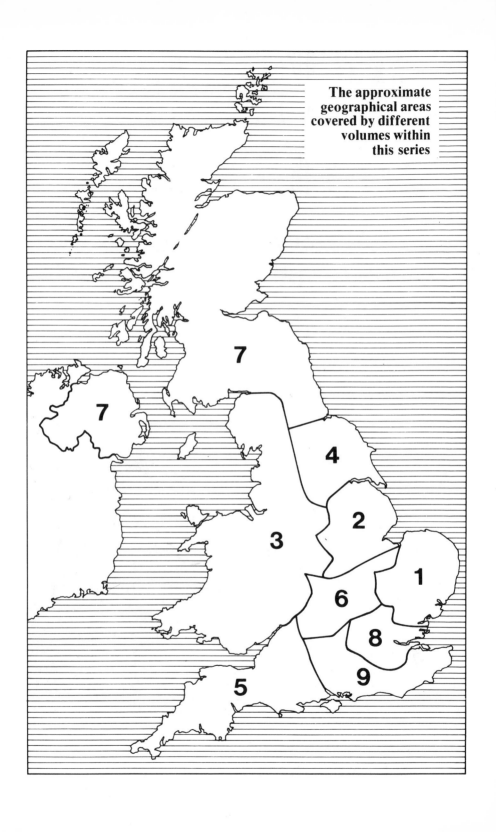

The approximate
geographical areas
covered by different
volumes within
this series

ACTION STATIONS

9. Military airfields of the Central South and South-East

Chris Ashworth

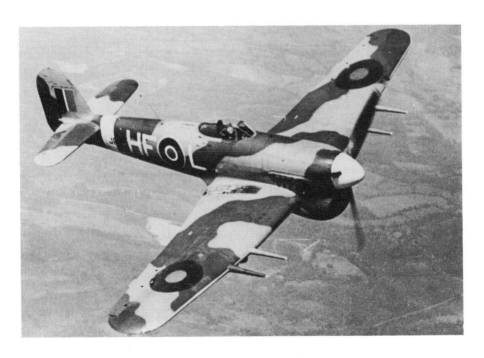

 Patrick Stephens, Wellingborough

Title page *Typhoons of No 183 Squadron were at Thorney Island during the early months of 1944* (Hawker Aircraft Ltd).

First published in 1985

British Library Cataloguing in Publication Data

Action stations.
  9: Military airfields of the Central South
  and South-East.
  1. Air bases—Great Britain—History
  I. Ashworth, Chris
  358.4'17'0941   UG635.G72

  ISBN 0-85059-608-4

Patrick Stephens Limited is part of Thorsons Publishing Group.

Photoset in 9 pt and 10 on 11 pt Times by MJL Typesetting, Hitchin, Herts. Printed in Great Britain on 100 gsm Fineblade coated cartridge, and bound, by The Garden City Press, Letchworth, Herts, for the publishers, Patrick Stephens Limited, Denington Estate, Wellingborough, Northants, NN8 2QD, England.

Contents

Introduction   4

Glossary   7

The first 100 years   10

Advanced Landing Grounds   25

Map of the airfields of South and South-East England   32

The airfields   36

Index of units referred to in the text   311

Introduction

My first sight of south-east England was the best possible—from the air on a beautiful August day. It was pure chance, for I was just one of many ATC cadets camping at Bircham Newton during the summer of 1944 and when my air experience flight came up it was not in the usual Dominie biplane, but in a Wellington XIII which was flying to Manston and back. I was put in the front turret out of the way and off we went across East Anglia and over the Thames Estuary. The thing I remember most about the flight was the fright I got when a P-47 Thunderbolt attacked us head-on. So convinced was I that it was a Fw 190 that had I known how to switch on the fully-loaded turret I might even have tried to open fire!

We joined the circuit and landed on Manston's wide and very impressive runway. What a view I had from that nose turret! I was told to be back at the aircraft by 15:30 hours, pointed in the direction of the airmens' dining hall and left to my own devices. My recollections are generally hazy, but I remember the thin dusty grass, the tattered appearance of the place, WRNS working on some Swordfish and Martinets, six Tempests taking off in echelon and another landing with one undercarriage leg still retracted—and vividly recall the exciting noise made by an aircraft that rushed into the circuit, landed and quickly taxied into a dispersal area, out of my view, behind some trees. My image as an aircraft recognition expert took another hard knock for I had no idea what it was, and some months passed before I found out that I had seen one of 616 Squadron's first Meteors. Altogether a wonderful introduction to the south-east and to Manston; certainly better than my next meeting with that runway, which was on a dark and dirty night flying a Shackleton. But that's another story, as are my subsequent visits to Tangmere, Thorney Island, Odiham and Farnborough.

It has not proved possible to treat the south and south-east as a neat geographical package because the number of airfields in the region has necessitated a separate London area book *(Action Stations 8)* which deals with those within an approximate 40 km radius of Charing Cross. The area surveyed in this volume is therefore crescent shaped, taking in a large portion of Kent, all of Sussex, half of Hampshire and parts of Wiltshire, Berkshire and Surrey. It just touches on Essex. While odd in shape it does have a general downland theme which strongly determined the way in which airfields were grouped and, to this extent, can be considered an entity.

Deciding what actually constitutes an aerodrome/airfield, especially during World War 1 when aeroplanes could, and did, use any reasonable sized, flat, grass field has been a problem. In general I have omitted any First World War Landing Ground or seaplane mooring which did not have permanent facilities, but have included airship sub-stations and World War 2 LGs used by AOP Austers for longer than a few days. My intention has been to provide sufficient information on each of the air bases to satisfy the interested onlooker and ex-serviceman, while encouraging the enthusiast to do further research in the local area. Such research should be particularly fruitful in the south-east of England which is well served with aeronautical museums and aviation groups dedicated to the preservation of relics and the gathering of information on all aspects of aviation. Prominent are the Kent Aviation Historical Research Society, the South Hampshire Historical Aviation Society and the Berkshire Aviation Group, while the British Airfield Research Group deals with the whole country and disseminates much information. Joining at least one of these societies is an essential prerequisite to deep research, together with visits to County PROs and libraries.

If this book is used for a tour of airfields in the area then the appropriate 1:50,000 Ordnance Survey maps will be very useful. They give much information on the layout of current airfields and disused sites where runways and taxiways still exist, while the *After the Battle* organisation publishes airfield plans in co-operation with the RAF Museum, these giving the detail necessary to locate individual buildings and outlying sites. Remember that nearly all such sites are private property, however, and permission is required before investigating them closely. Active airfields, particularly military ones, may have restricted areas and close examination may be unwise because of the security problems of this day and age. Where viewing facilities are available they are recorded in the text.

Almost unique to this area is the confusing tendency to use the same name for quite different sites. In a couple of cases airfields used or built post-war have adopted names previously used for defunct aerodromes; it is easy to jump to the wrong conclusions, but I have tried to point out the major pitfalls.

Much of the information in this book has been obtained from articles and new items collated over many years, or from official records held by the Air Historical Branch (MoD), the Fleet Air Arm Museum, Yeovilton and the Public Records Office, Kew. I gratefully acknowledge the help given by the staffs of these organisations. In addition I have had tremendous assistance from a large number of private individuals and this has been a source of encouragement as well as providing me with invaluable information. The facts have come from many sources, though the interpretation of them is solely my responsibility. I am very conscious that the choice of photographs used in a book of this type is extremely important. I have been well served in this respect by the staff of the Imperial War Museum, the Fleet Air Arm Museum, the RAF Museum, the RAE Farnborough and the Department of the Environment (Air Photo Unit), while other prints have been provided by private individuals and commercial firms.

Information and/or photographs have been provided by M. Asquith, the Automobile Association, G.G. Baxter, D. Benfield, Wing Commander D.E. Bennett, RAF (Retd), Squadron Leader D.L. Bird, RAF (Retd), J. Blezzard, Chaz Bowyer, M.J.F.Bowyer, P.H. Butler, C.C.H. Cole, D.G. Collyer, Captain J. Cross (Museum of Army Flying), Mrs P.A. Dufeu, N.W. Gillman, P.H.T. Green, H. Holmes, G.S. Leslie, L.J. Lovell (FAA Museum), E.B.

Morgan, J.A. McGivney (The Chilbolton Observatory), M.W. Payne, G. Richards, M. Roberts, B.R. Robertson, Royal Aircraft Establishment, Short Brothers Ltd, D.J. Smith, R.C. Sturtivant, Flight Lieutenant G.R. Sunderland, RAF (Retd), South Eastern Newspapers Ltd, J.C. Temple, Flight Lieutenant A.S. Thomas, RAF, C.H. Thomas, K.J. West and A.C. White.

I thank them all but feel I must single out the help afforded by R.N.E. Blake, BA, MRTPI, FRGS, a senior lecturer in Town & Country Planning, who has made a particular study of disused airfields and generously opened his records to me. Without his aid, my research would have been immeasurably more difficult. Last, but not least, I record my gratitude for the support I received from my wife Margaret throughout the many months of research and drafting entailed in writing this book—it has been very much a team effort.

R.C.B.Ashworth
Padstow
February 1984

Glossary

AA Anti-Aircraft.
AACU Anti-Aircraft Co-operation Unit.
AAP Aircraft Acceptance Park.
AAS Air Armament School.
AASF Advanced Air Striking Force.
AC Aero Club.
(AC) Army Co-operation.
ACRC Aircrew Reselection Centre.
ADEE Air Defence Experimental Establishment.
ADGB Air Defence Great Britain.
ADU Air Disarmament Unit.
AEF Air Experience Flight.
AES Air Electrical School.
AF Air Force.
AFB Air Force Base.
AFC Air Force Cross.
AFDU Air Fighting Development Unit.
(P)AFU (Pilot) Advanced Flying Unit.
AHU Aircrew Holding Unit.
AI Airborne Interception radar.
ALG Advanced Landing Ground.
AMWD Air Ministry Works Department.
Annie Anson aircraft (slang).
ANS Air Navigation School.
AONS Air Observer Navigation School.
AOP Air Observation Post.
APC Armament Practice Camp.
ASC Air Support Command.
ASR Air Sea Rescue.
AST Air Service Training.
ASWDU Air Sea Warfare Development Unit.
ATC Air Traffic Control *or* Air Training Corps.
ATDU Air Torpedo Development Unit.
ATS Air Training Squadron.
AVM Air Vice Marshal.
A/W Airways.
AWRE Atomic Weapons Research Establishment.

BAF British Air Ferries.
BAFO British Air Forces of Occupation.
(BAT) Beam Approach Training.
BEAC British European Airways Corporation.
BEF British Expeditionary Force.
BG Bomber Group.
BOAC British Overseas Airways Corporation.
Bogies Unidentified aircraft (slang).
Bomphoon Bomb-carrying Typhoon (slang).
BW Bomb Wing.
CAA Civil Aviation Authority.
Cab Rank Standing fighter patrol on immediate call for close tactical support.
CACU Coast Artillery Co-op Unit.
CAF Canadian Air Force.
CAG Carrier Air Group *or* Civil Air Guard.
CAM Catapult Aircraft Merchant (ship).
C&M Care and Maintenance.
CBE Commander British Empire.
Channel Stop Air operations to stop German shipping passing through the Straits of Dover.
Chanak Crisis Preventive action in Turkey, 1922.
C-in-C Commander-in-Chief.
Circus Fighter-escorted bombing raid to attract enemy response.
CND Campaign for Nuclear Disarmament.
CO Commanding Officer.
COA Cunliffe Owen Aircraft.
Combination Tug and glider with towing rope attached.
Co-op Co-operation.
Cross Bow Bombing operations on V-1 flying bomb installations.
CWS Co-operative Wholesale Society.

D-Day   June 8 1944—invasion of Northern France.

DCM   Distinguished Conduct Medal.

DFC   Distinguished Flying Cross.

DFM   Distinguished Flying Medal.

Diver   V-1 flying bomb.

DIY   Do-It-Yourself.

DME   Distance Measuring Equipment.

Doodlebug   V-1 flying bomb (slang).

DSC   Distinguished Service Cross.

DSO   Distinguished Service Order.

DZ   Dropping Zone.

Eagle   RAF fighter squadron manned largely by American volunteers.

ECFS   Empire Central Flying School.

EFTS   Elementary Flying Training School.

ELG   Emergency Landing Ground.

Erpr   Erprobungsgruppe.

E&RFTS   Elementary and Reserve Flying Training School.

Exercise Spartan   Large scale Army/RAF training exercise, 1943.

E/W   East/West.

E&WS   Electrical and Wireless School.

FAA   Fleet Air Arm.

FBG   Fighter Bomber Group (USAAF).

FEW   Fighter Escort Wing.

FEAF   Far East Air Force.

FG   Fighter Group (USAAF).

FIDO   Fog Investigation and Dispersal Operation.

FIS   Flying Instructors' School.

FIU   Fighter Interception Unit.

Flak   Fliegerabwehrkannonen—German anti-aircraft gunfire.

FRU   Forward Repair Unit (RAF).

FRU   Fleet Requirements Unit (FAA).

FPP   Ferry Pilots' Pool.

FS   Fighter Squadron (USAAF).

FTS   Flying Training School.

FW   Fighter Wing.

Gee   British navigation aid using ground transmitters and an airborne receiver.

GR   General Reconnaissance.

GRU   General Reconnaisance Unit.

GS   General Service (hangar).

GS   Gliding School (ATC).

GSU   Group Support Unit.

GTS   Glider Training School.

(HD)   Home Defence.

HE   High Explosive (bomb).

HGV   Heavy Goods Vehicle.

HMT   His Majesty's Transport.

HP   Handley Page.

HQ   Headquarters.

Hurribombers   Hurricane fighters carrying bombs (slang).

IHTU   Inter-Service Hovercraft Trials Unit.

JG   Jagdgeschwader—German fighter group.

Jim Crow   Reconnaissance patrols by armed fighters.

JOAC   Junior Officers' Air Course.

Kagohl   German bombing unit based in Belgium 1917-18.

KB   Kite Balloon.

KG   Kampfgeschwader—German bomber group.

LAA   Light Anti-Aircraft.

LG   Landing ground.

LG   Lehrgeschwader—German trials/training unit.

LZ   Landing zone.

MAP   Ministry of Aircraft Production.

MC   Medium Case (bomb).

MCA   Ministry of Civil Aviation.

(Met)   Meteorological.

MT   Motor Transport.

MU   Maintenance Unit.

Musketry   Anti-submarine patrol over Bay of Biscay.

NAAFI   Naval, Army and Air Force Institute.

NAFDU   Naval Air Fighting Development Unit.

NATO   North Atlantic Treaty Organisation.

NCO   *Non-Commissioned Officer.*

Noball   Rocket and flying bomb sites.

N/S   North-South.

(NT)   Night Training.

OC   Officer Commanding.

OCTU   Officer Cadet Training Unit.

OCU   Operational Conversion Unit.

OFU   Overseas Ferry Unit.

Ops   Operations.

Operation Anvil   Amphibious invasion of southern France.

Operation Jubilee   Combined operation at Dieppe, August 1942.

Operation Market   Airborne operation, Arnhem and Nijmegen, September 1944.

Operation Neptune   Amphibious phase of *Overlord*, June 1944.

Operation Overlord   Overall name for invasion of Europe, June 1944.

Operation Rutter   Abandoned attack on heavy guns at Dieppe, July 1942.

Operation Starkey   Feint and large-scale operation, Pas de Calais, September 1943.

Operation Steinbeck   Luftwaffe raids on London, 1944.

Operation Torch   Invasion of French North Africa, October 1942.

OTU   Operational Training Unit.

PAC   Parachute And Cable (installation).

Panhandles Circular 'frying-pan' type aircraft dispersals.

PIR Parachute Infantry Regiment (US Army).

PoW Prisoner of War.

PR Photographic Reconnaissance.

PS & IOW Portsmouth, Southsea and Isle of Wight.

PSP Pierced Steel Plank.

PX Post Exchange (American canteen/shop).

Q-site Flashing lights to represent airfield at night as a decoy.

RAAF Royal Australian Air Force.

R&SU Repair and Servicing Unit.

RAE Royal Aircraft Establishment.

RAeC Royal Aero Club.

RAF Royal Air Force.

Ramrods Day bomber raid escorted by fighters.

Rangers Deep-penetration flight to engage targets of opportunity.

RAS Reserve Aeroplane Squadron.

RCAF Royal Canadian Air Force.

RE Royal Engineers.

Rebecca Aircraft equipment for locating *Eureka* beacon

Recce Reconnaissance.

Reflex American Strategic Air Command bomber detachments on ground alert at overseas bases.

RFC Royal Flying Corps.

RFS Reserve Flying School.

Rhubarb Low-level strike operation against targets in occupied Europe.

RLG Relief Landing Ground.

RNAS Royal Naval Air Service.

RNVR Royal Naval Volunteer Reserve.

RNZAF Royal New Zealand Air Force.

Roadsteads Fighter operation against shipping.

Rodeo Fighter sweep.

Rover Armed reconnaissance against chance targets, usually shipping.

RS Reserve Squadron.

R/T Radio Telephony.

SAR Search and Rescue.

SBAC Society of British Aircraft Constructors.

SFTS Service Flying Training School.

SHAEF Supreme Headquarters Allied Expeditionary Force.

SoAG School of Aerial Gunnery.

SoFC School of Flying Control.

SoGR School of General Reconnaissance.

SoN&BD School of Navigation and Bomb Dropping.

SoNC School of Naval Co-operation.

SoTT School of Technical Training.

SSQ Station Sick Quarters.

StG Stukageschwader—Ju 88 flying unit.

Strafe Low level gunnery attacks on ground targets.

SU Servicing Unit.

(T) Training.

TAC Tactical Air Command (USAAF).

Tac/R Tactical Reconnaissance.

TAF Tactical Air Force.

TAG Telegraphist/Air Gunner (FAA).

TBR Torpedo Bomber Reconnaissance.

TCG Troop Carrier Group.

TCS Troop Carrier Squadron.

TCW Troop Carrier Wing.

TDS Training Depot Station.

TDU Torpedo Development Unit.

Tiffie Typhoon aircraft (slang).

TS Training Squadron.

TTU Torpedo Training Unit.

UAS University Air Squadron.

UHF Ultra High Frequency.

USAAF United States Army Air Force.

USAF United States Air Force.

USAS United States Air Service.

VHF Very High Frequency.

V-1 Vergeltungswaffe 1—the Fieseler 103 flying bomb.

VIP Very Important Person.

VOR VHF Omni-directional Receiver.

VR Volunteer Reserve.

WAAF Women's Auxiliary Air Force.

WAEC War Agricultural Emergency Committee.

WD War Department.

Window Metal foil dropped to confuse radar image.

WRAF Women's Royal Air Force.

WS Wireless School.

W/T Wireless Telephony.

Y-Service British organisation monitoring German radio transmissions to and from aircraft.

ZG Zerstorer—German twin-engined fighter unit.

The first 100 years

The proximity of London ensured that many of the first British excursions into the air would be made in the south and south-east of England, and the area duly saw the birth-pangs of both military and naval aviation. The first military balloon was constructed and flown at Woolwich Arsenal during 1878, but when the War Office handed over development of the art, and the training of new balloonists, to the Royal Engineers in 1882, the unit moved to the School of Military Engineering at Chatham; and this ancient garrison town was soon witnessing experiments in aerial reconnaissance, photography and signalling. These early *ad hoc* arrangements were regularised during May 1890 by the formation of the Balloon Section, RE, but space soon became a problem and in 1892 the unit was transferred to Aldershot. The Boer War accelerated expansion and during the early 1900s the factory and school both moved to Farnborough where the first British dirigible balloon was completed in 1907 and the flamboyant Colonel S.F.Cody, an American engaged for work with man-carrying kites, started experimenting with aeroplanes. He made the first sustained powered aeroplane flight in Britain on October 16 1908, using a part of Farnborough Common that is now within the confines of the Royal Aircraft Establishment. This Government airfield can therefore be claimed as the oldest flying site in the country still in use.

The first site actually prepared as an aerodrome was at Shellbeach (Leysdown) on the Isle of Sheppey, the result of a joint effort by the Aero Club of Great Britain and Short Brothers Ltd, the balloon and aeroplane manufacturers. It was used by J.T.C. Moore-Brabazon (later Lord Brabazon of Tara) when he became the first Briton to make a powered flight in this country

The Gamma *airship and shed at Farnborough* (FAA Museum A/Ship 91).

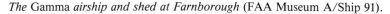

in May 1909. Others soon followed and military and naval chiefs were forced to take a greater interest in aviation as its potential became apparent.

The Air Battalion of the Royal Engineers was formed on February 28 1911 with its HQ at Farnborough, where it had two small airships. The Admiralty had already flirted unsuccessfully with airships but, after a number of naval officers had received pilot training on aeroplanes at Eastchurch, the formation of a flying school was authorised in December 1911. Following general unease about aeronautical advances made by France and Germany it was decided to build a chain of defensive air stations along the east coast and the Royal Flying Corps was formed on May 13 1912. The Air Battalion and Naval Flying School were both absorbed by the new organisation, which established its HQ at Farnborough, the Admiralty clinging firmly to Eastchurch.

The principal manufacturer in the region was still Short Bros, but in 1912 the ship-building firm of J. Samuel of Cowes, Isle of Wight, decided to open an aircraft department and across the Solent the eccentric Noel Pemberton-Billing purchased a yacht building yard at Woolston and tried turning his theories into practice. He had little success, but his firm did provide the start for the great Supermarine company. Other small-scale manufacture developed at Bognor, Eastbourne and Shoreham where several flying schools flourished.

Below *The SE 1, which went into the Royal Aircraft Factory as a Bleriot tractor mono-plane and reappeared early in 1911 as a canard pusher biplane. It crashed on August 18 1911 killing Lieutenant Theodore J. Ridge, the Assistant Superintendent at Farnborough* (Hampshire Country Library).

Bottom *The Pemberton Billing PB 1 takes to the water at Woolston for its unsuccessful flight trials in 1914.*

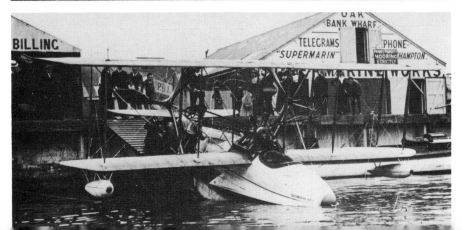

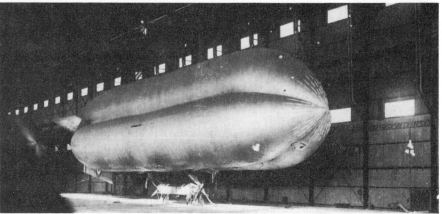

Top *The Supermarine works during World War 1—with an AD flying boat outside ready for launching* (Vickers via E.B. Morgan).

Above *A 'Coastal' airship in the main hangar at Kingsnorth giving some idea of the huge size of these sheds* (FAA Museum A/Ship 51).

Top right *Prominent amongst the seaplane manufacturing centres was Cowes—this strange looking AD Type 1000 floats on the River Medina just off the J. Samuel White slipway in West Cowes* (RAF Museum P10809).

When World War I started in August 1914, the RFC had seven squadrons. Hurriedly re-organised, five of them were despatched to France to operate with the BEF, crossing the Channel from a small landing ground near Dover. The Admiralty had just regained full control of the Naval Wing, now renamed the Royal Naval Air Service and Grain was about to be joined by a new seaplane base at Westgate. Operational airships were already at Kingsnorth and more stations were soon developed, some of them on private aerodromes requisitioned during the autumn, which were generally used as flying schools. The start of Zeppelin raids in January 1915 produced attempts at retaliation but most RNAS effort was concentrated on escorting shipping through the Dover Straits and across the Channel.

The RNAS maintained War Flights for defence of their bases, while seaplane and airship patrols were extended as the submarine war reached its first climax in August 1915. This coincided with the regrouping of British air stations under the Senior Naval Officer in the area, and the south-east was split between the

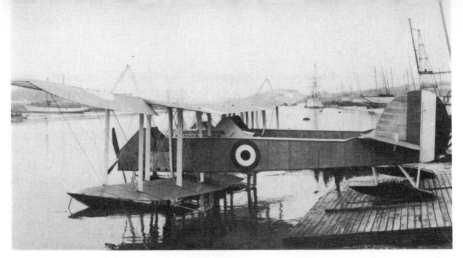

Above *Standing room only—a troopship on the Folkestone-Calais route* (Air Marshal Sir Victor Goddard via D.G. Collyer).

Below *The sinister looking SS40, known as the* Black Ship, *returns to Kingsnorth in November 1916. Intended for nocturnal flights over the German lines to drop agents it was actually used for recce work* (Air Marshal Sir Victor Goddard via D.G. Collyer).

Nore, Dover and Portsmouth Commands. The Dover Command, under
Admiral R.H.S. Bacon, was particularly aggressive, using aircraft and
seaplanes from the Dover area during a bombardment of Zeebrugge and for
general gun-spotting.

As the war dragged on, demands on the RFC escalated. The training task
mushroomed and, as new squadrons were formed and sent overseas, the trickle
of replacement machines going to France became a steady stream. More
aerodromes were required and when the home-defence commitment was
transferred from the Admiralty in 1916, the organisation was completely
overhauled, No 50 Squadron being formed at Dover to guard the south-east.
Available landing grounds (LGs) were graded Class I, II or III, depending on
their suitability for normal or emergency use, and aircraft were sent to the
former whenever required. Later in 1916 the HD squadrons were split into three
Flights and permanently detached to Class I LGs, No 50 Squadron using
Bekesbourne, Detling and Throwley, while the HQ used a large house at
Harrietsham (where, despite reports, there was no aerodrome). When patrols
were extended westwards, No 78 Squadron was formed, with its HQ at Hove; it
also operated detached flights.

Zeppelins were not the only problem; German aircraft also made 24 small-
scale raids between Christmas 1914 and the beginning of 1917. Most of these
either flew over Kent, or attacked targets in the area, and many lives were lost.
Desperate efforts were made to intercept these raiders but without success. In
retrospect it is easy to see why, for the performance of the defenders was often
inferior to that of the attackers and was rarely better.

The Isle of Sheppey in the north and Romney Marsh in the south were well
equipped with armament-practice ranges and Manston became a major training
school for the Handley Page 'Bloody Paralyser' (0/100). Kingsnorth developed
into an Admiralty production factory and Capel became an airship-assembly
unit, as well as remaining an operational station.

German bombing aircraft took a leap forward with the development of
Grossekampfflugzeuge (large combat aircraft) which led to the formation of
Kampfgeschwader 3 with Gotha G IV twin-engined bombers. With the specific
function of strategic bombing, Kagohl 3 (as it was usually known) operated as
an independent unit from bases in Belgium. Their first attempted raid on
London went badly wrong when the weather turned against them and some of
the 22 Gothas bombed Lympne aerodrome and Folkestone town instead,

A black-painted BE 2C single-seat 'night fighter' at Eastchurch 1916-17 (J.M. Bruce/
G.S. Leslie collection).

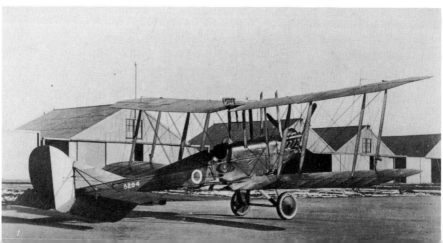

causing extensive damage, killing 95 and injuring nearly 200. Seventy RFC and RNAS defenders took off in pursuit but most failed to catch the speedy Gothas, and only one was definitely shot down—by an aircraft from Dunkirk. The British public reacted violently and argument about alleged shortcomings was still reverberating on June 13, when 20 Gothas reached London in perfect weather and returned to Belgium unscathed. They dropped 72 bombs which killed 162 and injured over 400 people.

Calls for action redoubled and No 56 Squadron was hastily recalled from the Western Front to spend an unproductive fortnight at Bekesbourne. No sooner were they back in France than the Gothas struck again and riots followed! Proposals for co-ordinated defences quickly emerged and at the end of July the London Defence Area came into being, with responsibility for the whole of the south-east from Harwich to Portsmouth. More and better aircraft were made available, Nos 61 and 112 Squadrons being formed in the area to operate behind a new gun line, alongside 50 and 78 Squadrons.

The continued expansion of the RFC and the arrival of the Americans in 1917 with promises of large numbers of aircraft to follow, led to plans for massive increases in flying-training facilities. Sussex, Hampshire and Wiltshire were beyond the normal reach of enemy aircraft and considered ideal for training, but current aerodromes could not accept additional pupils, so new sites had to be found. Large Training Depot Stations were built in Sussex for the Americans, while Hampshire and Wiltshire found themselves with more RFC wireless, navigation and bombing schools.

Aircraft manufacture had also expanded rapidly, the established firms increasing their factory space and output, while May, Harden & May Co Ltd took over Admiralty sheds at Hythe, Hants, for flying boat construction and Fairey Aviation were similarly accommodated at Hamble Point. Avro developed their new factory near Hamble village, though plans for a 'garden' site had to be abandoned.

Formation of the RAF on April 1 1918 resulted in the country being divided geographically into Areas. No 1 Area included Kent, Sussex and Berkshire, with No 5 (Marine) Group under its command, while No 2 Area covered Wiltshire, Hampshire and the West Country with No 10 Group, Portsmouth, its main marine component. Titles quickly changed to South-Eastern and South-Western Areas, but their tasks remained essentially the same, marine operations concentrating on anti-submarine work. Airship escort to convoys was

Taken from the SS8, this view of HM Kit Balloon Ship Menetaus *shows the stowage arrangements in the forward hold* (Air Marshall Sir Victor Goddard via D.G. Collyer).

Top *An airfield that never was—the site of the Electrical Wireless School at Flowerdown in 1927* (RAF Museum P9770).

Above *The 1918-style buildings at Flowerdown—still in good condition in April 1983.*

Top right *Siskin IIIAs of No 1 Squadron outside the hangars at Tangmere in the halcyon days of the late 1920s* (via J. Bartholomew).

Above right *Stamford Hill dominating the Eastchurch scene in 1929. The odd assortment of hangars remained throughout the active life of the aerodrome* (Wing Commander D. Allison via P.H.T. Green).

supplemented by kite balloons, and inshore patrols by aeroplanes flying from small, strategically placed Landing Grounds were introduced.

With the Zeppelin all but defeated, the improving home defence forces were able to concentrate on German Army aeroplanes which, flying at night, made 20 raids and dropped 50½ tons of bombs during 1917-18. These attacks continued until May 19/20 1918 when 41 bombers set out, but only 13 reached London. Six were shot down and others crashed on return to Belgium—a disaster for the Germans which caused them to turn to softer Continental targets. On August 5 five Zeppelins approached the coast, but after seeing *L70* shot down in flames, the other crews turned away. The defenders had won.

With the Armistice of November 1918, many of the American TDS bases were abandoned incomplete, but the region could boast a total of 55 flying

establishments. They ranged from spacious airfields to tiny LGs, huge airship bases to isolated moorings secreted in wooded vales, solitary seaplane slipways to flying-boat docks. The inevitable retrenchment followed and in September 1919 the South-Eastern and South-Western Areas were amalgamated as Southern Area with all remaining units under its command except those of No 10 (Marine) Group, which was renamed Coastal Area. On April 1 1920 the Northern and Southern Areas became Inland Area, and after the infamous 'Geddes Axe' of 1922 there were just 11 active bases in the area of south-east England covered by this book. Farnborough continued as a centre for experimental flying, but only Worthy Down and Andover survived on the Hampshire downland, with Gosport and Lee-on-Solent on the coast. Manston, Eastchurch, Grain and Hawkinge held sway in East Kent with Lympne in use as a cross-Channel airport but, apart from Shoreham, the region in between was an aeronautical desert. Around the Solent desultory business was continued by Avro, Fairey, Saunders and Supermarine.

The closure of Grain in 1923 proved to be the low point, for things were stirring and, with the formation of Air Defence of Great Britain on January 1 1925, Tangmere was reactivated, and an Army Co-operation summer camp established at Odiham the following year. The remainder of the 1920s and early '30s were years of careful consolidation. The few airfields under Air Ministry control were gradually improved, well-designed permanent buildings replacing temporary wartime structures, and slow progress was made with aircraft design

and equipment. A great deal of effort went into detection devices, the concrete acoustic mirrors still to be seen along the Kent coast being the impressive evidence of one of the more expensive attempts at early warning (see *Kent's Listening Ears* by David Collyer for a full and absorbing account).

Manufacturing staggered along on prototype contracts and a few short production runs, all the major firms surviving into the 1930s. Woolston slowly developed as a marine airport and civil aviation generally was showing signs of revival with the opening of Eastleigh (Southampton), Portsmouth, Shoreham and several small club aerodromes.

Finally accepting in May 1934 that the League of Nations was ineffective against dictators, the Government announced plans to increase substantially the strength of the RAF over the next five years. This meant more men and aircraft—and thus more airfields. The Volunteer Reserve was formed in 1936, units being established at several civil airfields in the area. Work started on a number of purely military aerodromes; Detling and Ford were re-activated, a landing ground was built at Lee-on-Solent, Odiham was upgraded and a brand-new station completed at Thorney Island.

Long split into the Wessex Bombing Area and the Fighting Area, the Air Defence of Great Britain (ADGB) became Bomber and Fighter Commands in July 1936, when Coastal Area was renamed Coastal Command and Inland Area reformed as Training Command. All played some part in the development of the south-east region, but it was Nos 16 and 17 Groups of Coastal and, overwhelmingly, No 11 Group of Fighter Command that took centre stage during the late 1930s. The expansion also revitalised the aircraft firms. New factories appeared at Hamble, Eastleigh and Portsmouth, while those at Cowes were expanded and Supermarine's at Woolston was rebuilt and an offshoot constructed at Itchen. Woolston relinquished its marine airport status, and a new terminal was opened at Hythe (Hants) in March 1937 when Imperial Airways started scheduled Empire flying boat services.

At the outbreak of World War 2 the region contained 16 operational military airfields, of which 13 were of First World War origin and only two had runways. In addition, ten civil aerodromes were available and these were quickly requisitioned. The few RAF flying-training organisations in the area were speedily removed and the newly independent Fleet Air Arm established itself strongly in West Sussex and in the south of Hampshire.

The Munich Crisis of September 1938 had provided the opportunity to test deployment to war stations, and the impetus to dust off aerodrome defence plans and air raid precautions, so final preparations were quickly completed in September 1939. No 11 Group stood braced for the expected Luftwaffe assault, its Hurricanes, Blenheims and Spitfires at readiness and the region divided into

Top left *A No 56 Squadron Hurricane at Ford in 1938* (P. Ward-Hunt).

Above left *The Hythe works of Vickers-Supermarine—originally Admiralty sheds used by May, Harden & May for flying boat production in World War 1—and in use by Imperial Airways when this photo was taken in 1938. A 'C'-Class boat is on the hardstanding and on the water is a Sikorsky S-42 of Pan American* (Wing Commander D.E. Bennett).

Left *Spitfires in production at Supermarine's (Itchen) Works during 1939. A little over a year later the factory was derelict—destroyed by the Luftwaffe* (Vickers Ltd via E.B. Morgan).

sectors, each with a main Sector Station, of which Tangmere was one. These were fed information from the Group Operations Rooms, using the still secret Radio Direction Finding (RDF) and the invaluable Observer Corps. Nerves were stretched by the sounding of air-raid sirens minutes after the declaration of war, and again on September 6 when the 'Battle of Barking Creek' revealed deficiencies in the raid-reporting organisation, but there was no enemy activity until late October and then only by small groups of reconnaissance bombers. Meanwhile, the Advanced Air Striking Force had gone to France, both Army Co-op and Fighter squadrons leaving from south-east airfields—so reminiscent of 1914.

Most of the fighter bases rapidly gained satellites, grass fields without facilities at first, but later able to accommodate whole squadrons permanently. After the sudden German thrust into France during May 1940 the Kentish airfields were used to give direct support to our forces in France, then cover the evacuation at Dunkirk, drop supplies to beleaguered troops in Calais and operate the short-lived *Back Violet* scheme. Fear of invasion followed and the airfields were used almost exclusively by defensive fighters and coastal aircraft

Top right *The experimental hangar at Hursley Park—established by Supermarine after evacuation from Woolston and Itchen during the autumn of 1940* (Vickers Ltd via E.B. Morgan).

Right *Inside the Hursley Park experimental hangar with trials Spitfires under construction* (Vickers Ltd via E.B. Morgan).

Below *Realistic dummy Blenheims, said to be on Thorney Island's decoy airfield at West Wittering. The crater-like object is a blemish on the print and the straight black lines are attempts to make the site appear camouflaged without actually succeeding* (Crown Copyright via P.H.T. Green).

covering convoys, Army Co-op and Coastal Blenheims attacking Belgian and French ports, and by Lysanders on coastal patrol. Scatter fields were hastily organised, and the area became littered with decoy sites, some complete with realistic aircraft models dispersed on them.

The region will always be synonymous with the Battle of Britain and rightly so, for it was No 11 Group and its famous Kent and Sussex airfields which bore the brunt of the Luftwaffe onslaught during the summer of 1940. Many of the airfields and radar stations were put out of action for short periods, Manston for rather longer. The towns in the region also suffered badly and the Supermarine Works were completely destroyed in a classic carpet bombing attack on September 26 1940. This resulted in dispersal of production, the design office and experimental shops going to Hursley Park near Winchester, while Spitfire parts were made in workshops, large and small, all over Hampshire and Wiltshire and fed to major component assembly lines in bus and car garages.

The tide slowly turned and the Luftwaffe was forced into night bombing attacks on large cities, though single aircraft continued to provide nuisance value by lurking in the vicinity of major airfields. The night-fighter force also became more effective as Ground Controlled Interception (GCI) equipment and tactics improved, and the RAF moved over to the offensive as Luftwaffe

strength declined following the launching of Operation *Barbarossa*, the German assault on Russia in June 1941. *Circus* operations, usually flown by Blenheims with a strong escort of Spitfires, had little early success, and *Roadsteads* resulted in horrific casualties from the wicked flak put up by German shipping. The greatest return came from the intruder operations pioneered by Boston crews operating from Ford, and other *Rhubarb* activities.

No major new airfields were built in Kent or Sussex and the construction of metalled runways in this region was belated, but planning for the stillborn Operation *Hadrian*—the invasion of German-occupied France optimistically proposed for the summer of 1942, resulted in the surveying and subsequent building of over 20 so-called Advanced Landing Grounds (ALGs) in the south and south-east. In Surrey a site at Dunsfold originally considered as an ALG became a full-scale bomber-type airfield and a whole series of similar bases were built in northern Hampshire, Berkshire and Wiltshire, intended for No 92 Group, Bomber Command, but used by the light bomber and transport forces of the RAF and USAAF.

The ALGs were not ready until the summer of 1943 and, in the meantime, all

Left *Hythe in post-war days as BOAC's flying boat base— soon to be abandoned for Berth 50 in Southampton Docks* (BOAC).

Below left *The 'gate guardian' at RNAY Fleetlands—the FAA maintenance unit uses nearby Lee-on-Solent as its test airfield.*

Right *Memorials abound in the south-east of England—this one is on the village green at Tangmere* (K.S. West).

Below *Few public houses reflect local aviation interests —but one that does is the new* Harrier *at Hamble close to the old Folland works now making parts for this famous V/STOL aircraft.*

available airfields in the south-east had been involved in the abortive Dieppe landings of August 1942 (Operation *Jubilee*). Anti-*Rhubarb* standing patrols against low-level fighter-bomber Bf 109s and Fw 190s making hit and run raids on coastal towns and airfields followed, but with little success until the introduction of the Typhoon—this aircraft also taking a major part in Operation *Starkey* in September 1943 and in the build-up of the Tactical Air Force during the autumn. Operation *Crossbow*, the attack on V-weapon sites in France, involved Mitchells, Bostons and Mosquitoes of No 2 Group, B-26s and P-47s of the IXth AF and aircraft of Nos 83 and 84 Groups flying from the region from November 1943 to April 1944. Then came preparations for D-Day and, by the end of May, the whole area was an armed camp swarming with men, guns, tanks, vehicles, aircraft and stores. The ALGs in Kent and Sussex had a few short weeks of hectic activity alongside the other fighter airfields, while further inland the big airfields of Berkshire and Hampshire were crowded with light bombers, transports and gliders. Even Lee-on-Solent was heavily involved, one of the few occasions when offensive operations were flown from a FAA shore base, though many naval aircraft had operated from RAF airfields throughout the war and continued to do so. During this period the hard-pressed airfields in the area also provided haven for many badly damaged aircraft, including four-engined bombers, the latter often a major headache.

As the Tactical Air Forces moved on to the Continent, the pressure on the south-east airfields slackened, though other units were moved forward and from the end of June 1944 defensive operations against the V-1 flying bombs intensified. Many of these weapons aimed at London fell short, and Kent in particular became Bomb Alley, many casualties being sustained. A significant part of Fighter Command's strength had to be diverted to deal with the *Divers* during the summer but by the autumn the worst was over, and the war was moving steadily away into the Continent. There was a flurry of activity by the airborne forces and supporting units during Operation *Market* but the number of operational airfields in the region had peaked at 68 during the summer. By the time the Germans capitulated in May 1945 all the ALGs had been closed down for several months and airfields such as Eastchurch, Detling, Hawkinge and Lympne were little used.

The rundown accelerated after the war. Requisitioned airports were returned to their owners and, as many of the other airfields were too small for satisfactory jet fighter operation, they were soon closed. Manston, Tangmere, Thorney Island and Odiham survived as operational bases, while Chilbolton and later Dunsfold were used by aircraft manufacturers for assembly and flight testing their products. The RAF also retained several famous airfields such as Andover, Hawkinge and Detling for support duties, while Blackbushe and, for a short time, Aldermaston, had important civil roles during the immediate post-war years. The Americans used Manston and Greenham Common for fighter and bomber operations respectively but by the mid-1950s there were scarcely a dozen active military airfields in the south and south-east.

Following the infamous 1957 Defence White Paper, the number was further reduced. It affected the Fleet Air Arm as well as the RAF and they pulled out of several airfields in the Portsmouth area leaving Lee-on-Solent as their only air station in the region. Fighter Command left completely, and with the Americans deserting Manston and Greenham Common the only operational military airfields were Thorney Island and Odiham, both transport support bases.

With the closure of Thorney Island in 1973 Sussex now has no military airfields, Kent has Manston fulfilling an emergency diversion and rescue role, while Hampshire can boast the truncated Lee-on-Solent in the south, Odiham in the north and Farnborough, which has again survived a recent attempt to close it. In Berkshire, Greenham Common is starting a new and controversial career as a cruise-missile base operated by the Americans.

Not one of the original aircraft factories remains, but British Aerospace is firmly established at Dunsfold and about a dozen airfields are used for various civilian operations, including one or two of the former ALGs. Most of the rest have reverted to agriculture or been built over. Signs of them can still be found and in some cases memorials mark the spot—such details can be found in the main body of this book, together with the history of each individual *Action Station*.

Advanced Landing Grounds

Numerous airfields described in *Action Stations 5* and this current volume are offically referred to as Advanced Landing Grounds and a few, such as Bolt Head and Friston, were perched out on headlands, and were genuinely used by Fighter Command as forward operating bases. The rest were built for a quite different purpose and it is with the development of these that we are concerned in this chapter.

The unexpected fall of France at the end of May 1940 left Britain and the RAF with many problems, not the least of which was the now exposed south coast and immediate hinterland, where fighter bases were barely adequate for defence purposes. The possibility of any of them being put out of action was a nightmare and this, coupled with the vastly increased training task, led the Air Staff to ask for 50 more airfields in June 1940. They wanted them *immediately* and all Station Commanders were required to seach for (and find) at least one ELG near their airfield, some for development as additional fully equipped bases, but most as grass-surfaced scatter fields where aircraft could be sent in the event of heavy bombing or actual invasion knocking out their home airfields. These scatter fields had no facilties and had to be available within two weeks—and many were.

In practice they were little used for their original purpose but some became genuine ALGs and others were reconsidered when Fighter Command went on the offensive in 1941 and planning staffs started work on Operation *Hadrian*, a proposed landing on the Pas de Calais. It was obvious that additional airfields would be required for such a venture, though hopefully only during the build-up and actual landings. It was therefore considered that basic facilities would suffice, by which was meant runways, refuelling and re-arming points, a few hardstandings, and Blister hangars for under-cover maintenance. The majority of the accommodation would be under canvas, with a small hutted camp for the C&M party.

These rudimentary airfields were called ALGs to give a measure of security cover, and 15 possible sites were selected in the Biggin Hill, Hornchurch, Kenley and Tangmere Sectors during April 1942. Six sites, at Hadlow, Marden Beeches, Rother Levels, Withersdale, Stelling Minnis and Wickham Breux were considered particularly promising, but the Permanent Aerodrome Board was not so enthusiastic, and it soon became apparent that the speedy development of even such temporary airstrips would be fraught with difficulty. Indeed, in the event, none of these favoured sites were developed at all!

As time went by the scheme became more ambitious and by mid-1942 the search for sites had been extended westwards to cover the whole area of the country south of a line Frinton–Reading–Weston Super Mare. With the postponement of *Hadrian*, the proposed ALGs became known as 'round-up' airfields, and now had to be ready by the beginning of March 1943. Each was to have two Sommerfeld Track runways of 3,000 ft (914 m) length at approximately 90 degrees to each other, a partial perimeter track, hardstandings, at a scale of one for every two aircraft, and two Blister hangars. Other buildings were still to be kept to a minimum and AA defences provided to satellite airfield scale.

Seventy-two possible sites were selected by the teams sent out during June and, by July 22, 36 of them had been chosen and were awaiting final acceptance. The use of some sites met with fierce opposition, mainly from the War Agricultural Executive Committee, and a few had to be abandoned. Others were developed into full-scale airfields (eg, Dunsfold) but a short list of 25 was agreed, of which 23 were built, all in the south-east or along the south coast of England. Two of them were designed for use by light bombers and were to have bomb dumps, though in the event they were used for fighter operations like the rest.

The specification of the chosen ALGs was slightly upgraded, the main runway ideally being 4,800 ft (1,463 m) in length, with a secondary 4,200 ft (1,280 m) strip, but a reduction of 200 ft (61 m) of each was acceptable providing the longest run was into the prevailing wind. Detailed surveys were completed during the summer of 1942 and with dispersal plans added by Fighter Command staffs late in the year, final authorisation followed during December.

Meanwhile, both the RAF and the Army had been planning the formation of airfield construction units, the latter basically for the building of strips on the

A typical Kentish ALG under construction during March 1943 and thought to be High Halden (RAF Museum W21/89/1).

Continent after the planned invasion, still called variously Operation *Hadrian* or *Round-up*. Despite manpower problems the first Royal Engineers' Construction Group was formed in June 1942 and carried out an exercise at Bottisham in Cambridgeshire, laying two 3,000 ft (914 m) 'Flightways' early in July. Training at Bottisham continued during August by which time it has been decided to use the RE's Airfield Construction Groups and the RAF units to build the ALGs in the UK to maintain interest and expertise. Hothfield Common Camp, near Ford in Sussex, became the main Army base, new Groups being formed from September onwards, while the RAF set up a large, tented camp at Ashford and sent out three officers and 200 men to each site.

Most of the ALGs were still planned for completion by the beginning of March 1943 and work on grading and clearing the sites was soon in hand, some also requiring the felling of large numbers of trees to provide adequate clearance either side of the strips and on the approaches. Despite some valuable help from American Engineer Aviation Battalions, the poor winter weather and shortages of materials prevented completion of most sites until later in the spring of 1943. Fortunately the build-up of the Tactical Air Force was also delayed and the first ALGs were not occupied until the end of June.

As already mentioned, the material used for the runways of these ALGs was Sommerfeld Track, a heavy steel netting held rigid by steel bars and rods secured in position by angled pickets. Developed by an expatriate Austrian, Kurt Sommerfeld, from the wire netting used in World War 1, it had been in production since August 1941 and was tested at Bottisham and again by No 16 Airfield Construction Group (RE) when they built strips at Lambourne (*SU350800*), Eastmanton Down (*SU340845*) and Red Barn (*SU276835*) during Exercise *Spartan* early in 1943. Left in position at Red Barn, the tracking was used by Mustangs of No 26 Squadron while it was on detachment there during

An excellent view of Sommerfeld Tracking being reinforced with square steel mesh at a USAAF ALG in use by P-47 Thunderbolts (USAAF).

March. These trials were successful, but experience of more intensive operations during the summer of 1943 revealed problems of wear and tear and new material specifications were devised to try and improve ease of production, transport, replacement and laying. British Reinforced Engineering Co Ltd developed a 3 in (76 mm) square mesh from the material used as reinforcement for concrete structures, calling it Square Mesh Track (SMT) or BRC Track. This was supplied in reasonably easily handled rolls but had an alarming tendency to form a bow wave in front of an aircraft taking off, finally cured by tensioning and increased picketing. It was widely used as replacement for Sommerfeld Track during the spring of 1944.

Attempts to use various forms of impregnated hessian to form a water-resistant surface were tested at Ashford and Dunsfold in 1943 but proved unsatisfactory in comparison with metal matting, and was downright dangerous in wet conditions when it was like a skid-pan. American Pierced Steel Planking (PSP) was much favoured when available. Simple to manufacture, store, transport and assemble, it was very effective when new, through costly to produce; however, in use on inadequately prepared base surfaces, the panels tended to curl at the edges with disastrous effects on tyres. Another American development was the Bar and Rod Track, lighter than PSP but more difficult to manufacture. It was made up in much larger panels, each section joined by clips to its neighbour. It was used largely for local reinforcement on taxiway bends and marshalling points.

The practice use of 13 of the forward ALGs during the summer of 1943 revealed other shortcomings. Tentage scales, which had been decided by trials at Brenzett during February 1943, proved inadequate, the dispersal of the transport of a mobile squadron (some 60 vehicles) was a constant headache, and the lack of complete taxiways, sufficient hardstandings and covered maintenance facilities were particular problems. There was never any intention of winter operations from the ALGs and, when the squadrons moved to more weatherproof quarters in the autumn of 1943 and the Airfield Construction Units had finished mobility exercises of their own, they set to work upgrading the ALGs. Eleven ALGs were earmarked for American IXth AF fighter-bombers and these were strengthened by their own Engineer Aviation Battalions who also erected Butler transportable hangars at most of the sites, either additional to, or in place of, the various-sized Blisters used on RAF strips. The taxiways were completed and up to 70 individual hardstandings were built, usually using one of the types of steel matting available, but occasionally rolled hardcore.

All the ALGs had to be ready for operations by April 1 1944, and units were forbidden to visit the sites by air until after that date, though some did send in advance ground parties late in March. Any available farm or cottage accommodation in the immediate area was requisitioned to supplement the tented camps which were generally established close to buildings — orchards were favourite sites in Kent. Central bomb stores were provided for each cluster of ALGs, typical ones at Ham Street and Smarden in Kent were deep in woodland, but ammunition and fuel storage was on the site, the latter usually of 18,000-gallon (81,720-litre) capacity.

Most of the ALGs served their purpose well, coping with intensive operations for three months or so before being deserted as the squadrons moved into France. A few had to be hastily repaired, the P-47 Thunderbolt being

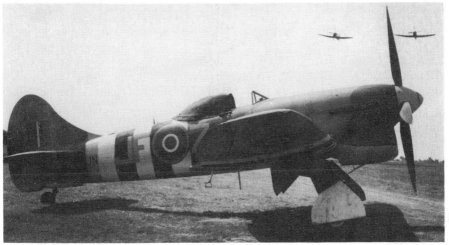

Top *This design of brick building with a concrete roof was common on ALGs and is thought to be an ammunition store. It is still extant at Chailey* (G.G. Baxter).

Above *A Tempest V of No 3 Squadron on the very successful Newchurch ALG in June 1944* (IWM CH14095).

particularly hard on the temporary surface, even the sturdy PSP wilting under prolonged operations by this brute aircraft. Considering the conditions, accidents were surprisingly few, but there were a number of ground collisions on the narrow taxiways, which were particularly difficult for Spitfire pilots, with their non-existent forward view.

When it was certain that the ALGs were no longer required, much of the usable PSP was ripped up and taken across to Normandy where it was in very short supply following unexpectedly poor weather. During September 1944 most of the temporary ALGs were declared surplus and work started on returning them to their former condition. Thousands of square yards of steel matting was lifted by the Works Flights, Blister hangars removed, stores collected and fuel dumps destroyed. This work went on into 1945 and in most cases was so thorough that only very close examination of a site reveals tell-tale

Top *Among the few remains of Lydd ALG is a concrete 'loop' road around which the technical site was developed on the eastern side of the landing ground* (G.G. Baxter).

Above *Newchurch was a comparatively well-appointed ALG and some of the communal site Nissen huts remain as farm buildings* (D.G. Collyer).

Below *Staplehurst ALG today with typically little evidence of any aeronautical connections except the square steel mesh forming the fence* (G.G. Baxter).

pieces of matting being used for fencing and the gaps in hedges, culverted streams, and strangely shaped woodland which indicates the line of the landing strips.

Information on individual ALGs in the south and south-east of England is given in the main section of this book and hopefully some flavour of what these now peaceful fields were like in the spring of 1944 comes across. Dusty or rain-sodden, depending on the changeable English weather, what they lacked in comfort they made up for in atmosphere. During those few weeks each was crowded with American or British fighter-bombers, noisily setting off on the short trip across the Channel to the battle area and returning in well under the hour for refuelling and re-arming, before repeating the whole dangerous process — again and again. Grim but exciting days.

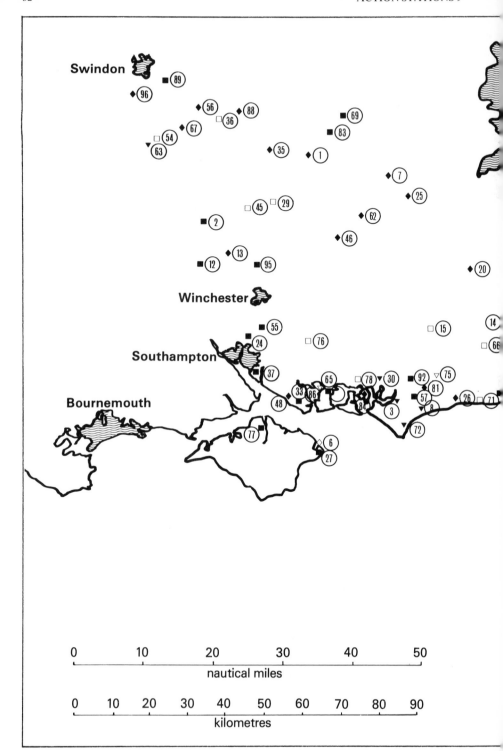

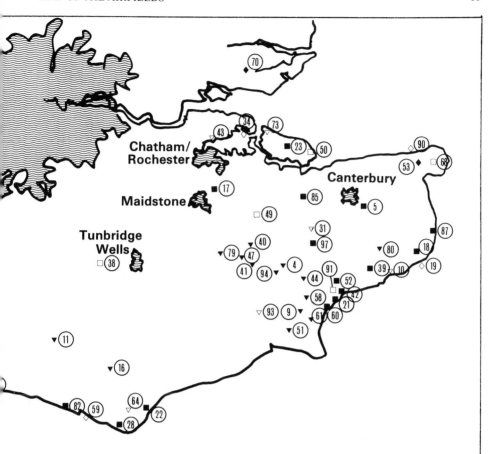

The military airfields of Central South and South-East England

Key

- ① Airfield number
- ◆ Airfield with tarmac runways
- ◇ Marine base
- ■ Grass airfield
- ▼ Airfield with metal track runways
- ☐ Satellite or emergency landing ground
- ▽ Airship or balloon base

Key to map on preceding pages

No	Name	County	No	Name	County
1	Aldermaston	Berkshire	49	Lenham	Kent
2	Andover	Hampshire	50	Leysdown	Kent
3	Appledram	Sussex	51	Lydd	Kent
4	Ashford	Kent	52	Lympne	Kent
5	Bekesbourne	Kent	53	Manston	Kent
6	Bembridge	Hampshire (IoW)	54	Marlborough	Wiltshire
7	Blackbushe	Hampshire	55	Marwell Hall	Hampshire
8	Bognor	Sussex	56	Membury	Berkshire
9	Brenzett	Kent	57	Merston	Sussex
10	Capel	Kent	58	Newchurch	Kent
11	Chailey	Sussex	59	Newhaven	Sussex
12	Chattis Hill	Hampshire	60	New Romney/	Kent
13	Chilbolton	Hampshire		Littlestone	
14	Coolham	Sussex	61	New Romney/	Kent
15	Cowdrey Park	Sussex		Honeychild	
16	Deanland	Sussex	62	Odiham	Hampshire
17	Detling	Kent	63	Overton Heath	Wiltshire
18	Dover/	Kent	64	Polegate	Sussex
	St Margarets &		65	Portsmouth	Hampshire
	Guston Road		66	Pulborough	Sussex
19	Dover/	Kent	67	Ramsbury	Wiltshire
	Marine Parade		68	Ramsgate	Kent
20	Dunsfold	Surrey	69	Reading/Coley	Berkshire
21	Dymchurch	Kent		Park	
22	Eastbourne	Sussex	70	Rochford	Essex
23	Eastchurch	Kent	71	Rustington	Sussex
24	Eastleigh	Hampshire	72	Selsey	Sussex
25	Farnborough	Hampshire	73	Sheerness	Kent
26	Ford	Sussex	74	Shoreham	Sussex
27	Foreland	Hampshire (IoW)	75	Slindon	Sussex
28	Friston	Sussex	76	Soberton	Hampshire
29	Frost Hill Farm	Hampshire	77	Somerton	Hampshire (IoW)
30	Funtington	Sussex	78	Southbourne	Sussex
31	Godersham Park	Kent	79	Staplehurst	Kent
32	Goring by Sea	Sussex	80	Swingfield	Kent
33	Gosport	Hampshire	81	Tangmere	Sussex
34	Grain	Kent	82	Telscombe Cliffs	Sussex
35	Greenham	Berkshire	83	Theale	Berkshire
	Common		84	Thorney Island	Sussex
36	Great Shefford	Berkshire	85	Throwley	Kent
37	Hamble	Hampshire	86	Tipnor	Kent
38	Hammerwood	Sussex	87	Walmer	Kent
39	Hawkinge	Kent	88	Wanborough	Wiltshire
40	Headcorn	Kent	89	Welford	Berkshire
41	High Halden	Kent	90	Westgate	Kent
42	Hythe	Kent	91	Westenhangar	Kent
43	Kingsnorth	Kent	92	Westhampnett	Sussex
	(Airship)		93	Wittersham	Kent
44	Kingsnorth (ALG)	Kent	94	Woodchurch	Kent
45	Larks Barrow	Hampshire	95	Worthy Down	Hampshire
46	Lasham	Hampshire	96	Wroughton	Wiltshire
47	Lashenden	Kent	97	Wye	Kent
48	Lee-on-Solent	Hampshire			

Key to symbols used on airfield maps

Local features

 Roads (important roads are numbered)

 Railway line

 Rivers and streams

 Outline of village or town built-up area

 Rocks or cliffs

 Wooded areas

 Earthworks and embankments

 Low tide line

Airfield features

 Concrete and tarmac runways and taxiways

 Steel mesh track runways and taxiways

 Aircraft dispersals

 Airfield buildings

Outline of airfield domestic sites

△ 50ft   Height of ground above sea level

The airfields

Aldermaston, Berkshire

SU600635. 1½ miles SE of Aldermaston village off A340

Associated in most people's minds with the Ban the Bomb marches of the 1950s, Aldermaston was the target of the Campaign for Nuclear Disarmament because it housed the Atomic Weapons Research Establishment, whose forbidding-looking buildings still sit squarely in the centre of the wartime airfield surrounded by acres of grass and miles of fencing.

Originally part of the large Aldermaston Court Estate, the site was chosen in 1941 for development as a bomber OTU with the standard three-runway layout, extensive dispersed enclaves and a large bomb dump. Opened by No 92

Group on July 1 1942, it was never occupied by the intended Wellingtons because it had already been earmarked for the USAAF. As soon as it was habitable, the 60th TCG moved in with four squadrons (10th, 11th, 12th and 28th TCS) of C-47 transports. First used for moving cargo, they were soon paratroop training, making the first American practice jumps over the United Kingdom on September 16 1942.

Aldermaston became USAAF Station

On the end of Aldermaston's main runway Horsas await D-Day in serried ranks with the 434th TCG C-47 tugs lined up on the PSP and grass alongside—an evocative June 1944 scene (USAAF via Mrs P.A. Dufeu).

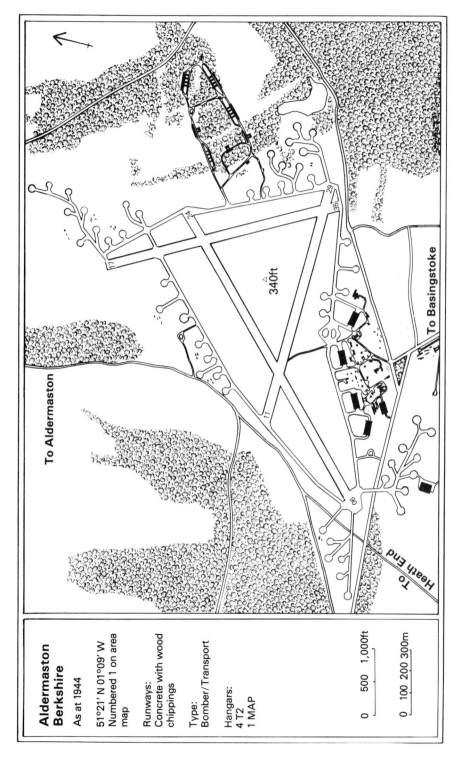

Aldermaston
Berkshire

As at 1944

51°21' N 01°09' W
Numbered 1 on area
map

Runways:
Concrete with wood
chippings

Type:
Bomber/Transport

Hangars:
4 T2
1 MAP

0   500   1,000ft

0   100 200 300m

To Aldermaston

To Basingstoke

To Heath End

340ft

17
24
29
35
11
09

467 on October 20 but the decision to open a second front in North Africa meant the transfer of the 60th to the XIIth AF. Crammed with troops, the C-47s left for Portreath and Operation Torch on November 6. The airfield returned briefly to RAF control to await the arrival of the 315th TCG which flew in via the northern Atlantic ferry route on December 12, having been delayed in Greenland by very bad weather. The C-47s/C-53s of the two squadrons (34th and 43rd TCS) were joined in February 1943 by a detachment of No 3 GTS, the only RAF unit to use Aldermaston. Their Master tugs and Hotspur gliders mingled with the Dakotas for nearly a month while Stoke Orchard was out of action. Soon afterwards the Americans received gliders of their own, Waco CG-4A Hadrians arriving unexpectedly during May.

The 315th sent 16 aircraft to Algeria in May to back up forces invading Sicily and they had not returned when the Group was transferred to the IXth AF and went to Welford in November 1943, the IXth Air Support Command HQ moving into Aldermaston Court later that month, taking over the historic home of the Congreve family.

The main technical site was now complete. Four 'T2' hangars and many temporary brick buildings were clustered near the Falcon Inn, while a self-contained MAP site lay south of the airfield off one of the 52 loop dispersals. This site had a large shed, taken over by Vickers in July 1943 for Spitfire assembly, using parts supplied by Reading and Newbury sub-contractors. The aircraft were then flight-tested from Aldermaston, production continuing until the spring of 1945, the site being finally closed on July 20 1946.

The 71st FW HQ moved into Aldermaston briefly and one of its Groups, the 370th, was temporarily based there with sleek twin-boomed P-38 Lightnings during February 1944. Meanwhile behind-the-scenes manoeuvring produced an extraordinary swap whereby the IXth ASC HQ changed places with the XIXth ASC by transferring the name plate but not personnel or equipment, the unit at

Above *The main technical site at Aldermaston with the* Falcon Inn *prominent in the bottom right-hand corner of the photo* (USAAF via Mrs P.A. Dufeu).

Left *Situated off dispersals on the south side of Aldermaston, this MAP hangar was used for Spitfire assembly. Note the Horsas in the background* (Vickers Ltd via E.B. Morgan).

Once Aldermaston's gymnasium-cum-church on the communal site, this Maycrete building still exists as Tadley Community Centre, surrounded by a modern housing estate (J. Temple).

Aldermaston Court becoming the XIXth on February 1.

Stability came at last when the 434th TCG arrived from Fulbeck on March 3 with its four squadrons (71st, 72nd, 73rd and 74th) of C-47s to continue intensive training with the 101st Airborne. On D-Day they towed 52 Hadrians carrying men and equipment of the 81st Airborne AA Battalion to a LZ a mile inland from *Omaha* beach. In bright moonlight the aircraft encountered flak over the French coast, losing one combination near Pont l'Abse to accurate ground fire. Forty-nine aircraft reached the LZ and cast off their gliders at 450 ft (137 m) in sight of the green landing *T*, but only six landed on the planned site, the rest losing it in the turn. The lead glider side-slipped over the trees on to the LZ, but the pilot touched down too fast and hit a bank. Strapped into a jeep in the cabin, the Assistant Divisional Commander, Brigadier General Don Pratt, broke his neck and died instantly. More lifts followed and the Group received a Distinguished Unit Citation and the French Croix de Guerre with Palm for its determination in getting the loads through in the face of heavy losses.

With the bridgehead established, the Group flew cargo in and wounded out while continuing training in preparation for Operation *Market*. On September 17 the 434rd TCG carried elements of the 82nd Airborne Division to Nijmegen and then flew re-supply despite appalling weather which disrupted operations until the 25th, by which time the venture had failed. More cargo/casualty flights followed before they crossed the Channel to a new base at Mourmelon-le-Grand on February 12 1945.

The IXth AF finally relinquished Aldermaston on June 15. Technical Training Command took over and moved in No 25 (RCAF) Aircrew Holding Unit, which sorted out men for further service in the fight against Japan, or repatriation to Canada. The unit disbanded in December and a C&M party moved in.

The airfield remained dormant until May 9 1946 when BOAC opened its Training HQ at Aldermaston. Dakotas and Oxfords from Whitchurch and Yorks from Ossington were brought in, later joined by Halifax, Halton and Viking aircraft. On January 1 1947 Aldermaston was loaned to the MCA as a temporary civil airport and BEAC joined BOAC to form Airways Training Ltd but, with a financial crisis looming, the school was closed down in November 1948.

Movements which had reached nearly 10,000 a month at the end of 1947 now rapidly dwindled, though reviving briefly when Eagle Aviation was withdrawn from the Berlin Airlift in August 1949 and set up its HQ at Aldermaston. Early in 1950 Eagle was informed that the company must leave by April because the airfield was being relinquished by the MCA. During the same month, the contractors moved in to start work converting the airfield into the Atomic Weapons Research Establishment. It was built in the very short time of two years, a number of existing organisations being brought together in the one facility, which used many of the original buildings in addition to the new site at Peak Farm.

Most of the communal and instructional buildings to the south of the airfield have been demolished to accommodate a large housing estate at Tadley, but the gymnasium/church survives as the Community Centre and the Gunnery & Crew Procedure Block is now the village cinema.

Photography or sketching of the AWRE area is *strictly forbidden* and too much interest in the old airfield is likely to be misunderstood.

Andover, Hampshire

SU328458. 2½ miles W of Andover on A303

Andover has the distinction of remaining almost unchanged in appearance after nearly 60 years in active RFC/RAF use. The station was built on 400 acres of nearly flat pasture land bounded by three roads, the most important now the A303. It was opened in August 1917, though the seven magnificent Belfast truss-roofed GS hangars and the wooden-hut accommodation were still far from complete. Personnel lived in tents with the aircraft housed in a row of Bessoneaux canvas hangars erected along the northern boundary.

Work-up of new bomber squadrons using the Salisbury Plain ranges was the first task of the new aerodrome, starting in September with Nos 104, 105 and 106 Squadrons, joined by No 148 in February 1918. The latter was the first to leave, taking its FE 2Bs to France in April, followed by No 104, but the others went to Ireland leaving Andover clear for Nos

207 and 215 Squadrons, which returned from operations with Handley Page 0/100s to convert to the much improved 0/400.

No 2 School of Navigation and Bomb Dropping (S of N & BD) formed on May 1 1918, equipped mainly with Bristol F 2Bs, but with DH 9s, DH 9As, FE 2Bs and 0/400s also on strength, the latter used exclusively by the night-training squadron of the school. The 0/400 crews also completed a special navigation course

Below *Andover in October 1918 with GS hangars still under construction, tents still in evidence, and alongside the northern boundary more Bessoneaux canvas hangars. On the field are Handley Page 0/400 and DH 9s of No 2 School of Navigation and Bomb Dropping (via A. Ferguson).*

Bottom *The brick administration and school buildings at Andover, 1918. In the background are the 'GS' hangars and a 0/400 (K.M. Robertson via B. Robertson).*

Top *A familiar sight outside the Andover hangars during the early 1930s—a Sidestrand of No 101 Squadron* (MoD H685).
Above *The proud 'owner' of this 'Shiny Twelve' Hart looks well pleased with his mount* (RAF Museum P7322).

in preparation for the projected assault on Berlin, cancelled when the Armistice intervened. Training continued into 1919, No 1 S of N & BD being absorbed in September and the combined unit renamed the Air Pilotage School three months later. It did not survive the post-war axe, being reduced to cadre on April 1 1920 and disbanded during December 1922.

No 7 Group formed at Andover on April 1 1920 to administer Army Co-operation squadrons and the RAF Staff

College which opened on April 3 1922 in a spartan brick hutment. No 11 Squadron re-formed in January 1923 with four DH 9As but moved to Bircham Newton in September and was replaced by No 2 (AC) Squadron from Farnborough. It left in March 1924 when No 12 Squadron arrived from Northolt with a few unwieldy Fawn day bombers. They were joined by the Bristol Fighters of No 13 (AC) Squadron during June and with No 12 at full strength, a Station HQ was formed on April 1 1925. The Wessex Bombing Area took over from No 7 Group on April 12 1926, No 12 Squadron celebrating this change by re-equipping with the famous Fairey Fox—the start of an outstandingly successful period for the unit.

September 1929 saw No 13 Squadron off to Netheravon, replaced by the bulky

Sidestrands of No 101 Squadron the following month, and Andover had its two bomber squadrons at last! No 12 Squadron carried out service trials on the Hart and Antelope, the former winning hands down. Both squadrons played their full part in the annual exercises and the RAF Displays at Hendon, while as a result of local Wessex Bombing Area trials, the Air Pilotage School was reborn on May 5 1933. On October 1 the Bombing Area was split in two, the new Western Area taking over the HQ and responsibility for Andover, Boscombe Down and Worthy Down.

In December 1934, No 101 Squadron moved to Bicester and the training unit, which had become the Air Navigation School in January 1935, was joined by No 142 Squadron. Their Harts took over the hangars vacated by No 101 Squadron, but in October accompanied the similarly-equipped No 12 Squadron to the Middle East as part of the build-up following Mussolini's invasion of Abyssinia. They were immediately replaced by two heavy bomber squadrons when Nos 9 and 214 moved in their stately Virginia Xs.

The Air Navigation School went to Manston and Western Area became No 3 (Bomber) Group on May 1 1936. Additional accommodation in the form of substantial brick barrack blocks was built and in August 1936 Nos 103 and 107 Squadrons re-formed with Hind day bombers. They were joined by Nos 12 and 142 Squadrons back from overseas, ousting the dark green-painted heavies, No 9 Squadron having received Heyfords whilst at Andover.

No 3 Group HQ moved to Mildenhall in January 1937 and was replaced by 2 Group from Abingdon, a more logical arrangement as all light bombers came under their jurisdiction. More Hind squadrons came and went, only staying long enough to reach full strength. Andover was soon left to its long-term residents, Nos 12 and 142 Squadrons and the Staff College. No 12 Squadron re-equipped with the disappointing Battle in February 1938, followed by No 142 Squadron in March. They spent the remainder of the year wrestling with unfamiliar retractable undercarriages, flaps and variable-pitch propellers, though accidents were surprisingly few.

No 2 Group HQ then moved to Wyton in April and the station found itself temporarily in No 1 Group. With international tension mounting, the Air Ministry issued instructions in May for stations to prepare full defence schemes and dispersal plans for the aircraft. This involved personnel in building gun positions and digging slit trenches—never popular occupations. In July, HQ Maintenance Command took over buildings vacated by No 2 Group, commencing a long association with Andover.

With the Munich Crisis at its peak, Nos 12 and 142 Squadrons were formed into No 76 Bomber Wing. Peacetime markings were removed from aircraft and the serials/codes toned down in preparation for the war which appeared imminent. The crisis passed, squadron life returning to something approaching normal, but beneath the surface preparations continued apace. The expansion of Maintenance Command was one sign, No 40 Group forming at Andover on January 1 1939, while 41 Group lodged in Kelly's Directories building at 81 Weyhill Road, Andover.

The Station transferred from Bomber to Fighter Command in May, coming under No 22 Group for Army Co-operation duties. The Battles left for Bicester and were replaced by Hectors and Blenheims of No 59 Squadron, re-equipping when moved from Old Sarum to become the operating unit of No 51 (AC) Wing.

On the day war was declared, No 42 Group was formed at Andover, the Staff College closed and No 51 Wing was warned for operations in France. The main ground party left on October 1 followed by the Blenheims five days later. Any respite was short-lived for, on October 21, No 2 S of AC was formed on the station, equipped with Blenheims and Ansons for training in low-flying, navigation, photography and Army Co-op tactics.

In November 1939 shortened staff courses restarted but were suspended again in May 1940 with the end of the Phoney War. The whole country braced itself for the Luftwaffe onslaught but the first attack on Andover was not until August 13 when five Ju 88s from LG 1 dropped ten bombs. The airfield, parade ground, SHQ and officers' quarters were hit, three men killed and six aircraft damaged. The following day a single aircraft dropped anti-personnel bombs killing two, then came a lull until January 11 1941 when a single HE and many incendaries were dropped. A decoy airfield was laid out at Hurstbourne, some seven miles to the east, but there is no evidence that it was effective.

The ground defences got a Ju 88 which attacked during March but more damage was done during April 1941 when two hangars had to be demolished after being wrecked. Half of No 2 S of AC was sent to Thornaby in July to form No 6 (Coastal) OTU, the remainder becoming the nucleus of No 42 OTU whose initial task was the conversion of Lysander crews to Blenheims, using Thruxton as a satellite. The next year was one of grinding endeavour, the appalling flying casualty rate being the most notable feature. Though No 42 OTU moved to Ashbourne in October, personnel strength kept-rising, for No 296 squadron had arrived with Whitleys, closely followed by No 170 with Mustangs, No 16 with Lysanders/Mustangs and 15 (P) AFU with Oxfords—a very mixed bag.

Army Co-op squadrons were frequent visitors during 1943, joined in June/July by 808, 809 and 879 Squadrons. They trained with the Army as No 4 Naval Fighter Wing using 60 Seafires. Andover

Apart from spaces left by the April 1941 bombing and new HQ buildings and quarters, Andover remained almost unchanged throughout its 60 years of active existence. Compare this 1973 scene with that of 1918 (MoD (Air) via A. Ferguson).

was very busy indeed that summer for the Seafires were back again in September to exercise with Austers of No 660 Squadron. Both 660 Squadron and 15 (P) AFU left in November, followed by the Naval Wing on December 7 1943.

Things were then quiet until the end of February 1944 when P-38 Lightnings of the 370th FG, USAAF, arrived from Aldermaston. The 71st FW HQ followed on March 1 and the IXth AF took over Andover formally two days later, as a forward operating base. The 401st, 402nd and 485th FS Lightnings filled the five main hangars and five Blisters dispersed around the field, for their Allison-powered twin-boomers were still lots of trouble! The undulating grass surface, with its maximum run of 3,900 ft (1,189 m) was fairly tight too, but the snags were ironed out, the Group trained hard and was declared operational on May 1. Its main tasks were dive-bombing radar installations and flak towers, mixed with close escort for bombers attacking bridges and marshalling yards. On D-Day the Group's aircraft provided cover for the Allied armada and spent the rest of the month on armed recce over the Cotentin Peninsula. They moved over to the Continent on July 20 and Andover's flirt with operational flying was over, the station returning to the RAF on the 29th. No 43 OTU gratefully vacated Oatlands Hill and moved in its Austers, joined later by a succession of newly-formed AOP squadrons,

the last leaving in June 1945.

With Maintenance Command and No 41 Group HQs both firmly entrenched, Andover remained open even after No 43 OTU moved to Middle Wallop in January 1948. The RAF Staff College returned and a Communications Squadron formed, the airfield being used for little except liaison flights for the next 15 years. This comfortable existence was shattered on January 1 1960 by the formation of No 225 Squadron which flew Sycamore and Whirlwind helicopters from Andover until moving to Odiham in November 1963.

The Western Communications Squadron was formed in 1964 with Pembrokes and Bassets, the latter soon withdrawn when it was found that the long propeller blades were carving a groove in the turf. On February 3 1969 the unit became No 21 Squadron, and standardised on the Devon. Mergers were commonplace. The Staff College left in December 1969 and in 1973 Maintenance Command joined with Technical Training and Transport Commands to form Air Support Command. Andover was retained as HQ which provided most of the trade for No 21 Squadron but 1975 Defence Review axed the squadron. When it disbanded on March 31 1976 the airfield was also closed.

With further streamlining, Air Support Command merged with Training Command on June 13 1977 and the Army took over Andover for use as the HQ of the Army Logistic Executive. The airfield is kept in good condition and is used by Middle Wallop units, both fixed-and rotary-winged.

Appledram, West Sussex

SU839018. 2½ miles SW of Chichester alongside A286

A large expanse of flat grassland, close to the Chichester Channel and with good road access from the nearby village of Appledram, was immediately attractive as a fighter ALG. A detailed survey was completed in June 1942 to requisition the land and prepare the site were given on December 10. Ministry of Agriculture objections were overruled and an RAF Airfield Construction Unit moved in during February to remove fences and obstacles and lay two Sommerfeld Track runways in the form of a crucifix. The work was completed by the end of May and Appledram was immediately occupied by a newly formed Typhoon fighter-bomber Wing (Nos 175, 181 and 182 Squadrons of No 124 Airfield) of the equally new Tactical Air Force. The aircraft were dispersed around the field and the personnel, both air and groundcrew, lived in tents as part of their training for mobile operations.

Nos 181 and 182 Squadrons were already well-established Typhoon fighter-bomber units, but No 175 had only converted to the aircraft in April and made its first sorties from Appledram on June 12, against Abbeville airfield. Operations against communications, installations and airfields were fairly intensive but Appledram could cope with a fully loaded

Some idea of the undulating surface of Andover can be gauged from this 1981 photograph. Note the airfield code 'AV' on the roof of the double 'GS' hangar and the small, but well preserved 'tower' (K.S. West).

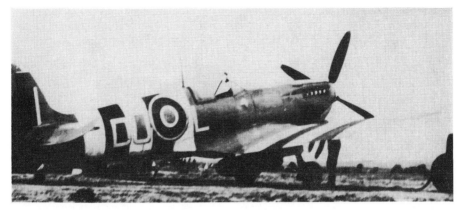

A Spitfire IX of No 312 Squadron at Appledram ALG just after D-Day 1944 (Leif Boel Hansen via R.C. Jones).

Typhoon and there was only one serious accident during their stay.

The ALG reverted to standby status early in July and was not used again until the Spitfires of No 134 Airfield (Nos 310, 312 and 313 Squadrons) 84 Group, arrived from Mendlesham on April 4 1944. In the meantime four Extra Over Blisters had been erected and a number of metal track hardstandings provided. The Czechs supplemented their damp tents by taking over a few farm cottages before starting their daily round of sweeps, bomber escorts and attacks on *Noball* sites.

On D-Day the Wing patrolled over the bridgehead without incident and Luftwaffe activity remained generally light. However, a number of Fw 190s were engaged and five destroyed, before the increasing threat from V-1 flying bombs caused the Czechs to be transferred to the ADGB and moved to Tangmere for anti-*Diver* patrols. They were replaced by the Poles of No 131 Wing (Nos 302, 308 and 317 Squadrons) also flying Spitfire IXs. They were soon on the offensive, dive-bombing forward German positions under Army direction, but went to Ford on July 16 to prepare for a move across the Channel.

No further use was made of Appledram ALG and it was derequisitioned on November 6, the farm cottages being released a week later. Two Flights of No 5027 Works Squadron moved in during January 1945 to lift the Sommerfeld Tracking, remove the Blisters and restore the land for farming. There is now no sign of its use as an airfield.

Ashford (Great Chart), Kent

TQ972402. 2½ miles SW of Ashford off A28

Known locally as Great Chart and not to be confused with the post-war Ashford Airport, this 400-acre site lay on flat grassland just west of Chilmington Green, in the apex formed by the A28 and a minor road to Stubbs' Cross. Development of an ALG was approved in September 1942, the dispersal plan agreed in December and the land requisitioned during January 1943 for completion by the beginning of March! Preparation was confined to grading, and the laying of a partial taxi-track and two Sommerfeld Track runways, parallel to existing roads in the form of a V. Chilmington Farm was earmarked for stores and equipment.

With the cancellation of *Hadrian*, the ALG was released for grazing until 2875 AA Squadron, RAF Regiment, arrived on August 11 1943 to set up gun posts. Two days later they were joined by No 129 (RCAF) Airfield and the Mustang 1s of Nos 414 and 430 Squadrons. Their reconnaissance role was interpreted rather loosely, No 414 Squadron engaging in night *Rangers* over France, and No 430 spending a lot of time on anti-*Rhubarb* sorties covering the south coast. The Royal Canadian Engineers took advantage of the RCAF presence to lay an impregnated-hessian landing strip similar to that tested earlier at Dunsfold, but it was just as unsatisfactory.

The Canadians left early in October, and were immediately replaced by an RAF Spitfire Wing displaced from Kingsnorth. During the ten days they spent at Ashford they flew top cover and diversionary fighter sweeps, but the most memorable

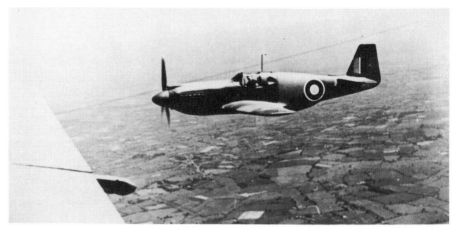

event had nothing to do with the enemy —the trouble was caused by Allies! At a temporary loose end, some pilots of No 126 (RCAF) Airfield were taken 'somewhere in Kent' with orders to avoid 'capture' and get back to Staplehurst by whatever means they could. The Canadians took these instructions literally and, spotting unguarded Spitfires on Ashford ALG, started two up and flew home. Questions were asked in high places, but to be fair the very nature of such temporary airfields made adequate security almost impossible.

Ashford was allocated to the IXth AF for fighter-bomber operations and required considerable strengthening

Above *A Mustang 1 of No 430 Squadron, RCAF, in August 1943—photographed from a Hudson over Kent while flying from Ashford ALG (via H. Holmes).*

Below *P-47D-27RE 42-26860 of the 406th Fighter Bomber Group at Great Chart (Ashford) in 1944. Note the steel mesh tracking, buckling under the pounding of Thunderbolt operations* (South Eastern Newspapers Ltd).

during the winter of 1943/44. A complete taxi track was laid, the number of hardstandings increased to 70, and the main runway extended and reinforced.

The HQ staff of the 303rd FW arrived on March 8, the 406th FBG assembled on April 4 and the 512th, 513th and 515th FSs, equipped with new P-47s, were declared operational on May 9 1944. The Group took a full part in the softening-up process prior to D-Day and on June 6 was very active over *Utah* beach, losing five aircraft during the day. Top cover continued until the beach-head was properly established then the Thunderbolts resumed armed reconnaissance, attacking gun emplacements, ammunition dumps and road/rail communications. The 513th FS claimed the first V-1 destroyed by the USAAF and also started equipping their aircraft with high velocity 5-in (127mm) rockets, a devastating weapon against armour.

The Americans planned to leave Ashford in early June but bad weather delayed completion of ALGs in France and the 406th was forced to stay until July 27 and the 303rd FW HQ into early August. Authority to release Ashford was given on September 15 and the site was cleared, then used by No 42 Group as a storage area. The work of reinstatement continued into the New Year and there is now little evidence of Ashford ALG except an unmetalled track parallel to the A28 road and some fences repaired with PSP.

Ashford (Lympne), Kent

See Lympne

Bekesbourne, Kent

TR205553. 4 miles SE of Canterbury on minor road
Requisitioned in 1916 as an ELG, this large sloping field just south-east of Bekesbourne village was first used by 'B'

Flight of No 50 (HD) Squadron, and despite its small size proved quite adequate for the FK 8s, Vickers ES 2s and BE 12s employed by the unit.

Action was extremely limited, but two BE 12s went up on November 28 1916 when a LVG biplane dropped bombs on London. The pilots saw nothing of the enemy, which was not very surprising as they would have to have been in just the right place at the right time to have any hope of an interception. After further daylight attacks on London during 1917 by Gothas of Kagohl 3, there was a public outcry, and two crack scout squadrons were ordered home from the Continent. No 56 Squadron arrived at Bekesbourne on June 21 but, ironically, the only daylight raid while their SE 5s were present was on East Anglia. The pilots spent a restful fortnight, returning to France on July 5. Two days later 22 Gothas bombed London!

In 1918 Bekesbourne was upgraded, the construction of two large Belfast Truss GS hangars and associated buildings being started in the north-western corner of the field, and a hutted domestic site erected close to Chalkpit Farm. The whole of No 50 Squadron moved in on February 8 and after the formation of the RAF took on additional training tasks.

By September the hangars were complete and work on the 98-acre site nearly finished. The squadron had 24 Camels, replaced by SE 5As in November. After the Armistice came a gradual rundown, No 50 Squadron being disbanded in June

Below *A mixed collection of No 50 (HD) Squadron aircraft at Bekesbourne in May 1917. They are a AW FK 8, a Vickers ES 1 and a BE 12, only the latter being any real use* (G.S. Leslie/J.M. Bruce collection).

Above *No 56 Squadron spent a frustrating fortnight at Bekesbourne in June 1917. Here one of their SE 5As is on standby alongside the wooden huts and canvas hangars of this small Home Defence aerodrome* (K. Muspatt via G.S. Leslie collection).

Left *An ELG during the early years of World War 2, Bekesbourne was illustrated in the Luftwaffe target handbook. The First World War 'GS' hangar is indicated at the north-western end of the field* (via D.G. Collyer).

1919 and the aerodrome relinquished in 1920. Suprisingly, Bekesbourne did not just fade away but was soon in use again as Canterbury Aerodrome. The Kent Flying Club was formed there and flourished in the 1930s, a section of the Civil Air Guard being established in 1938.

Bekesbourne closed at the outbreak of the Second World War, but re-opened in the desperate days of May 1940 as a *Back Violet* airfield. With the Air Component of the BEF in danger of being overrun in France, the Air Ministry devised a scheme whereby aircraft would be based in south-east England but operate from ALGs in France. Lysanders of No 2 Squadron arrived at Bekesbourne on May 20 and, joined by some No 13 Squadron aircraft, they carried out armed recces over France, largely without loss, though one Lysander was destroyed when it returned with three hang-ups, the bombs exploding when they dropped off during landing.

Operations in France ceased after the Dunkirk evacuation and No 2 Squadron went to Hatfield on June 8. Bekesbourne, small and vulnerable, was then liberally obstructed with strakes and abandoned.

Returned to its owner after the war, the remaining GS hangar was later used as a warehouse while some aerodrome buildings were converted into bungalows. A municipal camping site encroaches, but Bekesbourne retains the uncanny feel of an aerodrome—one can easily visualize the scene as a Camel climbed away into the dusk on yet another nocturnal patrol.

Bembridge, Isle of Wight (Marine)

SZ642887. 3½ miles SE of Ryde off B3395

As part of the Solent defence scheme, a sub-station of Calshot was set up on Bembridge Point during 1915, enabling seaplanes from the main base to operate from the Isle of Wight on occasion. The facilities were spartan, just a hardstanding and a slipway into Brading (now renamed Bembridge) Harbour where the seaplanes were usually moored.

During the autumn of 1916, the Admiralty decided to base four Short 184 floatplanes permanently at the substation so that a patrol could reach out 60 miles (97 km) from the island. The machines arrived in November and Bembridge joined the re-organised Portsmouth Group on January 1 1917 operating on the orders of the Naval C-in-C. A base was built consisting of two standard seaplane sheds and a number of huts fronting the hardstanding, officers living in the Spithead Hotel and ratings in an adapted coastguard station.

Operations could be decidedly tricky in adverse weather for the floatplanes were required to take-off and alight in open water to the north-west of St Helen's Fort and taxi to and from Brading Harbour. There was much monotony and little action, but it was a Bembridge-based Short which, on October 18 1917, came as close to sinking a submarine as any when the unit CO, Flight Commander McLaurin, and his observer spotted a surfaced U-boat and scored a direct hit with a 100 lb (45 kg) bomb. It was observed to submerge with a 30-degree list to port and was not seen again, but could not be confirmed as a kill.

On April 1 1918 the Portsmouth Group became No 10 Group, RAF Warsash, but the change made little difference to the seaplane units, determined as any to retain their naval traditions. After considerable confusion caused by several changes of plan, the unit at Bembridge became Nos 412 and 413 Flights of No 253 Squadron in August 1918. The establishment was 12 Short 184s and 190 men, but it is doubtful whether this number was ever attained.

No 253 Squadron was disbanded on May 1919, though the station remained open until September and was possibly visited by Calshot-based machines from time to time before final disposal in 1920.

Blackbushe (Hartfordbridge Flats), Hampshire

SU805595. 5 miles W of Camberley on A30

Rough common ground known as Hartfordbridge Flats was used for a demonstration of early airborne forces in January 1941, probably because of its easy access from London. The weather prevented the *ad hoc* collection of gliders from Haddenham (Thame) making the cross-country journey, but eight parachutists were dropped from a Whitley and a prototype Hotspur glider from nearby Farnborough was towed across the Flats by a Handley Page Heyford—quite a sight in itself. Whether this event attracted the attention of the surveyors, or whether it had already been chosen, is not known, but the site became a fully-fledged airfield, first known as Hartfordbridge (sometimes Hartfordbridge Flats) and later as Blackbushe.

The site was requisitioned in October 1941 and McAlpines started work on a standard three-runway bomber-type airfield soon afterwards. Progress was aided

When this photo was taken on October 1, 1942, Hartfordbridge was not officially open but already in use by the RAE (RAF Museum W13/6/4).

by the light soil, but not by the RAE at Farnborough who, despite considerable opposition from Army Co-operation Command, insisted on using it for glider trials while it was being built. Already hazardous, these experiments were made additionally exciting by the presence of a huge concrete mixer close to the main runway and large numbers of lorries moving haphazardly about the airfield, which was already being extended south of the A30 trunk road.

Hartfordbridge was officially opened by No 70 Group on November 1 1942, the advance party from Odiham taking over the first sites a week later. These were then used by RAE personnel and, with no other accommodation ready and no power at any of the sites, No 171 (AC) Squadron delayed moving in its Toma-hawks and Mustangs until December 7. Three weeks later it disbanded to form the nucleus of No 430 Squadron, which promptly left for Dunsfold. Hartford-bridge was left to the RAE, the Blenhein Flight from Odiham and the contractors, still removing their huts and levelling the middle of the airfield.

PR Spitfires and Venturas of No 140 Squadron moved in from Mount Farm on March 12 1943, were joined by No 16 Squadron at the end of June, and were soon operating as No 34 (PR) Wing. Nearly all the dispersed sites had now been handed over and were needed, for the first of many diversions arrived during the early hours of July 4 when two Wellingtons of No 196 Squadron, a Halifax of No 76 and another from No 158 Squadron landed—the latter's under-

Bostons were prominent equipment of units at Hartfordbridge. 'F' for Freddie, Mk IIIa of No 88 Squadron is seen here in typical day bomber weather (RAF Museum P11991).

carriage collapsing on touch-down. Meanwhile, trials of Horsa and Hamilcar gliders continued, these including rocket-assisted take-offs and experimental towing of the heavyweight Hamilcar by two Halifaxes. On July 13 1943 a Ju 88 slipped into the airfield—it was from Farnborough, carrying out night-flying tests with a Halifax and a Mosquito!

Indications of increased activity came with the complete closure of the main London-Basingstoke road for a whole month from August 16, the Bostons of Nos 88 and 107 Squadrons, and Venturas of No 21 Squadron arriving to form a No 2 Group Wing for Operation *Starkey*. Operating from the western end of Hart-fordbridge, they bombed marshalling yards, ammunition dumps, airfields and a power station, No 107 Squadron losing three Bostons in the latter attack.

Hartfordbridge was now a self-accounting No 2 Group station and after *Starkey* No 21 Squadron was replaced by No 342 (Free French) Squadron, making the Wing completely Boston-equipped for the first time. Determined attempts to disrupt French power supplies were made on October 3 when No 88 Squadron set off for the Distre electricity-distribution centre, No 107 Squadron attacked a transformer station at Orleans and the Free French sent 11 Bostons to bomb another transformer farm at Chevilly. Several aircraft were lost to flak but six transformers were destroyed and others damaged, paralysing rail communications over a wide area until steam locomotives could be found to replace useless electric units. Despite better aircraft and tactics, flak losses were still high—sometimes disastrously so, but the Wing kept up the pressure, concentrating during November on the V-1 *Noball* sites in Northern France, which had been painstakingly identified from reconnaissance photographs.

Fighter Command was disbanded on November 15 1943 and the tactical elements, which included all the units at Hartfordbridge, joined the new TAF organisation. No 140 Squadron received a few Mosquito PR IXs during the month and started to pass its Spitfires to No 16, which was in the process of converting to the more potent Mk XI. Both these No 34 Wing squadrons were engaged in re-photographing Western Europe so that up-to-date maps could be produced ready for the invasion.

In December the Bostons started operating as No 137 Airfield, *Noball* site destruction remaining their primary task until February 1944 despite persistent bad weather. No 107 Squadron moved to Lasham on February 3 and was replaced later in the month by No 226 Squadron from Swanton Morley. No 226 had Mitchells, however, and it was found more satisfactory for them to operate with their Dunsfold counterparts so, though they remained at Hartfordbridge, they took little part in No 137 Airfield activities.

No 140 Squadron had supplemented its Mosquito PR IXs with some PR XVIs and by February these were ranging far and wide over the Continent, at the same time training hard with *Gee* and *Rebecca* radar-navigation aids to improve night and bad-weather photography. On April 7 No 34 (PR) Wing went to Northolt and so Nos 16 and 140 Squadrons missed the visit from the Supreme Allied Commander and other top brass. General Eisenhower spoke to No 137 Airfield crews, congratulated them on recent operations against V-1 sites and gave them some idea of their part in the forthcoming invasion of Europe.

The big day was obviously close, for No 322 (Dutch) Squadron brought in Spitfire XIVs for defensive patrols over southern England to prevent preparations being photographed by high-flying German reconnaissance aircraft. Early in May, they were joined by the Mosquito NF XIIIs of No 264 Squadron, the two units forming No 141 Airfield. No 264 Squadron was soon in action against a small force detected coming in over the south coast on May 14. Flight Lieutenant C. M. Ramsey, DFC, shot down a Ju 88 near Alton, but then became disorientated and the crew baled out, the navigator being killed. The next night an Me 410 was shot down, but this flurry of activity was soon over and pilots of No 322 Squadron went on offensive patrols over the Continent to relieve the boredom.

There was precious little boredom for the bomber crews who were softening up gun positions and disrupting the French transport system as well as continuing attacks on V-1 sites. Early in June the Bostons were fitted with special tanks and smoke-laying dischargers in their bomb bays and, with personnel confined to camp during the afternoon of the 5th, the crews were informed that they would be operating at first light the next morning. Despite a strong wind, the smoke was well laid and gave the landing force some respite for the loss of two Bostons, one to flak, the other hitting the sea after laying smoke. That night 12 Bostons attempted to bomb Mezidon but were hampered by their lack of navigational aids, and crews found a daylight attack on the 21st Panzer Division in the Foret de Chambecq on June 12 much more satisfactory. Similar attacked followed, particularly successful being that on strongpoints in the Moneville Steel Works, near Caen on the 22nd. These had held the Army's advance up since June 10 and were plastered with 500- and 1,000-lb (227- and 454-kg) bombs by the 72 Mitchells and Bostons, whose efforts brought congratulations from the 51st Highland Division—a unit not known for giving praise lightly.

After inspection by Queen Wilhelmina and Prince Bernhardt of the Netherlands, No 322 Squadron went to West Malling on June 20 to join No 148 Wing in the battle against the V-1. No 141 Wing was then disbanded, No 264 Squadron continuing to fly night patrols from a quiet corner of the airfield until July 26, when it too departed for anti-*Diver* operations.

No 2 Group raids continued day and night throughout July when losses were surprisingly light. Their Majesties the King and Queen visited on July 14 and decorated 80 members of the station.

The full strength of No 2 Group was concentrated for Operation *Market*, the airborne attempt to capture the bridges at Nijmegen and Arnhem. No 137 Wing led Mitchells of No 139 Wing in a daylight attack on the Ede barracks on September 17 but the weather was poor and the bombing scattered. Continuing bad weather prevented any more assistance to the beleaguered troops and spirits were low at Hartfordbridge until the 26th, when they successfully bombed a road/rail bridge at Cleve—their first raid on Germany.

Casualties from the fighting on the Continent were now being flown into the United Kingdom for base hospital treatment, Hartfordbridge becoming one of the main reception airfields because of its good road access and the number of hospitals in the area.

On October 8, the 2nd TAF ordered the light-bomber Wings to the Continent and No 137 left for Vitry en Artois (B50) on October 17. Mosquito FB VIs of No 138 Wing (Nos 107, 305 and 613 Squadrons) arrived from Lasham but poor weather hampered operations until they too moved to the Continent, going to Cambrai/Epinoy (A75) on November 19 1944. Two days later the third 2nd TAF Mosquito Wing (No 136) formed when No 418 Squadron arrived from Hunsdon and was joined by No 605 from Manston. Previously very successful ADGB night-intruder units, they immediately started intensive training for their new tactical role and were well advanced on December 2 when the cumbersome name of the airfield was changed to Blackbushe.

No 136 Wing first operated on December 31 when 19 Mosquito FB VIs bombed and then strafed targets in the Ardennes. Attacks continued in this battle area and, on February 22 1945, an all-out offensive was launched against German communications. Called Operation *Clarion* and said to involve 9,000 aircraft, it was intended to destroy the transport system of Germany, No 136 Wing flying 39 sorties and dropping 56×500 lb (227 kg) bombs on targets of opportunity in north-eastern Holland and north-western Germany. Flak was heavy and the Wing lost eight aircraft and crews, including Wing Commander J. Wickett, CO of No 418 Squadron. Other units' losses were also high and the damage, although extensive, was not as crippling as had been hoped. On March 15 No 136 Wing moved to Coxyde (B71) in Belgium, the last operational 2nd TAF unit to go the Continent.

Blackbushe now transferred to No 46 Group, Transport Command, receiving No 167 Squadron from Holmsley South on March 27. Equipped with 25 Warwick C IIIs, this squadron operated freight and passenger services to the Continent for No 110 Wing. On April 4 1945 they were joined by a re-formed No 301 (Polish) Squadron, who received Warwicks during May but moved to North Weald on July 2 for operations. No 167 Squadron added Ansons for services to the Channel Islands, the Casualty Air Evacuation Unit continued bringing in personnel from the Continent and the South Africans commenced repatriation, using Dakotas. No 162 Squadron Mosquitoes arrived from Bourn to try out an express delivery service, free-dropping mail and newspaper containers on airfields. British newspapers were soon arriving in Cairo, Rome, Naples and Athens before breakfast! No 167 Squadron also extended its routes and now served Prague, Vienna, Paris, Naples and Brussels daily, Malta three times and Gibraltar twice weekly. The Warwicks proved unsatisfactory, No 167 Squadron being disbanded in February 1946 when BEA took over the No 110 Wing services.

Meanwhile, an experimental all-weather transport operation by Dakota crews of No 24 Squadron, Hendon, had commenced between Prestwick and Blackbushe. The 385-mile (620-km) route was chosen because it encompassed some of the worst British weather while the airfields provided a connection between the Atlantic terminal and London, and were well equipped with aids. The All-Weather Service started on September 16 1945 and was an outstanding success. Only two of the 728 planned flights were cancelled and there were no diversions, FIDO being used to assist five landings at Blackbushe. A refurbished manor house at Hartney Whitney provided a comfortable transit hotel.

Danish Airlines (DDL) commenced services to Copenhagen and Stockholm on September 6 and No 311 (Czech) Squadron Liberators started repatriation flights to Prague at the end of the month, and were involved in a tragic accident on October 4 when an aircraft crashed immediately after take-off, killing all 23 people on board.

The United Kingdom end of the Air Delivery Service moved in from Northolt during January 1946 but it was past its

Photographed by No 58 Squadron soon after re-opening as a civil airport, Blackbushe shows few changes from its wartime days (DoE/Crown Copyright).

peak and the unit disbanded on April 20. No 160 Staging Post started operations on May 5, responsible for an increasing number of ferry and special VIP flights including frequent visits by Field Marshal Montgomery en route to Camberley Staff College for conferences, while the crew of the famous *Aries* used the facilities at the start of their record-breaking flight to New Zealand in August 1946. No 162 Squadron was disbanded on July 14 leaving Blackbushe without based units, but this did not prevent an excellent Battle of Britain display in September 1946.

On November 15 1946, the airfield was officially closed, 11,444 aircraft and 63,934 passengers having used Blackbushe since Transport Command took it over in March 1945. A C&M party remained and it was transferred to the MCA on February 15 1947 and re-opened as Blackbushe Airport.

British Aviation Services had been established since 1946 and they were soon joined by other charter operators led by their associates, Silver City, Airwork and Air Contractors. The FIDO system was completely rebuilt to incorporate the latest improvements which provided a much quicker, and therefore more economical start-up. Among the few other improvements made by the MCA was the construction of a new terminal building alongside the A30 near the threshold of R/W 32 and the provision of a large tarmac apron by the simple expedient of filling in the grass centres of two Special Loop dispersals. A domestic area for airport workers, which included a club, canteen and living quarters, used an ex-RAF site to the north-east of the airfield.

Many aircraft were ferried through Blackbushe at this time, including such plums as Israeli Mosquitoes and Pakistani Furies. The rebuilt FIDO was given a demonstration test run and, on November 30 1948, its first (and, as it turned out, only) civil operational burn when it was used to enable an Airwork Viking under Crown Agents charter to take-off. The 90 ft (27 m) visibility was increased to nearly 2,400 ft (732 m) by partial use of the equipment.

Civilian participation in the Berlin Airlift occupied the aircraft of several Blackbushe firms, Airwork, Silver City and Westminster amongst them. On return some companies found it hard to find work for their aircraft, while others prospered. Airflight, under its mercurial owner, AVM D.C.T. Bennett of Pathfinder fame, moved into the airport from Langley in August 1949 and specialised in pilgrim and immigrant flights as Fairflight. Airwork received contracts from the War Office to fly families of Service personnel to the Middle East, and also provided the nucleus for No 622 Squadron which re-formed at Blackbushe on December 15 1950. The sole transport unit of the RAuxAF, equipped with Valettas, it was manned by a small number of regular personnel, and volunteers from the local airline companies. Both Valettas and requisitioned Vikings were to be flown in an emergency, but the squadron proved difficult to manage and was disbanded on September 30 1953.

The FIDO installation was again overhauled during 1952 and put on standby for the Manston unit, but not used and was dismantled in 1960. Airwork thrived on the military contracts and four Handley Page Hermes were purchased for use on MoD trooping flights to the Canal Zone and Kenya. Like many others seen at Blackbushe, these aircraft flew in military markings when going to Egypt.

Mr Harold Bamberg bought the Blackbushe-based Aviation Services from Britavia in November 1952 and moved his Eagle Aviation into the airport. It became Eagle Airways in July 1953, one of the

first companies in the package tour industry. Blackbushe was now firmly established as an aviation enthusiasts' Mecca for there were many visitors, both civil and military, in addition to the based operators. Hastings and Beverleys were frequently to be seen picking up troops for parachute training on the nearby DZ at Frensham, while each September the airfield was filled to capacity with an amazing selection of aircraft bringing in visitors to the SBAC Farnbrough Air Display.

US Navy aircraft were no strangers to Blackbushe either, R6D Liftmasters of VR-1 and VR-22 routing through, while the smaller R5D Skymasters of VR-24 made a twice-weekly circuit of Europe carrying mail and passengers between US Navy facilities. Martin Mercators and variants of the P2V Neptune were frequent visitors and during 1955 a US Navy liaison unit arrived from Hendon. As FASRON 200 it operated a twice-weekly service to Mainz-am-Rhein, West Germany, and a weekly PX run to Aldergrove in Northern Ireland using R4D-8s (Super Dakotas). They used a new hangar built on Yately Common to the north-east of the airfield, complete with a large hardstanding and interconnecting

The US Navy 'facility' meant many visitors to Blackbushe from that service, providing spectacular 'close-ups' of taxiing aircraft such as this P2V-5F of VQ-2 seen near the Terminal Building during the 1950s (Military Aircraft Photos).

The airport terminal building is now used as a club headquarters, restaurant and air traffic control

taxiways which joined the airfield perimeter track near the threshold of R/W 26.

Smaller companies sprang up and died just as quickly, while Eagle Airways steadily expanded to become the major operator. Meanwhile local opposition grew apace, especially in Yately. At the end of 1960 the Ministry announced that the airport would close. Eagle Aviation moved to London Airport, Airwork and Dan Air went to Gatwick and the US Navy to West Malling. Blackbushe officially closed at midnight on May 31 1960. This might have been expected to end the story, but the protagonists had reckoned without AVM Bennett. The eastern end of the airfield had been built on common land, but the rest was privately owned and was sold to the Air Marshal. Yately Common was cleared and fenced off, but against bitter opposition the remainder was re-opened in 1962 as a club and executive aircraft airfield, using the western end of the old terminal as the air traffic control and club facility.

The main runway had been resurfaced in 1956 and the usable 4,232-ft (1,920-m) strip was in good condition while the subsidiary strips were satisfactory for occasional use. Hangars, and the majority of other wartime buildings, had been removed, so aircraft had to be parked in the open and Blackbushe remained under constant threat from the vocal local lobby, planning permission for any new installations being refused.

In 1973 Bennett sold the 354-acre airfield to Douglas Arnold, a self-made millionaire who had developed a passion for rebuilding Second World War aircraft. The everyday use of the airfield by training, club and executive aircraft has continued, controlled by Aviation Services Ltd, while Arnold has developed Warbirds Museum of Great Britain Ltd in temporary buildings at the western end of the airfield. Other popular but less praiseworthy operations have been a Sunday Market, and in July 1978 a pop festival which attracted more spectators than the Football Association Cup Final!

For some years plans for a permanent museum building were thwarted by the threat of a compulsory purchase order, but in 1980 Arnold's appeal finally succeeded, and work started in June 1981, hangars and a museum being erected on the south-western side of the airfield. The future of Blackbushe now seems secure and it is certainly worth a visit, for there is usually plenty of activity and the unexpected on view. In the past this has meant a line of CASA 352s (Spanish-built Ju 52/3ms), four or five B-25 Mitchells, or a CASA 2 111 (the next best thing to a He 111). Who knows what might be there on your visit?

Bognor, West Sussex

SU915005. 1½ miles NW of Bognor Regis on B2166

Plans were well advanced in 1928 for a municipal airport between Bognor and Rose Green, but it failed to materialise and the land lay dormant until covered by the West Meads housing estate. Unable to find the reported municipal site in 1942 the surveyors chose a stretch of prime farmland immediately north-west where their ideal layout of two runways at right angles and of the required length could be constructed.

By September 1942, Bognor was on the short list, the detailed report submitted early the following month being approved and Air Ministry authority issued on December 10. During January 1943 the Ministry of Agriculture pressed hard for the land's retention but was overruled and the requisition order went ahead. Work on grading the land, felling isolated trees and laying the SW/NE and NW/SE Sommerfeld Track strips was pressed forward through the winter and, after the closing of the B2166 at Morells Farm and destruction of several minor tracks, the ALG was opened on June 1 1943, parented by Tangmere.

Intended as an exercise ALG for squadrons of the embryo Tactical AF, it was immediately in use by No 122 Airfield which arrived with Nos 122 and 602 Squadrons, joined by No 19 Squadron later in the month. They practised ground-attack techniques and carried out fighter sweeps in support of day-bomber raids. At the beginning of July, No 122 Airfield disappeared as suddenly as it had arrived and Bognor lay deserted until upgrading commenced in the autumn. Taxi-tracks were extended and an increased number of hardstandings provided, while the number of Extra Over Blister hangars was doubled to four in preparation for the intensive operations expected prior to and during the invasion of the Continent.

No 132 Airfield of No 84 Group, 2nd TAF, arrived from North Weald on the last day of March 1944 to work-up No 66 and two Norwegian squadrons, Nos 331 and 332, as a Spitfire IX fighter-bomber Wing. This involved visits to APCs, but they also managed to take part in offensive operations, the first *Ranger* by No 332 resulting in six enemy aircraft being destroyed during a strafing of Juvincourt airfield, Paris, on April 11.

Although largely a tented camp, No 132 Airfield was lucky at Bognor for there was more suitable property in the area than usual and some personnel were thus able to avoid the worst rigours of an English Spring.

On D-Day and for the following fortnight No 132 (Norwegian) Wing flew beach-head patrols interspersed with attacks on V-1 sites, finding the Allied AA gunners nearly as dangerous as the Germans, such was their appallingly bad aircraft recognition. On June 14 the Wing escorted Lancasters of Bomber Command making daylight raids on German positions which were holding up the advance in Normandy, and the following day started fighter sweeps at Wing strength.

No 132 Wing moved to Tangmere on June 21 but there was no respite at Bognor for it was immediately replaced by No 83 Group Support Unit. This organisation, with its stock of replacement pilots and over 100 immediate reserve aircraft, had been at Redhill, right under the flight path of the V-1s which were now coming over in ever-increasing numbers. Many of the flying bombs fell short of London and an explosion amongst the packed lines of aircraft at Redhill would have been disastrous, so a hasty move was made and Bognor was soon swamped by Mustangs, Typhoons and Spitfires. Also in from Redhill were ambulance Ansons of No 1310 Flight. During July they carried blood plasma into the Normandy bridgehead but, replaced by Dakotas, the Flight disbanded at the end of the month to become No 83 Group Communications Squadron. All this activity inevitably brought accidents, a Mustang III crashlanding on August 9, while on September 11 another made a hasty arrival with an engine fire and collided with an aircraft awaiting take-off clearance, resulting in the death of the pilot.

No 83 GSU moved to Thorney Island over September 25–26 and Bognor ALG was no longer needed. Property in the area was released during November and a Works Flight was soon engaged in removing the steel matting and reinstating the whole site for handover to the owners early in 1945. The road system has now been restored and, apart from the encroachment of the West Meads estate on the southern end, all the land has reverted to agriculture. There are no obvious signs of its wartime occupation.

Brenzett (Ivychurch), Kent

TR015280. 3 miles NW of New Romney off B2070

Built on 300 acres of Romney Marsh in the triangle formed by the B2070, B2081 and a minor road between Brenzett village and Ivychurch, this ALG was unusual in having its two runways in the form of a cross on the cardinal headings. Recommended by the Aerodrome Board as one of the best sites because the approaches were good, and there was local accommodation, Brenzett was approved by the Air Ministry in July 1942 and work on detailed plans and requisitioning formalities went swiftly ahead.

Dispersal and defence proposals were agreed and final authority for No 4 Works Squadron to start construction was issued on December 10. The work involved demolishing a bungalow, burying telegraph wires and closing two minor roads, in addition to considerable infilling of ditches. Moat House and the surrounding buildings on the eastern side of the ALG were taken over as accommodation.

Known locally as Ivychurch Landing Strip, the ALG was scheduled for completion on March 1 1943 and later that month was used for tentage-scaling trials prior to the deployment of fully mobile units to temporary airfields of this type. With two Sommerfeld Track runways, two Blister hangars and a few huts, but very little else, the ALG was released for grazing until September, when it was suddenly activated because Kingsnorth ALG was found to be in need of urgent repair. No 122 Squadron of 122 Airfield flew in its Spitfire IXs on September 14, but returned to Kingsnorth two days later. Brenzett then remained largely deserted until early 1944 when a programme of

A Second World War hut at Brenzett during 1969—thought to be one of the few ALG buildings on the site (D.G. Collyer).

general improvement of all ALGs was undertaken. When complete it had steel mesh taxiways, four large hardcore dispersals and five standard Blister hangars.

Brenzett appears to have remained unused during the build-up to D-Day except to accommodate ground signals units, but it was presumably on standby for air operations if needed. It came into its own when the battle against the V-1 flying bomb reached its height. Tempests and Spitfire XIVs had already been diverted on to Anti-*Diver* operations, and now it was the turn of the Mustangs. Nos 129 and 306 (Polish) Squadrons of 133 Wing, 84 Group, arrived from Ford on July 8 1944, followed two days later by 315 (Polish) Squadron. The next two months were hectic, with pilots living, eating and sleeping in tents alongside their aircraft, hardly thinking of anything except flying bombs. They were soon in action, 306 Squadron having their first success on July 12 when three V-1s were destroyed; by the time the worst was over, 133 Wing had accounted for 179 of these unpleasant weapons. They also managed to fit in a few other operations where their long range capabilities were vital, such as escorting Beaufighters of Coastal Command on a shipping strike off Norway, when they destroyed eight intercepting fighters for no loss.

The Wing put up 36 Mustangs for a *Rodeo* on August 18, No 315 Squadron pilots sighting an estimated 60 Fw 190s taking off from airfields around Beauvais. They swept into the attack, claiming 16 in a running fight and losing only one Mustang, but the pilot was their redoubtable leader, Squadron Leader

Herbaczewski, one of Poland's most brilliant wartime pilots. He was posthumously awarded the *Virtuti Militari* Class IV, the country's highest combat decoration.

Despite intensive flying and rapid deterioration of the ALG there were remarkably few accidents at Breznett, even when the Wing returned to its long-range bomber-escort role, penetrating deep into enemy territory. It also took part in Operation *Market*, escorting transports and glider combinations to Arnhem before moving to Andrews Field on October 10 1944.

The ALG and its accommodation was released by 11 Group in December 1944, and work started on clearing and renovating the site. The land returned to its owners in 1945 and with roads also restored there was soon little evidence of the airstrip except a few gaps in hedges and a concrete bridge or two across streams.

Using a building on the edge of the ALG which had been a Womens' Land Army hostel during the war, the Brenzett Aeronautical Museum was founded in 1972. It contains an interesting display ranging from pieces of Battle of Britain aircraft and engines to a 4½-ton Dambuster bomb. It is well worth a visit, though check first, for the museum is currently threatened with closure and it may be that the officers' quarter named *Brenzett* at Biggin Hill will be a more permanent reminder of this largely forgotten airfield.

Capel (Folkestone), Kent

TR260389. 2 miles NE of Folkestone alongside A20(T)

On February 4 1915, the German Admiralty declared unrestricted submarine warfare in the waters around the British Isles. A taste of German determination had already been given late in January and the British Admiralty reacted quickly. Not only were submarine bases in Belgium attacked but convoying was introduced in coastal waters, and new airship stations surveyed and built.

The Dover Straits was a natural shipping bottleneck and a submariners' dream. It therefore became top priority for an airship base and a site was speedily chosen at Capel le Ferne, high on the cliffs between Folkestone and Dover. Work started on clearing the site and erecting sheds during April, the first using the foundations of a bus garage as a base. Such was the urgency that, although far from complete, the station was commissioned on May 8 1915, the ratings being accommodated in four houses on the edge of the village while the officers took over Abbots Cliff House.

The first equipment consisted of the ex-Army ships *Beta*, *Delta* and *Gamma* but it was intended to operate the new SS Airships from Capel and, the day before the commissioning ceremony, the first of this type, the *SS1*, was sent down from Kingsnorth (Thames Estuary). Incredibly, this task was entrusted to young Flight Sub-Lieutenant R. S. Booth who had just completed his basic training, this delivery flight being his first cross-country! He was delayed in starting and it was dusk when he arrived over Capel where the landing party had laid out an illuminated arrow to indicate the direction of the wind. Booth took the arrow to indicate the direction of landing and therefore approached downwind, overshot the mooring party and collided with telephone wires alongside the main road. The wires tore the

The SS12 patrol airship alongside No 1 Shed at Capel, August 1915 (P. Liddle via G.S. Leslie).

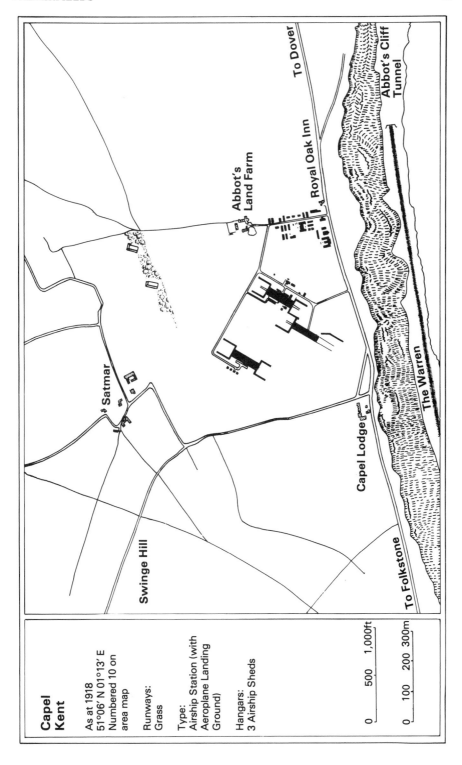

**Capel
Kent**

As at 1918
51°06′ N 01°13′ E
Numbered 10 on
area map

Runways:
Grass

Type:
Airship Station (with
Aeroplane Landing
Ground)

Hangars:
3 Airship Sheds

Swinge Hill

Satmar

Abbot's
Land Farm

Royal Oak Inn

To Dover

Abbot's Cliff
Tunnel

The Warren

Capel Lodge

To Folkstone

0   500   1,000ft

0   100   200   300m

envelope and in moments the *SS1* was ablaze, pilot and passenger jumping out on the very edge of 450 ft (137 m) cliffs. Amazingly, they escaped with minor burns.

It was an inauspicious start but the unit soon recovered and by the end of June four airships were in service on convoy patrol. When the first shed was complete and an attempt made to walk-in an SS type it wouldn't fit—the shed had been built to accommodate the smaller *Beta* type! The problem was soon overcome—a trench was dug in the floor centre into which the gondola car was lowered down a slope from ground level. This also allowed easier inspection of the envelope and supposedly resulted in the universally adopted name of 'Blimp' for coastal airships, because of the noise made when officers tested the tautness of the fabric.

Capel became one of the main assembly bases for the SS Type and, in the autumn of 1915, took over the construction of these airships from Kingsnorth. Rebuilds were also carried out, notable amongst them the *SS10* which had crashed into the Channel on September 10 1915. Just after midday on January 23 1916 a German seaplane appeared overhead Capel and dropped five bombs. They missed the sheds, but this audacious attack in broad daylight and the sight of another seaplane the following day, caused more than a few jitters.

The SS airships could stay airborne throughout the daylight hours, but they were extremely uncomfortable for the crew. During 1916 a pusher type car was designed and built at Capel and, when fitted to a SS envelope, it was found to be very much better than the standard cramped and draughty cockpit. The new airship became known as the SS *Zero* and was soon in production.

Convoys were also protected by kite balloons, and some of these were kept at Capel, while landplanes paid occasional liaison visits. Convoy escorts were usually uneventful but for the crew of the *SSZ1* there was excitement when a conning tower suddenly appeared at two miles' range. They attacked as the submarine submerged, two bombs being dropped on the swirl. A large patch of oil mixed with air bubbles immediately started to spread and as ships in the area moved in, Captain N. Grabowsky flew *SSZ1* back to Capel, loaded up with more bombs and returned to the scene. He dropped another 65 lb (30 kg) bomb on the oil patch but could only claim the submarine possibly damaged.

The *SSZ1* went to Dunkirk in September 1916 but other airships replaced it at Capel and during 1917 the cross-Channel transports on the Folkestone-Boulogne run were regularly escorted. When the RAF took over in April 1918 the station became part of No 5 Group, which embraced the whole of the Dover area. Now officially known as Folkestone, the Capel airship base had three large sheds fitted with windbreaks at each end and five operational SSZ ships on strength, in addition to others under construction or repair. Personnel were accommodated in extensive wooden hutting close to the Royal Oak Inn, and at the sub-stations at Godersham Park and Wittersham. At the end of the war Folkestone had seven SSZs and two SSTs (a twin-engined version) in operation, but with the Armistice the tempo slackened, and despite the proven efficiency of the small non-rigid airship in coastal waters they were gradually withdrawn. Capel/Folkestone was closed in 1919, the land and buildings being passed to the Disposal Board in August 1920.

In 1933 the old Capel station was used for an air display and the one remaining airship shed, visible for miles, was used as a turning point for many a pre-war air race, and for the Folkestone Trophy Race resurrected briefly in the immediate post-war years. During World War 2 the site was used for a wireless station, monitoring frequencies used by German aircrew during the Battle of Britain, and one mast survives. The Blue Channel Caravan Park occupies part of the original site and uses airship shed foundations as hardstandings on which the lowered floor section is still plainly visible.

Opposite page top to bottom
Perhaps the dazzle painting was overdone? The SHQ site under construction (Folkestone Local Collection).

Three airship sheds, the wind break for No 3 under construction (Folkestone Local Collection).

The Blue Channel Caravan Park occupying the foundations of one of the airship sheds at Capel (D.G. Collyer).

An irresistible tailpiece—a sad looking partially-inflated SS airship at Capel (Folkestone Local Collection).

Chailey, East Sussex

TQ370192. 3¼ miles E of Burgess Hill on minor road

Built on Bower and Great Homewood Farms in heavily wooded Sussex Weald countryside, the two landing strips making up Chailey ALG were laid with the intersection practically on the minor road from Godleys Green to Plumpton Green, and were extremely well camouflaged by trees. In common with other ALGs, the site was surveyed early in 1942, the plans being sent to Fighter Command for final approval and the addition of dispersals on December 28. The land was requisitioned in January 1943 and work started very soon afterwards with an expected completion date in June. High tension cables had to be buried and trees felled but the demolition of the Plough Inn on the western boundary was undoubtedly the most unpopular decision locally.

Sommerfeld Track runways and connecting taxiways were laid, but it was otherwise an extremely rudimentary site with no domestic accommodation, being intended solely for occupation by mobile squadrons living in tents. During the autumn and winter of 1943/44 the land was released for grazing while four Blisters were erected and three large hardcore dispersals constructed. It was not re-opened until April 1944 when No 131 Airfield, No 84 Group, 2nd TAF, consisting of three Polish squadrons, moved in on the 26th from neighbouring Deanland.

The three squadrons, Nos 302, 308 and 317, had been practising with 500 lb (227 kg) bombs on their Spitfire IXs, and they were soon engaged on *Rangers* over France, attacking communications, airfields and military installations. Operations were largely without loss, though a No 308 Squadron Spitfire was destroyed and another badly damaged by intense flak during a *Rhubarb* south-west of Dieppe on May 21. Accidents at Chailey were also rare and mainly caused by the steel matting which tended to ride up and tear tyres to ribbons—the Spitfire being particularly prone to this damage. On May 15, No 131 Airfield became No 131 Wing and when the Wing Leader was summoned to a top-level conference on June 2 everyone guessed that things were moving at last. Invasion stripes were painted on the aircraft and personnel confined to camp, though this must have been a little difficult under canvas in the woods!

No 131 Wing's task on D-Day was low-level cover over the beach-head and this continued for the rest of their stay at Chailey though some anti-*Diver* patrols were also flown. The Wing moved to Appledram on June 28 in the general surge forward as coastal airfields became available and Chailey's short operational career was over. Probably the last aircraft to use it was a Lysander of No 161 Squadron which force-landed there on October 18 1944 and was written off in the process. Pressure to release the site was already being applied, but the main interest was to recover the steel tracking and this was taking the Works Flight longer than expected.

Chailey was officially derequisitioned by No 11 Group on January 20 1945 and with the area cleared, the position of the runways can now only be determined by gaps in hedges. Only one building remains, a brick structure with a flat concrete roof. Similar to solitary brick buildings on other ALGs (see Coolham), its purpose remains obscure but it could have been an ammunition store.

Chattis Hill, Hampshire

SU335355/SU320355. 2½ miles W of Stockbridge on A30

A windy hill on the Downs above the River Test does not recommend itself as an aerodrome, yet Chattis Hill performed this duty during both World Wars. The site on Houghton Downs (*SU335355*) was prepared during the summer of 1917 and first occupied by Nos 91 and 93 Squadrons, both newly formed on September 1 1917, and joined by No 92 Squadron a fortnight later from London Colney. No 91 Squadron was used for wireless training, employing a variety of Corps reconnaissance aircraft such as the BE 2C, FK 8 and RE 8, while Nos 92 and 93 were intended as fighter-training units, the former with Avro 504Ks, Pups and Spads, and the latter with SE 5As. Bessoneaux hangars were erected near Chattis Hill House alongside the main road and a tented camp was established on the western side, but many of the personnel were billeted in Stockbridge, the officers using the Grosvenor Arms as their Mess. The 120-acre landing field sloped markedly towards Chattis Hill House and was not very satisfactory, the area around the hangars becoming a morass and the rest badly rutted.

Despite these poor conditions, the RFC persevered and only No 92 Squadron was extracted from the Chattis Hill mud, going to Tangmere in March 1918. The other two were joined by No 34 TS from Castle Bromwich and No 43 TS from Ternhill, both equipped with Avro 504Ks and a small number of Camels. They got down to the serious business of flying training early in April 1918 as the School of Wireless Telegraphy arrived from Biggin Hill. A couple of months later the latter organisation absorbed No 91 Squadron and started short courses for pilots and observers, and somewhat longer ones for W/T officers and mechanics.

More rationalisation occurred on July 15 when the two TS became No 43 TDS as part of No 34 Wing, No 8 Group. Established with 36 Avro 504Ks and 36 Camels, No 43 TDS also had a few obsolete Pups, used by the instructors for weekend and leave jollies to avoid having to go by train!

An American Construction Unit moved in to build a more permanent station. This involved the erection of six 180 × 100 ft aeroplane sheds and an Aircraft Repair Shed on the main technical site, while quarters and messes were built for the men on the eastern side of the field, and accommodation for WRAFs near Houghton Down Farm.

The clash of interests between the TDS,

Looking west across Chattis Hill in July 1941. The Spitfire assembly sheds can just be seen in the woods, but the 'gallops' very successfully disguise the current use of the large field (via E.B. Morgan).

whose Avros and Camels were continually buzzing around the circuit like angry bees, and the staid Wireless School machines trailing yards of wire, was the source of much anxiety but in fact there were no incidents. Personnel had moved into hutted accommodation just before the Armistice, but the technical site, including the hangars, was not completed, the Americans immediately stopping work. Flying also stopped while station personnel went into Southampton to celebrate.

After Christmas 1918, aircraft were flown in for storage from other aerodromes in the area, but there was little check on them and many were used until unserviceable and then broken up. Chattis Hill was still open in June 1919 but winding down, and it was abandoned later that year or early in 1920. The unfinished hangars were dismantled and the huts auctioned, leaving just concrete bases (*SU331354*) and a single MT garage building later converted into a bungalow.

For 20 years the Downs resounded to nothing more warlike than the galloping hooves of exercising racehorses. Then, when the Supermarine factories at Woolston and Itchen were bombed, the plans already made for dispersal of Spitfire production became top priority and were extended to include assembly airfields to supplement Eastleigh. The Southampton area choice was Chattis Hill where the assembly sheds could be erected in the woods on the northern edge of the First World War aerodrome, and the gallops immediately to the west used as the test and delivery airfield (*SU320355*). It was hoped the tracks made by horses would disguise the new use of the field which was large enough for Spitfires without any immediate changes, while the

The Chattis Hill assembly sheds with Spitfires hidden under the trees (Vickers Ltd via E.B. Morgan).

sheds would be camouflaged by clearing just sufficient woodland to lay the foundations, pulling back the trees with ropes while prefabricated sections were assembled, and then allowing them to spring back into their natural position and break up the factory outline.

Supermarine took over the site in December 1940 and the first Spitfires were completed three months later, most of them being flown out by the ATA based at Hamble. Initially a detachment of No 1 Ferry Pilots' Pool, the Hamble unit became No 15 FPP in September 1941 when established with female pilots. Their Anson and Argus taxi planes became a common sight at Chattis Hill, which was also designated as their emergency base in the event of invasion.

Production assembly of Spitfires remained the task of Chattis Hill for the rest of the war, the only change in its appearance being the felling of trees to provide a better approach to the strip, when the war was well advanced and the need for secrecy not so important. Flying ceased in 1945 but the assembly sheds were not immediately relinquished by Supermarine and the site was not closed until May 31 1948. The sheds were later removed and the foundations used for many years as a dump for roadstone by the County Council. These foundations and a few brick buildings deep in the woods are the only remaining signs of a very important World War 2 airfield—little known then, and largely unrecognised since, as an *Action Station* in its own right.

Chilbolton, Hampshire

SU392383. 1 mile S of Chilbolton village, off A3057

Intended as a dispersal site for the bomber base being built at Middle Wallop, the 145 acres of land requisitioned from Manor Farm in 1939 lay on a plateau of some 300 ft (91 m) above the River Test and picturesque Chilbolton village. Work on the site was confined to the removal of hedges and some levelling to produce a large well-drained grass area.

By the time the work was completed, Middle Wallop was a Fighter Command Sector Station in No 10 Group with four squadrons on strength and it was a considerable relief when the Hurricanes of No 238 Squadron were dispersed to Chilbolton on September 30 1940. Heavily engaged in defensive operations, No 238 Squadron continued in the front line during October, a Bf 110D of ZG 26 being shot down near Portsmouth on the 1st, and during the October 7 attack on Westland's Yeovil factory another Bf 110 and a Ju 88 of II/KG 51 were destroyed, for the loss of one squadron Hurricane.

Activities tailed off during November as the Luftwaffe turned to night raids, but No 238 Squadron remained at Chilbolton throughout the winter until finally stood down on May 1 1941 in preparation for a move to the Middle East. No 308 (Polish) Squadron Spitfire IIAs appeared briefly during June 1941, soon replaced by No 501 Squadron who employed their Spitfires on convoy patrols and night interceptions, the CO gaining a rare nocturnal success by shooting down a German bomber over Portsmouth. They left for Ibsley in August and were replaced by another ex-Auxiliary squadron, No 504, working up after the loss of 'A' flight to No 81 Squadron, before changing places with No 245 Squadron. The latter went on the offensive with their new Hurricane IIBs, employing them on *Roadsteads* over Northern France. When the weather got too bad for this work in December, No 245 Squadron moved to Middle Wallop and the pilots tried their hand at night flying.

It was decided to upgrade Chilbolton, though it remained grass-surfaced. A concrete perimeter track was laid, and a number of fighter hardstandings were built, some with double blast pens. Technical accommodation included three Blister hangars and more land was obtained for domestic sites, the airfield being declared a full No 10 Group satellite in April 1942.

While being rebuilt, Chilbolton served as a RLG for Army Co-op Tomahawks of No 41 OTU, Old Sarum, this unit continuing to use the airfield until November 1942 when it was transferred to No 70 Group and immediately reduced to C&M. On December 7, No 38 Wing took over and Chilbolton became Netheravon's satellite in place of Shrewton. The Night Flying Flight of the Glider Pilots' Exercise Unit moved in their Tiger Moths, joined during January 1943 by the remainder of the unit. The air resounded to the noise of straining Bristol Mercurys as Master II tugs hauled a never-ending stream of Hotspur gliders into the air.

Exercise *Spartan*, the largest military exercise held to date in the British Isles, took place during February/March 1943. It involved all home-based Army Co-operation and ground attack units in mobility exercises and field operations, Nos 174 and 184 Hurricane Squadrons arriving at Chilbolton on March 1 for 12 days under canvas. With the end of *Spartan*, Chilbolton lapsed into comparative slumber, soon made absolute when the airfield returned to No 70 Group on April 21 for redevelopment prior to hand-over to the USAAF. The GPEU returned to Netheravon on May 8 1943 and Works and Bricks moved in to supervise a complete rebuild of the airfield. More land to the south-west was obtained bringing the total to 345 acres, and allowing the construction of a standard three-runway airfield. Forty-eight loop type hardstandings were dispersed around the extended perimeter track and two 'T2' hangars joined the Blisters.

Chilbolton returned to No 10 Group,

Fighter Command, on June 1 and, with work on the airfield complete, it re-opened on December 6 1943 for occupation by the IXth AF. Their first permanent unit, the 5th Tactical Air Depot from Zeals, was joined by the 368th FG which arrived from Greenham Common on March 15 1944. The three squadrons in the Group (395th, 396th and 397th FS) flew P-47 Thunderbolts and were soon in action bombing and strafing airfields, bridges, trains and V-weapon sites in Northern France, intensifying operations as the invasion date got closer. When it came they were very active in support of the landings, making a special effort on D + 1 when V Corps was pinned down on the beach. Concentrating on five German gun positions, they successfully neutralized them with 1,000 lb (454 kg) and cluster bombs. Operations continued from Chilbolton until June 19 when the Group became one of the first to be transferred to France.

The airfield was then used by USAAF transports bringing in wounded American servicemen from the Continent on transfer to a large temporary hospital east of Stockbridge. IXth TCC operations were also mounted from Chilbolton, the 442nd TCG moving in from Boreham on re-assignment to the 53rd Wing on September 11 and making large-scale supply flights to Normandy the next day. The three squadrons (303rd, 304th and 305th TCS) remained at Chilbolton, the base being sealed on the 14th when troops of the 501st and 506th Parachute Infantry Regiments began to bivouac on the airfield. Shortly after 10:00 hours on September 17, 45 C-47s from the 442nd took off, part of the first wave taking the 501st PIR to a DZ near Veghel for Operation *Market*, the attempt to break through into Holland. Despite suppression by escorting P-51s, flak was heavy as they started their run in to the DZ but the drop pattern was good and the troops were soon in possession of Veghel town. A second wave of 45 aircraft from the 442nd followed with an excellent drop of the 506th PIR near Zon, and the following day the 442nd towed Hadrians to LZs in the Nijmegen area. They then transferred to Greenham Common for further back-up missions, using Chilbolton as a servicing base. The Group moved to the Continent in October but ambulance flights continued into Chilbolton and, on Christmas Day 1944, dozens of C-47s suddenly arrived to fly out the 17th

Chilbolton photographed in October 1946 when occupied by No 3MU. The typical bomb dump layout is plainly visible on the south side, as are the old fighter pens built in 1940 when it was little more than a large grass field (DoE/Crown Copyright).

Airborne to plug the gap made by Von Rundstedt's forces in the Ardennes. So sudden was the order to move that many troops were only able to grab pieces of Christmas turkey as they left their camp at Barten Stacy. A trail of discarded bones along the road to the airfield marked their route!

Chilbolton returned to the RAF in March 1945 when No 41 OTU re-appeared, this time as a complete unit. Flying Hurricanes, Spitfires, Masters and Martinets, the OTU was still engaged on fighter recce training, disbanding on June 26, when No 61 OTU, Keevil, took over the task.

Chilbolton now became a forward air-field in the Middle Wallop sector of No 11 Group. No 183 Squadron, which had recently relinquished its Typhoons, arrived to join the resident No 26 Squadron in converting to the superb Spitfire XIV. No 26 Squadron left for the Continent in August, exchanging places with No 247 which used Chilbolton to convert to the new Centaurus-powered Tempest II, followed by No 183 which abandoned its Spitfires to join No 247 in forming the first Tempest II Wing. This was intended for Tiger Force operations against Japan under the leadership of Wing Commander R.P. Beamont, but the end of the war stopped that and the Wing remained at Chilbolton, taking part in the Battle of Britain flypast in September and Exercise *Funfair* in November. No 183 was renumbered No 54 Squadron and found itself converting pilots destined for Middle East units, while No 247 Squadron was earmarked as the first Vampire squadron.

Geoffrey de Havilland gave an impressive display of the Vampire I during March 1946 and later that month the first aircraft arrived for No 247 Squadron. Shortly afterwards an unusual ceremony took place, involving the presentation of a Tempest II, *MW833*, to No 54 Squadron. In May 1941, a member of the RCAF had conceived the idea of using the sixpence a day awarded to the recipients of the DCM to form a fund from which an aircraft could be purchased. The donation scheme was agreed and No 54 Squadron was chosen to receive it and, at last, the fund had raised enough to buy a Tempest. It was dedicated on behalf of Canadian soldiers and airmen, and named *Canadian*

The Gnat trainer prototype at Chilbolton during its early flight trials, 1959 (Folland Aircraft Ltd).

DCMs. The squadron left for Odiham on June 26 followed by No 247 two days later, together with the Servicing Echelons and No 1007 Servicing Wing. Left behind was a C&M party, a few German PoWs, and personnel from Nos 3 and 49 MUs. The latter departed on July 4 after clearing up their site, leaving No 3 MU in occupation, the airfield parented by Middle Wallop, until November 1946 when it was abandoned.

In February 1947 Vickers-Amstrong Ltd transferred their Flight Test Centre from High Post, which was rapidly becoming untenable as the A & AEE Boscombe Down expanded. They erected an assembly shed alongside a 'T2' hangar on the south side of the airfield, allowing the remaining sites to become derelict, though there was so little accommodation in the local area that some technicians were forced to 'squat' in ex-RAF huts.

Most early test work at Chilbolton concerned the Attacker but development work which finally led to the ill-fated Swift started in December 1948 when the Supermarine 510 made its first flight from Chilbolton, and it continued in use for trials work on the Supermarine 535, and

on the Swift itself.

The Swift development programme was hampered by many problems and it was not until February 26 1953 that ground staff were rewarded with a sonic bang aimed at the airfield from the prototype —this being the required proof of successful barrier penetration in those days. It was also in 1953 that Folland Aircraft Ltd moved into Chilbolton, taking over the ex-RAF 'T2' hangar on the eastern side of the airfield, initially for storage and then, following construction of the diminutive Fo 139 Midge, as a Flight Development Unit. The Midge arrived in August 1954 and was used for pilot evaluation until it crashed on September 26 1955 after failing to get airborne properly.

With the rapid rundown of Swift production in the mid-1950s, Supermarine decided to relinquish Chilbolton and left in 1957. Folland retained the airfield to continue trials on their Gnat fighter and pre-production trainers, the first of which commenced flight testing at the end of August 1959. Several more Gnats were flown before Folland moved to Dunsfold in 1961 and Chilbolton again lay abandoned.

Work started in 1963 on the construction of an observatory for the Radio Research Station, Slough, using the runway intersection as the foundations, and it was opened on April 14 1967 by the late

Top *The massive 'dish' of the Chilbolton Observatory now dominates the centre of the old airfield* (Appelton Observatory).

Above *The Bellman hangar on the south side of Chilbolton in use as a grain store, August 1981* (K.S. West).

Rt Hon A. Crosland. The Out-Station has undergone several changes of name over the years, and is now called the Rutherford Appleton Laboratory of the Science & Engineering Research Council, the Chilbolton Observatory being used for communications' research and tropospheric propagation trials.

The remainder of the airfield was sold by auction and the Supermarine assembly sheds converted into a grain store. A dispersed communal site to the east of the airfield is still in good condition as are parts of the runways. In 1979 a crop-spraying firm, Agricopters Ltd, bought a

3½ acre plot on the edge of the airfield and now operates several helicopters and a light aircraft—flying has returned to Chilbolton.

Coldharbour (Egerton/Headcorn), Kent

See Headcorn

Coolham, West Sussex

TQ125222. 6 miles SSW of Horsham

Built on open farmland just south of the River Adur and close by Coolham village, this ALG was surveyed in 1942 and the site plans, approved in December were issued to the Works Construction Unit on January 31 1943. The land was taken over against strong opposition from the Ministry of Agriculture but work went ahead to grade the site and lay two Sommerfeld Track runways, the main SE/NW one being 4,500 ft (1,372 m) long. In July 1943 re-alignment of a perimeter track was undertaken to save Farley's farmhouse but other property had to be removed and considerable tree felling took place before completion. When the construction team moved out, the ALG was cleared for grazing and not used until the build-up for *Overlord* was well advanced.

It was opened on April 1 1944 when Nos 306 and 315 (Polish) Squadrons of No 133 Airfield arrived from Heston. They were joined by No 129 Squadron two days later, the RAF unit immediately starting conversion to the Mustang III while the Poles continued training. Unfortunately this was not without loss, a Mustang of No 315 Squadron breaking up in the air and another of 306 Squadron crashing while attempting an overshoot after hitting the ground on the approach. The first operational sorties from Coolham were on April 26 when 129 and 315 Squadrons went on a sweep over Beauvais. No 306 Squadron joined in three days later and throughout May the squadrons were heavily involved in *Ramrods* and *Rangers*. Though intended as a tented camp, both Sauceland and Farley's farmhouses were used for accommodation and, with the village close at hand, Coolham certainly proved one of the more comfortable ALGs.

On May 15 the airfield became No 133 Wing of No 84 Group, 2nd TAF, all three squadrons being highly tuned by the end of the month after flying many sorties

Very similar to the sole remaining building at Chailey is this brick and concrete hut at Coolham ALG—anyone know its precise purpose? (M.L. Asquith).

deep into Occupied Europe and becoming proficient at dive bombing. As invasion forces hit the Normandy beaches early on June 6, No 133 Wing Mustangs were standing by to escort the second wave of tugs and gliders. The Luftwaffe was generally conspicuous by its absence but No 129 Squadron caught a Fw 190 trying to get amongst the glider tugs and it was quickly shot down.

Low-level reconnaissance and *Ramrods* followed, an intensive sortie rate being maintained for days in the face of very effective German flak which produced heavy losses, for the Mustang was peculiarly vulnerable to AA gunfire. Such damage following an attack on tanks south of Cherbourg resulted in an almost unique rescue. Warrant Officer T. Tamowicz of No 315 Squadron was seen to force-land in marshland by his CO, Squadron Leader E. Horbaczewski, DSO, who promptly landed on a half-constructed airstrip nearby, borrowed a Jeep, drove to the crash site, then waded out and extricated the injured man from the aircraft. Back at the airstrip both squeezed into the cockpit of the Mustang which Horbaczewski flew back to England where amazed groundcrew watched two pilots get out of a cockpit only just large enough for one. Accidents also continued to take their toll, a bomb dropping off and badly damaging a taxying Mustang of No 129 Squadron at Coolham on June 15, while two days later another aircraft hit trees on take-off.

With better airfields available as units moved to the Continent, No 133 Wing started transferring to Holmsley South on June 22 and was completely clear of Coolham four days later. In their place came another No 84 Group unit, No 135 Wing (Nos 222, 349 and 485 Squadrons), whose Spitfire IX fighter-bombers hit

German forward troops around the steadily extending beach-head during their five days at Coolham.

The departure of No 135 Wing meant that the short, hectic career of Coolham ALG was over. External gun sites were cleared in October 1944, but release of the airstrip was delayed into the New Year while steel mesh was lifted. Perhaps this was just as well for, on January 19 1945, a USAAF Liberator made an emergency landing. After repairs it was flown out on the 26th and with the remaining Sommerfeld Tracking removed, the ALG soon reverted to agricultural use.

Present day evidence of the land's wartime use is confined to lengths of perimeter tracks used as farm roads and a solitary brick building which was probably a defence post, or an ammunition store.

Cowdray Park (Midhurst), West Sussex

SU925203. 2½ miles E of Midhurst on minor road

Overlooked by the South Downs on one side and the 919 ft (280 m) Blackdown on the other, Cowdray Park, one of the loveliest estates in Southern England, is an unlikely spot for a landing ground of any sort, but pre-World War 2 Lord Cowdray used his polo field as an occasional aerodrome, usually referred to as Midhurst or South Ambersham. It was on gently sloping ground between the railway and a minor road from Selham to South Ambersham which provided a maximum landing run of 2,250 ft (686 m) E/W and 1,650 ft (503 m) N/S.

With a steadily increasing aircraft

storage problem at Lee-on-Solent and the constant threat of German air attack on south coast airfields, the Admiralty decided to disperse stocks in a similar fashion to that adopted by RAF MUs—to satellite LGs. They chose the South Ambersham field, renamed it Cowdray Park, and commissioned it as part of *Daedalus* in June 1941. No obvious Service-design buildings were erected, control being exercised from a single HQ bungalow on the south side of the road. There was also a small workshop, medical dispensary, fuel bunker, ammunition store and 25 Dutch Barn hangars dispersed widely both north and south of the road. Each barn was 20 ft (6 m) by 40 ft (12 m), capable of concealing one or two aircraft with their wings folded. Domestic accommodation for one officer and 43 men was obtained in South Ambersham.

The landing ground was usually obstructed and aircraft were never left out on the field, being moved into a Dutch Barn immediately after arrival and only coming out for engine runs, or on departure. Cowdray Park remained in use for the remainder of the war and there are reports of its use for circuits and bumps by Proctors during 1944/45. It was paid off on September 30 1945 and after a short period on C&M the site was cleared and returned to the estate.

Deanland, East Sussex

TQ523118. 4½ miles NW of Hailsham off B2124

Surveyed during 1942, Deanland was one of the series of ALGs built for the projected 1943 invasion of Europe. The plans were approved in December and the land,

Looking east across the site of Deanland ALG in April 1943. The removal of hedges and the grading is plainly visible, but this ALG was obviously still without Sommerfeld Track or any other facility (RAF Museum W12/17/1).

including a dispersed gun site, was requisitioned early in 1943. It included pasture either side of the Golden Cross to Ripe road which itself was closed on March 2 1943. Initial preparation work, including grading and the removal of hedges, was then completed and the ALG cleared for grazing.

No 16 Airfield Construction Group of the RE arrived on July 2 1943 to upgrade the ALG. Two Sommerfeld Track runways were laid in the form of a cross, together with extensive steel plank taxitracks. Later, four Over Blister hangars were erected and four 200 ft (61 m) by 100 ft (30 m) concrete hardstandings laid, but there was no domestic accommodation. Deanland was for mobile squadrons using tents.

A landing was made two days after completion of the first runway, but it was not planned—a wounded Spitfire pilot had put down on the first place he saw. Then, on September 6 1943, a B-17F Fortress of 306th BG, VIIIth AF, crash-landed at Deanland after becoming lost and short of fuel during a raid on Stuttgart. Officially the ALG remained closed until April 1 1944—under the watchful eye of RAF Friston.

The Poles (Nos 302, 308 and 317 Squadrons) of No 131 Airfield, 84 Group, 2nd TAF, moved in on opening day and, with tents pitched, got down to the strange business of operating their Spitfire IXs from a forward airstrip. Only recently converted to the fighter-bomber rôle, they trained hard, but also managed some escort work and even the odd *Ranger* before being moved to Chailey on April 26 as part of their mobility training.

Three days later No 149 Airfield arrived from Castle Camps to look after three squadrons, Nos 64 and 611 from Coltishall and No 234 from Bolt Head. They provided escorts for the Bostons and Mitchells of No 2 Group, and the B-26 Marauders of the IXth AF, which were busy softening up the defenders of the Atlantic Wall. Occasional light relief was provided by train-busting and anti-shipping strikes when the low-level performance of their obsolescent Spitfire Vs could be used to the full.

On D-Day itself, No 149 Wing (redesignated from 'Airfield' on May 15) was operating at full stretch over the beach-head. No 611 Squadron was airborne at 03:00 hours and laid claim to being the first British fighter unit over the American *Gold* and *Omaha* beaches. No 234 escorted tugs and gliders and also bombed German forward positions, but none of the pilots saw any Luftwaffe activity until June 10 when Squadron Leader W.A. Douglas, DFC, the CO of No 611 Squadron, shot down a Ju 88 at night.

Deanland was uncomfortably placed on the V-1 route to London and the almost constant firing of AA defences, day and night, made sleep almost impossible. It was a relief when they landed for refuelling and rearming on Normandy airstrips, and a tonic when No 149 Wing moved to the West Country to re-equip.

After a lull lasting almost a month, Nos 91 and 322 (Dutch) Squadrons arrived from West Malling with Spitfire XIVs to continue their very successful war against the V-1 flying bomb. Deanland thus enjoyed a permanence rewarded by the construction of messes and some Nissen hut sleeping accommodation in the woods to the east of the airstrip. On August 16 No 345 (Free French) Squadron moved in from Shoreham and with the worst of the *Diver* menace over, the three squadrons started preparing for transfer to the Continent. This turned out to be a leisurely process and it was not until October that they moved out of Deanland and re-assembled at Biggin Hill. A month later the ALG closed and a Works Flight was soon lifting the Sommerfeld Tracking. The site was released on January 12 1945, but the road-closure order was not revoked until August 1947!

Tracking in the woods now forms the roadways of Deanland Wood Caravan Park and a number of hardstandings are used for farming activities. There are also reports of light aircraft using the strip occasionally.

Detling, Kent

TQ812594. 4 miles NE of Maidstone on A249

Tuesday, August 13 1940, was *Adler Tag* (Eagle Day), the start of the Luftwaffe's main assault on the south-east of England, as a prelude to invasion. The day passed quietly at Detling, but soon after the main evening meal started, with airmen and airwomen crowding the messes, 40 Stukas of LG 1 struck, having slipped through to dive-bomb without hindrance while escorting Bf 109s of JG 26 occupied Fighter Command. When they left, hangars were wrecked, all three messes badly damaged and the airfield extensively cratered. A total of 67 Service and civilian personnel died in the raid, a direct hit on the Operations Block killing the Station Commander. Twenty-two aircraft, mostly Ansons, were destroyed and others damaged, but none were fighters —the declared objective of the attack. Two WAAFs subsequently received the Military Medal for bravery, both remaining on duty throughout the bombing. Almost superhuman efforts got the essential services and Ops Room working by next morning, but it was a severe shake-up for the personnel, many of whom were locals.

In heavily wooded country up on the North Downs, the airfield at Detling resulted from a survey for air defence landing grounds made by the Directorate of Works early in 1915. Levelling of the rough turf was still in progress when a detachment of four Curtiss aeroplanes arrived in June, but these aircraft proved useless as fighters and, at the end of 1915, formed the nucleus of the RNAS Strategic Bombing Wing. Sopwith 1½-Strutter single-seat bombers started arriving late in February 1916 and the unit was renamed No 3 Wing, RNAS, two months later. It moved to Manston at the end of May when Delting was reduced to C&M.

The aerodrome remained dormant until transferred to the RFC on April 3 1917, when a detached Flight from No 50(HD) Squadron moved in. Flying BE 2Cs and BE 12s, this unit made day or night patrols over Kent whenever German airships or aeroplanes were reported in the area—but without success. They were replaced by the Camels of No 143 Squadron which formed at Detling on February 8 1918 and used the well-established Bessoneaux canvas hangars and accommodation tents which had served since the aerodrome opened. Development of the 95-acre site had started, however, two hangars being erected during the year, and the squadron was very active during the final series of German aeroplane attacks which culminated in a heavy night raid on May 18 1918 when 43 bombers set out for London. They were met by 84 defenders, among them the CO of No 143 Squadron, Major F. Sowrey. Near Maidstone he intercepted a Gotha and damaged it, the *coup de grâce* being given by a crew from No 141 Squadron. It was the only Detling victory but the German 3rd Bombing Squadron lost ten aircraft that night and never flew over Britain again. No 143 Squadron

received SE 5As but as the water-cooled engines took too long to warm up, the unit reverted to Camels, later receiving Snipes. It lingered on until disbanded on October 31 1919, Detling being abandoned the following December.

Farmland until the 1930s, Detling was selected as an Expansion Scheme station and rebuilt, with the then standard technical and domestic sites located near Binbury Manor. The grass aerodrome was developed to allow a maximum NE/SW landing run of 4,200 ft (1,280 m) and re-opened on September 14 1938 in No 6 (Auxiliary) Group of Bomber Command. No 500 (County of Kent) Squadron arrived from Manston and soon equipped with Hinds. On November 1 Detling transferred to No 16 Group, Coastal Command and No 500 followed suit, becoming a general reconnaissance squadron. Ansons arrived in March 1939, the Auxiliaries soon becoming accustomed to the peculiarities of twin-engines and retractable undercarriages.

Some 15,000 people flocked into Detling on Empire Air Day. Fiercely partisan, most of them were there to see the newly comouflaged Anson's of Kent's own squadron, soon to be embodied in the RAF as preparations for war accelerated. No 500 Squadron started patrols over the North Sea on September 3, and were soon involved in convoy work, but there was little action or excitement throughout the winter of 1939/40.

Things changed rapidly, however, with the German blitzkrieg of May 1940, the Ansons switching to operations off the French coast, and covering the Dunkirk evacuation at the end of the month. As the small boat armada crossed the Channel the Ansons searched for threatening E-Boats and even dive-bombed enemy-held harbours, so desperate was the situation. Losses mounted and some No 500 Squadron aircraft were fitted with extra guns and armour, while more Ansons and crews were provided by the Coast Artillery Co-operation Unit and a detachment from No 48 Squadron.

The number of aircraft at Detling rose dramatically when No 4 Squadron Lysanders and a veritable flood of naval aircraft arrived. Swordfish of 825 Squadron and Albacores of 826 carried out anti-submarine patrols, night recce, E-Boat attacks, bombardment spotting and even day bombing in the Calais area. Spotting during the bombardment of Calais was among the many hazardous

Above *Ansons of No 500 Squadron, Detling, in formation over Kent just before World War 2* (R.A. Budd).

Right *A vertical of Detling taken by the Luftwaffe in August 1939. The technical/ domestic site has been highlighted* (via D.G. Collyer).

operations by 825 Squadron, one aircraft under attack by two Bf 109s evading so violently that the observer was lost overboard. The Skuas of 801 and 806 Squadrons supplemented the fighter forces over Dunkirk beaches, while Blenheim fighters from Nos 235 and 254 Squadrons, which also arrived at the start of the Dunkirk evacuation, acted as a strike force.

No 500 Squadron flew to exhaustion during May. On the night of May 30/31, an Anson with bomb hang-ups developed engine trouble and crash-landed on the airfield. Hearing the noise, Corporal Daphne Pearson pulled on her clothes and ran from her billet towards the burning

aircraft, meeting two airmen staggering away from the wreck half-carrying a third. She took over from the dazed men and dragged the badly injured airman over a ridge, just as the Anson exploded about 90 ft (27 m) away. Her richly deserved Empire Gallantry Medal was later exchanged for a George Medal.

June 1 was a good day for Detling. No 254 Squadron shot down a He 111 and, when a No 500 Squadron Anson was attacked by nine Bf 109s they had such difficulty gauging the speed that one drew ahead of the lumbering 'Annie'. The pilot promptly shot it down with his single forward-firing gun, while the gunner hit another. Both Blenheim units returned to

their North Sea bases a few days later, but four Skuas and five Rocs of 801 Squadron, escorted by 12 Hurricanes, bombed gun emplacements at Cap Blanc Nez on June 21 and another Bf 109 fell victim to No 500 Squadron three days later.

No 53 Squadron, transferred from Army Co-op to Coastal Command, arrived from Gatwick early in July for attacks on French ports, but lost eight Blenheims during the *Adler Tag* raid on Detling when, in addition to the heavy death toll, 94 were injured. Immediate action was taken to accommodate all non-essential personnel off the station, while the aircraft were dispersed amongst trees and bushes. The original naval units had left before the raid but 812 Squadron arrived from North Coates with their Swordfish just in time to experience a new series of air attacks. These started during the afternoon of August 30 and continued until September 2 when an attack by 30 Do 17s wrecked a hangar and put the airfield out of action for a couple of hours. The pilot of a 111 Squadron Hurricane who landed with engine trouble as the raid developed had a very unhappy time—but survived!

Routinely covering inshore convoys, No 500 Squadron also went on shipping strikes for which some aircraft were fitted with a 20 mm cannon in the belly. When fired the effect was traumatic for those inside—presumably it frightened the enemy just as much! 812 Squadron went to St Eval in November and No 53 Squadron's Blenheims moved to Thorney, leaving Detling to the Ansons until the Swordfish returned in January for recce

A view north-east across Detling in September 1942. Filled in bomb craters are visible, as is the damage to the main technical site. The NE runway extension and dispersed Blister hangars are also identifiable (RAF Museum W13/5/3).

sorties over French ports—a task lasting two months. No 500 Squadron ceased operations on April 8 1941 and converted to Blenheim IVs, which it took to Bircham Newton at the end of May.

On the badly damaged technical and domestic sites, most of the original brick structures had now been demolished and replaced by temporary huts. A single Bellman was erected on the site of No 2 hangar and 14 Blisters were positioned on extensive new dispersals to the south of the main road and in the north-east corner of the airfield.

A detachment of Swordfish from North Coates, known as 816X Flight, moved in for anti-submarine patrols, but also found itself bombing gun positions on the French coast during April while, in June, 'D' Flight of No 2 AACU arrived from Gosport with Hectors, Sharks and Rocs to tow targets for naval gunners. The Swordfish detachment became 821 Squadron in July and soon went to Donibristle. Ansons re-appeared in February 1942 when No 280 (ASR) Squadron came from Thorney Island, but they only stayed until July before moving to Langham.

Detling was a tight airfield for large, heavy aircraft but on October 9 one of the first four-engined visitors certainly proved that it was usable in an emergency. Twenty miles west of Dunkirk a 92nd BG B-17E flown by Lieutenant Wiley was in collision with another Fortress. Two engines were disabled and a fuel tank ruptured but, after jettisoning his bombs, Wiley struggled back to the English coast and made a safe landing at Detling, quite an achievement under the circumstances.

The airfield remained a backwater, quietly transferring to Army Co-operation Command on January 1 1943. No 26 Squadron brought in its Mustangs before moving on to Stoney Cross for Exercise *Spartan*, and No 1624 Flight was re-formed from part of No 2 AACU to fly the Defiants and Martinets now replacing the earlier hotch-potch of obsolete types.

In March, Detling got its first taste of the Polish Air Force when No 318 Squadron formed with Hurricane Is as a fighter-reconnaissance unit for operations with the 2nd (Polish) Army Corps. They were not a happy bunch, considering recce work second rate and their mounts out of date. Disbandment of Army Co-op and transfer to Fighter Command on June 1 made little difference and the Poles' humour was not improved by the sight of Mustang Is of Nos 4 and 26 Squadrons, based briefly for operations during July. No 318 Squadron left for the Middle East on August 17 aboard the SS *Empress of Australia*, No 655 (AOP) Squadron going to North Africa at the same time in a much less glamorous ship, the SS *Indrapoera*. Equipped with Austers, 655 had arrived at Detling from Gatwick in April 1943 and spent the next few months training.

During October the three squadrons forming No 125 Airfield, Nos 132, 184 and 602, arrived from Newchurch as No 15 Fighter Wing, commanded by Wing Commander R. D. Yule, DSO, DFC & Bar. No 184 Squadron was unique in being equipped with Hurricane IVs, the other two having Spitfire IXs. The latter were used mainly on bomber escort work while No 184 found few targets for its bombs until it started to attack *Noball* sites in the New Year.

No 125 Airfield transferred to the 2nd TAF on November 15 1943 and No 1624 Flight re-formed as No 567 Squadron at the beginning of December. Heavy rain caused water-logging but bomber escorts continued unabated and the occasional fighter sweep sometimes tempted the Luftwaffe, as on December 21 when 40 Fw 190s pounced on the two Spitfire

squadrons near Cambrai. Two No 602 Squadron pilots were lost but a couple of '190s were shot down in the mêlée which followed.

The mines laid around the airfield during the invasion scare days of 1940 were lifted by Royal Engineers during the night of January 6 1944 and the following day the Spitfires were covering the withdrawal of B-17s and B-24s from attacks on communications in Western Germany. Four P-38 Lightnings had landed short of fuel on December 30, and were now followed by a B-17 Fortress of the 100th BG on January 21 1944 and a Liberator from the 446th BG, which belly-landed on the main runway on the 29th on return from Frankfurt. There was renewed Luftwaffe activity too, single-aircraft nuisance raids occurring almost nightly.

The two Spitfire squadrons changed places with No 118 and 453 Squadrons on January 18. No 184 was now undergoing Typhoon familiarisation, but continued to use the Hurricane on a few operations before moving to Odiham on March 6 for full conversion. No 453 Squadron flew its first mission in 2nd TAF on February 11, escorting B-26s; No 118 returned to ops three days later, but did not stay long and in March Nos 132 and 602 Squadrons returned, refreshed by Scottish air and ready for the run-up to the invasion. Fitted with bomb racks, the Spitfire IXs' main work was attacking V-1 sites, but escorts still continued. The Wing moved to Ford on April 18, being replaced a month later by an ADGB Spitfire Wing from Hornchurch (Nos 80, 229 and 274 Squadrons) which took on the familiar escort, fighter sweep and armed recce routine right through the period around D-Day.

On June 21 a V-1 came down on the north-eastern perimeter of the airfield, blowing out most of the windows of the camp. As if in reply the fighter-bomber Wing was moved out the next day and replaced by Nos 1 and 165 Squadrons for operations against the flying bombs. The speed and small size of the V-1 made it very hard to intercept, and its explosive load was lethal if it blew up during the final stages of an attack. Added to this were the dangers of collision with other pilots stalking the same *Diver*, balloon barrage cables and indiscriminate AA fire which rarely stopped while fighters were pursuing their quarry. No 1 Squadron flew their first anti-*Diver* patrols on June

24 and success came three days later. Others followed though, with the Spitfire IX only just able to catch a V-1, it was not easy. One pilot chased a flying bomb from Beachy Head to Gatwick before he caught it and succeeded in blowing off its port wing. As he turned away he hit a balloon cable which spun his Spitfire right round before the wing tip broke off and he was able to make a shaky landing at Gatwick.

Both squadrons moved to Lympne mid-July and were replaced by Nos 118, 124 and 504 Squadrons, who reverted to bomber escort and *Ramrods* for a month before dispersing. Detling then hosted Nos 1 and 165 Squadrons again but, with V-1s getting fewer, they returned to escort work in August. The pilots were briefed for a special op on September 17, escorting airborne forces on Operation *Market*. For the next nine days they flew intensively, covering transports re-supplying the troops on the ground. Then it was back to routine escorting until the middle of December when, with No 567 already gone, the fighter squadrons dispersed. Detling ceased to be an operational station on December 18 1944.

Grass airfields were surplus to requirements and in theory Detling was reduced to C&M on January 1 1945. In practice No 1336 Wing, RAF Regiment, moved in to run the Air Disarmament School using Nos 2814, 2878 and 2749 RAF Regiment Squadrons as staff. The authorities were afraid that Nazi fanatics would continue to resist after the German surrender. Detling was therefore laid out as a demonstration centre with booby-trapped buildings and equipment, while German-speaking personnel, dressed in German uniforms, gave Air Disarmament Unit trainees experience in dealing with

unpleasant situations they might face in Germany. What an outsider observing these activities made of them, can only be left to the imagination—they probably thought it was a film set!

On October 1 1945 the station was taken over by No 60 Group and No 75 Signals Wing established there in April 1946. No 141 Gliding School was formed and Southern Signals Area replaced the Wing at the end of 1946. It closed down in June 1947 leaving the airfield to the gliders, No 141 GS being replaced by No 168 GS in 1949 when the Reserve Command Gliding Instructors' School was formed. The latter became the Home Command Gliding Instructors School a year later and remained until November 1955.

During 1951–52 the station was occupied by a couple of Bomb Disposal Flights, but the gliding schools were the mainstay until January 1955 when No 1903 (AOP) Flight returned from Korea and moved into Detling with Auster AOP 6 aircraft to support 1 Infantry Division. When it moved to Feltwell in February 1956 and No 615 GS (No 168 renumbered) went to Kenley, the small station HQ was disbanded and the airfield reduced to C&M on April 1 1956.

Kent Gliding Club continued to use the airfield until they found a permanent site at Challock, but the C&M party was withdrawn on December 17 1956 and Detling became inactive, parented by West Malling until de-requisitioned on

Inside the Detling Bellman—a Slingsby Gull of Home Command Gliding Instructors School, June 1950 (P.H.T. Green).

October 1 1959. The Kent County Council acquired some land from the original owners to establish the County Agricultural Ground, Pye took over the old W/T station, and an Airways VOR/DME transmitter was located on the airfield.

The Bellman hangar and some smaller buildings are used by an industrial estate. Less obvious items remaining are the concrete pill boxes still guarding the perimeter, and the overgrown shelters which are so much a part of any Second World War airfield.

Dover (St Margarets/Swingate Down), Kent

TR335432. 2 miles NE of town alongside A258

As tension mounted in Europe during the early summer of 1914 the War Office was busy planning the despatch of the RFC to France, in the event of war with Germany. They needed a jumping off point in the south-east corner of England, and chose a site already used by aviators, on Swingate Downs high above Dover town.

When war actually came in August, No 6 Squadron RFC, donated its aircraft to other units and was sent to Swingate to clear a landing ground, organise fuel supplies and build a workshop. By the evening of August 12 the machines of Nos 2, 3 and 4 Squadrons had reached Dover and were ordered to France the next day, leaving one Flight of No 4 Squadron *in*

A Nieuport 10 of RNAS Dover at Swingate in 1916 with BE 2Cs and semi-permanent huts and hangars in the background (C.H. Brisley via D.G. Collyer).

situ for patrol work. The first machine across was as BE2A of No 2 Squadron, flown by Lieutenant H.D. Harvey-Kelly, who left Swingate at 06:25 hours and landed safely at Amiens two hours later. The rest were equally successful, the start of a flood which lasted over four years.

The strange collection of Henri Farmans, Avro 504s and BE8s that was No 5 Squadron, followed a few days later and, with the departure of the detached Flight at the end of the month, Dover LG was left deserted—the RFC had no more aeroplanes fit to send! The BE2Cs and RE5s of a revitalised No 6 Squadron staged through in October but then came a long break while new aviators were trained. The LG was converted into a proper aerodrome and when No 15 Squadron arrived in May 1915 it was well established with a long row of wooden sheds along the southern edge of the aerodrome, on top of those famous white cliffs. It was officially called Dover (St Margaret's), but more often known by its local names of Swingate or Langdon.

Officially preparing for overseas, No 15 Squadron was actually used as a training unit, continually losing pilots to front-line squadrons to replace losses. It also had to maintain one BE2C and pilot on standby each evening for anti-Zeppelin fighter patrols and No 9 Squadron was similarly employed, following its arrival in July 1915.

While work went ahead on more accommodation to house a flying school, the aerodrome became temporary host to the Machine Gun School for a month, before it moved to Hythe during November. No 12 RS was also formed at Dover but left immediately for Thetford and it was No 13 RS, raised on November

27 1915 as part of No 6 Wing, which became Dover's training unit.

When Nos 9 and 15 Squadrons left for France in December, No 13 RS took over the home defence commitment, but work-up of new units continued at Dover. The exposed position on top of the cliffs resulted in many accidents to the BE2Cs used for advanced training by No 13RS, several machines even falling over the cliffs onto the beaches below by over-running their landings! Training continued however, No 20 RS forming on February 1 1916, while No 49 Squadron acted as an advanced training school from April, to try and keep pace with the horrifying casualty rate experienced in France.

The near immunity enjoyed by Zeppelins finally persuaded the War Office to sanction specialist RFC home-defence squadrons. No 50 Squadron formed at Dover on May 15 1916 as one of these, becoming part of No 18 (HD) Wing the following month. Only variants of the unsuitable BE2C were available, but at least the pilots could concentrate on the role and success came nearer, though not near enough as Captain T.W. Woodhouse of No 50 Squadron found on August 24 as he strove to reach the L32, held in the Dover searchlight beams. The Zeppelin commander turned away into cloud but Woodhouse continued to climb and was rewarded with another glimpse of the silver cigar still some 2,000 ft (610 m) above him. In desperation he emptied a drum of ammunition at the huge envelope only to see the tracer fall short. While struggling to reload, Woodhouse lost the airship and, bitterly disappointed, gave up and allowed the probing searchlights to lead him home.

In October 1916 No 50 Squadron HQ moved to a mansion at Harrietsham and

A DH 4 at Swingate Downs—the airman is wearing an early form of life-saving jacket which looks extremely uncomfortable but was very necessary (C.H. Brisley via D.G. Collyer).

the Flights dispersed, leaving Dover to the training unit. No 20 RS had gone to Wye in June 1916, and No 49 Squadron became a bomber unit when RE7s were delivered during December. Using surplus personnel, No 64 RS formed early in April 1917 but left for Narborough almost immediately and, on June 1, the long-serving No 13 Training Squadron (re-designated from Reserve Squadron) swopped places at Yatesbury with No 62 TS. No 86 Squadron arrived from Shoreham as an advanced training unit in September and two months later No 49 Squadron crossed the Channel as an operational DH4 bomber unit. It was replaced by No 110 Squadron, but they only stayed a few days before going to Sedgeford where they changed places with No 65 TS.

The upshot of all this shuffling was that Dover (St Margaret's) became a two-squadron Training Station and work commenced on enlarging it. In place of the original corrugated iron-clad wooden sheds, five permanent hangars and an aircraft repair shed were built, together with more accommodation huts. Following the formation of the RAF, Training Depot Stations were introduced resulting in No 62 TS going to Houndslow and No 65 being expanded to become No 53 TDS on July 15 1918. The TDS was established with 24 Avro 504Ks and 24 Camels, the personnel strenth increasing to 570. By the summer of 1918 the station covered 219 acres and work had started on yet more accommodation, nominally for another

TDS, but in practice it was the Marine Operational Pilots' School which was formed at Dover to give specialised instruction on anti-submarine and convoy work, using either the DH6 or DH9, whichever was to be used operationally. The intended establishment of DH10s and Vimys was cancelled with the Armistice. Both 53 TDS and the Marine Operational Pilot's School closed during 1919 and soon after the cadre of No 3 Squadron disbanded in October, the aerodrome was closed to all except aircraft in distress.

The landing ground was derequisitioned in 1920, but the sheds were retained longer for storage purposes, then auctioned and removed. The site remained empty until 1938 when the wooden lattice towers of one of the first operational Chain Home radar stations appeared. It was also the location of a Chain Home Low station which despite bombing in 1940, remained in operation until some years after the war ended. Three of the radar towers have been retained for use by the Eurovision TV network and microwave communications system. On one of the old hangar floors a small granite plinth has been erected. A plate bears the following inscription: *'The Royal Flying Corps contingent of the 1914 British Expeditionary Force consisting of Nos 2, 3, 4 & 5 Squadrons flew from this field to Amiens between 13 & 15 August 1914'*—it is the only RFC memorial, simple but very moving.

Dover (Guston Road), Kent

TR325430. 1¼ miles NE of Dover town alongside A258

Amongst the air stations planned by the Admiralty in November 1912 was an aerodrome at Dover, needed to help defend the recently approved naval base in the harbour, as well as provide a departure point for France.

Progress was slow, for all available funds were rapidly expended on aircraft, repairs and the development of the first four air stations already building. By June 1913 a site between the old Fort Burgoyne and the Duke of Yorks' Military School had been selected, and the provision of aircraft sheds on a purpose-built aerodrome of some 55 acres was being considered. Its position 400 ft (130 m) above Dover on the fairly flat top of a hill was not ideal but had the overwhelming advantages of being on Government-owned land and in the right place.

Still incomplete at the start of World War One, the needs of the newly established RNAS base at Dunkirk and assumption of the UK air-defence task in September hastened its completion, and it was ready for a detachment of No 2 Squadron, RNAS, early in December. They soon returned to Eastchurch, replaced in January 1915 by No 1 Squadron, RNAS, which used the new aerodrome to complete its training and carry out the air-defence task.

The activities of Zeebrugge-based submarines was already worrying the Admiralty and on February 10 they assembled a motley collection of 30 machines at the Dunkirk and Dover bases with the intention of giving the German naval base a day to remember. The serviceable ones set off for Belgium on the 11th but bad weather prevented all but one from reaching the target. They were more successful on the 17th when seven floatplanes and 17 aircraft bombed Ostend and Zeebrugge dock installations but the largest bombs used weighed 100 lb (45 kg), so it was little more than a token effort.

An early Avro 504 at Guston Road, Dover during 1915. The hangar is of the type pioneered by Short Brothers at Leysdown (RAF Museum P948).

At the end of February 1915, 1 Squadron, RNAS, moved to Dunkirk leaving behind the Dover Defence Flight. This formed the nucleus of 4 Squadron, RNAS, on March 25 1915, but moved to Eastchurch leaving the aerodrome, now known as Dover (Guston Road) to develop as a training base.

The four original canvas hangars had now been supplemented by more permanent aeroplane sheds on the western side of the field with wooden accommodation huts and messes on the other side of the Dover-Guston road overlooking the entrance to the railway tunnel. It was a compact if rather cramped station equipped in October 1915 with seven BE2Cs, three Bristol Scouts, four Curtiss JN3s, three Sopwith 1½ Strutters, two Avro 504Bs, a couple of Vickers and eight dismantled Moranes.

No 5 Wing, RNAS, commanded by Squadron Commander Spenser D.A. Grey, was formed at Dover in March 1916 and almost immediately went to Coudekerque for operations, while back at Dover new pilots were trained for the type of work in the area. In July a big, but unsuccessful, effort was made to put the Tirpitz Battery out of action, continuous fighting patrols being flown from Dover and Dunkirk for two days to protect spotter aircraft plotting the fall of shot from a 12 in (30.5 cm) Dominion gun.

No 6 Squadron, RNAS, formed up at Dover on November 1 1916 only to take its Nieuport Scouts to Petit Synthe the following month, but the Dover Defence Flight remained in business, using black-painted BE2Cs for night work. Operations were on a wonderfully *ad hoc* and relaxed basis, it being recounted that a RNAS pilot waiting for passage to France volunteered to take a machine up during a raid alert on April 24 1917 only to crash the heavily-laden BE into the roof of the Duke of York's School, killing the observer. During 1917 really practical fighter scouts appeared at last and from time to time they were joined by RNAS squadrons resting from the Western Front.

No 218 Squadron formed on April 24 1918 with DH9s but moved over to Petit Synthe a month later, leaving Guston Road to use the same type of aircraft for inshore anti-submarine and coastal convoy patrols. In August 1918 the aircraft and crews of the former RNAS stations at Dover and Walmer were re-organised as No 233 Squadron, the DH9 element at Guston Road become No 491 Flight. Their efforts, combined with other units, virtually closed the Straits of Dover to German submarines, the six DH9s flying intensively until the Armistice. By January 1919 the Flight had been moved to Walmer and Dover (Guston Road) was virtually abandoned, though it was not finally closed until 1920.

There is no sign of the aerodrome now, most of it being covered by a large housing estate built in the late '70s for the Services.

Dover (Marine Parade), Kent (Marine)

TR326414. ½ mile from Dover town centre
Surely best known during World War One for the Royal Navy's romantic-sounding Dover Patrol, the town also boasted a seaplane base which barely covered two acres, but which held a prominent position in the area.

Dover's first sight of a military seaplane was probably on July 13 1912 when Commander Charles Samson, one of the RNAS pioneers, moored his Short S41 in the harbour overnight while returning to Harwich from the Portsmouth Naval Review, but despite selection as the site of a hydro-aeroplane (seaplane) station during 1913 nothing happened until the old torpedo-gunboat *Niger* was sunk off Deal pier by the submarine *U12* on November 11 1914. Though desperately short of floatplanes, the Admiralty then ordered Squadron Commander Bromet to take two Wight Navy planes to Dover and open up a base there. He arrived with Flight Commander Bigsworth on November 18 and requisitioned a skating rink on Marine Parade as a shed for the seaplanes. He also arranged for a slipway to be built enabling them to be man-handled up the beach and across the road. Despite the machines' unsuitability and the small, overcrowded harbour, which prevented take-off or alighting inside the breakwater, some flying was achieved, but they could do nothing at night, or during the day if the submarines kept their heads down, and sinkings continued unabated.

During December 1914 Bromet was instructed to keep two machines at readiness in case German seaplanes attacked coastal towns in the area. This must have provoked a hollow laugh, for it meant both his seaplanes and crews would always be on watch, and quite what the

Navy plane was expected to do, even if it got airborne in time, remained un-explained. Fortunately they were soon replaced by a variety of early Short seaplanes and, after the heavy sinkings of May 1915, by the much improved Short 184. In August 1915 most of the operational flying was transferred to Dunkirk, Dover assuming a training and repair role for which two additional standard 100 ft by 90 ft Admiralty sheds were erected alongside the skating-rink building, and a second slipway constructed.

In October 1915, Dover marine base had four Shorts, one FBA flying boat, seven Babies, two Schneiders and a single White & Thompson floatplane on strength, the scouts having been introduced to prevent German Navy seaplanes and airships interfering with Dover Patrol activities.

The rough sea and swell conditions at both Dunkirk and Dover led to the workshops devising an improved Short 184, which had enlarged main floats and streamlined wingtip floats and which was officially known as the Dover Type 184. New pilots spent a month at Dover learning about the special difficulties of the area before going over to Dunkirk.

With the formation of the RAF in April 1918 the Dover-based seaplanes joined No 5 Group and assisted in the Zeebrugge raid of April 22/23 by diverting enemy attention from the approaching naval forces. They then renewed their efforts against the U-boats and their combined air/sea patrols clearly started to take their effect, for few U-boats passed down the Channel after May 1918. In July there were four operational Short 184s at Dover

and, the following month, they and their crews were re-formed as No 407 Flight of No 233 Squadron, RAF, which had its HQ on Marine Parade and its other Flights at Dover (Guston Road) and Walmer.

No 233 Squadron was officially disbanded on May 15 1919 but it is probable that the Marine Parade base had already been vacated on March 26. The site was de-requisitioned in 1920 but Dover Harbour remained an official RAF flying-boat alighting area during the 1920s and 1930s and was occasionally visited by the current operational types. They made no use of the slipways and the area was not used at all during World War Two.

The Admiralty sheds soon disappeared but the ex-ice-skating rink stood until the late 1970s when it was demolished during a road-improvement scheme. Nothing now remains of the RNAS base, but its approximate position can be gauged from the nearby statue of C.S. Rolls which celebrates that pioneer's double crossing of the Channel on June 2 1910.

Dunsfold, Surrey

SQ027361. 6 miles SE of Godalming on A281
Set in beautiful heavily-wooded Surrey countryside, the stretch of pasture land just to the east of Dunsfold village attracted the attention of the Fighter

Dunsfold still without hangars and other essential accommodation a few days before handover in October 1942 (RAF Museum W13/6/5).

Command team surveying for ALGs and the Airfields Board, who saw it as a full-scale Army Co-operation aerodrome. The Airfields Board won and the site was requisitioned in April 1942 for development as a three-runway standard-pattern station with extensive dispersals on the eastern and southern sides.

Construction was largely undertaken by the Royal Canadian Engineers, who handed it over on October 16, but the domestic sites and airfield services were delayed by lack of materials, so it was not officially opened as RAF Dunsfold until early December 1942.

No 39 (Army Co-op) Wing, RCAF, moved in immediately, a detachment from No 400 (RCAF) Squadron arriving on December 4, followed next day by the whole of No 414 (RCAF) Squadron. Both squadrons flew Mustang Is and spent the first few months rushing off on detachments to Middle Wallop and the far south-west of England. They were joined by the newly formed No 430 (RCAF) Squadron on January 12 1943 and the whole Wing took part in Exercise *Spartan* during March, operating from a tented camp in the woods.

No 403 Repair & Servicing Unit used the facilities of Dunsfold from May 1943, though billeted at Alfold, and during the same month the Royal Canadian Engineers laid an experimental runway on the airfield. This was 3,600 ft (1,097 m) long and 150 ft (46 m) wide and consisted of 2-ply impregnated hessian, rather like heavy roofing felt, which was laid on a prepared surface and rolled flat. On June 23 a demonstration of this material was given, numerous take-offs and landings by aircraft up to the size of a Wellington being followed by deliberate damage to the surface. The hole was then filled with hardcore and a new covering applied—all in less than an hour.

With the disbandment of Army Co-operation Command on June 1 1943, Dunsfold became a fighter station with the units earmarked for the Tactical Air Force. The change in role to fighter reconnaissance was made official at the end of June and the accent on mobility was emphasised by the squadrons being grouped under Airfields. Nos 414 and 430 Squadrons moved to Gatwick while No 400 stayed at Dunsfold as the nucleus of No 128 Airfield, their first success coming on July 8 when two Mustangs from No 400 Squadron stumbled across a Fieseler Storch whilst attacking locomotives in Northern France.

The move of Nos 464 and 487 Squadrons' Venturas into Dunsfold was cancelled when it was decided to re-equip these units with Mosquitoes and, when No 128 Airfield transferred to Woodchurch on July 27, the airfield was left empty except for the aircraft of No 403 R&SU. A fortnight later, an advance party from Foulsham heralded the arrival of Mitchells of Nos 98 and 180 Squadrons which flew in on August 18 1943. Requisitioned property at Hall Place and Stovolds' Hill Farm was re-opened for the crews and the station rapidly filled up as Bomber Command diversions became common.

The first Dunsfold operation by the Mitchells was on August 23 when 24 aircraft bombed St Omer railway-marshalling yards. Early in September they

Mitchells flew from Dunsfold from August 1943 to October 1944. Sugar, a Mk II of No 180 Squadron, was a typical example of this very effective day bomber (RAF Museum P10392).

concentrated on Boulogne docks for Operation *Starkey*. By late October, 88 pilotless aircraft launching sites had been identified in northern France, and they were assaulted by No 2 Group Bostons and Mitchells, starting on November 5 with an attack on the large installation near Mimoyecques, south-west of Calais.

From December 1943 to February 1944 these *Crossbow* attacks were top priority and the Dunsfold Squadrons, now formed into No 139 Airfield as a self-contained mobile unit, were well to the fore, joined on February 18 by No 320 (Dutch) Squadron from Lasham. The V-1 sites, now generally known as *Noball* targets, were difficult to locate and heavily defended but towards the end of March 1944 other targets made a welcome re-appearance. On May 7, No 139 Airfield HQ went under canvas, leaving just a holding party to run Dunsfold, and a week later the airfield was transferred to No 11 Group, ADGB. No 139 Airfield became No 139 Wing, 2nd TAF, but continued to operate from Dunsfold as a lodger, with the *Overlord* task of night attacks on static targets.

During the night of June 6/7, 60 Mitchells were despatched against German communication bottlenecks, these attacks continuing each night until June 10, when a tank concentration was discovered at the Panzer HQ of Château de la Gaine. A large-scale operation was immediately laid on, 40 Typhoons and 71 Mitchells setting out, escorted by Spitfires. The Typhoons poured in rockets from low level, the Mitchells of Nos 98, 180, 226 and 320 Squadrons following with 436×500 lb (227 kg) MC bombs from 8,000 ft (2,438 m), the target disappearing in flame and smoke. It was a great success, reconnaissance showing that buildings and vehicles had been badly damaged and it was later learnt that General Von Dawans, German Chief of Staff, and his entire entourage had been killed.

With the bridgehead secured the Mitchells were switched to attacks on fuel and ammunition-supply dumps but, as usual, the accurate German flak took its toll. Not all losses were due to direct enemy action however, for there was a series of accidents at Dunsfold; especially unpleasant was one on September 8 1944 when a No 98 Squadron Mitchell landed with two 500 lb (227 kg) hang-ups in the bomb-bay. They exploded on touchdown, killing the entire crew and badly damaging the runway.

The bad weather during the autumn of 1944 hindered operations and also forced a move back into winter quarters for the whole of No 139 Wing. Attempts to support the Arnhem landings were badly disrupted and when the Wing did get through, No 98 Squadron was intercepted by Fw190s, resulting in two Mitchells being shot down—the first losses to fighters of 2nd TAF medium-bomber units since its formation ten months earlier.

A general order for Mitchell bombers to move to the Continent was issued on October 8 and No 139 Wing was the first to go, leaving Dunsfold for B58 Melsbroek the next day. Only a C&M party and a Works Flight remained until January 7 1945, when No 83 Group Support Unit (Training Section) arrived from Tangmere, followed by the rest of the unit from Westhampnett in February. Dunsfold became a satellite of Odiham on January 15 1945, but remained as a reserve airfield in the Tangmere Sector until May, when it was transferred to Nether Wallop.

The end of the war in Europe produced a tremendous upsurge in aircraft movements. From May 8 Dakotas poured into the airfield carrying ex-PoWs from German prison camps. A record 160 aircraft arrived on the 9th, but the daily count was often over 100, and by the end of the month 44,474 ex-prisoners had passed through Dunsfold. The operation continued until June 25, some of the later flights bringing in Canadian soldiers on the first leg of their repatriation.

The Group Support Unit became the Disbandment Centre in August 1945, No 16 Squadron becoming one of its candidates when it returned from the Continent on September 22 and was disbanded less than a month later—when two other squadrons were told to take over its number plate! The GSU moved to Lasham on October 24 and No 88 Group HQ arrived from Norway for disbandment.

No 667 Squadron also put in a brief appearance before disbandment and the rundown was then rapid, the station being reduced to C&M, parented by Tangmere, on February 2 1946. Declared an inactive site in August 1946, it was transferred to Technical Training Command on September 2 and leased by Skyways Ltd soon afterwards as their main base. One of their Lancastrians caught fire in a hangar at Dunsfold during the evening of

December 8 1946, but though it was totally destroyed the hangar was untouched. At the height of the Berlin Airlift the Skyways work force at Dunsfold reached over 1,200, but this number was drastically cut during late 1949 and in March 1950 the company went into voluntary liquidation.

Skyways re-formed with a much-reduced fleet and continued to use Duns-

Top *Dunsfold photographed by No 82 Squadron in April 1947 when Skyways Ltd was in residence. Several Yorks and a Lancastrian can be identified* (DoE/Crown Copyright).

Above *The first Sea Harrier with the British Aerospace complex at Dunsfold in the background—the main assembly shops have been built in between the two wartime 'T2' hangars* (British Aerospace).

fold, though the airfield now had a new champion in Hawker Aircraft Ltd, who took over the tenancy of Dunsfold in 1950 and built up a final-assembly and experimental-flight facility using the two existing 'T2' hangars as a basis for expansion.

Trials of early-production Sea Hawks were followed by the Hunter, the first of many variants of this superb aircraft lifting off from Dunsfold on May 16 1953. The Ministry of Civil Aviation took over the airfield from the Air Ministry at the beginning of 1960 and in 1961 the production testing of Gnats was transferred from Chilbolton. Dunsfold is, however, synonymous for Harrier. Starting with the P 1127's first tentative hover on October 21 1960 right up to the current Sea Harrier, all British development, assembly and testing of this family of vertical-take-off aircraft has been at Dunsfold, throughout a tortuous series of company name changes. Currently the British Aerospace factory at Dunsfold is preparing for the production of the next generation of Harriers, the Anglo-American AV-8B/Harrier GR5.

In addition to the two original 'T2' hangars, which are now hardly recognisable amongst the British Aerospace buildings on the north-east side of the airfield, there are still many Nissen huts and Maycrete buildings scattered about, some in use, others derelict. Close study of the airfield is likely to result in questions being asked by security personnel, but the company holds an annual Families' Day which is well worth attending.

Dymchurch (Hythe/Palmarsh) Kent

TR127330. 2½ miles SW of Hythe alongside A259 (T)

Located at Palmarsh on the edge of the Romney Marsh, the naming of this First World War aerodrome resulted in considerable confusion, not least for the Services themselves. The RFC Machine Gun School moved from Dover to Hythe on November 27 1915 to take advantage of the better facilities available on the gunnery ranges near the town. The unit HQ was set up in the Imperial Hotel, Hythe, but the BE2C, RE7 and Vickers FB5 aeroplanes were housed at Lympne, occasionally flying off the range itself. The unit became the School of Aerial Gunnery on September 3 1916 and as activity increased, it was decided to move the Kite Balloon Section further away from the ranges. In November, a site was selected near the Dymchurch Redoubt, for which an annual rent of £1 per acre was provisionally agreed with the farmer. Centred on *TR125319* this site was large enough for two balloon sheds and a winch, the ancient redoubt being taken

No 1 (Auxiliary) School of Aerial Gunnery at Dymchurch in 1917 (RAF Museum P012599).

over as accommodation. By the time the War Office finalised the lease, the farmer had had second thoughts and was demanding 30 shillings an acre plus rates. Almost unbelievably the finance branch did not haggle, paying up in full!

A move of the Aerial Gunnery School to Loch Doon was planned, but after much work on the Scottish site it was abandoned. Fighter pilots' training went instead to Turnberry and, in January 1917, the unit at Hythe became No 1 (Auxiliary) School of Aerial Gunnery and concentrated on two-week courses for observers. With other uses for Lympne already agreed, the school had to find a new aerodrome as close as possible to the ranges. A site almost alongside the kite balloon base was selected and rapidly developed, Lympne being vacated in February 1917. Twelve Bessoneaux canvas hangars were erected on a technical site in the south-east corner, but there was little personnel accommodation, the unit sharing the Napoleonic Redoubt with the kite balloon operators.

The new aerodrome was variously known as Hythe and Palmarsh, but its official title was Dymchurch, presumably to distinguish it from other establishments at Hythe. It was ideally placed for the ranges but quickly became flooded in the winter and was subject to sudden sea mists. The aeroplanes were frequently subject to forced landings, usually ending up in a drainage ditch somewhere on the Marsh.

In March 1918, the unit was renamed No 1 (Observer) School of Aerial Gunnery, which certainly described its function more accurately and, just before the Armistice, it moved to a better aerodrome at New Romney. Dymchurch then became an emergency LG for aircraft on the Hythe ranges, but closed when the School went to Manston. Soon afterwards instructions were issued for the disposal of land and buildings, the site being cleared during 1920.

The famous Romney, Hythe and Dymchurch miniature railway cut the old aerodrome in two, and the southern part is rapidly disappearing as gravel is extracted. The old kite balloon site is a Holiday Centre.

(Note: A site at Dymchurch was selected as a possible Fighter Command ALG during April 1942 but was not proceeded with. Its proposed position is unknown but it was not the same site as the First World War aerodrome, nor Littlestone—a pre-war civil airfield actually at St Mary's Bay.)

Eastbourne, East Sussex
TQ625015 2 miles N of Eastbourne

Bleriot's cross-Channel monoplane was exhibited at Eastbourne in 1909, sparking off great enthusiasm for aviation in the town, though financial realities soon tempered it. In September the local press reported the formation of the Eastbourne Flying Club and plans for an aerodrome on the Crumbles east of the town. Neither project got off the ground but two years later the enterprise of a Frederick Fowler, who bought up the assets of the McArdle & Drexel Flying School of Beaulieu, led to the construction of a 50-acre aerodrome on Willingdon Level, just to the west of St Anthony Hill. The site, though flat, was low lying and cut into small pieces by a large number of drainage ditches. These were covered by wooden boarding and a second-hand corrugated iron shed was re-erected on the site. One or two Bleriots were then brought across from Beaulieu on a trailer. The Eastbourne Flying School was officially opened on

Left *A gunnery school AW FK 8 in a ditch on the edge of Dymchurch (Pelmarsh)* (Late Sergeant F. Young via D.G. Collyer).

Right *A Sopwith Camel fitted with a camera gun rests outside the Bessoneaux hangers at Eastbourne* (R. Vann via Chaz Bowyer).

December 1 1911, Fowler teaching himself to fly the aircraft, and attempting to ferry one from Beaulieu before taking his certificate on January 16 1912.

Fowler joined forces with a pioneer aviator, Frank Hucks, to form the Eastbourne Aviation Co on February 18 1913. A site on the Crumbles was leased from Lord Willingdon and a seaplane factory built. This consisted of a large hangar on the seaward side of the main road to Pevensey, a turntable and a rail track down to the high-tide line.

The Admiralty became increasingly interested in these activities during 1913 and in June they leased a shed at the aerodrome and later subsidised the construction of two more hangars at the Crumbles factory (*TQ635019*). The school flourished and many famous aviators visited, including Commander Samson, RN, who arrived on March 7 1914 in the 140 hp Short biplane, whose 60 ft (18 m) wing span made it easily the largest machine to land on the small aerodrome.

When war was declared in August 1914, private flying was suspended and the airfield was taken over by the Admiralty as a training school. Rapidly extended to take in the whole of St Anthony's Hill, the western boundary was pushed out as far as Lottridge Drove, on land leased from the Duke of Devonshire. The Crumbles factory was put on full production, starting with a small batch of BE2Cs for the RNAS, and later building 150 Avro 504A and 504Ks for the RFC, but its main activity was repair work for the Admiralty.

The aerodrome became a premier *ab initio* RNAS training base with a large range of types in use. In 1915 these included Avro 504s, Bleriots, Caudrons, Curtiss Jennys, Grahame Whites, Henri Farmans, Maurice Farmans, Short 'pushers', White & Thompsons and a solitary BE2C, but by mid-1916 only Maurice Farmans and Curtiss JN4A Jennys were employed.

Despite continuing problems with the drainage ditches, flying operations were maintained throughout the war, the RNAS handing over to the RAF on April 1 1918. The latter continued the Aeroplane School, transferring No 54 TS from Castle Bromwich on July 6 to provide the nucleus for No 50 TDS. Aircraft types were then standardised as Avro 504K, DH9 and DH9A, the trainees being intended for day bomber squadrons on the Western Front.

After the Armistice, No 50 TDS declined though it was still active in July 1919. By November the airfield was empty and, complete with sheds and living accommodation, it was handed back to Major Fowler early in 1920. The Air Ministry licensed the field for civil flying and supplied some financial support, but this ceased in December. Shortly afterwards Fowler had to close St Anthony's which then reverted to agriculture.

The repair contracts which had kept the Eastbourne Aviation Co so busy were abruptly cancelled at the end of the war. The upsurge in joy-riding using Avro 504L and Short 184 seaplanes from the beach near the Royal Hotel kept the company alive until 1921, and attempts were made to manufacture motor vehicles. These failed and a receiver was appointed in 1924, with the Eastbourne Corporation later purchasing the factory buildings.

Most of the aerodrome buildings have disappeared over the years, but one RNAS hangar still exists as a furniture store and the original guardroom is now a private house. Part of the aerodrome is still agricultural land, but the Lottbridge Drove Industrial Estate has encroached on the western side and may soon engulf the old hangar.

Eastchurch, Kent

TQ985695. 1½ miles S of Eastchurch village

Flushed with the success of its new aerodrome at Eastchurch, and with the enthusiastic backing of Mr Francis McClean, the Royal Aero Club offered the Admiralty free flying instruction for naval officers in November 1910. The Admiralty did not fall over themselves to accept this remarkably generous offer, somewhat grudgingly choosing four officers from 200 volunteers in February 1911. They had to be unmarried, become members of the RAeC at their own expense and not fly on Sundays!

One of the original four went sick and it was Lieutenants E.L. Gerrard, R. Gregory, A.M. Longmore and C.R. Samson, who reported at Eastchurch on March 1 1911, having been given six months leave of absence on full pay. Horace Short provided technical instruction for which the Admiralty paid £20, while George Cockburn became their flying instructor. The aircraft were pusher biplanes with an incredible number of struts and flying wires, the pupil crouching precariously behind the pilot following through on the controls, before being launched off on their own. Instructional flying could only be undertaken in light winds which invariably meant the early morning or the evening and led to frustrating delays, but with only two minor mishaps all four gained their RAeC Aviators' Certificates during April/May 1911. They immediately started spreading their enthusiasm by taking their brother officers flying on every opportunity. Naval aviation, soon to be in the forefront

The Short factory and private owners' sheds at Eastchurch in 1911 (Short Brothers Ltd).

of experimentation and the development of new ideas, was off the ground.

Flying at Eastchurch had started at the end of July 1909, when the Hon. C.S. Rolls started using Stamford Hill for tests of his Short-built glider, and the adjoining level grassland was soon being considered as a new flying ground, Leysdown having proved unsatisfactory. Francis McClean purchased the required 400 acres, giving the Aero Club exclusive rights to the site for a nominal £1 annual rent.

The new aerodrome was a great success for, although low-lying and close to marshland, it was comparatively well-drained and free of the numerous ditches and dykes which abound on the Isle of Sheppey. March 1910 saw the first flight of the remarkable Dunne D5 tailless pusher biplane at Eastchurch, and McClean invited Short Brothers to move their whole works over from Leysdown. During May they did so, quite literally, re-erecting their Leysdown sheds at Eastchurch, the useful Short S 27 becoming the first production machine to be built in the new factory. More buildings followed, and soon there were seven large sheds and a repair shop on the aerodrome, which developed as a rather fashionable centre for the wealthier members of the flying fraternity.

The four naval airmen had progressed to short cross-country flights by the summer of 1911 but when the six-month agreement expired on August 31 the

Admiralty were unprepared and it was only after considerable pressure by two of the pilots, Lieutenants Samson and Longmore, that their Lordships agreed in October to set up a school and to purchase two Short biplanes from McClean. This public-spirited gentleman generously loaned several other machines to the Navy, Samson and Longmore remaining at Eastchurch for trials' work while four more officers started the flying course.

In February 1912 the Admiralty facilities at Eastchurch were expanded. Ten acres of ground close to the RAeC sheds were leased and work started on six large sheds and three portable canvas hangars for the Naval Flying School, formed the previous December. By the beginning of 1912 the School was commanded by Captain Godfrey Paine, RN, and for administration was on the books of HMS *Actaeon*, the torpedo-training ship at Sheerness.

With the formation of the RFC in April 1912, Eastchurch was established as the Naval Wing HQ. Paine was nominated as the Commandant of the CFS at Upavon and given a fortnight to obtain his flying brevet before taking up the post on May 1. He promptly informed Lieutenant Longmore that it was his job to see that the certificate was secured—it was—and the dashing Samson was put in charge at Eastchurch.

Samson's enthusiasm and energy resulted in enormous advances being made at Eastchurch which not only undertook most Naval Wing personnel training, but also acted as a depot for pilots awaiting posting and experimented with wireless, bomb-dropping and night flying. By June 1913 five of the sheds had been enlarged and others rented from private owners, while the aerodrome became known as HMS *Pembroke II* parented by Chatham naval barracks (HMS *Pembroke*). Twenty-four officers and 41 men had completed training and more were undergoing instruction, and the Admiralty was steadily working at separating the Military and Naval Wings of the RFC. It took a year, the RNAS being formed on July 1 1914. The Spithead Review, when most of the available naval aeroplanes flew over the Fleet, gave the RNAS the chance to concentrate and the landplanes then went to Eastchurch for mobilisation. The Eastchurch Squadron was formed by Commander Samson and, by the end of July 1914, No 4 Squadron, RFC, had also arrived to reinforce naval coastal patrols, while the Eastchurch War Flight prepared to defend the Sheerness and Chatham bases.

War fever gripped the whole of Sheppey, every report of German agents receiving an enthusiastic response from Samson, who sent out lorries containing officers armed to the teeth, to deal with them. He also collected a variety of weapons for aerodrome defence and Eastchurch entered the war easily the best-armed flying station in the United Kingdom, though aircraft were ill-equipped. Most had no armament at all, pilots going up with a revolver, or accompanied by a Royal Marine with a rifle.

At the outbreak of war on August 4, Samson's Eastchurch Squadron was detached to Skegness with seven seaplanes while the RFC unit moved to Dover, leaving the War Flight and Naval Flying School at Eastchurch alongside Shorts' small factory.

No 2 Squadron, RNAS, formed with two Bristol TB 8 biplanes, but was soon flying many of the assorted machines on the aerodrome, Eastchurch being formally requisitioned on December 22 under the Defence of the Realm Act. When the Germans announced new measures against shipping around the British Isles in February 1915, attacks on their bases in Belgium were increased, part of 2 Squadron transferring to Dover for this task. No 4 Squadron, RNAS, arrived from Dover for more training soon after formation and, like 2 Squadron, was redesignated a Wing in June. No 2 Wing went to Dunkirk in August, ostensibly to replace 1 Wing, RNAS, so avoiding the first bombing raid on Eastchurch, made erroneously on August 8 by the commander of the naval airship *L10*, who thought he was bombing London. A stick of 12 bombs fell across the aerodrome but only broke windows. The two pilots on patrol from Eastchurch saw nothing in the darkness—both attacker and defenders had their problems!

All RNAS units were still operating an incredible variety of aircraft. At Eastchurch in October 1915 the school had two Avros, five Caudrons, six Bleriots, two Curtiss JN3s, two Bristol TB 8s, three Grahame Whites, six Maurice Farmans, five Shorts and three Sopwiths. No 4 Wing had four Avro 504Bs, six BE2Cs, two Tabloids, some of which were used by the War Flight. It is easy to see why trained mechanics were at such a premium!

The official trials of a most significant aeroplane started at Eastchurch in January 1916 when the Handley Page 0/100 bomber arrived. This was the 'bloody paralyser' demanded earlier by the ebullient Commander Samson and, despite the inevitable teething troubles and the limitations of Eastchurch, the prototype was soon demonstrating its potential.

The Admiralty approved the enlargement of Eastchurch early in 1916 and new sheds were erected on the east side. The Flying School was temporarily closed whilst the work was in progress, opening again on May 1 by which time a SHQ was functioning and a gunnery school was being formed, the War Flight now having a number of Bristol Scouts and night-flying BE2Cs.

Although Home Defence was now a War Office responsibility, Eastchurch put up aircraft during the night of September 23/24 1916 when 11 Zeppelins of the German Naval Airship Service set out for targets in East Anglia and London. Two of them were shot down but not by East-

church pilots, who had their usual bad luck.

The War Flight disbanded in February 1917 and Eastchurch then concentrated on flying training for pilots and observers, and technical instruction for a growing number of mechanics, but the outcry following the first Gotha raid on London resulted in a Flight of Camels being sent from France during June 1917. They were active during the morning of July 7 when 22 Gothas of Kaghol 3 approached London. Two Camels, piloted by Flight Commander Draper and Flight Lieutenant Watkins engaged the enemy over Chingford but both suffered jammed guns—Eastchurch bad luck again.

With the death of Horace Short on April 6 1917, the Eastchurch works were sold to the Government and the aerodrome underwent further expansion in the autumn in readiness for the amalgamation of the RNAS and RFC on April 1 1918. No 58 Wing, RAF, was formed at Eastchurch on that day, the ground instructional school of the old Gunners &

Above *The haphazard layout of Eastchurch is clearly seen in this 1924 oblique* (RAF Museum P8392).

Left *An HP 0/100 at Eastchurch with Stamford Hill in the background* (G.S. Leslie/J.M. Bruce collection).

Bottom left *Camel F4017 in a highly colourful paint scheme. It belongs to No 204 TDS, Eastchurch* (via Chaz Bowyer).

Observers School remaining, while the flying side, known as the Aerial Flying and Gunnery School, re-formed at Leysdown. The Naval Flying School, Eastchurch later became No 204 TDS with the usual Shorthorns, DH 5s and Avro 504s for *ab inito* training and Camels, Snipes and DH 9As for advanced instrucion.

At the end of the war, Eastchurch covered some 600 acres of which 50 were occupied by buildings. There were 29 aeroplane sheds of incredible variety ranging from six 200 ft × 100 ft hangars down to 12 50 ft × 55 ft wooden huts. No 1 Observers School was about to restrict its output to specialists in Fleet work and be renamed No 2 Marine Observers School (Fleet Reconnaissance), the associated Ground Armament School providing classroom instruction on weapons, while the separate Boys Mechanics School trained 600 lads a time on a nine-month metalworkers course.

Flying activity on the station slowly faded as disbandment of units took place during 1919 and, as the ground instructional units were sorted out, the Armament School emerged supreme. It became the Armament and Gunnery School on April 1 1922, the airfield being used by aircraft of the squadrons on courses or flying on the Leysdown ranges.

No 207 Squadron arrived fresh from the Chanak Crisis with its DH9As in October 1923 to take part in several experiments, notably in bombing trials, with R/T gear and with the testing of completely ineffective engine silencers. A transfer to No 23 Group on April 1 1926 and the delivery of Fairey IIIFs to No 207 Squadron during 1927/28 disturbed the station little but, during the autumn of 1929, the purposeful-looking Horseleys of No 33 Squadron arrived and No 207 Squadron went to Bircham Newton. Within six months No 33 Squadron proudly received the first Hawker Harts to enter service, but moved to Bicester in November 1930, leaving Eastchurch to the gunnery school.

In January 1932 the unit was renamed the Air Armament School, and was joined by a No 22 Group lodger, the Coastal Defence Co-operation Flight. The latter moved to Gosport in May 1932 but the AAS gradually expanded, its importance warranting the formation of a separate Armament Group on February 1 1934 with its HQ at Eastchurch. A Station Flight was established in November 1936 for use by staff officers visiting Armament Practice Camps and the unit became No 1 AAS on November 1 1937 in preparation for the formation of No 2 AAS on July 1 1938 when, with two independent units at Eastchurch, a SHQ was established.

On August 15 1938 No 1 AAS moved to

Manby, No 21 Squadron arriving from Lympne on the same day to commence conversion from Hinds to Blenheims. A fortnight later No 48 Squadron, relieved of its training task at last, flew in its Ansons from Manston to concentrate on its general reconnaissance role. In common with the rest of the RAF, these squadrons and the Station were brought on to a war footing during the Munich Crisis. Eastchurch was transferred to No 16 Group, Coastal Command, in November, though No 21 Squadron and No 2 AAS remained as lodgers.

In March 1939, No 21 Squadron moved to Watton and, with mobilisation in August, No 48 went to its war station at Thorney Island. A forward airfield was no place for a training unit so No 2 AAS went to Pembrey and, on September 1 1939, Eastchurch was temporarily reduced to C&M. It was revitalised by the arrival of the first batch of exhausted and bewildered Polish AF groundcrew during December 1939 and the opening of the Polish Training Centre. At Eastchurch the Poles recuperated while being sorted out into their equivalent RAF trades. Many only required short conversion or refresher courses, but others had to be completely retrained and by March 1940 nearly 1,300 Poles were at Eastchurch. With the German advance into France in May the training units were again removed from the south-east, the Poles going to Blackpool. The airfield was then used by a detachment of Blenheim IVs from No 59 Squadron which, joined by No 53 in June, flew tactical recce over what was left of the fighting in France before being pulled back to regroup and be transferred to Coastal Command.

Eastchurch was now used to mount raids on shipping and barge concentrations in German-occupied ports of France and Belgium, first by detachments, then from early August 1940 by the whole of Nos 12 and 142 Squadrons whose Battles were based at Eastchurch for these hazardous operations. Blenheims of No 53 Squadron were also using Eastchurch and Spitfires from Nos 19 and 266 Squadrons were present when the Luftwaffe chose to strike on August 13. Two formations, each of 15 Do 17s from KG2, came in from the south just after 07:00 hours and dropped over 100 HE and incendiary bombs on the airfield. Most of the tightly clustered hangars received hits, one containing No 266 Squadron Spitfires bursting into flames. One Spitfire was quickly consumed but three others were saved, pushed out by brave ground crew. No 53 Squadron lost five Blenheims, and the station suffered severely, the operations block being destroyed, airmens' and officers' quarters badly damaged and much equipment lost. Sixteen people were killed and 48 injured in the attack which caught the defences napping. Fighter Command reacted quickly, however, and Nos 74, 111 & 151 Squadrons shot down four of the unescorted bombers as they withdrew.

Back at Eastchurch the station quickly recovered, and was operational again within ten hours. The Battles were more carefully dispersed, but more attacks by the Luftwaffe on Eastchurch made further operations difficult and it was effectively put out of action on September 2 when attacked by 12 bombers, part of a large force which swamped the defences early in the afternoon. One bomb hit the explosives dump and 350 250-lb (112 kg) bombs exploded. The NAAFI and administration buildings were wrecked, water mains and sewers badly damaged, while power and communications were cut. A hangar was hit, six aircraft destroyed and casualties reached four killed and 12 wounded.

The cumulative effects of the raids resulted in virtual evacuation of the airfield. Administrative personnel went to requisitioned property at Wymswold Warden and the sick quarters moved into Eastchurch village. The Battles and personnel of Nos 12 and 142 Squadrons were withdrawn to Binbrook and the airfield remained unused until September 16. Eastchurch suffered the occasional visit from single Luftwaffe aircraft for the next six months, the heaviest attack being during the night of April 19/20 1941 when two parachute mines were dropped causing loud explosions but no casualties and little damage except to windows.

Little use was made of Eastchurch until Technical Training Command took over in June 1941. The RAF Artillery School then made use of the repaired permanent accommodation and the wide open spaces surrounding the camp, joined by No 1 Parachute & Cable Establishment in September 1941. Courses on this 'Heath Robinson' equipment were given until the unit closed down in October 1942.

Flying was almost non-existent until June 1942 when No 124 Squandron started using Eastchurch as a forward operating base on detachment from

Gravesend. They were replaced by No 401 (RCAF) Squadron, possibly for the cancelled Operation *Rutter*, but when *Jubilee* was mounted in August it was the base for Spitfires of Nos 65 and 165 Squadrons.

On August 19 No 65 Squadron was called out at the ghastly hour of 03:30 and 50 minutes later its aircraft were taxying out to escort the first bombers over Dieppe. These sorties were uneventful, but it was a different matter during the Wing's second mission of the morning. On top cover No 65 Squadron intercepted and shot down two Do 217s, while No 165 became involved lower down, claiming one and damaging another. During the seaborne withdrawal, the squadrons were out again, No 65 again intercepting Do 217s, while No 165 claimed damage to a Ju 88. Neither squadron sustained any casualties so it was a pretty successful detachment which came to an end on August 20.

Eastchurch relapsed into its normal unexciting state and for no very obvious reason the station was transferred in October 1942 to No 72 Group, Army Co-op Command, the Artillery School remaining as a lodger. During March 1943 the large-scale Army co-operation Exercise *Spartan* involved No 184 Squadron operating from a tented camp at Eastchurch for part of the time. At the conclusion of the exercise the nucleus of the command system was retained by transforming *Z* Group HQ into No 83 Group and the lower formations into Airfields. No 122 Airfield was formed at Eastchurch on April 1 1943 to operate Nos 132, 174 and 184 Squadrons with Nos 602, 3035 and 3082 Servicing Echelons on an independent Wing basis, No 1493 Flight moving in with Martinets to tow targets for them.

On May 1 1943, Eastchurch was again transferred, this time to No 54 Group, and a combined Aircrew Re-selection Centre was formed, its job being to consider personnel for other aircrew categories or ground trades after being found unsuitable during training or on operational units. With the departure of No 122 Airfield and No 1493 Flight, the airfield was again under-utilised but the need for more intensive squadron armament training was recognised and No 18 Armament Practice Camp was formed during October 1943, equipped with Master IIIs. No 291 Squadron and, later, No 567 Squadron detachments, provided drogues for air-to-air firing. For its new

task the unusual L-shaped airfield was put back into an operational state. Three Bellman hangars were erected to replace the wrecked sheds and 51 PSP dispersed hardstandings were laid.

Though certainly not on the official USAF list of emergency LGs, Eastchurch found itself a haven for several stricken American fighters and bombers during 1943-44. Perhaps the most dramatic arrival was on January 24 1944 when a badly damaged 100th BG B-17 turned up, escorted by two Thunderbolts. Despite the loss of the lower part of the rudder and a gaping hole where the rear turret used to be, Lieutenant Valesh eased *Hang the Expense* gently on to the final approach and made a good landing—only to become bogged down on the muddy surface. The mangled tail became one of the most widely publicized photographs of a battle-damaged Fortress. It was assumed that the gunner had been killed but actually he was a POW, after being blasted out of his seat and pulling his parachute ripcord!

From January 1944 onwards the APC provided rocket-firing courses for Typhoon pilots, a total of six complete squadrons being passed out before D-Day. A further three underwent refresher training during July before transferring to the Continent, No 18 APC moving to Fairwood Common in August 1944 leaving the Aircrew Reselection Centre in occupation. The station continued to provide lodger facilities for two single-engined fighter squadrons as a secondary function, though in practice this was not required and the RN Mobile Recording and Analysing Unit (765 Squadron) arrived on detachment, joined in September by No 567 Squadron for Army and naval co-op work.

No 765 Squadron left in September 1945 but the reselection work went on until the end of August 1946. The ACRC moved to Bircham Newton and Eastchurch reverted to C&M on September 1 1946, parented by West Malling, and was reduced to an inactive site in April 1947. After lying derelict for some time the permanent camp buildings to the northeast of Stamford Hill were taken over by the Home Office in June 1950 and converted into an open prison, while the flying field reverted to agriculture. One wonders if the present inmates feel any more confined than the generations of trainees who have passed through the gates of Eastchurch to endure its isolation

and the heavy discipline imposed on pre-war recruits.

In the village, at the junction between the road leading to the camp and the main A250, stands a memorial to the RAeC pioneers whose activities at Eastchurch from 1909 to 1914 put themselves and the aerodrome at the forefront of early British aviation.

East Dean (Friston/Gayles), East Sussex
See Friston

East Grinstead (Hammerwood), East Sussex
See Hammerwood

Eastleigh (Southampton), Hampshire
SU450170. 1½ miles S of Eastleigh town on A335

Best known in aviation circles as the place where the prototype Spitfire made its first flight on March 5 1936, Eastleigh has had a long but rather troubled history. The North Stoneham Farm water meadows between the River Itchen and Wide Lane (now the A335) first saw powered flight in 1910 when a local man, Rowland Moon, managed to coax his home-built 20 hp tractor monoplane into the air. During 1910/11 the field was also briefly used by Grahame White and Maurice Tetard but it then faded from the scene until 1917 when the War Office decided to expand the RFC Depot in Leigh Road into an Air-craft Acceptance Park. The farm was requisitioned and work started on the

Above *This vertical of May 1946 shows up the 'L' shaped LG at Eastchurch. The foundations of three bombed hangars can be seen on the eastern side (DoE/Crown Copyright).*

Below *Inside one of the First World War General Service hangars at Eastleigh—the wooden Belfast-truss roof is still well preserved (K.S. West).*

construction of four large hangars and five storage sheds alongside the Eastleigh-Southampton railway line.

On April 30 1918, the US Secretary of the Navy approved a plan for air operations by a special unit against German submarine bases in the Zeebrugge area of Belgium. This unit, later known as the Northern Bombing Group, needed an assembly base for the flood of American-built bombers expected during the summer of 1918. The Americans rejected various sites in France and on July 4 approached the Air Ministry for facilities in Britain. They were offered the half completed AAP at Eastleigh and immediately accepted for, being close to Southampton docks, it was ideal.

The Americans found the hangars nearly complete, about a third of the storage sheds ready and living quarters for about 300 men prepared for occupation. The airfield itself was usable with most roadways already surfaced. Informed that they could take over on July 20, arrangements were made to transfer supplies from France and divert incoming equipment from America. Naval Air Station Eastleigh was commissioned on July 23 and tents and many more huts sprang up alongside the railway.

The promised American-built DH-4s did not appear on time so the Commander, US Naval Aviation Forces, did a deal with the British obtaining 54 DH 9As in exchange for Liberty engines. Sent to

Eastleigh in crates, these aircraft were assembled, flight-tested and then ferried across the Channel for distribution to 10th Bombing Group units.

Within ten weeks of the Americans arriving, Base *B*, as Eastleigh was called, was carrying out major repair work as well as assembly. The original sheds had been joined by 21 more, while most of the personnel had been re-housed in solid wooden huts. A visiting Board of Officers declared Eastleigh the most successful USN aviation station they had inspected, but it was only just getting into its stride when the Armistice came on November 11 1918. Assembly work ceased four days later and Base *B* started to receive equipment for despatch back to the States. The US Navy finally withdrew on April 10 1919 when Eastleigh was handed back to the RAF.

The hangars were used for storage, and the accommodation for squadron demobilisation until January 20 1920, after which the rundown accelerated, stores and some of the buildings being auctioned and the station closing in May 1920.

The Handley Page company had briefly tried a newspaper service in May 1919 but initial optimism soon evaporated and it was a shipping consortium that took over the buildings in 1921 as the Atlantic Park Hostel, to house European immigrants awaiting shipment and a new life in the USA. While the hostel was in being the airfield was officially closed, but actually became an unlicensed LG; in 1926 Surrey Flying Services used it for joy-riding, carrying over 3,600 passengers.

Public interest in municipal airports at the end of the 1920s prompted South-

Jersey Airways' DH 86A Express G-ACYF *outside the World War 1 'GS' hangars at Eastleigh, 1937* (M. Purcell via A.S. Thomas).

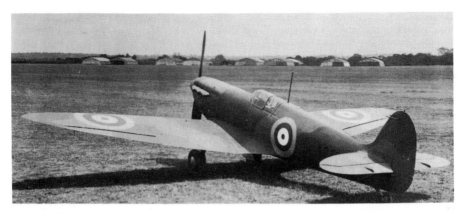

ampton authorities to start looking for a
site. Eastleigh was the obvious choice and
the Corporation bought 100 acres of the
land in 1929 and started protracted
negotiations for the Atlantic Park Hostel
buildings.

The Corporation's plans were publicly
disclosed in January 1932 and work was
put in hand to bring the airfield up to
standard. Meanwhile, Vickers-Armstrong
Ltd had expressed interest in using the
field for flight testing and, in July, RAE
staff inspected it on behalf of the Air
Ministry. It got their qualified approval
and Supermarine acquired facilities in
September.

Eastleigh was officially re-opened in
November 1932. The Hampshire Aero
Club moved in their three DH Moths
from Hamble immediately afterwards and
attempts to attract air services were made.
These bore fruit during 1934 when Jersey
Airways commenced operations and in
May 1935 Railway Air Services started a
service from the Midlands—a firm
indication of improving fortunes.

In July 1935 Audaxes of No 4 and 13
Squadrons held their summer camp at
Eastleigh and agreement between the Air
Ministry and Southampton Corporation
for part of Eastleigh to be used by Fleet
Air Arm units was negotiated. Ten acres
in the north-eastern corner of the airfield
were allocated and work started on
wooden-hutted accommodation and
canvas Bessoneaux hangars. 802 Squadron spent a few weeks at RAF Eastleigh
before embarking on HMS *Glorious* in
August 1935 and 800, 801 and 822
Squadrons were there when the station
was renamed RAF Southampton on
August 1 1936. The agreement was
originally for three years, limited to 20
weeks annually, but with the deteriorating

The first production Spitfire 1 K9787 *at
Eastleigh in May 1938 with the
Bessoneaux hangars of RAF Eastleigh in
the background* (Vickers Ltd).

international situation these restrictions
were dropped and RAF squadrons also
used the facilities.

Meanwhile, the Supermarine Aviation
Works (Vickers) Ltd had leased two of the
hangars and formed a flight-test centre,
primarily for the Spitfire, though the
Walrus did its landing trials there and the
Vickers Venom was based there for manufacturers' tests. Air Service Training was
outgrowing Hamble and, in February
1937, started a satellite school on the airfield—Eastleigh was getting steadily
busier.

During May 1937 some 40 naval aircraft
used Eastleigh for the Spithead Review
and the airfield was open to the public on
Empire Air Day. In June, Vickers
(Supermarine) Aviation Ltd put on a
private display at which the Spitfire,
Walrus, Wellesley and Wellington
prototypes were demonstrated followed
by a flypast by Stranraer and Scapa flying
boats—not bad for one company! Vildebeestes of No 22 Squadron arrived for a
four-month stay, joined for exercises in
September 1937 by their sister unit, No 42
Squadron. They were followed early in
1938 by Ansons of Nos 224 and 269
Squadrons on detachment for two and a
half months.

The Portsmouth, Southsea and IoW
Airways Co supplemented their income by
flying Couriers by day and a GAL Mono-
spar by night, giving Army gunners and
searchlight operators much-needed
aiming practice, while on the other side of
the airfield other nocturnal activity was

underway. A carrier dummy deck was laid out, complete with lights, to enable pilots from HMS *Courageous* to practice night landings.

In March 1938 a new Expansion Scheme increased Spitfire orders by another 200, which only served to provoke more acrimony, for sub-contracting was already causing hold-ups. It was to be a continuing problem with output slow to build up, despite the successful first production flight on May 14.

A subsidiary of the British American Tobacco Co had been formed during 1937 to manufacture the unique Burnelli Flying Wing. The name of the company was changed to Cunliffe-Owen Aircraft Ltd in May 1938 when work was well advanced on a factory at Swaythling on the southern edge of the airfield, and despite little interest from potential customers the firm pressed on with their own version.

The Air Ministry became responsible for air traffic facilities in April 1938 and a hangar large enough to take five Ensigns was completed. Further development, in particular the construction of a terminal building, was, however, delayed and later cancelled. 814 Squadron FAA was formed on November 21 equipped with 12 Swordfish for service aboard *Ark Royal*, but general naval activity was light and it was the first flight of the Cunliffe Owen OA-1 from Eastleigh on January 12 1939 which provided the main attraction. This coincided with the completion of their factory and they moved out of Hangar 2 on the airfield. This was promptly taken over by Supermarine, their Spitfire assembly lines having outgrown Hangar 1 where they had been established since 1936.

The Eastleigh base became HMS *Raven* on July 1 when the Swordfish aircraft of 811, 812 & 821 Squadrons arrived. They all embarked during August leaving *Raven* available for an Observer & Signals School which was forming as war was declared and civil flying ceased.

Camouflaging of buildings started immediately and Nimrod and Osprey biplane fleet fighters formed an airfield defence force at readiness by the side of the road forming the northern boundary. The flying element of the school became 758 Squadron and, equipped with Ospreys and Sharks, was soon engaged in airbourne instruction for TAGs. It was joined in October by 780 Squadron providing refresher courses for ex-civilian and reservist pilots using Tiger Moths, Harts and Sharks, and in November by

759 Squadron, intended as a Fighter School using Skuas and Rocs.

An operational squadron, 806, formed on February 15 1940 with Skuas and Rocs, and after rapid work-up left at the end of March for Hatston and operations over Norway. It was replaced by 760 Squadron formed on April 1 as a Fleet Fighter Pool with Skuas, Rocs and Sea Gladiators. 806 Squadron returned briefly during June and was back again in July/August to re-equip with Fulmar fleet fighters.

Meanwhile, AA defences were supplemented by No 924 Balloon Barrage Squadron which arrived at Eastleigh on June 29 1940 after service in France. It was not long before they claimed their first victim unfortunately it was a No 1 OTU Hudson which hit a cable during August. With the Battle of Britain in full swing, No 266 Squadron Spitfires spent a couple of days at Eastleigh and on August 24 the Luftwaffe paid their first visit, dropping a stick of eight bombs on the southern perimeter of the airfield. A more successful attack, from the German viewpoint, was on September 11 when six bombers dived on the Swaythling works of Cunliffe Owen and scored nine direct hits, badly damaging the factory.

Within days the FAA squadrons were moved out. 759 and 760 Squadrons went to Yeovilton on September 16, leaving 758 and 780 Squadrons to move to Arbroath and Lee early in October.

Using a landing Hudson to guide them through the balloons, three He 111s swept low over the airfield on October 8 1940. Thirty-eight 50 kg (110-lb) bombs fell within the perimeter, others in Eastleigh town where the GEC works were hit, but this time the defences were not caught napping, one of the bombers being hit and crashing near Chichester. More raids followed during November but had little effect for Spitfire production had been reduced to a trickle following the destruction of the Woolston and Itchen works and only gradually built up again as parts started to flow in from Southampton dispersal sites. Eastleigh was never again the major source of Spitfires.

The RNAS base now became a ground training station which gradually increased in size and importance. An incendiary attack on April 17 1941 just missed HMS *Raven* but, when the Luftwaffe singled out Eastleigh 14 months later, considerable damage was done, though with personnel in shelters, casualties were light.

The Observers School (Part 1) had been joined by a number of artificer training courses and a storage unit for reserve aircraft. Personnel numbered about 900, but hangarage was reduced to just one Bessoneaux, the reserve aircraft being housed in one of the large sheds on the civil side.

Cunliffe-Owen was now heavily involved in the modification and repair of a variety of aircraft, many of them American machines shipped in for final assembly and flight testing. Experimental and development work was done in the shops opposite the crematorium, one of the early contracts being the conversion of the Hudson for ASR work carrying Uffa Fox's airborne lifeboat. The company gained a reputation for work on Coastal Command aircraft, following the Hudson with the general-reconnaissance versions of the Halifax and Lancaster. Another big job was the modification of Typhoons for operation from dust-laden airstrips on the Continent.

COA Ltd also received sub-contracts from Westland for new-build Seafire IIIs, but though they had already modified 118 Spitfires into Seafires it took them nearly a year to produce their first aircraft, due to problems involved in setting up a production line. A total of 350 were built at Eastleigh before production moved on to the Seafire XV (of which 134 were completed) and the Mk XVII (20 built).

Over on the RNAS side, the Air Medicine School was sharing the facilities with fire-fighting trainees, and from July 1944 with the Safety Equipment School, which used 716 Squadron to provide flying experience in Barracuda and Wellington aircraft, until disbanded in August 1945. The Air Medicine School had already gone to Farnborough, and the Fire Fighting School moved to Gosport later in the year. On September 10 1945 Channel Island Airways re-opened Jersey and Guernsey services to Southampton with six Rapide flights a day, but the FAA retained control of the airfield until April 1946 when *Raven* was finally paid off.

The airfield was de-requisitioned the following month, and the MCA took over its operation. The Cierva Company was using Cunliffe-Owen production facilities at Eastleigh to build its first helicopter, while the latter company was still modifying Lancasters for Coastal Command. They had also started construction of an attractive feeder airliner.

Private flying was allowed again and

RNAS Eastleigh in April 1945. The Supermarine and Cunliffe-Owen factories are on the western side of the airfield with HMS Raven *on the east (FAA Museum A/Stn 87).*

the Hampshire Aero Club was soon flying, while Channel Islands services slowly increased their load factors. On October 18 1946, the two Tiger Moths of Southampton UAS arrived from Worthy Down and provided a small Service presence for a few months before moving to Hamble. During 1947, Vickers Supermarine transferred their remaining flying activities to Chilbolton and South Marston, though retaining facilities until December 1957.

The first flight of the Concordia was made on May 19 1947. It performed well, a second prototype was built and production started. Unfortunately, new regulations and the poor economic situation were against the company and in November it was announced that production must halt. In fact the company abandoned its aeronautical interests completely, the plant and factory being auctioned during 1948. They were bought by the Ford Motor Company who later used the factory for Transit van production.

This left Cierva in the lurch because Cunliffe Owen had started construction of the monster W 11 Air Horse helicopter and they had to find new production facilities. Naturally this slowed the project and the first flight was not until December 8 1948. A second prototype was complete and work proceeding on the W 14 light helicopter when the first Air Horse crashed. The problem could have been resolved, but confidence was lost and with it the company's backing. Fortunately, Saunders-Roe wanted additional facilities in the Southampton area and took over both the Eastleigh factory and the W 14 Skeeter project in January 1951.

Meanwhile, the commercial side of the airport was having its ups and downs, the general lack of aids and difficult operating conditions inhibiting growth, though Silver City did start car-ferry services in 1951. In an attempt to improve the situation the airport was extended to the north and a general clean-up removed the remains of the Fleet Air Arm hutted camp and all the original buildings except the four GS hangars and four adjacent sheds, now converted into freight/passenger handling accommodation. Modern warehousing replaced the sheds alongside the railway and the main NNE/SSW runway was extended from its wartime 3,800 ft (1,158 m) to 5,050 ft (1,539 m) the surface remaining grass.

The Saro company put the Skeeter into production and pioneered the larger Scout/Wasp, before being bought out by Westland in 1959. The following year the production line was transferred to Hayes, the Saro Division lingering on at Eastleigh for a year or so before closing.

The MCA decided that the airport was uneconomic and proposed withdrawal of all facilities. The corporation objected and in May 1961 the airport reverted to them. They immediately leased it to Southampton Airport Ltd, who are still running it 22 years later. Silver City Airways returned and when their routes were retained by British United in January 1962, the corporation finally agreed to build a single 5,653 ft (1,723 m) concrete runway linked to a large hardstanding outside the terminal. It was opened in January 1966 enabling British United (CI)

to enjoy considerable success with the London–Channel Islands rail/air link using the railway station alongside the airport. The company continued to maintain its position as the Airport's main operator through several name changes, its supremacy reinforced when British Airways suddenly pulled out in 1980, by which time it was part of the Air UK group. Air UK now also fly to Amsterdam, while Aurigny, the other main airline, concentrates on the Channel Islands. In addition to the Hampshire School of Flying there are currently several other small operators.

Egerton (Coldharbour/ Headcorn), Kent
See Headcorn

Farnborough, Hampshire
SU856538. 2 miles NW of Aldershot on A325

No one with the slightest interest in aviation can fail to have heard of Farnborough, though most people's acquaintance with the airfield will be confined to a few hectic September days during the Society of British Aircraft Constructors' Show. This has been held at Farnborough since the late 1940's, first annually and more recently biennially. Although a very important event in the aviation calendar, the SBAC Show is a small and comparatively short-lived part of the Farnborough story, which started on the present site in 1905 in the following way.

After two years with the Royal Engineers at the School of Military Engineering, Chatham, the Balloon Factory was moved to the garrison town of Aldershot. Here it was established in the Stanhope Lines, just east of the present A325 and south of the Basingstoke Canal (*SU863522*), with the acknowledged balloon expert, Lieutenant Colonel J.L. Templer, responsible for design, manufacture, development and training. It was a rather nebulous set-up until April 1 1897, when the Balloon Factory was recognised by the War Office as a separate organisation and a Balloon Section was created as a properly constituted RE unit with an independent CO.

The outbreak of the Boer War two years later put a tremendous strain on the Balloon Factory, accentuated by the

Boxer Rebellion in China. The pressure to move the factory to less cramped quarters became irresistible when it was decided to construct a balloon dirigible (later more commonly known as an airship), but finding a suitable location proved difficult and, as a temporary measure, a transportable airship shed was built on the northern end of Farnborough Common, some two miles from the Balloon Factory. Here there was plenty of room to manoeuvre an airship, which was all that was envisaged back in 1904.

Quaintly described as an Elongated Balloon Erecting House, the airship shed was an imposing structure, 160 ft (49 m) long and 72 ft (22 m) high, completed in May 1905. Meanwhile, estimates for the removal of the whole factory to the temporary site had been submitted and the iron-framed balloon house was carefully dismantled and re-erected alongside the airship shed during the autumn of 1905. Two gas holders and a number of smaller buildings were also transferred but the main workshops were newly constructed in 1906—the temporary site was rapidly becoming permanent.

The Balloon Sections had become Companies in April 1905 and a year later were amalgamated at Farnborough to form the Balloon School. The factory, now with Colonel J. E. Capper as Superintendent, completed the envelope for the Army's first dirigible. This flew as the *Nulli Secundus* on September 10 1907, to be followed, with varying success, by the *Nulli Secundus II*, the diminutive *Baby* and the larger *Beta, Gamma* and *Delta* airships.

Meanwhile, Samuel Franklin Cody was given a contract as a civilian Kite Instructor in February 1905 and moved with the balloon units to Farnborough where he was also responsible for kite manufacture. From this grew an interest in glider-kites, a development firmly, but unofficially, backed by the Superintendent who was also instrumental in getting Lieutenant J. Dunne into the Balloon Factory during 1906 to work quietly on his tailless glider projects. All Dunne's practical flying trials were made elsewhere but Cody, now with reluctant official permission, started construction of his Wright-type Flyer in the airship shed during October 1907. Lack of a suitable engine delayed the project and it was not until September 1908 that taxying runs took place in a clearing on Jersey Brow. Further trials were made on Laffan's Plain and Farn-

borough Common, the latter being used on October 16 1908 for the first sustained flight by an aeroplane in the British Isles. Cody started from Swan Inn Plateau, later the site of the RAF Officers' Mess, and took off north-westerly towards Cove Common reaching a height of about 35 ft (10 m). In avoiding trees, his port wing tip hit the ground and the machine crashed, though with little damage and no injury to Cody.

Official reaction was little short of staggering. Colonel Capper was lukewarm and a sub-committee of the Imperial Defence Committee came down firmly in favour of airships, recommending that experimental work on aeroplanes should cease. Both Cody and Dunne were dismissed, but allowed to keep their machines and use War Department property. In 1909 Cody built his own workshop and hangar on Laffan's Plain where he continued to fly until his fatal accident there on August 7 1913.

With the appointment of the energetic M.J.P. O'Gorman as the first civilian Superintendent of the Balloon Factory in October 1909, substantial additions were made to the facilities starting with workshop extensions and continuing with two more airship sheds during 1910 and 1911. By this time it had been officially admitted that the stopping of aeroplane work was a mistake and in April 1911 the name was changed to the Army Aircraft Factory. Significant advances were made with aeroplanes, largely through subterfuge, repairs to French imports becoming reconstructions, whose only connection with the original was the engine!

The Air Battalion of the Royal Engineers formed on February 28 1911, the HQ No 1 (Airship) Company being established at South Farnborough at the beginning of April. With two small airships on charge, the unit remained unchanged until the Royal Flying Corps (Military Wing) was born on May 13 1912, when it became No 1 Squadron, RFC, with two Flights of kites added to its strength. A large RFC workshop and No 2 Squadron, equipped with early BE biplanes, were created at Farnborough the same day. The BEs were housed in individual T-shaped canvas tents but the Royal Aircraft Factory continued to expand both its permanent buildings and test-beds.

No 4 Squadron, RFC, was formed in August 1912 at Farnborough with a variety of aeroplanes including one of

Above *The airship* Gamma II *flies past new hangars at Farnborough in 1910* (Hampshire County Library).

Right *The main factory area at Farnborough in 1914, looking west over the airship hangars towards the RFC sheds. In the foreground is the 'whirling arm' used for propeller trials* (B. Lowe via B. Robertson).

Cody's biplanes, but progress was slow and it was No 2 Squadron which made the greatest strides. In January 1913 they transferred to Montrose in Scotland by air. An epic journey by the standards of the time, Captain A.H. Longcroft, with Captain F.H. Sykes as passenger, made it in one day, landing at Alnmouth to refuel—a British record for a non-stop flight by a two-seater. Others took rather longer, but significantly they all got there in the end. No 4 Squadron completed a rather shorter journey in June 1913 when it moved to Netheravon and No 5 replaced it at Farnborough the following month. The build-up continued during 1914 with the creation of Nos 6 and 7 Squadrons, though a shortage of men and machines prevented the latter being more than a cadre.

On May 1 1914, all airships were transferred to the Naval Wing and No 1 Squadron, RFC, became the RNAS Airship Detachment, remaining at Farnborough until Kingsnorth was ready in March 1915. The Military Wing concentration camp at Netheravon during June and July 1914 denuded Farnborough of RFC aeroplanes and by the time they returned war was imminent. Almost the entire RFC went to France during August.

Major J.H.W. Becke finally started preparing No 6 Squadron for active service on October 4 and the first echelon went to Belgium three days later, commanded by Captain H.C.T. Dowding (later AOC-in-C Fighter Command during the Battle of Britain). With a similarly motley collection of machines, No 7 Squadron moved to Netheravon later in October 1914 to continue training and Farnborough settled down to what would now be termed a second-line role.

On the RFC side of the camp, the workshops became the Flying Depot, the nucleus of a repair organisation which developed into an Aircraft Park, while an offshoot of No 6 Squadron became a Reserve Aeroplane Squadron, a new source of trained pilots. It soon boasted a variety of Maurice Farman variants, Bleriot XIs and BE2s—in fact anything rejected for overseas service. With the formation of a second school at Brooklands, the original unit became No 1 RAS in November, the same month as the expanding RFC split into Wings. The Administrative Wing formed at Farnborough to control the RFC Depot, the Records Office and Aircraft Park on the station, and all the Reserve Aeroplane Squadrons. The latter were now given the added task of forming up new operational squadrons as personnel and equipment became available. The first such service squadron was No 10 in June 1915; this activity continued at Farnborough until, as No 1 RS, the unit moved to Gosport in April 1916.

By this time a number of standard RFC sheds replaced the canvas tents, more workshops had been built to the west of the factory, and the present Officers' Mess and quarters erected. Rows of workmen's cottages were appearing north of the factory, together with Pinehurst Barracks, a hutted camp for airmen close to Farnborough Park.

Despite adverse criticism it remained War Office policy to design and manufacture their own aircraft at the Royal Aircraft Factory, though an ever-increasing proportion of the activity was devoted to research and development. Construction was generally limited to prototypes but expansion of the RFC coupled with heavy losses did result in small batches of FE 2B night bombers, RE 8 reconnaissance machines and SE 5A fighter scouts being built in the new workshops between the original sheds and the Pinehurst cottages. Personnel, who had numbered 1,250 at the outbreak of war, had now increased to over 5,000.

On the research side, the experiments largely concerned armament and aerodynamics. Two wind tunnels were built during 1916/17 and trials included work on aircraft spinning.

The RFC repair workshops developed into No 1 (Southern) Aircraft Repair Depot which undertook anything up to complete rebuilds, while Nos 53, 70, 100 and 101 Squadrons were either formed up or mobilised at Farnborough during 1916 and 1917. The School for Wireless Operators formed on August 24 1916, becoming No 1 Wireless School in October 1917, using AW FK 3s, FK 8s and later Bristol F 2Bs for flying experience. They operated from hangars on Jersey Brow and when the School of Photography moved in, they used the same hangars, though their HQ was in a special building in the southeast corner of the airfield. The aerodrome now covered some 286 acres, taking in Cove Common and the levelled Laffan's Plain, which gave a very long landing run SW/NE, and adequate distances in other directions.

At the end of the war No 1 (Southern) ARD was handling DH 4s, DH 9s, DH 10s, SE 5As Dolphins and Martinsyde F 3s, covered 80 acres and employed over 3,000 men and women. The Wireless School was about to leave for Flowerdown, but the School of Photography was running courses for air mechanics, camera repairers and photographic officers, this work continuing into the difficult post-war retrenchment period.

Following the formation of the RAF, the factory was renamed the Royal Aircraft Establishment in July 1918 and work went ahead on Rafborough, a large housing estate for workers at Cove. Production of aircraft by the RAE ceased with the Armistice, the Establishment concentrating on research work for which it was now admirably equipped. By June 1920, the staff had been reduced to 1,380, but the following year the RAE absorbed the Instrument Design Establishment from Biggin Hill and the Airworthiness Department of the Air Ministry. An illustration of how far some researchers were perpared to go is given by the cool courage of Major G.H. Norman who deliberately set fire to his SE 5A to test a French fire-extinguishing system. The extinguisher worked but the resultant smoke blinded him and he crashed on landing. Though apparently unhurt, he suddenly collapsed and died later.

The RAF Repair Depot became a storage organisation and the inevitable contraction produced a series of command changes. At the end of the war, Farnborough was in the South Western Area which became No 7 Group, Southern Area, on September 20 1919. Southern and Northern Areas combined in April 1920 as Inland Area and it was into this organisation that No 4 Squadron was reborn, equipped with Bristol Fighters. At first sight, Farnborough would seem a strange location for one of the few operational squadrons in the UK, but No 4 was an Army Co-op unit, and what better place to be than next door to Aldershot? A Flight went to Ireland from November 1920 to January 1922 to operate against the Sinn Fein and in September the whole unit was embarked in HMS *Ark Royal* and transported to Turkey for the so-called Chanak Crisis. A year later No 4 Squadron was back at Farnborough in one of the famous black sheds, close to the RAE buildings and Cody's Tree, co-operating with the Aldershot Command in artillery spotting, photography, bombing and ground-strafing exercises.

No 7 Group was renumbered No 22 within Inland Area on April 12 1926, its HQ remaining at Farnborough responsible for the School of Photography, Experimental Section, RAE and No 4 Squadron in addition to Army Co-operation units at Andover, Larkhill and Old Sarum. No 4 Squadron was re-equipped with the Atlas in 1929, which served as a stop gap until the very useful Audax became available in February 1932.

Meanwhile, the facilities of the RAE were again improved. A 660 ft (201 m) seaplane test-tank was under construction in 1931 and three years later the very impressive 24 ft (7.3 m) wind-tunnel was opened, enabling full-scale tests to be made on both aircraft and engines. Considerable practical test work was done on flight refuelling between 1931 and 1938, while development of pressurised flying suits and breathing equipment was started as part of investigations into high-altitude flight. Trials were made in 1936 using a specially built Bristol 138A monoplane on which Squadron Leader F.R.D. Swain gained a new World Altitude Record of 49,967 ft (15,230 m) during a two-hour flight on September 28. After further modification, and spurred on by Italy regaining the record, Flight Lieutenant M.J. Adams succeeded in reaching 53,937 ft (16,440 m) in this extraordinary single-engined aircraft.

The station was transferred to No 24 Group on July 10 1936 and No 4 Squadron's long stay at Farnborough ended in February 1937 when it went to nearby Odiham, being replaced by No 53 (AC) Squadron, a specialist night-reconnaissance unit. Within a year it too, had joined the Odiham Wing. No 1 Anti-Aircraft Co-operation Unit moved in from Biggin Hill on April 11 1938 and expansion of the unit started, two new Wallace-equipped Flights being formed at Farnborough.

Farnborough reverted to No 22 Group control on June 1 1938 with the School of Photography as a lodger. The AACU Flights moved about in a most confusing manner, depending on the requirements of armament practice camps, but the HQ remained at Farnborough with A Flight, which spent the winter of 1938/39 converting pilots onto the latest target tower, the Henley. Further expansion took place in April 1939 but all moved to APCs the following month, leaving just the unit HQ, the RAE and the School of Photography at Farnborough when war was declared in September 1939.

Further Henley Flights were formed on No 1 AACU and late in February 1940 three aircraft went to Abbeville in France for co-operation with BEF AA batteries, probably the nearest the ill-used Henley got to the front line. They returned to Farnborough four weeks later and in April the strength of No 1 AACU increased again—it was now a very large, unwieldy unit.

The RAE was naturally very interested in German aircraft development and in addition to examination of pieces of wreckage they took every opportunity to evaluate flyable Luftwaffe machines. A Bf 109E was quickly obtained for this purpose, but a Bf 110 had to be built up from two aircraft which had crash landed during July 1940. The Luftwaffe also began taking an active interest in Farnborough, but a night raid apparently aimed at the RAE on August 2 was unsuccessful and an attempted attack by Ju 88s

Above *The scene at the corner of Sydney Smith Avenue near the main office block of the RAE after the Luftwaffe attack of August 16 1940* (RAE 32162).

Left *Taken a few days after the August 1940 bombing, this oblique shows new buildings under construction while the bomb damage has been made safe and the roads cleared. The partially protected Cody's Tree can be seen in the bottom left hand corner near the camouflaged sheds* (RAE 86476).

Below *Perhaps one of the more startling RAE experiments—the Avro Manchester prototype undergoing catapult-accelerated take-off tests at Farnborough* (RAE 42321).

The Farnborough runway layout in November 1941 at the start of a massive development programme which continued throughout the war and into the 1950s (RAE 38215).

of KG 54 on August 13 was foiled by defending fighters. A German bomber did penetrate to Farnborough the following day, but under rather different circumstances. It was a He 111H-1 of 5/KG26 which had been brought down near Dalkeith by a No 602 Squadron Spitfire on February 9 1940. Repaired, it was flown south to Farnborough on August 14 by Squadron Leader H. Wilson of the RAE. Such a trip, always hazardous because of the problem of informing all defences, was made even more dangerous by the loss of its Hurricane escort, but it arrived safely and did a considerable amount of flying with the RAE before despatch to the AFDU.

It was on August 16 1940 that the only bombs of the war fell on the establishment. Eight Ju 88s dropped 20 HE bombs, half of which hit the RAE, the rest exploding amongst local housing. Most of the staff were in shelters, but the roof of one concrete strongpoint collapsed, killing three employees, and the RAE was badly disrupted for three days. Some of the departments were dispersed, while the Experimental Flying Department formed a Defence Flight consisting of a Spitfire, two Hurricanes and a Gladiator.

During the autumn, the RAE was transferred to the Ministry of Aircraft Production, thus severing direct links with the RAF for the first time. Under the Director, W.S. Farren, activities expanded and its mandate was widely interpreted, while increased flying and the higher-performance aircraft now employed resulted in the construction of the first runways. Army Co-operation Command was formed at Farnborough in December 1940 but No 71 Group and the Command HQ soon moved out, leaving No 70 Group in control of the station and the AACU.

Only the bare outline of the RAE's work during the war can be given. Highlights were the successful development by the Instrument Department of bomb-sight and camera equipment which transformed Bomber and Coastal Commands, while work on gyro gun-sights by the Armament Department reached fruition and did wonders for Fighter Command. Equally important were supply-dropping and glider-towing techniques painfully hammered out by the Aerodynamics and Armament Departments, rocket-projectile development and the work of the Chemistry Department reducing aircraft losses from fire.

When a scheme for catapult-launched fighters to provide cover in mid-Atlantic was dreamed up, the RAE was told to produce the hardware. Twenty-five days later Wing Commander H.J. Wilson was demonstrating the system to Admiralty and Air Ministry officials. The first CAM ship was fitted with a catapult in April

Wing Commander J. Unwin (left) stands in front of a 'hack' Magister at Farnborough during 1942. Behind are the office block, airship shed and machine shops (Wing Commander J. Unwin via P.H.T. Green).

1941, by which time pilots and ground crew were already appearing at Farnborough for training using Fulmars. Over 60 launches were made without incident.

During the summer of 1942 the main SW/NE runway underwent considerable extension into Laffan's Plain, though flying continued unabated, added to by No 653 Squadron, which arrived from Old Sarum in August to join No 53 Wing. Using Taylorcraft C/2s at first, it had a full complement of 20 Auster AOP 1s when it went to Penshurst on September 7 1942.

No 1 AACU was broken into separate Flights in October 1942 and a detachment of No 7 AACU arrived to carry out local target-towing work. Farnborough returned to No 24 Group control in October 1943 and the AACU detachment was absorbed by No 577 Squadron in December, later joined by part of No 287 Squadron, while detachments from Nos 285, 290 and 667 Squadron at intervals for silent co-op with No 3 Royal Artillery Training Group, Blackdown.

At the RAE, testing and evaluation continued unabated and, because they were often exploring the unknown, the flying was anything but routine. During 1943–44, the Experimental Flying Section started investigating phenomena concerned with high-speed flight, following up wind-tunnel research data. Using Spitfires, they carried out full-power dives from 40,000 ft (12,192 m), Squadron Leader J.R. Tobin reaching an indicated Mach 0.92 in a Spitfire XI at the end of 1943. Squadron Leader A.F. Martindale, AFC, continued this work in 1944, during

which he suffered a catastrophic failure of a propeller, resulting in the reduction gear being torn out of the aircraft, but he was able to glide the 20 miles back to Farnborough saving the aircraft and its recording instruments.

By the end of 1944, the main SW/NE runway had been extended to 6,150 ft (1,874 m) and the supplementary 22/04 had been replaced by a new N/S concrete one of 3,000 ft (914 m) which made up the traditional tringular format with the original NW/SE strip. The 22/04 runway remained in use for experimental aircraft, mainly naval aircraft on dummy-deck trials.

With the end of World War Two, the commitments of the RAE were reduced. Work on piston engines was dropped and gas-turbine development transferred to the National Gas Turbine Establishment at nearby Pyestock, while rocket research was moved to Westcott. In April 1946, the RAE was transferred to the MoS and was joined in August 1947 by the ETPS, moved out of Cranfield to make room for the College of Aeronautics. A month later the RAE opened its gates to the public for perhaps the first time. Intended for employees and friends, over 4,000 people turned up to tour the departments and view the aircraft assembled alongside the new control tower.

When the airfield was also transferred to the MoS on June 1 1948, No 1 School of Photography moved with its Ansons to Wellesbourne Mountford and the ETPS took over their buildings for offices and a separate mess. The RAF units that remained included the Institute of Aviation Medicine and the Meteorological Research Flight, which had arrived in August 1946 with two Mosquito PR 34s and two Halifax VIs. The rather *ad hoc* RAE communications set-up developed into a formal Air Transport Flight during 1947 and received Devons in March 1949. These same aircraft, slightly updated, are still in service.

The SBAC Show was held at Farnborough for the first time in 1948 using very temporary tentage, but as the event became more permanent, so did the facilities, until the present-day conglomeration of chalets on the rising ground to the south of the main runway appeared in the 1960s.

Steady development of the airfield continued despite much of the flying being transferred to Bedford (Thurleigh) where the approaches are much less obstructed. The main runway was further extended and is now 7,814 ft (2,382 m) long while considerable rebuilding of dispersal areas has been undertaken. The research laboratories have also undergone updating, their tasks having included major advances in airfield lighting and the enquiry into the Comet disasters of 1954. The ETPS, with its fleet of interesting aeroplanes, moved back to Boscombe Down in January 1968 resulting in a considerable reduction in Farnborough's airborne traffic. This was partially restored when No 664 Squadron of the Army Air Corps re-formed from Nos 8 and 21 Flights and a variety of smaller units and, during October 1969, took up residence with Sioux and Scout helicopters in a purpose-built hangar. Apart from taking its share of Northern Ireland detachments and exercise deployments, the unit remained at Farnborough until re-formed as No 656 Squadron in March 1978.

Meanwhile, the Met Research Flight has worked its way through specially instrumentated Hastings, Varsity and Canberra aircraft and now employs the strange-looking Hercules W 2 (illustrated in *Action Stations 1*) while the Experimental Flying Department operates two squadrons at Farnborough—Western Squadron flying for the weapons, structures and engineering physics departments and Southern Squadron, which is concerned with avionics, radio, cockpit ergonomics and fly by wire controls development.

No 656 Squadron operated its Scouts and Gazelles for No 6 Field Force and had a fairly adventurous time while based at Farnborough, sending helicopters to Rhodesia from December 1979 to March 1980 to cover the independence handover, and to Hong Kong in support of No 660 Squadron. The unit moved to Netheravon on March 12 1982.

A year earlier it had been announced that MoD (PE) could no longer justify three research airfields and that Farnborough would be sold in 1985, though the RAE buildings would be retained. This plan produced much local opposition and in July 1982 it was decided that MoD would keep the airfield but release 50 acres for use as a general aviation enclave. The position of the SBAC Show is currently assured up to the 1986 display, and though the famous black sheds so beloved of commentators have been pulled down, many of the original buildings, some much modified, remain among their newer brethren. So does Cody's Tree, though this is now merely a metal replica of the pioneer's hitching post. Until recently so little was known about the early days at Farnborough that even the plate attached to the tree's plinth commemorating Cody's first flight has had to be amended—several times! A less well-known link with the past is the RAE Museum, a fascinating collection of items involved in the history of the establishment over the years. Not open to the public on a regular basis, sympathetic consideration will be given to requests for visits from genuine historians and researchers.

It now appears that this historic airfield, the oldest still active in the UK, has survived its latest crisis—let us hope it is with us for many years to come.

Folkestone (Capel), Kent
See Capel

Folkestone (Hawkinge), Kent
See Hawkinge

Ford, West Sussex
SU995029. 2⅜ miles W of Littlehampton on A2024

It was a frustrating business flying night fighter Blenheims during the autumn of 1940. There were plenty of targets over south-east England but unsuitable aircraft and unreliable equipment meant opportunities for interception were few. At Ford, No 23 Squadron crews fumed and finally got permission to try another way to deal with enemy bombers—by locating their airfields and attacking aircraft when they were taking off or landing. This sounds easy but proved difficult and though six Blenheims were over France during the first night, nothing was seen. With experience came successes, the first on January 2 1941 when Flying Officer P.S.B. Ensor sighted an aircraft near Caen with its navigation lights on. He followed it as far as Dreux where he closed and opened fire at 300 ft (92 m) range. Hits were observed on the tail, identified as belonging to a He 111 and, presumably thinking their attacker was a Luftwaffe fighter pilot, the crew fired a recognition flare. Ensor fired again but ran out of ammunition before he could claim a kill. It was a start, however, and after re-equipment with Havocs, No 23 Squadron gained a well-deserved reputation for being the intruder experts.

Officially known as Ford Junction, but more often as Yapton, this aerodrome was one of the large number of training stations authorised in 1917. The plans for a typical TDS on the 85-acre site between the villages of Yapton and Ford were approved in November 1917 and work started early in 1918, German PoWs building most of the camp. The technical site, on the west side of the aerodrome, was clustered around six 1917-pattern brick-walled, wooden-roofed hangars and a large aircraft-repair shed.

While still in the preliminary stages of construction, Ford Junction was earmarked for the United States Air Service to use for training on the American-built Handley Page 0/400 bombers expected to arrive in large numbers during the summer of 1918. The first flying, however, was by No 148 Squadron, RFC, which brought its FE 2B night bombers over from Andover on March 1 1918 and helped form No 149 Squadron two days later. No 253 Squadron was scheduled to move in two of its DH 6 coastal anti-submarine patrol Flights in May, but this plan was cancelled and No 148 Squadron left for France, followed by No 149 on June 2. Work then concentrated on preparing the aerodrome for the Americans, who took it over on August 15 as Field No 1 in the Chichester Area of the Night Bombardment Section, American Expeditionary Force. The hangars and a special Handley Page erection building were still unfinished, so when personnel moved in, early in September, they erected a row of eight Bessoneaux canvas hangars in front of the main technical site. The 92nd Aero Squadron arrived from the USA late in the month and received Farman F 40 pusher biplanes while the 140th and 326th Aero Squadrons were formed at Ford with a few BE 2Cs and American-built DH-4s respectively.

The Night Bombardment Training School, intended to teach night navigation by radio direction, opened on September 15. Delays in sending Standard Aircraft Corporation-built 0/400s from the States continued and, instead, ten sets of components were diverted from the National Aircraft Factory No 1, Waddon. The Armistice was signed before the first course was completed or the first machine assembled and everything came to a sudden halt.

On November 15 1918, the motley collection of Aero Squadron aircraft was

Bristol F 2B at Ford Junction in 1919. Probably a machine of No 50 Training Squadron which was based there at the time (G.S. Leslie/J.M. Bruce collection).

flown to nearby Tangmere and two days later all USAS personnel moved out, leaving Ford clear for the RAF to demobilise squadrons. The first was No 144 which arrived in December, followed early in 1919 by Nos 10, 97, 115 and 215 Squadrons. All soon disbanded except No 97 which was re-equipped with DH 10 twin-engined bombers and despatched to India the following July.

The main hangars were completed and No 50 TS had a short revival at Ford during 1919, but with the disbandment of the last of the demob units in December the station was virtually deserted and closed in January 1920.

It was ten years before flying returned to Ford. DW Aviation renovated two of the hangars in 1930 for the production of Dudley Watt DW 2 biplanes, but this plan came to nothing. With one eye on the publicity value of the name, the Ford Motor Company leased the airfield from July 1931 to use as a maintenance base during efforts to increase sales of their Trimotor aircraft. Only a handful were imported before the company ceased airliner manufacture and, in June 1932 Rollason Aviation moved their flying training organisation in from busy Croydon. They operated as the South Downs FC while Alan Cobham rented a couple of the hangars from Ford for winter storage and refurbishing of his barnstorming aircraft.

With the demise of the Ford operation in 1934, National Aviation Displays Ltd took over and Sir Alan Cobham developed the airfield as his HQ. As popularity of the aerial circus waned he established Flight Refuelling Ltd for develop-

ment work using the AW 23 and HP 51 prototype bomber transports. A pair of Harrows were later prepared as tankers at Ford for refuelling trial with Short C-boats, aimed at getting the flying boats across the Atlantic non-stop.

After Audaxes of Nos 4 and 13 (AC) Squadrons had used Ford during a Brigade exercise in 1936, the Air Ministry acquired the airfield, the Air Estimates including £109,000 for the construction of a hutted camp and hangars for a School of Naval Co-operation. Standard wooden huts and five Bellmans were built on additional ground purchased to the east of the original airfield. RAF station Ford was opened on December 1 1937 in No 17 (Training) Group of Coastal Command and a month later the school moved from Lee equipped with Sharks and Swordfish.

The part-timers of Nos 500 and 601 Squadrons held their annual summer camps at Ford during 1938 but, on May 24 1939, the airfield was formally transferred to the Admiraly and commissioned as HMS *Peregrine*, the training unit being renamed the RN Observer School. The aircraft were divided between three squadrons, 750, 751 and 752, and for the next year their ancient biplanes could be seen plodding out over the Channel on navigation exercises. Even before the Dunkirk evacuation it had been recognised that the area was unsuitable for a training unit and as soon as possible 750 and 752 Squadrons were moved to a still incomplete Yeovilton leaving 751 Squadron with the newly formed 753 (Air Target Training) and 779 (Armament Training) Squadrons at Ford. Flight Refuelling Ltd still occupied their hangars on the western side of the airfield

Soon after Ford re-opened as an RAF station in December 1937 this No 56 Squadron Hurricane visited—probably for Empire Air Day 1938 (P. Ward-Hunt).

carrying out aircraft repair work but their presence embarrassed the Admiralty and they finally moved to the Morgan Motor Works at Malvern during May 1940, leaving the AW 23 and two Harrows stored at Ford. A number of front-line naval squadrons also used the airfield for work-up, but only training units were resident on August 18 when the Luftwaffe decided to eliminate it—apparently under the impression it was a fighter base.

The attack came after a morning of heavy raids on airfields further east and a few minutes after an all clear had been sounded at Ford. Twenty-eight Ju 87s of II/StG77 broke away from a large formation approaching the Isle of Wight, and while defending fighters waited over the anticipated targets the Stukas rained bombs on the virtually unprotected airfield. A huge pall of thick black smoke proclaimed direct hits on fuel installations, two hangars, MT and stores sheds, the ratings' and POs' canteens and many huts, both wooden and Nissen. Of aircraft in and around the hangars, 17 were wrecked, including all three belonging to Flight Refuelling. A further 26 were damaged while the casualty list showed 28 killed and 75 wounded, with many more badly shocked by the suddeness of the attack. Spitfires of No 602 Squadron, Westhampnett, intercepted the Ju 87s as they withdrew and managed to shoot down three and badly damaged another before being set upon by the Bf 109s of III/JG27. One Spitfire pilot had to bale out and three others crash-landed, one on Ford airfield itself.

No 793 Squadron was disbanded immediately and plans for the FAA to leave Ford were accelerated, though not before 828 Squadron was formed with Albacores in September, at about the same time as No 23 Squadron, RAF, moved its Blenheim If night fighters in from Collyweston. HMS *Peregrine* was paid off on September 30 1940, and the following day Ford was on the strength of No 11 Group, Fighter Command—perhaps Luftwaffe intelligence staffs now felt vindicated, but four raids during October were minor, only one resulting in any significant damage.

The last naval unit, 751 Squadron, left for Arbroath in December and when the Fighter Interception Unit brought its Blenheims and Beaufighters in from Shoreham it was the start of a long period of intensive trials work on night fighter and intruder tactics, often frustrating, but

finally crowned with success. No 23 Squadron re-equipped with Havocs in March 1941 and their intruder operations became more adventurous, every bomber airfield from Gilze-Rijen in Holland to Caen in France being visited during the next few months.

All-weather operations were helped by the construction of two tarmac runways of 6,000 ft (1,828 m) SW/NE and 4,800 ft (1,463 m) NW/SE, together with extensive new taxi-tracks to the west of the original airfield. Blast pens were built, as were a number of Blisters dispersed around the perimeter track to supplement the Bellmans and the one GS hangar refurbished after the Stuka attack. All the accommodation was temporary except for married quarters now used as billets.

On June 7 1942, No 605 Squadron, which had been decimated in the Dutch East Indies debacle, was re-formed at Ford, the one-off Owlet dual trainer giving the pilots experience of tricycle under-carriages before they took over Bostons and Havocs from No 23 Squadron. They started ops on July 14 with an attack on marshalling yards at Caen but most of their personnel were not combat ready and, for Operation *Jubilee*, all but two crews were detached to Hunsdon. This was not noticeable at Ford, for No 88 Squadron appeared in their place and this high-spirited bunch were more than a little intrigued to find notices in their sleeping quarters which read, *If you need a mistress, ring the bell*. Incessant ringing soon rent the air but to no avail—it was a requisitioned Girls Boarding School. No 107 Squadron Bostons, plus two from No 418 (RCAF) Squadron, were cheek by jowl with Hurri-bombers of No 174 Squadron, all crowded into Ford by August 18 ready for the combined-operation assault on Dieppe planned for the following day.

Boston crews were woken early and the first off were four from Nos 88 and 107 Squadrons, briefed to join up with ten aircraft from No 226 Squadron (Thruxton) and drop 156 × 100-lb (45 kg) phosphorus smoke bombs to screen the ships as they approached the beaches. Five minutes later six more Bostons of No 88 Squadron, each carrying three 500-lb (227 kg) and 16 40-lb (18 kg) bombs set off to bomb the massive Rommel gun position which dominated the eastern approaches to the port, while a mixed formation from Nos 107, 418 and 605 Squadrons attacked the Hitler and Göring batteries to the

One of the famous Ford 'intruders'—a Mosquito II of No 605 Squadron in 1943 (IWM CH19476).

south-west. The Germans were alert and the aircraft met heavy flak, several receiving hits. Hurricanes followed the Bostons, to dive-bomb the gun positions and strafe the nearby airfield at St Aubin.

Back at Ford the ground-crew, particularly the armourers, laboured on aircraft turnrounds. Bostons and Hurricanes made two, and sometimes three, sorties against the gun batteries during the day, the Bostons finishing with another smoke screen to cover the retreating ships.

No 141 Squadron had arrived at Ford on August 10, but took no direct part in *Jubilee* until the Germans made scattered raids on southern England, when a Beaufighter shot down a Ju 88. Ford was attacked during the evening, one Boston being destroyed and two damaged, and a single Fw 190 dropped three bombs which blast-damaged two Beaufighters. In the air, No 174 Squadron had lost six Hurricanes, and Nos 88 and 418 Squadrons a Boston each with others damaged. One Fw 190 was claimed by a Boston gunner—but *Jubilee* could not be rated as a Ford success.

When fully operational, No 605 Squadron started establishing a reputation for intruder work while No 141 tried intercepting daytime fighter-bomber attacks on south coast towns. It was very much a matter of luck, the only success being a Do 217 which hit a gasholder at Bognor on December 16 1942 while trying to evade Flying Officer Cook—who didn't fire a shot!

No 141 Squadron swopped places with No 604 Squadron at Predannack on February 18 1943 and a month later No 605 went to Castle Camps to finish conversion to Mosquitoes. They were replaced by No 418 (RCAF) Squadron, no strangers to Ford, who now converted to Mosquito IIs and entered one of their most successful intruder periods, doubling their previous score of seven in four months.

No 604 Squadron was replaced by No 256 on April 24 and they wasted no time, destroying a Do 217 off Worthing four nights later. After converting to Mosquito XIIs, another night raider was accounted for on June 11, but none of the night-fighter squadrons stayed long, No 256 departing in August just after a raid on Portsmouth by 91 bombers during which the CO, Wing Commander G.R. Park, shot down a Do 217. No 29 Squadron arrived early in September with Mosquito XIIs, the crews being very upset when ordered not to cross the Channel because they risked compromising their new AI sets. The start of Operation *Steinbock* on the night of January 21/22 1944, when the Luftwaffe despatched 447 aircraft against London, perked them up, however. No 29 Squadron scrambled 13 Mosquitoes and despite trouble with *duppel* (German *window*) were able to claim a Fw 190, one of nine destroyed that night. The raids continued and the squadron had its most successful night on February 24 when a He 177, a Do 217, two Ju 88s/188s and probably a Me 410 were shot down for the loss of their CO, Wing Commander R.E. Mack, DFC. Five days later they were withdrawn to Drem and replaced by No 456 Squadron from Fairwood Common. Newly equipped with Mosquito XVIIs, which had improved radar, this Australian unit shot down a Me 410 near Horsham on April 20, followed three nights later by a Ju 88 over Swanage, and no less than three Ju 88s on the 25th during an attack on Portsmouth.

Meanwhile, Ford was prepared for use by the Allied Expeditionary Air Force, the FIU moving to Wittering early in April where it was joined by 746 Squadron. Mustangs of Nos 19, 65 and 122 Squadrons, No 83 Group, operating as No 122 Airfield, arrived from Gravesend on April 15 and immediately started flying *Rangers*. Four aircraft of No 122 Squadron penetrated to the Swiss border on the 23rd, arriving over Dole/Tavaux airfield just as eight He 111s joined the circuit. It was a turkey shoot, six of the bombers being shot down, while a Gotha Go 242 transport and another '111 were damaged.

Late in April the Mustangs were fitted with bomb racks and on May 2 Nos 65 and 122 Squadrons dropped 36 500 lb (226 kg) bombs on Nantes/Grassicourt marshalling yards during their first fighter-bomber operation. They moved to Funtington on May 14 to practice operations from an ALG and were replaced by Spitfires of No 125 Airfield (Nos 132, 453 and 602 Squadrons). They were used for offensive sweeps over France, Belgium, Holland and even south-west Germany, bomber escorts and attacks on *Noball* sites.

On May 15, the day Airfields became Wings, the Canadians of No 144 Wing (Nos 441, 442 and 443 Squadrons) joined No 125 at Ford. Recently equipped with Spitfire IX fighter-bombers, the Canadians had a very hectic three weeks preparing for D-Day by flying *Roadsteads, Rodeos* and *Ramrods* during which they dive-bombed railways, airfields and radar stations, nine direct hits being scored on a *Warzbürg* installations at Cap d'Antifer during a Wing attack.

On June 6 all the Ford squadrons took part in the fighter umbrella over the invasion forces. In the days that followed they provided low-level cover over the beachhead and then turned to ground attack in support of forward troops. After dark, the pressure was maintained by 15 night fighter squadrons, among them No 456 at Ford. On June 7 they intercepted five He 177s, between Cherbourg and Le Havre and shot down four of them, while the next night three more were destroyed.

This carnage continued until the squadron was diverted to anti-*Diver* (V-1) work on June 24, but it was July 9/10 before the first could be claimed. No 96 Squadron arrived from West Malling on June 20 and continued its success with flying bombs, its Mosquito XIII crews destroying 49 by the end of the month. Further kills were made, though it was neither safe nor simple to get in a successful attack on this small target travelling at between 320 and 350 mph (515-563 km/h). If it blew up, damage to the Mosquitoes' coolant radiators was almost inevitable.

On June 10, No 453 Squadron started to use the dusty strips prepared by the REs in the beach-head, but it was No 144 Wing which was the first to transfer to the Continent, moving to B3 (St Croix-sur-Mer) five days later. The last No 83 Group unit in England, No 125 Wing, left for the Continent on June 25 and was promptly replaced at Ford by No 133 Wing (Nos 129, 306 and 315 Squadrons) of No 84 Group. They were engaged in intensive armed recce over the battlefield and suffered heavy losses until transferred to anti-*Diver* operations for which they moved to Brenzett. No 131 (Polish) Wing (Nos 302, 308 and 317 Squadrons) which had been languishing at Appledram and Chailey ALGs, moved in to continue co-operation with the army in France while preparing to join them at B10 (Plumetot) on August 3. There was then a short respite before the arrival of No 132 Wing (Nos 66, 127, 331 and 332 Squadrons) with more Spitfires on August 12, but they too were only preparing for France and went to B16 (Villons les Buissons) on August 20.

With the excitement over, No 96 Squadron moved to Odiham in September and the FIU and 746 Squadron returned, becoming part of the newly formed Night Fighter Development Wing which flew Mosquitoes, Beaufighters and a variety of naval aircraft. No 456 Squadron sent a detachment to Manston during September/October for the Arnhem débâcle and subsequent operations in Holland, but the unit was at full strength at Ford when anti-V-1 patrols started again on November 5. These were against He 111s being used as aerial launchers, the first squadron success coming on November 19, but No 456 Squadron was withdrawn at the end of December 1944, leaving the airfield to the Development Wing. The Ranger Flight and Fighter Interception Development Squadron both made some operational flights, but the early months of 1945 saw the gradual transfer of the Wing to Tangmere, completed in July 1945.

Ford ceased to be a No 11 Group station on July 31 1945 and was transferred to the Admiralty, being re-commissioned as HMS *Peregrine*. 746 Squadron remained and was joined by the newly formed 720 Squadron which operated as a photographic school using four Ansons and some Barracudas. 746 Squadron was absorbed by 787 in September but naval strength continued to build up at Ford, two front-line units forming that month, 811 Squadron with Mosquitoes and 813 with Firebrands. Conditions at Ford were poor with little hangarage available, the aircraft having to be dispersed among the old fighter blast pens. This situation got worse as more second-line units, mostly concerned with advanced training on

twin-engined aircraft, joined the strength of *Peregine*.

Despite this, No 161 GS of the ATC moved in from Burgess Hill early in 1946, by which time Flight Refuelling Ltd had also returned from Staverton, remaining until June 1948 when the company transferred to Tarrant Rushton. Shortly afterwards, 804 and 812 Squadrons completed their initial work-up and moved as a Carrier Group to Eglinton. Ford was then closed so that a large-scale refurbishing programme could be completed as quickly as possible. The runways and taxiways were resurfaced, a large concrete hardstanding laid and three new hangars erected, while the technical and domestic sites were cleaned up and partially rebuilt.

RNAS Ford re-opened in March 1950 and the following month 703 Squadron moved in from Lee-on-Solent as the Service Trials Unit, with 771 Squadron as

Taken a year after the airfield re-opened in March 1950 this vertical by No 540 Squadron reveals new dispersals and a cleaned up airfield—but also that many Blister hangars and fighter blast pens remain (DoE/Crown Copyright).

a FRU. Both operated a very mixed bunch of naval aircraft and were finally amalgamated on August 17 1955 as 700 (Trials & FRU) Squadron. They were joined by a stream of front-line naval squadrons, working-up prior to embarking in a carrier, or on return from a commission. Ford was the parent station for the four squadrons making up HMS *Eagle*'s Air Group for many years.

In June 1951, No 1840 Squadron, RNVR, arrived from Culham with Firefly aircraft and, a year later, Ford became HQ of the Channel Air Division. Perhaps the most significant event, however, came in August 1951 when 800 Squadron became the first operational naval unit equipped with jet fighters. Eight Attackers were received at Ford prior to going aboard *Eagle* as part of the 13th CAG in March 1952. With its sister squadron, 803, it returned many times to Ford before disbanding in June 1954.

A new Petty Officers' Mess was completed in 1956, as the first stage of a major rebuilding programme which was not completed for, although 700X Squadron formed as the Intensive Trials Unit for the Scimitar on August 27 1957, the introduc-

tion of this large, heavy fighter was really Ford's swansong. Reductions in the FAA announced in the 1958 Estimates and availability of larger and better equipped airfields meant Ford's closure was inevitable, despite its pleasant and convenient location. With the work of 700X completed and the departure of the parent squadron to Culdrose on September 19 1958, flying ceased.

HMS *Peregrine* was paid off on November 13 1958 but many of the buildings remain in pristine condition because they were retained when the main camp near Ford village was transferred to the Home Office as an open prison. The control tower and Bellman hangars were demolished, as were most of the First World War buildings on the eastern side, but others, including the three large hangars erected in 1951, survive for use by two industrial estates. Kendellstone occupy most of one, while the other was used by Miles Aviation & Transport (R&D) Ltd for aircraft overhaul from 1964 until the firm moved to Shoreham in November 1971. Flying ceased for a while, but then revived, part of the airfield being used as an unlicensed LG until 1980 when

Left A recent photograph of Ford viewed from the north-west shows that the general appearance is little changed despite the claims of agriculture (N.D. Welch via D.J. Smith).

Below One of the Ford Extra Over Blisters in 1982 (M.L. Asquith).

Ford finally closed.

The A2024 road from Littlehampton to Yapton has been restored and a large housing estate encroaches on the western side of the old airfield. Stretches of runway and perimeter track still survive which, together with the still obvious airfield buildings, allow most of the outline to be traced. Ford is a place of memories.

Foreland, Isle of Wight

SZ654877. ½ mile S of Bembridge off B3395

The U-boat offensive close inshore around the British Isles reached a new peak in the spring of 1918 and it was decided to supplement seaplanes and airships with landplane 'scare' patrols, designed to keep submarines submerged rather than destroy them. Certainly the majority of the aircraft employed could do little more, for their offensive capability was minimal. To enable them to be on the scene quickly and to provide a reasonable endurance on patrol, the aircraft bases' had to be spread around the coast —one of them was at Bembridge on the extreme eastern tip of the Isle of Wight.

It was built on 51 acres of fairly flat ground at Lane End, Bembridge, and known as Foreland or New Bembridge. The aerodrome was quickly in use for there were no permanent buildings, the aircraft being housed in Bessoneaux hangars and the personnel in the town. Conditions were pretty miserable when the weather was bad. The original intention was to have one Flight at the Brading LG (just inland from Foreland), one at Telscombe Cliffs and a third at Foreland, making up a squadron, but these plans were changed and by early June the 12 DH 6 two-seat biplanes were at Foreland/ New Bembridge, co-operating with floatplanes long established in Brading Harbour. In August 1918 the unit was re-organised as Nos 511 and 512 Flights of No 253 Squadron, which was part of No 10 (Operations) Group, Warsash.

The DH 6s, universally known as the 'Clutching Hands', were unsuitable for over-water flying—but they were all that was available to the Marine Groups of the newly formed RAF. The aircraft plodded monotonously up and down their patrol lines off the coast, with little to report and even less action, but the measures introduced to combat the submarine menace did work, for shipping losses were soon

showing a significant decrease. After the Armistice there was little flying and the Flights were disbanded on January 21 1919. Disposal instructions for the site were issued during the autumn of 1919 and it was relinquished early in 1920. No evidence of its presence now exists, the site having been completely built over years ago.

Friston, East Sussex

TV534982. 4½ miles W of Eastbourne off A259

Known pre-war as Gayles and sometimes as East Dean, this private landing ground was first referred to as Friston when used by Hawker Audax Army co-operation machines off Nos 2 and 4 Squadrons for exercises with an Army brigade during August and September 1936. It is also believed to have accommodated pre-war Auxiliary Air Force camps but then lay dormant until designated a Fighter Command ELG during the summer of 1940.

A dog leg-shaped piece of fairly level grassland with a maximum NE/SW landing run of 5,020 ft (1,532 m), its position on top of the Seven Sisters cliffs made it ideal for this purpose. It was also well placed as a forward satellite airfield and in May 1941 an upgrade to this standard was authorised. Parented by Kenley, its use was still largely confined to fighters in trouble and ASR Lysanders on detachment from the Shoreham Flight, and it was closed during the winter while the work went ahead. With bulk fuel and ammunition storage built and accommodation huts erected, Friston re-opened on May 15 1942, still under Kenley.

The first residents were moved in on May 31—Spitfires which arrived by lorry and were assembled on site, for they were dummies! Surrounded by Bofors guns, they were bait for the Luftwaffe—who ignored the trap. The ambush was soon abandoned for preparations were under way early in June to receive Hurricanes of No 253 Squadron from Hibaldstow. Stores and equipment arrived and marquees were erected, the ground crew arriving by transport Harrows on the 12th, the aircraft following the next day.

On June 14 they were joined by Hurricanes of No 32 Squadron from West Malling and started operating as a Wing, though there were many problems, not least of them caused when contractors moved in to level the site and only left a usable 240 ft (73 m) wide strip. The reason for the sudden move of the Hurricanes to Friston was never revealed to the crews, but rumours were rife, especially after the aircraft were painted with zebra-like identification markings on July 4. It was all for Operation *Rutter*, which was intended to knock out the heavy gun positions overlooking Dieppe, but abandoned after an unsuccessful Army exercise.

The squadrons returned home on July 7, leaving one battle-damaged Hurricane behind; this became a target when two Bf 109s made a belated appearance two days later. Each dropped a 500 lb (227 kg) bomb, cratering the N/S landing strip and causing blast damage to the SHQ and a Nissen hut. They then strafed the airfield, cannon fire hitting a newly erected Blister hangar and the wretched Hurricane. The damage was still being repaired when a number of No 602 Squadron Spitfires, accompanied by three Battles, two Mustangs and a single Henley arrived for a firepower demonstration which attracted some 5,000 official spectators.

On July 20 the Kenley Wing started sending in detachments to provide dawn and dusk cover against low flying fighter-bombers, resulting in a nasty accident two days later when No 402 Squadron Hurricanes were scrambled just before first light and one collided with a tractor, killing two airmen who had been collecting glim lamps.

Following pressure from the Russians, the Dieppe raid was reinstated at the end of July as Operation *Jubilee*. Much of the *Rutter* plan was retained and Nos 32 and 253 Squadrons returned to Friston. Both were at readiness by 03:00 hours on August 19, Squadron Leader E.R. Thorn, DFM, leading 12 Hurricanes of No 32 Squadron off at 04:45 hours, followed by No 253 Squadron, who concentrated on the gun emplacements on Dieppe's western headland, losing one aircraft to the intense flak. More attacks on machine-gun emplacements followed later in the day. Flight Lieutenant J.L.W. Ellacombe, DFC, was hit but managed to bale out and landed alongside the last ships leaving Dieppe, while Squadron Leader D.S. Yapp managed to get back to Friston in time to lead a Section on a patrol over base following reports of enemy aircraft in the vicinity.

Friston was also host to several lame ducks, proving beyond doubt its ELG role. Shot up over Dieppe, Flight Lieutenant J.E. Scott was the first arrival, his No

614 Squadron Blenheim making a belly landing which ignited his smoke bombs and set the aircraft alight. The gunner was killed in the crash, but the badly burned Scott pulled out his unconscious observer, Sergeant W. Johnson, then got clear by rolling down the burning wing. Unfortunately Johnson succumbed to his injuries, but Scott recovered in hospital. Two Hurricanes made successful force-landings and a No 71 Squadron Spitfire ended up near the still-burning Blenheim, joined in the afternoon by a recce Mustang from No 239 Squadron which just made it across the Channel with a leaking oil tank. The operation as a whole may have been a disaster but Friston had a good day!

Many more aircraft used Friston as an emergency strip during the autumn of 1942, but the residents were confined to detachments from No 412 (RCAF) Squadron, Kenley. Their Spitfires used it from November until January 1943 when the grass surface became too soft for safe operation.

On March 14, just after midnight, Kenley Ops warned Friston of approaching raiders who dropped flares over the airfield. Two HE bombs exploded near the requisitioned house used as an Officers' Mess, while the flares and following incendiaries started two large gorse fires, one near the communal site to the north-west and the other by the Blister hangar at the western end of the main landing strip. Raids by low-flying Fw 190 and Bf 109 fighter-bombers on south coast towns reached serious proportions in the spring of 1943 and, to try and counter them, Griffon-powered Spitfire XIIs of No 41 Squadron were moved to Friston on May 27, though the grass surface was far from ideal for this variant. Cockpit readiness stand-bys started two days later, but it was June 4 before there was any action—18 Fw 190s spotted racing towards Eastbourne. Eight Spitfires were scrambled just in time to break up the attack, forcing some bombs to be jettisoned. Two Fw 190s were shot down, one by No 41 Squadron, the other by the AA defences. Another attack developed on June 6 but then things slackened and the XIIs went on *Jim Crow* patrols over the Channel before being replaced on June 21 by No 412 (RCAF) Squadron whose Spitfire Vbs were used for *Ramrods* and *Rodeos*. They were the first of a string of squadrons engaged in such sorties throughout the remainder of 1943

Spitfire IXs of No 349 Squadron dispersed on a bleak, snow covered Friston during February 1944 (IWM CH12434).

and into 1944. With the onset of autumn, the diversions increased and included many four-engined aircraft of Bomber Command making desperate emergency landings.

For the first time the airfield was used by a resident squadron throughout the winter, No 349 (Belgian) Squadron arriving on October 22 1943 to fly its first operations since arriving in Britain. On December 13 the SHQ, situated in The Gayles, caught fire and the adjutant and orderly room staff, together with the 24 WAAFs accommodated in the building, lost everything they possessed. A new SHQ was established at Tree Tops, East Dean, while the squadron struggled on against appalling weather. However, no less than 68 emergency landings were made during January 1944, and the Luftwaffe also visited on the 21st to drop one delayed-action bomb.

No 349 Squadron built up the sortie rate again in February, and as the facilities improved Friston became self-accounting, though still parented, now by Biggin Hill. Accommodation of various types was available for 1,248 RAF and 152 WAAF personnel and two Over Blisters were in use for servicing. There were still no hardstandings, however, and the only hard surface was a perimeter roadway which joined the approach road to The Gayles.

On March 11 1944, No 41 Squadron Spitfire XIIs returned to replace No 349 on *Ramrods* and *Rhubarbs*. They found the airfield no easier than before, a taxying aircraft being blown over during a gale and another crashing while trying to land. The squadron unsuccessfully chased a number of reconnaissance aircraft and covered for two ASR amphibians before

thankfully departing for Bolt Head on April 29.

The VIIIth AF was now carrying out heavy daylight raids on targets in France, and badly damaged B-17s and B-24s became a common sight at Friston despite it being one of the most unsuitable strips imaginable. Most were just a problem to shift off the landing area but others, like a B-24 of the 44th BG on March 16, crashed and burned on the airfield—a tragic sight for the fire-fighters just could not cope with such large aircraft.

Tangmere now took over parenting duties and a No 11 Group ADGB Wing led by Wing Commander D. Kingaby, DSO, DFM and two Bars, was established at Friston. Flying Spitfire Vbs, Nos 350 (Belgian) and 501 Squadron started working-up on Army exercises and, as D-Day approached, commenced all-out attacks on offshore shipping, communications and airfields. On May 20, a German aircraft dropped a solitary bomb near the main runway and put the airfield out of action for several hours, but most of the problems were concerned with accommodation which was so tight that it was planned to start putting WAAFs under canvas as well as airmen.

On June 6 the Wing was over the beachhead early, but few enemy aircraft appeared and it was June 8 before No 501 Squadron shot down a Bf 109, while No 350 flew 1,192 operational hours during the month and had only one contact. Again the station found itself overwhelmed by emergency landings—it seemed that everyone made for Friston. This continued throughout July into August, while the threat posed by V-1 flying bombs resulted in the more potent Spitfire XIIs and XIVs of Nos 41 and 610 Squadrons replacing the Vbs at Friston on July 2 for anti-*Diver* operations. Their scores mounted steadily, though No 41 had only marginally better performance than the quarry and was replaced on July 11 by Mustang IIIs of No 316 (Polish) Squadron. They destroyed 50 V-1s by the end of July and continued this work until August 25, when replaced by No 131 Squadron from Culmhead. The peak of the V-1 offensive was now over and the new residents were concerned with bomber escorts and sweeps interspersed with coastal patrols. The diversions still kept coming but were now usually for weather, as on September 8 when facilities were stretched to the limit by a steam landing of 22 C-47s. No 610 Squadron moved away for *Market Garden* escort work and, with the action getting further away, No 131 Squadron ceased operations on October 31 1944 and prepared for transfer to India.

Friston now returned to its original role of ELG, but was not very busy. No 7 Fighter Command Servicing Unit arrived early in 1945 and there was a flurry of activity when Austers of No 666 (RCAF) Squadron appeared on April 18 and stayed a little over a month before crossing the Channel to join the First Canadian Army at B77 (Gilze-Rijen) in Holland.

Friston was reduced to C&M on May 25 1945, parenting being transferred to Dunsfold on June 8 and to Tangmere on February 15 1946 before the airfield was derequisitioned on April 8.

The ban on civilian gliding had been lifted in the interim, but when the Southdown GC checked their old site at Devil's Dyke they found it dangerous after use as a battle-training area. They agreed terms with the owner of Friston and gliding started on the cliff-top airfield soon after its release by the Air Ministry. In 1948 the club's hangar was moved to Friston and soon housed their two SG 38s, the Cadet 2 Tutors and a Slingsby T 21B. The club stayed for nine years of successful cliff soaring at Friston before the tenancy agreement ended in March 1955 and they moved to Bo Peep Hill, some ten miles away. For some years a Nissen hut close to the RAC box on the A259 was a reminder

The outline of Friston LG is clear on this 1950 photograph despite the passage of five years since military occupation. 'Gayles' is on the edge of the airfield, centre right (DoE/Crown Copyright).

of a once busy airfield, but all evidence has now disappeared.

Frost Hill Farm, Hampshire

SU517525. 1½ miles N of Overton alongside B3051

A large stretch of open downland immediately east of the B3051 and 420 ft (140 m) above sea level, Frost Hill Farm was earmarked as the scatter field for Odiham in 1940, one of a series of large grass areas selected as suitable places for aircraft to land if south-eastern airfields were put out of action or captured.

During the summer of 1940 it was covered with wigwams made of poles to prevent enemy landings, but easily removable to allow friendly aircraft to find a haven. As far as is known, Frost Hill Farm was not used during the Battle of Britain but, when the Franco-Belgian School at Odiham was looking for a forced-landing ground in December, it was pressed into use. Flying by Magisters, and occasionally Lysanders, continued into 1941.

In June 1942 it was surveyed as one of the so-called ALGs in readiness for an increased number of fighter operations planned for 1943, a main 4,800 ft (1,453 m) NW/SE wire mesh runway with a subsidiary 3,000 ft (914 m) E/W strip being proposed. The site was selected as a low-priority ALG in July and the two Sommerfeld Track runways laid during 1943. No buildings were erected and as far as is known no subsequent use was made of this ALG.

At the end of the war the steel mesh was lifted and much of it buried in an old gravel pit at nearby Nutley Bottom, small pieces of it being recycled by locals for chicken runs. Maintenance Command took over the site and temporarily stored bulk fuel alongside the prehistoric Harrow Way. Today, helicopters from Middle Wallop use the field for training, and it probably sees more aeronautical activity —and mushroom picking—by military men than ever it did during World War Two.

Funtington, West Sussex

SU790085. 5 miles W of Chichester off B2146

Some of the ALGs on which so much effort was expended during 1943 failed to earn their keep, but Funtington was certainly not one of them. It was occupied continuously for 4½ months during 1944 by whole Wings on non-stop operations —one of the most successful of the temporary airfields.

In residence over the D-Day period was No 122 Wing (Nos 19, 65 & 122 Squadrons) of No 83 Group, equipped with Mustangs modified for dive bombing. It was a busy time, the Wing spending the fateful June 6 covering Coastal Command Beaufighters on anti-U-boat patrols and escorting the second wave of troop carriers and tug/glider combinations as they flew across the Channel to their allotted DZ and LZs. The next day was spent on armed recce and it was the 8th before the Wing encountered the Luftwaffe. The CO of No 65 Squadron, Squadron Leader D.F. Westenra, DFC, spotted Fw 190s and went after them, shooting down one himself, Flight Lieutenant R.A.E. Millom and R.L. Sutherland also claiming one apiece.

No 65 Squadron were bounced over the beach-head by Bf 109s on June 10, losing two Mustangs, but Flight Lieutenant Collyns redressed the balance somewhat by getting a '109 and damaging a second. Half an hour later, six Mustangs of No 19 Squadron got involved in a dogfight with five Bf 109s claiming three of them; in the afternoon six No 65 Squadron aircraft, having dive-bombed a small German convoy, intercepted a formation of Bf 109s and destroyed one. Intensive operations continued from Funtingdon until June 15 when No 122 Wing went to Ford to prepare for the Continent.

Funtingdon had been selected as an Operation *Hadrian* LG during the summer of 1942, the report issued in October suggesting that the felling of part of Jubilee Wood, the closing of a minor road and a little grading was all that would be required to produce a good site. The basic layout was quickly approved and detailed surveying completed by the end of December. Early in January 1943, the Ministry of Agriculture asked for the land to be relinquished but this was refused and the finalised plans, including dispersals, were issued on February 7. They called for a main Sommerfeld Track runway of 4,800 ft (1,464 m) roughly parallel to, and just south of, the present road between Funtington and Aldsworth, and a subsidiary of 3,600 ft (1,097 m) running SSE from Racton Park Farm towards Jubilee Wood.

Funtington was ready for occupation

by the late summer of 1943, the newly formed No 130 Airfield (Nos 4 & 268 Squadrons) moving in from Odiham on September 15 with Mustang I fighter recce aircraft to experience the rather primitive conditions of an ALG. All servicing was out on the open and accommodation was in tents. Offensive recce over France was the main occupation despite generally poor weather. A successful train-busting *Ranger* was flown on September 25 but the following day two No 268 Squadron Mustangs were attacked by seven Fw 190s, attempts by No 4 Squadron aircraft to help being defeated by heavy flak.

The Mustangs returned to Odiham early in October 1943 and work went ahead during the winter on newly authorised improvements, including the construction of taxiways, additional hardstandings and erection of four Extra Over Blister hangars. The work was completed on schedule and the ALG formally handed over on April 1 1944 for occupation by the 2nd TAF. No 143 Airfield HQ arrived the same day, followed over April 2/3 by its newly operational Canadian squadrons, Nos 438, 439 and 440, flying the heavyweight Typhoon fighter-bomber. Led by Wing Commander R.T.P. Davidson, No 143 Airfield concentrated on dive-bombing *Noball* sites in northern France, but left for Hurn on April 19/20; it was immediately replaced by No 144 Airfield which consisted of Nos 441, 442 and 443 (RCAF) Squadrons, flying Spitfire IXs. No 442 spent most of the time on an APC at Hutton Cranswick but the other two squadrons flew intensively on bomber escorts led by the renowned Wing Commander J.E. 'Johnny' Johnson, DSO, DFC and Bar. Two days after their arrival, a sweep by 24 Spitfires from Funtington in support of USAAF Fortresses and Liberators resulted in a dogfight during which six Fw 190s were shot down. Unfortunately the CO of No 441, Squadron Leader G.U. Hill, DFC and two Bars, had to bale out and became a PoW and Flying Officer Sparling was shot down and killed.

Intensive *Roadsteads, Rodeos, Ramrods* and *Rangers* followed, No 442 Squadron rejoining the Airfield on May 2, and it was a fully worked-up unit which transferred to Ford on the 15th. Despite the notorious reputation of Sommerfeld Tracking for damaging Spitfires, and the non-stop operations, accidents had been few, the worst being on May 8 when a No 422 Squadron aircraft swung on landing

and collided with two other Spitfires. All three were write-offs.

It was No 122 Wing, No 83 Group which took over Funtington on the day that Airfields were redesignated. Two days later, on May 17, five Mustangs of No 65 Squadron and two from No 122 refuelled at Coltishall and then set off across the North Sea to Aalborg in Denmark, 400 nm (732 km) away. They achieved complete surprise and were soon shooting up an amazing collection of aircraft, claiming five Ju 88s, one He 177, one Bf 109, two Ju W34s destroyed and two Arado 196 floatplanes damaged at their moorings, while Flight Lieutenant Barrett, who did not return, was believed to have got another Bf 109. Flight Sergeant R.T. Williams was also shot down but, after hiding for a week, he escaped via the underground to Sweden and was repatriated, claiming a further two Ju W34s and a He 177, and to have shared a second with Flight Lieutenant Barrett. Perhaps the most surprising part of this very successful *Ranger* was that the pilots could identify a Ju W34, for this ancient warrior was unlikely to have featured in many recognition lessons.

More *Rangers* followed while the squadrons went in turn to Southend for a bombing APC, completed on June 4 with the return of No 65 Squadron, just in time for D-Day and the battle already described.

The Typhoon squadrons of No 123 Wing (Nos 198 and 609) Squadrons and 136 Wing (Nos 164 and 183) of No 84 Group replaced them, but only spent five days at Funtington during the latter part of June, presumably to acclimatise to living under canvas and to check their equipment before moving to the Continent via Hurn. No 145 (French) Wing of No 84 Group (Nos 329, 340 and 341 Squadrons) arrived from Merston on June 22 to continue their bomber escort work and sweeps over France using Spitfire IXs. They started refuelling and re-arming in Normandy, using B3 for a sweep of the Evreux area on June 29 when a formation of eight Bf 109s and Fw 190s was attacked. The Wing Leader, Wing Commander Crawford-Compton, was credited with one of each type, while Lieutenant Guignard of No 340 Sqaudron claimed another Fw 190.

The Frenchmen's visit was just as fleeting as that of most of their predecessors at Funtington. They went to Selsey on July 1 and three days later were replaced by No

135 Wing also of No 84 Group and flying Spitfire IXs. The three squadrons, Nos 222, 349 (Belgian) and 485 (RNZAF), flew in from Coolham and escorted day bombing Lancasters, Halifaxes, Mitchells, Bostons and Mosquitoes. A new Wing Leader, Wing Commander Harries, arrived mid-July, bringing with him No 33 Squadron from No 134 Wing as the fourth unit of an enlarged Funtington Wing. They had a particularly successful day on July 26 when escorting 36 Mitchells and 24 Bostons to Alencon. Over 30 German fighters tried to get through to the bombers and a dogfight ensued resulting in claims by three pilots totalling three Bf 109s and a Fw 190.

No 135 Wing went to Selsey on August 6 and was replaced immediately by the four Spitfire IX squadrons of No 132 Wing (Nos 66, 127, 331 and 332) from Tangmere. They were also involved on bomber escort work but carried out bombing and ground strafing when circumstances permitted, before following the familiar trail to the Continent via Ford. Suddenly the field was silent and deserted—the local inhabitants could hardly take it in, the departure was so sudden.

The airfield was de-requisitioned by No 11 Group on December 13 1944 and work went ahead to clear the site. It is believed that the Blisters and their immediate surrounds were retained for storage for some months but the airfield soon returned to agriculture.

Gayles, (East Dean/Friston), East Sussex
See Friston

Godersham Park, Kent
TR049504. 2½ miles N of Wye

On the principle that all one's eggs should not be in one basket, airship mooring-out stations were developed, usually sited some distance inland from the parent base and in heavily wooded, hilly terrain. Godersham Park was just such a site, a sub-station of Capel-le-Ferne, Folkestone. The moorings were to the west of Godersham village in a dry chalk valley protected from the prevailing winds by King's Wood. It was usual to moor out one SSZ airship at Godersham Park from the late spring 1918, but the base was abandoned soon after the Armistice. Remains of the concrete mooring blocks have been found at the site, which can be rediscovered quite close to the North Downs Way by the more energetic searcher.

Below left *A partially deflated SSZ airship in the 'hide' at Godersham Park* (Folkstone Local Collection).

Below *An SSZ airship deep in the trees at Godersham Park mooring-out station* (Folkestone Local Collection).

Goodwood (Westhampnett), West Sussex

See Westhampnett

Goring-by-sea, West Sussex

TQ114036. 2 miles NW of Worthing alongside A2032

To provide training for airmen of the United States Army Air Service, a number of new aerodromes in the south-east of England were surveyed during the spring of 1918. One of those accepted was at Goring-by-Sea. Intended as a three-squadron TDS, the plan called for the erection of six large, and one very large (Handley Page assembly), hangars and an aeroplane repair shed alongside the Chichester to Brighton railway line which formed the southern boundary, with hutted accommodation in the north-west corner of the site, close to the road and Ham Farm. Roughly square in outline, the 168-acre flying field gave landings runs of about 2,700 ft (823 m) in most directions.

Work on the site had not started by August 1918 and the aerodrome was never occupied; indeed, the Armistice may have caused abandonment before construction began. The whole site has long since formed part of the built-up area surrounding Worthing.

Gosport, Hampshire

SU590010. 4 miles W of Portsmouth off A32

Although the Solent was, as now, a naval domain in the 1800s, it was the War Office which was responsible for its defence. To help discharge this responsibility the Army purchased 1,500 acres of land at Gosport in 1857 and built two massive red brick forts, Rowner and Grange, to cover the land and sea approaches to Portsmouth. Between the forts lay a fine stretch of level grassland intended to rival the best parade grounds of Europe.

By the end of the 19th century the power of contemporary naval guns made the Gosport defences virtually useless, but the forts remained in use and in 1909 a group of naval officers designed, built and attempted to fly a pusher biplane off the grass, but they wrecked it. Other enthusiasts had no more success and interest faded, leaving the forts to the Royal Garrison Artillery and the grass to grazing cattle.

The Military Wing of the RFC gradually expanded during 1912/13, squadrons being formed as men and machines became available. Aerodromes were needed and, in November 1913, the land between, and to the west of Forts Rowners and Grange—known as Grange Camp Field—became the almost automatic choice in the Portsmouth area. Work to remove ridges and furrows started in February 1914 and, with tent shelters erected for the machines, No 5 Squadron, RFC, moved in from Netheravon on July 6 equipped with Maurice and Henri Farmans, Avro 504s and the SE 2 Bullet. The men joined the aircraft in tents, but neither stayed long, the squadron being mobilised as part of the British Expeditionary Force at the outbreak of war.

Gosport was left virtually deserted for nearly two months, the RFC having neither aircraft nor personnel to man it. However, the formation of two RNAS squadrons for military duties had been authorised, and Squadron Commander A.M. Longmore was detailed to commission No 1 Squadron, RNAS, on October 15 at Fort Grange equipped with four Bristol Scouts. Ground crew were recruited by scouring local garages and factories, grabbing anyone suitable. Little over a month later the aircraft were flown to Farnborough and put on a train to Gosforth, but most of the squadron returned in December and were able to form *A* and *B* Flights with Avro 504s and Sopwith Tabloids before being despatched to Dover in January 1915.

Unhappy about the RNAS take-over, the War Office had already sent the newly formed BE 2C-equipped No 8 Squadron to Gosport. Within days No 13 Squadron was formed there, followed by No 17 Squadron on February 1, all three units coming under the newly constituted 5th Wing. Accommodation in Fort Grange was ready in March, just in time to cope with an influx of personnel following the authorisation of separate training Flights on all home-based Service squadrons to help overcome the chronic shortage of pilots. No 8 Squadron avoided this unpopular duty by going to France on April 15 but by August lack of accommodation in Fort Grange was again limiting the formation of additional units. The RFC therefore took over Fort Rowner on September 24 1915 when No 22 Squadron moved in, while No 23 Squadron was formed to take up space in Fort Grange

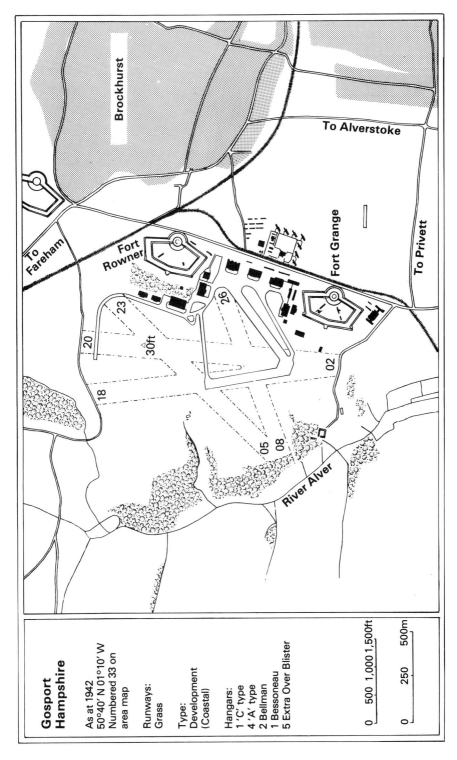

Gosport
Hampshire

As at 1942
50°40' N 01°10' W
Numbered 33 on
area map

Runways:
Grass

Type:
Development
(Coastal)

Hangars:
1 'C' type
4 'A' type
2 Bellman
1 Bessoneau
5 Extra Over Blister

Brockhurst

To Alverstoke

To Fareham

Fort Rowner

Fort Grange

To Privett

23

20

30ft

18

26

02

05

08

River Alver

0   500 1,000 1,500ft

0   250   500m

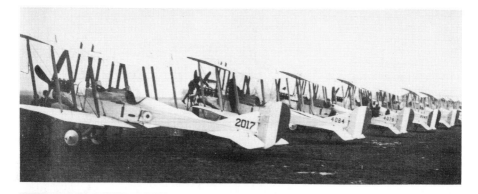

alongside Nos 13 and 17. The new units were extremely short of aircraft, new ones only being obtained by scrounging, and the work-up of the units was slowed by milking of both pilots and machines to form the nucleus of new squadrons or to replace casualties in France. No 23 Squadron, who had included some night flying in their training, also found themselves providing most of the pilots when the 5th Wing was ordered to allocate seven BE 2Cs for anti-Zeppelin patrols from Northolt, Joyce Green, Suttons Farm and Hainault Farm.

During October, No 13 Squadron went to France and the 5th Wing, complete with Nos 14 and 17 Squadrons, prepared to depart for Egypt, being replaced in November by the 7th Wing HQ. Two new squadrons, Nos 28 and 29, were formed from Nos 22 and 23 and started training on an odd collection of Avro 504As, Caudron G IIIs and BE 8s, while in mid-December the Wing also became responsible for Nos 4 and 11 RAS at Northolt and the newly formed No 16 RAS at Beaulieu.

Gradually the aircraft situation improved, No 22 Squadron re-equipping with FE 2Bs in January 1916. No 23 Squadron also received FE 2Bs which they

Top *No 13 Squadron was formed and trained at Gosport in 1915—and their BE 2Cs are seen lined up prior to flying to France in October 1915* (IWM Q50964).

Above *The scene from Fort Grange in 1916. The haphazard collection of aircraft stand outside the line of sheds backing onto the railway* (RAF Museum P755).

took to France on March 16, followed a week later by No 29 Squadron which had received DH 2 scouts earlier in the month, and on April 1 1916 by the long-suffering No 22 Squadron. Meanwhile, No 45 Squadron had formed at Gosport on March 20 with the usual collection of cast off machines for work-up before moving to Thetford in May.

This pattern of working-up squadrons and providing the nucleus of new ones continued throughout 1916, with Nos 41, 56 and 60 Squadrons forming at Gosport in this way. There was, however, a significant development when No 1 RS moved in from Farnborough on April 7 and No 27 RS formed on May 22 1916—the start of a proper training organisation which was to revolutionise teaching methods a year later.

By this time the original canvas hangars had been supplemented by a long line of wooden sheds alongside the road forming the eastern boundary between the two forts, and more substantial hangars started to appear at each end of the aerodrome together with workshops and flight offices. By the end of 1916 the whole unit was devoted to training and a number of Reserve squadrons for Canadian operations were formed, while Gosport units also provided personnel to start-up the training organisation at Yatesbury.

On December 24 1916, Major R.R. Smith-Barry left No 60 Squadron and was given command of No 1 RS. While in France he had been appalled by the standard of the pilots arriving at the Front, and had formulated a number of what were then revolutionary ideas—now was his chance to try them out. When he arrived, the standard equipment was Avro 504As, Maurice Farman Longhorns and Shorthorns and the staff were still accommodated in the dungeon-like forts. He quickly changed all that, renting a country house named Alverbank as No 1 RS mess, getting rid of the lumbering Farmans and splitting the squadron into three Flights, *A* with Avro 504s, *B* with BE 2Cs and *C* with Moranes and Bristol Scouts, later replacing the BEs with dual-control 1½-Strutters. Indeed, it was dual

A Camel of 'F' Flight, Special School of Flying, outside Fort Grange, Gosport in 1918 (via Chaz Bowyer).

demonstration and instruction following a laid down set of exercises with solo consolidation which was central to the Smith-Barry method. Having proved this to his own satisfaction, he started agitating for proper instructors courses and in May 1917 wrote a set of training notes. There was still the problem of communication since hand signals were often misunderstood and, after various schemes using telephone equipment proved useless, Smith-Barry tried a modified speaking tube and met with immediate success —the Gosport Tube was born and remained in daily use all over the world for the next 30 years.

After a practical demonstration, General Salmond sanctioned the formation of a Special School of Flying at Gosport, Nos 1, 25 and 55 TS being amalgamated for this purpose early in August. The establishment was six Flights, five to train qualified pilots as instructors, the sixth to teach courses of pupils *ab initio* flying using Fort Rowner as a mess and HQ. The student instructors lived in Fort Grange, the staff relinquishing Alverbank to join them.

The success of the system was soon apparent and early in 1918 all TS were instructed to change to the Gosport training methods, their instructors being sent to the SofSF in batches. While these changes were taking place one or two service squadrons had been formed at Gosport and a detached Flight from No 78 Squadron, Hove, had flown BE 12s on Home Defence duties. Later, part of No

39 Squadron using Bristol Fighters took their place, the strength of this unit being increased on January 31 1918 when it became the School of Aerial Co-operation with Coast Defence Batteries. It worked with the Coast Artillery School at Golden Hill, while remaining responsible for the defence of the Portsmouth area against Zeppelin attack.

When the RAF was formed on April 1 1918, Gosport was placed in No 2 Area, commanded by No 8 Group, Southampton. For a short while the unit at Gosport became No 1 SofSF, but in July each area was given its own training organisation and it was renamed the South-West Area

Flying Instructors' School. Smith-Barry had already left, having fallen foul of higher authority, but his methods were retained and, indeed, form the basis of the present syllabus at the RAF Central Flying School and many foreign air force training schemes.

Above *An instructors' hack at Gosport— a dragon painted Bristol M1C monoplane* (via R.W. Elliott collection).

Below *A general view of the Gosport hangars looking north-east—probably in 1918* (H.A. Vasse via P.H.T. Green).

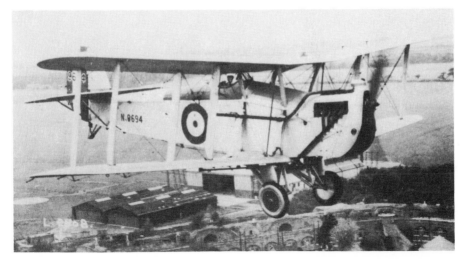

Blackburn Dart N9694 overflies Fort Rowner, Gosport, in November 1928 (RAF Museum P11938).

Other changes were taking place. On May 31 a Special Experimental Flight was formed at Fort Grange for research work with the RN Signals School, Portsmouth, and No 10 TS moved in from Lilbourne during July. The importance of Gosport was increased during August by the formation of the Development Squadron. This deliberately vague title covered work on torpedoes, for which six Sopwith Cuckoos were established. In September the School of Aerial Co-operation moved out, being replaced at Fort Rowner in October by the Anti-Aircraft Defence Flight.

HQ Gosport was formed on October 28 1918 to deal with this unwieldly collection of units but with the Armistice came an immediate reduction in activity. No 10 TS and the Defence Flight started closing in December and the South West Instructors' School was disbanded on February 26 1919. This was followed by transfer of the station to No 10 (Operations) Group on March 1 and the disbandment of HQ Gosport on May 15.

Gosport's future was very uncertain until June 1919 when it was confirmed as the torpedo school. In September it was formally listed as a permanent No 10 Group, Coastal Area station and No 186 Squadron was re-formed for development work using Sopwith Cuckoo and Bristol F 2B aircraft. A Coastal Battery Co-operation Flight formed in March 1920 but

further re-organisation the following year resulted in its demise and during September 1921 the station became known as RAF Base Gosport, controlling the activities of No 210 Squadron (re-formed from No 186 on February 1 1920), an Observer Training Flight, a Composite Flight and the Development Flight. In October 1922 No 3 Squadron moved its DH 9A and Westland Walrus biplanes down from Leuchars, by which time the Observer Training Flight and Composite Flight had left. More upheaval came on April 1 1923 when Nos 3 and 210 Squadrons disbanded, the former splitting into Nos 420, 421 and 422 Flights and the latter into Nos 460 and 461 Flights.

The first Blackburn Dart single-seat torpedo bombers joined the Developmental Flight in the spring of 1922 and this aircraft became synomonous with Gosport, Nos 460, 461, 462, 463 and 464 Flights being added to the strength when not embarked on carriers. D Flight was formed in 1925 with Darts to teach pilots torpedo dropping techniques, in particular the art of flying 15 ft (4.6 m) above the waters of the Solent while aiming the whole aircraft at the target. However, the aircraft will probably be best remembered for making the first ever night landing on a carrier—after preliminary training at Gosport. Meanwhile, the Fleet Spotter Flights had been re-equipped with the incredibly cumbersome-looking Avro Bison and Blackburn Blackburn biplanes and it was not until 1928 that the first Fairey IIIfs were taken out of the Gosport store and issued to the FSR Flights. In May 1929 wholesale renumbering of these

Flights took place, about the same time as the Bisons were completely usurped by IIIfs, the Blackburns having to wait until June 1931.

Permanent hangars were now replacing the wooden sheds on the eastern boundary and new brick barrack blocks enabled the men to move out of the two dreary forts in April 1930. When the Base Training Squadron was formed, *D* Flt (Torpedo Training) was joined by *A* (Army & Navy Co-operation), *B* (Telegraphist Air Gunner training) and *C* (Deck Landing). A later addition was *E* Flight which carried out experiments for the Air Ministry, in co-operation with *D* Flight.

Replacement of the sturdy Darts of Nos 460, 461 and 462 Flights by the equally well-liked Ripon started in August 1929 but was not completed until 1933. In May 1932 the Coast Defence Co-operation Flight arrived from Eastchurch with Fairey IIIfs and was promptly renamed the Coast Defence Training Flight. Three months later it became No 1 CDT Flight when two similar units, Nos 2 and 3, were formed at Gosport. There was another major change in April 1933 when pairs of Flights were re-formed as squadrons, Nos 442 and 449 becoming 821 Squadron and Nos 461 and 462 amalgamating to form 812 Squadron.

During October 1934, *A* and *B* Flights of the Gosport training organisation moved to Lee-on-Solent and *D* and *E* were renamed *A* (Torpedo Training) and

An impressive line-up of RAF and FAA aircraft at Gosport on the occasion of the Silver Jubilee Naval Review, July 1935. Sharks, Baffins, Seals, Osprey, Nimrod and Vildebeest aircraft can be identified (FAA Museum A/Stn 56).

B (Torpedo Experimental) Flights, the existing *C* Flight remaining as the Deck Landing and Flying Practice Flight. In April 1935 the base became RAF Station Gosport and the Coast Defence Training Flights were amalgamated to form the Coast Defence Development Unit. This situation did not last long, the unit being disbanded in December 1936 leaving just No 1 Coast Artillery Co-operation Flight in operation.

A Flight has received Baffins in January 1935 and one of these gained a certain notoriety for the Base Training Squadron when its pilot flew around the French liner *Normandie* on June 22 1935, struck one of the derricks and crashed on the fore-deck. Jammed in position, it was only retrieved by an RAF working party when the ship reached Le Havre.

In December 1936, No 17 Group assumed control of Gosport and, on January 18 1937, 813 Squadron commissioned on the airfield with nine Swordfish before embarking in HMS *Eagle* the following month. Other FAA squadrons were shore-based at Gosport for short periods, usually while re-equipping.

Coastal defence exercises were undertaken by a No 42 Squadron detachment during January 1938 and in September, with the Munich Crisis at its peak, No 10 Mobilisation Pool was formed while the Torpedo Development Unit grew out of *B* Flight in November. When Lee-on-Solent was transferred to the Admiralty in May 1938, HQ No 17 (Training) Group moved to Gosport where it was joined by No 2 AACU, the recipient of Skuas the following month.

At the beginning of the war, Gosport housed the Group HQ, the Training Squadron, Torpedo Section, Storage Unit, No 2 AACU and No 1 CACU, although the latter was soon off to Thorney Island. *H* Flight of No 1 AACU arrived on detachment from Biggin Hill on September 20 with three Battles for work with the ADEE Christchurch and remained until June 1941, while *A* Flight No 2 AACU continued co-operation with the RN Anti-Aircraft School, Eastney.

The Training Section of the TDU left for Abbotsinch in March 1940 when the Experimental Department became the Air Torpedo Development Unit and steadily expanded under the control of the MAP. The airfield also expanded, the two tarmac runways, 2,100 ft (640 m) SW/NE and 1,650 ft (504 m) N/S, built largely for carrier landing practice pre-war, being abandoned and replaced by four grass strips, the longest 4,650 ft (1,417 m) N/S though the more frequently used SW/NE run was only 150 ft (46 m) shorter. This unusual, possibly unique, reversion to grass enabled the larger torpedo bombers and test aircraft to be operated, amongst them early Bothas and Beauforts. The four 'A' Type and single 'C' Type hangars were joined by two Bellmans near Fort Rowner and more accommodation was built between the forts to the east of the airfield.

In April the station workshops were transferred to No 43 Group and were renamed the FAA MU, while the ATDU carried out secret work on torpedoes and ran courses for armament fitters. The same month ATDU Beaufort expertise was put to good use when No 42 Squadron arrived for conversion. Training was interrupted by the Dunkirk evacuation when the aircraft escorted the armada of

Right *The new 'C' Type hangar near Fort Rowner dominates the airfield in this oblique taken from a No 103 Squadron Hind in 1938—this hangar still stands* (Wing Commander D.E. Bennett).

Below *A Hurricane 'running-up' outside one of the 'A' Type hangars at Gosport during January 1939* (J.W.G. Wellham).

little ships across the Channel, but the squadron was declared operational in June and left for Wick.

No 22 Squadron underwent an intensive torpedo course in July but had returned to North Coates before the Luftwaffe took an interest in Gosport. This started on Monday, August 12, when 15 Ju 88s of KG51 dive-bombed the airfield. A more serious raid followed on August 16 when 12 Ju 88s escorted by Bf 110s dived out of the sun to drop 250 kg and 50 kg (550 and 110 lb) bombs and strafe the airfield. Several hangars and other buildings were wrecked, six servicemen killed, nine aircraft were destroyed and ten damaged. It was while trying to intercept the Bf 110s that Hurricanes of No 249 Squadron were bounced by Bf 109s and Flight Lieutenant James Nicolson won Fighter Command's only VC.

On August 18 the Germans put up all 109 available Stukas, escorted by 157 Bf 109s. They were thought to be making a repeat visit to Tangmere but instead split into four distinct formations, 22 Ju 87Bs of 1/Stg 3 making for Gosport. Despite the heaviest AA fire the station could muster, they calmly circled the airfield and, selecting a target, entered their devastating dive, dropping bombs from about 700 ft (213 m). They could not miss. Many buildings were wrecked and two more hangars damaged, while four aircraft were destroyed and five damaged. Fortunately, adequate warning meant the personnel were in shelters and there were no casualties. Although the damage was considerable, Gosport remained usable but it was not a fighter station, and took no part in the battle for air supremacy then raging over south-east England.

No 86 Squadron formed on December 6 1940 but had moved its Blenheim IVs to Leuchars before bombs again fell on the airfield, Gosport being showered with incendiaries on March 10/11 and 11/12 during heavy night raids on Portsmouth. Meanwhile, the ATDU continued expanding, the HQ and design offices moving into Moat House, while the Ashley Wallpaper Works in Gosport provided much-needed additional machine shop facilities. The ATDU had its own Marine Craft Unit to operate range safety launches and torpedo recovery pinnaces in Stokes Bay, and during 1942 Wellingtons, Hampdens, Beauforts and single Albemarle, Beaufighter and Manchester aircraft were in use though most of the routine torpedo drops were made by

Swordfish, for RAF equipment, and Albacores for naval weapons. The Wellingtons were testing extending stabilisers so that two torpedoes could be carried while Beauforts and Hampdens concentrated on sighting problems. Mines and depth charges were also tested, mainly by Hampdens and the Manchester respectively.

The first torpedo Beaufighter arrived at the ATDU in May and was quickly on test, carrying out trial drops and air firing with the 'tin-fish' attached. Its potential was already obvious when a tragic accident robbed the unit of its CO. With Flying Officer Davenport at the controls and Wing Commander Shaw standing behind gaining air experience, the aircraft took off for a torpedo drop over the Stokes Bay range. At about 200 ft (61 m) one of the engines cut and the Beaufighter rolled on to its back and plunged into the ground just short of houses at Alverstoke. Both pilots were killed instantly.

By now the FAA MU had become No 3502 Servicing Unit but continued the same work while No 2 AACU was still threading its way through the ever-hazardous balloon barage defences of Portsmouth and Southampton. On August 23 1942, Gosport transferred to No 16 Group and 22 Hudsons of No 608 Squadron arrived to be fitted with long-range tanks by No 3502 SU. They were replaced by 19 similar aircraft from No 500 Squadron in mid-September, both squadrons going to Gibraltar for Operation *Torch*.

The first Torbeau unit, No 254 Squadron, brought its converted Mk IV aircraft into Gosport for six weeks' torpedo training in October, prior to joining the first Beaufighter Strike Wing at North Coates. Three days later the Hudson VIs of No 48 Squadron arrived from Sumburgh—for the tank modifications and overhaul by No 3502 SU, who were now responsible for major servicings on Nos 48, 233 and 608 Squadron aircraft.

No 2 AACU transferred to No 70 Group on February 14 1943, *A* Flight being renamed No 1622 (AAC) Flight and remaining at Gosport as a lodger equipped with Defiants, Gladiators and a single Roc. During the year the ATDU workshops, badly damaged by bombs in 1940, were rebuilt and No 3502 SU continued its overhaul work on Hudons, responsible for the Gibraltar squadrons (Nos 48, 233 and 520) and No 1407 (Met) Flight from Reykjavik, Iceland.

'Torbeau' trials aircraft of the Air Torpedo Development Unit, Gosport (IWM MH4558).

On December 1 1943, Nos 1622 and 1631 Flights were combined to form No 667 Squadron, which was based at Gosport with Defiants to tow targets for the RN gunnery schools. They were joined by Hurricanes for gun-laying practice and supplemented by a few Barracudas in May 1944.

A reborn 764 Squadron had joined the ATDU in February 1944 largely for torpedo trails with early Firebrands but, in general, life on the station was pretty stable despite the intense activity in the vicinity of Gosport as the build-up for Operation *Overlord* went on. Indeed, D-Day itself was almost an anti-climax, personnel feeling very much outsiders until No 49 MU started receiving salvaged aircraft from the Continent, brought into Southampton by sea.

Oxfords joined No 667 Squadrons in June 1944 and the Defiants were gradually replaced by Vengeances from October. Early in January 1945 the naval strength increased when 708 (Tactical Trials) Squadron moved in from Lee while runway resurfacing took place. They spent three months at Gosport on Firebrand trials, and the airfield was also used by Harvards, Masters and Fireflies from Lee during this busy period.

No sooner had the FAA returned to Lee than a conference was held to discuss the hand-over of Gosport to the Navy. Although delayed by uncertainty following the German capitulation, it changed hands on August 1 1945, becoming HMS *Siskin*. The ATDU and No 667 remained as lodgers, administered by RAF Thorney

Island, but the FAA lost no time moving in units, 707 Squadron on August 14 with Ansons and Avengers, followed by 711 (FRU) with Mosquitoes and Martinets and 778 Squadron from Arbroath during September.

The immediate post-war period was one of turmoil. In October, 764 Squadron disbanded and No 667 Squadron moved to Dunsfold early in December. 707 and 778 Squadrons had also left by early spring 1946, partially replaced by 727 Squadron which re-formed for Sub Lieutenant and Royal Marine officer training courses in May. 771 Squadron moved out in April 1947 and the way was clear for a virtually fresh start when 705 Squadron was re-formed at Gosport as the sole operator of FAA helicopters. Sikorsky R-4s were collected and 705 Squadron commissioned on May 7 1947, commanded by Lieutenant K. Reed, RN, mustering seven Hoverflies, seven pilots and 30 ratings. From this small beginning grew the current comprehensive helicopter operations of the FAA. Officially 705 Squadron was the Naval Helicopter Training Unit but it soon found itself carrying out trials and providing aircraft for radar checks and VIP communications work.

No 720 Squadron transferred from Ford on July 1 1947 and continued flying its four Ansons for the RN School of Photography. It returned to Ford later in the year but was back at Gosport in May 1948 until amalgamated with 711 Squadron on January 5 1950. In that same month 705 Squadron received a number of Dragonfly (licence-built S-51) helicoptors and during June 1951 the RN Operational Helicopter Flight was formed from 705 Squadron personnel and left in *Warrior* for Singapore during July. The unit's success in the Far East resulted in an order for Sikorsky HRS-2s and the formation of 848 Squadron at Gosport in October 1952. The American-built machines arrived by ship at Southampton on November 18 and within eight days had been transported to Gosport by lighter, stripped of anti-corrosion protection, and were flying. Such was the rush to get them into action in the Malayan campaign against Communist rebels that the squadron was embarked in *Perseus* with ten Whirlwind 21s on December 12 1952.

In May 1953 the Hiller HTE-2 entered service with 705 Squadron and proved an instant success—the first good helicopter for *ab initio* instruction. American-built Whirlwind 22s followed in the autumn, eight of them equipping 706 Squadron. On October 29 1953 this unit went to Northern Ireland but returned to Gosport on March 1 1954 and two weeks later was renumbered 845 Squadron, charged with working-up the Whirlwind as an anti-submarine helicopter using dunking sonar.

With retrenchment in full swing after the Korean War, spending on defence was cut and it was decided to close Gosport during 1956. Equipped with Hillers and Whirlwinds, 705 Squadron moved to Lee in November 1955, leaving the ATDU as not only the longest-established flying unit at Gosport, but also the last. It went to Culdrose early in 1956, ending 38 years'

association with the station. The airfield was closed in May 1956 and HMS *Siskin* paid off during June, though 705 Squadron continued to use Gosport as a RLG for several months.

On May 28 1958 a memorial plaque was unveiled to mark the RNAS, FAA and RAF association with the area, which is now largely covered by extensive naval housing estates. The airfield is only recognisable by the modified 'A' Type hangars along the eastern boundary and the 'C' Type just to the west of Fort Rowner and close to the modern HQ buildings of HMS *Centurion*. These hangars are still in use by various naval units, but Gosport's long association with flying has ended. Never an operational station, its contribution as a training and trials airfield has been outstanding despite its out-moded accommodation and difficult flying conditions. It is one of those airfields which developed rather than was planned—but is remembered with affection by all its old boys.

Grain (Port Victoria), Kent

TQ885745. 1½ miles S of Grain village

Isolated, and comparatively safe from prying eyes, this site on the marshy Isle of Grain, was chosen by the Admiralty in 1912 as one of their first seaplane bases. An extensive area of foreshore was purchased and a slipway cut through the sea

The much modified 'A' Type now known as the 'Watt' hangar and in daily use at Gosport (K.S. West).

wall, giving access to land on which sheds were to be built, while a number of coastguard cottages were taken over for the personnel—on the understanding that they provided the lookouts!

Grain was commissioned on December 30 1912 with Lieutenant J.W. Seddon, RN, in command and, because of the absence of seaplane facilities at Eastchurch, was soon carrying out development work on hydro-aeroplanes as the Admiralty quaintly termed them. During 1913, £20,000 was budgeted on improvements and new sheds, and in August Grain officially replaced Eastchurch as the principal air station in the Sheerness Naval District, charged with the air defence of the Thames Estuary. To test the usefulness of a Naval Wing base and its seaplanes a concentration camp was planned at Grain during 1913, but this had to be abandoned, the station having an unexpected trial when the CO was ordered to search for the missing submarine *A7* off Plymouth on January 21 1914. Squadron Commander Seddon left Grain in a Maurice Farman floatplane at 09:15 hours and flew around the coast towards Plymouth. He landed at Calshot to refuel and finally alighted in the Sound at 16:40 hours after 5½ hours in the air. A gallant effort, but the time scale was unlikely to inspire confidence.

A poor photo but it does show the original Grain seaplane sheds and the Medway slipways. The marshy state of the ground which later became Grain airfield is also apparent (via Chaz Bowyer collection).

During 1914 all available seaplanes were assembled at Felixstowe, Yarmouth and Grain, the latter responsible for patrolling the Estuary as far out as the North Hinder and Galloper lightships. The first patrol was on August 9 but most flying was expended giving cover to ships transporting the BEF to France. The unreliable engines of the period meant this work could be extremely hazardous. On December 17, Squadron Commander Seddon with Leading Mechanic R.L. Hartley as passenger set out in a Short Type 830. An hour and a half later the engine failed and they landed on the water. Attempted restarts failed and the port float was carried away, Hartley climbing out on the starboard wing to counter-balance it. When the starboard float went the seaplane started to break up and they were finally picked up by the crew of the Norwegian SS *Orn* eight hours after ditching.

Used as a holding unit for reserve Short and Sopwith seaplanes for the forward bases at Westgate and Clacton, the emphasis at Grain shifted away from front-line operations, and a number of very rough grazing fields were joined up to form an aerodrome by boarding over numerous dykes. Bessoneaux hangars joined the seaplane sheds inside the sea wall and early in 1915 the Royal Naval Aeroplane Repair Depot was commissioned at Grain under the command of an engineer officer, Squadron Commander G.W.R. Aldwell. The Depot was housed in an ex-Salvation Army Congress Hall, which had been transported to the Isle of Grain and re-

erected a few hundred yards to the west of the original station, the site (TQ879741) being named Port Victoria.

At the end of 1915 the Experimental Armament Section was established alongside the Repair Depot, and early in 1916 the Seaplane Test Flight was added to the organisation. The Air Department proposed that an Experimental Construction Section should be formed to give the RNAS its own 'Farnborough' and this scheme was accepted by the Admiralty, the combined unit becoming the Marine Experimental Aircraft Depot.

The Grain Depot at Port Victoria grew in size steadily, using three large sheds, while the Test Flight became a separate organisation with hangars on the main Air Station. The latter was now little more than an Acceptance Depot, though it did continue to administer the whole of the Marine Experimental Aircraft Depot.

Work on the airfield concentrated on landing trials by Sopwith Pups and 1½-Strutters using a dummy deck, a number of ingenious solutions being tried including various arrangements of arrester wires. Meanwhile, the Experimental Construction Department started modifying a Sopwith Baby to improve its take-off performance, though the extra drag badly affected its maximum speed. This aircraft was designated the PV 1 (for Port Victoria) and was quickly followed by an anti-Zeppelin fighter which flew in June 1916 but suffered from poor lateral control. The PV 3 was a two-seat fighter landplane project, and the PV 4 a seaplane version which was not a success.

When responsibility for the supply of

Above *Officers' quarters at Grain built around requisitioned property, September 1917* (FAA Museum A/Stn 99).

Above right *The diminutive PV 7 and PV 8 Kittens at Grain with a Curtiss R-2* (Captain D.S. Glover via P.H.T. Green).

Right *The 2F1 Camel prototype heavily armed with Le Prieur rockets and an upper wing Lewis gun while undergoing trials at Grain, April 1917* (via Chaz Bowyer collection).

Below right *A DH 4 heavily festooned with hydrovanes and flotation bags for ditching experiments at Grain* (via R.W. Elliott collection).

aircraft was transferred to the Ministry of Munitions in January 1917, the organisation at Port Victoria came under close scrutiny and closure was recommended. The Admiralty has always had the habit of ignoring such advice from outsiders, however, and not only was the PV 5 single-seat fighter seaplane completed but the depot was asked to build a small aeroplane capable of being carried aboard torpedo-boat destroyers and similar small craft. The resulting PV7 Grain Kitten had a span of 18 ft (5.5 m) but, powered by the inadequate 35 hp ABC Gnat, was not a success. A rival design produced at Eastchurch fared better when tested in September 1917 as the PV8. The Port Victoria design team now tackled another single-seat fighter in the same category as the PV2. It first flew in December 1917 as the PV9, but its 150 hp Bentley BR1 engine caused continual problems.

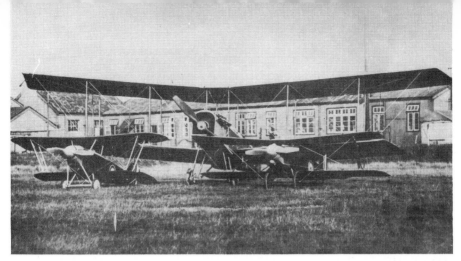

During 1917, a Sopwith B1 single-seat bomber was delivered to Port Victoria with instructions to turn it into a two-seat fleet reconnaissance aircraft for carrier operations. The design staff suggested it would be easier to build a new aircraft based on the machine, and the Admiralty finally agreed, but insisted on the B1 conversion as well. The Armistice prevented any further development—and it proved to be the last type produced by the depot.

While this interesting series of prototypes were being produced, the Experimental Armament Depot and Test Depot had not been idle. The armament experts evaluated British and German equipment, including such strange contraptions as the Davis recoilless gun and the Rankin anti-Zeppelin explosive dart, while flight testing of both land and seaplanes was pursued with great enthusiasm. These involved such diverse items as flotation bags, hydrovanes, W/T sets and hydrophones—the latter to detect submarines under the water—while deck landing experiments continued relentlessly. Seaplane testing was often held up because of launching difficultes, and among the more bizarre schemes dreamt up by the dynamic Squadron Commander Busteed was launching them from railway flat trucks using the aircraft's engine power to reach flying speed. He rated this method of getting airborne as 'great fun'!

By the autumn of 1918 the number of sheds had reached 15, most of them just behind the sea wall which was now cut by three slipways. A large accommodation camp had been built just south of Grain village for the staff which numbered about 1,480. After the war, work proceeded at a relaxed pace but when Orfordness closed in 1921 the Armament Experimental Squadron moved in. The testing of flying boats, in particular the Saunders Valentia, the Short Cromarty and the Fairey Atalanta went ahead slowly, the latter probably the last *new* type at the depot, for on March 17 1924 the Marine Aircraft Experimental Unit moved to Felixstowe and Grain/Port Victoria was closed down after nearly 12 years of interesting and lively experimentation.

Nowadays the old aerodrome lies in the shadow of the massive oil terminal, the railway spur to Port Victoria has been extended along the river bank to facilities near the rebuilt pier, and there is a power station on the site.

Great Chart (Ashford), Kent
See Ashford

Greenham Common, Berkshire
SU500645. 2 miles NE of Newbury off A339(T)

The 101st Airborne Division, US Army, crossed the Atlantic in September 1943 and camped around Newbury. For the

'A', 'B', 'C' and 'D' sheds at Grain with the engineering shop which is being extended, September 1917 (FAA Museum A/Stn 101).

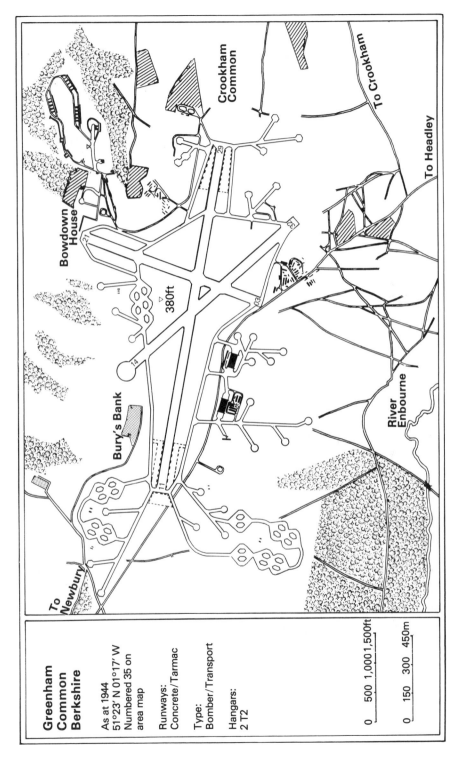

Greenham
Common
Berkshire

As at 1944
51°23' N 01°17' W
Numbered 35 on
area map

Runways:
Concrete/Tarmac

Type:
Bomber/Transport

Hangars:
2 T2

0   500 1,0001,500ft

0   150   300 450m

To Newbury

Bury's Bank

Bowdown
House

380ft

Crookham
Common

To Crookham

To Headley

River
Enbourne

next eight months they worked and played hard, virtually taking over the famous Berkshire town as the roar of C-47 Dakota troop carriers from Membury, Welford, Ramsbury, Aldermaston and Greenham Common filled the air day and night. Then early in June 1944 the troops suddenly deserted Newbury—it was an eerie feeling, full of expectancy.

At Greenham Common the airborne troops assigned to the 438th TCG were all inside the perimeter which was ringed with armed guards. With the decision on *Overlord* made, General Eisenhower drove to the airfield during the evening of June 5 to join General Lewis H. Brereton, Commander of the IXth AF, watching the first paratroopers leave aboard *Birmingham Belle*, airborne at 22:48 hours in the hands of Colonel J.M. Donaldson, CO of the 438th. Another 80 C-47As followed at 11-second intervals—at night! Each formation was led by a specially trained pathfinder crew in aircraft equipped with the British navigation aid Gee. From the Wing assembly area they flew to 'Flatbrush', the Command departure point for Operation *Neptune*. Descending, they headed out over the Channel at 500 ft (152 m) over a vessel acting as checkpoint 'Gallop', then turned for 'Hoboken', a position off the Cherbourg peninsula. From here Stirling bombers continued to fly south dropping bundles of *window*, while the C-47s turned east and climbed to 1,500 ft (457 m) past Guernsey and Alderney from where they experienced light flak. Heavier flak greeted them as they crossed the French coast at 'Muleshoe' and aircraft were hit. Down again to 700 ft (213 m), the leaders identified the DZ by Gee, and at 00:16 hours on June 6 1944 the first paratroopers jumped into Normandy near Carentan—the invasion was on.

Lying on a ridge some 380 ft (116 m) above sea level, and two miles from Newbury on a pockmarked area of heath

Hadrians wait at Greenham Common for Operation Overlord, *June 1944* (USAAF via D. Benfield).

and scrub, Greenham Common airfield was first surveyed early in 1941 as a satellite for the proposed bomber OTU at Aldermaston. Authority to requisition was given in May 1941 and because the land was poor there was none of the usual opposition from farming interests. Development of a standard OTU pattern airfield with a 5,988 ft (1,825 m) main E/W runway went ahead steadily. Several minor roads crossing the common were closed but the main Newbury-Basingstoke road was fitted with barriers and guard huts where it bisected the technical site and crossed the approaches to several of the dispersal areas. A small instructional site was built alongside the main road south-east of the airfield and further out were the very dispersed accommodation sites, some of them on Sydmonton Common. The WAAF sites, wire-fenced, were clustered around Bowdown House and Grove Cottage to the north-east, adjacent to the bomb dump and sewage works, which smacks of discrimination—fortunately they remained unused by the ladies.

The airfield was nearing completion in the summer of 1942, by which time the priority had changed and Greenham Common became one of the many sites earmarked for USAAF occupation. Indeed, the first unit at Greenham after the opening-up party was the HQ staff of the 51st TCW who arrived from the USA in September 1942. They stayed until going to North Africa for *Torch* in November when responsibility for the airfield was transferred from No 92 to No 70 Group, RAF, and Greenham was opened for flying the following month by a detachment from No 15 (P) AFU newly arrived at Andover. Joined by No 1511 (BAT) Flight on April 28, 1943, the AFU flew Oxfords

An Airspeed Horsa being towed to its destination at LZ'W' near Ste Mere Eglise. The formation of 50 gliders coded Elmira *was a support mission for the 82nd Airborne* (US Air Force).

on pilot training until the end of September when the airfield was required by the Americans. Greenham Common became USAAF Station 486 on October 1 1943 and was finally handed over to the VIIIth ASC, USAAF, on November 8. Its first task was the re-equipment of the 354th FG, IXth AF which arrived on November 4 to collect brand-new P-51Bs, the first Merlin-powered Mustangs to enter service in the European theatre. They only stayed a week before moving to Boxted, the first of a string of units to use Greenham briefly while the IXth AF settled down. Others included the HQ of the 70th FW which swopped places at Boxted with the 100th FW on December 6, the latter displaced at Greenham on January 13 1944 by the 71st FW HQ and one of its Fighter Groups, the 368th, which used the airfield to work up on P-47 Thunderbolts.

On February 22 1944, the 53rd TCW arrived to take over most of the 50th TCW elements in a general re-organisation completed in March. The 71st FW began its operational career on March 14 with a fighter sweep by the 366th and 368th FGs along the French coast, but this was the only one they made from Greenham, for they moved to Chilbolton the next day to make room for the troop carriers of the 438th TCG which arrived on March 16. Their introduction to Britain had been a fantastic muddle, a series of orders and counter-orders sending them wandering about the country like gypsies. By the time they reached Greenham Common their morale was at rock bottom, but with a heavy and successful training programme came a steady

improvement and they were declared operational in April.

To accommodate the C-47s, more of the very efficient loop hardstandings were built to supplement the original panhandles, bringing the total available to 50. Extensive steel track marshalling areas were laid at each end of the main runway, allowing gliders to be positioned on the runway with tugs still able to manoeuvre alongside for mass stream take-offs. Two 'T2' hangars remained the only covered servicing accommodation on the base but special long buildings were constructed for storing and inspecting the towing cables. By the beginning of June all four squadrons of the 438th TCG (87th, 88th, 89th and 90th TCS) were fully trained for paratroop drops and glider towing, day or night, and were given the task of leading the airborne forces to Normandy on June 5/6. They acquitted themselves so well during the first drop of the 101st Airborne Division, and subsequent Hadrian and Horsa gliders tows, that they received a Distinguished Unit Citation for their efforts. Re-supply missions followed and, when landing strips became available, they hauled freight, returning from the battlefield with casualties.

In July 1944 the 438th sent a detachment to Italy to take part in the invasion of Southern France, dropping paratroops on August 15 and then towing in Hadrians carrying reinforcements. They returned to Greenham at the end of August after freight lifts around Italy and in September the whole Group helped supply the Third Army as it pushed across France before taking part in Operation *Market* when 90 aircraft dropped elements of the 101st in the Eindhoven sector on Sunday, September 17. This major operation was followed by resupply sorties into the battle areas, the 439th and 442nd TCGs also flying from Greenham, and two missions to Bastogne were flown by the 438th during the surprise German offensive in the Ardennes, which started on December 16 1944 and caught the Americans off-balance.

During February 1945, the 438th started moving to Prosnes in France, the 53rd TCW HQ joining them towards the end of the month. American ground echelons retained Greenham until the end of the war in Europe when it was handed over to Transport Command, leaving a small USAAF detachment at the supply depot near Thatcham. In August the airfield was transferred to Technical Training Command and the runways obstructed while No 13 Recruit Centre used the accommodation to train entrants during an eight-week 'square bashing' course. After five such courses Greenham was declared surplus and closed down on June 1 1946, becoming an inactive site in Maintenance Command, parented first by Welford and later Andover.

Though periodically used by Army units as a training camp, the airfield buildings quickly became derelict and were gradually demolished for use as hardcore by local builders. There was a strong feeling in the locality that the Common should be restored to its original condition, but the Cold War of the 1950s put a stop to that remote possibility. American strategic bomber bases in the UK were agreed between the governments and Greenham Common was included in the second group of airfields chosen to house these detachments. American survey teams moved in during February 1951 amid increasingly wild rumours, which continued until the Air Ministry confirmed that Greenham was to become a bomber airfield. Control passed to Bomber Command, a small RAF party reopened the station, and then things moved fast. On April 23 the 7501st Air Base Squadron was designated the administrator of Greenham Common under the overall control of the 7th AD, 3rd AF, USAFE, and the 804th Engineer Aviation Battalion immediately started to rebuild the airfield.

Greenham Common was formally handed over to the 7th AD on June 18 1951, by which time it had become known locally as Tent City because of the vast array of canvas on the site. The wartime buildings, including the two 'T2' hangars, were all demolished and the whole area regraded to allow the construction of a massive 10,000 ft (3,048 m) runway laid E/W on top of the existing one, but extended at each end. Parallel taxiways

had extensive spur hardstandings, which partially used the old subsidiary runways as foundations. A large technical and domestic site was built on the south side, the A339 being diverted to lie along the edge of the ridge and through Packmoor Copse. Several buildings, including two pubs, had to be demolished and 44 families rehoused.

The peak of the construction work was during the summer of 1951 but the rebuilding was not complete until September 1953 when Greenham was declared available for *Reflex* operations by B-47 Stratojets. The new runway had been unofficially christened a few days earlier by a No 614 Squadron Vampire which force-landed short of fuel, but the first operational use was in March 1954 when 2,200 men moved in and a detachment of 303rd BW B-47s arrived from Davis Monthan AFB, Arizona—the first of the 90-day rotations from the States. Unfortunately the aircraft quickly proved too much for the runway which began to break up, and the Wing had to move hastily to Fairford to complete its *Reflex*.

After the runway was reinforced Greenham became the home of the 3909th Air Base Group in April 1956 when designated for KC-97G tanker deployments. The 97th Air Refuelling Squadron arrived at the end of the month and soon revealed another problem with the Common, flint stones which continually worked their way to the surface and damaged the propellers. The only solution was almost constant sweeping of the runways and taxiways.

The first full BW deployment with 45 B-47 aircraft commenced in October 1956 when the 310th arrived from Schilling AFB, provoking an immediate outcry. Not only were the aircraft extremely noisy on take-off, but also on landing due to a technique which involved high power against the drag of a tail parachute. Coupled with almost continuous running of generators and ground testing of engines, the noise was almost unbearable in Newbury. Although PR exercises helped, local opposition steadily increased, reinforced in March 1958 by a very nasty incident on the base. A B-47 experienced engine trouble on take-off and the crew had to jettison two full 1,700-gal (7,728 l) underwing fuel tanks. They missed the designated safe area on the base, one hitting a parked B-47 and other going through a hangar roof and bursting inside. The resulting fire burned for 16 hours despite the efforts of the Base Fire Detachment and help from RAF Odiham and USAF Welford. The final toll was two dead and eight injured, two B-47s destroyed and a hangar gutted.

The next month the 90-day detachments were replaced by a three-week *Reflex Alert* rotation during which the bombers did not fly, thus reducing the noise and the number of tankers considerably. There was more local concern when the runways and dispersals were further strengthened for the mighty B-52 bombers, but none were ever based at Greenham. From August 1960 they made periodic training visits but more excitement was caused by the arrival of a B-58 Hustler in October 1963, for this four-jet delta bomber was an impressive sight by any standards

Reflex operations by B-47 BWs and their attendant KB-97s continued until April 1 1964 when SAC policy changed and Greenham Common was returned to RAF control on July 1. The French withdrawal from NATO resulted in what was euphemistically described as the French Relocation of Assets (Freloc), and Greenham was re-opened during January 1967 as a storage annexe for Welford. It was subsequently upgraded and became a NATO standby base operated by the 7551st Combat Support Group under the control of 3rd AF HQ, South Ruislip. Greenham was then used for several *Reforger* (ie, reinforcement) exercises and in March 1976 the swing-wing F-111Es of the 20th TFW moved in for three months while the runways at Upper Heyford were re-surfaced.

Dozens of B-47E bombers 'rotated' through Greenham Common during the 1950s and early '60s (Military Aircraft Photos).

In March 1978 it was revealed that the British Government was considering a request for Greenham Common to be re-activated as a base for KC-135A air-refuelling tankers and work went ahead resurfacing the runway and repairing buildings, many of which had again fallen into disrepair. The predictable outcry from local residents greeted this plan, and it had an effect, for in October it was announced that there would be no aircraft permanently stationed at Greenham until the 1980s, and then they would be a quiet type. On January 1 1979, the 7273rd Air Base Group was formed, and a USAF Base Commander appointed, though in common with other American bases it remained a MoD establishment, with a RAF unit commander who also acted as liaison officer.

Following the NATO decision in December 1979 to deploy cruise missles in Europe it was announced on June 17 1980 that Greenham Common would be one of the two British bases. Ninety-six missiles would be stored in purpose-built underground shelters but in the event of war would be dispersed in the surrounding countryside on trailers. Inevitably these preparations drew renewed protests from local environmental groups, soon swamped by the Campaign for Nuclear Disarmament (CND) who supported a Women's Peace Camp established at the main entrance to the airfield in October 1981. At the time of writing this is still in existence through experienceing increasing local opposition because of the cost to ratepayers and poor condition of the camp.

Apart from occasional exercises by US Army helicopters using Greenham as a base, and infrequent aircraft visits in connection with the continued standby role, flying activity has centred on the

series of very successful International Air Tattoos which have been held on the airfield since 1973. From 1977 they have been biennial, growing steadily to become major displays with over 200 aircraft taking part. In May 1983, C-5A Galaxies started moving in equipment for the first cruise missile squadron, the 11th TMS, which received its first weapons in November. Whatever one's attitude to nuclear weapons and the missiles themselves, one must give the MoD credit for sticking to their promise of 1978—the missiles are making a lot less noise than the protestors. Hopefully they will stay that way.

The only remaining evidence of the wartime station, the bomb dump and the few sites north of the Burys Bank road, are fast disappearing in the undergrowth. The rest was bulldozed during the restruction in 1951-53 but, like the flints, bits will probably reappear from time to time.

Great Shefford, Berkshire

SU360730. 4 miles NE of Hungerford alongside A338

Some 1½ miles south-west of Great Shefford village and bounded on the southern side of the Ermine Way and the A338, this site was a large expanse of fairly flat ground chosen in 1940 as a scatter field for the aircraft at Woodley, near Reading. Woodley was the factory airfield of Phillip & Powis Aircraft Ltd who were building Masters and Magisters and also operated No 8 EFTS, an important flying school equipped with Tiger Moth and Magisters. Thus it was a likely target for the Luftwaffe, and in the event of invasion would have been deliberately obstructed to prevent enemy landings. In either event the plan was to fly all serviceable aircraft to Great Shefford, the scatter decision being taken if Woodley appeared directly threatened.

Reports of spies and paratroopers were legion in 1940 but as far as is known Great Shefford was not used until August, when on several occasions just before the sirens started wailing, all the aircraft on the Woodley flight line started up and took off, disappearing in a westerly direction. It would seem certain that they were making for Great Shefford, though it is just possible that they went to Sheffield Farm, then under development as a RLG.

With the threat of invasion subsiding and bombing becoming more unlikely, Great Shefford was redesignated an ELG

for flying training units in the area, remaining available until the end of the war when it was quickly relinquished. At no time were there any buildings or facilities at Great Shefford so there is no present day evidence to connect this large field close to the M4 with its wartime usage.

Guston Road (Dover), Kent

See Dover (Guston Road)

Hamble, Hampshire

SU477077. 4 miles SE of Southampton on B3397

When someone blithely refers to Hamble in an aeronautical context it is as well to ask, *which* Hamble?, or at least, *when?*, for the small peninsula contained by Southampton Water, the Hamble River and the Southampton-Portsmouth railway line has supported three quite distinct aerodromes, and as many marine bases, since 1913. It is a complicated story.

The first LG at Hamble was simply a grass field known as Browns which the Admiralty used during 1913 for the convenience of visitors to Calshot who arrived in landplanes, and were then ferried across the Water. The same field was used by Harry Hawker to win the £500 Mortimer Singer prize for amphibians on July 8 1913 with the co-operation of Lieutenant Spencer Grey, RN, the official observer, who got the wheels to come down for the five landings at Hamble with a well-aimed kick. However, the LG's main claim to fame was probably a visit on September 2 by Mr Winston Churchill, First Lord of the Admiralty, when he experienced a flight in a RNAS Sopwith tractor biplane piloted by Spencer Grey. Mrs Churchill was also taken up and while her husband fretted, fearful for her safety, she is reported to have enjoyed her flight tremendously.

Little more was heard of landplanes at Hamble for over a year, but things had been stirring on the river bank for some time. In 1912 the Hamble River Engineering Co and the yacht builders, Luke & Co, joined forces to design and construct a large floatplane. Named the HLI, it was shown incomplete at the 1914 Olympia Aero Show but then quietly faded from view and by the outbreak of war in August 1914 the project was moribund. The company's two sheds on Hamble Point were requisitioned by the Admiralty

Top *Avro's 'Garden City' factory on the original aerodrome at Hamble* (A.V. Roe & Co Ltd).

Above *A representative of Avro's most famous trainer with Southampton Water as a backcloth* (A.V. Roe & Co Ltd).

in December 1914 and presumably used for storage. When Fairey Aviation started looking for a suitable site to erect and test floatplanes manufactured at Hayes, Middlesex, late in 1915, they were offered these sheds, accepted them with alacrity, and immediately embarked on expansion. The existing wooden slipway was extended to permit launching of seaplanes at all states of the tide, and new erecting shops were built—on 4 ft (1.2 m) high concrete posts because the marshy ground was prone to flooding. Under the management of Brice G. Slater, sub-contracted Short 827s were assembled and then flown from Southampton Water by test pilot, Sydney

Pickles, who also dealt with Short 166 floatplanes manufactured by Westland Aircraft at Yeovil and sent by rail in crates.

Meanwhile, A.V. Roe had decided that the *ad hoc* expansion taking place at his Manchester factories was unsatisfactory, and decided to build a custom-designed unit in more pleasant surroundings. His choice fell on the Southampton area and he toured around looking for what would now be called a 'green field' site. He found it at Hamble where firm grassland stretched down to the edge of Southampton Water. He telegraphed his co-directors and within a fortnight the 100-acre field and a portion of the foreshore had been purchased, and a Garden City on the lines of Bournville was planned. Work on the factory, a large rectangular building with floor space unimpeded by the usual roof supports and with full span doors, was soon under way, followed by the first of 350 houses for the

staff. Unfortunately only part of the works, and 24 of the houses, were completed when the Government took control of building materials and the work had to stop. This prevented Roe's dream of moving down lock, stock and barrel from Manchester and restricted the use of Hamble to a design and experimental centre. The first new Avro machine to be assembled there was the Pike twin-engined bomber, flown by F.P. Raynham during May 1916 and later involved in an extraordinary escapade when a young Roy Dobson (who became the firm's managing director) crawled along the fuselage top to restore the centre of gravity during trials at Martlesham Heath. In September 1916 the design team, headed by Roy Chadwick, arrived and work at Hamble steadily increased as new projects saw the light of day.

The Fairey factory at Hamble assembled nearly all seaplanes produced by the company during the war, including the Campania, Hamble Baby and Fairey III series, while Avro carried out never ending trials on various machines and also built a number of 504Ks late in the conflict.

An upsurge in flying boat production late in 1917 forced the Admiralty to authorise the construction of No 1 (Southern) Marine Acceptance Depot to handle the products of the south coast firms. A site between Hamble Point and the Avro aerodrome on Southampton Water was chosen and construction of 12 large sheds and two slipways commenced (*SU478061*). By the beginning of September 1918 the sheds were partially complete, as was a railway spur from the main line, but with the Armistice

One of Avro's unsuccessful products, the 530 two-seat fighter outside the factory at Hamble (A.V. Roe & Co Ltd).

construction ceased. The sheds were demolished during 1919, the site later becoming an oil tank farm for which the railway line was completed.

For the aircraft companies the end of the war brought massive cut-backs in orders and the early 1920s were a very thin time for them all. Both Fairey and Avro just survived, the former's floatplane design and construction work culminating in the 1930s with the neat little Seafox which was both designed and built at Hamble, while Avro kept going with developments of the famous 504 and new design prototypes. These covered the whole spectrum from the diminutive Baby single-seater to the truly massive Aldershot, one version of which had a 1,000 hp Napier Cub as its powerplant, while even the standard production machine had a 650 hp Rolls-Royce Condor.

By the mid-1920s it was obvious that the Avro aerodrome was too small for safe testing of the heavier military machines coming out of the assembly shops. Early in 1926 the company invested in 200 acres of land between Satchell Lane (now the B3397) and the railway, these fields being transformed into a new airfield by Hunters, the well-known seedsmen. The Cierva Autogiro Company was formed at this time, and Avro built the first two machines ordered by the Air Ministry, using Avro 504K fuselages fitted with the Cierva rotor system. Company interest in this novel form of flying lasted many years, despite a serious accident on

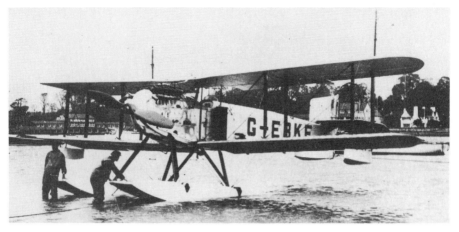

Above *The British Guinea Fairey IIID G-EBKE after launching at Hamble* (Fairey Aviation Ltd).

Below *The AST 'fleet' displayed outside the hangar at Hamble during 1934. Included are Avians, DH 9J, Cutty Sark, Avro Five, 504s, Atlas, Avro 621, 626 and 631 Cadet, plus a solitary Siskin* (via A.W. Wood & P.H.T. Green collection).

Hamble (South) airfield in February 1927 when a rotor broke and Frank Courtney was lucky to escape serious injury.

All landplane flying was transferred to Hamble (North) as the new aerodrome was called, the original Avro field being relegated to autogiros, engine testing and slipway access. In August 1926 the Hampshire Aero Club re-formed and took premises on Hamble (North) for their two DH Moths.

A.V. Roe sold his interest in the company in 1928, control passing to J.D. Siddeley of Sir W.G. Armstrong-Whitworth Aircraft Ltd during May. The design and development staff were transferred to Manchester and Cierva took over the Hamble design office while the works continued building a few Avians, the Antelope and various autogiros.

The Armstrong-Whitworth-operated Flying School for Reserve Officers at Whitley, Coventry, was an important part of the company's business, and J.D. Siddeley decided to offer similar facilities to civilians. Production of the Atlas and initial work on the Atalanta air liner precluded any expansion at Whitley, but with Hamble underutilised, the obvious answer was to move the Reserve School south and add a civilian element.

Air Service Training Ltd was formed for this purpose in 1931, taking over all the facilities at Hamble, the old Avro factory becoming little more than a workshop. Training started in April when new buildings and hangars were still being built at the southern end of Hamble (North), and the school was formally opened by HRH Prince Henry, Duke of Gloucester, on June 25 1931. The aircraft in use were Avians, Tutors, Atlases, twin-seater Siskins and even the odd DH9J, the latter fitted with ex-airliner Jaguar engines. The courses included *ab initio* instruction for overseas Service pilots.

The Cierva Company moved out, followed by the Hampshire AC in November 1932 when Eastleigh became available. AST then had Hamble to themselves, the Reserve School becoming No 3 E&RFTS in April 1933 under an Air Ministry rationalisation plan. Civilian-registered aircraft were retained, 12 Tutors and 17 Cadets being in service during 1935 when 8,828 hours were flown by the company on RAF training. During November AST received a Calcutta to enable them to start training Imperial A/Ws crews. This continued for a while using two Cutty Sark amphibians as well, but these were transferred to No 3 E&RFTS alongside several other redundant civil air transports when navigational training was introduced in 1937. The following year Harts, Hinds and even some Battles reached the unit when advanced training was added to the reserve task, while the navigation trainers added Army co-operation to their list of duties.

During February 1936, British Marine Aircraft Ltd was formed to manufacture Sikorsky S-42 four-engined flying boats under licence, work starting on a large factory using a 120-acre site on the shores of Southampton Water (*SU469072*) to the west of Hamble (North) airfield. Construction of the first machine progressed slowly and was finally abandoned in the face of competition from Short Brothers and difficulties in obtaining materials and staff. Early in 1937 an amalgamation with Westland was strongly tipped but this fell through and instead H.P. Folland, formerly chief designer of Gloster, became Managing Director. By the end of the year the factory was complete and Imperial Airways were using the main erecting shop for maintenance work on their Short Empire flying boats whilst various sub-contracting work, primarily from Supermarine, had been obtained. The name was changed to Folland Aircraft Ltd and during 1936 original design work started on a flying test-bed for various high-powered aero engines then under development.

Armstrong Whitworth had now received orders for a new airliner which could not be manufactured at Coventry because the factory was bursting at the seams with Whitleys. The jigs and tools were therefore transferred to the old Avro factory on Hamble (South) which inevitably led to delay, compounded by design changes requested by the customer, and it was not until January 23 1938 that the prototype Ensign was taxied across the road on to the airfield, to make its maiden flight the next day. The company's flight tests were done at Coventry, but production continued at Hamble, 11 being delivered by the outbreak of war in September 1939.

VR training ceased immediately and the unit became No 3 EFTS, equipped with 32

Avro Cadets and two Link Trainers (ground-bound instrument procedure trainers), 29 QFIs and eight ground instructors. Like the maintenance men, all were civilians. No 1 Supplementary School of Wireless Training was also formed, tasked with taking in 60 trainees a week for a 16-week course, while the EFTS spent the first two wartime months training new flying instructors. Blacking out the aerodrome buildings, gun post siting and camouflaging the airfield was completed by late September. The aircraft were also camouflaged on their upper surfaces, but retained their civil registrations. *Ab initio* courses restarted early in November and on the 20th No 11 AONS was formed, initially using an odd collection of civil aircraft including Avro Fives, Avro 652s, Wessexes, Dragonflies and Airspeed Envoys.

As the last Ensign left AST, the two prototype Albemarle bombers started assembly at Hamble from parts supplied by other factories in the Group. Completed early in 1940, the first was wheeled across Stachell Lane on to the airfield in March for engine tests and taxy runs. During a run on March 20, Armstrong-Whitworth's chief test pilot. C.K. Turner-Hughes, suddenly realised he was going too fast to stop. He lifted the Albemarle off, using the full 2,900 ft (884 m) length of the airfield, and staggered round the circuit for a very shaky landing. Another 10 ft (3 m) was added to the wing span before a second and more satisfactory attempt to fly was made.

The increasing Spitfire ferry task in the Southampton area resulted in *A* Section of No 3 Ferry Pilots Pool, an Air Transport Auxiliary unit, moving into Hamble

on June 1 1940, but the number of barrage balloons was also increasing and making life very difficult for the training units. It was decided to move them out as soon as possible, a decision strengthened by an attack by a single He-111 which dropped four bombs just outside the perimeter on July 12. Nos 3 EFTS and 11 AONS both left for Watchfield on the 20th, and the wireless school closed down soon afterwards, it performance having been unsatisfactory.

Folland were now busy producing components for Blenheims and Beauforts and were to go on to Beaufighter, Buckingham, Mosquito, Wellington and Sunderland sub-contracting in addition to their main preoccupation—Spitfire assemblies. AST were similarly engaged, becoming the largest fighter repair base in the country. The work continued throughout the war, repaired Spitfires totalling 3,400, in addition to contracts for the conversion of machines to Seafires, Mustang development and large assemblies for the Albemarle. AST also found time to convert 60 Hurricanes for use as catafighters from merchant ships against the dreaded Fw 200 Condor during the Battle of the Atlantic.

Most of these repaired or modified aircraft were ferried out by the ATA, whose organisation at Hamble was re-designated No 1 Sub Ferry Pilots Pool in November 1940 and in July 1941 became No 15 FPP. Quite a stir was caused when the first women pilots arrived on the unit, but the novelty had worn off by the time Miss M.W. Gore became the CO, and the last male pilot had left. Initially the accommodation was very poor, just two rooms in a hut on the airfield, but by the summer of

Left *Looking north across Hamble (South) towards the North airfield in 1934. The old Avro factory is on the left with the new AST hangar on the North field alongside the housing estate* (via A.W. Wood & P.H.T. Green collection).

Right *Further development of Hamble is apparent in this 1938 view. There is extensive new hangarage for the school, and the fourth Ensign G-ADSU is being readied for flight trials outside the old Avro factory* (Wing Commander D.E. Bennett).

Folland's work at Hamble included the development of the Spitfire floatplane. Several aircraft were used, including this Mk Vb which later saw service in the Middle East (Folland Aircraft Ltd).

1942 the 30 pilots, three ops officers, two adjutants, typists, maps officer, four drivers and canteen staff occupied a complete building, while 20 engineers were responsible for a fleet of five Ansons and six Argus 'taxis', which ferried pilots between airfields. The bulk of the work involved clearing aircraft from Eastleigh, Portsmouth, Christchurch, Chattis Hill, Marwell Hall, Worthy Down and last, but not least, Hamble itself. After delivery the pilots either flew another aircraft in, or were ferried back by Anson to Worthy Down, were they awaited clearance into the Southampton defence zone—a worrying and time-consuming business.

The remainder of the war was spent in quiet but steady achievement at Hamble, but with the cessation of hostilities came changes. No 15 FPP was disbanded and early in 1946 a sorry sight were the Ensigns which were flown back to their birthplace to moulder for a year before being broken up. Early in 1947 Tiger Moths of Southampton UAS arrived from Eastleigh and by the summer AST were busy providing flying training for both British and foreign students. They also secured Air Ministry contracts, not only servicing the UAS aircraft but also opened No 14 RFS on August 14 1947, equipped with Tiger Moths and Ansons. The unit maintained local Reserve pilots in flying practice.

The Fairey Aviation works at Hamble Point, which had been busy on sub-assembly and repair work throughout the war, was transferred to the associated boat-building firm, Fairey Marine, in 1945 but repair work on aircraft continued and in 1948 a production line of ten Fairey Primer light two-seaters was laid down—though only two were completed.

Target-towing variants of the Firefly were being produced as late as 1955, but work then tailed off, one of the last tasks being the refurbishing of Swordfish *G-AJVH* as a flying museum piece. It later reverted to military markings and is currently a popular item at air displays as part of the RN Historic Aircraft Flight based at Yeovilton.

Air Service Training carried out a series of conversions to Lancasters, Lancastrians and Lincolns for jet engine testing, the last one a Lancaster which was delivered to Sweden in 1951. The company also continued its tradition of assembling prototypes for other Hawker Siddeley Group members, when the Javelin T 3 dual trainer was completed at Hamble—but it was transferred to Brockworth by lorry for its maiden flight in August 1956. AST also overhauled and maintained the ex-BOAC Sunderland flying boats of Aquila Airways. Most were kept in reserve or for spares, standing forlornly on beaching trolleys near the Hamble slipway or moored in Southampton Water. The Sunderlands were gradually replaced by Solents, Aquila entering 1957 with four of these graceful aircraft. They became hopelessly uneconomic, however, and the company ceased operations in the United Kingdom at the end of September 1958.

It was Folland Aircraft Ltd which did the most work, sub-contracting on a wide selection of Hawker-Siddely aircraft, while also undertaking original design and development. The Folland Midge was built at Hamble during 1953-54. Its name described it perfectly for it was so small that it went on the back of a lorry, fully assembled, to Boscombe Down for its first flight! It was followed in 1955 by the Gnat fighter, an aircraft supported by the MoS and put into small-scale production at Hamble for the Finnish, Yugoslav and Indian air forces. The RAF was interested in a two-seat variant, and this went into full-scale production at Hamble where major components for over 100 were manufactured between 1959 and 1965. During the autumn of 1959 Folland were completely absorbed by Hawker Siddeley and the following year the company undertook some hovercraft work on behalf of the Group.

Meanwhile, changes had occurred on the flying side. Ansons previously operated by 783 Squadron, Lee-on-Solent, on behalf of the Naval Air Signals School, were moved to Hamble in November 1949 when AST obtained the contract. They continued to plod around the Solent area for the next four years until the Air Signals School closed in November 1953. More Ansons appeared when No 1 Basic Air Navigation School was formed by AST during January 1951 to teach RAF National Servicemen aircrew volunteers the basic art of navigation. The school started courses in February and worked up to a pupil strength of 80 before reductions in NS training and the Reserve

Chipmunks of No 2 Air Experience Flight spent some time at Hamble during the post-war years (C.P. Russell-Smith).

commitment resulted in No 1 BANS being closed in June 1953, followed by No 14 RFS two months later.

The loss of these three contracts in 1953 was only partially offset by increased civilian training using a fleet of Chipmunks which had started to supersede earlier aircraft in 1952. They were joined by Hiller 12Bs in August 1955 and Piper Apaches in 1957. The UAS also used Chipmunks, and in 1958 was joined by No 2 Air Experience Flight whose aircraft were used by cadets of the Sussex, Hampshire, Wiltshire and Dorset ATC Wings and 19 CCF units.

In 1960 the Hawker Siddeley Group disposed of AST and the school's facilities were taken over by the State-run College of Air Training. A two-year course for budding airline pilots was started using 18 Chipmunks and six Apaches, on which each student flew 150 and 75 hours respectively. The college was housed in the old AST buildings and accommodation was provided close the the airfield. The Chipmunks were partially replaced by Cherokees in November 1966 and two years later Beech Barons displaced the Apaches. In February 1970 the Barons were moved to Hurn where better operational facilities were available, leaving Hamble clear for primary training. The college maintained a high standard, but the fluctuating requirements of the two State airlines made it difficult to match output with needs.

The college was at a particularly low ebb in 1975 when the RAF found themselves with an urgent requirement for asymmetric training and basic airways flying for 75 pilots a year. The contract went to the College of Air Training, the

Barons being brought back to Hamble in August 1975, and flown by RAF students for the next two years.

With the RAF contract complete, the college again started training pilots for British Airways but it was a reduced commitment, and with further retrenchment at the end of the 1970s the number on the courses became totally uneconomic. In 1982 British Airways withdrew their support and both the college and the airfield were sold to a private consortium, Hampshire Airfield Properties Ltd. Specialist Flying Training Ltd, headed by Air Marshal Sir Peter Wykeham, which operated the college on behalf of the consortium, put the Cherokees and half the Barons into store, restarting operations with two Chipmunks and six Barons, while actively pursuing the development of the Vickers T67M and NDN Firecracker trainers.

In the meantime, Southampton UAS received Bulldogs early in 1974 and with No 2 AEF (which retained the Chipmunk), moved to Hurn in 1979, thus cutting the last military connection with Hamble.

During 1983 Specialist Flying Training transferred all activities to Carlisle and the College of Air Training had to call in the Receiver early in 1984. Trading ceased on February 14, 32 aircraft being sold by tender while other assets went by action on May 16, the airfield going to a property developer. Other tenants received eviction orders and flying virtually ceased during

Hamble Point on a foggy day in April 1983. Fairey Allday now occupy the former Fairey Aviation site on which several aircraft hangars still remain amongst the more modern buildings—and the many yachts.

the summer. The old Fairey factory at Hamble Point is concerned solely with boats, the Avro airfield and Admiralty Acceptance Depot are part-covered by Shell oil storage tanks while the old factory, still with its distinctive square chimney, forms the central part of Petters Works (*SU477068*). The British Marine Aircraft/Folland factory, however, is still pat of British Aerospace and makes sub-assemblies for Harriers and Hawks, thus maintaining one strand of the Hamble story intact. The locals have a constant reminder of this activity in the *Harrier* public house, for the gaily painted sign depicts the aeroplane—not the bird. Sadly it appears that the art of flying training, the other activity which made Hamble famous, has finally succumbed to rapacious house builders.

Hammerwood, East Sussex

TQ440391. 3 miles E of East Grinstead off A264

Often referred to by the Army as East Grinstead, the rather nebulous airstrip at Hammerwood was longer-lasting than most of the Air Observation Post squadron bases set up in south-east England to accommodate units being prepared for the Second Front.

Two landing strips were laid out on grassland at Bower Farm which was almost completely surrounded by woodland and extremely well camouflaged. No 660 Squadron, No 84 Group, arrived from Andover on November 20 1943, set up its HQ in Hammerwood House, and operated detached Flights at Holyte and Ashington, whilst getting used to functioning from mobile camps and exercising with Army formations in the area.

In March 1944 the improved Lycoming-

powered Auster AOP IV replaced the
Gipsy-engined Mk III and the following
month the squadron moved to Westenhangar. They were replaced by No 659
Squadron, working up as part of No 83
Group and already equipped with the
Auster IV. Practice AOP work intensified
as D-Day approached, followed by an
anxious wait before crossing the Channel
to join the Army in the field. This they did
on June 14 1944 when they reached Cully,
and Hammerwood was soon just a fading
memory for the Army AOP aviators and
their RAF tradesmen—airmen were responsible for the Auster maintenance
during the war!

Hartfordbridge Flats
(Blackbushe), Hampshire
See Blackbushe

Hawkinge (Folkestone), Kent
*TR213395. 2 miles N of Folkstone on
A260*

No 32 Squadron flew into their forward
airfield of Hawkinge soon after mid-day
on August 12 1940. While their Hurricanes were refuelled the pilots relaxed on
the warm grass, some talking quietly,
others sleeping, for they were already very
tired. At 14:30 hours they were airborne,
replacing No 610 Squadron on a standing
patrol, necessary because five radar
stations had been damaged that morning.
Back after an hour, the scramble call
came at 16:45 hours—reports were in of
aircraft forming up over the French coast.
While No 32 Squadron patrolled off
Margate, the enemy, 15 Ju 88s of II/
KG76, headed for Dungeness at 5,000 ft
(1,524 m). Near Dymchurch they split into
two groups, one making for Lympne, the
other for Hawkinge where they arrived in
a shallow dive, completely unannounced,
the airfield defenceless except for three
Lewis guns and a single 20 mm Hispano
cannon.

   With bombs exploding, officers,
NCOs, airmen, airwomen and civilians
dived into slit trenches and held their
breath. The first bombs cratered the airfield, the rest hit the technical site causing
the massive end doors of No 3 hangar to
collapse, blew up the main equipment
store and two of the married quarters used
for airmen's accommodation. A large
workshop caught fire and it was a chaotic
scene which greeted personnel as they
clambered out of their hidey-holes. The

raid was over so quickly that some could
hardly believe it had happened, but they
were soon tackling fires and searching for
victims. Five were killed and another
seven badly wounded, but fortunately the
Watch Office was still usable, for half of
No 32 Squadron, low on fuel, were
already requesting permission to land.
Carefully threading their way between the
28 craters on the field, all five got down
safely, a considerable relief because four
Hurricanes on the ground had been
damaged in the raid. Getting the airfield
operational again was the top priority,
and despite the risks from unexploded and
delayed action bombs, this was achieved
overnight, three Hurricanes taking off
next morning for a dawn patrol.

   It was a couple of days before the debris
was cleared and the Station Commander
began to look happier, but not for long
because, during the morning of August
15, another attack developed, about 16
Stukas of IV/LG1 breaking away from a
much larger formation as they crossed the
coast. As they took up their pre-dive positions they were set upon by Hurricanes of
No 501 Squadron and Spitfires from No
54, quickly losing four of their number.
The Bf 109s promptly intervened, shooting down two Spitfires and two Hurricanes, but the squadrons undoubtedly saved
Hawkinge from total destruction. Things
were bad enough, No 5 (Handley Page)
hangar being demolished by a 1,100 lb
(500 kg) bomb and a barrack block used
by Sergeant Pilots badly damaged. During
the afternoon Hawkinge received a visit
from He 111s of KG1 and Do 17s of KG2,
but no significant damage was done,
except to the defenders' nerves.

   These were the first raids on Hawkinge,
and arguably the worst—certainly personnel were aware that they were in the front-
line by the end of that week in August
1940!

   Aviation had come to Hawkinge much
earlier, however, for in 1912 a Dutchman,
W.B. Megone, started building a flying
machine in a corrugated iron shed in the
corner of a field at Barnhouse, just to the
west of the village. It managed a few hops
but nothing more and in September 1914
the shed lay locked and abandoned—
Megone had disappeared. With the real-
isation that the war was not going to be
over quickly, the War Office started
scouring the whole of Kent for suitable
aerodrome sites. The needs of the supply
route to France resulted in particular
attention being paid to the Dover-

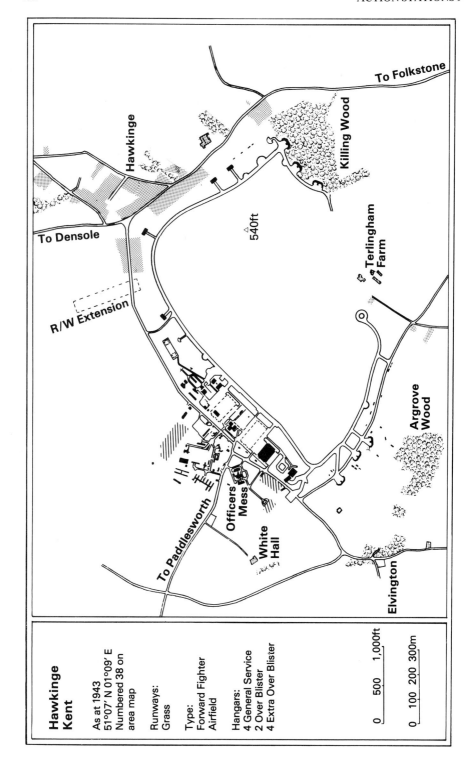

Hawkinge
Kent

As at 1943
51°07' N 01°09' E
Numbered 38 on
area map

Runways:
Grass

Type:
Forward Fighter
Airfield

Hangars:
4 General Service
2 Over Blister
4 Extra Over Blister

To Folkstone

Killing Wood

Hawkinge

To Densole

540ft

R/W Extension

Terlingham
Farm

Argrove
Wood

To Paddlesworth

Officers'
Mess

White
Hall

Elvington

0   500   1,000ft

0   100 200 300m

Folkestone area but it is said that the village postmaster was instrumental in getting Hawkinge considered. In any event the site, high up on the Downs above Folkestone, was approved and the Megone field and adjoining pasture on Lord Radnor's estate, a total of 166 acres, were acquired by the War Office.

There is uncertainty about when RFC personnel started to arrive at Folkestone, as the LG at Hawkinge was first named. One authoratitive source suggests September 1915, but No 1 Squadron, RFC, used Folkestone for its crossing to France early in March so, unless this refers to some other site, such as Capel, Megone's field would appear to have been in RFC use from the end of February 1915. No 1 Squadron crossed without incident, but others were not so lucky, a No 7 Squadron RE 5 bursting into flames at Folkestone in April while No 8 Squadron lost two BE 2Cs in crash landings on the aerodrome a week later. By the autumn of 1915 Folkestone (Hawkinge) was definitely in being, with rows of tents and three Bessoneaux canvas hangars gracing the skyline. Compasses were notoriously inaccurate so to assist pilots in crossing to St Omer two circles were cut in the turf. When lined up, they pointed the aircraft straight at the French aerodrome.

More permanent sheds and accommodation huts were built during 1916 and the Despatch Section gradually settled down to dealing efficiently with the ever-growing numbers of aircraft passing through to replace the horrendous losses in France. In January 1917, HQ 21st Wing, RFC, decided that the aerodrome would be renamed Hawkinge to prevent

One of the 'GS' hangars at Hawkinge approaching completion in 1919 (via B. Robertson).

confusion with the airship station at Capel. The unit thus became the Aeroplane Despatch Centre, Hawkinge, later developed into No 12 Aircraft Acceptance Park (SE area), which by the end of the year consisted of a Park HQ, two Erection Sections and one Storage Section and was to be the final despatch station for all machines going to France, relieving Lympne AAP entirely of this task. With nine General Service hangars and two running sheds on the north-west side (covering most of Megone's original field) and very adequate landing runs of 2,400 ft (732 m) E/W and 2,000 ft (610 m) N/S, Hawkinge was ideally placed for its task, though the sheds took so long to build that when aircraft were delayed in transit they had to be tied down around the perimeter. Late in 1918 two more sheds of the Handley Page type were being constructed along the north-east side, while an extensive hutted camp had sprung up on the other side of the road between Hawkinge and Paddlesworth.

The AAP was nearly complete at the Armistice, but the pace then slowed and it was some time before the Handley Page sheds were finished. The work of the Acceptance Park gradually wound down but the accommodation was used by Nos 38 and 83 Squadrons which returned from the Continent on February 14 1919, parked their aircraft and awaited demobilisation.

Earlier in the year the Belgian Government had requested help in alleviating the chronic shortages of food and clothing in some parts of the country. An air parcel service was started between Hawkinge and Ghent on February 1, organised by Aircraft Transport & Travel Ltd but using RAF DH 9s flown by Service pilots. The Army then allowed mail for the occupation forces to be flown across the Channel and late in the month No 120 Squadron

moved in from Lympne. The *C* Service was inaugurated on March 1 by four DH 9s of *B* Flight which left on schedule with 24 mailbags to link up with the Continental service at Maisoncelle. Unfortunately, this good start was followed by a spell of atrocious weather and flying was impossible on ten days of the month. The UK terminal returned to Lympne in July, the hangars at Hawkinge being required for storage of Handley Page V/1500 bombers and many smaller types awaiting scrapping.

The AAP was disbanded in July, followed by No 120 Squadron in October 1919 when the airfield became inactive, though the disposal work continued. During February 1920 the station was taken over by the RAF Section of the Inter-Allied Commission of Control but nominally became a fighter base when No 25 Squadron re-formed at Hawkinge on April 20 1920. Though the only fighter squadron in the UK, it was a cadre unit which took on charge the 127 Snipes, 14 0/400s, 21 V/1500s, one Bristol F 2B and two Avro 504Ks still stored in the hangars, and only had sufficient personnel to fly the two '504s. However, it gradually built up and was getting properly established, equipped with the best of the Snipes, when the Chanak crisis developed and No 25 was rushed off to Turkey in September 1922. No 56 Squadron was at Hawkinge from November but moved to Biggin Hill in May 1923. No 25 Squadron got back in October 1923 and remained for 15 years while working through famous fighter biplanes such as the Grebe, Siskin, Fury, Demon and Gladiator, before suddenly

Above *A view north-west across Hawkinge during October 1933* (RAF Museum P1562).

Above right *A familiar sight at Hawkinge during 1935-37 were the Audax Army Co-op biplanes of No 2 Squadron* (RAF Museum P7775).

changing to the heavy brigade in the form of Blenheim Ifs during December 1938.

Hawkinge was brought up to Wing strength when No 17 Squadron re-formed during April 1924 with the inevitable Snipes but, after re-equipping with Woodcocks, they moved to Upavon in October 1926, and the station reverted to its former state, the Squadron CO also being the Station Commander. The leisurely pattern of peacetime training provided the officer pilots with an enviable existence, but the airmen were also an elite bunch. Apart from annual practice camps, air-to-air firing was confined to camera guns but aerobatics, formation flying and air-to-ground firing were practised assiduously, much of the latter on the Lydd and Hythe ranges.

The Wessex Area Storage Unit, the AAP by another name, was formed at Hawkinge early in 1926 and used for the acceptance of new aircraft from the manufacturers, holding them for scheduled squadron re-equipment or accident replacements—it was the forerunner of the modern MU.

Summer camps for Auxiliary and Reserve squadrons became an annual event from 1930 when No 602 (City of

Glasgow) Squadron visited, their Wapitis flying a record 451 hours while at Hawkinge. The following year the Air Ministry started a rebuilding programme which lasted until 1933. Two barrack blocks, an Educational/Barrack block, NAAFI, Officers Mess, Sergeants Mess and Airmens Dining Hall were constructed, together with married quarters. Hardly had the bulk of this work been completed, than a Horsley of No 504 Squadron returning from the bombing ranges on August 7 1933, lost power on the approach and landed on top of No 4 hangar (the easterly single-bay GS shed). The landing was masterly and the crew scrambled clear, but escaping fuel started a fire and very quickly the whole hangar and six Blackburn Darts stored inside were ablaze—and completely gutted.

After the station facelift and with the RAF Expansion Programme in full swing, it was no great surprise when a convoy of lorries arrived from Manston on November 3 1935. They were directed to No 3 hangar and soon afterwards Audax biplanes of No 2 (AC) Squadron appeared overhead and landed. Hawkinge now had its second permanently based unit resulting in the formation of a SHQ and transfer to No 22 Group, Inland Area. The new squadron started almost non-stop Army co-operation exercises with local formations and were soon acknowledged low-level experts.

During the Munich Crisis No 25 Squadron moved to its war station, while at Hawkinge the station defence scheme was activated and buildings darkened with camouflage paint. No 2 Squadron was in

the throes of converting from Hectors to Lysanders so already had its hands full, but the crisis passed and No 25 Squadron returned to prepare for the Blenheim. The wet grass of a rather small airfield was not the best operating surface for a night fighter but it was still with mixed feelings that No 25 Squadron went to Northolt on August 22 1939—it was obvious that war was looming. When the newly formed No 613 (City of Manchester) Squadron arrived at Hawkinge for their summer camp the tension could be felt and the outbreak of war was almost a relief, though its effect on Hawkinge was most unexpected. After No 2 Squadron made its planned move to France on October 6, the station was transferred to Training Command as No 3 Recruits Training Pool! The parade square soon resounded to the sound of marching feet, but the airfield lay deserted.

The 5th Buffs Territorials moved in to man the few Lewis guns forming the defences, slit trenches were dug and sandbags stacked round doors and windows, while the buildings and roads were re-camouflaged and 'hedges' painted on the airfield. This miserable task went on until December so it was with satisfaction that the uncertain arrival of a Hurricane detachment from No 3 Squadron was noted—the pilots couldn't decide which was the boundary hedge! There was little activity for the Hurricanes and heavy snowfalls brought things to a standstill during January 1940. The recruits pool was closed in February and Fighter Command took over, though No 3 Squadron had left a few days earlier, and were replaced by No 16 Squadron Lysanders from Old Sarum and the Pilotless Aircraft Section from Henlow. The Lysanders launched into exercises with local Army units before moving to France during April.

During February 1940 two radio specialists were instructed to establish a listening post at Hawkinge. Given an old hut, Flight Lieutenants Scott Farnie and Allway set up their local purchase HF receivers and started listening. They heard nothing for two months, then in mid-May German transmissions came through loud and clear. Fortuitously, they discovered a linguist on the camp, and soon had a team of German-speaking WAAF maintaining a 24-hour watch. They outgrew the hut, moved into Maypole Cottage in the village, and after the fall of France, transfered to less vulnerable accommodation away from the airfield. It was the start of the world-wide *Y* Service which contributed greatly to the success of the codebreaking and intelligence services.

Use of Hawkinge as a forward satellite returned with a detachment of No 17 Squadron from Debden on April 17, and they were still present when the Phoney War ended with the German breakthrough into France and the Low Countries on May 10. The Hurricanes were joined by detachments of Blenheim fighters from Nos 25 and 604 Squadrons, which flew standing patrols over the rapidly changing battle front in France, and even managed to shoot down one or two aircraft. Nine days after the blitzkrieg started, communications in France had broken down. The Air Ministry took control and formed a Rear HQ at Hawkinge commanded by AVM C.H.B. Blount. He planned to bring the Air Component aircraft back to south-east England (designated *Back Violet*) but operate them in the lower Seine area (*South Violet*) using ALGs in France. In the event the plan was overtaken by the speed of advance and all Kentish airfields, including Hawkinge, became jammed with escaping Lysanders, Hurricanes, Blenheims and Battles. The majority were refuelled and sent rearwards to regroup, a few were repaired, and others were scrapped on the spot. When Operation *Dynamo*, the evacuation of British forces through Dunkirk, started on May 27, Blount's HQ at Hawkinge collated information using reports from Army Co-operation aircrew and the *Y* Service— a little known but vital part in an operation which was almost miraculous in its success.

On May 25, No 613 Squadron, who had been ferrying Lysanders to France, found themselves back at Hawkinge with a sterner task. Still partially equipped with Hector biplanes, they sent six of them to attack a battery of heavy field guns threatening the beleaguered garrison of Calais. Despite accurate flak they returned without loss, repeating the process the next day—and again they all got back. On the 27th the Lysander Flight joined the Hectors in a desperate supply drop to the Calais defenders, going in at 200 ft (61 m) escorted by Skuas of the FAA. Again they all survived German fire but one Hector crash-landed near Dover, killing the gunner. These were the only operations by Hectors, No 613 Squadron being withdrawn shortly afterwards. Hawkinge then became a forward airfield in the Biggin Hill sector, a detachment of No 245 Squadron Hurricanes being looked after by the permanently based No 11 Servicing Flight.

Work started on six double fighter pens, three on the western boundary across Gibraltar Lane, and three in Killing Wood at the south-eastern corner of the airfield. Renewed efforts were made to improve airfield defences for Hawkinge was particularly vulnerable—it could be seen from France on a clear day! The eight Lewis guns were joined by four 20 mm Hispano and one 20 mm Oerlikon (salvaged from a ship), and the Army provided some Bofors in the immediate vicinity, while at the end of June the incredible (and largely useless) Parachute & Cable device was installed. More trenches and shelters were dug, road blocks set up and vital installations mined, while work went ahead on pill boxes and three Pickett Hamilton retractable forts.

When the Luftwaffe opened its offensive early in July it was the Hurricanes of No 79 Squadron which were on standby at Hawkinge. Small groups of heavily escorted bombers came over the Channel at intervals to attack merchant ships, with the obvious intention of bringing the RAF to combat. No 79 Squadron were early victims, losing their CO and two other pilots when surprised by free-ranging Bf 109s. Being bounced so easily was an obvious sign of acute fatigue and they were moved north on July 10. Hawkinge was then used during daylight hours by Hurricane squadrons in rotation though a slightly different shape appeared on July

19 when 12 Defiants of No 141 Squadron flew in for their first taste of forward airfield operations. The morning was quiet but lunch was interrupted by the mournful wail of Folkestone's sirens and the Defiants were scrambled soon after the Luftwaffe started an attack on Dover harbour. Only nine got airborne, climbing in sections of three towards Cap Gris Nez to catch the returning German bombers. Almost immediately ten Bf 109s of II/JG2 *Richthofen* Geschwader dived on them out of the sun, completely routing the squadron. While the gunners desperately tried to track the '109s, a second Staffel attacked head on. In less than a minute four Defiants were shot down and another abandoned on fire. The arrival of No 111 Squadron Hurricanes saved the rest, four Defiants struggling back to Hawkinge, of which two survived the landing. No 141 Squadron had been effectively destroyed in one engagement.

The first raids on Hawkinge have been described already, but they did not stop there. The tannoy blared out its air raid warning again on August 18 and as personnel took shelter six Do 17Zs, escorted by Bf 109s, came in low over the village. Bullets flew in all directions as the Germans strafed the airfield and the defences fired back. Little damage was done and in the respite which followed repairs were made and the airfield generally cleaned up. A formation of about 50 aircraft approached on September 1. Most attacked Lympne, but five dived on Hawkinge, dropping eight 275 lb (125 kg) bombs which hit the already wrecked No 3 hangar and blew a small building to bits. It was decided to disperse some sections of the station, while work was started on a decoy Q-site at Wooton, and plans made for a rest camp at Hockley Sole, to be known as Hawkinge *D*. Landings by parachutists or glider-borne troops were expected daily and everyone, including non-combatants like cooks and clerks, was issued with a rifle on September 6, and told to make every round count if the camp was attacked—there was no more ammunition!

By coincidence a German did arrive that day, but after his experiences he had little fight left in him. Feldwebel Werner Gottschalk of 6/LG2 had been escorting bombers over Chatham when his Bf 109 was turned onto its back by a bursting AA shell. He was then attacked by British fighters near Canterbury and as he made for the sea, his engine stopped. He turned

along the coast and, sighting an airfield, put the wheels and flaps down to make a perfect dead stick landing at Hawkinge. When the swastika markings sank in, the defenders, who had been on red alert for a week, opened up on the aircraft from all sides. Gottschalk led a charmed life for he survived the fusilade uninjured and was captured in one of the hangars.

September 7 1940 is generally known as the date the Luftwaffe switched its daylight attacks to London, but started much as usual, the low-level attacks by Bf 109s and '110s on Hawkinge, the main event. In all they dropped 18 bombs, hitting the Officers' Mess, No 1 hangar and the SHQ. One soldier was killed and 12 station personnel injured while the last bomb fell on a village shelter, killing six civilians. It was a small but nasty attack, leaving more craters to fill in on the sorely tried airfield, which looked more like a building site. Clouds of dust rose on every take-off, enveloping the whole camp like a blanket.

By October the Luftwaffe had virtually ceased conventional daylight bombing and was using Bf 109 and '110 fighter-bombers instead. Six Bf 109s appeared over Hawkinge at mid-day on the 9th making a lot of noise but fortunately only hitting already abandoned buildings. Similar raids, often by single aircraft, followed and, though they did some material damage, their biggest effect was upon personnel, always on edge awaiting an attack.

Spotting incoming Luftwaffe formations using a Spitfire was so successful that No 421 Flight was formed with nine aircraft on November 15, as the first Hawkinge-based unit for many months —and an unexpectedly useful one despite the decreased Luftwaffe activity in the area. The pilots spotted shipping for No 2 Group and also disrupted the activities of the long-range guns on Cap Gris Nez.

Aircraft recognition was never the AA gunner's strong point and with the added jitters produced by fighter bomber attacks, approaching a south coast airfield unannounced was a risky business. On November 2 1940 it nearly resulted in the loss of a bomber VC. Flight Lieutenant R.A.B. Learoyd flew a Hampden down to Hawkinge for a presentation at his home town of New Romney. Before landing he circled the town several times at low level, this strange behaviour resulting in trigger-happy gunners firing and hitting Hampden *P1176*. Learoyd quickly retracted the

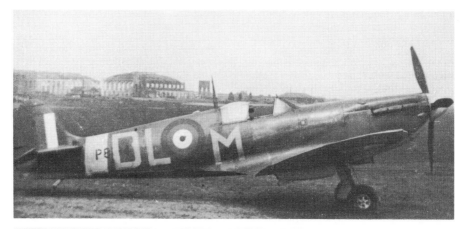

undercarriage and flew at low level and high speed to Detling where he landed with an injured crewman—and completed the journey by car!

The success of No 421 Flight resulted in an upgrading as No 91 Squadron on February 16 1941 and the pilots even managed to shoot down the odd fighter bomber, as well as continue their spotting duties. The Battle of Britain had demonstrated the inferiority of British sea rescue services compared with those of the Germans and with Fighter Command going on to the offensive attempts were made to remedy this by flying in a Lysander daily from the *B* Flight detachment of No 4 Squadron, at Manston. It was present on May 16 when the station was attacked four times by marauding Bf 109s, killing one airman and injuring five, demolishing two shelters and caving in the roof of No 2 hangar damaging two Spitfires and the CO's hack.

A   dedicated   ASR   Flight   of   two

Top *Spitfire IIA of No 91 Squadron in April 1941 with the gutted Hawkinge hangars as a backcloth* (G.R.S. McKay).

Above *A damaged Spitfire of No 71 Squadron at Hawkinge during August 1941 with an ASR Lysander to the rear* (RAF Hawkinge).

Lysanders fitted with sea markers and dinghies was formed at Hawkinge in June, joined by two Walrus amphibians in August, and finally became *B* Flight of No 277 Squadron on December 22 1941 when air-sea rescue became big business. Of the original hangars only one was now usable, but with the perimeter track complete three Extra Over Blister hangars were dispersed around the airfield. Nos 65 and 41 Squadrons arrived at the end of June 1942 for *Rhubarbs* and *Rodeos* over France but were suddenly withdrawn on July 8, and the next arrivals were for Operation *Jubilee*, the combined Services landing at Dieppe. Every airfield in the south-east bulged at the seams, Hawkinge being sealed early on August 18 when the resident Nos 91 and 277 Squadrons were joined by Spitfires of Nos 416 and 616 Squadrons. The Jim Crows of No 91 Squadron were to reconnoitre the Channel between Ostend and Le Havre continuously to ensure no surprise attacks by the German Navy on the landing ships, while the visitors were to be part of the top cover.

Three Spitfires of No 91 Squadron were away on their first sorties by 06:00 hours and an hour later Nos 416 and 616 were over Dieppe at 12,000 ft (3,658 m). On their second mission Nos 416 and 616 Squadrons saw some 50 Fw 190s and a lone Do 217 which was destroyed, while four Fw 190s were claimed damaged. More action was reported in the afternoon with No 416 Squadron attacking seven Ju 88s seen approaching the ships, claiming one probable and five damaged. No 616 Squadron lost a Spitfire during combat with Fw 190s, but the pilot was subsequently rescued. Meanwhile, No 91 Squadron kept up their cover, finding two HSLs on fire and escorting three more to the English coast despite being jumped by eight Fw 190s. In case the Luftwaffe tried an all-out attack on the crowded airfields the CO then led off ten Spitfires for a defensive patrol between Folkestone and Hastings. It had been a very busy day at Hawkinge, with almost non-stop refuelling and re-arming by groundcrew.

No 91 Squadron was out early on the 20th searching for missing pilots, while the visitors prepared to leave for their home bases. The Luftwaffe was also scouring the Channel and one Spitfire failed to return—so there was some satisfaction in the destruction of a Do 24 flying boat, which exploded as it hit the water. When No 91 Squadron moved over to Lympne on November 23 the airfield was left practically deserted until they returned early in January 1943. They left again during April for conversion to the Griffon-powered Spitfire XII, but were replaced by their sister squadron, No 41, who were soon in action, shooting down a Fw 190 on April 27 during the first encounter with this formidable aircraft.

When No 91 Squadron returned on May 21, No 41 left for Biggin Hill, leaving the old Hawkinge unit to resume its Jim Crow activities, and to cope with the Fw 190 fighter-bombers now making life a misery in south coast towns. They could outpace most Spitfires, but not the Mk XII, whose low-altitude-rated Griffon engines were ideal for the task. This they demonstrated on May 25 by shooting down five Germans in a chase across the Channel, but with a lull in the enemy's tip and run activities the Spitfire XII squadrons formed a bomber support Wing and moved to Westhampnett at the end of June 1943.

No 501 Squadron had already taken over the Jim Crow work, while the airfield had a new role forced on it. More and more B-17 Fortresses and B-24 Liberators were reaching the English coast badly damaged, or with seriously injured men aboard, as USAAF daylight operations over Europe increased. Their pilots were prepared to put down anywhere, however unsuitable, and in company with all forward airfields, Hawkinge became host to a steady stream of these four-engined aircraft. It was hardly large enough for them when fully serviceable so with engines out, hydraulics shot away, or no brakes, some of the landings were hazardous in the extreme. Bomber Command also joined in, one of the first arrivals being a No 460 Squadron Lancaster on two engines, which joined the circuit early in the morning of July 9 1943 after a raid on Cologne. After the road fencing had been removed to give access to the extension, and several attempts, the pilot got it down on the N/S runway. Unfortunately he wasn't lined up properly, and with brakes squealing the aircraft was only stopped when it demolished a Nissen hut. From the wreckage were taken six severely injured men, only one of them able to walk unaided.

In addition to the runway extension, three more Blister hangars and nine large hardstandings were approved during 1943, when No 501 Squadron's early weather/shipping recces were often extended into France, especially after the receipt of some Spitfire IXs in November. They shared Hawkinge with a string of Spitfire VB-equipped squadrons, Nos 313, 322 and 350 being prominent, these units spending varying periods at this forward base for *Ramrods* and *Rhubarbs* until April 1944 when the fighters departed, leaving Hawkinge to the ASR unit. Their Spitfire IIs and Walrus aircraft had been joined by some Sea Otters in November 1943, and it was one of the latter that was involved in a dramatic rescue on March 18 1944. A No 2 Group Mitchell of No 320 (Dutch) Squadron was forced to ditch just a few miles off the French coast. Good drill enabled the whole crew to get out before the aircraft sank and they were quickly spotted, the Sea Otter being put down alongside. The Dutchmen were soon aboard but the amphibian was so overloaded it could not take-off, and for four hours the pilot taxied towards the English coast until finally met by an ASR launch.

On May 14, No 157 (GR) Wing of No 16 Group, Coastal Command, moved to Hawkinge. A week later 24 Grumman Avengers of 854 and 855 Squadrons, FAA, arrived, the locals hardly able to believe their eyes at the sight of these pot-bellied monsters in place of the trim fighters. The Wing started patrols on May 31, part of the intensive *Channel Stop* operation designed to deny the whole area to U-boats and German surface vessels alike. Hawkinge was ideally placed, but not really suitable for the aircraft, as was discovered on June 5 when a fully-loaded Avenger of 855 Squadron crashed on take-off. The maximum load was immediately reduced to 1,500 lb (680 kg) and with black and white invasion stripes liberally applied, intensive anti-submarine searches were flown by day, and anti-shipping patrols at night. They saw little because the *Channel Stop* was so effective, only one U-boat being attacked during June, but with the introduction of *Rovers* off the coast of Holland, Belgium and northern France early in July there was more action. 854 Squadron made a number of successful attacks on shipping, and a rear gunner shot down a flying boat on July 9.

As soon as Thorney Island was available, No 157 (GR) Wing moved there and Spitfire XIVs of Nos 350 and 402 Squadrons moved into Hawkinge for anti-*Diver* patrols during August. No 350 Squadron gained its first V-1 success on August 15 and the next day No 402 destroyed three, one almost overhead their dispersal at Hawkinge! The Spitfires also took part in *Rangers* during which No 350 destroyed a Ju 188 over Brussels on August 19, and *Ramrods*, some of the latter as cover for the Arnhem airborne landings.

The V-1 menace largely over, the Griffon Spitfires departed at the end of September and were replaced by a series of Merlin-powered Spitfire IX squadrons which spent most of their time on bomber escort work, with the occasional long-range sweep over Germany. This work continued until the German surrender on May 8 1945, as did Hawkinge's other pre-occupation, dealing with distressed bombers. Some of the latter were desperate in the extreme, but none more so than the 388th BG B-17 which suddenly appeared over Killing Wood during the afternoon of January 5 1945. During an attack on central Germany the port inner engine had been shot away and the pilots killed. The navigator was flying the aircraft and he would not, or could not, close the throttles fully, coming across the grass on each approach too fast, and then crabbing horribly as he overshot. There was no doubt that he would crash, it was just a matter of when, and where. Finally he threw the aircraft at the ground and it tore through a fence, hit a bank and broke in two, killing four of the crew. The tail gunner and the heroic 'pilot' survived; the very shaken spectators returning quietly to their work.

No 277 Squadron was also going quietly about its business. During November 1944 a Warwick detachment from No 276 Squadron was absorbed by the home-based unit and thus became the largest aircraft to be operated permanently from the station. Not for long though, re-organisation resulting in No 277 Squadron being disbanded mid-February 1945 and replaced by a detachment of No 278 equipped with Walrus and Sea Otter amphibians.

Life at Hawkinge became very quiet, though the arrival of ex-PoWs for processing kept the staff busy. On June 13 No 657 Squadron, an anti-aircraft co-operation unit, moved in from Hornchurch but did little flying, most of the time being spent modifying Vengeances as replacement for their Martinets. In August it was decided temporarily to base an Armament Practice Station at Hawkinge while a permanent location was found. No 567 Squadron left and No 3 APS was formed, their first customers being No 234 Squadron whose Spitfire IXs arrived in August 27, followed by Nos 1 and 132 Squadrons in September. They proved to be the last, for the APS moved north, the No 278 Squadron detachment disbanded, and Hawkinge was reduced to C&M on November 7 1945.

No 166 GS used the airfield at weekends for ATC gliding during 1946, but in the spring of 1947 Hawkinge was transferred to No 22 Group, Technical Training Command, and was re-opened on June 1 as the WAAF Technical Training Unit. Com-

The sadly dilapidated guardroom at Hawkinge in 1982. Most of the rest of the camp buildings have now been demolished (M.L. Asquith).

manded by Group Officer N. Dinnie, WAAF, the Station soon became spick and span again and in May 1948 the few males on the station rubbed their eyes in disbelief, as 14 members of the WAAF Flying Branch arrived for a weekend course. All ex-ATA pilots, they wore both aircrew brevets and Pilot IV rank badges. The following month the first WAAF officer cadets arrived for OCTU courses. On February 1 1949 the WAAF became the Womens Royal Air Force and Hawkinge the depot for the new organisation.

During December 1955 the Home Command Gliding Centre had transferred to Hawkinge as a lodger unit, tasked with giving seven-day courses to potential ATC gliding instructors. Their gliders were housed in Bessoneaux hangars along the eastern boundary, a storm in January 1948 causing considerable damage to the canvas structures and their wooden inmates, though most were repairable. Airwomens' basic training was moved to Spitalgate in 1960 and in July the station became the WRAF Officer Cadets Training Unit. Further re-organisation resulted in the OCTU moving to Jurby, Hawkinge being closed on December 8 1961, and reduced to C&M on January 3 1962.

The technical site was put up for auction during the autumn of 1963 but the rest of the station mouldered quietly until June 1968, when it became a gigantic set for the film *Battle of Britain*. Hangars miraculously reappeared on the sites of the original GS Belfast sheds together with dispersal crew huts and all the paraphernalia associated with aircraft of the 1940s. Zwicky fuel bowsers, oil carts and trolley accumulators surrounded the largest number of Spitfires gathered together for many years, but the film crews left as quickly as they had come, and the airfield again reverted to pasture.

Recently the airfield was partially ploughed and many buildings have been demolished, but several of the dispersal pens survive, together with a number of pill boxes and one of the rare Pickett-Hamilton retractable forts. Some of the barrack blocks have been turned into flats and houses built around them, while the Officers' Mess is now a hostel.

A Spitfire, on static display at the main gate for many years, was removed before the station closed, but a memorial stone dedicated to all who served there is still situated near the site of the gymnasium, close to Aerodrome Road. More recently a museum had been opened by the Hawkinge Aeronautical Trust in the old operations building. This contains a large collection of remains of British and German aircraft recovered from sites in Kent, together with equipment and uniforms of the type worn by personnel in 1940. This worthy non-profit making venture is open on mid-week afternoons during July and August, and selected days from Easter until the end of September—it is well worth a visit.

Headcorn, Kent

*TQ880460. 8 miles W of Ashford on
minor road*

One of the first ALGs to be chosen by
Fighter Command, Headcorn was originally known as Coldharbour after a farm
of that name. It was subsequently rejected
because of the difficulty of dealing with a
number of ponds on the site, but when the
proposed ALG at Paddock Wood was
abandoned, Headcorn was reconsidered
and in August 1942 a modified plan was
adopted which recommended a N/S strip
of 3,600 ft (1,097 m) and an E/W runway
of 4,140 ft (1,262 m) which took in large
portions of Barham's Mill, Kingden and
Weeks Farms. Telegraph wires were to be
buried, a barn and oast house at the
southern end demolished, and a few trees
lopped. Apart from construction difficulties, Headcorn was considered a good
site, with natural camouflage provided by
the well-wooded general area.

The completed plans included a partial
perimeter track and showed the Sommerfeld Track runways laid out in the rough
shape of a cross. The go-ahead was given
in December 1942 with the completion

Right *Close inspection of this oblique,
taken in March 1943, reveals runways laid
out in the form of a cross at Headcorn
ALG (RAF Museum W21/89/7).*

Below *Five months later Headcorn was
the temporary base for Spitfires of Nos
403 and 421 (RCAF) Squadrons. This rare
photo was taken from Kingsdown Farm
by a Mr Palmer. Tents and MT vehicles
can be seen in front of the dispersed
Spitfire IXs (via G. Richards).*

due by June 1 1943. Despite the heavy
going, construction was completed during
the early summer of 1943 when Headcorn
was taken over by the Biggin Hill sector of
No 11 Group and first used by the HQ of
No 17 Fighter Wing, RCAF, which formed there on July 4 1943 to administer Nos
126 and 127 Airfields. The HQ probably
used local accommodation but when Nos
403 and 421 Squadrons flew their Spitfire
XIbs in from Lashenden on August 20,
and were joined by a detachment of No
405 Repair & Salvage Unit, they were
completely tented except for their orderly
rooms. All maintenance was carried out in
the open, with the object of testing their
mobility and equipment.

No 127 Airfield provided Wing facilities
at Headcorn and was almost exclusively
engaged on *Ramrods*—escorts to medium
bombers, being particularly active during
Operation *Starkey* early in September. On

In September 1983 the Canadians returned and at a small ceremony Air Marshal 'Johnny' Johnson unveiled this memorial to the 106 men of No 127 (RCAF) Wing who died (G. Richards).

the 6th, 12 Fortresses, a Mitchell and a Marauder all landed at Headcorn off ops, much to the consternation of No 127 Airfield HQ, overwhelmed by this influx of heavy metal. However, the strip was finally cleared and ops continued, probably the most successful mission being on October 3 when a *Ramrod* was flown, Mitchells of No 320 (Dutch) Squadron being close escorted by four Spitfire squadrons, while No 127 Airfield flew a diversion in the Roye area. The ruse worked and they had a bitter fight with German fighters, seven of which were shot down by No 421 Squadron for the loss of one Spitfire, while No 403 Squadron claimed two more of the enemy.

The Canadians returned to winter quarters at Kenley on October 14 1943, and work to bring Headcorn up to a new standard was soon under way. Allocated to the IXth AF, USAAF, they rebuilt and extended the runways, surfacing them with US Steel Planking to take the punishment meted out by the heavyweight P-47 Thunderbolt. Complete taxiways parallel to the runways were constructed and the PSP hardstandings increased to 70. An American steel-framed Butler combat hangar was assembled on the site by an Engineer Aviation Battalion to provide some protection for major technical work on the rather temperamental P-47s. Headcorn was required for occupation by April 1 1944, but in fact was not used until the 13th when the 362nd FG of the 100th FW, IXIth TAC, arrived. The three squadrons (377th, 378th and 379th) flew in from Wormingford and were soon heavily engaged in attacks on communications in northern France and Belgium in preparation for the invasion.

On June 6/7, the 362nd FG escorted C-47As of the Combat Carrier Wings dropping paratroops and equipment over Normandy, and then spent days on close-support work as the Americans battled their way out of the beach-head. Called up by ground controllers to knock out individual hard points and pockets of armour, the P-47s undertook both strafing and dive-bombing missions against heavy flak. Many aircraft returned with

extensive damage—fortunately the Thunderbolt could absorb a lot of punishment for this was very dangerous work.

When landing strips became available in Normandy, the tactical air forces moved over the Channel, 362nd FG going to A-12 (Lignerolles) on July 2 1944. The rear party cleared up and left five days later. Within a week it was confirmed that Headcorn was no longer required, and that the Americans could lift the PSP and take it to the Continent, where it was urgently required.

Authority to de-requisition both land and buildings was issued in September and work started to remove all tele-communications, WD stores and remaining steel tracking. Headcorn quickly returned to farming but its general outline can be deduced fairly easily in an area generally dotted with old oak trees and thick hedges. An officers' married quarter (now privately owned) at Biggin Hill was named after Headcorn postwar. There was nothing else to associate it with its wartime past until recently, when three maple trees were planted at Headcorn (often called Egerton by the locals) to commemorate Canadian pilots of No 127 Airfield killed flying from the ALG in 1943. This has caused some controversy because very confusingly the wartime Lashenden ALG is now called Headcorn airfield—it has no connection with the Egerton site, except a common purpose.

Headcorn (Lashenden), Kent
See Lashenden

High Halden, Kent
TQ890397. 7½ miles WSW of Ashford on minor road off A28

One of a conglomeration of Advanced Landing Grounds which erupted in the Ashford area during 1943, High Halden was surveyed during the early summer of 1942 and had been accepted by July 22, despite local warnings that the land selected quickly became waterlogged. The full report issued in September suggested a NE/SW landing strip of 4,020 ft (1,225 m) which could possibly be extended to 4,800 ft (1,463 m), and a WNW/ESE strip of 4,200 ft (1,280 m). Extensive tree felling and lopping, telegraph wires buried, and the requisitioning of large portions of Brickhouse, Haffenden, Dents Cates and Oldhouse farms would be required. The final site plan approved in December revealed the landing strips in an unusual open V layout, made necessary by the way the land fell away both east and west of the 400-acre site. Work had already started with the object of completion by June 1 1943, and changes to the positioning of two Blister hangars and a hardstanding requested by Fighter Command in January did not delay it in any way.

High Halden was designated a standby ALG, and on completion was released to local farmers for grazing until the late autumn of 1943, when the improvements authorised for all such temporary airfields were started. It was allocated to the US IXth AF and it is probable that their Engineer Aviation Battalion construction gangs rebuilt it, relaying and extending the NE/SW runway to 5,400 ft (1,646 m) using US Steel Planking and building complete taxiways in Sommerfeld Tracking, together with holding platforms at the end of each runway and 70 hardstandings. This work was to allow the operation of the heavily-loaded P-47 Thunderbolt fighter-bomber and was required to be complete by April 1 1944 when the IXIth TAC was due to take over the ALG.

The 358th FG, which consisted of the 365th, 366th and 367th FS, moved in from Raydon, Essex on April 13, and after settling into their tents started dive bombing, concentrating on marshalling yards and airfields in France. These attacks intensified during May, though a few bomber escorts were also flown and on D-Day the Group protected C-47s of the Combat Carrier Groups as they flew in to their DZs on the Contentin Peninsula. On completion of the airborne assault the 358th returned to interdiction, attacking bridges, trains, vehicles and troop concentrations—anything that moved!

As soon as there was room in Normandy, the 358th FG moved their P-47s to Cretteville (A-14) on July 3. The American IXth AF rear party left soon afterwards and High Halden lay deserted.

Normally this would have been the end of the excitement—but not for High Haldon. Early in August, at the height of the anti-*Diver* campaign, the CO of No 616 Squadron accepted it as a forward operating base for the unit's short range Meteor 1s, and a small detachment moved in from Manston. Usually operating in pairs, the Meteors took on V-1 flying bombs which had penetrated the outer fighter and gun screen, and it was while on one of these sorties that Flight Sergeant D.A. Gregg got lost in bad weather on August 14. Short of fuel, he tried to land at Ashford ALG but crashed on the approach. Three days later a No 130 Squadron Spitfire crash-landed at High Haldon and was written-off when it went off the end of the strip. This was probably the last aircraft movement at High Halden for it was closed shortly afterwards, and on September 15 authority was given for the derequisition of the land after the Americans had recovered the PSP, and all equipment, hangars and stores had been removed.

During January No 1 Flight of No 5027 Works Squadron was reinstating the site, and it was returned to the original owners soon afterwards, and has remained farmland ever since. The only trace of its wartime usage is a widened track leading to the boundary of the ALG which was used as the camp entrance.

Hythe (Dymchurch/Palmarsh), Kent
See Dymchurch

Hythe, Kent
TR157341. ½ mile W of Hythe

Considerable confusion exists over the location of various military bases in the Hythe area, largely because at one time or another they have all been referred to by the town's name. The School of Aerial Gunnery, for instance, had its HQ in the town but its aerodrome was at Palmarsh, and though often called Hythe, it was officially listed as Dymchurch and is so described in this book.

However, in March 1918, as part of the intensive efforts made that year to combat the German submarine threat around the British Isles, an operational Kite Balloon base was established on a nine-acre site squeezed between the Parkfield district of Hythe and the large Shorncliffe rifle range. Four canvas balloon sheds and a workshop were erected together with a number of wooden huts for offices. There was no living accommodation, the 148 officers and men on establishment being billetted in the town.

Officially known as No 14 Kite Balloon Base, Hythe, the unit operated in No 5 Group, RAF, its four operational balloons being used for convoy protection under the control of Vice Admiral, Dover Patrol. With the Armistice the base was closed and the site had long been completely built over.

Ivychurch (Brenzett), Kent

See Brenzett

Kingsnorth, Kent (Airship)

TQ810725. 5 miles NE of Rochester off minor road

Most of the early British work on airships was done at Farnborough under the auspices of the War Office, but the Admiralty had formed a small Naval Air-

Kingsnorth Airship Station showing the domestic site and one of the enormous sheds (G.S. Leslie/J.M. Bruce collection).

ship Branch in September 1912. By June the following year, an airship base was being constructed on the Hundred of Hoo, a peninsula between the Thames and the Medway conveniently close to the Chatham naval base and the new air station at Grain, and already government property. In October 1913 it was agreed that the Admiralty should have sole responsibility for powered lighter-than-air craft, and in January 1914 they took over the airships, some of the personnel and temporarily, the sheds and airfield at Farnborough. Work continued on the Hoo, where the partially complete station was commissioned as Kingsnorth in April 1914. Covering a large expanse of low-lying ground two miles east of Hoo village, it was soon the most important airship station in the country, as well as the biggest, and the Admiralty became seriously concerned for the safety of the site despite its isolation. Attack by potential enemies was considered but of more immediate threat were the Suffragettes, for whose wilder elements the large wooden shed was thought a tempting target.

The Naval Airship Branch was absorbed by the RNAS when the latter formed on July 1 1914. Little over a month later the nation was at war and Kingsnorth had the *Astra Torres* (Airship No 3) standing by to repel attacks by hostile airships on Chatham and Sheerness. Quite how the CO, Wing Commander N.F. Usborne, was supposed to do this with one non-rigid dirigible and a stock of four Hale grenades was not made clear, so it was just as well that the expected attack by the superior German airships did not materi-

alise. Airship patrols over the Thames Estuary were started and, joined by a *Parseval* (Airship No 4), regular daily flights were made between Dover and Calais while the British Expeditionary Force was crossing to France during August.

The large double-bay airship shed was now complete, and work went ahead on a second shed and the rest of the station. A railway spur was built into the camp and a hydrogen production plant constructed, while to the north-east wooden huts were erected for personnel accommodation.

Usborne played a central part in the successful development of the non-rigid airship as an operational machine. He was told by Admiral Fisher on February 28 1915, that some small airships were needed to operate against German submarines and, just as important, they were needed immediately. There was no time for the usual lengthy design and development work, so after discussion at Farnborough, a BE 2C fuselage was attached to a Willows envelope and within three weeks the resultant airship was undergoing trials at Kingsnorth. After initial tendency to hunt at maximum speed due to elevator overbalance, the SS type (Submarine Scout) as she was called, was a great success and the Admiralty promptly placed orders for 50 of them. Usborne arranged for the envelope to be made by waterproof garment manufacturers, while new cars were designed by Airships Ltd and Armstrong Whitworth. The latter type, closely resembling the original BE 2C fuselage, was favoured and most of them were manufactured by Frederick Sage & Co Ltd of Peterborough. They were transported to Kingsnorth for marrying to the envelopes—the north Kent airship station had found its niche.

During March 1915 the remaining design staff and equipment at Farnborough were transferred to Kingsnorth, and a training school was opened to cope with the massive increase in air and ground crew needed to operate these new non-rigids. Immediately the SS1 was flying properly work started on a larger, longer endurance ship and this duly appeared as the *C* Type, or Coastal, at the end of May 1915. It was basically an *Astra Torres* envelope with a car made from two Avro 504 front fuselages spliced together, and initially it proved quite a headache. With the bugs ironed out, however, it was obviously a big improvement over the SS-type and Kingsnorth were ordered to build

30 from subcontracted parts, resulting in assembly of the remaining SS airships being transferred to Barrow, Folkestone (Capel) and Wormwood Scrubs in September 1915.

The training task grew steadily during 1915, airships in use during October including the veteran *Astra Torres*, a RAF type and three SS. There was also a BE 2C on strength, for an ambitious anti-Zeppelin fighter scheme instigated by Wing Commander Usborne. The plan was to attach the BE 2C to a SS-type envelope through a release mechanism, so that the aeroplane could be taken to height quickly, then detach and attack the Zeppelin, while the SS envelope sank slowly back to earth following the operation of a rip valve activated as the BE departed. The first test of the combination in August 1915 showed that more work was needed on the control system, and it was February 2 1916 before a further trial was attempted, this time by Usborne accompanied by Lieutenant Commander de Courcy W.P. Ireland. The AO 1 (Airshiplane), as it was called, had reached about 4,000 ft (1,219 m) when the onlookers saw the BE separate. It turned right over as it fell away, throwing Ireland out, then continued to tumble until it crashed in the goods yard of Strood railway station, killing Usborne. This tragedy ended these particular trials with non-rigids, but a similar scheme was later tested using a rigid airship.

By the end of 1915, 36 trainee pilots had passed out as fully fledged airship captains. Numerous maintenance and handling ratings had also completed courses and 16 SS-Type non-rigids were in commission. Design work on new craft had also continued, construction of six NS (North Sea) Types being approved in January 1916, followed by an order for six of the long-endurance SS Pusher (SSP) which were expected to stay airborne for a full 17-hour patrol.

Despite the death of Wing Commander Usborne, experiments also continued, trials of an airship on tow by a surface vessel being resumed in March 1916, using part of the landing ground marked out to represent the stern of a destroyer. In dummy tests a *C*-Type was secured to the vessel, the crew changed and the airship refuelled, and this was successfully repeated off the Thames Estuary using the light cruiser *Canterbury*.

Thirty-two Coastals were built at Kings-

A 'Coastal' Type airship starting out on patrol from Kingsnorth in April 1916 (G.S. Leslie/J.M. Bruce collection).

north during the year, four of these going to Russia and one to France, but the rest joined the RNAS and quickly made a name for themselves as the most successful non-rigids of all. Another 56 pilots were turned out, but it was with relief that training was handed over to RNAS Cranwell at the end of the year. Kingsnorth was then able to concentrate on its assembly, repair and design work, becoming known as the Airship Constructional Station (Non-Rigid).

The first SSP was on trials in January 1917, followed in February by the famous North Sea type which was nearly twice the size of the SS-type. Improved Coastals were under construction in 1918 but by November production was concentrated on the SS Twin with 47 under construction. This programme was rapidly cut back at the end of the war and only the four most advanced were completed—the rest scrapped.

The non-rigid airships lingered on for a few months after the war but it was decided that aircraft were more effective and the airship stations were gradually closed down during 1919. Kingsnorth and its huge sheds, the largest of which was 700 ft (213 m) long, 150 ft (46 m) wide and 98 ft (30 m) high, was soon deserted and just faded away. The station was dismantled

during the early 1920s and the whole 570-acre site is now occupied by a large power station—which retains the Kingsnorth name.

Kingsnorth, Kent, (ALG)
TR025380. 3 miles SE of Ashford on minor road

Lying in thick woodland and named Kingsnorth after the hamlet to the north-west, this site was one of the many in the area provisionally selected as an Advanced Landing Ground in the spring of 1942. Accepted in July, subject to re-alignment to allow two 4,500 ft (1,372 m) wire mesh runways to be laid, a satisfactory report was made in September, though it was obvious that considerable work would be required and several minor roads would have to be closed.

The final plan called for a T-shaped runway layout aligned NW/SE and involved the felling of a large portion of Buresland Wood and the pulling down of two buildings at Cheeseman's Green, while the whole of Bliby would be absorbed by the ALG in addition to a hefty chunk of Brockman's Farm. Chequertree and Brockman's Farms were considered suitable for HQ, stores and living accommodation, and were recommended for take-over with the land. The site plans went to Fighter Command in October and Kingsnorth was earmarked as a training ALG for mobile squadrons, priority being given in January 1943 to ensure its com-

pletion by the following June. The site was flat and required little grading, but suffered from waterlogging during the wet winter months. However, the two Sommerfeld track landing strips and a partial access track had been completed by June, the hardstandings prepared and Blister hangars erected. The roads which had been closed were utilised as access tracks to refuelling stands, tented camp areas and dispersals on the edge of Butterland Wood.

The recently formed, and oddly named, No 122 Airfield became the first occupant when Spitfire Vbs of Nos 65, 122 and 603 Squadrons arrived from Selsey and Bognor on July 1 1943 to start tactical work-ups. No 602 Squadron managed to grab a cottage as their HQ although their orderly room was in a marquee in the grounds of the house occupied by the Airfield HQ, which must have been somewhat confusing!

The Squadrons continued their *Rodeos* over northern France in addition to the disliked bomber escorts. The Spitfire Vb was no longer really acceptable for escort work, as was proved when No 602 Squadron got into a fight with a mixed force of Bf 109s and Fw 190s. They were outfought and could only claim two for the loss of four Spitfires. In the middle of August No 602 Squadron transferred back to No 121 Airfield and was replaced by 19 Squadron from Newchurch. The

Kingsnorth units converted to the much better Spitfire IX at this time, while still maintaining operations, on which they were joined by the Hurricanes of No 184 Squadron for a few days.

The ALG deteriorated rapidly during September 1943 and No 122 Airfield dispersed for two days while a Works Service Corps relaid the runways. They were back on September 17, and five days later two aircraft from 65 Squadron collided over the ALG during a formation break. Apart from this, there were few accidents despite the primitive operating conditions. The Airfield left on October 5 well pleased with its work at Kingsnorth, which was handed over to the construction units for improvements, these consisting largely of increasing the number of hardstandings.

Early in 1944, Kingsnorth was allocated to the Americans for use by the IXth AF, and Engineer Aviation Battalion personnel arrived to re-lay the runways with pierced planking and extend the taxiways so that the heavyweight P-47 Thunderbolt fighter-bombers would not get bogged down in the soft turf. A transportable metal-framed Butler combat hangar was also erected by *A* Company of the 816th Engineer Aviation Battalion as a combined exercise/operational requirement, and the base was ready for occupation by the flying squadrons by April 1 1944.

The 36th FG, 303rd FW, XIXth TAC, moved in four days later under the command of Lieutenant-Colonel Van H. Slayden. The 22nd, 23rd and 53rd FS ferried in their P-47s and prepared to do battle with the UK weather, the conditions made more apparent by the unannounced arrival of a battle-damaged B-24 of the 44th BG which crash-landed on April 18 and took some shifting off the strip. Operations started in May 8 1944, the first missions being the usual mixture of armed recce, escort and interdiction. On D-Day itself the 36th FG patrolled landing areas and beach-heads, and during the days that followed flew exhaustive close support dive bombing and strafing missions which continued right up to the breakout of St Lô on July 20. The 36th had moved over the Channel to A-16 (Brucheville) three days earlier leaving only the remains of a 93rd BG Liberator on Kingsnorth ALG.

The rear party soon followed but, as soon as it was confirmed that the ALG was no longer required, the Americans were back, ripping up the PSP for use on the Continent, where there was a desperate shortage.

Disposal authority was issued in September 1944 and a Flight from No 5027 Works Squadron moved in to dismantle Blister hangars, remove the remaining Sommerfeld steel mesh, and restore the land as near its original condition as possible. This work was completed early in 1945 and the land returned to its former farm owners. The road system was soon replaced and there is now no evidence of wartime use except for missing bits of hedge where runways and taxiways crossed the roads, while the postwar removal of more woodland has considerably changed the appearance of the area.

A tangible, though distant, reminder of Kingsnorth is provided by naming a Biggin Hill married quarter after it—one of several less well-known wartime Kent airfields commemorated in this way.

Larks Barrow, Hampshire

SU455505. 1½ miles NW of Whitchurch alongside A34(T)

No 57 on the list of possible sites, Larks Barrow, which tooks its name from a tumulus ½ mile to the east, was chosen in June 1942 as one of the second line ALGs. It was a large grass area of some 500 acres bounded on the east and south by railway lines and to the north by Bradley Wood. The report suggested that two 4,500 ft (1,372 m) landing strips could be laid, but that preparation would be slow because of the heavy grading work needed on the sloping ground, and the amount of tree felling necessary.

Despite this somewhat gloomy report, a full survey was made during the autumn of 1942. This detailed the partial destruction of Down Farm, which was close to the intersection of the proposed strips, extensive tree cutting in Cowdown Copse and the burying of telegraph wires along the railway line. Dispersed sites were suggested in the vicinity of Hogdigging Cottage and Cholesley Farm where good cover was available.

The site was formally accepted on December 10, but how much of the proposed work was actually done is uncertain. At the beginning of 1943 the Air Staff at the Air Ministry declared Larks Barrow surplus to requirements but this may have been countermanded, only to be cancelled later in the year. Certainly it was never used by Fighter Command or the 2nd TAF, and it is probable that no Sommerfeld Tracking was laid. However, it has been reported as a relief landing ground for flying training units in the area, probably as an unmanned forced landing practice field for Andover or Worthy Down.

The present A34(T) uses much of the original course of the old railway line between Newbury and Winchester, including the embankments and cuttings, but cuts across the south-east corner of the ALG site to avoid Whitchurch. There is no sign of its rather nebulous use by the RAF or FAA during World War 2, and no evidence has been found supporting reports of its use as a scatter field during 1940.

Lasham, Hampshire

SU677435. 4 miles NW of Alton off A339

The famous pin-point attack on Amiens jail by the Hunsdon Wing during February 1944 confirmed the 2nd TAF Mosquito VI squadrons' ability to destroy a single building, and soon they were all at it. From Lasham No 138 Airfield joined in on April 11 when six aircraft from No 613 Squadron, led by Wing Commander R.N. Bateson, attacked and destroyed the Dutch Central Population Registry housed in the Kunstzaal Kleizkamp Art Gallery in the centre of the Hague. Here the Gestapo kept records of Dutch families and decided who should go to concentration or forced labour camps, and who to torture when reprisals were sought for the activities of the patriots.

The Mosquitoes flew to Swanton Morley for refuelling and crew briefing, using detailed models of the five-storey building. After take-off they flew at 50 ft (15.2 m) over the North Sea, keeping below radar cover, climbing to 4,000 ft (1,219 m) as they approached the Dutch coast, then into a shallow dive to attack in pairs, at two minute intervals to allow the 500 lb (227 kg) delayed action bombs time to detonate. Bateson skimmed the rooftops on the run in to the target, and achieved complete surprise and success, Flight Lieutenant P.C. Cobley seeing his leader's bombs going 'in by the front door'. After circling Lake Gouda, Squadron Leader C.W.M. Newman led in

Flight Lieutenant R.W. Smith to drop incendiaries through the smoke, followed by Flight Lieutenant V.A. Hester and Flying Officer R. Cohen, the latter disappointed when his bombs hung up despite two further runs. Such was the confusion on the ground that AA fire was spasmodic and only Newman's Mosquito was hit and slightly damaged. Reconnaissance later showed the building completely destroyed but neighbouring houses untouched—it was a classic attack.

Requisiton of farmland for an airfield in the heavily wooded rolling hills between Basingstoke and Alton was authorised in September 1941. It was intended as a satellite for the bomber OTU then being constructed at Aldermaston, and the plans showed a standard three-runway layout with a complete perimeter track and extensive dispersals, some of them in the woods. The site was contracted to McAlpines, who made rapid progress, despite having to divert the A339 road away from Lasham village, using the route of a disused section of the Basingstoke and Alton light railway. The major building work, including the four 'T2' hangars, a large technical area, and dispersed accommodation sites, was well advanced by the autumn of 1942 and Lasham was taken over by No 38 Wing, Army Co-operation Command, on November 9, the OTU plans having been cancelled.

Lack of essential services and the slower than expected build-up of airborne forces meant that Lasham remained unused by aircraft until March 1943, but a number of Canadian ground units were present on January 2 when the airfield was bombed and machine-gunned by a single aircraft, thought to be a Do 217. The advance party of No 4165 AA Flight arrived eight days later!

No 175 Squadron spent two days at Lasham in March living under canvas for mobility training as part of No 124 Airfield, *Z* Group during Exercise *Spartan*. This big Army exercise involved virtually all single-seat fighter and Army co-op units, and No 412 (RCAF) Squadron also appeared briefly while operating detachments at Hurn, Odiham and Lasham. On April 1 1943, *Z* Group became No 83 Group and No 124 Airfield was put on a permanent basis using No 2 Group personnel, No 412 Squadron and 3085 Servicing Echelon from Fighter Command. They were joined by the Typhoons of No 181 Squadron on April 5, then replaced by Spitfire Vbs of No 602 Squadron until the arrival of Nos 182 and 183 Squadrons to form a Typhoon Wing. During late May, No 175 Squadron replaced No 183, and on June 2 the whole Airfield went forward to Appledram ALG.

On the previous day, Army Co-operation Command had disbanded and Lasham was temporarily transferred to No 10 Group, Fighter Command, then to No 70 Group, before No 2 Group, Tactical AF, took over on August 28 1943. Two days later No 320 (Dutch) Squadron arrived from Attlebridge where it had worked up on Mitchells, followed by Foulsham SHQ staff, transferred en bloc to provide admin services. No 320 prepared for Operation *Starkey*, but were unable to take part until September 9 when they made their first operational sorties from Lasham, 11 Mitchells attacking long-range guns at Boulogne. With *Starkey* over, the Dutchmen joined in on the usual round of raids on railway

Viewed from the south-east, Lasham is seen here in October 1942 just before handover by the contractors (RAF Museum W13/6/1).

marshalling yards, airfields, bridges and, from November onwards, *Noball* sites; the number of sorties gradually increasing towards the end of 1943.

On October 12 they were joined by No 613 Squadron, a Mustang unit from Snailwell which immediately started converting to Mosquito VIs, and the Lasham squadrons were grouped under No 138 Airfield HQ when No 305 (Polish) Squadron arrived on November 18 from Swanton Morley, also converting to Mosquitoes. The juggling act was completed by No 107 Squadron, which ceased Boston operations at Hartfordbridge during January 1944, and moved to Lasham to join the Mosquito Wing on February 3, No 320 Squadron going to Dunsfold 15 days later.

The whole of No 138 Airfield was operational by March 15 when No 107 Squadron flew its first Mosquito mission, an attack on a *Noball* site. These were the priority target at this time, though No 613 Squadron was also used on night bomber support work and for a few *Rangers*, despite appalling weather over the Continent. Proof that aircraft recognition was still not all it might be was given when an American P-51 Mustang shot up a No 107 Squadron Mossie. The Mosquito pilot, by coincidence also an American, crash-landed on a south coast beach, traced his assailant by his code letters, drove to his base, discovered the culprit, and left him unconscious!

The primary role of the Mosquitoes during *Overlord* was to attack communications by night, maintaining a contin-

Mosquitoes were synonymous with Lasham during the war—here a Mk VI of No 305 (Polish) Squadron has its engines 'run-up' before another mission (via J.D.R. Rawlings).

uous patrol in their areas. They started at 22:00 hours on June 5, 98 Mosquitoes being despatched that night from Nos 138 (Lasham) and 140 (Gravesend) Wings, and they bombed villages, roads and rail junctions all over Normandy, causing chaos. On the 6th they were again out in force attacking anything that moved, this work continuing whenever the weather allowed.

Pin-point target attacks, a natural follow-up from the earlier V-1 site successes, were mounted whenever required. On July 30, Group Captain L.W.C. Bower, with AVM B.E. Embry (the AOC) as his No 2, led five Mosquitoes of No 138 Wing in an attack on a château used as a rest centre for U-boat crews. The target appeared deserted but it later transpired that 400 Germans were killed, similar successes attending raids on other châteaux housing SS troops and a saboteurs' school.

No 138 Wing had flown 2,319 sorties in the 72 days since D-Day, a remarkable achievement by any standards. Operations continued at a high sortie rate, but a special effort was made on September 17 in support of Operation *Market*. Nos 107 and 613 Squadrons were briefed for low-level attacks on individual houses in Arnhem. Each aircraft dropped four 500 lb (227 kg) MC bombs in the face of heavy flak, No 107 Squadron losing two aircraft, but some direct hits were confirmed.

The weather now severely limited operations and little was done until the Wing moved to Hartfordbridge at the end of October 1944. No 84 Group Support Unit, responsible for providing aircraft and crew replacements to the operational squadrons, moved from Thruxton to Lasham on November 27, the airfield itself being transferred to No 11 Group, Fighter Command, and becoming a satel-

lite of Blackbushe on January 15 1945, with No 84 GSU as a lodger. From December 1944, first Spitfire and then Typhoon squadrons brought their aircraft into Lasham for disposal. In August the GSU was renamed the Group Disbandment Centre and a fortnight later Lasham was transferred to the same Group, nominally becoming a BAFO base. No 83 Group Disbandment Centre arrived from Dunsfold on October 24 and, when No 49 MU moved in from Faygate during February 1945, the airfield was again quite active.

A month later, arrangements were made for General Aircraft Ltd to occupy two 'T2' hangars and adjacent buildings to carry out Mosquito overhaul and conversion contracts, and flight trials on their tailless gliders also took place from Lasham. No 49 MU took over the tasks of No 71 MU Little Horwood when the latter disbanded in November 1947, but early in the new year Maintenance Command decided to leave Lasham and urged the Air Ministry to sanction its abandonment.

One of the GAL experimental gliders crashed during February 1948, killing the company's famous test pilot, Robert Kronfled and, despite No 49 MU completing its move to Colerne on June 7, trials of the incredibly ugly Mosquito TT 39 target tug continued for a while. Lasham was closed on October 26 1948, becoming an inactive site in Fighter Command, parented by Odiham.

In the early 1950s permission for gliding at Lasham was obtained and the number of clubs quickly mushroomed. The 1955 National Gliding Club championships were held there during July-August, by which time gliders shared the airfield with Dan Air Engineering Ltd, the maintenance organisation of the charter airline which had moved in earlier in the year.

The airfield was transferred from the Air Ministry to the Ministry of Aviation on July 15 1961 and, although since then many of the individual gliding clubs have foundered, the Lasham Gliding Centre has prospered, and the championships have become an almost annual event. During the mid-1960s, Staravia set up a massive aircraft scrapping facility at Lasham situated opposite the main entrance to the Gliding Centre. This became a mecca for enthusiasts interested in bits of aircraft but the dump was slowly cleared and nothing now remains of this unsightly mess. Dan Air have extended their activities and now carry out mainten-

ance for other companies as well as their own. They also have an active Preservation Group who have an example of the York, Dakota, Comet 4 and Ambassador, all types operated by the company in the past. A separate organisation, the Second World War Aircraft Preservation Society, took over a former dispersal hut on the north-east corner of the airfield in January 1979 and now have a number of postwar machines in display. Their collection therefore hardly matches their name but it can be viewed most weekends and there is no charge for admission, though any financial assistance is naturally welcome.

The Ministry retains the control tower which is surrounded by radio installations making up an out-station of the RAE Farnborough in conjunction with a unit at Cobbett Hill, both places being quiet in the electronic sense, and hence suitable for the transmission and reception of radio signals.

Lashenden, Kent
TQ855425. 9 miles SE of Maidstone on A274

Much of the interior of Kent is hilly and heavily wooded, but west of Ashford there is a comparatively flat area which naturally attracted the attention of the Airfields Board and their survey teams in their 1941-42 search for suitable sites. Unfortunately it is also fairly low-lying ground with many meandering streams and isolated ponds and thus becomes easily waterlogged. The advantages outweighed this one drawback, however, and ALGs sprouted in all directions during 1943. One of the most successful was alongside the River Beult and close to the Tonbridge-Ashford railway line, the site being named Lashenden after the nearby hamlet.

Lashenden was provisionally accepted as a site for one of the second-line ALGs in July 1942 and by September had been designated as one of two light bomber bases for Operation *Round-Up*, these being the only ones with type-designed bomb storage facilities. Work on the site was expected to be limited to the felling of a few scattered trees and the burial of telegraph wires in addition to normal grading, while it was unusually well provided with accommodation. Ebenezer and White Horse Farms were considered suitable for stores and workshops, Shenley

Farm as a MT yard, while the house and the hall were requisitioned as living quarters.

The ALG plans were approved in December 1942 and work went ahead throughout the winter, Lashenden having been chosen as a training base for the proposed mobile squadrons and thus receiving priority alongside Lydd and Kingsnorth. Two Sommerfeld Track runways were laid, the main WNW strip of 4,800 ft (1,463 m) lying between and roughly parallel to the river and the minor road from Smarden to Waterman Quarter. This road was cut by the N/S 4,200 ft (1,280 m) subsidiary strip which had a notably poor overshoot area at its northern end—the river.

The newly formed No 127 (RCAF) Airfield moved in from its comfortable quarters at Kenley on August 6 1943. The next day Nos 403 and 421 Squadrons arrived, the road party having taken 4½ hours to make the 45-mile journey. They were safely under canvas by nightfall and ready the next day to continue flying *Ramrods* for No 2 Group bombers, while getting used to their mobile equipment. The squadrons only stayed 12 days before moving on to Headcorn. Apart from the loss of No 403 Squadron's CO, Squadron Leader W.A.G. Conrad, DFC, posted missing on August 17, the attachment was comparatively uneventful until the very last mission. Then the Spitfires were engaged by some 12 Bf 109s south-west of

A P-51B Mustang of the 356th FS, 354th FG, Lashenden (via H. Holmes collection).

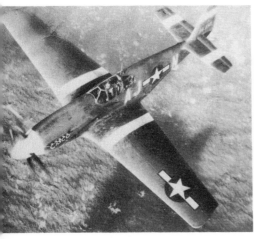

Abbeville and Flight Lieutenant A.C. Coles of No 403 Squadron shot down one, while Flying Officer A.E. Fleming of No 421 Squadron damaged another.

With the departure of No 127 Airfield, the ALG was returned to the airfield construction organisation for upgrading. More hardstandings and a taxi strip connecting dispersals with the runways were built. This work continued into 1944, enlivened by the arrival of a P-47 Thunderbolt of 4 FG which crash-landed on the strip after battle damage on January 29. Lashenden was already earmarked for American use during the Second Front, the 100th FW, XIXth TAC, arriving on April 15 and doubtless taking over the accommodation available in Shenley Hall and House. They controlled the 354th, 358th, 362nd and 363rd FGs, the 354th joining them at Lashenden from Boxted on April 17. This Group flew the very successful Merlin-engined Mustang, the P-51B, the three squadrons, 353rd, 355th and 356th, quickly settling into their tented camps in the apple orchards and farmyards around the ALG, and resuming their long-range escort work for B-17s and B-24s of the VIIth AF.

By the time they reached Lashenden, their escort tactics were finely honed, and a mission to Magdeburg, just 80 miles short of Berlin on May 28, when they claimed 19½ enemy aircraft for the loss of two Mustangs, was little more than routine. By the end of that month they had flown 93 missions during which the Group claimed 324 Luftwaffe aircraft destroyed, 39 probables and 212 damaged, losing 67 P-51Bs and 63 pilots in the process. In the heat of battle, claims are often exaggerated, but there is little doubt that the 354th inflicted much heavier casualites than they sustained. While at Lashenden the Group received a well-deserved Distinguished Unit Citation for this work.

From May 15 onwards the 354th FG expanded their repertoire to include fighter-bomber operations. They dive-bombed and strafed airfields, gun positions, vehicles and railway engines as part of the concerted Allied effort to produce a breakdown in the German communication system throughout Northern France, Belgium and Holland. Much to their disgust, the 354th were held in reserve on D-Day itself until the late afternoon when they escorted glider combinations to their LZs. They made up for it afterwards, though, by days of dangerous close-

support work, for though little was seen of the Luftwaffe the German flak was as lethal as ever.

With Lashenden directly between the V-1 launching sites in France and their target, London, the Group became involved in the anti-*Diver* campaign and several missiles were destroyed during June, Lieutenant J. Powers of the 355th FS bringing down 2½ (one shared) in one sortie. Meanwhile, on the Continent, frantic efforts were being made to get airstrips into operation. The 354th FG were among the first units across the Channel, going to A-2 (Criqueville) on June 23 after a very successful two months in Kent, the last of 1,000 Americans to occupy the strip departing six days later.

Above *The P-51B* Little Chris II *of the 353rd FS, 354th FG, Lashenden is prepared for another sortie. Note the crudely painted 'invasion stripes' under the wings* (South Eastern Newspapers Ltd).

Below *A Whirlwind HAS 7 of the Air Museum at Lashenden in September 1977 —now known as Headcorn airfield! In the background is a more 'operational' Aztec awaiting its next charter* (R. Clare).

By early October 1944 the War Agricultural Executive Committee was pressing for the release of the ALG, and work soon started in removing thousands of square yards of steel mesh, dismantling Blister

hangars and renovating land and buildings. The land reverted to agriculture in January 1945, but in the 1970s some 160 acres at the western end of the original ALG began to be used as a light aircraft strip. Weald Air Services Ltd was formed in 1973 for air taxi and executive charter work, the company also operating pleasure flights during the summer months. As the airstrip became more popular, so the usual environmental protestors grew more vocal, culminating in closure orders by the Maidstone & Ashford Borough Councils. An appeal was lodged and strong support received from private individuals and other airfield operators, resulting in Lashenden being licensed for machines up to 12,500 lb (5,670 kg) and the withdrawal of the enforcement orders.

The operator is Shenley Farms (Aviation) Ltd and the airfield is officially known as Lashenden/Headcorn, but more generally as just Headcorn. This is logical, but is also the cause of much confusion with the nearby wartime Headcorn ALG. Currently, Headcorn Flying School, Weald Air Services and a microlight organisation are based there, alongside a number of privately owned aircraft and the Lashenden Air Warfare Museum. The latter is open on Sundays during the summer months, and features a Fi 103 flying bomb amongst a fascinating variety of aviation archaeological items found in the local area.

long time, and seems set to remain an active airfield for the foreseeable future, despite a recent lessening in importance.

The spring of 1917 saw a renewed U-boat offensive around the coasts of Britain, unprecedented in its ferocity. Shipping losses were horrendous, and among the counter-measures taken was the provision of more patrol seaplanes. This meant more crews were needed—quickly! The seaplane training unit at Calshot could not be expanded so it was decided to build a brand new school on Holy Island, off the Northumbrian coast. While surveys went ahead, the Calshot CO was instructed to establish a temporary sub-station somewhere on the Solent to increase his immediate training capacity. He selected a site on the western edge of Lee-on-Solent town, where a shallow cliff led down to a gently shelving gravel beach. Work on the site, restricted to essentials, started in July. Portable Bessoneaux canvas hangars were erected in Westcliffe Paddock, MT and stores sheds were built on the playing fields of Wykeham Hall alongside the mens' tented camp, and three nearby houses were taken over as messes and classrooms. The officers were billeted in the town.

The Naval Seaplane Training School was officially opened on July 30 1917, the day the CO, Squadron Commander D.C.S. Evill, RN, two other officers, and 30 men arrived from Calshot. Courses started at the end of August, pupils travel-

Lee-on-Solent, Hampshire

SU560020. 2½ miles NW of Gosport off B3385

Intended to be purely temporary, RNAS Lee-on-Solent has lasted a surprisingly

The seaplane base at Lee-on-Solent in November 1918 showing the two hangar complexes and slipways. The floatplanes offshore are Short 184s (FAA Museum A/Stn 170).

ling daily from Warsash barracks for ground instruction at Lee, the flying commencing on September 22 using six Short 827 floatplanes. The system employed to get the machines into the water was extremely laborious. From the Bessoneaux they were wheeled up a ramp on to a trolley which ran on rails to the cliff edge. Here they were lifted by crane on to a similar trolley on beach rails and rolled into the water. This time-consuming performance was acceptable as a temporary measure, but in November 1917 the Holy Island scheme was scrapped and Lee became permanent. More domestic accommodation was immediately taken over, and sites selected for aircraft sheds covering 30 acres on the landward side of Marine Parade. A single slipway cut through the cliff was completed early in 1918, work continuing on a double one leading down from the new sheds.

On April 1 1918, Lee-on-Solent was transferred to the newly formed Air Ministry and became No 209 TDS in No 10 Group, RAF. The TDS operated two training squadrons with a capacity of 100 pupils on courses lasting 7-8 weeks. By the end of June the strength of the unit had reached 31 staff officers, 95 pupils and 550 men with 36 machines in use, the establishment being 24 floatplanes and 48 small flying boats. The apparently open beach was surprisingly well sheltered by the Isle of Wight in most weather conditions and, with the double slipway coming into use during September, the TDS was just getting into full swing when the Armistice was declared. Personnel strength peaked at 827 in December 1918 when the aircraft available were 24 Short 184 and two Short 827 floatplanes and 27 FBA and 16 Norman Thompson NT2B flying

Another view of Lee showing the main slipway (far left) and in the centre a large crane for lifting machines up the cliff (G.S. Leslie/J.M. Bruce collection).

boats, but all training ceased on January 1 1919. No 209 TDS and the station were run down rapidly as demobilisation took its toll.

After much deliberation it was decided that Lee would be retained for the much-reduced peacetime air force and, on June 16 1919, the RAF & Naval Co-operation School was formed, the name being simplified a month later to RAF Seaplane School, Lee-on-Solent. The course remained much the same as before, and initially used the same Short 184 floatplanes. During the autumn a crash course was given to 27 pilots urgently needed for service in North Russia, but the general turmoil and budgetary cuts forced policy changes, the station being reduced to C&M at the beginning of December 1919.

Lee was re-opened on June 1 1920, again as a seaplane training base, each trainee reporting individually for a course tailored to his needs. The following month No 10 Group HQ moved in from Warsash and the unit became the School of Naval Co-operation & Air Navigation. The authorities could not leave the name alone, however, for in April 1921 it became the RAF Seaplane Training School, just three months before the first RN observer course started with Fairey IIIds as the standard training aircraft. It was intended to have two five-month courses per year, but in January 1922 a similar course was introduced for RAF seaplane pilots so that they could double as fleet observers when required. In May

1923 came yet another title change—to the School of Naval Co-operation—and in November the RAF and RN observer courses were combined. The intermittent seaplane handling courses were suspended in January 1924, the station then being devoted entirely to fleet observer training, disturbed only by Fleet exercises in which the School took an active part, and more surprisingly, by experimental work. Tests of W/T-controlled Fairey IIIds started and trials of the Flycatcher floatplane were also carried out at Lee. In January 1925, 444 Flight was formed for fleet spotter duties using three Fairey IIIds stressed for catapult work, which resumed when the Flight returned from the Far East in July 1929. Lee was also the shore base of the Parnall Peto undergoing trials aboard the ill-fated submarine *M-2*. 443A Flight became the seaplane training unit in 1930 when catapulting of all sorts became a major pre-occupation, 443 and 444 Flights working up with Fairey IIIf/Flycatchers and Fairey IIIds respectively, before embarking on battleships and cruisers.

The Schools' Co-operation Flight also completed conversion to the Fairey IIIf in February 1930, followed by the reborn Floatplane Training Flight in June 1931. Bigger organisational changes were occurring, however, No 10 Group being disbanded on January 18 1932 when the HQ of Coastal Area moved to Lee from its previous home in Central London and took over the building now known as Eagle Block. More land, immediately behind the seaplane hangars, was purchased and, at the end of September, work started on the construction of an aerodrome complete with new barrack blocks, administration and technical buildings, which included a Type 'A' hangar. Two Queen Bee drones destined for HMS *Achilles* became the first aircraft to land, the airfield being formally taken over from AMWD on October 25 1934.

The S of NC now underwent a complicated re-organisation which involved some units from Gosport. The six IIIfs and three Moths of *A* Flight, Gosport, were absorbed by *A* Flight, Lee, which now undertook seaplane and landplane training. *B* Flight, Lee, was formed from No 2 (Training) Flight for naval observer training, and Gosport's *B* Flight (five IIIfs, five Seals and a Ripon) became *C* Flight, Lee, for telegraphist air gunner training. Later, on July 15 1935, *D* Flight

A view of Lee airfield in 1938 when the 'C' Type hangar was being constructed (Wing Commander D.E. Bennett).

was formed to train Air Observers' Mates.

To reduce the pressure on Lee, the FAA Floatplane Base units, 407 and 444 Flights, took their Ospreys to Mount Batten in June 1935 and, during the 2½ years they were away, more changes took place. Coastal Area became Coastal Command in July 1936 and Nos 16 (Reconnaissance) and 17 (Training) Group HQs were formed at Lee at the beginning of December, when No 1 Gunnery Co-operation Flight became No 2 AACU. In September 1937 the S of NC was again re-organised: *A* Flight became the Communications Flight, *B* Flight was renamed *A* Flight, *C* Flight was re-designated *B* Flight, a new *C* Flight formed and only *D* Flight remained intact. All these training Flights had between eight and ten Sharks on strength.

Changes generated by the rapid expansion of the RAF during the mid-30s continued, the S of NC going to Ford on January 1 1938 when a SHQ formed at Lee to administer the remaining diverse units on the station, now the shore base for Home Fleet catapult Flights and a number of FAA front-line squadrons. Another building programme started during the year with more domestic and technical accommodation, including a ten-bay Type 'C' hangar. No 18 Group HQ formed on the station in September —surely a unique situation with Command and the three Group HQs all on the same wretched airfield! It was not for long, however, No 16 Group going to Chatham and No 18 to Donibristle a couple of months later, leaving No 17 Group to share Lee with the Command HQ, No 2 AACU, the Communications Flight, Floatplane Training Flight (from Calshot in April 1938), the Storage Unit and a Fleet Requirements Unit. Swordfish-equipped front-line FAA squadrons visited frequently and in March 1939 No 15 Group HQ formed at Lee.

On May 24 1939, Lee-on-Solent was transferred to the Admiralty and was commissioned as HMS *Daedulus*, No 17 Group HQ moving to nearby Gosport while No 15 Group went to Plymouth in June. Flag Officer (Air) Home formed his HQ in Wykeham Hall during July with HMS *Daedulus* (Lee), HMS *Raven* (Eastleigh), HMS *Peregrine* (Donibristle), HMS *Kestrel* (Worthy Down), HMS *Merlin* (Ford) and HMS *Malabar* (Bermuda) under command. No 2 Observers School was established at Lee using Sharks of 753 and 754 Squadrons for the flying phase, while improvements on the airfield included the completion of a narrow perimeter track encompassing the firm turf, and joining the maintenance area to a row of four Bellman hangars erected on the western side of the airfield.

Coastal Command HQ moved out on August 7 1939, by which time the Floatplane Training Flight had become 765 Squadron flying Walrus, Swordfish and Seafox aircraft, and a Service Trials Unit (778 Squadron) had been formed. Just before war was declared, 710 Squadron was formed at Lee with Walrus amphibians but almost immediately moved to Mount Batten and Lee was left just its training units. No 2 Observers School was

now flying the Swordfish and Walrus alongside its old Sharks, while floatplanes of 765 Squadron, housed in the First World War sheds by the dual slipway, continued to operate from the open beach, as they had since 1918.

Frantic shelter construction, camouflaging of buildings and digging of slit trenches, gun and picquet posts took precedence during September 1939. A deck landing training squadron, 770, using a motley selection of Moths, Sea Gladiators and Skuas, appeared in November; 781 Squadron was formed as a communications unit flying Walruses and Swordfish, and 778 Squadron, currently flying Swordfish, Rocs and Skuas, prepared for the arrival of their first new trials aircraft, the Fulmar fleet fighter. It finally appeared on May 10 1940 the very day the Germans started their Blitzkrieg advance in France. During the Dunkirk evacuation, most of the Observer School aircraft were involved in support duties, but afterwards it was obvious they would have to move out of what was now a front-line war zone. Unfortunately the FAA were still building their training airfields in the rear areas, and the more immediate result of the collapse in France was the arrival of 763 (TBR Pool) Squadron from Worthy Down in June and a sudden influx of Albacores for 829 Squadron, which formed that same month.

A Swordfish of the Floatplane Training Unit alongside the old control 'tower' at Lee in 1938 (RAF Museum P1582).

The Walrus Flight of the Seaplane Training Unit, re-formed as 764 Squadron in March, went to Pembroke Dock in July, and 778 Squadron moved to the incomplete Arbroath. They were just in time to avoid the air raids. Portsmouth was a major target and a few stray bombs exploded in the Lee area, resulting in reported attacks on the airfield being very confused. There is certainly no doubt that a reconnaissance overflight on August 8 was followed by a deliberate attack on the 16th, when part of a large force of Ju 87s approaching the Isle of Wight made straight for Lee. Despite a desperate effort by No 213 Squadron, whose Hurricanes flew at top speed all the way from Exeter to help hard-pressed No 11 Group units, severe damage was caused. Three hangars, including two of the new Bellmans, were destroyed and six aircraft burnt out. There were no casualties, for the warning had been sufficient for all personnel to reach the shelters.

The mess was soon cleared up, so it was the balloon barrages, and hostile attentions from both friend and foe, which finally forced out those training units which needed exercise areas over the Channel. The TBR Pool (763 Squadron) went to Arbroath in October, followed by No 2 Observer School (753 and 754 Squadrons) in December, these being replaced by 780 Squadron displaced from Eastleigh and the commissioning of 702 Squadron for duty aboard armed merchant cruisers using the diminutive Seafox.

The New Year saw the formation of 771 (Fleet Requirements) Squadron flying a weird collection of obsolescent aircraft, and the start of the task which was to occupy most the station's effort for the rest of the war—the formation and work-up of newly commissioned operational squadrons, and the re-equipment of others. A few were fighter units, but it was the TBR squadrons with which Lee-on-Solent became synonymous, in particular those flying Swordfish, though the Albacore was also well represented.

Out on its own was the Vought Chesapeake dive bomber, taken over from French contracts, and which equipped 811 Squadron in July 1941. It flew well, but was underpowered, requiring too long a take-off run for escort carrier use. After a few short months savouring luxurious enclosed cockpits, the squadron returned to the rigours of the Swordfish, and Lee's dalliance with the dedicated dive bomber was over.

In June 1942 a Night Fighter School was set up using Fulmars and Anson (AI-equipped) aircraft and during the summer Lee was enlivened by the arrival of Seafire and Sea Hurricane squadrons on work-up. It was now that the limitations of the airfield became really apparent and a 3,000 ft (914 m) 24/06 tarmac runway was laid, backed up by a subsidiary 2,400 ft (762 m) 13/31 strip, while 12 blast pens were built off the perimeter track. At the end of the year a Blind Approach Development Unit (739 Squadron) was formed with a Swordfish and Fulmar on strength. Later, Oxfords and Ansons were received, the unit moving to Hinstock in February 1943.

Re-arming with the extraordinary Barracuda was started by 810 Squadron in the spring of 1943. Other squadrons followed, and again the airfield showed itself wanting. Land up to the Lee-Fareham road was acquired and the airfield extended eastwards. The E/W runway was re-aligned and lengthened to 3,300 ft (1,006 m), the main runway extended to 4,500 ft (1,372 m) and a new N/S 2,970 ft (905 m) strip built. Extensive new dispersals were laid to the east and north, liberally equipped with 12 Mains and eight Fromson-type 60 ft × 70 ft naval hangars, each capable of housing several aircraft with their wings folded. It was probably at this stage that the present ATC tower replaced the original one outside the Type 'A' hangar, but the presence of installations, once on the eastern side of the airfield but now in the middle, must have been of constant concern to the Commander (Air) and his controllers.

The Barracuda now reigned supreme at Lee, squadrons being formed into TBR Wings before embarking in their carriers. The work continued into 1944 when the station also had an *Overlord* commitment, which built up steadily as D-Day approached. Elements of No 3 Fighter Wing (808, 886, 897 Squadrons) equipped with Seafire IIs arrived at Lee-on-Solent during January 1944, but spent long periods away on specialist courses until March, when they were joined by the newly formed 885 Squadron. By April they had re-equipped with Seafire L IIIs and Spitfire Vbs and, when similar Spitfires belonging to Nos 26 and 63 Squadrons, RAF, and VCS7 of the US Navy, arrived at the end of the month, they formed a unique Air Spotting Pool known as No 34 Recce Wing, 2nd TAF, commanded by Commodore E.C. Thornton, RN. By June 1 1944 this Wing had 101 Seafires and Spitfires plus the Typhoons of No 1320 Flight at Lee and, as if this was not enough, three Mustang squadrons, Nos 2, 268 and 414, crowded in just before D-Day—what a target for the Luftwaffe!

Hastily daubed with invasion stripes during June 3, the Wing stood ready, the first pair of Seafires taking off at 04:40 hours on D-Day to seek likely naval gunnery targets, one pilot acting as spotter, the other as protector. With the Mustang visitors contributing 96 sorties, the total for the day came to 435, by far the highest number achieved by any of the TAF bases. Losses were three Seafires, three Spitfires and a Mustang. The enemy obviously found the attentions of the Air Spotting Pool annoying, for enemy fighters seemed to take a particular interest in them, breaking through the top cover provided by American P-47s and RAF Spitfires to attack them. Lieutenant-Commander S.L. Devonald, RN, OC 885 Squadron, had to ditch alongside an LST on June 7 while Lee's Commander Flying, Commander J.H. Keene-Miller, RNVR, became a PoW when bounced by six Bf 109Gs. A Spitfire V of No 26 Squadron was hit by flak while spotting, but at least one Bf 109 was destroyed by Lieutenant R.M. Crosley, DSC, using a mere 40 cannon shells, thus ably demonstrating suitability for his post of Wing Air Gunnery Instructor!

Similar action followed whenever the weather allowed, but from June 15 the calls on the Pool's services became fewer as Army firepower in the bridgehead built up. When Cherbourg fell, VCS7 was withdrawn, followed by No 63 Squadron at the end of June, but No 26 and the Naval Wing continued operations, switching to anti-midget submarine searches as gunnery targets became fewer. 808 and 885 Squadrons shared in the destruction of a number of these potentially dangerous pests before No 3 Naval Fighter Wing disbanded on July 15. The four squadrons were reduced to two, these going to Ballyhalbert early in August, but No 26 Squadron, RAF, soldiered on at Lee, rejoined for a period by No 63, until October 6 1944 when it moved to North Weald. Lee-on-Solent was then left to its Barracudas, and the various communications aircraft of the evergreen 781 Squadron.

No 1791 and 1792 Squadrons formed in March and May 1945 respectively with night fighter Fireflies, but both soon moved to Inskip as Lee took on more training responsibilities. Perhaps the biggest surprise, however, was the sudden disbandment of 781 Squadron. Its work was taken over by a detachment of 782 Squadron which coped with VIPs, and 799 Squadron which combined ordinary communications work with refresher flying for TAGs using Sea Otters, Expeditors and Avengers.

The slipway was abandoned early in 1946 when marine operations finally ceased, but with the rebirth of 781 Squadron in June the activity on the airfield hardly flagged. The splitting of the communication task had proved a mistake. A new departure was the shorebasing of HMS *Triumph*'s squadrons, 800 with Seafire XVIIs and 827 with Fireflies, but with the start of the Carrier Air Group system in September 1946, they moved to Eglinton to form 13 CAG.

At the beginning of 1947 Lee accommodated 781 (Southern Communications) Squadron with Expeditors and Rapides, 799 engaged on refresher flying, the Martinet target-towers of 771 Squadron, and parented the Naval Air Sea Development Unit (703 Squadron) at Thorney Island. They were joined by 807 Squadron, fresh from Army exercises in BAFO, during mid-January and by most of the fixed wing element of 771 Squadron in April. 783 moved south from Arbroath in May, and the fighter section of the Service Trials Unit (778 Squadron) returned with Seafires and Sea Furies.

Naval Air Command held a display of the latest FAA aircraft and equipment in June 1947, and the following year 703 Squadron moved in from Thorney Island, absorbing the duties of 778 and replacing 799 Squadron, which went to Yeovilton. During July 1948 the 51st Miscellaneous Air Group was formed with 771 and 783 Squadrons under command, the latter flying ASH-equipped Ansons. The former brought in its heavy twins, Mosquitoes and Sea Hornets. The Firebrands of 813 Squadron became a familiar sight at Lee while Ford was closed for modernisation. In January 1950, 771 Squadron took over the tasks of 720 Squadron, Gosport, but went to Ford with 703 when it re-opened in April, leaving 781 the main unit at Lee. 813 Squadron was very much the permanent lodger due to problems with the Firebrand which seriously restricted sea time but did not seem to affect their

Postwar photograph of Lee-on-Solent when 781 Squadron was the major flying unit and they occupied the hangars in the north-west corner (FAA Museum A/Stn 118).

startling demonstration of a mass rocket-assisted take-off during the 1950 Air Day.

No 781 Squadron steadily grew in size and variety of tasks. By 1951 it was not only providing VIPs with comfortable transport but had an Instrument Flying Examining Flight, a Training Flight and a SAR section using Ansons, Oxfords, Harvards, Fireflies, Sea Furies, Sea Otters and even a couple of Meteors. During 1952 the station was given a facelift, many of the wartime structures being removed, and on November 21 HM the Queen visited Home Air Command, witnessing a flypast of representative naval aircraft. On the same day 771 Squadron absorbed the Junior Officers' Air Course—a sort of Air Experience Flight equipped with a couple of Sea Princes.

No 813 Squadron finally returned to Ford for re-equipment with Wyverns in February 1953 while, in the background, planning was well advanced for the biggest event in the history of Lee, the Coronation Review of the Fleet Air Arm. Lee was the temporary base for many of the 327 naval aircraft taking part and was also responsible for overall control of the whole formation flypast. Swordfish *NF389* joined the Station Flight for the occasion, and remained a firm favourite at displays for the next ten years.

No 820 Squadron disembarked from *Theseus* with Fireflies in October 1953

before going to Eglinton to re-equip with Avengers in the New Year. Three Sea Balliols joined 781 (FOAC) Flight in April 1954, supplemented the following month by three Sea Vampires, thus providing the students with something more than a mere passenger ride. The first operational Gannet anti-submarine unit, 826 Squadron, formed at Lee on January 17 1955, remaining until May when it embarked in HMS *Eagle*, but it was the arrival of numerous helicopters during November that held greater significance.

Hillers, Dragonflies and Whirlwinds of 705 Squadron moved in from Gosport, while 845 Squadron re-formed at Lee with Whirlwind 22s. The latter were largely concerned with anti-submarine trials and spent little time at Lee, but 705 Squadron hardly moved out of the circuit, training new helicopter pilots and developing new techniques until January 1958 when it went to Culdrose.

More changes came early in 1956 when 781 Squadron was severely cut back, losing all its tasks except communications and JOAC air experience sorties. A Helicopter Flight of 700 Squadron was formed in March 1957 as the Whirlwind HAS 7 IFTU, the aircraft and crews going to 845 Squadron in October when they embarked in *Bulwark* for NATO exercises. In a surprise move, two new squadrons were formed, 701 Squadron taking over the

trials work of 705 Squadron and responsibility for SAR Whirlwind and Dragonfly
helicopters aboard carriers, while 702
Squadron took charge of the JOAC
Flight. Almost immediately 702 Squadron
transferred to Ford and 701 lasted less
than a year—but in that time carried out
mine-sweeping trials with HMS
Burnaston, towed the same vessel using
the sweep gear, did Type 194 sonar tests
and, in August 1958, tried towing a glider
with a Whirlwind 3—which sounds a
recipe for disaster. The squadron also
provided SAR helicopters for the
Portsmouth area until disbanded in
September 1958.

The accommodation at Lee-on-Solent,
much improved during the postwar years,
was under-utilised and the station was
developed as the FAA's major technical
training establishment. The Air Electrical
School started to move over from Worthy
Down during 1959, Lee becoming HMS
Ariel on October 31 in recognition of its
new status, though the Naval Air
Command in Wykeham Hall retained
Daedalus as its title. The move of the AES
was completed during October 1960, by
which time 781 Squadron was operating
its first Whirlwind HAR 22 on communications duties. The Sea Heron was
introduced in October 1961, when
servicing of the fixed-wing fleet was transferred to Airwork Ltd, who also became
responsible for the day-to-day running of
the airfield under Royal Navy direction.

The slipway came back into use with the
formation of the Inter-Service Hovercraft
Trials Unit in 1962. This unit examined
the use of the hovercraft in military roles,
the machines being hangared in the old
First World War sheds. In the autumn of
1965 the station again became HMS

*A Dragonfly HR 3 of 705 Squadron, Lee-
on-Solent, 1953* (Military Aircraft
Photos).

Daedalus, with 781 Squadron and the
IHTU on strength, together with an
increasing number of ground units. 800
ratings and WRENs paraded for the
Freedom of Gosport ceremony when it
was granted to the station in 1966, by
which time 781 Squadron had four Sea
Devons, three Sea Herons, two Whirlwinds and a Sea Hawk on strength. The
first Wessex was delivered in June 1969,
by which time the solitary Sea Hawk had
disappeared and the squadron had settled
into a straightforward communications
role.

As Naval Air Command HQ moved to
Yeovilton during the autumn of 1970, so
the Air Engineering School completed its
staged transfer from Arbroath and
absorbed the Electrical School. Meanwhile, training on hovercraft had been
introduced in 1968 and the 'Trials' part of
the title was dropped, the strength of the
unit reaching one SRN 3, two SRN 5s,
two SRN 6s, and one of the very large BH
7s, a craft weighing 50 tons.

The SAR commitment from Beachy
Head to Start Point was taken over from
the RAF in February 1973, when three
Whirlwind HAR 9s joined 781 Squadron.
They were soon in the thick of rescuing
the usual crop of carefree yachtsmen and
careless holidaymakers in addition to
doing their proper job—assisting airmen
and mariners in distress.

The Army and RAF withdrew from the
IHU during 1974, and it was re-commi-
sioned at Lee on January 1 1975 as the
Naval Hovercraft Trials Unit, involved in

testing the machines for mine counter-measures work.

Wessex 5s joined the SAR Flight in 1977, one of them kept at 15 minutes' readiness from dawn to dusk for 365 days a year—the usual scramble time being 2½ minutes from call to take-off! During 1979 the Flight dealt with 161 call-outs and assisted in the rescue of 95 people, and that was a pretty average year. The communications side of the squadron was now covered by the Sea Herons which had kept up their weekly bus-stop tour of FAA stations for years, while the Devons spent more and more time on other tasks such as fishery protection, oil pollution surveillance and checks of ships thought

to be contravening the traffic rules in the Dover Straits. Three VIP communications Wessex 5s were operated in the green and white livery of Naval Air Command and were soon known affectionately as Green Parrots.

Not even 781 Squadron could escape the axe for ever and, on March 31 1981, it was disbanded. Its Herons and Devons were distributed around the few remaining RNAS stations while the three SAR Wessex remained at Lee, sharing the airfield with the RN Gliding Club, a Chipmunk and helicopters on test from Fleetlands. It was the end of an era but Lee-on-Solent is by no means dead. The Air Engineering School always has some 650 men under instruction and maintains hangars full of obsolete aircraft, including such gems as the Swordfish *NF389*, long-since retired from Station Flight service. A multitude of smaller support units, such as the Naval Air Trials Installation Unit (NARIU) and the RN Accident Investigation Unit (AIU), proliferated.

Below *The well preserved Type 'A' hangar at Lee—ready for the 1983 Air Day* (K.S. West).

Bottom *The magnificent tower at Lee—sadly under used by 1983* (K.S. West).

The centre-piece of the impressive Fleet Air Arm Memorial at Lee-on-Solent.

It is somewhat ironic that the largest aircraft to use the old slipway waited until the 1980s. After storage at Calshot, the ex-Antilles Air Boats Short Sandringham, *Southern Cross*, was taxied across the Solent and brought ashore at Lee in 1981. When it became clear that it would never fly again, the elegant old flying boat was sold to the Science Museum. After more negotiations it was agreed that it should become the centrepiece of the new Southampton Hall of Aviation and, on March 1 1983, the Sandringham was eased across the main coast road, down the slipway, on to a pontoon, and towed to Berth 30 in Southampton Docks.

The long association between Lee and the Swordfish is commemorated by the naming of a public house just outside HMS *Daedulus*, while those who made the ultimate sacrifice in RNAS service are remembered at Lee—their names inscribed on the impressive memorial at the south-east corner of the air station.

Lenham, Kent
TQ898528, ½ mile N of Lenham village off A20(T)

Flying at Lenham started in 1930 when the Kent Gliding Club made the village their HQ, keeping their gliders in a garage and using fields on the north side of the A20 before progressing to the adjoining slopes of the North Downs. This activity ceased at the beginning of the war and in June 1940 a dummy airfield, almost certainly using the same fields, was built as a decoy for Detling. Dummy Blenheims, known as Target Planes, were dispersed around the site, which quickly had the desired effect for it was bombed on June 22, though how the residents of the village felt about this success is not recorded. Q-site lighting was added in the autumn to attract the attention of night bomber crews, and many have been responsible for the destruction of a No 49 Squadron Hampden which force-landed at Lenham early on October 17 1940, killing one and injuring three of the crew.

Despite the declining strength of Luftwaffe raids as the war progressed, the Lenham Q-site remained active, the old gliding site finding itself hosting the Auster IIIs of *B* Flight No 653 Squadron briefly during March 1943 while the unit was nominally based at Penshurst. They were followed in April by *C* Flight of No 655 Squadron, employed on Army exercises from Lenham while their HQ was at Detling, this being a time when these units were practising operating from unprepared fields under battle conditions.

The temporary strip was soon quiet again, only to be awakened during the mini-blitz of January/February 1944 when the Q-site was again bombed. With the end of the war Lenham was quickly cleared and reverted to agriculture.

Leysdown (Shellbeach), Kent
TR040698. ½ mile SE of Leysdown-on-Sea on minor road

Recognised as the first flying field in Kent to be prepared as such, Leysdown (or Shellbeach) had a good claim to be considered the first aerodrome in Britain. The potential of the site was first realised by Griffith Brewer, a well-know balloonist and the British agent for the Wright Brothers. He had a high opinion of the balloons made by the Short Brothers at Battersea and when they negotiated licence production of Wright aeroplanes, he suggested the flat marshy ground between Leysdown village and Shellness Point on the isolated Isle of Sheppey, as the ideal place for their assembly sheds and aerodrome. Griffiths was friendly with prominent members of the Aero Club and also recommended the Sheppey area as suitable for a club aerodrome. The result was that Short Bros purchased land at Shellbeach on which to build a factory, and Frank McClean of the Aero Club obtained the flying rights over several hundred acres of the adjoining marsh. He also purchased a farm, known as Mussel Manor, for use as a clubhouse.

Work started on the site in February 1909, the first building for Short Bros being erected in March. It was an adaption of a standard 120 ft (36.5 m) by 45 ft (13.7 m) corrugated iron-clad shed produced for general purposes by William Harbrow Ltd of St Mary Cray, Bromley, and had four sliding doors on one side, which gave a clear opening 40 ft (12.2 m) wide. Other buildings of similar construction went up for Club members, and McClean started construction of a bungalow alongside his hangar. A number of abandoned cottages near the coastguard station were refurbished and by June 1909 overnight accommodation was available at the Manor.

Meanwhile, J.T.C. Moore-Brabazon commenced flying his Voisin and the Wright brothers themselves visited the site, expressing satisfaction with all they saw. The first Flyers were delayed by lack of suitable engines and it was a Short-Wright glider, designed for the Hon C.S. Rolls, which became the first machine to be completed in the Shellbeach factory—

Short Brothers works at Leysdown in May 1909 (Short Brothers Ltd).

but it was taken to a hill at Eastchurch for flight trials!

By August 1909 Short's second shed was nearing completion and they employed 80 men at Leysdown, some living in workmens' cottages erected nearby. Determined to win the *Daily Mail* £1,000 prize for the first all-British aircraft flown by a Briton to complete a circuit of more than a mile, Moore-Brabazon ordered a machine from Shorts. It was a slightly modified version of the Flyer, which finally flew with a Green engine and on October 30 got round the course—at an average height of 10 ft (3 m)! He was soon improving on this, but the flying ground at Shellbeach was far from satisfactory. It suffered from numerous ditches scarring the surface, was liable to flooding, and was so rough that the Short Wright Flyers had to be fitted with wing tip skids.

These problems prompted the pioneers to move to the Eastchurch landing ground originally intended as the satellite for Leysdown. They were followed by Short Brothers, who moved their factory in May 1910 after six Short Wright biplanes had been built. Construction work and flying continued at Leysdown however, Rolls and Cecil Grace improving their skills steadily until the former's tragic death at Bournemouth on July 12 1910. Shorts also conducted floatplane experiments there until 1913, though most production seaplanes were being launched at Sheerness.

With the expansion of the Naval Flying School at Eastchurch the Leysdown LG was used for emergency forced landings until 1917 when bombing and gunnery ranges were established off-shore. It was then redeveloped as a 115-acre aerodrome, though still retaining its odd dog-leg shape. The haphazard collection of buildings built in the pioneering days were

not disturbed, merely added to by standard WD wooden huts, a large aircraft shed, and two Bessoneaux canvas hangars. Aircraft of the Gunnery School were moved in from Eastchurch, the unit being redesignated the Pilots & Observers Aerial Gunnery and Aerial Fighting School (SE Area) when the RAF was formed on April 1 1918. This awkwardly named school was equipped with 12 Avro 504Ks and six DH 4/9s and catered for a total of 50 pupils giving pilot and observer cadets training in gunnery and bomb dropping, while W/T operators and engineer mechanics selected for flying boats also attended the gunnery courses.

After the Armistice the school rapidly ran down and was closed in 1919. The station remained open to administer ranges used by aircraft from Eastchurch, a small range party operating it as a sub-unit of the main Armament School. The grass landing strips, NW/SE 2,100 ft (640 m) and NE/SW 1,200 ft (366 m) were kept clear for emergency landings by aircraft on the ranges and this situation continued throughout World War 2, the unit being particularly busy while No 18 APC was active at Eastchurch.

The aerodrome remained MoD property for many years after the Second World War, though Mussel Manor was released, becoming a country club renamed Muswell Manor, and part of the airfield nearest Leysdown was used as a caravan site. By 1978 the rest of the site had been cleared and the whole property was up for sale but it was 1981 before disposal took place.

Leysdown LG in 1918 when housing the Pilots & Observers Aerial Gunnery and Aerial Fighting School (quite a mouthful!) (RAF Museum P7660).

Littlestone (New Romney), Kent
See New Romney

Lydd, Kent
TR015230. 2½ miles NW of Lydd on minor road

Lydd was another of those places in the south-east of England which has spawned several flying sites, all named after the town and most associated with the weapons ranges which have long been established in the area. Aviators arrived as early as 1886 when the Royal Engineers, wishing to test their newly acquired balloons for artillery observation, moved a detachment into Lydd Camp. The balloon trials continued into the 1900s but had apparently ceased when No 3 Squadron, RFC, appeared early in 1914 with a detachment of four aeroplanes to continue the gunnery experiments started at Shorncliffe Camp, Hythe.

With the outbreak of war, Lydd Camp was fully occupied with training courses and it was not until the formation of a RFC Training Brigade during April 1916 that aviation returned to the town. Again it concerned balloons, No 2 Balloon School being formed in July on a site immediately north of Lydd between the present B2076 and Dering Farm (*TR037212*), a position from which students could practice what they had been taught by observing activities on the ranges.

Soon afterwards, 60 acres of Dering Farm were requisitioned as an aeroplane LG. It was a rough square 1,800 ft (549 m) by 1,800 ft to the west of the farm (*TR032208*) developed for an Artillery Co-operation Flight working with guns on the range, and in full operation by January 1917. In August of that year the

Alongside the approach road to Lydd ALG from Hawthorn Corner is one of the few remaining signs of wartime use—a Nissen hut (D.G. Collyer).

aerodrome was designated a SE Area 3rd Class LG as an emergency night landing field for the newly formed No 112 (HD) Squadron. It thus became one of a network of such LGs equipped for use by home defence units battling with unreliable engines and indifferent weather information, as well as the enemy.

The Balloon School closed in September 1918 and the Artillery Co-operation Flight quickly disbanded following the Armistice. No 53 (HD) Wing soon relinquished Lydd as an ELG, and in November pilots were instructed not to land there, so that the site could be cleared prior to return to its owners as farmland.

In 1940 a decoy airfield was built at Midley, some two miles north-west of Lydd, and this *D* Site attracted the attention of the Aerodrome Board early in 1942. It was selected as one of the more promising ALG sites in May, accepted in July and fully surveyed in September 1942. It was described as having excellent approaches to the proposed NE/SW and NW/SE strips, but conversely had no cover and very poor road access across Walland Marsh. Considerable piping of ditches would be required, and the War Agricultural Emergency Committee had strong objections to any of the few available buildings being used.

The site plans went to Fighter Command in November for the dispersal scheme to be added, a simple task in this instance because whatever they did the ALG would be impossible to disguise. There were strong reservations about this,

and about the difficulties of adequate drainage, but these objections were overruled and construction of Lydd ALG went ahead. Indeed, Midley as it was known as locally, was given priority in January 1943, intended as a training field for mobile fighter units.

The airfield covered much of Newland, Upper Agney and Scotts Marsh farms but in deference to the WAEE carefully skirted round the farmhouses and Midley cottages. Apart from extensive drainage piping and filling of ditches, the site was easy to prepare and with Sommerfeld Track runways laid, Lydd was ready in plenty of time for the arrival of No 121 Airfield at the end of June 1943. The three Typhoon squadrons came from Merston (No 174), Appledram (No 175) and Selsey (No 245) and spent the summer at Lydd working up as a team. Communal messing was provided in Nissen huts on either side of the approach road from Hawthorn Corner and Squadron HQs were set up in farmhouses, but personnel lived in tents and most maintenance was done in the open using workshops on wheels. No 175 Squadron continued its fighter-bomber operations, joined by No 174 Squadron from July 14 when No 182 Squadron (124 Airfield) was escorted to Poix. No 245 Squadron started with Army support training but went operational on July 27 concentrating on escorts to 'Bomphoon' squadrons before indulging in *Ramrods* and some night *Rhubarbs*. The whole Airfield took part in Operation *Starkey* in September, helping to give cover to the invasion force.

On September 15 they got a taste of their own medicine when Lydd ALG was bombed, but there were no casualties and no interruption in the dive bombing of targets in France and Holland. Inevitably, all three squadrons had losses, some through accidents at Lydd, for the steel mesh tracking did not stand up well to constant pounding by the heavy fighter bombers, and was not improved when a bomb fell off a No 174 Squadron 'Tiffie' during landing. It was therefore with some relief that the Airfield packed up dripping tents, sorted out sodden clothing and moved en bloc to the comforts of Westhampnett, their winter quarters.

Five Blister hangars were erected during the winter, and additional work, including the completion of access tracks, was undertaken. Most of it was in vain, for Lydd remained in reserve, only occupied by ground echelons and the RAF Regiment during the busy spring and summer of 1944. By September Lydd lay deserted. Authority to de-requisition was given by No 11 Group on December 13 1944, work starting on the removal of metal tracking and Blister hangars early in 1945. There are still a few signs of the land's wartime occupation in the form of a Nissen hut, said to have been the office/living quarters of OC No 121 Airfield, and some concrete in the vicinity of the cookhouse, but the site has completely reverted to agriculture.

Lympne, Ashford, Kent

TR115355. 2½ miles W of Hythe on B2067

The morning of Monday, August 12 1940, dawned crystal clear, ideal for a hastily planned but concerted attack on the south coast radar stations which were proving such a thorn in the Luftwaffe's side. Made by small groups of Bf 110s from Erprobungsgruppe 210, the raids caught Fighter Command completely off guard. They were brilliantly executed and three stations, those at Dover, Pevensey and Rye, were temporarily put out of action. In the confusion that followed, 15 Do 17s of 1/KG2 had little difficulty in approaching Lympne unobserved, coming in low over Romney Marsh and lifting up over the escarpment formed by the old sea cliffs, to drop 141 bombs on the airfield. The three pairs of GS hangars, which had stood in the south-west corner of the airfield since 1918, received direct hits as did the SHQ, the Cinque Ports clubhouse and many accommodation huts. One airman was killed and two badly injured, 13 civil aircraft were consumed by fire in No 2 hangar, and repair work was hindered by delayed-action bombs. Station personnel, led by the CO, Squadron

Leader D. Montgomery, were only just getting to grips with the situation, when Luftflotte 2 struck again, dropping some 240 bombs. Nearly a third fell outside the perimeter, but considerable additional damage was done and the airfield badly cratered. More delayed action and unexploded bombs made rescue work hazardous, and the survival of two wounded No 54 Squadron pilots who force-landed their Spitfires amongst the craters was little short of miraculous. Lympne was out of action—but it was a poor target for the Luftwaffe. No service aircraft were present during either attack, and its temporary loss had no effect on Biggin Sector operations.

The aerodrome at Lympne originated as a flying field for the Machine Gun School, Hythe. Land between The Roughs and the present B2067 road, directly south of Folks Wood and east of the village, was selected in October 1915 but after work had started on reseeding, it was found that the lower portion of the field became a swamp after winter rain and would require extensive drainage. The War Office abandoned the site and by March 1916 had chosen a new area to the north-west of the village between Otterpool Wood (now Harringe Brooks Wood) and the lane to Otterpool Manor. It was then decided that Lympne would be needed as a night ELG for the Home Defence organisation so extra land to the east was requisitioned. After a few small adjustments the newly acquired land became the main aerodrome site to which was added a tented camp on the western edge of Lympne village.

By October 1916 the aerodrome was well advanced, with Bessoneaux canvas hangars erected and technical buildings starting to appear. Lympne Castle had become the Officers Mess and the airmens' tents were being replaced by wooden huts erected on allotment gardens to the south of the road—which must have strained relations with the villagers. In the meantime, the Machine Gun School had become the School of Aerial Gunnery, Hythe, and the aerodrome was busy with FE 8, FE 2B, AW FK 8, Camel and RE 8 aircraft flying to and from the nearby ranges.

In January 1917, Hythe became No 1 (Auxiliary) School of Air Gunnery, part of which operated from Lympne as the Advanced Air Firing School. Plans were laid for No 8 Aircraft Acceptance Park to be formed at Lympne, and early in the

Above *A Bristol F 2B, an RE 8 and a BE 12 outside the GS hangars at Lympne* (Captain D.S. Glover via P.H.T. Green).

Below *'Off the the Front'—an SE 5A leaves Lympne for France in 1917* (Captain D.S. Glover via P.H.T. Green).

year work started on the storage accommodation, six General Service sheds being supplemented by 11 corrugated iron sheds, workshops and offices sited close to the road along the southern boundary. The AAP hangars were only partially built when the aerodrome was bombed on May 25 1917, the Gotha crews of Kagohl 3 venting their frustration on Folkestone town and Lympne aerodrome after being defeated by the weather en route to London.

No 8 AAP became involved in ferrying aircraft to France, but was also responsible for carrying out modifications called for by HQ Expeditionary Force in France, with a monthly output of some 40 machines. It was intended that No 8 AAP would concentrate on this task once the AAP at Hawkinge was fully operational,

but the Armistice intervened before either establishment was complete.

Meanwhile, the 175-acre flying field with landing runs approaching 3,000 ft (914 m) had been designated a 1st Class LG in 1918 by No 53 Wing. No 50 (HD) Squadron Camels used it as an emergency aerodrome and other units also enjoyed the facilities, No 120 Squadron forming as a DH 9 day bomber unit on January 1 1918, joined by No 98 Squadron from Old Sarum in March. The latter only stayed a month, but was almost certainly replaced by the Day & Night Bombing and Observation School which continued the de Havilland theme by employing all three of that famous designer's single-engined bombers, the DH 4, DH 9 and DH 9A.

No 120 Squadron was joined on February 16 1919 by the cadre of No 108 Squadron but, by the time the FE 2Ds of No 102 were flown in from the Continent during March most of No 120 Squadron's aircraft and men were at Hawkinge for the cross-Channel mail link. The presence of the AAP prevented any immediate closure plans and indeed extensions north-east were being negotiated during April.

Nos 102 and 108 Squadrons officially disbanded on July 3 and No 120 Squadron started flying the mail service from Lympne on the 16th. The dwindling commitment meant that it could easily be handled by civil aviation however, and No 120 Squadron ceased mail flying on August 2, the detachment returning to Hawkinge.

The Air Ministry now faced a problem —they had two excellent aerodromes in Hawkinge and Lympne within a few miles of each other—and only needed one. British compromise finally came to the rescue and they kept both, but allowed Lympne to be used for civil aviation. The North Sea Aerial & General Transport began a Leeds-Lympne-Amsterdam cargo service with Blackburn Kangaroos on March 6 1920 but the anticipated aviation boom did not materialise and the service was soon withdrawn. For a time the War Office considered using the hangars for storage but in December 1920 they finally withdrew from the scheme and Lympne entered the doldrums for the first, but not the last time. It survived to become a fully-fledged customs airport with a wireless station and a 30-mile aerial lighthouse and was used as a reporting point and an emergency LG for aircraft on the London-Paris air route.

Lympne was really put on the aviation map when it was chosen as the venue for a competition to find the British single-seat machine which could travel furthest on one gallon (4.54 l) of petrol using an engine of 750 cc or less. The Duke of Sutherland offered a £500 prize and the

Daily Mail capped this with a £1,000 prize for the longest motor glider flight of more than 50 miles over a 15-mile triangular course, open to any nationality. Some very ingenious solutions resulted, the competitors assembling at Lympne during the first weekend in October 1923 to perform the mandatory transportation test. This involved removing or folding the wings, manhandling the machine for a mile along a road and passing through a gate. This presented an unexpected problem for the DH 53 Humming Bird—the tailplane had a greater span—quickly solved by sawing off the tips. Those really were the days! The competition attracted many spectators and was full of drama, ably assisted by the weather.

With the closure of Grain in March 1924, Short Brothers took hangar space at Lympne and used the aerodrome as their landplane flight test facility during the rest of the 1920s, a fascinating selection of types making their maiden flights.

The Air Ministry laid down the rules for the 1924 Light Aeroplane Competition and also supervised the 1926 event when the *Daily Mail* offered £5,000 in prizes. The attractive little Hawker Cygnet was the winner and aircraft such as the Bluebird, which later became useful club aircraft were eliminated. It was obvious that though the competitions provoked

Lympne in the late 1920s when it was a civil aerodrome—looking east (via B. Robertson collection).

much ingenious design and were thoroughly enjoyable, they were not cost-effective in practical results. The DH Moth was already showing the path the light aeroplane movement should take and the 1926 contest was the last.

During 1927 the RAF showed interest in Lympne using it for the tented summer camps of Nos 600 and 601 Squadrons, the latter during August with six DH 9As and four Avro 504Ns. Stories about the off-beat activities of these auxiliary squadrons were already legion, and lost none of their fascination when it became known that the officers were being entertained by Sir Philip Sassoon at his seaside residence, Porte Lympne. The following year two Horsleys and a Bison of the Night Flying Flight arrived for a short detachment from Biggin Hill but, with the formation of the Cinque Ports FC, the Air Ministry seemed to lose interest and it was to be another eight years before the RAF returned. After a flurry of activity during which the Gurnards were flight tested in May 1929, Short Brothers found other airfields closer to Rochester and they also left Lympne. Fortunately a new phase had already opened, Lt Pat Murdoch, SAAF, having left at the end of July 1928 on an attempt to beat Alan Cobham's UK to the Cape record. He was successful and it was not long before Lympne was virtually the official starting point for Cape flights. The personalities involved included the Duchess of Bedford in 1930, Jim Mollison in 1931, Amy Johnson 1932, and Captain W.N. Lancaster in April 1933. The latter disappeared over the Sahara and was not found for 29 years!

International rallies such as that held in August 1935 were also popular events, but the climate was changing and in February 1936 came one of the last record-breaking attempts from Lympne when Flight Lieutenant 'Tommy' Rose set out to beat Amy Mollison's time to the Cape. He had his share of ill-fortune but his time of 3 days, 17 hours, 38 minutes handsomely beat the previous best. For good measure he gained the Cape-UK record on the way back.

With existing Service aerodromes over-stretched as the expansion of the RAF took effect, it was no great surprise when an advance party of airmen arrived on October 28 1936 to open up Lympne as a temporary No 1 (Bomber) Group station. Hawker Hind day bombers of Nos 21 and 34 Squadrons flew in on November 3 and a SHQ was formed. The First World War metal-clad sheds on the southern boundary and most of the wooden huts had long since gone, but the remaining Belfast Truss hangars were more than adequate and temporary living accommo-dation was provided for the personnel.

It had been intended to transfer the station to No 2 (Bomber) Group in December 1937 but this was deferred and later cancelled. Instead the Hinds left in the summer of 1938 and on October 1 Lympne was reduced to C&M. This was very temporary, but in view of the airfield's excellent forward position the next move was surprising. Instead of join-ing Fighter Command it went to No 24 Group, Training Command, re-opening as the School of Clerks, Accounting, on October 17. In practice the school did not stay long and on May 24 1939 the station was transferred to Fighter Command—but as a No 22 Group unit in readiness for handover to the Admiralty! It commis-sioned as HMS *Buzzard* on July 1, six Skuas and three Rocs disembarking from HMS *Ark Royal* the following week. With nine Skuas the squadron re-embarked in the *Ark* during September 1939 and Lympne promptly re-commissioned as *Daedalus II*, an out-station of Lee-on-Solent. A naval Air Mechanics School was formed and recruits, wearing unfamiliar navy bell-bottoms, jackets and caps, swarmed over the village.

Private flying ceased with the outbreak of war and most of the light aircraft were flown away to Sywell, leaving a few lock-ed securely in No 2 hangar. Lympne seemed strangely isolated from the war, the airfield silent and unused until, following the German breakthrough into Belgium and France early in May 1940, Lysander and Blenheim aircraft of the AASF retreated across the Channel, many descending upon Lympne. The Blenheims of Nos 18, 53 and 59 Squadrons were quickly dispersed to the less vulnerable airfields of Watton and Andover, and No 2 Squadron Lysanders went to Bekesbourne and Croydon. The Lysanders of Nos 16 and 26 Squadrons remained at Lympne which became one of the *Back Violet* bases set up by the Air Ministry after communications in France broke down. They flew Tac/R sorties over Dunkirk until evacuation was completed early in June, and also maintained a detachment at Rouen Boos airfield. On May 26/27, No 26 Squadron took part in the epic drops of water and ammunition to the British garrison holding out at Calais. Even more unlikely visitors appeared on May 31 when French AF Bloch 152 fighters of GCII/8 refuelled at Lympne. Eight of the pilots were briefed to give top cover to six Vought 156Fs (Chesapeakes) of the Aeronavale which were to bomb Gravelines, but communications on the ground and in the air were confused. They did not meet up and returned later to France. Right in the middle of all this activity, the Air Mechanics School was moved to Newcastle-under-Lyne, the Admiralty returning Lympne to the Air Ministry on May 23.

The *Back Violet* organisation disbanded, and the Lysanders moved away from Lympne which became a forward satellite airfield in the Biggin Sector of No 11 Group, Fighter Command. Squadron detachments flew in to be held at readiness during daylight hours, looked after by a small permanent Technical Flight. The Luftwaffe first took an interest on July 3, scattering bombs over the area without doing very much damage. A lull followed until the August 12 raid which badly damaged the Station, and a few isolated bombs fell on the 13th. Two days later another major assault developed after two heavily escorted formations of Stukas crossed the coast between Dover and Dungeness. About 40 Ju 87s from II/StG1 made for Lympne and dive-bombed unopposed. They achieved their usual good results under such ideal conditions, and very few of the buildings left unscathed after the earlier attack survived this one. Electricity and water supplies were cut, the SSQ received a direct hit, and the airfield was littered with fragmentation bombs.

Lympne was out of action for 48 hours and only fit for emergency use until early September. Personnel, and whole sections

such as the SSQ, Accounts and the Orderly Room were evacuated to houses in the area and for the rest of the war Port Lympne was the Officers' Mess, French House the Sergeants' Mess and the airmen were fed in Lympne Palace. WAAFs were housed in the village and at Bellevue, which doubled as the MT Section, while the NAAFI was in the village hall. Further small scale attacks were made on the airfield during September and Lympne took no active part in the Battle of Britain, though a number of British fighter pilots successfully force-landed badly damaged aircraft on its battered turf.

In practice little use was made of Lympne until the spring of 1941, when No 91 Squadron dispersed one Flight from Hawkinge to reduce the risk from German fighter-bombers and hedge their bets on the weather for both airfields were rarely affected by low cloud or mist at the same time. With fighter sweeps over France increasing, it was decided to bring Lympne up to full satellite standard and work started on dispersed hardstandings, a fighter pen and the erection of three Blister hangars, to supplement the temporary accommodation alongside the Bellevue estate. Squadrons based at Biggin Hill were occasionally moved forward to operate from Lympne for a day. At the end of June 1942 No 72 Squadron spent a week on the satellite, but it was Operation *Jubilee*, the ill-fated

Lympne in August 1942 viewed from the south-west. The 'GS' hangars have disappeared after the attentions of the Luftwaffe and have been replaced by 'Blisters'. Painted 'hedges' break up the outline quite effectively (RAF Museum W13/1/7).

combined services assault on Dieppe, which confirmed that Lympne had a vital part to play.

For this operation, Nos 133 and 401 (RCAF) Squadrons moved in from Biggin mid-August 1942 and both had a very exciting time. No 133, an American volunteer Eagle squadron, had been something of a headache in Fighter Command, but in four missions on the 19th, all led by the acting OC, Flight Lieutenant Don Blakeslee, DFC, the pilots proved themselves. At 07:20 hours they took off with orders to patrol Dieppe, getting into a dogfight with Fw 190s during which the OC and Pilot Officer W.H. Baker each shot one down, and another was claimed probable. The Canadians followed with an escort to B-17s of the 97th BG over the Abbeville/Drucat fighter base, after which they broke away and attacked Fw 190s and Do 217s over Dieppe. One Fw 190 was shot down and another damaged, but honours were even, for a Spitfire pilot had to bale out and another brought his aircraft back to Lympne so badly damaged it was immediately written off.

Quickly refuelled, armed and briefed, No 133 were away again at 10:15 hours to provide top cover. Again they tangled with the Luftwaffe, claiming a Ju 88 and two Fw 190s during a wild fight. Airborne on their third mission at 12:25 hours, they attacked six Do 217s just as they started bombing ships offshore, shooting one down. No 401 Squadron was intercepted by Fw 190s over Dieppe and lost two Spitfires but after licking their wounds they went with No 602 Squadron to cover the returning ships—an uneventful patrol which concluded their day. No 133 Squadron escorted the invasion fleet during the final stages of withdrawal. Inconclusively attacked by Fw 190s they landed back at Lympne at 20:55 hours—the last fighter unit down, tired but content. *Jubilee* was over, and the squadrons soon left, activity at Lympne dropping markedly until Spitfire Vbs of No 65 Squadron flew in from Drem for a heavy week of sweeps, patrols and *Rhubarbs* early in October. No 91 Squadron moved in for similar work on November 23 while continuing Jim Crow activities, returning to Hawkinge during January 1943.

As a result of successful use during *Jubilee*, Lympne was further upgraded so that prolonged operations by a two-squadron Wing could be mounted. More PSP dispersals were provided on the northern side and south-eastern corner, together with an additional Blister hangar and the distinctive note of the Sabre engine fitted to the temperamental Typhoons of No 1 Squadron was first heard in March. Transferred from Biggin Hill to try and deal with low-level fighter-bomber Fw 190s, their standing patrols did have a measure of success, though proving generally boring. The move to Lympne was very popular, however, not least because of the splendid accommodation enjoyed by both NCOs and officers. The airfield itself was not so good, being a tight fit for a Typhoon, and the first of several accidents occurred on March 19 when the pilot of *DN335* overshot on landing and overturned. The Typhoon was not a favourite with the local population, for the Sabre engine gave so much trouble on cold start-ups, that the groundcrew had to run them at intervals throughout the night!

No 245 Squadron helped with the anti-*Rhubarb* work for six weeks or so during April/May, after which No 1 Squadron started escorting the bomber-Typhoons now using Lympne as a forward operating base. No 609 Squadron arrived during August and declared themselves impressed both by the sea of mud which, even in high summer, greeted them at the dispersals, and by the messing standards.

During late August/early September both units were involved in Operation *Starkey*, an unsuccessful spoof intended to tempt the Luftwaffe into large-scale combat. In the autumn, servicing personnel were formed into Nos 6001 and 6609 Servicing Echelons, a move viewed with disfavour by air and groundcrew alike, and seemingly of no practical value. The first of a number of emergency crash landings by VIIIth AF B-17s and B-24s also occurred. With wounded men aboard or in dire trouble, pilots landed on the first possible airfield, however unsuitable. This was understandable but a terrible headache for the Station Commander—one four-engined bomber on its belly could effectively block the airfield for hours.

No 609 Squadron concentrated on long-range low-level intruder operations while No 1 started fighter-bomber work, a distinctly hairy occupation off Lympne's grass runways, the longest only 4,200 ft (1,280 m) in length. The first *Ramrod* was flown on November 10 1943 by 18 Bomphoons escorted by No 609 Squadron. After crossing the Channel at 50 ft (15.2

m) they rocketed up to 11,000 ft (3,353 m) to dive down on to construction sites (later revealed as V-1 launch pads) at Martinvaast in Belgium. After several successful *Rangers*, No 609 Squadron left Lympne in December and were promptly replaced by rocket-firing Hurricanes of No 137 Squadron, engaged on extremely dangerous anti-shipping strikes. They moved to Colerne to re-equip with Typhoons in the New Year, but were back early in February 1944 just as the long-established No 1 reluctantly went to Martlesham Heath—they had found an almost holiday atmosphere at Lympne despite the difficult operating conditions.

No 137 Squadron flew their first 'Tiffie' escort on February 8 and in March started fighter-bomber work themselves, before leaving again for conversion to rocket firing! Spitfires returned, No 186 Squadron becoming operational on tired old Mk Vbs before being renumbered No 130, and leaving at the end of April 1944 to make way for something more potent—a complete ADGB Spitfire IX Wing from North Weald which arrived on May 17 for pre-invasion sweeps and bomber escorts over France. All three squadrons (Nos 33, 74 and 127) started fighter-bomber operations with a raid on the Douai marshalling yards, but on D-Day escorted glider combinations and then transferred to interminable beach-head patrols. When the V-1 campaign reached its height, No 74 Squadron was diverted to anti-*Diver* interception, and the whole Wing dive-bombed *Noball* sites before leaving Lympne early in July on transfer to 2nd TAF.

They were replaced by a Czech Wing consisting of Nos 310, 312 and 313 Squadrons but they moved on after a few *Ramrods* and *Roadsteads* and Nos 1, 41 and 165 Squadrons arrived on July 11 for anti-*Diver* operations. A complete re-organisation of the defences resulted in ADGB fighters being given two patrol lines, one in mid-Channel and the other inland over the Kentish Weald with the gun-belt on the coast between them. This took some getting used to, but despite the marginal performance advantage of the Spitfire IX scores mounted, helped by exploits such as that of Flying Officer Davy, who shot down four V-1s in a day.

Nos 1 and 165 Squadrons went to Detling on August 10 and with the gradual slackening of the V-1 offensive as *Noball* sites were overrun, No 41 Squadron resumed sweeps over the Continent. After

conversion to the potent Spitfire XIV in September, they extended their armed recce patrols specifically to intercept jet-propelled Me 262 fighters, now becoming a serious problem for the VIIIth AF. They were joined by Nos 130 and 610 Squadrons, the new Spitfire XIV Wing taking part in supporting sweeps during the airborne landings at Arnhem (Operation *Market*). The *Elephants* (No 130 Squadron) left Lympne at the end of September and were replaced by No 350 (Belgian) Squadron for more *Ramrods*, the Wing proving very successful against German MT in the battle zone.

The intended October transfer of the Lympne Wing to the Continent as part of 2nd TAF was delayed by appalling weather and so Nos 41, 350 & 610 Squadrons continued their sweeps and escorts of returning heavy bombers until December 4 when they flew to Belgium to replace other squadrons in No 127 Wing, No 83 Group, 2nd TAF. With the war moving away, Lympne reverted to its emergency LG role until April 1945 when Spitfire XVIs of Nos 451 and 453 (RAAF) Squadrons arrived to finish the war on day bomber escorts before transferring to Hawkinge. Lympne ATC was withdrawn on May 22 1945 and the airfield reduced to C&M soon afterwards.

Lympne was transferred to the MTCA on January 1 1946 and the Cinque Ports FC re-opened during April. Air Kruise was formed during the summer for pleasure flying but the most important postwar event was the loading of a 16hp Armstrong Siddeley Lancaster car aboard Bristol Freighter *G-AGVC* on July 13 1948 for transit across the English Channel to Le Tourqet—the inaugural flight of what was to become Silver City Airways' most famous route. Closed for the winter, the service was soon a roaring summer success, the demand for car space increasing every year, resulting in a hangar, similar in appearance to a Super Robin, being erected on one of the old General Service shed bases. Other concrete foundations were used for cargo and as parking areas for the Freighters.

Silver City introduced Dakotas on an expanded network of scheduled services during 1953 but that same year torrential rain revealed Lympne's Achilles heel, the airfield rapidly becoming a quagmire, flying having to be transferred to Southend Airport. The company had already complained about the facilities at Lympne without success and when rain

This page top to bottom
One of Lympne's uninvited guests—a badly damaged B-17 Fortress of the 379th BG in February 1944 (L.P. Boucher via C.H. Thomas).

Typhoons of No 137 Squadron and Spitfires of No 403 (RCAF) Squadron in the snow at Lympne during January 1944 (L.P. Boucher via C.H. Thomas).

L.P. Boucher and his 403 Squadron Spitfire during operations from a snow-covered Lympne during February 1944 (L.P. Boucher via C.H. Thomas).

again caused chaos in the autumn they announced their intention to construct their own airfield near Dungeness. They had carried 54,600 cars and 208,457 passengers during 6¼ years operation from the airfield, their last service leaving on October 3 1954.

The loss of Silver City was a body blow. Revenue dried up and the airfield was closed to commercial traffic on October 31. Put up for sale, no purchaser could be found for the whole site so the Ministry started selling bits to previous owners. Meanwhile, Eric Rylands of Skyways Ltd came up with an idea for coach/air operations to Europe and chose Lympne as suitable for his Dakotas. He obtained the use of the main airfield site on a long lease, and it was re-licensed in 1955 when Skyways was awarded the London-Lympne-Beauvais-Paris coach/air/coach route. Services started on September 30 and Rylands finally succeeded in purchasing the whole airfield, persuading local farmers to part with their land. The cheap travel concept proved very successful, being extended in 1958 to include Lyon, Brussels and Antwerp as destinations, and resulting in the formation of Skyways Coach Air.

By 1960 the Dakota was losing appeal and Skyways chose the Hs 748 as a replacement, the first of three arriving at Lympne for route proving in November 1961. Scheduled flights started the following April, one of the aircraft being lost on July 11 1965 when it cartwheeled on landing at Lympne and ended up on its back, a complete write-off, but amazingly no one was seriously injured. A replacement aircraft was soon found, and Skyways built up a very successful little business.

Rain and fog still caused operating problems and during the winter of 1967 a single 4,400 ft (1,341 m) concrete NW/SE runway was laid, the airfield being renamed Ashford Airport in April 1968. A new terminal building was completed in April 1969, but the economics of the operation began to go wrong and on January 20 1971 Skyways Air Coach suddenly ceased trading. The fleet of four Hs 748s and three DC-3s were grounded at Ashford (Lympne) but ten of the senior employees put in a bid for the company and the '748s, which was accepted. The DC-3s were transferred to Air Freight Ltd and scheduled services using the Hs 748s resumed on February 8 1971 by the renamed Skyways International. A year later Dan Air made a successful offer for the company and took up a short lease on the airfield, flying the coach air service from Ashford to Beauvais until October 31 1974 when they moved to Lydd (Ferryfield).

Business Air Travel, Skyfotos and the Cinque Ports FC also moved over to Lydd and Ashford (Lympne) was left with a few privately-owned aircraft and, more recently, a parachuting school. Plans to convert the southern half of the airfield into a golf course have been stopped and something of a revival in Lympne's

fortunes is under way. Part of the industrial estate on the airfield was taken over by Luscombe Light Aircraft in 1982 to build the Valiant two-seat canard microlight and its military version, the Rattler. Another building is now occupied by the East Kent Memorial Flight whose aim is to rebuild ex-Royal Navy aircraft to flying standard. They have started with a Sea Fury and have ambitious plans for a Sea Hornet—which is certainly worthy of support.

Evidence of wartime usage is rapidly disappearing, being limited to the large concrete bases of the old hangars, a single Blister, the 1942-style control tower, and a few huts near Bellevue. The post-war airport is more in evidence with the runway, taxiway, two hangars and other buildings alongside Otterpool Lane extant. Some are used by light aircraft which fly from an area in the south-east corner of the original airfield. Port Lympne, the wartime Officers' Mess, is now part of Howletts Zoo Park and Wildlife Sanctuary.

Manston, Kent
TR333662. 2 miles W of Ramsgate off A253 road

They are out! The news spread like wildfire! No need in February 1942 for anyone remotely concerned with Operation *Fuller* to ask what was meant. They knew it could only refer to the German battle cruisers *Scharnhorst* and *Gneisenau*, which had been brooding in Brest for months, but were daily expected to break out.

Intelligence assessment was that they would make a dash up the Channel under the cover of darkness and British plans were made accordingly, with the Beaufort torpedo-bombers of Coastal Command positioned, so it was thought, to cover all eventualities. For several reasons, however, they were thin on the ground, and the Admiralty were keen to augment them. Only the newly formed 825 Squadron, working up on Swordfish at Lee-on-Solent, was available. On February 3 1942 the OC, Lieutenant Commander Eugene Esmonde, RN, was tentatively asked whether he could take on the German ships if they attempted passage of the Dover Straits. It was taken for granted this would be at night or very early in the morning, so he agreed, although his crews were not operational. The six available Swordfish were at Manston the next day,

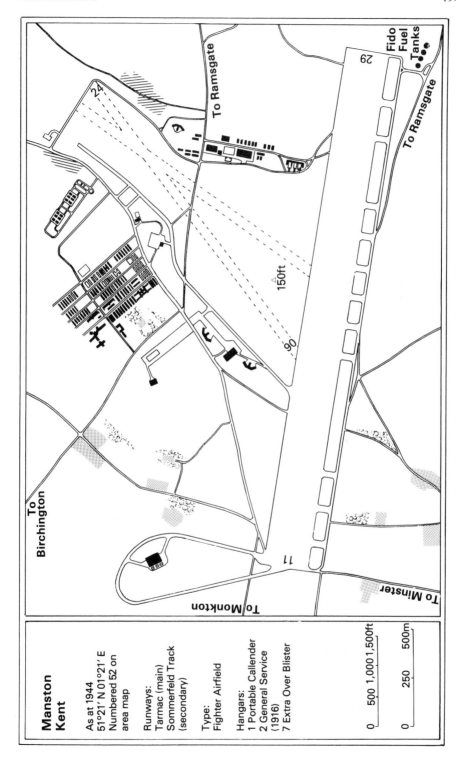

Manston
Kent

As at 1944
51°21' N 01°21' E
Numbered 52 on
area map

Runways:
Tarmac (main)
Sommerfeld Track
(secondary)

Type:
Fighter Airfield

Hangars:
1 Portable Callender
2 General Service
(1916)
7 Extra Over Blister

0   500 1,000 1,500ft

0   250   500m

To Ramsgate

To Ramsgate

To Minster

To Monkton

To
Birchington

Fido
Fuel
Tanks

29

150ft

90

24

11

crews briefed to expect the break-out during the next no moon period.

Esmonde was warned at 10:55 hours on February 12 that there was unusual German surface activity and that there might be a target for his crews. He immediately ordered his squadron to readiness and had the torpedoes set to run deep, though there was no real suspicion of the target type until 30 minutes later when Group Captain Victor Beamish and Wing Commander R.F. Boyd returned from their bad weather cross-Channel sweep with the dramatic news.

Promised fighter cover, Esmonde agreed to try an attack though a daylight operation against such ships had little chance. Five squadrons of Spitfires were tasked as escorts and diversions, with a rendezvous over Manston at 12:25 hours. This was less than an hour ahead but time was running out if the Swordfish were not to be faced with a tail chase into the North Sea. Esmondes' crews were incapable of the classic crescent formation attack so he had to brief them to follow in line astern, despite the advantage this gave enemy AA gunners and fighters.

Esmonde was now informed that the fighters would be delayed—but he could not afford to wait. The six Swordfish lurched off at 12:20 hours to be joined by 11 Spitfires of No 72 Squadron. Within minutes the tiny force was set upon by Fw 190s and Bf 109s and, while the Spitfires tried to hold them off, the Swordfish lumbered on into a smoke screen and a horrifying barrage from destroyers, E-boats and even the 11-in guns of the battle cruisers. Esmonde's Swordfish was hit first, the whole of the starboard lower mainplane outboard of the interplane struts being torn away and the aircraft set on fire. He continued his run, dropping his torpedo just before control was lost and the Swordfish went into the sea.

With the leader gone, enemy fighters concentrated on Sub-Lieutenant B. Rose and his Swordfish were raked by cannon fire, killing the gunner and holing the main fuel tank. With a failing engine, he dropped his 'fish' in the direction of the ships and ditched. Sub-Lieutenant C. Kingsmill dropped his torpedo as close as he dared, but as he turned away the top cylinders of his Pegasus engine were shot away and he too was forced into the water. Led by Lieutenant J. Thompson, the second wave of three Swordfish were seen under heavy fighter and AA attack going in over the inner screen of escorts.

None of their torpedoes found their target and neither Swordfish or crews from this 'vic' were ever seen again.

There were five survivors, Sub-Lieutenants Rose, Lee, Kingsmill and Samples and Leading Airman Bunce. The four officers were awarded the DSO, Bunce the CGM. Lieutenant Commander E. Esmonde, DSO, DSC, received the posthumous award of the Victoria Cross, the other gallant men who lost their lives the only other possible award, a Mention in Despatches. The sacrifice had been in vain, except perhaps as an example to other combatants. In addition to public tributes at the time can be added a statement found in the German War Diaries. . . 'a handful of ancient planes, piloted by men whose bravery surpasses any other action by either side that day'.

By 1942 Manston was an important airfield and was to go on to greater things, but it had very small beginnings; for it resulted from the problems experienced by anti-Zeppelin patrols at Detling and Westgate in 1915. The RNAS looked about for a safer night LG and settled on a large field near Ramsgate. A large packing case, equipped with a telephone and bunks, was set up on the site for two duty Air Mechanics. When advised that an aeroplane had taken off they laid out a paraffin flare path and sat back to wait for the firing of a Verey cartridge overhead. They then rushed out and lit the flares in readiness for the tricky business of a night landing.

The field, known then as Manstone LG, was improved in February 1916 when two wooden huts and a demountable hangar were erected. The permanent move of the Westgate landplanes to the ELG was proposed in March, and agreed late in April. Further land was requisitioned and work started on better facilities, though personnel remained under canvas for some time.

Meanwhile, the night defence unit at Detling had become the nucleus of No 3 (Aeroplane) Wing and as soon as Manston became available the Wing moved in with a motley collection of trainers and four 1½-Strutter bombers. The second prototype Handley Page 0/ 100 'paralyser' arrived for trials with the Wing, Eastchurch having been found too small, and later in June the Westgate War Flight transferred to Manston with six aircraft and about 50 men.

Training of No 3 Wing continued, though the drain of 1½-Strutters to the

Mens' quarters at RNAS Station, Manston, 1917—rows of wooden huts (P. Liddle via G.S. Leslie).

RFC, desperately short of aircraft following the start of the Somme battles, made progress very difficult. However some aircraft and crews had reached Luxeuil by the end of July 1916, and the testing of the 0/100 was going ahead, if only slowly. Two were retained as the nucleus of the Handley Page Training Flight in September and plans made for all RNAS production aircraft to be equipped and armed at Manston before delivery to France. This required a massive expansion in hangarage and personnel, work starting on rows of wooden accommodation huts for both officers and men.

The training echelon of No 3 Wing left for France in October 1916 followed by the first 0/100s for the unit, leaving just the Handley Page School, Modification Centre and the War Flight at Manston. During November the War Flight was reduced in size to provide pilots for a RNAS squadron going to the Western Front, but the unit retained its agressiveness, a Bristol Scout attempting an interception of a LVG reconnaissance aeroplane on the 28th and another hostile machine being sighted during a dawn patrol on February 16 1917. It outran the defender and with such incidents increasing, daylight standing patrols were introduced, Manston being responsible for a line between Ramsgate and Whitstable.

During spring 1917, part of the pilot training school at Eastchurch was transferred to Manston and formed the nucleus of the War School, equipped with Avro 504s and a variety of service types to

provide advanced instruction on aircraft which the pilots would be flying operationally—a sort of OCU. A spate of air raids by Gothas kept the War Flight busy, their efforts rewarded on August 22 when a Kagohl 3 machine was brought down at Vincents Farm, in sight of the airfield.

Shortage of trained Air Mechanics became acute during 1917 and with Crystal Palace bursting at the seams the Admiralty selected Cranwell and Manston as main instructional units for the RNAS, the latter known as the Southern Training Base. Personnel flooded in during the autumn, new construction of huts not keeping pace. To complicate matters it was decided that Manston would become a permanent Station and work started on schools' buildings, workshops and additional aircraft sheds.

A Flight of four 0/100s arrived from Redcar on October 2 1917 to form *A* Squadron, RNAS. Reinforced by newly delivered aircraft, the Squadron left for Ochey fifteen days later, and it was reluctantly agreed by the Admiralty that the Handley Page Training School should also move because of concern that the units' night flying could cause false alarms and confusion amongst the Home Defence forces charged with the sensitive business of protecting London against the night bomber. It was transferred to Stonehenge in January 1918 leaving Manston short of flying units, but the decision to go ahead with five so-called underground hangars was still taken that same month.

With the formation of the RAF in April 1918 came the establishment of a three-squadron day bomber training unit, No 203 TDS, and after the big German offensive in March increasing calls for reinforcements resulted in the War School becoming a Pilots' Pool. In July, for

reasons unexplained, No 203 TDS was renamed No 55 TDS and soon afterwards the War Flight was absorbed by the newly-formed No 219 Squadron which had its HQ and floatplanes at Westgate, but three Flights at Manston, Nos 555 and 556 with DH 9s and No 470 with Camels. The latter was intended for escort of both DH 9s and the Short 184 floatplanes.

The large aerodrome was still under-utilised and with shortages in France, No 2 School of Observers was formed with a through-put of 500 pupils per month, No 55 TDS being moved to Narborough on September 12. The personnel strength of the Station rose to 2,539 (750 of whom were pupils) and 125 aircraft were operated.

Apart from the underground hangars which were never finished, the Station was virtually complete at the end of September 1918 with eight large, and one small, aircraft sheds, two MT sheds and three large workshops which together with numerous single storey wooden huts covered 100 of the 680 acre aerodrome. The Pilots' Pool moved to Joyce Green in October and the Armistice on November 11 1918 brought a sudden reduction in flying activity though both No 219 Squadron and the Observers School con-tinued in operation, the latter finally closing in September 1919. It was briefly replaced by No 1 (Observers) School of Aerial Gunnery from New Romney but No 219 Squadron outlasted the lot, linger-ing on until February 7 1920.

Keeping Manston as a peacetime station meant that with the end of the 'emer-gency' the requisition of property had to be converted into purchase. As usual there was one awkward owner—an elderly German lady! Miss Luhn and three other German invalids had been obliged to move from Pouce's House early in the

F1 Camels of the War Flight at Manston, June 1918 (G.S. Leslie/J.M. Bruce collection).

war, but were now allowed back into the coastal area. She wanted her house back, but unfortunately it was in the middle of the aerodrome and earmarked as the Station Commander's House. Letters passed to and fro between Ministries and Miss Luhn, but it was the end of 1919 before she finally gave in and submitted her compensation claim alongside more compliant locals.

During October 1919 it was decided that the School of Technical Training (Men) would move from Halton to Manston. Accommodation previously used by the Gunnery School was refurbished, training courses recom-mencing in May 1920 using the ample workshops and hangars. The cadre of No 6 FTS arrived from Spitalgate during May 1921 and in September started using the airfield to provide refresher flying for pilots going overseas, on aircraft types such as Avro 504Ks, Snipes, Bristol Fighters and even a few Vimy and DH 10 heavies.

The 1921 rail strike resulted in 80 officers and some 600 men of the Reserve being mobilised at Manston, but the swingeing Geddes Axe of 1922 cut deep, No 6 FTS being disbanded in April, the wireless station dismantled, and the S o TT courses reduced in size. Of more immediate interest to trainees though was the state of the parade square, which was visibly sinking in the middle under the pounding of marching feet. This was due to subsidence of the wartime shelters built underneath, but unfortunately for the recruits it was quickly repaired, and with a modest expansion in 1924, money was voted for married quarters and the removal of the remains of the semi-underground hangars.

On March 31 1924, Bristol Fighters of No 2 (AC) Squadron arrived from Andover and the next day the paltry UK fighter defences were strengthened by the reforming of No 3 Squadron at Flight strength. Their five Sopwith Snipes had just been assembled when the squadron received orders to recrate them and move to Upavon. The new location seemed strange for a fighter unit, but the explanation was simple—they were changing places with No 9 (B) Squadron who couldn't get their Vimys into Upavon's narrow hangars.

Manston transferred from No 1 to No 23 Group on April 1 1926 and got involved in another work stoppage the following month—the General Strike. Officers and men were sent to London to help defend the Stores Depot at Kidbrooke and No 9 Squadron, now flying the lumbering Virginia, took part in the distribution of the Government newspaper, the *British Gazette*. Manston was back to normal by June and Oxford UAS training in July was followed by the first Auxiliary Air Force summer camp, No 600 Squadron bringing their DH 9As from Northolt for a fortnight under canvas.

The administrative and domestic sites at Manston in the 1920s. The Virginias belonged to No 9 Squadron (via P.H.T. Green collection).

No 2 Squadron, still equipped with Bristol F 2Bs, went to the Far East from April to October 1927 and did not get rid of its ancient warriors until January 1930 when AW Atlas biplanes arrived. After six years at Manston No 9 Squadron went to Boscombe Down in November but the ubitiquous Virginias were soon back, for on March 1 1931 a Special Reserve squadron, No 500 (County of Kent), was formed. The half regular, half reserve, formula succeeded in Kent, helped by a naming policy, the first Virginia X being christened *Isle of Thanet* by the Mayors of Margate and Ramsgate on June 4. By October local men were joining the reserves in substantial numbers, and a year later the aircraft strength stabilized at six Virginias and two Avro 504N trainers.

The station was transferred from No 23 to No 22 Group, Inland Area, on October 1 1932 and Fairey IIIFs of 821 and 822 Squadrons spent a short time at Manston during 1933 while disembarked from HMS *Courageous* and HMS *Furious* respectively. The first Empire Air Day held in May 1934 attracted over 6,000 people. It was followed in July by the annual air exercise when Nos 500, 501 and 503 squadrons all gathered at Manston to provide an auxiliary bomber force for 'Southland', working with regular bombers stationed in the Salisbury Plane area and opposed by fighters of 'Northland' at Biggin Hill and North Weald. How limited it now sounds, but it was typical of the 1930s.

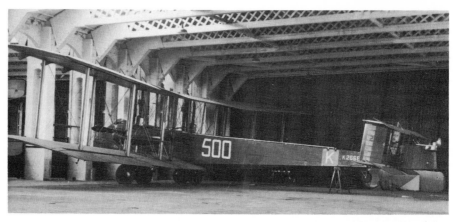

A No 500 (County of Kent) Squadron
Virginia X in one of the Belfast truss-
roofed 'GS' hangars at Manston (via R.S.
Sturtivant collection).

On July 1 1935 the training school
became No 3 S o TT (Men) and was
increased in size, reflecting the need for
more technicians as the RAF expansion
really took effect. Changes on the flying
side were also apparent, No 2 Squadron
going to Hawkinge in November to make
room for the School of Air Navigation,
formed by combining the Air Pilotage
School at Andover with the Navigation
School from Calshot. It came into being
in January 1936 using a variety of aircraft
including the Saro Cloud amphibian. The
personnel strength of the station rose
rapidly, new huts were erected and other
buildings converted into billets, but
despite this more beds had to be crammed
into existing accommodation severely
reducing each man's precious territory.
No 500 Squadron became a light bomber
unit in January 1936 when its elderly
Virginias were replaced by Harts. Five
months later further re-organisation
brought the Reserve squadrons into line
with the Auxiliaries and the unit became
No 500 Squadron, AAF, though it
remained firmly associated with Kent.

No 48 Squadron was responsible for
providing the flying for the S of AN and
greeted the arrival of Ansons in March
with considerable relief, the Cloud having
proved a disappointment. The Anson was
unique at this time as the only monoplane
in full squadron service, and the first
equipped with a retractable under-
carriage. This was manually operated, and
as anyone familiar with the Anson 1 will

recall, required 172 turns of a handle to
raise or lower it. The squadron was
nominally a coastal reconnaissance unit
but in practice its first two years at
Manston were almost entirely devoted to
coping with the flood of pupils, plus some
night flying for the ADEE Biggin Hill. It
also provided the nucleus for No 206
Squadron in June 1936 and No 224
Squadron during February 1937, before
the Air Navigation School became
responsible for its own flying, and No 48
Squadron was able to retreat to Eastchurch in September 1938 and become an
operational unit.

During the Munich crisis the personnel,
now so numerous that 700 had to live in
tents, were busy digging trenches, siting
gun posts, camouflaging aircraft and
buildings, setting up bomb and ammunition dumps. At the end of September, No
500 Squadron took its Hind day bombers
to Detling leaving Manston to concentrate
on training as the build-up continued.
More temporary accommodation huts
were built, and on August 24 1939 the
pressure was such that No 616 Squadron's
summer camp was cut short. General
mobilisation was ordered on September 1
which meant complete upheaval. Living
out personnel were brought into camp,
the defence scheme initiated, the S o TT
courses dispersed and the S o AN moved
to the safety of St Athan.

For a few days Manston reverted to
C&M, then No 3 Squadron Hurricanes
arrived from Croydon on detachment,
and 816 and 818 Squadrons, FAA,
formed up on Swordfish. Nos 235 and 253
Squadrons re-formed at Manston on
October 30, temporarily with Battles,
though both were intended as Blenheim
fighter units. This choice of unit numbers

seems incredibly inept, almost designed for confusion, but they both survived, No 235 transferring to Coastal Command with Blenheims in February 1940, while No 253 Squadron was given Hurricanes and went to Northolt.

Clear of training units, Manston was transferred to Fighter Command on November 15 1939 and welcomed Hurricanes of No 79 Squadron and a detachment of No 600 Squadron Blenheim IVfs as the first based fighters for many years. They were soon in action, the first kill going to No 79 Squadron on November 2, two pilots catching a Do 17 ten miles off the coast. The AI-equipped Blenheims were used at night in an unsuccessful attempt to catch He 115 floatplanes mining the Thames Estuary. Many of these mines were a magnetic type and while work went ahead to provide ships with a degaussing belt, a small number of Wellingtons were fitted with a 48 ft (14.6 m) diameter magnetic coil fed from a Ford V-8 engine driven generator. They equipped No 1 General Reconnaissance Unit (a cover name) at Manston, the plan being to fly at low level over the Estuary with the deliberate intention of setting the mines off! No one knew what the effect would be when Squadron Leader H.A. Purvis, escorted by fighters and with a rescue launch in the area, made the first sweeps on January 8 1940. One mine was exploded, but no further successes were recorded until the 13th. Heavy snowfalls at Manston held up further operations until February 10 when efforts were redoubled. Mid-March the Wellingtons began formation sweeps over the North Goodwins and got another mine on April 8. No 3 GRU formed in April but went to Thorney Island almost immediately, and with the departure of the original unit to the Middle East in May, Manston's involvement in this dangerous occupation was over.

Day fighter cover was continued by detachments from Nos 32 and 79 Squadrons on alternate weeks while No 600 Squadron changed places with *B* Flight of No 604 at Northolt on May 15. The latter was heavily engaged on standing patrols inland from Dunkirk during the evacuation, unseen by the troops complaining bitterly about the absence of the RAF. Aircraft started to filter back from France, those landing at Manston including most of No 504 Squadron's Hurricanes and some Lysanders of No 13 Squadron. Most were passed quickly on after refuelling to regroup further inland, but some No 615 Squadron pilots were attached to No 604 Squadron as *G* Flight, with the job of local airfield defence using a number of Gladiators.

It was a period of confusion but gradually things were sorted out. In June direct communication with the Sector Station at Hornchurch was established, a decoy airfield was built on the Ash Level marshes two miles south-west, and everyone at Manston was encouraged by No 604 Squadron's first night success, a He 115 shot down off the French coast. They were almost immediately replaced by No 600 (City of London) Squadron who sent three Blenheims on intruder operations over St Pol and Arras airfields on June 20, the day they arrived at Manston.

On July 3 a small force of Do 17s nipped over the beach and sprinkled light bombs on the landing area—damaging a grass mower. The day fighter detachments were used to cover coastal convoys in between interminable standbys, but early on Sunday July 7 *B* Flight No 54 Squadron found itself scrambled to intercept a 'bogey'. A single He 111 was spotted, but lurking in the background were Bf 109s which attacked the Spitfires unseen, shooting down two and damaging a third. This favourite Luftwaffe ploy was used very successfully until the RAF abandoned their rigid 'vic' formation for the more controllable 'finger four'. Up to three day fighter squadrons were now using Manston daily as a forward airfield to relieve pressure on the main bases as No 11 Group was strengthened to cope with increased Luftwaffe activity.

Things were hotting up and a switch from convoy to airfield attack was anticipated—it came on August 12. At Manston, Spitfires of No 65 Squadron were taxying out for a routine patrol soon after midday when all hell was let loose. Without warning, Bf 110s of the brilliantly led Erprobungsgruppe 210 shot across the airfield, dropping bombs and strafing as they went, while almost simultaneously 18 Do 17s of KG2 bombed from medium altitude. The airfield erupted in clouds of chalk dust and smoke as the raiders made their escape leaving a workshop destroyed, two hangars badly damaged, a Blenheim written off and several Spitfires damaged. The spectacular dust cloud convinced the Germans that Manston had been completely destroyed, but though badly cratered it was actually back in operation 24 hours later.

A repeat performance by Erpr 210 came two days later. Four hangars were badly damaged and three Blenheims destroyed, but there was some consolation in the success of the AA defences, *ad hoc* though they were. A 20 mm Hispano rigged up by No 600 Squadron in their dispersal brought down one Bf 110, and the Royal Artillery manning a 40 mm Bofors got another, but the weary airmen had 50 more craters to fill in and morale, already at a low ebb, began to falter. There was no respite from the low level attacks which daily caused more damage and casualties. No 600 Squadron was withdrawn on the 21st, but the fight continued until August 24 when events made the situation untenable.

As mid-day refuelling of No 264 Squadron's Defiants was completed, warning came of another raid. The crews struggled into their aircraft and were just taking off when the first bombs fell. They had no time to form up and three Defiants were quickly shot down, all six crewmen being killed. On the ground the situation was just as bad, with seven killed, buildings on fire and the airfield littered with unexploded bombs. Hardly had clearing up started, than a second raid developed, resulting in more severe damage, particularly to living accommodation. All communication with Sector and Group was lost until valiant efforts by Post Office engineers, working in a large crater alongside an unexploded bomb, restored essential contact. The Station Commander's report resulted in Manston being abandoned, except as an ELG. The men of No 12 Servicing Flight camped in nearby woods for the next eight days, while clerks worked from the CO's house and nearly everyone else was moved to Westgate.

The Prime Minister, Mr Winston Churchill, visited on the 28th to see the damage for himself. The 'Bulldog' was unhappy about the apparent lack of effort being made to get the airfield serviceable again, and as usual had a remedy. He suggested mobile teams trained to carry out raid repairs, and with the transport and equipment to do the job. The Works Flights were thus born!

The station was back in limited operation by the second week of September and at the end of the month a couple of Lysanders from No 4 Squadron arrived to co-operate with high-speed ASR launches at Ramsgate. The Luftwaffe also paid periodic visits though little further damage occurred and more excitement was caused by a forced landing by Oberleutnant Walter Rupp in his Bf 109E-4 of III/JG53 on October 17 after combat with Spitfires of No 603 Squadron. Five weeks later a fighter-bomber Bf 109E-3 of II/JG5 put down after Leutnant Wolfgang Teumer was intercepted over the Thames Estuary, this aircraft being repaired and used for trials work.

Despite Manston's vulnerability, No 92 Squadron was moved forward from Biggin Hill early in January 1941, and were quickly successful with their cannon-armed Spitfire Vbs, Flying Officer A.C. Barkley shooting a He 111 into the sea on February 3. The Blenheims of No 59 Squadron arrived for reconnaissance and night bombing of French ports and No 74 Squadron replaced No 92 for offensive sweeps just before a nasty attack by 15 Bf 109s, which damaged barrack blocks, a Spitfire and the airfield.

In April 1941 a Flight of No 101 Squadron Blenheim IVs arrived to try out a new scheme designed to deny the Dover Straits to enemy shipping during daylight. Even with fighter protection, attacking shipping was a hazardous business, and the first attack, made on April 28 against trawlers off Calais, set the pattern, one of the three Blenheims being shot down. Occasionally came success, the first claim a 2,000-ton vessel off Ostend on May 2, but they were few and the accumulated losses were alarming. *Channel Stop* was temporarily halted on May 9 but restored at the end of the month when No 110 Squadron were the victims. On July 15 it was decided to support the No 2 Group Blenheim detachments at Manston with a dedicated Hurricane fighter unit. The first was No 242 Squadron, responsible for silencing the guns while the Blenheims went for the supply vessels. The whole force approached at very low level—wave-top height—the Hurricanes zooming up to 1,500 ft (457 m) during the last mile or so to dive on to the escorts, while the Blenheims lifted to mast height for the bombing run and Spitfires tried to keep off enemy fighters.

Meanwhile, detachments of Hurricanes from No 3 Squadron operated a Night Flight, Havocs from No 23 Squadron were intruding over France with increasing success and No 239 Squadron spent more and more time at Manston, first with Lysanders on ASR standby and later for fighter-recce sorties over Belgium using Tomahawks—the airfield was really back in business.

The *Channel Stop* continued into September, but with fewer targets presenting themselves and the flak ships more numerous, the Blenheims were withdrawn during the month. Between January and September 1941, Manston-based squadrons had sunk 44,600 tons of shipping and damaged another 27,500 tons—but at a terrible cost in aircrew. The four-cannon Hurricane IIcs of No 615 Squadron swopped places with No 242 Squadron and spent the next two months roaming about on *Rangers* and *Rhubarbs* attacking anything which presented itself off the French and Belgian coasts.

Wing Commander R.P. Gleave assumed command of Manston in October 1941 with instructions from the AOC to turn it into an operational station. He immediately set about tidying up, getting the burnt-out remains of hangars and workshops removed and refurbishing the airmens' accommodation using salvaged materials. More squadrons moved in, one of them flying Airacobras, which had the engine mounted amidships driving the propeller through a long shaft which passed between the pilot's legs—not universally popular! The aircraft proved unsatisfactory, more success attending the Hurri-bombers of No 607 Squadron which also arrived in October, and immediately set about targets in France.

The grass airfield had now been extended, lengthening the E/W and NE/SW landing runs to 4,800 ft (1,463 m) and 5,700 ft (1,737 m) respectively, the latter cutting the public road through the camp. This helped, but with an increasing number of 'lame duck' bomber aircraft

Hurricanes of No 174 Squadron lined up at Manston in May 1942—presumably for an inspection—but what an inviting target! (IWM CH5627).

making emergency landings, a strong case for a substantial runway with proper lighting was made, unfortunately with no immediate result. Detachments of Beaufort torpedo bombers were also making their appearance at Manston, while Hurricane IIcs continued their sweeps and short range anti-shipping work, No 32 Squadron taking over from No 615 in November.

The *Scharnhorst* and *Gneisenau* break-out on February 12 1942, a disaster for 825 Squadron, was a bitter let-down for the RAF Beaufort crews. Hastily arranged briefings for Nos 42 and 217 Squadrons gave their rendezvous with supporting bombers and fighters as Manston, but mismatched radio frequencies and generally poor ground communications between various units reduced their efforts to a shambles. Several crews only discovered what was happening by landing at Manston and being rebriefed!

No 174 Squadron was re-formed at Manston on March 3 from a nucleus provided by No 607 and promptly took over their job, the first target being at Berck-sur-Mer on the 28th. The same month saw the arrival of the first WAAF, accommodated in the Ursuline Convent at Westgate, but employed in the catering section at Manston. They were part of the CO's morale-boosting plan and were an immediate success, for restrictions on movement in the coastal defence zone had made off-duty activities very limited.

The Hurri-bombers of No 174 Squadron were joined in their intruding by regular detachments of No 23 Squadron Havocs, while four Typhoons of No 56 Squadron were on standby from the end of May in case Canterbury became the subject of a *Baedeker* raid. The Typhoon's resemblance to the Fw 190 became a serious problem, two being shot down by No 401 Squadron Spitfires early in June. The familiar black and white

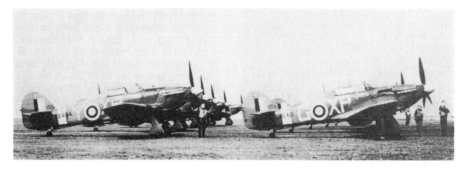

stripes soon appeared under the wings as a recognition feature.

The North Weald Wing was now using Manston as a forward base for Spitfire Vbs on *Rhubarbs* and No 23 Squadron, fully equipped with Mosquito IIs, finally moved across from Ford early in August to continue long-range intruding over the Continent. On August 14 1942 the whole of the North Weald Wing (Nos 242, 331 and 332 Squadrons) flew into Manston for Operation *Jubilee*, and were joined by No 403 (RCAF) Squadron from Catterick and eight Mustangs from the Gatwick fighter-recce Wing. On the 19th the Mustangs were off at 05:30 hours and half an hour later the airfield reverberated as the engines of 36 Spitfires burst into life and Wing Commander F.D.S. Scott-Malden, DFC, led out his Wing for their first patrol of *Jubilee*. They arrived over Dieppe just as the Luftwaffe reacted and the top cover Norwegians of Nos 331 and 332 Squadrons were soon embroiled in a terrific dogfight with some 20 Fw 190s and Bf 109s. Between them they claimed five Fw 190s destroyed and three damaged for the loss of two Spitfires. Lower down, No

A Luftwaffe recce photo of Manston dated July 1942—they were still around! (via D.G. Collyer).

242 Squadron were not involved, but the Canadians arrived at the tail end of the fight and shot down two German fighters, losing three Spitfires in the process.

On their second patrol the Norwegians joined up with the Canadians over the ships, and again a fight started as heavily escorted Do 217s approached. Between them they claimed three Dorniers and two Fw 190s destroyed and others damaged, OC No 403, Squadron Leader L.S. Ford, DFC, having no difficulty in getting his '190 confirmed—it fell to pieces, parts hitting his wingman. The Norwegians were out again in the afternoon, a head-on meeting with Typhoons having tragic results when a pilot fired almost automatically and the Tiffie went straight into the sea. Recovering from this disaster, the two Spitfire squadrons intercepted some Do 217s and damaged several.

With the assault ships well on their way home things had quietened down when Nos 242 and 403 Squadrons arrived at tea-time, but Squadron Leader Ford led his men over the French coast and got his second confirmed kill of the day when another Fw 190 went down in flames. A final patrol by Nos 331 and 332 Squadrons was uneventful, as was the scramble by No 242 Squadron to intercept reported intruders over the south coast, a quiet end to a busy day during which Manston-based Spitfires probably saw more action than any other RAF fighter units. Apart from the unhappy incident of the Typhoon it was also very successful, and there were several monumental parties that night.

The Spitfires left the following day to be replaced by four Albacore biplanes! These were from 841 Squadron, FAA, engaged in mine laying and flare dropping, the latter for RAF night strikes on enemy shipping.

The USAAF had discovered Manston, the first badly shot-up bomber to find refuge being a B-17 of 1 BW during the afternoon of August 24, but it was the night-time diversions which gave the most trouble and the Station Commander's worst fears were realised on August 28/29. It started when the Northolt-based Polish Fighter Wing diverted in 45 Spitfires at dusk. They had just been refuelled and serviced when a Wellington of No 305 (Polish) Squadron crash-landed on the flare path. Three more Wellingtons and three Stirlings landed safely off bomber operations and then, with the flare path still blocked, another Stirling called for an

Typhoons of No 609 Squadron at dispersal at Manston, May 1943 (IWM CH9822).

emergency landing. Told to aim to the right of the lights he moved over too far and swept through the line of Polish Spitfires and into the Albacore dispersal. With one Spitfire a blazing wreck and debris in all directions, another Stirling arrived on a straight in approach, desperately short of fuel. He also landed too far to the right, missing the Spitfires only to hit a large wooden hut before running into a hangar. Two more bombers, one so short of fuel that it couldn't taxy, landed before the night was through, and the scene the following morning was almost indescribable. One Stirling was embedded in a hangar, another sat on top of a flattened Albacore while the remnants of two Spitfires lay scattered about. The report, backed by photographs, did, however, get approval in principle for a crash runway.

No 174 Squadron, still on limited operations with its outclassed Hurricanes, was joined by the Whirlwinds of No 137 Squadron in September 1942. Newly equipped with bomb racks, these attractive but troublesome aircraft made their first fighter-bomber attacks from Manston on October 31 when they went to Etaples, and lost three Whirlwinds to flak. Manston itself also improved its AA defences, becoming one of the first stations to receive RAF Regiment gunners and they had quick success, shooting down a Fw 190 of 10/JG26 on October 10. Another upsurge of Luftwaffe activity with low level attacks by both Fw 190 fighter-bombers and Do 217s, resulted in

Typhoons of No 609 Squadron arriving for a week of experimental standing patrols from Manston. In practice they stayed for nearly nine months, the pilots accommodated at The Nook in Westgate, and using a former girls' school, Doone House, as their off-duty mess. With Squadron Leader R.P. Beaumont (later famous as a Typhoon/Tempest Wing Leader and Canberra/Lightning/TSR-2 test pilot) as OC, it could not be expected that No 609 Squadron would be satisfied with standing patrols, and in November they started offensive *Rhubarbs* at night! They concentrated on German troop trains with some success, and also managed to counter some of the similar nocturnal activities of Fw 190s.

While *A* Flight of 832 Squadron was embarked in HMS *Victorious* for Operation *Torch, B* Flight Albacores were at Manston supplementing the anti-shipping work of 841 Squadron. Anyone observing their departure a month later was probably convinced that the ancient biplanes were carrying some form of bizarre secret weapon on their underwing racks. Actually they were essential items of personal kit—the crew bicycles! 823 Squadron, transferred from Tangmere at the beginning of 1943, stayed for six months, continuing highly dangerous nightly shipping strikes. Not all the danger was provided by the enemy—one 841 Squadron Albacore which suffered engine failure on take-off careered across the wet grass, through a fence, across a road, to be finally stopped by the main guardroom, which it moved several feet in the process. Amazingly, no one was killed.

No 137 and 609 Squadrons, now roaming the Continent whenever the moon shone, were joined by the Typhoons of No 198 Squadron in March, initially to fly escort to Whirlwinds on day trips, but starting *Rhubarbs* themselves in April. That same month a very 'hush-hush' ground party arrived carrying carefully concealed equipment which disappeared into a closely guarded hangar, followed by a number of boffins—one of whom was Barnes Wallis of Vickers-Armstrong. They were conducting trials of a bouncing bomb code-named *Highball* which started on April 13 with drops of the spherical wooden-skinned weapon on Reculver Sands, from Mosquito IV *DK290*. Twenty-three were dropped without great success, and similar problems beset the larger *Upkeep* weapon when Lancaster trials followed a few days later. It was not until the end of the month, and only three weeks before the famous Dambusters' attack on the Moehne, Eder and Sorfe dams, that the production bomb worked for the first time!

Hardly a night went by without distressed bombers arriving at Manston, often guided in by the *Darky* emergency homing system. Even the Germans joined in, Underoffizier Heinz Ehrhardt bringing in his fighter-bomber Fw 190A-4/U8 of 1/SKG10 early on May 20, under the mistaken impression he had crossed the Channel and was landing at St Omer. A month later another aircraft from the same unit was presented intact to the RAF by a disorientated Unteroffizier Werner Ohne who mistook Manston's identification beacon for his home airfield.

Other Fw 190 pilots were not so lucky. A strong force of fighter-bombers intruded over Kent in June 1 and 12 of them were spotted by No 609's standing patrol after a Margate gasometer blew up. Although hit by enthusiastic AA fire, Flight Lieutenant J.C. Wells pursued them at low level and shot down two before his ammunition was exhausted. Flying Officer L.J. Davies saw another four strafing the streets of Broadstairs and caught one, the pilot baling out. He then saw six more streaking low over the water and shot down the 'weaver'. He broke away as tracer flashed past and in the turn glimpsed three more Fw 190s, gave chase and with his last few rounds set fire to a straggler over Ostend. The AA defences got another, resulting in a very satisfactory six-nil score.

The contract for the massive 9,000 ft (2,743 m) long, 750 ft (229 m) wide runway, a 6,000 ft (1,829 m) dispersal loop and 12 crash bays, was let to John Laing & Son Ltd, work officially starting on June 15 1943. Flying off a temporary strip on the eastern side and the PSP-reinforced NE/SW grass runway continued unabated, indeed it increased when the USAAF realised Manston's potential as a forward operating base for P-47 Thunderbolts, designating it Station 351.

In June No 137 Squadron had been replaced by No 184, equipped with Hurricanes. This apparent retrograde step was offset by their armament, for they were Mk IVs equipped with eight rockets—a mighty punch, first demonstrated against shipping off Cherbourg on June 17. They continued similar small-scale attacks until No 137 Squadron returned in August, accompanied by No 164. Also armed with Hurricane IVs, they formed a Wing, No 137 with 40 mm cannon-equipped aircraft, while No 164 favoured rockets. Again operations were on a small scale, their most celebrated an attack on the lock gates at the entrance to the Zuid Beveland canal, when they managed to destroy one massive gate.

Typhoon fighter-bombers of No 3 Squadron also arrived in June and the following month No 56 Squadron replaced No 609, but only stayed a month before No 198 Squadron joined No 3 as the second resident 'Tiffie' unit. Operation *Starkey*, the ill-fated spoof attack, had little impact on Manston, the main tasks remaining *Rhubarbs* and anti-shipping strikes, 823 Squadron Albacores joining in the latter at night from early September. When 841 Squadron disbanded in November, six of their aircraft were taken over by the RAF as *A* Flight of No 415 (RCAF) Squadron, while No 1401 (Met) Flight arrived with Spitfire VIs and continued weather reconnaissance over Europe.

Most missions now involved support for VIIIth AF operations, usually while the bombers were extricating themselves from German fighter attentions after a raid, but *Rhubarbs* were flown at every opportunity. By the end of the year the Hurricanes had been withdrawn and No 3 Squadron, which had concentrated on *Roadsteads* during the autumn, went to Swanton Morley. No 609 Squadron returned, to join forces with No 198 in clouting everything in sight. Probably their biggest success was on January 30 1944 when seven Typhoons of No 609 Squadron destroyed three enemy aircraft in the air and another two on the ground, while six of No 198, jumped by Fw 190s, claimed nine of them. The Wing score of 43 for the month was three-quarters of the No 11 Group total—Manston was riding on the crest of a wave.

In February 1944 No 3 Squadron reappeared, and at the end of the month a large vehicle convoy entered the station. No 123 Airfield, No 84 Group, 2nd TAF, had arrived to assume command of the three Typhoon squadrons. It was a time of turmoil, however, for there was almost constant changeover of squadrons, and both Typhoons and the Airfield had left by April 1.

Meanwhile, the massive task of runway construction had continued non-stop and at 14:25 hours on April 5 it was brought into operation. Some idea of the magnitude of the project may be gained by a few statistics. Over 370,000 cubic yards of soil had been excavated and replaced by hardcore topped by 379,000 sq yds of 7 in thick concrete on the main runway, and a further 462,000 sq yds of tarmac for taxiways and dispersals, using over 600 men and 149 lorries to lay it. At each end of the runway was a cleared grass overrun of 1,500 ft (457 m) and Mk II lighting, and the fuel piping for FIDO had also been installed. It did not take long to justify the expense and effort, 56 emergency landings being made in the first three weeks of operation. The Servicing Wing, always over-stretched, was now being assisted by

The FIDO fuel tanks alongside the Ramsgate Road (Air Ministry PRB 12885).

an American contingent to cope with USAAF aircraft, and a detachment from No 86 MU. They used the remaining two GS sheds and single Callender portable hangar for maintenance work, supplemented by seven extra-over Blisters dispersed around the airfield.

No 137 Squadron were back again at the beginning of April, this time with Typhoon fighter-bombers, soon converted to rockets for anti-E- and R-boat operations in the Channel. A week later No 605 Squadron moved its Mosquito VIs to Manston for night intruder work over Dutch and Belgian airfields, but more startling was the formation on the station of No 155 (GR) Wing, No 16 Group, Coastal Command. Comprising black-painted Swordfish from 819 Squadron and portly Avengers of 848 Squadron, the Wing was intended to prevent the Germans moving desperately needed fuel into France by coastal tankers, following the rail and road disruption caused by 2nd TAF and USAAF intruders.

The Swordfish used ASV Mk X radar to seek out their targets, which were then dealt with by the eager rocket-firing Typhoon pilots of No 137 Squadron. The Avengers concentrated on the Scheldt Estuary end of the route and made E- and R-boats their speciality. As D-Day got closer, the pressure increased and Beaufighter Xs of No 143 Squadron arrived from North Coates on May 23 for anti-E boat patrols, sometimes operating with flare-dropping Albacores of No 415 Squadron, but more often free-ranging.

At the beginning of June, No 605

Squadron was concentratng on French airfields and AA gun/searchlight batteries, but had a roving commission on D-Day when 18 Mosquitoes were out over the Continent, looking for anything that moved—and finding a Me 410 near Evreux. Anti-shipping patrols were intensified, No 143 Squadron making six attacks on E-boats in June 7, while No 137 was transferred to Army support work once the troops were ashore.

Meanwhile, Manston was coping with even more bomber diversions, some being hard to deal with, like the B-24 which accidentally jettisoned eight bombs while making an emergency landing on June 13. This was not a good day, a 500 lb (227 kg) bomb exploding aboard a dispersed Mosquito causing casualties, and the first V-1 flying bomb impacting in south-east England. Two days later a No 605 Squadron crew, Flight Lieutenant J.G. Musgrove and Flight Sergeant Samwell, met a V-1 head-on, turned round and shot it down—the first airborne *Diver* to be destroyed by the RAF. Together with No 137 Squadron Typhoons and many other fighter units, No 605 were immediately transferred to anti-*Diver* patrols, the Mosquitoes proving one of the more successful types, the Manston squadron alone claiming 36 by the end of the month.

No 415 Squadron, still heavily engaged on anti E-boat and shipping patrols, also laid smoke and spotted for coastal bombardment. On July 10 the Albacore Flight suddenly became No 119 Squadron, but they remained at Manston and hardly had time to notice. Two days later Manston upped its personal score of Luftwaffe aircraft to six when two Bf 109G-6s quite separately joined the circuit and landed, but the 21st was probably more noteworthy because of a new sight and sound, the arrival of two Meteors of No 616 Squadron. The unit's Spitfire VIIs moved in from Culmhead on the same day, but were soon relinquished as more Meteors arrived. They were declared operational on July 26 but it was over a week before success came—in a remarkable way.

On patrol over Tonbridge, Flying Officer 'Dixie' Dean spotted a V-1. He attacked head-on but the cannons refused to fire. He turned, caught up and, easing his wing beneath that of the flying bomb, used the disturbed airflow to tip the V-1 over, toppling its gyros—it crashed five miles south of the town. A few minutes later Flying Officer Rodgers got another V-1 in a more conventional manner, the bomb blowing up violently in front of him.

The anti-*Diver* forces were further strengthened by the arrival of Tempest Vs. These potent aircraft, operated by No 501 Squadron mainly at night, proved very effective against the V-1 and accounted for 33 by the end of the month, Flight Lieutenant Bonham getting four in one patrol. More Tempests joined in when Nos 80 and 274 Squadrons arrived, though as the V-1 sites in France were overrun the numbers coming across the Channel decreased markedly. The Tempest Wing then reverted to armed recce over France while No 504 Squadron's Spitfire fighter-bombers strengthened the Coastal Command forces, preventing interference with cross-Channel reinforcement shipping by E-boats. Thus at the end of August 1944, three Tempest, one Meteor, one Mosquito, one Spitfire, one Beaufighter and an Avenger squadron were operational from Manston, while at the same time the station was dealing with a flood of emergency landings.

Early in September 97 Horsas were towed in by Albemarles of Nos 296 and 297 Squadrons for Operation *Comet*. This was cancelled but the gliders and airborne troops stayed to make use of the broad runway on the 17/18th when they went to Arnhem in two lifts, the Tempest Wing being used on flak suppression for Operation *Market*. No 146 Wing, 2nd TAF, spent a few days at Manston awaiting suitable airfields on the Continent, and on September 25 a No 11 Group Spitfire Wing (Nos 118, 124 and 229 Squadrons) arrived to carry out intensive bomber escort work.

Landing between two rows of unsheilded petrol burners was few peoples' idea of fun at any time, but with a crippled aircraft and possibly a wounded pilot it could be extremely hazardous. However it was better than trying to land in fog, and the newly operational FIDO helped 19 crews to get down safely during September alone, and saved many more in the winter months ahead.

The Fighter Wing underwent the usual changes, No 229 Squadron being replaced by No 91 at the end of October, and No 118 by No 1 Squadron mid-December, by which time No 1401 (Met) Flight was using three Spitfire IX (Met) which it took to Belgium in January 1945. The resident Mosquito night fighter unit also changed when No 406 Squadron arrived from Cologne with Mk XXXs. These flew standing patrols over enemy fighter airfields during bomber raids and night *Rangers*, the latter universally popular.

On February 27 1945 the Czech Wing (Nos 310, 312 and 313 Squadrons) moved in from Bradwell Bay with Spitfire IXs to continue *Ramrods* and bomber escorts right up to the end of the war. The last major operation was escorting 446 Lancasters and Halifaxes to Wangerooge on April 25, but they also flew cover for the forces re-occupying the Channel Islands in May 1945.

A flurry of activity during the last few weeks of the war included the arrival of the ungainly Barracudas of 822 Squadron for anti-midget submarine patrols over the Scheldt Estuary in case of a suicide mission by fanatics. Only one was sighted, and that had been abandoned. It was a rather anti-climatic end to the war in Europe, during which Manston-based aircraft officially sank 123 enemy ships and destroyed 234 aircraft and 161 V-1s.

No 29 Squadron replaced No 406 in June and when the Czechs left for Prague late in August with brand-new Spitfire IXs, the night fighter Mosquitoes held operational sway at Manston until the end of October when they too departed. The rather nebulous No 567 Squadron, which flew Oxfords, Spitfires and Vengeances in a desultory fashion for the benefit of anti-aircraft gunners, was joined by No 130 Squadron on that unit's return from Norway in November, but both suffered from Fighter Command's lack of interest in the station with the formation of No 91 Staging Post, and its authorisation as a RAF & Civil Customs Aerodrome on April 1 1946. One of the first users of these facilities were Yorks of the reborn Skyways Ltd on contract to the Anglo-Iranian Oil Company, while diverted RAF Dakotas started appearing in increasing numbers. It was no surprise when No 46 Group, Transport Command took control on July 15 1946, No 130 Squadron having already left for Acklington.

Dakotas of No 46 Squadron arrived from Stoney Cross in October 1946 to continue their schedules, but had hardly settled in before an advance party was ordered to Abingdon and the whole unit was there by the end of the year. The Staging Post continued to process personnel and freight, and in May 1948 was joined by No 1 Overseas Ferry Unit from Pershore. The OFU delivered aircraft to the Middle and Far East until July 1950 when it moved to Chivenor, following a decision to transfer Manston to the American 3rd Air Division for use by SAC fighter escort Wings. The 7512nd Air Base Group moved in on July 11 1950, and three days later Manston was transferred from No 46 to No 11 Group, Fighter Command, RAF interests being preserved by a small liaison team and air traffic control section under an RAF Station Commander.

Within days Republic F-84E Thunderjets of the 20th FB Wing arrived on detachment from Langley Field, SC, followed on rotation by the 31st FEW in January 1951 and the 12th FEW six months later. A detachment of SA-16 Albatross and SB-29 Fortress aircraft of the 9th ARS arrived in April 1951, and when SAC units departed in November the 3rd AF, USAFE took over, the F-84Es of the 123rd FBW, Kentucky Air Guard, moving in. The Americans built new hardstandings on the east side by the control tower and split the wide runway into three sections using the centre lane as a 200 ft (61 m) wide landing strip and the sides for taxying. On July 10 1952, the 123rd was de-activated, aircraft and some personnel being used to re-form the 406th FBW (512, 513 and 514th FBS). Soon afterwards the 66th ARS was formed from the air rescue detachment. A year later, in November 1953, the 406th received the long awaited Sabre, becoming a Fighter Interceptor Wing in the process. The RAF kept one Chipmunk in the Station!

The 512th FS moved to Soesterburg in November 1954 and was replaced four months later by the 92nd FS from Bentwaters, but a bigger disturbance occurred in August 1955 when an American airman awaiting trial went berserk. Breaking into the armoury he lay in wait for the USAF military police commander, then suddenly opened fire on a police billet and sprayed passing cars indiscriminately. A RAF Corporal was shot dead before the gunman commandeered a car and drove to Broadstairs. After a tense manhunt he was shot on the beach at Joss Bay.

Manston became a Master Diversion airfield in April 1956, remaining open day and night, 365 days a year, to accept aircraft in emergency, or unable to land at their destination due to weather problems. Six months later the USAF took complete control of the base, including air traffic control and operated it until the 406th FW was de-activated during May 1958. The

airfield was returned to RAF Fighter
Command on June 30 and reduced to
C&M on August 1 1958. The emergency
value of its magnificent runway was
undeniable, but the noise, particularly of
the Sabres, had generated considerable
opposition and it was not re-opened as a
Master Diversion airfield in No 11 Group
until March 28 1959.

Parented by West Malling, it hit the
headlines when an operations clerk, alone
in the tower, successfully homed in four
Belgian aircraft on emergency diversion.
He coped so well that he was awarded an
AOC's commendation.

A limited number of civil operators
were accepted, the closure of Blackbushe
resulting in Silver City making Manston
its main base, aircraft and staff moving
over during April 1959. They used the
SHQ building initially, but later
transferred to the eastern end of the
airfield which became known as the civil
side in January 1960 the Air Ministry
Fire Service formed its Civil Training
Establishment at Manston and customs
facilities were provided later in the year,
generating more traffic, including air
trooping and training flights by BEA.

RAF personnel strength was given a
boost by the arrival of *D* Flight, No 22
Squadron in March 1961 for SAR around
the Thames Estuary. The two Whirlwind
helicopters were soon in business, but as
usual it was the rescue of holidaymakers
which provided most of their trade, rather
than their primary tasks. With the airfield
intended as a standby base for bomber
aircraft it was logical that Bomber
Command should operate it and on
October 1 1962 Manston was transferred
to No 3 Group, the Central Training

*North American F-86D of the 415th FS,
406th FIW, USAF, based at Manston in
1957* (Military Aircraft Photos).

Establishment being taken over at the
same time. The establishment, already
gathering an impressive collection of
obsolete aircraft in its fire fighting and
rescue training compounds, promptly
introduced more courses, and during 1963
RAF/ATC activities were further
increased by the formation of No 615
Gliding School in March and the arrival of
No 1 Air Experience Flight's Chipmunks
in April.

Trials on Pyrene Foam laying equipment, designed to reduce the fire risk
from wheels-up landings started during
1963 and Manston became one of the
three airfields in the country having the
facility on call. It was used for the first
time in May 1964 when a No 543 Squadron Valiant from Wyton made a successful arrival on the foam strip.

Air Ferry Ltd commenced operations
on March 30 1963 using two Vikings and a
DC-4 and were building up trade when
sold to Air Holdings in 1964. They
continued flying from Manston, joined by
Invicta Airways in 1965 and with civil
traffic increasing markedly, work on a
new hangar and terminal was started on
the civil side, and the gliding school was
moved to West Malling.

With reducing Bomber Command
interest the station was transferred to No
19 Group, Coastal Command, during
August 1967. The Master Diversion
facility was retained, the CTE and No 1
AEF remaining as lodgers.

Early in June 1968 Manston was

A F-84F of the 77th FBS, 20th TFW based at Manston, but seen here at a display at Burtonwood, 1957 (Military Aircraft Photos).

invaded by the Luftwaffe, when two Heinkel He 111s and 15 Bf 109s swept in over the Channel and landed. As already recorded, aircraft wearing swastikas had visited Manston before, but not with so much advance publicity, crowds flocking to see these aircraft. Actually they were licence-built Spanish CASA 2 111s and HA 1112s in for inspection by the ARB before taking part in the film *Battle of Britain*—all Merlin-powered but looking surprisingly authentic!

Air Ferry closed down on October 31, and despite widespread rumours that the airfield was to become London's third airport all that happened was that Invicta also reduced schedules early in 1969 and it was announced that the ASR helicopters were to be withdrawn at the end of March. There was the inevitable outcry, but they still went. Agitation continued and two years later the Board of Trade contracted Bristows to provide two Whirlwind helicopters on standby at Manston for civil rescue duties in co-operation with the Coastguard. After another three years RAF helicopters returned in the form of two yellow-painted Wessex 2s, these operating as *D* Flight of No 72 Squadron until No 22 (SAR) Squadron was re-equipped with the same aircraft in June 1976— then the Manston detachment became their *E* Flight.

Regular visitors were Sea Devons of 781 Squadron from Lee-on-Solent, operating in support of HM Coastguard's Channel

radar surveillance unit at Dover, while military diversions have continued at a steady rate despite the withdrawal of the foam laying equipment in September 1980.

Manston entered the 1980s still a joint-user Master Diversion airfield, with No 22 Squadron's Wessex and the four Chipmunks of No 1 AEF, the only visible signs of active RAF occupation. The large aircraft compound belonging to the Air Force Department Fire Service Central Training Establishment and Spitfire XVI *TB752* are, however, probably more interesting to the aviation enthusiast. This Spitfire arrived at Manston in June 1956 as a gate guardian and became a magnet for camera-totting American servicemen. In July 1967 it was joined by Javelin *XH764* (reserialled *XH639*) and later by Canberra *WE168*. The Spitfire deteriorated and in 1978 was taken to Rochester Airport for restoration by the Medway Branch of the Royal Aeronautical Society. It returned in pristine condition and was placed in a weatherproof memorial building. The Cortex runway mines laid in 1940 and which defied all efforts to find them eight years later, were finally discovered in 1982 and lifted, using very sophisticated equipment. There is now less chance of being blown up by our defences, but no guarantee that the odd German bomb in not still lurking undetected.

Manston is an interesting place, steeped in aviation history, and very accessible. The A253 follows the line of the old southern taxiway close to the main runway, and the B2190 cuts across the camp dividing the control tower from the airfield. A number of the buildings

The Manston 'gate guardian' Spitfire LF XVI outside Station HQ in May 1967.

erected in World War 1 survive, including the Station HQ and some of the hangars. The platform and a small length of the rail spur built in 1918 is still visible, and the foundations of the one semi-buried hangar that was partially constructed have been used by Allard Grange Farm for many years. Another hangar was transferred from Westgate and is used to house the gliders of No 617 GS which came from Bovingdon in 1972. The present Officers' Mess was originally Pouces' Farmhouse, the Station Commander now living in a tastefully renovated cottage called Homecroft. It is a sobering thought that though only a mere shadow of its former self, Manston is now the only operational RAF airfield in Kent.

Marine Parade (Dover), Kent
See Dover (Marine Parade)

Marlborough, Wiltshire
SU193678. 1 mile S of Marlborough off A346

Aerodromes have been built in some odd and unlikely spots but Marlborough LG must surely be unique in at least one respect—it was on top of a railway tunnel!

Opened as an unlicensed private aerodrome by the Earl of Cardigan in 1935, this L-shaped, smooth grass field was on a saddle which sloped away sharply both north and south, but gave an E/W run of some 1,800 ft (549 m) and N/W of 1,500 ft (457 m). The Earl was the enthusiastic owner of Avro 504N *G-ACZC* for a number of years, keeping it in a hangar

alongside the A346 road where it was joined by other privately-owned machines.

In January 1936, against considerable local opposition the Central Flying School, Upavon, started using the LG on certain weekdays for forced landing training. Apparently the feared disruption for Marlborough College did not occur because RAF usage continued, mainly by Avro Tutors but also by more exotic types, a Fury biplane crashing on the LG in May 1939. Private flying ceased in September 1939 but the strip remained open, CFS making increased use of the facility. This, coupled with less experienced students, resulted in more accidents, but Marlborough LG remained in use until early 1942 when it was finally abandoned in favour of nearby Overton Heath. It was not re-opened after the war, but the hangar still exists.

Marwell Hall, Hampshire
SU510210. 3½ miles NE of Eastleigh town on A333

By 1941 work on both British and American aircraft in the Cunliffe Owen Aircraft factory at Swaythling, Southampton, was in full swing, the company having design authority for the modification of several types of aircraft, in addition to repair contracts. Increasing output brought its own problems for Southampton was surrounded by very effective balloon and gun defences, aircraft requiring individual clearance to fly in the zone, resulting in wasted time and frustration for pilots delivering machines to the factory, or taking them out to MUs.

Cunliffe Owen's Managing Director, Mr R. Hayes, lived at Marwell Hall, a large house with extensive grounds some four miles to the north-east of Eastleigh airport, and just outside the balloon barrage. It was decided to establish a flight test base on the estate, and to hide it from the Luftwaffe by using the natural camouflage provided by the heavily wooded area. By carefully joining two fields together, cutting gaps in hedges and a line of trees, and closing the minor road between the A333 and Hurst Farm a satisfactory grass runway was prepared, roughly E/W in direction. Robin hangars, some 20 in number and each capable of accommodating four Spitfire-sized aircraft, were erected in the woods surrounding the strip, or in positions which allowed their disguise as farm buildings, while part of the Hall and the whole of Hurst Farm were used for staff accommodation.

Marwell was opened in September 1941, aircraft modified at the Eastleigh factory being flown in by company test pilots and prepared for collection. Ferrying to and from Marwell was handled by the ATA, who used the cellars of the Hall as crew rest rooms and the old cheese room as administrative offices.

The first aircraft at Marwell were Spitfires and Blenheims, some of the former being modified for naval use by the addition of arrester hooks and other gear at Marwell itself. American types included Bostons, Hudsons and the heartily disliked Airacobra. The latter showed a marked reluctance to get airborne from

One of several remaining 'Robin' hangars at Marwell Hall—this one is near Hurst Farm and is used to store agricultural implements.

the grass strip unless a very strong wind was blowing.

Strong winds also caused problems, though. If blowing across the strip, which was only 600 ft (61 m) wide at one point, they could make landing impossible, while over the trees unpleasant turbulence resulted. All these difficulties were accentuated when Cunliffe Owen started modifying Halifaxes for Coastal Command and it was decided to deliver them into Marwell where they were parked under the trees. Many of the ATA pilots were women and some of the more experienced and able were cleared to fly four-engined types. Although the sight of women pilots soon ceased to cause a stir, few people really got used to seeing them climb into a Halifax with just a flight engineer for company, start up, taxy out and take-off between those lines of trees while being buffetted by a gusting crosswind. It was no job for a weakling!

This work reached a peak during 1943 with the company also busy on continued modification of American types, including Venturas and Liberators, and on the production of Seafires. With the risk of bombing at Eastleigh much reduced, Cunliffe Owen moved out of Marwell in 1944 and Air Service Training took over the accommodation to carry out design work on Mustang and Mitchell modifications, for which AST was the daughter firm. There was little flying involved and with the end of the war the staff returned to Hamble. The small firm of Willmott & Manser Experimental Aircraft then used the Hall for a short while before moving to Beaulieu, after which the land reverted to agriculture.

The Hall is now a zoological park, its

Above *Near the Marwell Zoological Park alongside the road is another 'Robin'—with a Mini to give scale.*

entrance close to that of the wartime LG. A Robin hangar near Hurst Farm is used for implements while another two on the roadside between Marwell Manor and Hurst Farm are in good repair. There are also a number of derelict hangars and some concrete foundations still visible, while the direction of the runway can be traced by the gaps in hedges and trees. Few of the visitors to the Zoo will have any idea they are on the site of a wartime airfield for Marwell Hall has preserved its semi-secret nature extremely well. During the war it was little known for it did not appear on RAF maps and was very difficult to locate even by inveterate 'Bradshawers' like the ATA. Fortunately Fisher's Pond, about half a mile to the west, was a distinctive stretch of water and gave pilots something to line up on when visibility was a problem. It was for these occasions, rather than for night landings, that a generator and runway lighting were installed in 1942.

Membury, Berkshire

SU308753. 3 miles SW of Lambourn alongside M4

Construction of this bomber OTU airfield was authorised in May 1941, it being typical in layout with a main SW/NE runway of 4,554 ft (1,388 m) and two sub-

sidiary runways, four 'T2' hangars, the usual technical area and dispersed domestic sites. The latter included a large instructional site north-east of the airfield alongside Ermin Street, the Roman road. It was nearing completion just as the US VIIIth AF started to flood into the country and Membury was immediately earmarked for their occupation. The airfield was formally taken over from the contractors by No 91 Group, Bomber Command and an opening up party sent from No 24 OTU, Honeybourne during August 1942. Many of the installations were not complete but sufficient domestic accommodation was available to receive HQ personnel from the strangely named VIIIth Ground Air Support Command on August 21, the USAAF designating Membury as Station 466.

Assigned units arrived in a rush early in September and comprised the 3rd Photographic Group, the 67th Observation Group and the 153rd Liaison Squadron. Nominally each of the Groups had four squadrons but fortunately all that arrived were several hundred half-trained men, six camera-B-17 Fortress and a few Piper Cubs. Nine F-4s (photo-recce version of P-38 Lightning) came later with the 5th Photo Squadron but they left with the 3rd PG during October. *Torch* prevented the

Below *Oblique of Membury looking north-west. Dated May 1943 it is soon after completion of the four 'T2' hangars (RAF Museum W21/101/4).*

units at Membury reaching their established strength, and at the end of the year the 67th Obs Group could still only muster 36 ex-31st and 52nd FG Spitfire Vbs, spread amongst the four squadrons (12th, 107th, 109th and 153rd).

A number of target-towing A-20 Havocs were received early in 1943, but the 67th was little more than a training unit for Spitfire pilots who were promptly posted elsewhere when qualified. By March tactical reconnaissance work had resumed, the Spitfires being used for training in observation, photography and artillery spotting during British and Canadian army manouevres, and the large-scale Exercise *Spartan* when Spitfire Vbs of No 19 Squadron, RAF, joined the Americans at Membury for three days under canvas.

In June the main unit became the 67th Reconnaissance Group and, although still largely a training organisation, small scale operations were performed during the summer by detaching pilots to RAF units for cross-Channel sweeps. The A-20 crews also took time off from dragging drogues for VIIIth AF bomber units, to fly on operations with the RAF. Two crews of the 153rd RS took part in a 12-aircraft attack by No 107 Squadron, RAF, on Schipol airfield in July 30, the Boston flown by Lieutenant McQuvie being lost when it suddenly broke formation and spun into the sea. In August the 2911th Bombardment Squadron (Light), Provisional, was formed with A-20Bs fitted with cameras, and the 67th carried out its first missions on August 18 when two aircraft joined in attacks on Lannion/Brest, operating from Exeter and escorted by Spitfires of No 610 Squadron, RAF.

By September the 67th RG was again concentrating on reconnaissance, but also checked out pilots of the 354th FG on P-51As in November prior to the fighter unit receiving Merlin-powered Mustangs. On November 13 the 67th RG was transferred to the IXth AF and a month later they left Membury for Middle Wallop.

Meanwhile, Membury had become the 6th Tactical Air Depot, IXth AF, and with the decision to move the 53rd TCW from East Anglia it was chosen as the base for a TCG, resulting in a priority need for a longer runway. Extension was only practical to the north though prevailing winds would have dictated a SW/NE direction, so it was the N/S runway which was lengthened to 6,000 ft (1,829 m), taking it almost up to Ermine Street. With

the airfield and all domestic sites finally complete No 70 Group, RAF, handed over Membury to the IXth AF on February 22 1944.

Six weeks earlier the 366th FG had assembled at Membury after crossing from the States by troopship. The three component squadrons (389th, 390th and 391st) collected their P-47 Thunderbolts and spent the next two months acclimatising before moving to Thruxton. Two days later, on March 3 1944, the 436th TCG (79th, 80th, 81st and 82nd TCS) arrived from Bottesford with C-47 troop and cargo transports. Under the dynamic leadership of Colonel A.N. Williams they immediately accelerated training with airborne forces, practising both paratroop drops and glider towing at low level and in formation at night in preparation for D-Day.

The Normandy lift code-named *Albany* was the Group's first operation, involving 90 aircraft in the carriage of paratroops of the US 101st Airborne Division, the first waves going in just after midnight on the DZ south-east of Ste Mere Eglise. No losses occurred, but many of the drops by the second wave were poorly positioned, and on return bad weather over Membury delayed landings. The 436th then took part in the second glider lift for the 82nd Airborne using two Hadrians and 48 Horsas to carry the 319th Field Artillery Battalion, who arrived in and around the LZ after dark on the 6th under heavy fire, but were soon in action. The re-supply for the 101st Airborne on D-Day + 1 also involved Membury, but it was by the 442nd TCG moved forward from Fulbeck because of base limitations. 56 C-47s took off in poor weather, and most dropped successfully but on the wrong DZ, the supplies being either lost or retrieved by the 82nd Airborne. One para-pack was prised loose by a crew chief hanging out of the aircraft with the radio operator hanging onto his ankles! The 436th TCG followed up with small scale glider and parachute supply drops very successfully and received a Distinguished Unit Citation for their efforts during *Overlord*.

In July a detachment of C-47s from the 436th went to Italy for Operation *Anvil/Dragoon*, paratroops and glider-borne troops being flown to positions inland from the assault beaches on August 15, to cut communications and isolate the German troops. After several re-supply missions and drops to Allied forces in northern Italy, the elements of the 51st

TCW returned to Britain late in August to prepare for the next major operation, *Market Garden*. Reverting to the 53rd TCW, the 436th flew the 506th PIR to a DZ near Zon in the Eindhoven sector to capture the vital Wilhemena Canal crossing on September 17 and three days later they were involved in a freight re-supply for the 82nd Airborne near Nijmegen. The final *Garden* mission from Membury was on D + 6 when gliders were towed to the same sector.

The 436th TCG now reverted to cargo transport work between Britain and France interspersed with more glider and paratroop training. They were working up for the Rhine crossings when they left Membury for Melun in France on February 25 1945, the airfield then lying dormant while equipment was transferred and the base tidied up, prior to takeover by No 47 Group, Transport Command, RAF. All Americans had left by mid-June and it was planned to re-open as RAF Membury on July 1 but this had to be delayed because of the poor condition of the station. The Dakotas of No 525 Squadron moved in from Lyneham on July 15 and with the arrival of No 187 Squadron in September the station prepared for its next major task; long range trooping to and from India which started on October 1 using procedures developed at Merryfield.

In February 1946, restrictions on the all-up weight of Dakotas cut the maximum load to 17 troops, later further reduced to 14 on the Istres-Castel Benito sector of the route, and with the availability of long-range four-engined transports the trooping commitment

ceased on March 17. The squadrons took over Continental mail and newspaper schedules which involved up to nine aircraft a day, increased further when they took over the Down Ampney task. On April 1 1946, Membury and its units transferred to No 46 Group, ten Dakotas from No 187 Squadron being detached to Bari to give support to the British occupation forces in July. Both Squadrons left during October 1946, No 187 to Netheravon and No 525 to Abingdon. Membury was closed and put on C&M parented by Welford. In April 1947 it became an inactive site, but was seriously considered as one of the SAC bases being built in the United Kingdom. It was rejected because of runway orientation problems, Greenham being chosen instead.

The Campbell Aircraft Ltd of Hungerford used Membury for flight testing their gyrocopters in the mid-1960s and moved in their workshops during 1967. Tests on the Campbell Cricket commenced in 1969, production building up to two per week before the company closed down in 1976.

Despite the M4 motorway crossing the northern end and the construction of a service area on it, Membury remains the most complete of Berkshire's 'hostility only' airfields with the possible exception of Welford. Many of the technical and communal site buildings remain, some in

Below *Seen in October 1982 from one of the old 'loop' dispersals is a 'T2' and silos belonging to Ridgeway Grain Ltd.*
Bottom *One of the many Maycrete finished buildings at Membury still in use—by light industry.*

use for light industry, while the control tower is an office block, and two of the hangars are used for storage/grass drying. Aircraft and glider overhaul has occupied the attentions of several small firms and private groups since the collapse of Campbell's and a limited amount of flying takes place from part of the runways.

Merston, West Sussex

SU885030. 1½ miles SE of Chichester off A259

Merston spent the whole of its active existence as a satellite of Tangmere. Only 2½ miles south-west of the main airfield the site was surveyed early in 1939 and the land requisitioned in July. Development included semi-permanent domestic quarters near Marsh Farm, administration and technical accommodation, the latter near the large nursery gardens on the west side of the airfield. A 30 ft (9 m) perimeter track encircled the roughly rectangular grass field.

By the time Merston was ready the Battle of Britain had come and gone. The autumn rains waterlogged the ground so its opening was delayed until the Spring of 1941 by which time six Over-Blister hangars and some fighter blast pens had been added. Established to operate one fighter squadron of the Tangmere Wing its first occupant, No 145 Squadron arrived on May 7 equipped with cannon-firing Spitfire IIbs, but was replaced on July 28 by No 41 Squadron which soon received Mk Vbs for *Rhubarbs*, the curiously named low level sweeps over occupied France.

No 41 Squadron moved to the West-hampnett satellite in December, probably because Merston was again suffering waterlogging, but returned on April 1 1942 and added bomber escort for raids over France to its repertoire. No 131 Squadron joined the Tangmere Wing in May, and operated from Merston making

Spitfire Vbs of No 131 Squadron at Merston, June 1942 (RAF Museum P1654).

it a two-squadron base for the summer, No 412 (RCAF) Squadron replacing No 41 in June for a hard working period of bomber escorts.

For Operation *Jubilee*, on August 19 1942, No 412 (RCAF) Squadron moved to Tangmere leaving No 131 alone at Merston. Their first sortie was a scramble to intercept aircraft approaching the south coast—which proved to be a Boston under attack by German fighters. It ditched off Shoreham and No 131 found itself escorting a Walrus to rescue the crew. At 08:50 hours the squadron was over the ships with the 309th FS of the USAAF giving low cover. They were continually harassed by Fw 190s but were able to claim one for no loss. An escort to Bostons of Nos 88 and 107 Squadrons around midday was followed by a top cover mission during which three Do 217s were intercepted. Two were destroyed and the other damaged. The day was rounded off by another scramble from Merston intercepting an incoming raid plotted off Selsey Bill. A motley collection of Luftwaffe bombers was soon spotted and No 131 Squadron waded in, shooting down a Ju 88 and badly damaging two Do 217s. One Spitfire was hit by return fire but managed a crash landing near Selsey. It had been a long and very mixed day, but No 131 Squadron were very satisfied—they had not lost any pilots.

Immediately after the Dieppe affair, No 131 and 412 Squadrons moved across to Tangmere and the 307th FS of 31 FG, VIIIth AF took over Merston as USAAF Station 356. They flew their Spitfire Vbs on bomber escort until transfer to the XIIth AF for Operation *Torch*. Flying ceased at Merston when the Americans left but with the prospect of heavier aircraft operating from the satellite during the Second Front it was decided to weatherproof the airfield. An Airfield Construction Unit moved in and two Sommerfeld Track runways and 20 hard-standings were laid during the winter of 1942/43. Both strips extended outside the original perimeter track, the 4,776 ft (1,456 m) SW/NE runway cutting a minor road flanking the western side of the

airfield, and also required the extension of the perimeter track to the north-east. Increased accommodation was also provided, allowing a total strength of 80 officers and 1,200 non-commissioned personnel, of which 60 were WAAFs.

Merston re-opened in May 1943 for No 485 (RNZAF) Squadron which moved its Spitfire Vbs over from Westhampnett and continued its punishing bomber escort work with these outclassed aircraft. At the end of May they were joined by the Hurricanes of No 184 Squadron. They were Mk IV fighter-bombers recently fitted with rocket rails and used Merston while the pilots practised RP firing on the ranges off the coast. On June 12 Typhoons of No 174 Squadron, also on work-up, replaced the Hurricanes, but they too had gone by the end of the month, and when No 485 left for Biggin Hill in July there was a temporary lull at Merston. It came to an end on August 7 when Nos 402 and 416 (RCAF) Squadrons of the Canadian Digby Wing were attached to No 11 Group for *Roadstead* operations. Joined by No 118 Squadron from Westhampnett later in the month,

Above *Spitfire Vb of the 307th FS, 31st FG at Merston in August 1942—note the smart 'Blisters' in the background (IWM CH17420).*

Below *'Slim' Kenny, RCAF, sits on the wing of his No 181 Squadron Typhoon at Merston in March 1944 (P.E. Tickner via C.H. Thomas).*

they accompanied Coastal Beaufighters in shipping strikes—a very dangerous occupation. The experiment ceased in October, the Wing split up and Merston prepared for use as an accommodation airfield for the Tactical AF in readiness for the invasion of Europe.

In October 1943 a Typhoon Wing (Nos 181, 182 and 247 Squadrons) arrived from New Romney, the pilots much appreciating the superior living quarters in Shopwyke House. No 181, equipped with rocket-firing aircraft, got off to a bad start when four were despatched to attack targets of opportunity south of Paris on November 13. One Typhoon was lost to flak, another just disappeared, and a third had engine trouble and crashed into the

sea during the return flight. Accidents also took their toll, a particularly nasty one occurring while Nos 182 and 247 Squadrons were converting to the bomber role, when a 500 lb (227 kg) bomb was dislodged during landing, exploded on impact and completely destroyed the aircraft.

On November 15 1943 the Wing was renamed No 124 Airfield to indicate its mobile function and with its sister outfit at Westhampnett was soon escorting bombers, making fighter-bomber attacks on communication and airfield targets, and increasingly assaulting the strange constructions which became known as *Noball* sites—the V-1 launching pads.

No 124 Airfield moved to Hurn at the beginning of April and were replaced by No 145 Airfield from Perranporth. This Free French Wing (Nos 329, 340 and 341 Squadrons) flew Spitfire IXs and immediately started extensive sweeps over France, suffering an early blow on April 26 when the Wing Leader collided with a No 329 Squadron pilot and both were killed. The aircraft received bomb racks in May and after training, commenced dive bombing. On D-Day the Wing flew low-level cover over ships and the bridgehead, and the following day intercepted a formation of five Ju 88s north of Caen, shooting one down.

On June 22 the Frenchmen moved to Funtington and an ADGB Spitfire IX Wing (Nos 80, 229 and 274 Squadrons) replaced them for a few days before making way for No 142 Wing (Nos 30, 303 and 402 Squadrons). Their Spitfires concentrated on escort of No 2 Group bombers but only remained until the second week of August 1944. They proved to be the last flying units to occupy Merston. Air Traffic Control facilities were withdrawn on August 21, and, still parented by Tangmere, the airfield was reduced to C&M, a Works Flight moving in to remove the Sommerfeld mesh track and restore fences.

On March 16 1945 Merston was handed over to No 103 Wing of the Rear Element of SHAEF for use by Air Disarmament Units. They used the accommodation to house 700 men for a few weeks and with the airfield cleared local farmers were given permission to graze it. The ADU had left by the end of May 1945 and in November 1945, buildings were handed over to the Admiralty and Blister hangars used for the storage of piles of surplus equipment accumulating after the war.

The Blisters have long gone and the land has been carved up into separate fields but part of the perimeter track and a few derelict buildings remains as silent evidence of another 'hostilities only' fighter airfield.

Midhurst (Cowdray Park), West Sussex
See Cowdray Park

New Bembridge (Foreland), Isle of Wight
See Foreland

Newchurch, Kent
TR045315. 7 miles SSE of Ashford on minor road

The most northerly of the four ALGs built on Romney Marsh, the strip at Newchurch was on flat land immediately west of the village, bounded on the east and south by minor roads connecting Oak Farm, Newchurch and Brookes Farm, and skirting Wills' farmhouse on the western side. Two Sommerfeld Track landing strips were laid at right angles to each other, nearly on the N/S and E/W cardinal headings with their intersection on the easterly side of the ALG near the village.

Like other ALGs in the area Newchurch was provisionally selected and approved during the early summer of 1942, and fully surveyed in September when it was determined that it would need little grading but that scattered trees would need felling and telegraph wires burying. The Rectory and Brookes Farm were earmarked for accommodation, with the MT park at the Rectory and a dispersal at the farm. The site plans were with Fighter Command by the end of October and, with the full dispersal arrangements agreed early in December, authority for work to commence was given on the 13th with the object of completion by March 1 1943.

It was agreed with the War Agricultural Executive Committee that once the construction teams had left the site Newchurch could be used for grazing, but this was soon interrupted by the arrival of the newly formed No 125 Airfield on July 2 1943. Initially consisting of Nos 19 and 132 Squadrons from Bognor and Gravesend respectively, the Airfield was immediately thrust into the bomber escort business, mainly for USAF light and medium bombers operating over France from East Anglia bases—nothing new for the two Spitfire Vb squadrons who were old hands at the game.

Most of the squadron personnel lived in tents on the ALG to practice self-sufficiency and test the equipment, but during July Orchard House, Bilsington, was taken over as additional accommodation. Unusually for ALGs a decoy site was built at Burmarsh some three miles to the east. During August No 19 Squadron was replaced by No 602 also with Spitfire Vbs, and No 125 Airfield was further reinforced by the Hurricanes of No 184 Squadron. The latter did not operate much but No 602 did, flying extensively on sweeps and bomber escorts, starting on August 15 with a raid by 19 Marauders of the 323rd BG, VIIIth ASC, USAAF, on Abbeville marshalling yards which was little better than disastrous. One aircraft dropped a bomb in a field near Redhill on the way out and flak in the target area upset the formation so much that all the bombs missed by miles. Several of these early sorties were dicey in the extreme, an escort to 21 Marauders of the 322nd BG on August 27 being especially so. In poor weather the bombers could not find the target, and flew about aimlessly before returning minus one of their number and with the Spitfires extremely low in fuel.

On September 4 the Luftwaffe made one of its rare appearances during the withdrawal of 36 Marauders of the 387th BG from Courtrai marshalling yards and No 602 Squadron shot down a Fw 190 during the ensuing mêlée. Operation *Starkey* saw the airfield providing top cover for the invasion force, but there was no action for the tired Mk Vbs, soon to be replaced by the long-awaited Spitfire IXs. They became operational on October 8 during an attack on Chievres airfield by 72 Marauders of the 322nd, 386th and 387th BG, by which time both navigation and bombing had much improved.

No 125 Airfield moved to Detling on October 12 and the ALG was improved by the extension of taxiways and doubling of the number of Blister hangars to four, though Newchurch remained unusual in that no hardstandings were provided, the grass being firm enough for dispersed aircraft. Newchurch was re-opened in April 1944 with the arrival of No 150 Airfield, No 85 Group, 2nd TAF, a unit intended for Tempest operations. In practice this new aircraft had been delayed and only No 3 Squadron was operational on arrival, No 486 (RNZAF) joining them on May 1, while poor old No 56 Squadron had to make do with a mixture of Spitfire IXs and Typhoons.

Led by Wing Commander R.P. Beamont, DSO, DFC, and Bar (already well-known but to become famous as a test-pilot) the Airfield began operations with pairs of aircraft on shipping recces. As confidence in the Tempest grew they strafed transport and airfield targets in France and, by D-Day, now as No 150 Wing, they were really ready to take on the Luftwaffe. Much to the pilots' disgust, the Tempest squadrons were retained for air cover over the beach-head and saw little action though 56 Squadron

Spitfire Vbs of No 132 Squadron at Newchurch during the summer of 1943— the poor state of the Sommerfeld Track is evident (A.E. Tamblin via M. Garbett).

Spitfires were used for close escort of glider/tug combinations during the afternoon of June 6 and again on the 7th.

The Tempest pilots got their chance on D-Day + 2 when 24 aircraft from Nos 3 and 486 Squadrons made a sweep from Le Havre to Cherbourg. As they crossed the coast in a shallow dive to maintain speed through the coastal flak, GCI radar reported unidentified aircraft 15 miles (24 km) ahead. Beamont spotted them moments later, some 5,000 ft (1,524 m) below. Taking No 3 Squadron down he identified the 'bogeys' as Bf 109s just as they broke violently port. After a full 360 degree turn Beamont got on the tail of a Messerschmitt and with a long burst of cannon fire hit it amidships. The Bf 109 pitched into a dive, smoking badly, but at that moment the Tempest was hit, a large hole appearing in the starboard wing. Beamont pulled out of the fight and made his way carefully back to Newchurch where he landed safely. When the others returned the full score proved to be four Bf 109s shot down and two damaged, without loss—a good start.

No more opposition was met during subsequent patrols but on June 13 a V-1 flying bomb was seen in the air, heralding a new era for the Wing which was transferred to ADGB on the 18th to tackle this new menace. They had opened their score on the 16th, Flight Sergeant M. Rose of No 3 Squadron claiming the first one, and by the end of the day eleven had been destroyed. They were not easy targets however, for they were very much smaller than a standard single-seat fighter, were fast, and flew comparitively low at about 2,000 ft (610 m). To ensure sufficient fire-power concentration the Tempests had to close to about 600 ft (183 m) which was dangerous if the warhead exploded. With typical energy and decisiveness, Beamont requested permission to reharmonise the guns to concentrate fire at 900 ft (274 m) and, when this was refused, went ahead anyway. The result was improved scores and less damage to the attacker—plus a 'rocket' from Command HQ.

No 56 Squadron scored their first anti-*Diver* success on June 18 when Flight-Lieutenant Bateman-Jones got one using a Spitfire IX, but they were already being re-equipped and became operational on Tempests in July. Dealing with 'Doodle bugs' at night was even more difficult. The hard-pressed Newchurch Wing was given the job, but day fighter pilots were

not trained for night ops and on June 25 two night fighter pilots from the FIU, Ford, were sent to Newchurch to convert to Tempests and see if they were any more successful. After three nights of frustration and ribald comment during which the weather defeated all attempts to fly, they had their revenge, shooting down four V-1s during three sorties. Under radar control and in reasonable visibility, the V-1s were easy to find at night for flames issuing from the jet pipe could be seen for miles, but ranging was a problem until a special sight was developed. Then, despite losses from both weather and engine failure, some pilots showed a real aptitude for this nocturnal activity, the FIU detachment commander shooting down seven during the night of July 23/24!

At the peak of the 'Doodlebug' attacks, life was no picnic at Newchurch. The noise of gunfire from nearby artillery batteries, coupled with aircraft continually taking off made sleep nearly impossible. Shrapnel frequently fell on the tented camp sites and dispersals, a hazard to personnel and aircraft, but fortunately the tempo gradually slackened during August. With the worst over, the Wing left for a rest on September 23.

De-requisitioning was authorised on December 13 and work to remove traces of military occupation was soon underway, the site being returned to its owners during 1945. One of the most successful ALGs was soon little more than a memory, and there is now virtually no sign of the strip, except a double width gateway on the eastern boundary which probably indicates the main fuel bowser entrance to the field.

Newhaven, East Sussex

TQ454002. ½ mile SE of Newhaven town

The first visit by a military flying machine to this busy little port was probably the involuntary arrival of the Short S45 floatplane early in July 1912 following engine failure when Lieutenant Spenser Gray was on his way from Sheerness to Portsmouth for the Naval Review. His report did not produce any immediate interest, indeed there was none until the upsurge in U-boat activity following the German declaration of unrestricted submarine warfare made in February 1917. The need to strengthen the Portsmouth Group of RNAS stations then forced a re-survey of the south coast for new seaplane bases, and a five-acre stretch of shingle foreshore on the eastern

side of Newhaven harbour entrance was amongst the sites selected.

At the top of the shelving beach, some 15 ft (4.5 m) above normal high tide, a double-fronted wooden hangar was built with a concrete hardstanding from which a wooden slipway led down into the sea. The men's quarters were wooden Army huts on top of piles behind the hangar while the officers lived in a collection of buildings at Bishopstone, the Tidemill becoming the Mess. On the main base various huts served as workshops and stores, three old railway carriages acting as offices and crewroom.

RNAS Newhaven opened in May 1917 as an offshoot of the main Calshot base, equipped with four Short 184 floatplanes. Flying took place from the open sea, but protected by the long breakwater from all but south-easterly winds. The location did, however, suffer from a heavy swell and improved Dover Type 184s with strengthened floats were supplied as soon as available. They flew their monotonous 4-5 hours patrols from first light until dusk whenever the weather allowed, but with little obvious reward for their efforts.

By the end of 1917 the strength had reached six Shorts and with the formation of the RAF in April 1918 plans were made to extend the base and equip it with still more floatplanes. A new steel-framed hangar was erected alongside the original one, together with a second slipway, an MT shed and more permanent workshops. A six acre site north of the railway line was also obtained and became known as the drill ground but may occasionally have been used as a LG for visiting aircraft.

In May the existing unit at Newhaven became No 408 Flight and a second

Above A steel framed hangar joining the original wooden sheds at Newhaven. In front are the railway carriages used as flight offices and crew rooms (FAA Museum Short 36).

Above right An 'improved' Short 184 pulled up on the shelving beach at Newhaven in 1918 (G.S. Leslie/J.M. Bruce collection).

Right The much rarer Fairey Campania also operated from Newhaven—here an aircraft of No 242 Squadron is 'readied' late in 1918 (RAF Museum P9338).

Flight, No 409, was allocated to the base. By July the Short 184s had been joined by a small number of the similar-looking Fairey Campania. Patrols were usually flown between Dungeness and the Isle of Wight and convoy escorts maintained through the same area. They were generally uneventful but on July 7 the crew of a Short 184 spotted a torpedo track while escorting a convoy off Hastings. They held their breath as it just missed the leading ship and were then astounded to see the U-boat surfacing, presumably intent on finishing off the victim with gunfire, unaware of the seaplane escort. As Lieutenant E.M. Ackery turned in to attack they were spotted and the submarine crew scrambled desperately into the conning tower. The observer, Lieutenant Dangerfield, dropped the 112-lb (50-kb) bomb and saw it hit the water about 6 ft (1.8 m) from the U-boat hull—there was a tremendous explosion and oil started coming to the surface—but it was not credited as a kill.

No 409 Flight was made up to strength in August 1918 when No 242 Squadron,

RAF, was formed to administer the two Newhaven seaplane Flights and a landplane unit at Telscombe Cliffs. There were no more incidents of note before the Armistice when No 409 Flight was disbanded, but No 242 Squadron (and it is believed No 408 Flight) continued to operate from Newhaven and still had six Short 184s and three Fairey IIIB seaplanes at the end of 1918. During 1919 it slowly wound down and was finally disbanded on May 15, the station being closed in the autumn and the buildings auctioned early in 1920.

Typical of coastal seaplane bases, Newhaven had few moments of glory but put in much hard endeavour. No one will ever know how many ships and lives were saved by the mere presence of those frail seaplanes over British coastal waters during 1917/19. In August 1922 the Short Cromarty and an F5 flying boat visited Newhaven during a tour of possible south coast anchorages by the staff of the

Seaplane Development Flight, but it was not selected as a reserve mooring. The site of the RNAS station has been completely cleared and remains a stretch of shingle virtually surrounded by water—it is difficult to visualise its busy past.

New Romney (Littlestone), Kent
TR089275. 2 miles NE of New Romney on A259(T)

This strangely shaped aerodrome was opened on August 1 1917 when No 3 (Auxiliary) School of Aerial Gunnery was formed at Littlestone/New Romney to increase the training facilities available for observer pupils.

The main part of the aerodrome was built at St Mary's Bay north west of the New Romney to Dymchurch road and the outlet of the New Sewer, while a portion of the triangular Littlestone golf course, to the south-east of the road, and more popularly known as the Warren, was also taken in as a landing ground (*TR085264*). Three hangars, two workshops and two MT sheds were built on the north-east side of the main aerodrome together with extensive hutted accommodation, and a mixed collection of corps recce and day bomber aircraft were soon hard at work giving air firing practice to pupils. How the pilots coped with three public roads crossing the aerodrome, even in days of much lower traffic levels, is best left to the imagination. Presumably most flying was done from the Warren unless the wind direction prevented it—in any event it must have been a highly inconvenient place to operate from.

On March 9 1918 the unit became part of No 1 (Observers) School of Aerial Gunnery formed by amalgamation with No 1 (Auxiliary) School of Aerial Gunnery, Dymchurch/Pelmarsh. The new organisation used both aerodromes until November 1 when it concentrated staff, students and Bristol F 2Bs, DH 4s, DH 9s, RE 8s and the inevitable Avro 504Ks at New Romney, which had proved the better LG despite its obvious problems.

The work continued at a reduced tempo after the Armistice but when the size of the post-war RAF was finalized it was announced that New Romney would be closed. During September the School of Aerial Gunnery moved to Manston and in November 1919 pilots were ordered to avoid landing at New Romney unless in emergency. Soon afterwards it was in the hands of the Government Surplus Property Disposal Board.

With the establishment of regular air services from Croydon to Paris and Brussels, civil ELGs were opened at intervals along the route. Lympne was the south coast customs airfield, but it was considered desirable to have a weather diversion available near by, and part of the Littlestone aerodrome was chosen. The Romney, Hythe and Dymchurch miniature railway had been laid across the original field during 1925 and so it was a rough rectangle of grassland inland of the track just north of Jesson Farm and St Mary's Bay station which was developed as the ELG.

Littlestone was maintained by the Directorate of Civil Aviation and came under the control of Lympne until the mid-1930s when, with larger and more reliable aircraft on the route, it was no longer considered necessary and became a private LG. It closed before the outbreak of war and has reverted to farmland. The part of the 1917-19 aerodrome between the railway and the main road is now covered by housing and a holiday camp while the Warren quickly returned to being a golf course, and remains one today.

New Romney (Honeychild), Kent
TR063269. 1½ miles N of New Romney off minor road

With the rejection of the coastal Dymchurch/New Romney site as a fighter ALG early in 1942, a new survey of the area was made and some 400 acres of farmland between St Mary-in-the-Marsh and the New Sewer (one of the main Marsh drainage channels) was chosen. Provisionally accepted in July 1942 it was fully surveyed in September when it was reported as having good approaches but poor cover, needing little grading but requiring telegraph wires to be buried. The main problem was expected to be the numerous streams dividing up the site which would need extensive piping and infill. Accommodation was comparatively lavish, Honeychild Manor being available for a communal site while several Army huts, currently occupied by a searchlight battery, would be sufficient for 50 men. There were also four cottages and a large galvanised steel shed near the Manor.

The plans were revised to allow realignment of the SW/NE landing strip so that the intended tent sites could be near the only road access but the final go-ahead was given on December 19 1942 and it was intended to complete the work by March 1 1943, so that New Romney could be used for training new mobile squadrons. Because of the impossibility of camouflage a decoy site was laid out at Romney Salts in the hope of confusing possible attackers.

With two Sommerfeld Track runways laid in the form of a cross the ALG was ready for occupation when the first TAF units were officially designated, No 124 Airfield arriving from Appledram on July 2 1943. The Typhoons of Nos 181 and 182 Squadrons were quickly dispersed around the field and the numerous vehicles used by these mobile squadrons were hidden in and around Honeychild Manor Farm which was taken over as the MT yard. The fighter-bombers, or 'Bomphoons' as the Press insisted on calling them, were joined by fighter 'Tiffies' of No 247 Squadron a week later when conditions were still chaotic in the camping sites due to the

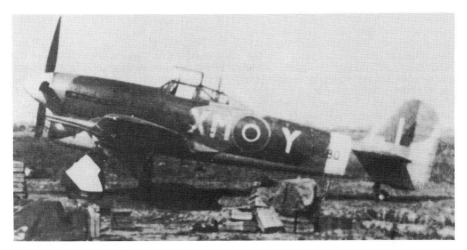

Typhoon 1b JP380 of No 182 Squadron amongst piles of fuel cans and other stores at New Romney (RAF Museum P1627).

effects of heavy rain. Operating as a Wing the three squadrons started dangerous anti-shipping strikes, No 247 Squadron being responsible for flak suppression while Nos 181 and 182 went in fast and low before pulling up and into a dive to drop their 500-lb (227-kg) bombs at point blank range.

In August No 247 Squadron spent a week at Attlebridge for Exercise *Snaffle* and then found themselves trying to stop the Luftwaffe fighter-bomber raids on south coast towns while their 'Bomphoon' brethren carried out similar *Rhubarbs* over the Continent, No 182 Squadron even trying a few raids at night. Rail and road communications, airfields and army camps, were the targets for dive bombing during September after the unsuccessful Operation *Sharkey*, but with the weather worsening it was time to find better quarters and No 124 Airfield moved to Merston early in October after a successful summer practising working from an airstrip. It had not been without losses of course, some of them accidents on the airfield. Perhaps the most spectacular was that of a No 182 Squadron aircraft which was stalled on the approach, and cartwheeled across the airfield shedding a wing, the tail and the engine. The pilot finished up on his back still firmly strapped to his seat and with nothing more than a few bruises! Less fortunate were two pilots of No 247 Squadron who collided over the airfield on August 15.

During the autumn refuelling hardstandings and a partial taxi track were built, and four Blisters erected, but New Romney remained a reserve ALG for the invasion of Europe, probably because of its exposed position. It was used to house ground signals units waiting to cross to France, and a servicing party to deal with emergencies. They had little trade and unfortunately were unable to do anything for one of their customers, a B-24 Liberator of the 466th BG which crash-landed with battle damage on July 17 1944 following the first tactical bombing operation over France by the VIIIth AF.

On November 1 1944 Honeychild Manor was damaged by fire, but soon afterwards New Romney ALG was de-requisitioned, a Works Flight spending some weeks clearing the site of steel mesh tracking, Blisters and the other paraphernalia required on even the most rudimentary airfield. The land was handed back to its owners during 1945, quickly reverting to farmland. There is now no evidence at New Romney of the ALG except some culverted streams and ditches. A slightly more permanent reminder is provided by the naming after the war of the Station Commander's house at Biggin Hill as *Romney*.

Odiham, Hampshire

SU740491. 6½ miles ESE of Basingstoke alongside A32

Soon after No 13 Squadron moved into Andover in June 1924 its crews were tasked with photographing large areas of the surrounding countryside to identify suitable exercise landing grounds. One of the more promising fields was on Down Farm, a mile south-west of Odiham town. It was particularly favoured because it was within easy travelling distance of Aldershot and R/T range of Farnborough, where communication experiments were being made. After inspection of the field by the CO, the land was purchased by the Air Ministry for use as a Summer Camp LG during exercises with the Army.

For a camp a fleet of lorries conveyed the equipment from Andover, tents being positioned on either side of the track between Down Farm and Snatchangers Farm for personnel and stores, while Bessoneaux canvas hangars were erected for the aircraft—simulating field conditions. From 1926 onwards the Farnborough-based No 4 Squadron shared the camps with No 13, both equipped with the ancient Bristol Fighter, then the rather unsuccessful AW Atlas, and finally the excellent Hawker Audax.

As the Expansion Scheme of the 1930s took effect, more airfields were needed and Odiham was a natural early selection. The Air Ministry purchased another 150 acres to add to the LG and the contractors, Lindsey Parkinson Ltd, began work in 1934 to clear the site for a three-squadron Army Co-operation airfield. The usual compact technical and domestic areas were built near the Alton road (A32) to the north-west of the roughly circular airfield, the buildings including tastefully designed Messes and 'H'-type barrack blocks, SHQ and technical stores, dominated by three 'C'-Type hangars. Construction work went well being finished by Christmas 1936 at a cost of £315,000, and RAF Odiham was handed over to No 22 Group on December 3, for use by No 50 (AC) Wing HQ—the first Home Establishment use of the Wing organisation since 1922.

Nos 4 and 13 Squadron's move to Odiham was completed in the middle of February 1937 despite the mud and water which were a permanent feature of that winter. The weather improved as the Audaxes were replaced by Hectors during May but whether the aircraft change was also for the better is open to doubt. Certainly the unfamiliar engines were temperamental and gave a great deal of trouble but the annual round of exercises with the Aldershot Command were soon under way, artillery spotting, recce, photography and ground strafing being the main occupations.

The station had more than its fair share of visitors, the inevitable result of being within easy travelling distance of London, but perhaps the most unlikely VIP of all visited on October 18 1937. This was General Erhard Milch, the German Secretary of State for Air, who came officially to open RAF Odiham, certainly the first time this honour had been afforded to a Luftwaffe officer—and despite changed circumstances, probably the last.

The following winter saw the arrival of a very odd-looking Whitley from RAE Farnborough. It had a massive beam

Above right *Blenheim IVs of No 59 Squadron lined up by the signals square at Odiham mid-1939—incidentally proving that runways existed there pre-war* (Group Captain J. Butterworth via Chaz Bowyer).

Below right *With the declaration of war No 59 Squadron changed its codes but the Blenheims still equipped the unit mid-1940* (M.D. Howley via A.S. Thomas).

Below *Audax of No 4 Squadron at Odiham in 1937 with newly completed station buildings of a typical 'expansion scheme' station in the background* (M. Purcell via A.S. Thomas).

mounted across the standard main under-carriage oleo legs carrying oversize Dunlop wheels—its object to test whether new bomber pattern grass-surfaced air-fields would be capable of sustained operations by the heavier aircraft under development. Trials began on January 4 1938 and immediately hit trouble, the aircraft becoming bogged down. Pulled on to firmer ground, it was successfully taxied at 24,000 lb (10,886 kg), later increased to 40,000 lb (18,144 kg) before being refitted with a standard under-carriage and flown back to Farnborough.

On April 8 1938 No 50 (AC) Wing was brought up to strength with the arrival of No 53 Squadron Hectors and it was this unit which took the brunt of the re-equip-ment upheavals at Odiham during January 1939. They took delivery of their first twin-engined Blenheim IV bombers while Nos 4 and 13 received the long-awaited Lysander. Much was expected of the latter, a high-wing monoplane with an impressive array of slow flying devices. Unfortunately, although certainly a great improvement on the Hector, it was a poor fighting machine, and over-enthusiastic pilots showing off its slow flying capabili-ties became involved in a number of acci-dents.

The waterlogging experienced during the first year of operation resulted in Odiham becoming one of the first airfields with concrete runways, these being ready by the spring of 1939.

Conversion of No 53 Squadron was rather slow, but their Hectors had all left by the end of June 1939 and the whole of No 50 (AC) Wing was on a mobilisation exercise in August—which became the real thing on the 23rd! No 4 and 13

Squadrons, earmarked for service with the BEF were put on immediate standby, packed and ready to go by September 3. In fact they waited restlessly for two weeks before their ground parties marched out of the camp to Hook station en route for Portsmouth and the Somme. The Lysanders left a few days later, having been beaten by No 53 Squadron which went to Plivot on the 18th.

Additional personnel, including the first WAAFs for duty in messes, stores and administration sections, now arrived followed by two ex-Auxiliary AF squadrons, No 613 with Hinds and No 614 with Hectors on October 2. The following day No 614 Squadron was split, *B* Flight becoming 614A which on October 11 became No 225 Squadron, equipped with Lysanders. No 613 Squadron converted to Hectors during November 1939 and all three were heavily engaged on exercises with the Army throughout the winter whenever the weather allowed. In March 1940 No 613 received some Lysanders, and when the German breakthrough came on May 10, both squadrons ferried reinforcement Lysanders to Amiens-Glisy to provide extra spotting aircraft for British and French gunners. No 613's remaining Hectors were detached to Hawkinge and carried out very gallant supply drops to the defenders of Calais later in the month.

During June No 613 Squadron was engaged in dawn and dusk patrols of a section of the south coast checking for infiltrators, while Nos 225 and 614 carried out the same task elsewhere. They were replaced at Odiham by the Blenheims of No 59 Squadron returned from France and No 110 (RCAF) City of Toronto Squadron who brought their Lysanders in from Old Sarum. No 59 Squadron soon went to Thorney Island and the Canadians were further strengthened when the Royal Montreal Regiment took over station defence until replaced by the Canadian Holding Company in August. No 110 (RCAF) Squadron spent the next months training hard with local Army units, using Lysanders supplied by the RAF, including one fitted experimentally with two 20 mm cannon.

After the fall of France scores of Belgian and French airmen arrived in Britain by a variety of unorthodox means, and No 1 Fighter Training Squadron of the Free French was set up at Odiham on August 3 equipped with a motley collection of liberated French aircraft,

mainly Bloch 151 and Dewoitine 520 fighters. Five days later they were visited by General de Gaulle, but the plan to operate a Free French squadron in Britain fell through and it went overseas instead.

The first German aircraft were seen on August 10 and two days later the airfield was a briefed target for an early morning raid by Ju 88s of KG54. They were intercepted by No 43 Squadron, however, and harried so much that they lost cohesion and missed their target. Indeed, the only attack which did develop was on the 15th, and that was a mistake—Ju 88 crews of LG1 being under the impression that they had attacked Andover! Little damage was sustained but a decoy was built at Froyle, some 3½ miles to the south.

On November 2 1940 the Franco-Belgian FTS was formed with 12 Magisters as basic equipment and a hotch-potch of more advanced types, including Lysanders and Blenheims, for service training. British accents were very much in the minority and few at Odiham knew, or cared, that the unit had been transferred from No 22 (AC) Group to No 70 Group on December 1 as part of the newly formed Army Co-operation Command. Accommodation was very tight as French and Belgian escapees continued to gather and many of the Canadians spent the winter in a tented camp set up at Long Sutton, 1½ miles to the south, with the more fortunate living at the Manor House in comparative comfort.

Meanwhile, the airfield was being turned into a vast building site as work started on re-laying the runways and providing a meandering perimeter track to connect them with the main hardstanding outside the hangars. While the work was progressing a Ju 88 jettisioned 12 bombs in the vicinity to get away from a Hurricane on March 23 1941, and three days later another was fired on by the gun defences as it flew low over the camp, but the station was not deliberately attacked—its charmed life continued!

No 110 (RCAF) Squadron was renumbered No 400 (RCAF) in March 1941 to avoid confusion with the RAF unit, the ineffective Lysander being replaced in April by the Tomahawk, an American aircraft which had not impressed as a fighter but possessed a good low-level performance. The runways were tested by a Havoc on May 17 but were not considered long enough, proposals for extensions immediately being discussed, while the Franco-Belgian FTS disbanded at the end of May because the flow of new recruits from the Continent had now slowed to a trickle which could easily be absorbed by RAF training schools.

Odiham transferred to No 71 Group, the operational component of the Command, in June 1941 and welcomed back an old friend when No 13 Squadron brought its Lysanders in from Hooton Park. Conversion to the Blenheim IV started immediately, though the last Lysander lingered until September.

More land to the east and north was acquired and a temporary runway laid while work, which involved the demolition of Isnams farmhouse, was pressed forward, further runway extensions having been authorized in September. When completed by an Airfield Construction Unit in 1942 the main E/W runway was 5,100 ft (1,554 m) in length, the SW/NE strip was 4,200 ft (1,280 m) but the SE/NW runway had been abandoned and was in use as an access track.

No 400 Squadron carried out its first operation on November 6 when two Tomahawks attempted a reconnaissance over France. It was spoilt by lack of cloud cover but the squadron steadily built up experience during the winter of 1941/42, while No 13 concentrated on low-level

A nice oblique of Odiham taken during October 14 1942 and revealing many aircraft scattered about on the grass in front of the hangars (RAF Museum W13/6/8).

bombing, gas spraying and smoke laying. More WAAFs arrived in January 1942 and were accommodated in The Priory, a large house in the main street of the town, some of them working at Clump House which was used as a hospital.

When the 1,000 Bomber raids planned by Bomber Command were agreed the net had to be flung wide to make up the numbers and even No 13 Squadron found itself involved. They joined No 2 Group Blenheims on diversionary intruder raids for the first two attacks, but for the third, five aircraft flew up to Wattisham and set off to bomb Bremen, the primary target. Four claimed success, the fifth being shot down over the Dutch-German border.

The units at Odiham underwent rapid changes during the summer of 1942. Tomahawks of the newly-formed No 171 Squadron arrived in July followed by the Blenheim IV/Vs of No 614 Squadron late in August. No 400 Squadron converted to the very effective Mustang 1 during July and were soon in action, the unit being detached to Gatwick in August for Operation *Jubilee*. No 13's Blenheims were also involved in *Jubilee*, going to Thruxton where longer runways allowed maximum take-off weights—enabling them to use their smoke laying expertise to the full. No 400 Squadron flew 20 recce sorties during August 19, alongside three other Army co-op Mustang squadrons. Operating in pairs, the aircraft covered the rear areas behind Dieppe checking German movements, and losing one

aircraft on the very last mission. When the operational units returned, No 171 Squadron moved back to Gatwick and No 13 Squadron rapidly converted to Blenheim Vs, ready to leave with No 614 on November 16 for North Africa and Operation *Torch*.

No 400 Squadron were joined at Odiham by two more Army Co-op Mustang units, Nos 168 and 239 Squadrons, but any idea of operating as a Wing was quickly dispelled by No 400 moving to Dunsfold and No 239 Squadron to Hurn early in December 1942. No 168 Squadron concentrated on Channel shipping and coastal targets, joined by the Hurricane IIbs of Nos 174 and 175 Squadrons in December 1942 and January 1943 respectively. The Hurricanes did not stay long, more Mustangs appearing during May/June 1943 when Nos 170, 268 and elements of No 2 Squadron moved in to join No 168 Squadron. On June 1 1943 Odiham and the based units transferred to Fighter Command, No 123 Airfield HQ arriving on the 21st and camping in the old bomb dump. On July 10 it took charge of all three Mustang units and became fully mobile on a new site to the north-east of the airfield. The task remained Tac/R, the Mustangs scouring northern France for radar stations, enemy HQs and supply bases. Night intruder and even interception patrols also added spice to life, but there was much shuffling of units and when Fighter Command was split into the 2nd TAF and ADGB on November 15 the units at Odiham were Nos 2 and 4 Squadrons. They moved out the next day to make way for No 511 Forward Repair Unit which arrived from Henlow and received its first aircraft for repair on December 4—a Spitfire IX of No 315 Squadron.

Two Typhoon units, Nos 181 and 247 Squadrons, spent a fortnight at Odiham at the beginning of 1944 for intensive attacks on *Noball* sites, and in February No 400 Squadron returned to complete a change-over from Tac/R Mustang to PR Mosquito/Spitfires. They were joined briefly by the Typhoons of No 184 Squadron working up after converting from Hurricanes, and the No 6 Mobile Field Photographic Section. No 400 Squadron restarted operations with Spitfire PR XIs and Mosquito PR XVIs in March, and was joined at the end of the month by Nos 168, 414 and 430 Squadrons which formed No 128 Airfield of No 83 Group, 2nd TAF, all living under canvas at Broad Oak

and Long Sutton. The Mustangs of the three Tac/R units added escort work for Spitfires and Typhoons to their other duties, recording the damage done by the strike aircraft. The Airfield became No 128 Wing on May 15 as operations intensified prior to the invasion of Europe.

The task of No 511 FRU gradually increased during 1944, personnel numbering nearly 3,000 by May, though not all at Odiham, for detached servicing parties were working on Halifax, Stirling and Albemarle glider tugs elsewhere, in readiness for Operation *Overlord*. Spitfire, Typhoon and Wellington modifications were top priority, and it was at this time that the 'T2' hangar on the south side, and another near Snatchangers Farm, were erected to give additional covered working areas for maintenance crews. The airfield was jammed with aircraft and personnel, and it was a relief when the camp was closed to outside contact—and it was obvious that D-Day was near.

The whole of No 128 Wing was very active on June 6, No 168 Squadron alone flying 36 Tac/Rs in support of the landings during 18 hours of continuous activity. Four Mustangs of No 430 Squadron were intercepted by six Fw 190s in the Evreux area and an aircraft was lost—this level of operations and losses continuing daily—relieved only by bad weather. On June 28 No 430 Squadron flew over to Normandy to operate from B-8, a dusty strip ripped out of farmland near Sommervieu, Bayeaux. They were followed by No 168 Squadron and Spitfires of No 400 Squadron, the Mosquitoes remaining at Odiham until August 14 when they left with No 414 (RCAF) Squadron, to catch up with what was now known as No 39 (Recce) Wing.

These moves did not reduce activity at Odiham very much for the work of No 511 FRU continued to mount, and No 130 Wing moved in from Gatwick on June 27, Nos 2 and 268 Squadrons operating Tac/R Mustangs while No 4 was equipped with Spitfire XIs. The HQ unit was renamed No 35 (Recce) Wing early in July when the Mustang pilots were searching for signs of enemy troop reinforcements, bunkers and transport parks, often flying 50-60 sorties a day, and No 4 Squadron continued to update the photo coverage of the Wings' sector of Normandy. No 2 Squadron departed for B-10 Plumetot at the end of July, followed by No 268 in August, when it was flying Typhoons operationally alongside Mustangs. A few days later No 4 moved its Spitfires to the Continent, and with part of No 511 FRU also crossing the Channel in the wake of the 2nd TAF, the pace at Odiham became a little less hectic.

Like all airfields in the south-east, Odiham received unexpected visitors throughout 1944 and up to the end of the war. Both Bomber Command and VIIIth AF aircraft lobbed in, damaged, lost, or short of fuel, the numbers building up considerably during the tactical bombing of France by the heavies in June/July 1944.

It was a strange feeling with no operational units present, unrelieved by the appearance of No 1516 (BAT) Flight, who moved in during mid-September. A few days later however No 96 Squadron arrived from Ford, their Mosquito NF VIIIs intended for anti-*Diver* operations. Previously one of the most successful units against these targets the Squadron found little trade from Odiham and disbanded on December 12 1944.

Meanwhile No 511 FRU, its main work done, disbanded on November 28, the remnants joining repair organisations on the Continent. No 604 Squadron, fresh from a rest at Predannack, spent most of December at Odiham, joined by the other No 147 Wing unit, No 264 Squadron on the 19th. Their Mosquito NF VIIIs carried out some patrols over Belgium and Holland, one crew shooting down a Ju 88. At the end of the year No 147 Wing moved to B51 (Lille/Vendreville), leaving Odiham with just the Oxfords of No 1516 BAT flight in residence.

Dunsfold was taken over as a satellite in January 1945 but activity at Odiham remained slight until ex-PoWs started to flood in by the Dakota load during April —for medical check-ups, re-kitting and documentation before being sent on leave.

On June 7 1945 the airfield was transferred from Fighter (No 11 Group) to Transport Command (No 46 Group) and the SHQ staff of Blakehill Farm moved in en bloc, joined three days later by No 233 Squadron. Their Dakotas flew to and from the Continent on regular schedules, supplemented in August by a six-aircraft detachment from No 437 (RCAF) Squadron. Among the items carried out were medical supplies, petrol and food, while they returned with troops and, it is said, the infamous collaborator 'Lord Haw Haw' who had nightly broadcast propaganda in English from Germany

throughout the war. No 233 Squadron found themselves on their way to the Far East on August 23 but were replaced by No 271 Squadron at the end of the month, both passenger and freight services being maintained.

In October 1945 it was No 271 Squadron's turn to depart, clearing the way for the whole station to be transferred to the RCAF on the 21st. Early in November No 120 (RCAF) Wing moved in to control Odiham and Down Ampney and No 437 (RCAF) Squadron arrived on the 15th leaving a detachment at B56 Evere to operate a shuttle service between the two airfields for Canadian units on the Continent. No 436 (RCAF) Squadron arrived from Down Ampney on April 4 and the two Dakota units continued schedules until suddenly disbanded, Odiham being handed back to the RAF on June 28 1946 as a No 11 Group unit in the Southern Sector.

During July three fighter squadrons moved in, Nos 54 and 247 Squadrons from Chilbolton with Tempest IIs and Vampire F 1s respectively, and No 130 Squadron from Manston with Spitfire IXs. This strange collection of aircraft did not last long, however, for after spending most of September at Molesworth, No 54 Squadron returned to join No 130 in converting to the Vampire F 1, the latter unit hardly completing training before it was re-numbered No 72 Squadron. The first Vampire Wing in the RAF, Odiham received the much improved Vampire F 3 in 1948, No 54 Squadron going on a goodwill tour of Canada and the USA in July, thus achieving the first jet fighter crossing of the Atlantic. Only just though, for 16 F-80A Shooting Stars of the 56th FG, USAF flew into Odiham from the States later that same month. Not to be completely outdone No 72 Squadron took its F 3s to an international meeting at Luxembourg and gave several displays of high speed aerobatics. At the end of 1949 the Wing was again upgraded with the FB 5 variant of the Vampire.

No 72 Squadron took its Vampire 5s to North Weald in March 1950 replaced by No 421 Squadron, RCAF, which picked up its loaned Vampires in January 1951 for ten months' training with the RAF prior to conversion to the Sabre back in Canada. Nos 54 and 247 Squadrons converted to Meteor F 8s during 1951/52 and spent to next four years at Odiham on these delightful aircraft, taking part in Fighter Command and early NATO exercises. It was about this time that the E/W runway was extended eastwards to 6,000 ft (1,828 m) in length with operational readiness platforms (ORP) on each end, and a new hardstanding and 'T2' hangar were built on the south side to replace the six wartime Blisters which had originally been dispersed around the airfield.

In the spring of 1954, Nos 54 and 247 Squadrons moved out temporarily while Odiham was prepared for its most spectacular event, the Review of the Royal Air Force by Her Majesty the Queen on July 15. A huge tented town was erected on the south side of the airfield to house the 3,000 officers and men brought into Odiham to do the preparatory work, while on the parade square a Bessoneaux hangar was erected to provide extra messing facilities. The 1,200 Service personnel and 318 meticulously marshalled aircraft on parade represented every RAF Command in Europe and some Commonwealth units, while overhead flew 47 separate formations at 30-second intervals, starting with a single Sycamore helicopter and finishing with a Supermarine Swift. A grand total of nearly 1,000 aircraft, of which 641 were in the air —a spectacle which will assuredly not be repeated in Britain.

With the station returned to normal, No 46 Squadron was re-formed on August 15 1954 with a mixture of Meteor NF 12s and '14s, to provide a night fighter element in the Wing. A year later the day fighter squadrons both received their long awaited Hunters, the initial Mk 1s soon being replaced by F 4s and in 1957 by the much superior Mk 6—though more defence cuts meant the disbandment of No 247 Squadron at the end of the year. Meanwhile, No 46 Squadron pioneered the mighty delta-winged Javelin all-weather fighter in front-line service and was operating a mixed force of Mk 2 and 6 variants when it was decided to disperse the Wing and close Odiham as a fighter station. On July 15 1959 No 46 Squadron went to Waterbeach and No 54 to Stradishall, and Odiham was reduced to C&M.

It was re-opened in Transport Command on February 15 1960, as No 38 Group HQ (which moved in during May) and the main UK base for RAF transport helicopters. Initially these were in short supply, but No 225 Squadron arrived from Andover with a mixed collection of Sycamores and piston-engined Whirlwinds and were joined on May 30 by the Pioneer and Twin Pioneer STOL aircraft of No 230 Squadron, which behaved almost like 'choppers'.

The twin-rotor Belvedere, later aptly named the *Flying Longhouse* by Borneo natives, was nursed into service by a Trials Unit which formed on July 1 1960, and became the nucleus of No 66 Squadron on September 15 1961. Two months later No 72 Squadron re-formed on this medium lift 'chopper', followed by the third and last squadron, No 26, in June 1962. No 66 Squadron had already gone to FEAF in May 1962 and No 26 went to Aden the following March, leaving No 72 Squadron at Odiham for transport duties with No 38 Group. It brought a new dimension to helicopter operations in the RAF and its achievements were legion, though none required greater precision than the lowering into position of the 80 ft (24.4 m) spire of the new Coventry Cathedral, followed by the even trickier 'flying cross', which took a week to fix on top because the wind had to be just right.

No 225 Squadron was fully equipped with the turbine-engined Whirlwind Mk 10 at Odiham in March 1962, followed by No 230 Squadron in June, but neither stayed long. No 230 Squadron went to Germany in January 1963 and No 225 to Malaysia at the end of that year to take part in the Indonesian Confrontation.

Meanwhile, Twin Pioneers deposed from No 230 Squadron joined Odiham Station Flight in January 1963 as a small training element, but more significant was the Wessex Intensive Flying Unit formed on July 1. After working up the RAF Wessex HC 2, the unit became the nucleus of No 18 Squadron in January 1964 and the training organisations for the Twin Pioneer, Wessex and Belvedere amalgamated to form the Short Range Conversion Unit in August, its first major task being the conversion of No 72 Squadron to the Wessex.

When the fixed wing element finished in July 1967 the unit became the Helicopter Operational Conversion Flight, initially with Wessex only, joined by the new Puma in January 1971. Retitling continued, the unit becoming the Air Training Squadron in May and finally No 240 OCU on January 1 1972. Throughout these changes the basic Wessex pilot course remained about six weeks in length, involving ground school and 30 hours flying.

Changes amongst the operational squadrons were also fairly complicated.

No 18 Squadron moved to Germany in January 1965, allowing the return of No 230 Squadron towards the end of November so that its Whirlwinds could be employed teaching support helicopter techniques to the Army. In March 1969 No 230 Squadron moved its Whirlwinds to Wittering and No 18 Squadron arrived at Odiham from Acklington at the end of July. For a year the two Wessex squadrons shared the same base, operating many small detachments throughout the country, before No 18 Squadron returned to Germany in August 1970.

On June 14 1971 No 33 Squadron re-formed with Pumas, followed by No 230 which had a Puma element at Odiham from October that year, while the main unit continued to operate Whirlwinds from Wittering. The squadron was fully Puma-equipped by the end of January 1972 and after No 38 Group HQ moved to Benson in May and an extended building programme was completed in June, Odiham entered a stable period which lasted eight years.

No 72 Squadron grew into the biggest Army support unit in the UK, having two operational Flights and a HQ, the latter coping with training, navigational requirements and administration. Every conceivable task was undertaken, including transport of troops, carriage of underslung loads, medevac, casevac, aerial observation and photography. Nos 33 and 230 Squadrons was also divided into three Flights and were completely mobile, having the added advantage of being airportable. They were quickly on the scene when the Turks landed on Cyprus in July 1974, provided almost continuous support for the troops in Belize and went out to Rhodesia/Zimbabwe during the transfer of power in that unhappy country. In addition the Pumas take part in every exercise which involves the British Army, and share the UK Mobile Force commitment. These are the military tasks, but the Odiham helicopter crews have caught the public eye many times over the years whilst aiding local authorities.

After many years of prevarication, the order for heavy lift Chinook helicopters finally went through, and naturally Odiham became involved as delivery of the hardware got closer. A Chinook Servicing School was formed and a shuffle of flying units commenced. No 18 Squadron was chosen as the first operational user and was replaced in Germany by the Pumas of No 230

Squadron during the autumn of 1980. The first Chinook arrived at Odiham in December and entered service with No 240 OCU, which promptly detached its Wessex element to form a separate Training Flight at Benson. The OCU got on with the task of converting crews for No 18 Squadron which re-formed on August 4 1981 but as the number of Chinooks at Odiham increased space became a problem, and in December No 72 Squadron moved its Wessex to Aldergrove to concentrate on its anti-terrorist role in Northern Ireland.

The Falkand Islands crisis and the despatch of the Task Force in April 1982 gave the Chinooks their first big test, the squadron ferrying equipment and stores to the ships as they sailed down the English Channel. Three of the four Chinooks embarked in the ill-fated *Atlantic Conveyor* were lost when the ship was set on fire by an air-fired Exocet, but the one survivor, which happened to be on air test at the time, did sterling work during the land battles for the islands.

The second Chinook squadron formed on September 1 1982 as No 7. Initially it shared aircraft with No 18 but by mid-1983 it had its own machines, some detached to the Falklands. No 18 Squadron moved to Gutersloh and Odiham entered 1984 with No 7 (Chinook), 33 (Puma) squadrons and No 240 OCU (Chinook and Puma) as the based units, well able to support the claim made on the large board at the main entrance, *Home of the Battlefield Helicopters*. It maintains its close links with Odiham town and exercises its right to march through Basingstoke following the granting of the Freedom of the Borough in 1968. The heady days of the 1960s when crowds of aviation enthusiasts gathered each September to watch aircraft from many armed forces bringing in personnel for the SBAC Show at Farnborough are over—though the airfield still receives some rare visitors on these occasions. It has not opened its gates for many years—if it does it is well worth a visit.

Overton Heath, Wiltshire

SU180657. 2½ miles S of Marlborough alongside A345

The increasing congestion at Upavon late in 1939 as the Central Flying School expanded started a search for RLGs and amongst those chosen was a stretch of open heathland at Clench Common, high

above the Vale of Pewsey and the ancient town of Marlborough. Preparatory work went ahead with the declared intention of opening Overton Heath LG on October 1 1940, but it suffered badly from water-logging and remained closed until April 1941 when it was inspected by the AOC. during a visit to the CFS. It is unlikely that it boasted much more than a windsock and a runway controllers' van at this stage, but in October it was being con-sidered as the location of a flying training research and development unit under the legendary R. Smith-Barry, back in uniform as a Squadron Leader. This scheme fell through, the task going to the ECFS when it formed at Hullavington and Overton Heath was then checked, and

Above *This vertical of Overton Heath taken on November 4 1946 clearly shows the line of the two Sommerfeld Track runways though the steel mesh has been lifted* (DoE).

Below *One of the 'Blisters' at Overton Heath—still in use for farming purposes in 1983* (K.S. West).

rejected, as a night flying RLG. With waterlogging making it practically un-usable, it was redeveloped by laying run-ways and providing facilities for permanent occupation.

No 5 Works Squadron commenced lay-ing two Sommerfeld Track runways in February 1942 and seven hangars (two

standard and five Over-Blisters) were erected around the field. A communal mess, barrack huts and stores were built in the southernmost corner alongside the road between Clench Common and Wootton Rivers, the unit having an establishment of two officers, three SNCOs and 80 men.

The CFS became No 7 Flying Instructors' School on April 1 1942 and when Overton Heath re-opened Oxford twin-engined trainers were in use, some of them based on the RLG. With the closure of New Zealand Farm in November 1943 Overton Heath assumed greater importance and more personnel, resulting in improved medical facilities. Fortunately the latter were not required on New Years' Day 1944 when the RLG received its largest visitor—a B-17 Fortress of the USAAF which force-landed on the steel mesh runway, without injury to the crew.

For a time Oxfords of No 1537 BAT Flight were attached from Upavon but with the end of the war in Europe, and takeover of Lulsgate Bottom as a satellite of No 7 FIS in July 1945, the unit abandoned Overton Heath at the end of August. It was retained as an inactive site until June 1948 when handed over to the Ministry of Agriculture & Fisheries. It is now farmland with one of the Blisters still in use, and at least one defence bunker still buried in the hedge.

Palmarsh (Dymchurch/Hythe), Kent

See Dymchurch

Polegate, East Sussex

TQ581035. 3½ miles NW of Eastbourne

The upsurge in German submarine activity around the British Isles and particularly in the Channel, was responsible for the establishment of several airship stations during 1915. Search for a suitable site in Sussex ended with the choice of 142 acres of meadowland just south of Polegate village. It was sheltered and had good access by both road and rail, ideal for airship operation.

Work started early in 1915 but the site, which was low lying, proved a nightmare for the contractors, the large airship shed built by Arrol Ltd remaining waterlogged for the best part of a year, despite all attempts to drain it. Officially opened on July 6 1915, the accommodation was far from complete, the officers living in two thatched cottages at Wannock, while the ratings were dispersed in billets at Polegate, Wannock and Willington. Things slowly improved, however, and by the end of 1915 three SS-Type non-rigid Blimps were in operation carrying out daily patrols along the Sussex coast under the control of Dover Command.

Early in 1916 a second wood and corrugated iron hangar was completed and the 14 officers and 137 ratings were moved into wooden huts clustered around the famous Polegate windmill. A special airship, the *SS40*, was assembled at Polegate in June 1916, painted black for clandestine operations at night over France. Nicknamed the *Black Ship*, she went to Boubers-sur-Canche near Arras in July, and carried out several night recces over the lines, but was not used for its intended purpose—the dropping of agents in enemy territory.

Parachute trials were also conducted during July. After a number of dummy drops using the Calthorp *Guardian Angel,* Sir Bryan Leighton volunteered to do a live test which was completely successful and eventually led to the introduction of parachutes in airships and later, aircraft.

Meanwhile, work on the base continued, concrete roads and paths replacing the muddy tracks, while a Gas Plant and nine gas holders were installed alongside the hangars.

In 1917 Polegate was transferred to Portsmouth Command and the improved SS Zero airship was introduced, six being in service by the beginning of September when Admiral Sir Stanley Colville, Commander-in-Chief, Portsmouth, was given a short flight in one. While he was airborne a freshening wind caused a general recall and soon three airships were battling to reach the mooring lines. The Admiral was retrieved safely, with first-hand knowledge of some of the problems of operating the ships. Real trouble was fairly rare however, losses being confined to the *SS30* on November 27 1916, *SS16* on October 6 1917 and two ships, the *SSZ7* and *'10* on December 20.

Consternation of a different kind was caused by the arrival of WRNS in March 1918, but they settled in well, taking over clerk, cook, driver and fabric worker duties. The RAF took over Polegate in April 1918, although the airships remained on Admiralty charge and this re-organisation resulted in the Group HQ moving to the nearby village of Hankham.

The success of the SSZ type of airship

The SSZ 30 *in front of one of the airship sheds at Polegate* (G.S. Leslie/J.M. Bruce collection).

was daily demonstrated on patrols, but was highlighted by the record endurance flight by *SSZ39* on August 11 1918. Setting out from Polegate it stayed up for 50 hours 55 minutes, the engine running throughout, all going well until the final stage when a strong headwind caused anxiety and resulted in only a gallon (4.54 l) of fuel remaining on landing.

In October 1918, when 11 SSZ Blimps were in operation, No 10 Group, Warsash, took control of Polegate and its sub-stations at Slindon and Upton, but after the Armistice the amount of flying was cut drastically and in 1919 the base was closed down. The majority of the sectional wooden buildings were auctioned and the hangars were demolished, leaving only the transport repair shop which is still intact. The concrete roads have been used for the large housing estate which now covers the site and joins up Polegate and Willingdon.

Portsmouth, Hampshire

SU670035. 2 miles NE of city centre off A2030

In 1924 a Portsmouth City councillor floated a grandiose scheme for a seaplane base in Langstone Harbour, an international airport on Portsea Island and a separate municipal airport on Farlington Marshes. It was way ahead of its time and nothing happened until 1929 when the Government announced that aerodrome construction qualified for assistance from the Unemployment Grants Committee. The Portsmouth Corportation gratefully took this opportunity to establish a municipal airport as part of a land reclamation project at Portsea Island and purchased a 275-acre farm near Hilsea railway station as a site. Work on grading and draining the land, demolishing part of the city's old fortifications, filling in the moat, and removing trees and hedges continued for the next two years, the airport being officially opened by Sir Philip Sassoon, Under Secretary of State for Air, on July 2 1932. It boasted a 204-acre landing area of perfectly flat grass and a large hangar and terminal building on the south side giving easy access to the city and other towns in the area.

The Portsmouth, Southsea and Isle of Wight Aviation Co Ltd had already started a ferry service to Ryde using a Westland Wessex three-motor monoplane and were soon also flying to Shanklin and Shoreham, doing aerial photography and offering flying tuition, having converted the original farmhouse into a clubhouse.

The corporation was very keen to attract industry to the area and offered extremely good terms to Airspeed Ltd of York. In September 1932 the company accepted the offer and work started on a corporation-financed factory on the airport at the beginning of December. Airspeed moved in during March 1933 bringing with them the nearly complete AS5 Courier prototype, two half-finished AS4 Ferries and a large collection of tools and jigs. The company's very survival depended on the Courier and much was the relief when Flight Lieutenant G.H. Stainforth, the well-known Schneider Trophy pilot, pronounced himself impressed by its handling and performance after its first flight in April 11.

A large Air Pageant was held in July 1933 and during the following month International Airlines introduced their 'Western Air Express' between Croydon and Plymouth calling at Portsmouth and Southampton en route, a service much appreciated by senior naval personnel.

Jersey Airlines was formed in December and started using DH Dragons from Portsmouth, followed by Provincial Airways in January 1934, presenting the onlooker with a very busy scene. Another hangar was built and leased to Jersey Airlines while aircraft inspection work was undertaken in a large shed. Custom facilities were introduced, and the Air Ministry provided a portable wireless station.

Airspeed were already in financial difficulty, however—in modern parlance they had a cash-flow problem—but needed to expand to survive. Finance was arranged by the corporation and a controlling interest acquired by Swan Hunter and Wigham Richardson, the Wallsend shipbuilders, enabling the company to go public as Airspeed (1934) Ltd. For an attempted non-stop flight to India by Sir Alan Cobham using the Courier, his Aerial Pageant Handley Page W 10s were modified as tankers by Airspeed, but the company interest lay mainly in the promising Envoy. This enlarged twin-engined variant of the AS 5, flew on June 26 1934 and was an immediate success. Amongst purchasers were the PS & IoW Aviation Co who used it to link their local services with Paris, and a development was a dual control trainer version in which the Air Ministry was taking a tentative interest during 1935.

The Yapton Aero Club formed at Portsmouth in March 1935 and during 1936 the Langstone Harbour flying boat terminal scheme was again under serious consideration. But the airport gained more prominence and some notoriety from the attempt on August 20 by two Airspeed employees to steal a Courier and fly it to Spain where the civil war was raging. They stalled it on take-off and it crashed into trees on the northern boundary, one being killed and the other convicted of theft.

More small airlines had come, and some had gone, by the time the City Council voted against the Empire flying boat base, stating that the offered Government grant of £400,000 towards to cost was insufficient.

Airspeed at last received instructions to proceed with a batch of 50 Oxford trainers and the prototype flew for the first time on June 19 1937. Further extensions were made to the Airspeed complex to cope with further large orders for the aircraft, first deliveries being made in November 1937.

Jersey Airways started making calls at Portsmouth on its London-Jersey route in February 1938 and in August the Portsmouth AC received a contract to train Civil Air Guard pilots. Such was the enthusiasm engendered by this scheme that by the end of the year they had flown more CAG hours than any other club in the country.

With the outbreak of war in September 1939 the airport was requisitioned by the Air Ministry. The PS & IoW aircraft were evacuated to Wales, the staff left behind being retained by the re-organised company, now known as Portsmouth Aviation. They received contracts for the repair and overhaul of RAF aircraft, this work continuing throughout the war while Airspeeds accelerated production of the Oxford and continued work on a number of interesting prototypes including the ungainly Fleet Shadower and a single-engined trainer somewhat reminiscent of the Harvard.

At 21:00 hours on May 10 1940, an Air Ministry staff officer phoned the Airspeed factory to warn of possible paratroop attack. The stunned reaction to this message triggered a query about defence arrangements, which the company described as consisting of three single Lewis guns manned by RAOC personnel and satisfactory arrangements for the supply of further troops. Whether this mollified the Air Ministry officials is doubtful, but it is certain that neither they, nor the company, could do much about it except obstruct the airfield nightly.

In June 1940 the de Havilland Aircraft Co bought out the Swan Hunter shareholding in Airspeed, the staff hardly having time to digest this change before the airfield and factory became the target for the Luftwaffe—by accident. Just after 17:00 hours on July 11 'bogeys' were detected approaching the Isle of Wight from the south and turned out to be 12 He

111s escorted by 12 Bf 110s making for Portsmouth, their target presumable the naval dockyard. Both Flights of No 601 Squadron were sent up from Tangmere and were soon in a running dogfight led by Flight Lieutenant W. Rhodes-Moorhouse. The naval AA gunners joined in and the raid was completely disorganised, at least one Heinkel spreading his load over the airport.

The damage at Airspeed was not extensive but it was deemed sensible to move the project design team to Hatfield out of the front-line, wisely as it turned out, for though there were no obviously deliberate raids on the factory attacks on Portsmouth naval installations often meant stray bombs on or near the airfield and on April 9 1941 one man was killed. Oxford production continued apace while Horsa freight and weapons loading trials started, using some of the prototypes assembled in the factory from parts made elsewhere. Sub-contracted production by furniture factories was a feature of this large all-wood glider, the drawings for which flowed out of the main Portsmouth office in profusion, though comparatively few complete machines graced the airport. Most Horsas were assembled and test flown at RAF MUs.

It is believed that Portsmouth acted as a satellite for Thorney Island, resulting in a number of large aircraft using the field, but undoubtedly the most impressive sight was provided by four-engined Halifaxes towing Horsas from the grass on trials work. An ATC Gliding School, No 163, had been formed as early as October 1943 and continued operating throughout the rest of the war using rather smaller gliders, but the main activity remained Oxford production, the demand for which was insatiable.

With the end of the war Oxford production soon came to an end, the last of 4,411 built at Portsmouth being delivered on July 14 1945. Schemes to enlarge and improve the airfield by laying a tarmac runway fell through, the Portsmouth Corporation being divided on the need for an airport. Portsmouth Aviation, however, re-established itself and resumed charter work in April 1946 using a DH Rapide, while Airspeed kept themselves busy with a profitable venture—the conversion of Oxfords into six-seat passenger aircraft known as Consuls. The first was produced in March 1946 and 161 were built alongside Oxfords refurbished for sale to a number of overseas air forces, notably those of Burma and Turkey.

In June 1946 No 62 Group, Reserve Command, took over No 163 GS but three months later the ATC moved to Gosport and the last tentative link with the Services was broken. The Langstone Harbour Development Scheme again came up in 1947 when a committee headed by Lord Pakenham recommended it in preference to Southampton, but a strong lobby from the latter city plus Government objections to development so close to the important naval base resulted in its rejection.

The Portsmouth AC started operations in May 1947, coinciding with the first large public air display held at the airport since the war. A month later Portsmouth Aviation flew their Aerocar, a twin-engined, twin-boom five-passenger light transport but it attracted no customers and production plans were abandoned.

The Wasp-powered Oxford V prototype at Portsmouth, May 1942 (IWM MH4184).

The airport was finally de-requisitioned in June 1949, and two years later Airspeed lost its identity completely when it was merged with de Havilland, a situation which in reality had existed since 1948. The Portsmouth factory then concentrated on the production of parts for the Ambassador, Comet and Vampire until it was closed in the mid-1960s.

Various small airlines provided services and in 1966 when Channel Airways' Hs 748s took over from Dakotas on the Ipswich-Southend-Portsmouth-Jersey route, the City Council was actually making a profit on the operation—for the first time since the airport opened in 1932. It was short-lived, however, for after a heavy rainstorm on August 15 1967 two Hs 748s skidded on the wet grass and went through the airfield boundary. No-one was seriously injured but it was a set back at the height of the holiday season and the proposed bus stop service to the north from Portsmouth was abandoned—it started from Southend instead.

More stringent restrictions on the use of grass runways were imposed by the CAA and the airport was soon without scheduled services. John Fisher, Chairman of the City's Docks & Airport Committee, tried to get the council to start their own airline but failed, and the decision was taken in 1970 to close the airfield altogether. This led to bitter controversy, Fisher resigned and with two businessmen formed JF Airlines in January 1971. They were moderately successful but the Council was determined to close the airport, this being achieved after the departure of the JFA Islander during the afternoon of December 31 1973. Further attempts to get it re-opened were all in vain and the buildings erected for Portsmouth Aviation Ltd were taken over to manufacture bus bodies while those formerly used by Channel Airways were demolished in 1980 to make way for housing development.

Through all these traumas the Hants & Sussex Aviation Ltd has remained at Portsmouth on the industrial estate, engaged in specialist overhaul work. In June 1983 the company received the ultimate accolade when Rolls-Royce transferred full responsibility for the design and support of the DH Gipsy series of engines to them.

The old control tower and terminal survive and two Bellman hangars provide further evidence of the former use of the site—and of missed opportunity.

Port Victoria (Grain), Kent
See Grain

Pulborough (Parham Park), West Sussex
TQ072147. 1 mile NW of Storrington

Overlooked by the South Downs and Amberley Mount where Jose Weiss carried out his early gliding experiments was Parham Park. During the 1930s, a private aerodrome was established immediately east of the Park and just north of the A283 road and in July 1940 the 100-acre site was taken over as a dispersal ELG for Tangmere. It is believed to have been used later in the war, probably just prior to D-Day, by one of the Auster AOP units.

Ramsbury, Wiltshire
SU269703. 4½ miles E of Marlborough on minor roads

The picturesque village of Ramsbury nestling alongside the River Kennet gave its name to another of the bomber OTU airfields which stretched in a long line across southern England. Grievous though they were, the losses suffered by Bomber Command were not as heavy as had been anticipated, and Ramsbury was among several similar airfields which could therefore be spared for the build-up of American forces during 1942.

Authorised for development as a satellite of Membury in May 1941, the plans for this hilltop site detailed a standard OTU airfield with the main 6,000 ft (1,828 m) runway pointing into the prevailing south-westerly. The construction was overseen by No 92 Group, Bomber Command, the bulk of the work being completed just in time for its assignment to the VIIIth AF on August 18 1942, the day the 64th TCG (16th, 17th, 18th and 35th TCS) started flying in its C-47s from the USA via the northern ferry route. Ground echelons of the 64th reached Ramsbury three days later and took over the dispersed sites as they became habitable, the technical facilities including two 'T2' hangars and a large number of panhandle hardstandings.

With the decision to delay the assault on Europe and start a second front in North Africa instead, the 64th TCG were immediately thrown into intensive training exercises with the 2nd Battalion of the 503rd Parachute Regiment. On September 14 the Wing transferred to the newly-formed XIIth AF and prepared to move to the Mediterranean for Operation *Torch*. Fully loaded with paratroops they flew out to Gibraltar on November 9 1942 via the Cornish ferry airfields.

Ramsbury was then transferred to No 70 Group, RAF, for use as a satellite of Andover. No 15(P)AFU moved in some of its Oxfords during December to provide advanced multi-engined training for pupils taught to fly under the Commonwealth Air Training Plan and unused to European weather conditions. Activity at Ramsbury increased substantially in July 1943 when the units' Flights previously at Grove arrived, and there were the usual crop of take-off and landing accidents, inevitable with this type of unit. One of the more bizarre was on February 19 when an unmanned Oxford ran away and collided with another of the same type—how it came to be unoccupied with the engines running can only be guessed at—a call of nature perhaps?

The RAF only had the use of Ramsbury while the bulk of American airborne forces were occupied in the Mediterranean, and moved out in October 1943. The airfield was transferred to American control on November 1 as USAAF Station 469, though further delays in the build-up of the TCGs meant that it was February 1944 before the airfield was permanently occupied—by the 437th TCG from Balderton, part of the 53rd TCW which took over Ramsbury from the 50th TCW late in February. Under the command of Colonel C.E. Hudgens, the 437th specialised in glider towing, working up to mass night formation flights involving up to 48 'combinations'. To facilitate the despatch of these glider streams, the ends of the main runway were flanked with steel planking, the interval between take-offs being reduced to seconds rather than minutes.

The Group (83rd, 84th, 85th and 86th TCS) spent D-Day towing Hadrians and a number of the disliked Horsas to Normandy. For the 82nd Airborne's first glider assault they flew 52 'combinations' behind the 434th (Welford), casting off the Hadrians just before dawn on June 6. Cloud and harassing anti-aircraft fire as they ran in over the coast broke up the formations and resulted in gliders being badly scattered, but there were few casualties. On return to Ramsbury 26 C-47s were immediately readied to tow a further eight Wacos and 18 Horsas on an evening reinforcement for the 82nd Airborne now fighting desperately with elements of the German 91st Infantry Division. More gliders were towed in on the 7th, after which the Group concentrated on re-supply.

Like other TCGs, the 437th sent a detachment to Italy during July 1944 to help the 51st TCW on Operation *Anvil*. This was the invasion of southern France, the main force going in at 04:30 hours on August 15, one hour after a successful pathfinder drop. Unfortunately, thick mist obscured the ground and, despite pathfinder beacons, many troops were dropped wide of the DZ. The 437th detachment flew a re-supply drop the following day and then moved freight around Italy until returning to Ramsbury on August 24.

For Operation *Market Garden* on September 17, the Ramsbury Group towed 70 Waco Hadrian gliders carrying men and equipment of the 101st Airborne Division to Zon in the Eindhoven sector. They experienced heavy opposition, six of the 64 C-47s which reached the German lines being shot down and two Wacos colliding over the LZ, so casualties were high. The 437th followed up with equally dangerous re-supply missions while a miniature paratroop operation was flown from Ramsbury on the 20th by 12 C-47s of the 442nd TCG carrying 75 mm howitzers and men of the 377th Parachute Field Artillery. The whole of the 53rd TCW then reverted to the standard freight shuttle to France and Belgium, the 437th TCG flying 'casevac' on the way back until February 25 1945 when, after just a year of very eventful operations from Ramsbury, they moved to Coulommiers/Voisins.

USAAF rear echelons continued to occupy the airfield until the end of the war when Ramsbury nominally reverted to No 70 Group, parented by Andover. The first RAF airmen posted in had a pleasant surprise—they were fed by the Americans and really lived it up until the last USAAF personnel left three days after the station was transferred to No 4 Group, Transport Command on June 8. There were no immediate indications of Ramsbury's future task but early in July it became a satellite for Welford and more dispersed sites were opened up, one of them as accommodation for Glider Pilot Regiment personnel.

Dakotas from Welford commenced 'circuits and bumps' at Ramsbury in September 1945 and on the 21st they collected eight Horsa II gliders from Cosford. More

Top *A Dakota IV of the Glider Pick-up Unit approaches with hook lowered to 'snatch' a Hadrian. This unit was at Ramsbury during October/November 1945* (Military Aircraft Photographs).
Above *Oversize Nissens in use as farm buildings at Ramsbury in October 1982.*

gliders arrived in October and Regiment training started in preparation for the Glider Pick-up Unit. The main air party, five Dakotas towing Hadrian gliders, flew in from Ibsley on October 29 and training started immediately. Their raison d'être was snatching a glider out of a field without landing! A special tow-rope was attached to the glider and laid out across the field with a pick-up loop stretched between two poles. The Dakota, fitted with a hook and winch system, picked-up the loop and snatched the glider off the ground. Apparently it was easier and smoother than it looked, but 1945 was a time of rapidly changing priorities and, with the end of the war with Japan, gliders took a back seat. The GPU disbanded on November 15, 1945 and at the end of the month Ramsbury was reduced to C&M status.

Not for long, however, for on January 22 1946 the station was transferred to No 23 Group, Flying Training Command, and F Flight of No 7 FIS, Upavon, moved in and commenced night flying using Oxfords. This continued until March 29 when the Flight returned to Upavon and operations ceased, the airfield reverting to C&M. It was held for several years as a surplus inactive site, parented first by Welford and then Yatesbury. When de-requisitioned the land returned to agriculture, a short portion of the southern perimeter track being employed as a minor public road to replace one closed during the war. The remainder of the paved surface was extremely well adapted to suit the requirements of a farm named Darrells, which was built on the intersection of the two short runways, and used the two 'T2' hangars and a number of the Nissen huts as farm buildings.

Large sections of the perimeter track and runways, the latter reduced in width, are in use as farm roads, leaving just the western portion of the main runway intact as a private landing strip. For a number of years the Balloon Stable, a hot air balloon organisation, was active but moved to Bedminister, Bristol, in April 1983 and there is now little aerial activity.

Above *Ramsgate airfield in August 1937 with aircraft lining up for the Thanet Aero Trophy race. The rare Latvian visitor in the foreground is a VEF1-12, but in the rear are RAF biplanes on summer camp at this small municipal aerodrome* (RAF Museum P2204).

Ramsgate, Kent

TR375673. 1½ miles N of Ramsgate town

Mention of an aerodrome at Ramsgate first appeared as early as December 1914 when the use of a field for two Home Defence aeroplanes was authorized. It would seem that the proposal was not actually taken up and it was 20 years later that campaigning by prominent councillors finally bore fruit and flying started in June 1935 from a site one mile west of Broadstairs. Two hangars and a control/clubhouse/restaurant were built in the south-western corner of the field, which provided an E/W run of 2,250 ft (685 m).

Crilly Airways and Hillman Airways both flew some services during the summer of 1935 but they were suspended in September and not restarted, despite the aerodrome being extended early in 1936. The Thanet AC was formed in April and the Airport officially opened on July 3 1937 operated by Ramsgate Airport Ltd on behalf of the corporation. Three RAF squadrons held their summer camps at Ramsgate during August and in 1938 the Aero club took part in the Civil Air Guard scheme, while Southern Airways operated a service across the Thames Estuary during the summer months. In common with other civil fields, the airport closed at the beginning of the war, but in 1940 it was back in use as a scatter field for Manston, fighters being dispersed there on several occasions. During a major raid on Manston during August 24 1940 some of the bombers attacked the small airport, cratering the field, but it was Ramsgate town that really suffered, numerous casualties resulting from the demolition of whole rows of seaside villas.

With the Battle of Britain over, but the threat of invasion still present, the aerodrome was obstructed and remained so for the rest of the war. It re-opened on June 27 1953 operated by Air Kruise Ltd on a lease from Ramsgate Corporation. The company started scheduled services

Below *A Luftwaffe recce photo of Ramsgate airfield dated June 1941—it can be seen immediately north of the built up area* (via D.G. Collyer).

through Lympne to Le Touquet and Ostend and later reformed the Ramsgate Flying Club and Skyphotos using a camera equipped Autocrat.

During the spring of 1958 Skyflights Ltd took over the operation of the airfield and a Hornet Moth was used for pleasure flights. At the end of the summer these activities ceased and flying remained at a low ebb until Chrisair started joyriding in 1961. The company moved in from Luton at the end of 1962 but transferred to Sywell in June 1963, and again little happened until East Kent Air Services formed late in 1967. They were also unsuccessful, and the airfield was closed for the last time in 1968.

The pleasant grass airfield is now the site of a large industrial estate with housing steadily encroaching on the remaining open ground.

Reading (Coley), Berkshire

SU711718. ¾ mile S of Reading town centre

During 1915 it was realised that the war was not going to be over quickly and that many more RFC squadrons would be required, bringing the War Office face to face with the need for an enlargement of

Wantage Hall, Reading—used during the First World War by the School of Aeronautics (J. Temple).

the training organisation. Before more training schools could be formed, however, instructors were needed and during December 1915 the buildings of University College, Reading, were taken over and the School of Instruction established.

It soon became, together with a similar school at Oxford, the initial training course for prospective pilots and observers and was renamed No 1 School of Military Aeronautics on October 27 1916. Yeomanry House, Castle Hill (now used by the Council and by Reading Museum) was the original HQ, the main classrooms were in Wantage Hall (*SU727724*), and accommodation was requisitioned in various parts of the town. By 1917 cadets were doing a four week course in artillery spotting, use of wireless, photography and machine gun instruction, practical training being provided by lodging old aircraft fuselages in trees lining Upper Redlands Road near Wantage Hall. This startling sight was only matched by the activities on playing fields alongside Elmhurst Road (*SU731723*), where wingless aircraft were used to provide taxying experience. It is probable that this instruction was combined with that given to trainees of the School of Technical Training (Men), which was also established at Reading. Advanced instruction for the latter took place at a small aerodrome built on lowlying ground near the River Kennet at

Coley, by joining up two fields alongside the CWS jam factory off Beverley Avenue. It is believed that the main aircraft in use was the Avro 504, but Martinsyde S1 biplanes and various Farman Longhorns and Shorthorns were also reported at Reading.

The field also served as a LG for visitors to both training organisations until September 1917, when the S o TT (Men) started its move to Halton. Coley Park remained open, for it is recorded that Captain Palethorpe, an RAE test pilot, force-landed there on November 23 1918 during a flight from Farnborough in the temperamental BAT Bantam.

The aerodrome, plagued by river fogs, fell into disuse after the war and the land was released. All trace of it and the jam factory have long disappeared. It is now the site of an industrial estate.

Rochford (Southend), Essex

TQ870895. 2 miles N of Southend off B1013

Southend had its fair share of aviation hopefuls in the early 1900s but apart from one Bleriot monoplane flight from a field which later became the Roots Hall football ground, they had had little success by August 1914 when experimentation came to a sudden end. It took the Zeppelin raids of spring 1915 to bring flying back to the town, the Admiralty being galvanised into action and immediately establishing eight forward landing grounds to counter airships making a landfall on the East Anglian coast. One of them was a large low-lying field between Southend and Rochford, a pair of aircraft being flown in before dark if a raid was anticipated from wireless intercepts.

Admiralty priorities were elsewhere, however, the defence of London and the south-east being left to newly qualified personnel with little or no night flying experience, primitive aids and well-nigh useless aircraft. At Rochford (also known as Eastwood) the aircraft used were apparently Bleriot XI trainers, presumably from Chingford or Eastchurch. The LG was soon operational, a Bleriot going up on May 31 in pursuit of the German Army Zeppelin *LZ38,* which was making the first airship raid on London. Unfortunately the Bleriot suffered engine failure at 6,000 ft (1,828 m) and ended up in estuary mud off Leigh-on-Sea.

Another attempted interception on January 31 1916 had the same dismal end, and in February home defence became a War Office responsibility. Rochford was transferred to the RFC on June 4 1916 and work started on hangarage and hutted accommodation on two sites, one bordering Eastwoodbury Lane and the other near Westbarrow Hall. There was little flying however until No 37 (HD) Squadron formed at Woodham Market in September 1916, the BE 2C/Be 12 aircraft of *A* Flight taking up residence at Rochford. They were joined by No 11 (Reserve) Squadron in January 1917 when it became the night training unit for the Home Defence forces. It was renamed No 98 (Depot) Squadron a fortnight later, and after a while took its pupils direct from Schools of Military Aeronautics, doing all their flying training at Rochford using Avro 504Ks and Pups. Standards were not exactly onerous—in addition to day training they had to make six night landings and fly for an hour at 6,000 ft (1,828 m) in the dark.

A Flight No 37 Squadron spent the 1916/17 winter and spring of 1917 on fruitless patrols, but put up two BE 2Ds against the *L48* during the night of June 16/17 when they basked in reflected glory, for it was Lieutenant P. Watkins of the Squadron's Goldhangar detachment who gave the mighty Zeppelin the coup de grâce. No 99 (Depot) Squadron was formed the same month to help with the increased number of trainees required for the expanding night fighter business. A few days later No 98 was re-designated No 198 (Depot) Squadron, for some yet undiscovered reason.

No 99 (Depot) Squadron had moved to East Retford by July 7 1917 when 22 Gotha twin-engined bombers of Kagohl 3 attacked London in daylight. A motley collection of defenders rose to meet them, including four newly delivered Sopwith 1½-Strutters from Rochford. Again success eluded *A* Flight which suffered the loss of an aircraft shot down by the gunner of one of the formidable bombers. 2nd Lieutenant J.E.R. Young was killed, and his observer Air Mechanic, C.C. Taylor, wounded in the crash.

With the formation of No 61 (HD) Squadron at Rochford on August 2 *A* Flight of No 37 was withdrawn to Stow Maries. Equipped with Sopwith Pups, the new squadron was in action ten days later against Gothas which turned back over the Thames Estuary and dropped their bombs in the Rochford area, two falling

Pups of No 61 (HD) Squadron at Rochford in October 1917 (P. Liddle via G.S. Leslie).

near the hangars and wounding two flight mechanics. The squadron got airborne and finally caught up with the raiders 40 miles (64 km) out to sea, but without positive result. This proved to be the only interception by No 61 Squadron throughout the war, though some of the pilots got a close, if brief, view of their adversary on December 6 when a badly damaged Gotha force-landed on the aerodrome. The crew were taken prisoner but soon afterwards the aircraft burst into flames, ignited by a carelessly-handled signal pistol!

Meanwhile, No 190 (Depot) Squadron had been formed in October 1917 equipped with DH 6s, BE 2Cs and Avro 504Ks to operate as the primary training unit, thus allowing No 198 to concentrate on the advanced phases of the course. Both were designated (Night) Training Squadrons on December 21 and took full advantage of the comparitively large size and open approaches of the 168-acre aerodrome.

A Flight of No 61 Squadron and its Pups were detached to form the nucleus of No 141 Squadron and departed to Biggin Hill early in February 1918, while the remainder of the unit faced the task of introducing the SE 5A into night fighter service. The aircraft was hopeless in the role because of the time taken to warm its water-cooled engine and the glare from the exhausts, but whether the latter had anything to do with the tragic deaths of Captain A.B. Kynoch of No 37 Squadron and H.C. Stroud of No 61, who collided during the night of March 7 1918, is open to conjecture.

No 190 (Night) TS moved to Newmarket on March 14 and when the RAF took over, Nos 61 (HD) and 198 (Night) TS were in residence as part of the 50th Wing. By September 1918 No 61

Squadron was responsible for the Stow Maries-Leigh-Yanlet Creek section of the new barrier patrol, but there was little activity and it was with relief that the pilots saw 24 Camels arrive to replace the disliked SEs the following month. The pugnacious little Sopwith also equipped No 152 Squadron, which formed up at Rochford before moving to France to join No 151 on the Western Front.

The station was now virtually complete having four large hangars, four MT sheds and sufficient living and working accommodation for some 600 men. No 198 (Night)TS was equipped with 24 Avro 504Ks, but after the Armistice the station started to run down, No 61 Squadron disbanding on June 13 1919 followed by No 198 in September. By this time civilian joy-riding had already started, three-seater 504Ks being flown from Rochford by Navarro Aviation. The RAF station was closed in 1920 and with the demise of joy-riding the land was released for agriculture.

There is some evidence of gliding from the site around 1930 and when the Southend FC moved to the Rochford Pony Track, pressure grew for the establishment of a municipal airport. Southend Flying Services Ltd was registered in December 1932 and, with commendable courage, the Southend Council purchased the big field the following year to bring it up to licensed aerodrome standard. Southend FS started local ferry services, joined by Crilly Airways in 1935 but by the time the airport was officially opened by Sir Philip Sassoon, Under Secretary of State for Air, on September 18 1935, both were losing money and withdrew soon afterwards, leaving the flying club and private owners in sole occupation.

Rallies and air displays provided much needed income and in the summer of 1937 No 602 Squadron Hinds were flown down from Glasgow for the unit's annual camp. Their Honorary Air Commodore, Lord

Stonehaven, inspected the camp and Air Commodore S. Goble, CBE, DSO presented the squadron badge recently approved by the King. No 607(County of Durham) Squadron also spent 14 days at Rochford during August of that year, their Demon two-seat fighters being inspected by AM Sir Hugh Dowding, already AoC-in-C, Fighter Command, and soon to have grimmer reasons to know of the airfield.

The RAF Volunteer Reserve, formed in 1936, was strengthened in the Southend area by the formation of No 34 E&RFTS at the airport early in 1939, Air Hire Ltd receiving the operating contract. The unit initially flew Tiger Moths, supplemented later by Harts and a few Ansons before it was closed down by No 50 Group on September 1, its equipment going to strengthen other EFTS.

A more warlike use for Southend had been tested on August 11 when No 54 Squadron moved into the airport as part of a practice evacuation of Hornchurch. This exercise took 3 hours 40 minutes to completed amidst considerable confusion, but the squadron was soon to become expert at it, for Rochford was a forward satellite in October 1939 and Spitfires of Nos 54 and 74 Squadrons shared the daytime standbys throughout that first autumn and winter of the war. The Flying Club buildings were used for domestic accommodation, personnel sleeping on camp beds in the recreation hall. While it was comfortable enough, there was little action and boredom soon crept in despite much AA co-operation flying and tactical exercises. Blenheims of No 600 Squadron also ventured forward from Hornchurch for a few days during October but Rochford was more suitable for Spitfires and remained their province, No 54 were replaced by No 65 Squadron in March 1940 but the routine remained the same until May when the Germans broke through in France.

No 616 Squadron relieved No 74 at Rochford on May 27 and within minutes of completing refuelling had 12 Spitfire Is airborne for a patrol between Dunkirk and Gravelines with other squadrons of the Hornchurch Wing. Their big day came on June 1, during a spell of frantic activity over the Dunkirk beaches. A tangle with Bf 109s resulted in two going down for the loss of one Spitfire while later in the day the squadron attacked German bombers over evacuation ships, claiming one Ju 88 and a He 111 destroyed and several

probables. No 74 Squadron were back at Rochford on June 6, and with the Dunkirk evacuation complete No 616 Squadron returned to Yorkshire.

A raid on the general Southend area during the night of June 18/19 provided the chance Flight Lieutenant A.G. 'Sailor' Malan needed to become the first British day fighter pilot to destroy an enemy aircraft at night. He took off soon after midnight and climbed after an aircraft held in searchlights—opened fire at 200 yds (183 m) and kept his finger on the firing button until down to 50 yds (46 m). With his windscreen covered in oil he watched the He 111 spiral out of the beam. Another He 111 was picked up and Malan closed to 250 yds (229 m) when he opened fire. The bomber started smoking heavily and then caught fire before crashing near Chelmsford. Both were credited to this outstanding pilot—others who tried to emulate him soon found out how difficult the Spitfire was to fly and fight at night.

No 54 Squadron replaced No 74 on June 25 and spent a month at Rochford before the North Weald Sector took over the airfield and No 56 Squadron Hurricanes started using it. Other squadrons made refuelling and rearming stops during the hectic days of August 1940 and on the 23rd Flight Lieutenant G.A.W. Saunders of No 56 Squadron, damaged a Do 17Z-3 of II/KG2 so badly that the pilot, Hauptmann Hans Bose, had to force-land on the airfield—a useful prize for the technical assessors and oddly reminiscent of the Gotha incident of 1917.

With the Luftwaffe concentrating their venom on Kentish airfields, Rochford seemed to bear a charmed life until early on August 25 when 27 He 111s of II and III/KG53 broke away from a large formation and made straight for the airfield. A fortuitous sighting by No 79 Squadron enabled Defiants of No 264 Squadron to be vectored onto the Heinkels but the two-seat fighters were badly mauled by crossfire from the bombers, and from their escorting Bf 109s waiting unseen up sun. Four Defiants were shot down and three others damaged and only Pilot Officer W. Carnaby, on his first meeting with the enemy, could claim victory over a He 111. The remaining Heinkels got through but heavy flak upset their attack and little damage was done until the afternoon when 30 Do 17s of II and III/KG3 flew up the Thames Estuary at 18,000 ft (5,486 m) under heavy Bf 109 escort. No 54 Squadron intercepted them and one of the escorts was shot down for the loss of a Spitfire, but the bombers again got through and this time they badly cratered the airfield, hit buildings and put power, water and telephone services out of action.

The airfield was again attacked on September 2, but little further damage was done and it remained serviceable. With the Luftwaffe turning increasingly to night operations Rochford was up-graded, and on October 28 1940 it became a night fighter station renamed RAF Southend and commanded by Wing Commander B. Embry—later rather better known as AM Sir Basil Embry, KBE, CB, DSO, DFC, AFC. The Defiants of No 264 Squadron, now transformed into night fighters, appeared in the Hornchurch Sector and spent a month at Southend. The poor lighting and surface of the airfield caused several accidents, one aircraft striking trees on the approach and another flying into the ground after take-off but, on November 23, spirits rose when Pilot Officer D. Hughes (later an AVM) intercepted a He 111 over Brentwood and damaged it. Almost certainly it would have been destroyed if the Defiant's turret hadn't jammed preventing Sergeant F. Gash from either rotating it or elevating the guns. Hughes tried to position the aircraft so that the bullets would hit the target—this would have been difficult enough in daylight, but at night it was well night impossible and the bomber escaped.

Four days later, No 264 Squadron moved to Debden and day fighter squadrons returned to Southend on rotation from Hornchurch. On January 7 1941 a single raider dropped eight bombs, three of which landed on the airfield but caused no casualties or significant damage, and two days later Southend became a forward base for offensive fighter operations. It was used by numerous No 11 Group squadrons, the Spitfires of Nos 54 and 64 Squadron becoming frequent visitors as *Circuses* became properly established.

On May 11 the station was strafed by 16 Bf 109s. The Operations Room and air-field ambulance garage were demolished, one airman was killed and several wounded, but the ground defences which now included three of the fascinating Pickett Hamilton retractable forts, a PAC installation and several gun positions, reacted well, shooting down one attacker

which crashed near No 1 hangar. Despite these and earlier attentions from the Luftwaffe, the accommodation on the station, though temporary, had improved considerably. Two Bellman hangars had been erected along the southern boundary and four Over Blisters were dispersed around the field which now had a peri-meter track connecting them with six large double blast pens originally built for Blen-heim/Beaufighter night fighters. The air-men's sleeping quarters, NAAFI, dining room and the technical and supply stores, were all Nissen huts of various sizes while the officers lived at Eastwoodbury, a large house at the south-west corner of the airfield.

No 611 Squadron, now equipped with cannon-armed Spitfire Vbs, took over Southend on May 20 1941 to continue the steady round of *Rodeos* and *Circuses.* They had one signal success, shooting down seven Bf 109s near Hazebrouck just before No 603 Squadron took over in mid-June. The latter were involved in the first day bomber raids by Stirlings but had gone when No 402 (RCAF) Squadron appeared on August 19 to pioneer a new role. At first their Hurricane IIbs were used on straightforward *Rodeos* and *Ramrods* but on November 1 the squadron carried out the first fighter bomber raid, attacking Berck-sur-Mer airfield with 250 lb (113 kg) bombs. Four days later they moved to Warmwell and Southend was without a resident, though still much used to extend the range of *Circus* operations over northern France and Belgium.

Part of No 313 (Czech) Squadron moved in early in February 1942 to carry out the unit's first *Rhubarbs,* joined on the 9th by No 1488 Flight which arrived from Shoreham with target-towing Lysanders to provide air-to-air firing practice for No 11 Group squadrons. Some Masters were received in March and the Lysander strength gradually increased, reaching 14 by the time the unit moved again in June 1942. Meanwhile, the familiar procession of Hornchurch Wing squadrons to Southend had resumed, with Nos 411 and 64 Squadrons taking their turn, until May 1 1942 when operational control passed to North Weald and No 403 (RCAF) Squadron appeared, involved like the rest in fighter sweeps and bomber escort work. After a fairly uneventful month they were jumped by some 30 Fw 190s on June 2 and badly beaten, losing six pilots. They were sent to Martlesham

Heath to recover and replaced by No 121 Squadron, one of the three rather unruly Eagle squadrons. They started well, destroying four Fw 190s on June 9, successfully shooting up a train, and on July 31 claimed seven German fighters for the loss of one Spitfire.

For the Eagle squadrons, soon to transfer to the USAAF, Operation *Jubilee* was their RAF swansong. After No 19 Squadron joined No 121 at Southend the camp was sealed and, at 08:41 hours on August 19, Squadron Leader P. Davies led off 24 Spitfire Vbs from the two units. They were employed on medium level cover for the landing ships and had a bad time over Dieppe at the hands of Fw 190s. Immediately on arrival they were attacked, losing four aircraft in quick succession, and though able to claim one Fw 190 destroyed and three damaged it was very much a German victory. The two squadrons were back over the ships at 12:20 hours but this time the skirmishes were inconclusive, as was the third combined mission when a probable Fw 190 was claimed—for the definite loss of a Spitfire. It had not been a good day for the Southend Wing. No 19 Squadron returned to Perranporth the next day, No 121 remaining until September 23 when the pilots flew to Debden to become the 335th FS of the 4th FG, VIIth AF, USAAF.

No 350 (Belgian) Squadron replaced them at Southend, still with Spitfire Vbs despite this variant's inferiority to the Fw 190. It was the weather however, which was the main reason for a marked drop in operations, few *Rhubarbs* and only the occasional *Circus* being flown. A reminder that the Luftwaffe could still hit back was provided by a sharp attack on the Southend area on October 26 1942 during which 100 houses were damaged. Swift work by No 2820 LAA Squadron, RAF Regiment, bagged a Bf 109 but unfortunately it crashed on No 350 Squadrons dispersal, killing a Belgian Warrant Officer and injuring two airmen.

No 453 (RAAF) Squadron arrived to fly convoy patrols and very occasional offensive sweeps during the autumn and winter of 1942/43, but with their departure in March operations from Southend virtually came to an end. Instead No 137 Squadron used the facilities to work up their new Hurricane IV rocket-firers during June and July, as the station prepared itself for an armament training role with detachments from Nos 287 Squadron and

6 AACU temporarily based. No 1488 Flt returned from Martlesham Heath on August 17 1943 with Masters, Martinets and Lysanders to continue its drogue towing, and became the nucleus of No 17 Armament Practice Camp when it formed on October 18. The main task was the conversion of Spitfire IX squadrons to fighter-bombing, starting with No 66 Squadron in November 1943. They were attached for 14-day bombing courses as part of pre-invasion training, followed by Mustang pilots of No 122 Wing, Funtington, who underwent a weeks' crash course in May 1944, No 65 Squadron completing its training on the very eve of D-Day!

No 17 APC were bystanders during the invasion, having no customers until July when Nos 74 and 127 Squadrons were converted to the bombing role. They were the last, however, for the extended balloon barrage set up against the V-1 flying bombs steadily encroached and on August 9 No 17 APC was moved to North Weald, leaving Southend to Nos 951 and 958 Balloon Squadrons. RAF Southend reverted to its original status as a satellite of Hornchurch on September 1 1944 but was little used, and with the V-1 menace virtually over, the Balloon Squadrons withdrew in February 1945 and the station was reduced to C&M, used only by No 71 MU to operate a Salvage Ferry Service. This was withdrawn on March 31 1946 and the station closed at the end of May, leaving a single Blister in use by No 148 Gliding School, ATC.

De-requisitioned in 1946, Southend was relicensed as a civil airport on January 1 1947, and four days later East Anglian Flying Services moved in to start *ad hoc* charter and joy ride operations. A Municipal Air Centre and Flying School was opened in March and an International Rally arranged to coincide with the official re-opening on August 9, 1947.

Freddie Laker's Aviation Traders made an appearance on the Southend scene during 1948 overhauling ex-BOAC Haltons which were sold to freight operators, many being used on the Berlin Airlift. The sudden end of the lucrative airlift contracts in 1949 meant over capacity and derelict aeroplanes were soon littering the field. Aviation Traders survived by manufacturing Bristol Freighters wing sections using a newly erected hangar, this association with the Filton-based company being further developed when their associate, Air Charter Ltd started the Channel Air Bridge in 1954 using Mk 31 Freighters to carry two cars and 12 passengers across to Calais.

Various other commercial operators flowered briefly at Southend before moving on, but East Anglian and Air Charter/Aviation Traders remained, and the gradually improving finances of the airport encouraged the authorities to start a massive improvement programme. This included a large hardstanding in front of a new terminal building, new taxi-tracks and two asphalt runways, 06/24 5,265 ft (1,605 m) in length and a subsidiary 15/33 of 3,712 ft (1,131 m), both extending outside the original perimeter track. This work was completed in 1956 when a Blister and the club hangar, numerous Nissens and other wartime buildings were still in use.

Meanwhile, the car ferry services had been extended and Mk 32 Freighters, capable of carrying three cars and 15 passengers, had been added to the fleet. Another venture was the purchase of all 252 ex-RAF Prentice trainers offered for sale. Starting in April 1956, many were flown into Southend over the next 18 months, the grass around Aviation Traders hangar becoming covered in them. They were not a Laker success for despite a low price the Prentice did not sell well, and most were scrapped in 1961.

Even more ambitious was the design and construction of a DC-3 replacement at Southend. First metal was cut in 1954 but progress was slow and not until July 1957 did the Dart-powered Accountant make its first 27-minute flight. It was subsequently demonstrated at the SBAC Show at Farnborough but with the Herald and Friendship going into production and recession looming the programme was abandoned in January 1958. Instead, Laker began looking for a new car ferry, finally settling on the Douglas DC-4 locally converted by Aviation Traders to enable vehicles to be loaded through the nose. Work started in October 1960 and the first Carvair conversion flew at Southend during June 1961. The remainder were completed at Stansted, but the forward fuselage sections were all manufactured at Southend, the aircraft entering service in February 1962 and quickly proving very popular.

East Anglian FS started using its alternative Channel Airways name in October 1962, and at the end of the year took over Tradair, thus adding a Viscount to the fleet. On January 1 1963 rationalisation within the British United Group produced further amalgamation and the operating company became British United Air Ferries, while Channel Airways introduced more Viscounts and in May 1965 started moving up market by ordering four new Hs 748s followed by four BAC-111s less than 18 months later—the first jet service being flown on June 26 1967.

Proposals for further runway lengthening were the subject of much controversy during the mid-1960s, the argument becoming complicated by local agitation about noise levels following the introduction of the BAC-111 and the ordering of Tridents by Channel in 1967. When the Ministry refused to allow further expansion, more Channel Airways services were moved out, and with severe competition being experienced from sea ferries, the car transport services of British Air Ferries were gradually run-down, the firm concentrating on cargo and passengers. On October 17 1971, however, the company was purchased by another aviation entrepreneur, T.D. Keegan, and services were again built up, receiving a boost after the demise of Channel Airways in February 1972 when BAF became the main operators at Southend.

Soon afterwards the museum which had languished alongside the railway line on the eastern boundary for several years was moved to a special compound on the southern side and publicly re-opened as the Historic Aircraft Museum on May 27 1972. Unfortunately the organiser went bankrupt, the museum being rescued by a property developer who erected an airport hotel, discotheque and exhibition hall, the latter housing the more fragile aircraft when not in use commercially. The arrangements did not prove satisfactory and at the end of 1982 it was decided to close the museum and sell off the aircraft —resulting in more controversy over ownership. The doors closed in March 1983 and the collection auctioned in May —the sad result of muddle and conflicting commercial interests.

For a time new CAA regulations looked like closing Southend to commercial operators altogether, but the problem was resolved and BAF still use the airport as their main base with British Midland also operating services. Amongst smaller concerns are the thriving Southend Light Aviation Centre, the Southend AC and Aspenair, while Aviation Traders continue to overhaul and modifying aircraft. Southend has seen more prosperous and exciting times, but it remains an interesting place which always holds out the chance to see surprise visitors, civil and military.

Rustington, West Sussex

TQ058020. 2 miles E of Littlehampton off A259

Located between Rustington and East Preston villages, this obscure aerodrome was originally opened in 1917 as a Day LG, probably for use by Gosport aircraft when engaged in gunnery practice.

In 1918 it was re-surveyed and accepted for development as one of a string of Training Depot Stations built along the south coast for the United States Air Service. It was a roughly rectangular site of 159 acres in the north-west corner of which six large aeroplane sheds capable of hangaring Handley Page 0/400s, two erection and repair sheds and an accommodation site were to be built.

The Handley Page erection building, which had a steel triangular truss roof, was nearly complete when the Armistice intervened and work stopped on the site. In October 1919 instructions were issued detailing the disposal of the buildings and relinquishment of the land, which has long been completely built over and is now known as West Preston.

St Margarets (Dover), Kent

See Dover (St Margarets)

Selsey, West Sussex

SZ865957. 5 miles S of Chichester along-side B2145

Used as a private aerodrome during the 1930s, an expanse of prime agricultural land on the southern edge of Pagham Harbour, alongside the village of Church Norton, was one of the many ALG sites surveyed early in 1942. It was adopted in the face of strong opposition from the Ministry of Agriculture and immediately became a priority location, having good approaches, a flat surface and a certain amount of accommodation available in the immediate vicinity. The land was requisitioned in July and a complete survey in October detailed a NE/SW landing strip of 4,200 ft (1,280 m) with a subsidiary SE/NW runway of 3,900 ft (1,189 m) in the form of a cross. Penhold Barn and adjacent outbuildings were listed for demolition and trees for felling at the south-east corner of the ALG, but

Norton Priory, Mitchards Croft and cottages near Coles Farm were earmarked for accommodation as well as an old aircraft hangar near the croft.

Authority for the ALG was given by Fighter Command in December 1942 and the final site plan issued on February 16 1943, work by a RAF construction unit starting immediately. Grading was confined to the removal of field boundaries and the Sommerfeld Tracking was laid in time for the arrival of the Spitfire Vs of No 65 Squadron at the end of May. They were joined the next day by Typhoons of No 245 Squadron, whose air and ground crew pitched their tents in the grounds of Norton Priory which was used as the unit HQ. Both units had just joined the embryo Tactical AF and were experiencing their first taste of living rough on a largely unprepared strip. At Selsey they formed the operational components of No 121 Airfield, the Spitfires continuing their bomber escort work, while the Typhoons concentrated on air firing and tactical training.

After a month the squadrons moved on, No 65 to Kingsnorth while No 245 Squadron went to Lydd. Selsey had been tested and had seen only one accident of note when a Spitfire Vb of No 602 Squadron stalled and crashed on the strip. During the autumn more work was done at Selsey. Four Extra Over Blisters were erected, metal tracking added and PSP temporary hardstandings laid around the ALG in readiness for its real work during *Overlord*. The site was re-opened on April 1 1944 and eight days later No 485 (RNZAF) Squadron of No 135 Airfield, No 84 Group, 2nd TAF, moved in followed by No 222 and 349 (Belgian) Squadrons, the latter fresh from an APC at Llanbedr. Their Spitfire IX dive-bombers were soon in action on armed recce over the Continent, softening up communication targets but also involved in bomber escorts.

Renamed No 135 Wing on May 15, its three squadrons were active on D-Day giving cover over the beach-head. On their third patrol No 349 Squadron intercepted a mixed force of Ju 88s and 188s near Caen and Sergeant Bragard was able to claim the unit's first confirmed kill, while Flying Officer Moreau shared a second Ju 88 with Flight Sergeant J. Moureau and three others were damaged. The whole Wing flew a low level patrol over the invasion beaches during the evening of June 8 and were rewarded by the sight of some 20 Fw 190s and 12 Bf 109s, all carrying bombs. These were intercepted by Nos 222 and 485 Squadrons and seven were claimed shot down. No 222 was again successful on the 10th when one of a pair of Fw 190s was shot down by Flight Lieutenant G.W. Varley and later that day No 349 Squadron achieved the distinction of being the first unit to land in the bridgehead when a Section refuelled and re-armed at B2 (Bazenville) landing strip. On June 13 the New Zealanders flew into B3 (St Croix-sur-Mer) to operate from the ALG during daylight hours, giving additional time on patrol.

No 135 Wing Spitfires carried bombs for the first time since D-Day on June 19, and also stepped up its bomber escort work before moving out of Selsey at the end of the month. They were immediately replaced by No 145 (French) Wing which consisted of Nos 329, 340 and 341 Squadrons, all flying Spitfire IX fighter bombers. While beach-head patrols remained the top priority, No 145 Wing also took part in escorts to heavy bombers attacking *Noball* sites in daylight. During such a raid on July 9 they saw P-47 Thunderbolts in combat with eight Bf 109s south-east of Dieppe. Led by Wing Commander Crawford-Compton, the Wing joined in, the Wing Leader and Commandant J.A.M. Fournier of No 340 Squadron each shooting down a Bf 109. Captain Boudier of No 341 Squadron got on the tail of another which was being attacked by a P-47 pilot, who promptly turned on Boudier and so badly damaged his Spitfire that the Frenchman was forced to bale out. To his chagrin he ended up as a PoW!

During a general re-organisation, No 74 Squadron joined the Frenchmen for a week in mid-July, but No 145 Wing left Selsey for Tangmere on August 6 and No 135 Wing (Nos 33, 222 and 349 Squadrons) re-appeared to continue bomber escort duties. To relieve the boredom they interspersed them with ground strafing but did not stay long, No 33 Squadron going to B10 strip on August 19 while the rest of the Wing moved to the relative comfort of Tangmere.

After a hectic 4½ months, Selsey's job was over for, though retained as a back-up field, it was not used again operationally and in March 1945 local farmers were given permission to graze sheep and cattle on the ALG. The site was de-requisitioned soon after the end of the war. The road into Church Norton was re-opened

and with the steel tracking lifted and Blister removed, the ground was restored to its near original condition. There is now virtually no sign of the existence of this very successful ALG, certainly one of the best in the south-west.

Sheerness, Kent
TQ913742/932748.

The historic port of Sheerness had early associations with aviation for the Naval Flying School at Eastchurch was first borne on the books of HMS *Actaeon* for administrative and supply purposes and it was from HMS *Africa*, positioned in the estuary off the dockyard, that Lieutenant Charles Samson, RN, made his historic take-off from a fore-gun turret platform on January 10 1912. This feat created a great impression amongst the assembled senior officers and the next day the Naval Flying School was visited by Admiral Sir Richard Poore, C-in-C The Nore, who made a short flight in the same Short S 38 and expressed satisfaction with the whole organisation.

On May 1 1912 the S 38 was back at Sheerness on a lighter and was hoisted aboard HMS *Hibernia* to be taken to Weymouth for the Naval Review where Samson again demonstrated a take-off, repeating the performance at the Portsmouth Naval Review in July.

Such experiments were largely forgotten by the Sheerness naval authorities by the time the threat of war turned into reality in August 1914, and it was not until 1917 that the town was again directly involved with flying. It then developed at two completely different sites, one a mile to the south of the dockyard (*TQ913742*) intended for Kite Balloon training under Admiralty control, and the other a mile to the east, a RFC establishment (*TQ932748*).

No 1 Balloon Training Base (SE Area) was right on the edge of Mile Town, just inland of the railway line, the 75-acre site cutting the minor road between Mile Town and West Minster. Five canvas balloon sheds were erected on the land side of the road, the kite balloons providing advanced training for observers after their preliminary course at No 1 Balloon Training Depot, Roehampton. The Base had an establishment of 306, of which 132 were pupils. It was soon churning out observers ready to go to sea, this work continuing under the command of Flight Commander B.E.P. Gregg after the unit transferred to RAF control in April 1918.

Meanwhile, the RFC established a 50-acre ELG for Home Defence units immediately to the east of Marine Town, one of a chain of rudimentary aerodromes intended for use by pilots in difficulty at night due to battle damage, unserviceability, fuel shortage or weather. The field, which had a maximum landing run of 1,200 ft (366 m) suffered from waterlogging but remained open for No 37 (HD) Squadron flying from Rochford, Stow Maries and Goldhanger sub-stations. During 1918 it was also employed as a day LG by aircraft operating with the Artillery Co-operation Camp at Sheerness.

Both units effectively closed down soon after the Armistice, though the Kite Balloon base was not finally transferred to the Admiralty for naval use until September 1919. Only part of this KB site has been built on during subsequent years but the 50th Wing LG has been used for an extensive schools complex.

Sheffield Farm (Theale), Berkshire
See Theale

Shellbeach (Leysdown), Kent
See Leysdown

Shoreham, West Sussex

TQ203055. 1 mile NW of Shoreham-by-Sea alongside A27(T)

It has taken over 71 years to escape from Shoreham airfield's perennial problem, a surface which became waterlogged immediately after a shower of rain. For nearly the whole of this time there has been flying at Shoreham though the site has moved several times before returning to its original position, hemmed in by the River Adur to the east, the London-Brighton railway line to the south and now the A27(T) to the north. After years of local opposition, the Brighton, Hove and Worthing Joint Municipal Airports Committee finally gained permission to lay a tarmac runway in 1981 which came into operation the following year.

First established as an aerodrome in February 1911, it boasted a 2,000 ft (610 m) landing run and generally good approaches though the river and railway embankment were certainly hazards for inexperienced pilots, and it was the Brooklands-Brighton race of May 1911, won by Gustav Hamel in his Bleriot, that put Shoreham on the map. A row of ten wooden sheds were erected alongside the railway embankment and on June 20 the airfield was officially opened by the Mayors of Brighton, Hove and Worthing. It was used as a compulsory landing ground for the ambitious Circuit of Europe, and by Horatio Barber when he made the first recorded cargo flight in the world carrying a number of Osram lamps to Hove aboard his Valkyrie biplane.

The Chanter flying school moved in from Hendon during November 1911 and another was founded by the Pashley Brothers, its claim to be a major training field being further strengthened when the Avro Flying School moved down from Brooklands in October 1912. They took over three permanent hangars and a new clubhouse, started test flying the Avro 503 seaplane from the River Adur in May 1913, but suffered a setback on June 29 when a pupil flying solo was killed in the Avro 500.

More unorthodox machines also appeared at Shoreham in 1913. The Radley England Waterplane, which had three 50 hp Gnome engines in tandem in the centre-section driving a pusher propeller, was one which performed well until the bottom of the starboard float was ripped out. James Radley and Gordon England then becoming involved in the extraordinary Lee-Richards Annular Wing Monoplane. Completed under tight security in Hangar No 7 it was successfully flown by Gordon England on November 23 1913 until the engine failed on the landing approach and the machine stalled, falling 50 ft (15.2 m) into telegraph wires, fortunately without serious injury to the pilot. Meanwhile, the Pashley Brothers founded the Sussex County Aero Club which rapidly became a popular rendezvous for the more affluent in the area, and while the number of pupils trained at Shoreham during 1913-14 was disappointing it laid a solid foundation for the aerodrome's wartime activities.

Shoreham was acquired by the War Office in August 1914 and taken over by the RFC the following month as a training field, the Pashley School being closed down after a few weeks of *ad hoc* operation. Lack of aircraft and instructors resulted in Shoreham remaining practically deserted until the nucleus of No 3 Reserve Aeroplane Squadron moved in on January 21 1915. They were soon flying the usual scratch collection of aircraft, the output of trained pilots not being helped by the formation of No 14 Squadron on February 3 from No 3 RAS personnel, or the requirement to maintain at least one aircraft available for home defence against Zeppelins. Things slowly settled down despite the formation of No 21 RS in May 1916, and its prompt departure to Egypt in the wake of No 14 Squadron.

The Training Brigade was de-centralised on January 10 1917, No 3 RS coming under Eastern Group Command. The inappropriate Reserve Squadron title became Training Squadron on May 31 when the unit was dealing with six-week ab initio pilot courses which included a minimum of three hours' dual and three hours' solo flying—a recipe for disaster.

No 86 Squadron is believed to have been formed at Shoreham on September 1 1917, but probably only in cadre form for it was at Dover nine days later, and it was No 3 TS, now flying some Avro 504s, which was still the main stay of the unit when the RAF was born. It finally left in July 1918 replaced by the South Eastern Area Flying Instructors School, a direct result of Major Smith Barry's work at Gosport. The unit used 19 Avros and two of each Service type in the Area to give 14-day instructor courses. Flying, though curtailed after the Armistice, continued until the FIS was disbanded early in 1919. Meanwhile, No 94 Squadron completed its work-up on SE 5As at Shoreham before going to France at the end of October 1918, and No 82 Squadron

Snipe E8213 Leicester *at Shoreham in 1919* (via C. Bowyer).

arrived for demobilisation in February 1919, but moved to Tangmere in May when the aerodrome was cleared for No 1 Wing, Canadian Air Force which had commenced its take-over early in April.

The CAF had been the victim of continual policy changes and among the first recommendations of the new Director of Air Services in February 1919 was the move of No 1 Wing, CAF, to a better airfield than their Upper Heyford base, and a change of aircraft from Dolphins to SE 5As for No 1 (Fighter) Squadron. Both requests were granted by the British Air Ministry, the move to Shoreham commencing on March 31 when No 2 (Bomber) Squadron left Upper Heyford, followed by No 1 Squadron on May 1 when their re-equipment was complete.

At Shoreham the Canadians took over the long line of hangars along the southern boundary and pitched their tents in the south eastern corner near their HQ building. Under the command of the distinguished ex-RNAS pilot, Lieutenant Colonel R. Leckie, the Wing settled down to a period of relative stability, No 1 Squadron happily adding a very mixed bunch of machines to their officially approved SE 5As, while No 2 Squadron were content to fly their DH 9As. Unfortunately the Canadians decided to abandon plans for a peacetime air force and ordered the aircraft and equipment to be dismantled and packed for shipment to Canada. No 1 Squadron disbanded on January 28 1920, followed by the Wing HQ and No 2 Squadron on February 5. The Packing Section completed its work in December 1921 and the aerodrome was then closed, reverting to grazing land.

In 1923, F.G. Miles persuaded Cecil Pashley to join him in forming the Gnat Aero Company and they leased a field on the seaward side of the railway for joy riding and training using an Avro 504K. Three years later they moved to a field west of the original aerodrome and formed the Southern Aero Club, the Gnat Aero Co becoming Southern Aircraft Ltd. A whole book could be written about their activities during the next ten years, but the early 1930s also saw a new enthusiasm for airports and Brighton, Hove and Worthing formed an Airport Committee and engaged Sir Alan Cobham to survey possible sites. His report favoured the original aerodrome expanded to take in land up to the main Worthing-Brighton road, F.G. Miles making a shrewd £3,000 profit when the land was purchased in 1933 for £10,000. A further £31,000 was allocated for the construction of a terminal building and hangarage in the area originally occupied by the pre-war sheds. Work on the contemporary style cement rendered brick terminal began in November 1934 and the following year Olley Air Services were appointed to manage the airport. On July 1 1935 the Southern Railway re-opened Bungalow Town Halt as Shoreham Airport Station and air services gained impetus when Railway Air Services included Shoreham in their time tables. They were well established when the terminal building was officially opened on June 13 1936.

The Air Ministry, in the middle of a major expansion of aircrew training in the mid-1930s, strongly favoured the increased use of civilian organisations, the Martin School of Air Navigation at Shoreham receiving a RAF Volunteer Reserve pilot training contract, starting on July 1 1937. Designated No 16 E&RFTS by No 26 (T) Group, the school was initially equipped with Ministry-supplied Tiger Moths, later supplemented by Harts, Hinds and even a few Battles. Standard Air Ministry wooden huts were erected near the clubroom as classrooms and offices for the school, and in May 1938 navigation training for bomber pilots was also moved to Shoreham, where the Martin School used civilian Dragon and Rapide biplanes to provide practical flying exercises during a 12-week course. In December 1938 the training of full-time observers replaced the pilot specialisation, but Martins' were not considered very efficient and in May 1939 the contract was transferred to Airwork at Staverton. VR pilot training continued until September 1 when, in company with many E&RFTS, No 16 closed down and its aircraft sent to enlarge EFTS's.

Cleared of training and club aircraft Shoreham was now used to maintain civilian air routes evacuated from Croydon. The national airlines of three neutral countries, KLM, Sabena and DDL were allowed to operate in and out of the airport, their aircraft having to suffer the indignity of camouflage netting while at Shoreham to hide their high visibility orange neutrality paint. The National Air Communications organisation ran a Shoreham-Tunis-Alexandria service using a DH 91 Albatross. This later extended to India, while Channel Islands services resumed in October and a flight joining Heston-Shoreham-Dieppe-Paris was also introduced. During February and March 1940 the services had to be transferred to Tangmere for several days because of flooding, and continental services ground to a halt in May when first Denmark, then Belgium and Holland were invaded. Finally the Middle East route was suspended following Italy's entry into the war on June 10 1940—and Shoreham's short life as an international airport was over.

Requisitioned by the Air Ministry as an advanced airfield in the Kenley Sector of No 11 Group, Fighter Command, Shoreham was little used except by Lysanders of No 225 Squadron on anti-invasion coastal patrols until August 20 when the Fighter Interception Unit became the first resident. Bombed out of Tangmere, its one surviving aircraft was joined by a second all-black Beaufighter on September 1, this becoming the first to fly an operational night sortie when Flying Officer G. Ashfield patrolled the south coast on 4/5th—and the AI failed. After one more sortie *R2059* went missing off the French coast during the night of September 12/13—a short but very typical operational career.

The FIU was joined on October 14 by No 422 Flight, a night fighter unit which flew Hurricanes with considerable success. Domestic accommodation on the airfield was non-existent, the Officers' Mess being the Sussex Pad Hotel, the Sergeants Mess and quarters were at Ricardo's Engineering Works, while most of the airmen were billeted on families in the area.

Having destroyed two enemy aircraft and damaged another, No 422 Flight

A Walrus amphibian of No 277 Squadron —the air-sea rescue unit which used Shoreham from December 1941 until August 1944 (RAF Museum P5016).

moved to Cranage in January 1941 when the FIU also left. The airfield was extended westwards by removing some buildings and the embanked road to New Salts Farm, before the Luftwaffe took an interest and bombing destroyed the main hangar during Spring 1941. The foundations were used for an Over Blister and three others were erected around the perimeter connected to large hardstandings on the east side by a narrow track.

In May 1941 a proper Air-Sea Rescue Flight of two Lysanders was established, these aircraft carrying a dinghy pack on each bomb rack and smoke floats under the fuselage. They were responsible for rescue work out to 20 miles and despite their slow speed quickly proved valuable in locating aircrew who had baled out or ditched in the English Channel.

Six more Lysanders arrived in October 1941 but were for No 11 Group Target Towing Flight which formed on the 25th to provide drogue targets for local fighter squadrons. This unit became No 1488 Flight on December 1 and the ASR Flight was also rationalised, becoming part of the new No 277 Squadron on the 22nd of the same month, the Shoreham Flight having three Lysanders and two Walrus. On February 9 1942 No 1488 Flight moved to Southend and in May Defiants arrived

to replace Lysanders with No 277 Squadron. More exciting were two Harrows which flew in ground crew and stores for No 253 Squadron, whose Hurricanes arrived shortly afterwards for Exercise *Tiger*. They only stayed a few days but were followed in June by Nos 3 and 245 Squadrons, moved forward for Operation *Rutter*. This was cancelled and the Hurricanes departed, only to return in great haste on August 14 when the combined operation at Dieppe was re-activated as *Jubilee*.

Pilots of both squadrons were up early on August 19 for they were to accompany No 43 Squadron in the first fighter strike. Things did not go well, for in the pre-dawn half light on an unfamiliar and badly lit airfield two aircraft collided and had to be left behind. The rendezvous with No 43 Squadron was more successful and 34 Hurricane IIcs were soon attacking gun positions overlooking the beaches on which the Canadians were about to land. Led in by Squadron Leader A.E. Berry, DFC, No 3 Squadron encountered heavy flak and Sergeant S.D. Banks was shot down, while No 245 Squadron were badly mauled, three aircraft failing to re-appear after the first attack. On the second run Squadron Leader H.H.B. Mould was badly shot up and only just managed to struggle back across the Channel, while Pilot Officer I.H. Behil scrapped into Friston streaming fuel. Only one No 245 Squadron Hurricane was still serviceable after the first mission but No 3 Squadron, quickly refuelled and re-armed, was off

A gunnery trainer dome was built on the northern perimeter of Shoreham in 1943 and is still in reasonably good condition (M.L. Asquith).

again at 07:50 hours with No 43 Squadron, this time escorted by Spitfires of Nos 310 and 312 Squadrons. Ground crew at Shoreham worked frantically on damaged Hurricanes and seven of No 245 got away at 12:55 hours for their second strike on gun positions. Making their strafing runs at 300 ft (91 m), the Hurricanes again came under heavy fire, several being hit but none lost, the squadron ending the day with three usable aircraft.

Nos 3 and 245 Squadrons returned to their bases at Hunsdon and Middle Wallop immediately after the Dieppe fiasco and No 277 remained the only based unit. On October 2 a Lysander crew from Hawkinge spotted a pilot in the sea off Cap Gris Nez and a Shoreham Walrus was sent to rescue him. Under fire from German coastal batteries and in constant danger from mines the pick up was successfully accomplished, earning DFMs for both the pilot, Sergeant T. Fletcher, and his gunner, Sergeant L. Healey.

On November 25 1942, Ford took over parentage of Shoreham and Spitfire IIs started to replace the unsuccessful Defiant early in 1943, greeted by the heaviest Luftwaffe attack of the war when over 100 incendiaries were dropped on or around the airfield on February 13 1943, but without causing serious damage. The near defenceless ASR amphibians were also regularly attacked, a particularly one-sided fight being on April 14 when a Walrus was intercepted by 15 Bf 109s. When the top mainplane was set on fire, Pilot Officer J. Barber was forced to alight heavily. The amphibian sank and the crew took to the water, inflating their dinghy when the Germans left. Fortunately it was another Walrus which reached them first, and they were soon back at Shoreham, little the worse for their experiences.

In April 1943 No 7 AA Practice Camp was formed to train RAF Regiment gunners, their plodding target-towing Lysanders becoming No 1631 Flight on August 1. Meanwhile the airfield was swarming with the Regiment and the accent on gunnery training was increased when No 18 Armament Practice Camp was formed on October 18. It moved to Eastchurch by the end of the year and the AA Flight amalgamated with No 1622 Flight at Gosport, operating from Shoreham as C Flight of No 667 Squadron.

A 3,600 ft (1,097 m) metal track strip was laid by the Pioneer Corps in February 1944 to reinforce the 03/21 grass runway, this work co-inciding with a spate of attacks by VIIIth AF heavy bombers on targets in France. Many of the B-17s and B-24s were badly shot up and in just one month (February 11 to March 12) seven Fortress and two Liberators chose to land at Shoreham. Though only one overshot the USAAF had to be urged not to use the field unless essential because of the damage they did to the surface, and the difficulty of getting these heavy bombers out again.

In March Shoreham was transferred to Tangmere as a forward satellite and the first Sea Otter rescue was made on the 5th, these amphibians having been dogged by unserviceability since their arrival in October 1943. Six injured Americans were picked up from a ditched B-24 south of Bognor Regis, and altogether 14 aircrew were rescued that day. Two days later, Squadron Leader Brown landed his Sea Otter in the Somme Estuary to rescue four Americans right under the noses of the Germans. Overloaded he was unable to take-off so taxied the amphibian all the way home—a distance of 76 miles (122 km)! The following month No 277 Squadron HQ arrived from Stapleford Tawney and on April 26 No 345 (Free French) Squadron flew in from Ayr with Spitfire

Vbs. After an air firing course, the squadron started operations on May 2 with defensive patrols along the south coast, ten days later flying its first *Ramrod* when it escorted the Bostons of No 342 (Free French) over France. It was the start of the busiest sustained period of military operation at Shoreham since World War 1, both Nos 277 and 345 Squadrons being extremely active during the next three months.

D-Day was heralded by mail censorship and a string of VIP visits which included the AOC No 11 Group and General P.J. Koenig, Commander of the Free French forces in Britain. No 345 Squadron flew four missions on June 6 covering the landings, and late in the day escorted long trains of tug/glider combinations carrying airborne trooops to their LZs behind the coastal defences. The squadron suffered its first loss on these operations, and more during the next two days while covering American beachheads. This work plus the occasional bomber escort or sweep was the pattern of operations for the next two months. On July 26 a sudden weather deterioration resulted in No 345 Squadron pilots making a hasty diversion to the beachhead ALG B2 (Bazenville) and an emotional reunion with their native soil. The squadron returned to Shoreham the next day, but transferred to 2nd TAF and Deanland on August 16. Most of the excitement at Shoreham was over, though the Spitfire Vs of the ASR squadron managed to shoot down the odd V-1 flying bomb in addition to their other duties, a first class effort in aircraft which could not overhaul a 'Doodlebug' in straight and level flight!

The Station HQ closed in September and the following month No 277 Squadron moved its Spitfire and Walrus aircraft to Warmwell, and its HQ to Hawkinge. Shoreham was reduced to C&M but when Tangmere became the Central Fighter Establishment on January 15 1945 a detachment was formed at Shoreham until Nether Wallop took over the airfield during March. It is believed that No 451 (RAAF) Squadron arrived with Spitfire XVIs on May 17 1945 for a short stay, but there was certainly little other activity until Shoreham was transferred to the Ministry of Civil Aviation on March 12 1946.

The South Coast FC was re-established and the airfield was officially re-opened on June 29 1946. The Government hoped that the airport would become part of an internal air service network, but there was little interest until 1951 when Shoreham reverted to the control of the Joint Airport Committee. It was leased to F.G. Miles Ltd, an aircraft repair and overhaul company, formed after the liquidation of the Woodley-based Miles Aircraft Ltd. They occupied most of the existing buildings and restarted aircraft design and prototype construction, the first product being the Miles M77 Sparrowjet which flew on December 14 1953. They also took over operation of the renamed Southern Aero Club. East Anglian Flying Services started local schedules to France and the Channel Islands but, when the company re-formed as Channel Airways on October 25 1962, services from Shoreham were dropped.

The Miles Student made its first flight on May 15 1957 but despite much interest

The unexploded bomb dropped in 1940 and discovered during excavations for the laying of the tarmac runway in 1981— now resides in the entrance hall of the terminal building (M.L. Asquith).

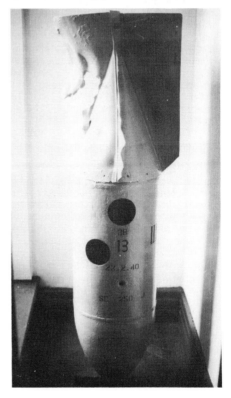

there were no orders and in October 1960 F.G. Miles Ltd was absorbed by Beagle Aircraft Ltd. A new factory was erected in 1962 and a number of Beagle B 206 light executive type aircraft plus a handful of experimental prototypes were produced, in addition to the 180 Pup club trainers completed before Beagle went into liquidation during February 1970.

Shoreham became a Municipal Airport again on May 15 1971 and the factory was taken over by Miles Aviation and Transport Ltd the following November—which must have given F.G. Miles some wry satisfaction. More recently a number of small air taxi firms have moved into Shoreham, and Spooner Aviation have operated a successful agency for Enstrom Helicopters since 1972. Other current organisations are Link-Miles who build flight simulators in the factory, the Southern Aero Club, Toon Ghoose Aviation flying school, Chelsea College of Aeronautical Engineering and Jersey European Airways who operate regular Channel Islands services.

The airfield has proved resilient despite its environmental problems. With a hard runway now in full operation it would seem assured of an enduring future. A number of wartime buildings are still in use, a gunnery practice dome remains near Honeyman's Hole, and less obvious are concrete pill boxes, gun emplacements and two retractable gun positions intended for use in case of glider-borne attack. The pre-World War 2 terminal must be one of the few 1930s style buildings still in daily use.

Slindon, West Sussex
SU952104. 6½ miles NE of Chichester

The renewed German submarine offensive early in 1918 resulted in increased operations by the RNAS airship bases along the south coast and the establishment of mooring-out stations to decrease the risk of weather interfering with patrols.

One of the Polegate mooring-out stations was at Slindon in a sheltered valley in Eartham Wood, between The Folly and the course of Stane Street, a long abandoned Roman road. Brought into use on April 28 1918, two SSZ ships were usually in operation at Slindon, which had a very good reputation as one of the best mooring-out sites in the Group. It was soon abandoned after the Armistice and there are no obvious remains in the wood.

Soberton, Hampshire
SU620155. ¾ mile SE of Soberton village off minor road

On a plateau just south-east of Soberton in a particularly hilly part of Hampshire this LG covered some 150 acres and provided two landing strips, NW/SE and N/S. It was prepared as a scatter field for Gosport during July 1940 when heavy air raids were daily expected on all the airfields in south-eastern England. Nothing is known of its actual usage but it was still listed as an ELG by the Air Ministry in 1944 and was used for a period during the 1950s as a practice forced landing field by Air Service Training Ltd of Hamble, before being relinquished in favour of Somerton, IoW.

It has now reverted to good arable land divided into fields by substantial earth banks and hedges and there is no sign of its transitory wartime purpose.

Somerton, Isle of Wight
SZ488944. 1 mile S of Cowes on A3020

When J. Samuel White & Co Ltd, the well-known Isle of Wight boat-builders extended their Aviation Department to include landplanes as well as seaplanes they sent them away for flight trials at first, and later used a field at Three Gate Cottages, Northwood. Neither solution was very satisfactory and so when invited to tender for 20 Short Land Tractor bombers early in 1916 they purchased 60 acres of arable farmland between Cowes and Northwood from the owners of Somerton Farm. While the task of clearing hedges and filling in ditches progressed, the Company decided that they could improve on the Short bomber by producing a landplane version of their Type 840 seaplane, and the proposed contract was held in abeyance awaiting the outcome of trials. Named Somerton, the aerodrome site and the newly erected hangar were inspected and approved by an Air Department representative on March 28 1916 and flight trials of the aircraft started early in April.

By the time production started a 20-acre site on the other side of the main Cowes-Newport road opposite the aerodrome had been obtained for new factory buildings. It was tooled up in time to cope with the conversion of some of the landplanes into seaplanes and the assembly of licence-built Short 184s. These were then trundled down a prepared path across the fields on trolleys and rolled down the bank into the Medina, to be towed down the river to the East Cowes slipways for flight preparation.

Samuel White built an extraordinary quadruplane scout which was flown at Somerton during 1916 and S.E. Saunders Ltd also produced the T 1 two-seat tractor biplane during 1917. Neither were successful, the latter company's landplane efforts being concentrated on Avro 504 production which were flight tested at Somerton, the aerodrome acting as an Air Park for IoW landplane production.

In 1918 the School of Aerial Co-operation with Coastal Artillery at Gosport, started to use Somerton as a day LG while working with gun batteries on the Isle of Wight. In practice it was more of an AA co-operation unit than a school, its 12 BE 2Cs and 118 personnel moving over to Wight aerodrome, as the RAF called Somerton, during September 1918. The Armistice had a stultifying effect on the co-operation unit and the White factory, the latter ceasing aircraft production on January 21 1919 and closing down the Aircraft Department completely in July. The Coastal Battery Co-operation, as it was now named, was still functioning at Somerton in August 1919 when it was decided to close and dispose of the air station, but it is doubtful whether there had been much activity for months.

It is believed that Somerton was operated as an unlicensed aerodrome during the 1920s, certainly it was used by Captain F.W. Merriam, AFC, for his unsuccessful gliding school which closed in 1923 and for his Aviation Bureau started in 1926. He used his Avro 504K for joy-riding during Whitsun in 1928, and it was the scene of initial flight trials of the attractive little Saunders A 10 fighter early in 1929. With the award of a sub-contract for Bluebird IV production in May 1929 Saunders-Roe started using it as a flight test and delivery airfield, augmented when Spartan Aircraft Ltd added Arrow, Three-seater and Cruiser production following their take over of the Somerton works on February 20 1931.

An operating company, known as Spartan Air Lines, was formed to fly services between Heston and Cowes from April 1933, partially to demonstrate the Cruiser on such routes. The following year Railway Air Services started a service into Cowes from Birmingham and Bristol using a Dragon, and in 1936 Spartan Air Lines was absorbed by British Airways.

Somerton (Cowes) remained the property of Saunders-Roe and when the war started it stayed open as the communications airfield, all other Isle of Wight aerodromes being closed. The Air Ministry were extremely concerned about the vulnerability of Somerton, its defences against surprise assault being confined to two unarmed watchmen. Two years later the airfield was under consideration as an ALG but the report, issued in June 1942, put it low on the priority list because, although two landing strips were possible, they were a barely adequate 3,000 ft (914 m) and the area was obstructed by buildings. In the event the site was rejected, the airfield remaining undisturbed, used irregularly by visitors to Saunders-Roe throughout the war. A Tiger Moth of No 41 Squadron was overturned by a gust of wind during take-off on September 14 1944 but other incidents seem to have been few.

During 1946 Somerton Airways was formed for charter work, the operation of Cowes AC, and were also responsible for the running of the airfield. In September 1947 they were taken over by Morgan Aviation who later undertook the lengthening of the main grass runway from 2,490 ft (759 m) to 3,600 ft (1,097 m). Somerton Airways was granted BEA associate status to operate scheduled services to Portsmouth and Southampton from May 1949, but the agreement ceased in April 1951 and shortly afterwards the company ceased trading and the airfield was closed.

In January 1951 Air Service Training Ltd of Hamble purchased the lease, intending to use Somerton for practice force-landings and possibly as a relief airfield. They withdrew when a cut back in flying training made the airfield superfluous, and the land was purchased by Plessey who built a factory on the site, retaining part of the original hangars. The Somerton Works still stand, almost unchanged in appearance from its First World War days with J.S. White and Co.

Southampton (Eastleigh), Hampshire
See Eastleigh

Southbourne, West Sussex
SU763065. 6 miles W of Chichester off minor road

Sometimes referred to as Emsworth, which is the nearest town, the proposed Southbourne aerodrome should not be confused with the pre-1914 landing ground near Bournemouth which was popular amongst early aviators for a brief spell.

Southbourne was intended as a Training Depot Station for a Handley Page 0/400 unit of the United States Army Air Service. It was considerably larger than most TDSs, covering some 247 acres of flat agricultural land between the parishes of Westbourne and Southbourne. Construction was well under way by the beginning of August 1918 with roads and essential water, sewage and power services virtually complete, and a start made on the large technical site alongside Southbourne village. This consisted of six large aeroplane sheds, an even larger Handley Page erection shed, an Aeroplane Repair shop, salvage shed and two MT buildings. A substantial domestic site was planned in the north-west corner near Lumley Farm.

Although scheduled for completion by November 1 1918, this proved optimistic and Southbourne remained unoccupied after the Armistice. The buildings were auctioned off in 1919 and the site returned to agriculture. It has stayed remarkably undisturbed since then, the only inroad being the construction of a new school on what was to have been part of the technical site at Southbourne.

Staplehurst, Kent

TQ810432. 8 miles SSE of Maidstone off A229

Situated on low-lying ground between Staplehurst and Headcorn, and just south of the River Beuit, this was the most westerly of the 12 Kentish ALGs. Surveyed during the spring of 1942, it was tentatively selected in July, but awaiting approval from the Air Ministry. A detailed survey was completed in September when the report stated that the site was capable of development with a 4,200 ft (1,280 m) main E/W strip and subsidiary N/S runway of 3,300 ft (1,006 m), both with good approaches. A few scattered trees would have to be felled and a cottage demolished, but some accommodation was available at Chickendon Farm, Spills Hill Farm and in several cottages in the immediate vicinity.

The site and aircraft dispersal plans were accepted and the go ahead given on January 19 1943, work starting almost immediately with a target completion date at the beginning of March. On completion Staplehurst ALG was cleared for cattle

grazing until the arrival of No 126 Airfield, No 83 Group, on August 6 1943, the 60-vehicle convoy taking 3¼ hours to travel the 40 miles (64 km) from Redhill. Spitfire Vbs of Nos 401, 411 and 412 (RCAF) Squadrons flew in the next day and were soon dispersed around the soft grass field with both air and groundcrew under canvas in farm orchards.

The first *Ramrod*, a close escort to 36 Marauders on August 8, was aborted by bad weather but others followed in rapid succession, some flown from Friston, and interspersed with fighter sweeps over France and the Low Countries. On September 8 the Airfield was cut off from outside contact and all personnel confined to the ALG for Operation *Starkey*. A heavy ground mist delayed things the next morning but the Canadians were patrolling the French coast just after 09:00 hours without incident. During a second mission they were inconclusively bounced by eight Fw 190s, and later escorted Bostons on an abortive trip to Courtrai. Altogether a disappointing day, but it did prove that the ALG could support intensive summer operations. Indeed the only trouble experienced throughout the Canadians stay was with the Spitfire tailwheel which had the habit of getting jammed in badly laid metal tracking and being torn off.

Perhaps the greatest excitement was produced by an escape exercise on October 10. Dropped at locations all over south-eastern Kent and told to use their initiative in getting back to Staplehurst the pilots did just that. Flying Officer J.T. Murchison and Pilot Officer R.M. Davenport stole unattended Spitfires from No 129 Airfield, Ashford, and Flying Officer D.P. Kelly took a Tiger Moth from the same ALG, and the fuss was just dying down when Flight Lieutenant W.R. McRae and Flying Officer T. Koch arrived back in an army bus liberated from a camp near Headcorn. There was much consternation and a few red faces after this incident! Three days later No 126 Airfield was in winter quarters at Biggin Hill.

The ALG underwent improvement during the winter, the runways being strengthened and complete taxy tracks laid together with 70 hardstandings in readiness for hand-over to the USAAF on April 1 1944. P-51Ds of the 363rd FG (380th, 381st and 382nd FS) of IXth Tactical Air Command arrived from Rivenhall early in April but, much to their

P-51D 44-63811 Big Mac *seen at Staplehurst with a group of 363rd FG pilots. It was the mount of Major J.R. Brown, Jr* (South Eastern Newspapers Ltd).

disgust, the pilots continued escorting heavy bombers of the VIIIth AF over Germany because of the superior range of the Mustang over the Thunderbolt. They felt like nursemaids to the B-17 and B-24 formations, though such sorties certainly did not lack action. On just two days during May the 363rd FG claimed 23 kills while on the 24th of the month, having failed to rendezvous with the bombers on a mission to Berlin, the 381st FS took the opportunity to strafe marshalling yards at Hanover and Nordhorn, and shot up 22 locomotives for the loss of four aircraft to the ever-effective German flak defences.

This escort work lasted until the end of May when the 363rd went on the offensive, attacking communications in Northern France. On D-Day itself they escorted troop carrier and glider formations before strafing enemy positions around the bridgehead, this continuing until July 1 when they moved to A-15, a hastily prepared landing strip at Maupertuis in Normandy. The USAAF rear party left Staplehurst four days later and the ALG was not used again, the War Agricultural Committee pressing for its de-requisition during October. With the steel tracking lifted for use on the Continent clearance of the site went ahead during the winter of 1944/45, No 11 Group releasing Staplehurst on January 18 1945.

The only sign of wartime occupation now remaining is a few short lengths of Army Steel Mesh repairing fences on the western boundary road, but another reminder is provided by the use of the name for one of the officers' quarters at Biggin Hill.

Swingate Down (Dover), Kent
See Dover (St Margarets)

Swingfield, Kent
TR240448. 6 miles N of Folkestone on minor road

High on the North Downs above Folkestone, Swingfield had long aeronautical connections, though only a couple of months activity in 1944 seems well recorded. About 50 acres of grassland between St Johns Farm and Park Wood was used as an unmanned emergency landing ground for No 50 (HD) Squadron from 1916 until the end of World War 1, when it was described as a 2nd Class LG roughly rectangular in shape with 1,500 ft (457 m) landing runs. Swingfield quickly reverted to farmland in 1919 only to be resurrected in the desperate days of May 1940 when it was used by Swordfish biplanes flying extremely dangerous spoof patrols over the Dunkirk beaches, trying to look like Gladiator fighters.

Early in 1942 it was surveyed as one of a chain of ALGs which later stretched from Kent to Dorset. The plans, accepted in mid-December, required more land to the east and north-east of the original site. Grading and the removal of numbers of trees starting almost immediately and on May 10 1943 the men of No 16 Airfield Construction Group, RE, moved in to lay two Sommerfeld Track steel mesh runways and erect two Blister hangars. The

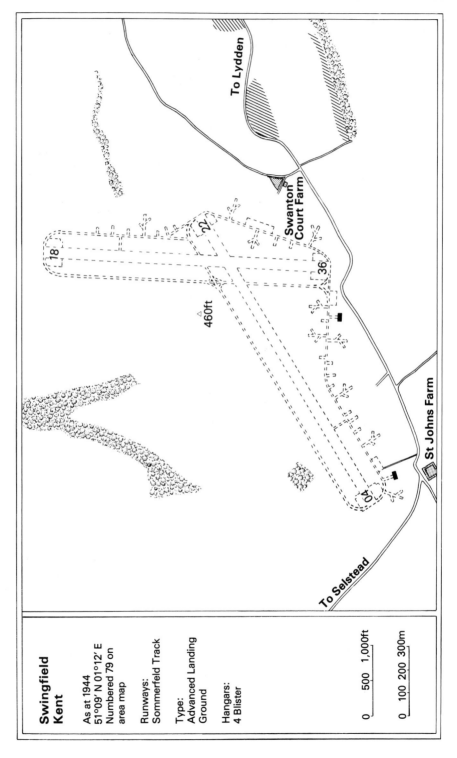

Swingfield
Kent

As at 1944
51°09′ N 01°12′ E
Numbered 79 on
area map

Runways:
Sommerfeld Track

Type:
Advanced Landing
Ground

Hangars:
4 Blister

0   500   1,000ft

0   100 200 300m

work was completed on June 16 when a Spitfire tested the strips, the site then being released for sheep and cattle grazing. In August 1943 it was decided to develop Swingfield to full ALG standards and during the autumn work started on strengthening the main 4,800 ft (1,463 m) NW/SW and secondary 4,200 ft (1,280 m) N/S runways erecting two more Blisters, and laying a complete taxi track and 14, later increased to 50, hardstandings.

Intended for use during the D-Day period Swingfield was not required and apart from occasional aircraft visits from nearby Hawkinge and some reported clandestine Lysander activity it remained empty until August 1944. At the beginning of that month more units arrived at Manston to strengthen the anti-*Diver* defences and with the place bursting at the seams the Coastal Command detachments were politely asked to leave! The Swordfish of 819 Squadron, operating with No 16 Group, RAF, promptly departed to Inskip, but the CO of No 119 Squadron inspected Swingfield on August 6, considered it suitable and moved 11 Albacores there three days later. They were rejoined soon afterwards by 819 Squadron, both units transferring to No 157 (GR) Wing which had its HQ at Hawkinge. On August 10 the first sorties were flown against enemy shipping, followed by smoke laying to cover the movements of convoys in the Channel.

819 Squadron manufactured a DIY flare path, a single line of electric lights, and both units then resumed their anti-shipping and E-boat role, the latter attacked mainly at night. One such attack was made on 11 unidentified targets off Gravelines on August 19 and another on five E- or R-boats off Calais on August 29, when at least one was hit and set on fire. On September 1 No 157 Wing co-operated with surface vessels against a force of 30 German vessels evacuating men from Boulogne, bombs being dropped in the face of heavy flak. One Albacore was shot down, and in similar attacks the next day No 119 Squadron lost their CO, Squadron Leader D.T.J. Davis, DFC. After laying a smoke screen on September 10 to cover heavy naval units shelling Le Havre, operations slackened off and both squadrons transferred to Bircham Newton on October 2 1944. The tented camp site was cleared and Swingfield returned to its role as an unused Fighter Command ALG—not being declared surplus until finally de-requi-

sitioned on April 28 1945 after metal tracking and the Blister hangars had been removed.

Tangmere, West Sussex

SU910060. 3 miles E of Chichester, south of A27(T)

There may have been an element of luck involved, but for the Fighter Interception Unit the night of July 22/23 1940 produced the breakthrough. Flying Officer G. Ashfield, Pilot Officer G.E. Morris and Sergeant R.H. Leyland were on patrol at 10,000 ft (3,048 m) when Poling CH radar station got a contact on a group of raiders crossing the coast at about 6,000 ft (1,829 m). Information on their progress was passed to Tangmere Sector operations room where the FIU's CO, Wing Commander G.P. Chamberlain, worked out an interception and acted as Controller. Ashfield turned his Blenheim If and increased speed in a shallow dive. Two minutes later Leyland got contact on his radar with the target at one mile, slightly right of the nose. He talked Ashfield into a closing position, while in the nose Morris strained his eyes looking into the darkness. Suddenly he saw the shadowy outline of a Do 17Z crossing their path ahead and slightly above the Blenheim. He shouted excitedly and Ashfield looked up, raised the nose and from 400 yds (366 m) fired a long burst from the four belly mounted guns. The Dornier swung to starboard, went into a dive and was lost to view. A few long moments later a sudden flare up on the surface of the sea south of Brighton marked the demise of the II/KG3 aircraft, and the end of weeks of frustration for night fighter crews—success for AI at last.

It has long been claimed that Tangmere aerodrome owed its existence to Geoffrey Dorman, later an eminent journalist, who on November 16 1916 force-landed his FE 2B at Bayleys Farm, while on a flight from Shoreham to Gosport. He flew the aircraft out the next day and his report suggested that the field would make a good landing ground. If the authorities did take note, they also took their time, for the necessary 200 acres were not requisitioned under the Defence of the Realm Act until September 25 1917. Work to clear the site started almost immediately, assisted by a party of German PoWs, and the aerodrome was well advanced in February 1918 when it was agreed to transfer Tangmere to the

United States Army Air Service on completion. The Americans decided to use Tangmere for a Handley Page TDS, the hangars having to be modified to accommodate these large aircraft, resulting in the planned June handover being delayed.

In the meantime, No 92 Squadron, RFC, used it for training on their SE 5As between March and July, when they went to France and were replaced by No 61 TDS, formed at Tangmere with Avro 504K and Bristol F 2B aircraft. It was also used as a LG by the School of Aerial Co-operation with Coastal Artillery, Gosport, until the Americans finally took over in September 1918. The seven GS Belfast Truss hangars and large HP shed were now nearly complete, together with a large amount of hutted accommodation, but continued delays in delivery of their 0/400s prevented the start of training before the Armistice. On November 17, USAS personnel moved in from Ford with a few BE 2Es, Farman F40s and DH 4s, but they were soon on their way back to the States, leaving Tangmere in the hands of No 61 TDS. Pupil training continued at a reduced rate during 1919 with the unit redesignated No 61 TS, while the airfield was used as a holding station for squadrons returning from the Continent, starting with No 41 Squadron on February 7. They all arrived without aircraft, except No 40 which still had its SE 5As. The squadrons either disbanded during the year or, when Tangmere was declared surplus, moved to Croydon, the last departing in December 1919.

The airfield was closed in 1920 but the Air Ministry retained the land and buildings and on June 1 1925 Tangmere re-opened as the Coastal Area Storage Unit which used the extensive hangarage. A Station HQ was formed on November 23 1926 and the airfield re-activated, No 43 Squadron moving its attractive Gloster Gamecock biplane fighters in from Henlow three weeks later. They were joined by a reconstituted No 1 Squadron on April 1 the following year, this unit being fully equipped with Siskin IIIAs in November 1927.

The two squadrons made Tangmere arguably the best fighter station in the country. During the summer a tropical routine was operated, flying starting soon after 07:30 hours and continuing nonstop until 13:00 hours, when virtually the whole Station stood down for the rest of the day. In this Tangmere was unique in the Home Establishment and the subject of much envy, but critics were silenced because Nos 1 and 43 Squadrons always managed to fly more than other units, and regularly beat them at gunnery practice camps and during exercises.

In June 1928 No 43 Squadron re-equipped with Siskins and the friendly rivalry between the two squadrons increased while the Station underwent a facelift with the building of permanent brick barrack blocks, messes and married quarters. Completed in 1930, the work resulted in a neat and comfortable station on the north side of the three remaining GS hangars, ARS and 330 ft (100 m) Handley Page shed. These faced a roughly rectangular grass aerodrome which had a maximum NE/SW landing run of 3,600 ft (1,097 m).

The *Fighting Cocks* received the superlative Hawker Fury in May 1931, No 1 having to conceal their envy for nearly a year before their similar mounts arrived. They were ready to perform at the Hendon Display alongside their rivals however, and such was the fame of Tangmere that Auxiliary squadrons vied with each other for the privilege of holding their summer camps on the station—it really was a golden time for the fortunate personnel on this aerodrome nestling between the South Downs and the sea.

The early 1930s were stable years at Tangmere but things changed rapidly in 1937 with the Expansion Scheme in full flood. Nos 72 and 87 (Fighter) Squadrons were formed in March followed by No 233 Squadron in May, the latter a No 16 Group 'lodger' flying GR Ansons. When the two new fighter units moved out in June they were replaced by another Anson squadron, No 217, from Boscombe Down. Another building programme started with new workshops, MT

Above *A Fury of No 43 Squadron outside the 'GS' hangars at Tangmere (RAF Museum P10420).*

Below left *Tangmere camp buildings in July 1935 dominated by the three 'GS' hangars, and nearest to the camera, the Handley Page assembly shed (RAF Museum P3933).*

Bottom *Blenheim 1f fighters of No 601 Squadron with crews awaiting inspection on a very unpleasant looking day at Tangmere (via A.S. Thomas).*

buildings, more barrack blocks and quarters and in 1938 the airfield was extended eastwards to increase the maximum run to 4,500 ft (1,327 m), and an asphalt perimeter track was constructed.

The Munich Crisis of September 1938 burst upon Tangmere like a thunderclap, air raid shelters were hastily dug all over the camp, hangars were camouflaged and the aircraft and crews brought up to readiness. The Furies were painted dark green and brown and were joined by four Demons, the sole night defence in the area. At the end of the month Prime Minister Neville Chamberlain waved his famous piece of paper and the country relaxed. Not so the RAF, for they were determined to make good use of the respite. No 1 Squadron got their Hurricanes in October followed by No 43 in November, and both started their work-up for the now inevitable conflict.

Tangmere was No 605 Squadron's war station and it duly arrived on August 27 1939 with six Hurricanes and ten Gladiators to replace No 1 which was earmarked for France as part of the Advanced Air Striking Force. No 43 Squadron found itself erecting barbed wire and from September 3 at readiness living in tents alongside their aircraft dispersed on the eastern side of the airfield. When the expected onslaught failed to materialise the alert state gradually relaxed and intensive training resumed. Changes were rapid, No 92 Squadron reforming with Blenheims during October and the old guard, No 43 Squadron, leaving on November 18 to reinforce No 13 Group. It was replaced by No 501 Squadron ten days later, and at the end of the year No 92 Squadron went to Croydon and No 601 arrived, Tangmere entering the New Year with three ex-auxiliary squadrons on strength.

They had ample time to prepare themselves and absorb new personnel, for this was the Phoney War period and boredom was the only real enemy. No 605 Squadron left for Leuchars in February 1940 while No 601, after a period leading groups of Hurricanes to France for re-equipment of the Gladiator squadrons in the field, finally received the aircraft themselves in March.

Both Jersey and Guernsey Airways used Tangmere as their mainland terminal for short periods during February and March while Shoreham was waterlogged, but

generally the airfield was quiet until the sudden German attack on France and the Low Countries on May 10 1940. Immediately No 501 Squadron was sent to Bethienville and *A* Flight of No 601 Squadron joined No 3 at Merville while No 145 Squadron, which had moved up from Filton, ferried Hurricanes to France and backed up the forces there whenever possible. Nos 501 and 601 Squadrons were badly mauled in France, but they did good work over Dunkirk beaches from May 27, *A* Flight of No 601 Squadron again operating from Tangmere.

No 43 Squadron was back at Tangmere and in action off Dunkirk on June 1. The nine Hurricanes were soon split up in a whirling mass of aircraft and when it was over claimed seven '109s and two '110s for the loss of two aircraft and one pilot— a successful baptism of fire. Hurricanes were common at Tangmere but not so six Vought 156F dive bombers of the Aeronavale which used the airfield to mount an attack on the Germans at Furness before returning to their base at Cherbourg. No 43 Squadron was almost decimated on June 7 but a fortnight later was operational again, still at Tangmere with No 145 and the whole of No 601 Squadron. No 1 Squadron returned on June 23 and for the next month the squadrons worked on their new pilots in preparation for the expected Luftwaffe attack on south-east England. Activity against coastal convoys and towns had already started and built up steadily through July as the Germans prepared for *Adler Tag* (Eagle Day).

At Tangmere, now with a fully operational Sector Operations Room, the Hurricanes of No 43 and 601 Squadrons, with No 145 dispersed at the newly completed Westhampnett satellite, provided the day fighter force while the Fighter Interception Unit, formed in April 18, had a few Blenheims. The attacks intensified from August 8 and Tangmere was strengthened with No 266 Squadron. They intercepted Ju 88s of 1/KG51 attacking Portsmouth on the 12th, and probably destroyed two of the bombers in the melee, but lost two Spitfires and were withdrawn for anti-shipping operations. The Germans were now turning their attention to the south-east airfields, attempting to overwhelm the defences by sheer weight of numbers. The third raid on August 16, more than 100 aircraft, reached the Isle of Wight at 13:00 hours.

Nos 43 and 601 Squadrons were already airborne as Ju 87s of StG2 (Stukage-

schwader 2) turned and made straight for Tangmere. Diving out of the sun they made a text book attack which left the Station in ruins. Two hangars were completely destroyed and the other three badly damaged. The station workshops, sick quarters, water pumping station, Y-Service hut and the Officers' Mess were wrecked and the tannoy, power, water and sanitation systems were all put out of action. All six Blenheims of the FIU were either destroyed or badly damaged, along with two Spitfires, seven Hurricanes and a Magister, while ten servicemen and three civilians were killed, and another 20 injured.

While the attack was at its height a damaged Hurricane landed between the bomb craters, immediately becoming the target for strafing and was soon an inferno. With great courage groundcrew extricated the terribly wounded pilot and he was rushed to hospital, only to die the next day. He was Pilot Officer William Fiske of No 601 Squadron, the first American volunteer pilot to lose his life for Britain. Meanwhile the squadrons took revenge on the Stukas, No 43 shooting down seven and damaging three for the loss of two Hurricanes, while No 601 Squadron destroyed two of the escorting Bf 109Es of II/JG2. All the remaining Hurricanes got down safely and *B* Flight of No 43 Squadron had five aircraft refuelled, re-armed and airborne again in under ten minutes. Tangmere remained operational throughout, but the Sector Operations room had to move to St James School in Chichester and the Officers' Mess to Shopwyke House near Goodwood. Some lessons were learnt, aircraft being better dispersed and provided with blast pens.

The FIU's one Beaufighter was moved to Shoreham on August 20 and a very weary No 601 Squadron changed places with No 17 at Debden for a so-called rest. It was soon back, however, in the almost constant juggling of units which Fighter Command performed to try and give pilots some respite from the relentless pressure of the front-line stations. After losing four Hurricanes on September 6, No 601 Squadron was withdrawn to Exeter and replaced by No 213, while No 43 Squadron swopped with No 607 from Usworth on the 8th, the latter's first operational patrol from Tangmere being a disaster, six Hurricanes lost in a battle with Bf 109s over Mayfield.

A decoy airfield was laid out at Gumber

Above *No 501 Squadron's CO's Hurricane stands outside a wooden flight hut at Tangmere late in 1940. In the background are HP 42 and Ensign airliners being used on transport duties* (via M.W. Payne).
Below *Opposite the main gate of the RAF station is Tangmere Cottage where SOE agents awaited transit to France by Lysander during the war* (K.S. West).

and when the day attacks were replaced by the night blitz at the end of September a Q-Site (dummy flarepath) was built at Colworth, two miles south of Tangmere. As the pressure slackened, No 145 Squadron arrived with Blenheim If night fighters. They changed over to intruder work when Beaufighters of No 219 Squadron appeared in December, but despite numerous opportunities the latter had no success and their morale hit rock bottom when Flight Lieutenant Smart of No 65 Squadron had the nerve to shoot down a German bomber over Portsmouth during the night of January 10—using a Spitfire! Things improved in the New Year, the OC, Squadron Leader J.H. Little, getting a Do 17 on February 17, and on the night of March 13 1941 No 219 Squadron had a very successful time, destroying four of the Luftwaffe bombers attacking Tangmere, and damaging another. A barrack block was destroyed in this raid, but there were no casualties. It was decided to disperse all non-essential personnel at night however, 400 airmen being moved into Goodwood Racecourse buildings and another 500 went to Bishop Otter College.

Meanwhile Nos 65 and 145 Squadrons went over to the offensive, sweeping the Channel and Northern France using Spitfire IIs, these activities being continued by Nos 122 and 616 Squadrons. By the summer of 1941 there was a very varied collection of units and aircraft at Tangmere. The detachment of No 23 Squadron from Ford was still present with Havocs, No 219 Squadron had Beaufighters, while two borrowed Army Co-op Lysanders had officially became the ASR Flight in May. The AA Co-op Flight was flying two Blenheims and a Lysander and No 1 Squadron was back, charged with the defence of Portsmouth and Southampton at night using Hurricane IICs in co-operation with Havocs of No 1455 flight, which had formed at Tangmere on July 7. These AI-equipped Havocs carried a searchlight in the nose to illuminate the target for formating Hurricanes to attack. Much time and effort was expended on this scheme, but it was too complicated to be practical and the end of 1941 the night flying expertise so painfully acquired by the Hurricane pilots was being used to seek targets over France.

Questions about other black-painted aircraft discreetly parked on the airfield from time to time were actively discouraged, for they were Special Duty Lysanders carrying agents of the SOE to and from France, where they landed in small fields in the dark. The first of these clandestine flights had been on October 19/20 1940 and, from March 1941, the aircraft of No 1419 Flight were frequent visitors. While awaiting final clearance the agents stayed

in Tangmere Cottage, a small house facing the main camp entrance. Rationalisation of the small units scattered about No 11 Group resulted in the AAC Flight becoming No 287 Squadron in November, and the ASR Flight at Tangmere being withdrawn during December to form part of No 277 Squadron, Stapleford Tawney.

Some reconstruction took place during 1941-42, the airfield being extended to the south-east and west and two asphalt runways, the longest with a run of 5,850 ft (1,783 m), were completed by Wimpey who also laid extended taxiways. The bomb blasted hangars were replaced by 16 Blisters dotted around the airfield.

Throughout the winter No 1 Squadron's long-range Hurricanes operated over France and also continued co-operating with the Havocs. In mid-June 1942 No 43 Squadron arrived from Acklington and took over early July from No 1 Squadron which left to re-equip with Typhoons. The *Fighting Cocks* were just getting settled into the routine when a visit from Air Chief Marshal Sir Sholto Douglas, C-in-C Fighter Command early in August started rumours of something big. These rumours were strengthened when No 87 Squadron's night intruder Hurricanes flew in from Charmy Down, followed by Spitfires from No 41 Squadron, the whole of the Ibsley Wing (Nos 66, 118 and 501 Squadrons) and No 412 Squadron. Only then did the OCs learn about *Jubilee*, the combined operation at Dieppe.

The Hurricanes of No 43 Squadron taxied out for take-off shortly after 04:15 hours on August 19 and joined up with Nos 3 and 245 Squadrons from Shoreham. With No 43's Belgian OC, Squadron Leader D.N.R.G. Le Roy Du Vivier, DFC, in the lead, they flew low across the Channel to attack gun positions west of Dieppe harbour. Though the first fighters to appear, the defences had been alerted

by smoke-laying Bostons and they met heavy flak, seven Hurricanes being hit, two of which were lost. At 05:45 hours it was the turn of the Spitfires, No 41 Squadron providing top cover for the Canadians of No 412 who patrolled over the assault ships for 30 minutes with only a minor skirmish with six Fw 190s to show for it. No 43 Squadron were up again at 07:50 hours, and with No 3 Squadron (Shoreham) and a Spitfire escort searched for E-boats reported to be threatening the ships—but found nothing. Gun positions south-east of Dieppe were attacked by Hurribombers of No 175 Squadron (Warmwell) followed in by No 87 Squadron, covered by Spitfires of Nos 41, 412 and 501 Squadrons.

Meanwhile, No 66 Squadron was held in reserve, but with the decision to withdraw from Dieppe they were called at last —to escort No 3 and 43 Squadrons' third mission and then patrol the anchorage before accompanying the surviving Hurribombers of No 174 Squadron (Ford) back across the Channel. More sorties followed during which No 41 Squadron had five Spitfires hit, their OC, Squadron Leader G. Hyde, failing to return, and shortly after 15:00 hours Nos 41, 118, 501 and the 309th FS (Westhampnett) set out to cover the returning ships, which they found being attacked by the Luftwaffe. Nos 118 and 501 Squadrons rushed in and two Do 217s were shot down for the loss of one Spitfire. The visibility now deteriorated rapidly and only four of No 501 Squadron managed to sneak into Tangmere, the rest landing at bases all along the south coast. So ended a fiasco for Combined Operations, but a generally successful day for Tangmere, which put up over 400 sorties.

Typhoon 1b of No 197 Squadron flown by the CO, Squadron Leader M.C. Holmes, DFC, from Tangmere in October 1943 (IWM CH11592).

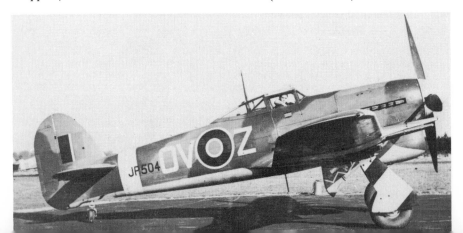

Just before *Jubilee*, Shopwyke House was handed over to the 31st FG, USAAF, at Westhampnett and the Officers' Mess was re-established at Tangmere. The airfield became host to a succession of Spitfire squadrons engaged on *Rhubarbs* and *Ramrods*, joined in September 1942 by Albacores from 823 Squadron for three months of costly anti-shipping patrols in the Channel. Typhoons of No 486 (RNZAF) Squadron arrived at Tangmere at the end of October to tackle the Luftwaffe fighter-bombers making low level attacks on south coast towns, ports and airfields and proved very successful in December when four Bf 109 and a Fw 190 were shot down. For good measure two Do 217s also went into the bag.

With a slackening of activity in the spring of 1943, the Tiffies went on the offensive, flying escorts to fighter-bomber *Ramrods* and *Roadsteads* joined by No 197 Squadron in March 1943. When No 486 Squadron started carrying 500 lb (227 kg) bombs for attacks on enemy shipping in the Channel and along the French coast, the Wing was strengthened by No 183 Squadron from Harrowbeer, and the temporary Operations Room at St James School had to move into larger premises—the Concert Hall of Bishop Otter College.

All three Typhoon squadrons played a full part in the spoof operation *Starkey* during the early days of September, but when No 197 Squadron converted to fighter-bomber operations No 183 Squadron moved out, and the Griffon-powered Spitfire XII Wing (Nos 41 and 91 Squadrons) transferred from the nearby Westhampnett satellite. They concentrated on *Rodeo* fighter sweeps but only once managed to attract the Luftwaffe. This was on October 20 when a mixed force of 25-30 Fw 190 and Bf 109s attacked out of the sun. The Spitfire pilots turned into the would-be 'bouncers' and after the battle claimed nine for no loss. As the year wore on the Spitfire Wing started escorting No 2 Group and American bombers to *Noball* (V-1) sites in France, these operations continuing into 1944.

As the bomber offensive mounted so the number of damaged aircraft making emergency landings at Tangmere increased. Weather diversions were also common and later the VIIIth and IXth Air Forces discovered the airfield. Usually the aircraft got down in one piece, though often on their bellies, but there were also incidents like the Halifax on November 19

1943 which ploughed into one of the hangars destroying itself, its crew, and six Typhoons of Nos 197 and 486 Squadrons. New medical staff soon became experts at Tangmere!

With the build-up of the 2nd TAF in readiness for the invasion, there was a general shuffle of units and in February 1944 the first No 84 Group Typhoon Wing formed at Tangmere as No 146 Airfield. No 197 Squadron was joined by Nos 183 and 257 Squadrons and led by Wing Commander D.E. Gillam, DSO, DFC and Bar, the Wing concentrated on ground attack, seeking out *Noball* sites in Northern France. Another change resulted in Nos 183 and 197 Squadrons being replaced by Nos 198 and 609 Squadrons on March 16. No 266 Squadron joined them a week later and on April 1 No 146 Airfield went under canvas in preparation for a move to Needs Oar Point ALG.

The six Canadian squadrons of Nos 126 and 127 Airfields, No 83 Group, moved in their Spitfire IXs, Nos 401, 411 and 412 Squadrons from Biggin Hill on April 12, followed by Nos 403, 416 and 421 Squadrons six days later. They flew a few *Rangers* but their main occupation was the dive bombing of *Noball* sites, Squadron Leader N. Fowlow's aircraft being destroyed when his bomb was hit by flak on April 19. Other activities included bomber escorts, during which they usually broke away to attack communications and airfield targets, No 416 Squadron destroying four railway engines on May 22 before being intercepted by six Fw 190s, five of which were claimed by the Canadians.

From dawn on June 6 the Spitfires went off in waves as part of a continuous umbrella over the invasion forces and then concentrated on providing cover for the forward troops, but there was little action. D-Day + 1 was a little more eventful, No 126 Wing following 12 Ju 88s as they dived on targets in the beach-head and though harassed by some P-47 Thunderbolts, cut the bombers to pieces and claimed eight. A patrol in the afternoon coincided with an attack by Fw 190 fighter-bombers and the Wing Leader, Wing Commander G.C. Keefer, DFC & Bar, led No 401 Squadron in and shot one down. The squadron claimed another, and the day was rounded off by No 411 Squadron sending down two more. No 421 Squadron operated from B-2 (Bazenville) on June 15, 12 aircraft meeting over 20 Fw 190s and Bf 109s that evening,

One of the post-war 'T2' hangars at Tangmere—in use for some years as an 'intervention grain store'—note the ventilators (M.L. Asquith).

claiming ten of them for the loss of one Spitfire. The next day the whole of No 127 Wing moved onto the Continent and two days later No 126 Wing were at B-2 (Beny-sur-Mer).

This allowed Nos 132 (Nos 66, 331 and 332 Squadrons) and 134 (Czech) Wing (Nos 310, 312 and 313 Squadrons) to move in from Bognor and Appledram ALGs. The Czechs spent a couple of days at B-10 (Plumetot) at the end of the month and then, leaving their aircraft and Wing designation behind, swopped places with the Lympne Wing on July 4. The Lympne Wing (Nos 33, 74 and 127 Squadrons) then became No 134 Wing as part of 2nd TAF, specialising in close support work with the forward troops. Meanwhile No 132 Wing spent most of its time escorting bombers over France and though these were usually uneventful they had several successful combats.

A surprise visit from HM King George VI and Queen Elizabeth livened things up, but late in July both Wings started to move to satellite ALGs and another Wing of No 84 Group, No 145 (Nos 74, 329, 340 and 341 Squadrons) arrived in August for escort work which included the DC-3 carrying Prime Minister Winston Churchill, and a B-26 Marauder containing the Supreme Commander, General Dwight Eisenhower. On August 19 No 145 Wing moved to France and was replaced by No 135 Wing (Nos 222, 349 and 485 Squadrons) who similarly crossed the Channel at the end of the month.

Suddenly it was quieter at Tangmere, despite the arrival of No 83 Support Unit with its replacement aircraft and pilots, and American transports flying in wounded for treatment at local Chichester hospitals. The GSU went to Dunsfold on January 7 1945 leaving Tangmere available for the reconstituted Central Fighter Establishment which officially assembled on January 15. Over the next few months it absorbed the Day Fighter Development Wing previously at Milfield, the Night Fighter Development Wing from Ford, the Fighter Leaders School, Wittering and

the Naval Air Fighting Development Unit. The NAFDU, usually known as 787 Squadron, flew some very strange aircraft including Barracudas, Avengers and the rare Grumman Tigercat which was at Tangmere in April 1945. To make room for the units from Ford, 787 Squadron moved to the satellite at Westhampnett in July, but the whole of CFE went to West Raynham in October 1945 and a refurbishing programme was undertaken. Three 'T2' hangars were built on the foundations of old bombed ones, and the tatty selection of Blisters were removed.

The sole flying unit was No 85 Squadron flying Mosquito XXXs, replaced by NF 36s in January 1946. On April 30 No 1 Squadron returned to their old stamping ground and it was not long before a large *1* embellished the side of one of the new hangars as they made their presence felt. Also in the limelight was a new High Speed Flight, formed on June 14 1946 to retain the World's Air Speed Record for Great Britain. A course was plotted between Rustington and Angerming and three pilots, Group Captain E.M. Donaldson and Squadron Leaders W.A. Waterton and N. Duke were chosen to fly Meteor IVs on the attempt. Two modified aircraft arrived in August and on September 7 Donaldson achieved 616 mph (991 km/h), putting the record out of reach of the Americans for a little while longer.

A month later No 1 Squadron re-equipped with Meteor IIIs, and No 222 Squadron arrived from Weston Zoyland with the same aircraft to form a new Tangmere Wing, No 85 Squadron providing the night element until April 1947 when it was replaced by a third Meteor day squadron, No 266. Three months later came a traumatic shock for No 1 Squadron, they lost their Meteors and became an instrument flying training unit equipped with Harvards and Oxfords! Common sense prevailed and on June 1 1948 they returned to the fighter fold with brand new Meteor F 4s, replacing No 222 Squadron at Tangmere.

No 266 Squadron became No 43 on

Among the many Meteor variants which graced Tangmere after the war were the NF 11s of No 29 Squadron.

February 11 1949 and the two old rivals were together again, this happy state of affairs existing when Geoffrey Dorman presented the Officers' Mess with the propeller damaged during his forced landing at Tangmere in 1916. Three months later the airfield was officially declared clear of mines—British ones laid in 1940 at the time of the expected German invasion. The standard Fighter Command Station establishment changed to one day and one night fighter squadron, and No 43 Squadron moved to Leuchars in November 1950 to be replaced by the Mosquito NF 36s of No 29 Squadron from West Malling. They received Meteor NF 11s in August 1951 and Tangmere remained an all-Meteor station for the next four years.

In October 1952 the Air Ministry announced that No 1 Squadron would receive its Standard during the following spring. It was a little late, for it had been granted by King George VI in September 1943, but the presentation parade was still the first of its kind when it finally took place on April 24 1953.

Neville Duke had been the reserve pilot on the 1946 High Speed Flight so it must have been particularly satisfying to return to Tangmere in August 1953 with the bright red prototype Hunter, specially modified for a record attempt over the same three kilometre course. In ideal conditions on September 7 he successfully raised the Absolute Air Speed Record to 727.63 mph (1,171 km/h), the equivalent of Mach 0.92 at sea level under the prevailing conditions.

Meteor F 8s and the need for rapid response to low level attackers brought operational readiness platforms (ORPs) at each end of the main runway and a large hardstanding in front of the hangars. No 34 Squadron re-formed in August 1 1954 and eighteen months later followed No 1 in receiving the excellent Sapphire-powered Hunter F 5. Both squadrons went to Cyprus in August 1956 to take part in the ill-fated Suez operation, returning to Tangmere in December. No

29 Squadron moved to Acklington on January 14 1957 leaving a nine-month gap in the night fighter coverage until No 25 Squadron brought its mixed bunch of Meteor NF 12/14s from West Malling.

It was not for long, for the decision to concentrate on defence of the V-bomber bases meant that Tangmere was in the wrong place. During 1958 all three squadrons were disbanded, and Tangmere was transferred to No 90 (Signals) Group, No 2 Ground Servicing Squadron and a Ground Radio Calibration Flight moving in to operate with Canberras of the reformed No 245 Squadron and the Varsities of No 115 Squadron which arrived in August and September 1958 respectively. The Canberra squadron was responsible for daily checking on early warning radars while No 115 Squadron Varsities calibrated navigation and approach aids in Britain and abroad.

In November 1958 No 90 Group was absorbed by Signals Command but this had little impact on the Tangmere units which plodded on with their rather mundane but essential tasks. On May 5 1960 the station received the Freedom of Chichester and in June of the following year relations with the local community were further cemented by the arrival of *B* Flight, No 22 Squadron and their bright yellow ASR Whirlwind helicopters. No 245 Squadron was rather unnecessarily renumbered No 98 Squadron on April 19 1963, and later in the year Signals Command units started returning to Watton and Tangmere was taken over by No 38 Group, Transport Command, on October 1 for use by their non-flying Support Unit which provided backing for the world-wide operation of the Group's mobile forces. The beginning of the end came when No 22 Squadron moved to Thorney Island in May 1964 leaving the airfield to No 623 GS and as a RLG for No 242 OCU which also used it for parachute training drops.

Transport Command was renamed Air Support Command on August 1 1967 and it was this authority which presided over

the closure of Tangmere. After a parade on October 16 1970, the married quarters were handed over to Thorney Island and the airfield reduced to C&M status on December 14. The Gliding School continued in operation until June 1975, by which time the airfield had been taken over by the Property Services Agency who auctioned it off in 1979. Early that year the Royal Engineers carried out anti-terrorist exercises in the Officers' Mess, blowing holes in many of the interior walls. The three 'T2' hangars were refurbished and, with air conditioning and humidity control equipment installed, were used for storage of surplus food by the European Economic Community for several years while the perimeter track was used for training by the Sussex Police Driving School. Demolition of many other buildings started in February 1983 as plans for an industrial estate took shape.

A plaque in the Hall of Bishop Otter College, Chichester, commemorates its wartime use by the RAF and nearer at hand the Tangmere Village Community Centre erected a memorial stone on the village green which was unveiled by the late Group Captain D.R.S. Bader, CBE, DSO, DFC, on December 18 1976. A number of enthusiasts established a Tangmere Aerodrome Memorial Museum and this was finally opened in June 1982 in a large hut on the airfield. After a successful first year an expansion was under way during the winter of 1983–84. It is well worth a visit, as is the *Bader Arms*, a new public house near Tangmere which has some interesting relics of the Battle of Britain period adorning the walls.

Telscombe Cliffs, East Sussex

TQ406017. 2½ miles W of Newhaven off A259

On September 25 1916 a Zeppelin commanded by the great Kapitanleutnant Heinrich Mathy, doyen of the German Naval Airship Service, avoided the Dover patrol and dropped his bombs on Portsmouth. Before this disturbing event it had been considered unnecessary to deploy Home Defence squadrons west of Romney Marsh, but as a direct result of this bold flight No 78 Squadron was formed with Flights at Chiddingstone Causeway, Gosport, and Telscombe Cliffs.

Perched 120 ft (36.6 m) above the sea on the chalk downs between Rottingdean and Newhaven the LG at Telscombe Cliffs was a 1,500 ft by 1,500 ft (457 m) square of grass with no permanent acco-

modation, the six BE 2C/BE 12 biplanes of No 78 Squadron living in canvas Bessoneaux hangars with the men in tents or billets in the nearby township. The Flight had a particularly bleak time through the winter of 1917 for the wind blew uninterrupted across the LG and the Germans never again penetrated so far west. After nine months No 78 Squadron was moved to Suttons' Farms, Essex, and Telscombe Cliffs LG was reduced to emergency field status for 6th Brigade home defence aircraft in difficulties.

The success of the convoy system and long range seaplane patrols introduced in 1917 forced U-boat commanders to change their tactics and move closer inshore to lurk off British ports. Shipping losses within ten miles of the coast escalated alarmingly and it was decided to try patrols by aircraft at 20 minute intervals to force U-boats out to sea again.

This required a lot of aircraft and the only ones immediately available were DH 6s, a low-powered two-seat trainer of little operational value. However the object

Above *DH 6s of No 242 Squadron outside the wooden sheds at Telscombe Cliffs in 1918* (RAF Museum P9339).
Below *A closer view of a DH 6 coastal patrol aircraft at Telscombe Cliffs in 1918. Its marginal performance was of great concern, but it was all that was immediately available* (RAF Museum P9337).

was not destruction of the U-boats, but to scare them off, and Telscombe Cliffs was one of a chain of LGs used by Flights of these aircraft. The Bessoneaux hangars were soon replaced by two aeroplane sheds on the eastern side of the LG, to which a new road was built from the coast road. The guard hut at the entrance doubled as a dining room for duty personnel and a number of Armstrong huts were built for the 30 men on strength, officers and NCOs continuing to be billeted out.

Intended as part of No 253 Squadron, the plan was changed and the Telscombe unit was temporarily known as *A* Flight, being re-designated No 514 Flight when it came under the control of No 242 Squadron, Newhaven, in August 1918. Flown solo as light bombers, or unarmed when carrying an observer, the DH 6s plodded back and forth along the coast for the rest of the war, their success only measurable by the reduced number of sinkings experienced in coastal waters.

No 514 Flight was disbanded on January 20 1919 and the LG was relinquished shortly afterwards. It reverted to farmland but was subsequently completely covered by the new town of Peacehaven.

Theale, (Sheffield Farm), Berkshire
SU650700. 3½ miles W of Reading on minor road off A4

Most airfields built during World War 2 have changed considerably since 1945, some are difficult to positively locate, but few have actually disappeared. Theale is one of the latter, most of it having been removed for gravel extraction, leaving a large expanse of water covering the area.

Bounded by the Kennet & Avon Canal to the north and minor roads to the west and south, this rough square of grass fields was requisitioned in 1940 for use by No 8 EFTS Woodley as Sheffield Farm

RLG. Expected in service during November, the newly sown grass was not ready until the following spring when a new unit was planned, operated by Phillip & Powis Aircraft Ltd under contract, as a *C* Type EFTS. No 26 EFTS was formed on July 21 1941 with an establishment of 24 Tiger Moths and 60 pupils, the latter split into two six week *ab initio* courses, overlapping by three weeks.

The airfield opened on August 14 and was renamed Theale the following day. Delayed by flooding it was still far from complete. Two Blister hangars were ready together with some of the office, store and crew huts, but the airmens' mess was still under construction and there was no water supply to the site. Most of the instructors were transferred from No 8 EFTS and all maintenance and other ground services were civilianised, under the overall control of No 50 Group. Sulhamstead House, about a mile from the airfield, was taken over to accommodate pupils and provide ground school lecture rooms, but it was not quite ready and the first course had to be delayed for six days.

Conditions on the airfield were still primitive but the first course commenced flying on August 21. With two Nissen huts as accommodation, *B* Flight started flying from a dispersed site in October 1941, and slowly the technical area near the village of Sheffield Bottom was completed around a 'T1' hangar. By July 1941 the hangarage consisted of the 'T1', two Over-Blisters and three Double Standard Blisters. Flooding was a constant threat, pumping being required in winter.

Tiger Moths remained the main equipment, with one or two Puss Moths, Hinds or Mentors on strength as communications aircraft. There were no night flying facilities, this being carried out at White Waltham, but there was a watch office, of a rare 1941 type. Accidents are inevitable at an EFTS, but seem to have been few at Theale, one of the worst being a collision on the approach on May 19 1942. The school changed over to grading in 1943, each pupil receiving about 12 hours dual flying, but this ceased in May 1944 and was superseded by assessment courses for would-be flying instructors, quickly marred by a nasty accident when *DE 261* crashed amongst Nissen hut sleeping quarters.

No 128 Gliding School formed during 1944, for ATC training using Slingsby Cadets and one of the Blister hangars, it remaining in operation after the end of

Vertical of Theale taken by No 541 Squadron on July 10 1946. The technical site is in the bottom left-hand corner of the field (DoE/Crown Copyright).

the war in Europe when Theale became the first EFTS to close down. Flying ceased on June 30 1945, Sulhampstead House was vacated on July 7 and two days later No 26 EFTS was disbanded, leaving Theale to the C&M party and with 28 Tiger Moths awaiting disposal instructions. An Aircrew Disposal Unit used some of the accommodation until December 14 1945 and the airfield was host to No 128 GS until 1948.

The gravel companies moved in when the site was de-requisitioned and now only only two areas of the airfield remain, the north-west corner on which stands a wooden house, and the south-west where part of the main technical site still stands. This includes a Nissen, two other huts, and the 'T1' hangar which is used to accommodate vehicles used on the adjacent residual gravel workings. The flooded pits, appropriate in view of the waterlogging experienced throughout its airfield use, are now used as a marine leisure centre for sailing and water skiing.

Thorney Island, Hampshire

SU760025. 2 miles S of Emsworth on minor road

The operational debut of the Beaufort was fraught with problems, but by September 1940 it looked as if the worst was over. Ports had been bombed, channels mined, *Rovers* completed, and at long last a torpedo strike made at sea. On the 17th six Beauforts of No 22 Squadron flew down to Thorney Island for another such operation.

After standing by all afternoon the crews were released, some leaving the camp, though most visited the station cinema. At Group they studied the weather and recce photographs and suddenly decided on something new, a set piece night attack on Cherbourg! Blenheims were to shower the port with incendaries and a torpedo attack was to follow in the light of fires produced by the bombs. The Beaufort crews were called to briefing by Tannoy broadcast and visits to local pubs, and all were finally rounded up, some so late they went straight to the aircraft.

The six torpedo bombers formed up in bright moonlight, but as cloud built up over the Channel they became separated and arrived independently, suprised to find shipping silhouetted against flaming dockside buildings, just as advertised. On their run in over the mole, pilots were dazzled by searchlights and distracted by heavy flak from forts surrounding the harbour, but four managed to drop their torpedoes. One was shot down and another was badly damaged, but successfully crash-landed at Thorney by Sergeant Hearn Phillips, who was taken aback when berated by a furious duty pilot for blocking the flarepath. Although last to attack, he was first back, but the other

Looking almost like a model, the newly completed Thorney Island is seen here soon after RAF occupation in 1938 (IWM HU8605).

four landed safely and flew back to North Coates the next day—doubtless reflecting on whether one merchant ship was worth the risks and losses involved.

RAF Thorney Island was just one of several airfields reputedly resulting from a crash or forced landing—but in this case there is some justification for the claim. A Hawker Fury crashed in a field close to St Nicholas Church during September 1933 and the accident investigation team reported the potential of the area to the Air Ministry. With plans for expansion already under way, the report bore fruit and surveyors were soon at work, the Portsmouth *Evening News* printing the first announcement of the intention to build a five-squadron aerodrome on the Island during the summer of 1935. The contractors moved in and the 1,450-acre site was cleared as work went ahead on the construction of six Type *C* hangars fronting the technical and domestic sites of a typical Expansion Scheme airfield covering the area north and east of the approach road to West Thorney village. Steel girders for the massive hangars arrived by rail in December 1935 and were off-loaded at Emsworth, making the final stage of the journey by lorry.

It had been intended to open the station on August 30 1937 for Coastal Command, but this proved optimistic and it was not until the end of the year that major construction work was complete, and the attractive red brick three-storey barrack blocks, administrative buildings and technical workshops could be properly appreciated. Large concrete hardstandings surrounded the hangars and the whole site was dominated by a 95 ft (29 m) water tower.

The airfield officially opened in No 16 Group, Coastal Command, on February 3

1938, the Vildebeeste III/IVs of No 22 Squadron flying in from Donibristle followed a day later by those of No 42 Squadron—the whole of the RAF's home-based strike force! Less than a month later the Station transferred to No 17 (Training) Group and the School of General Reconnaissance formed at Thorney to teach over-sea navigation to embryo GR pilots. The first two courses were transferred from the SoAN, Manston, together with an instructor nucleus. Sharks, Nimrods and Ospreys were soon replaced by Ansons for the flying phases of the course, the school being responsible for training 200 pilots annually.

His Majesty King George VI visited the station on May 9 1938, but the main event of the year was the Munich Crisis in September. No 42 Squadron was despatched to its war station at Thornaby, while No 22 Squadron's aircraft were placed in sandbagged dispersals and fully armed with live torpedoes. Immediately after the crisis, Ansons were ferried out to Abu Suier, Egypt, via Thorney for No 4 FTS, 15 leaving during October, followed during March-May 1939 by batches of Blenheims on transit to Habbaniya.

Meanwhile Thorney Island had reverted to No 16 Group control on November 1 1938, with the SoGR a No 17 Group lodger, and was to remain an operational Coastal station for the next eleven years despite many radical changes of task and occupant. No 42 Squadron moved to its new base at Bircham Newton on August 12 1939 and was replaced by the Ansons of No 48 Squadron who started anti U-boat patrols over the Channel on September 3 alongside the Vildebeestes of No 22 Squadron. Six Ansons searched the area for the German liner *Westerland* on September 9, and two Vildebeestes attacked a U-boat in October—but had no success—it was not yet realised that the standard 100 lb (45 kg) bombs were incapable of denting a submarine hull even with a direct hit!

The anxiously awaited Beauforts arrived in January 1940 and for the next few months No 22 Squadron concentrated on working up these complicated aircraft, leaving No 48 Squadron's Ansons to do all the work in the Channel area, assisted by similar aircraft from No 1 Coastal Artillery Co-operation Unit, which had arrived at Thorney soon after the outbreak of war. Meanwhile the airfield was extended by taking in land south of the road to West Thorney, resulting in the station occupying virtually the whole of Thorney Island and the evacuation of nearly all the remaining villagers.

On April 8 1940, No 22 Squadron left for North Coates and No 42 Squadron returned to work-up on Beauforts, though doing much of its flying from Gosport. At about the same time Coastal Blenheim squadrons started to make short appearances at Thorney as operations dictated, none of them remaining anywhere for long. With Thorney Island getting crowded the SofGR took its Ansons to Guernsey on April 22, and No 1 CACU moved back to Detling to leave the airfield clear for operational squadrons. During the Dunkirk evacuation No 48 Squadron Ansons joined No 500 Squadron in dangerous anti-E-boat patrols off the beaches, and Swordfish of 818 Squadron covered the armada of little ships bringing back troops from Dunkirk.

A Vildebeeste IV of No 42 Squadron, carrying the CO's pennant on the tail, seen at Thorney Island before the war (M. Purcell via A.S. Thomas).

Magnetic mines caused a great deal of trouble at this time and following successful operation over the Thames Estuary using Wellingtons fitted with a 48 ft (14.6 m) diameter magnetic coil suspended from nose, tail and wings, a unit known as No 3 GRU arrived at Thorney on May 24 with three of these aircraft. It remained for two months, disbanding when degaussing equipment had been fitted to the majority of ships.

In June 1940 a detachment of Blenheim fighters arrived from No 235 Squadron, Detling, joined by more from No 236 Squadron the following month when they engaged in Channel patrols. They shot down several enemy aircraft whilst covering convoys and attacks on French ports, the latter the main preoccupation of No 59 Squadron, a Blenheim IV bomber unit also at Thorney.

The Luftwaffe took little notice of Thorney Island until August 13 when a stray Ju 88 dropped four bombs on the airfield without doing significant damage. Three days later another Ju 88 was more successful, hitting a hangar and destroying four aircraft, but the big day came on August 18. Shortly after 14:00 hours four large formations were seen approaching the Isle of Wight, one of which turned and headed for Thorney Island. It consisted of 28 Ju 87Bs of I/StG77 escorted by a strong force of JG27 Bf 109Es. As the Stukas were taking up their classic line astern circle they were set upon by Hurricanes of Nos 43 and 601 Squadrons, and three bombers went down on the first pass. The set piece attack on Thorney was broken up, but the German pilots persisted and succeeded in badly damaging two hangars, destroying three aircraft and damaging another. A fuel dump was hit, as was a shelter resulting in slight injuries to five civilian workmen—the only casualties in the attack. Three Blenheim fighters of No 235 Squadron took off and followed the raiders out to sea. They claimed two, the unlucky Germans then running into Spitfires of No 152 Squadron off the Isle of Wight, and altogether ten I/STG77 Stukas were shot down and five damaged, one beyond repair—a disaster for the unit and, when added to the losses sustained by the other Ju 87 formations, it spelled the end of United Kingdom operations for the much vaunted aircraft.

An evening raid by three Ju 88s on August 23 caused little damage, but unfortunately two Spitfires of No 602 Squadron collided in low cloud while trying to intercept them, and the same type of aircraft was indirectly responsible for the loss of one of a formation of three Blenheim Ifs of No 235 Squadron on patrol over the Solent from Thorney Island the following day. They were attacked by Hurricanes of No 1 (RCAF) Squadron having been mistaken for the rather similar looking Ju 88—not the first, or the last case of poor aircraft recognition during the war!

By September 1940 only the Blenheims of Nos 59 and 235 Squadrons remained at Thorney but 812 Squadron Swordfish soon appeared, and carried out six weeks of very successful shipping strikes and anti-U-boat patrols. In November No 53 Squadron joined No 59 for bombing raids on French ports which continued until February 1941, aimed at the barge concentrations still posing an invasion threat. Further spasmodic raids by single hit and run bombers kept the defences of Thorney on their toes, a 1,100 lb (500 kg) bomb hitting the bomb dump on December 5, but fortunately failing to explode. Two hangars were damaged by a Ju 88 on February 18 1941 but five further small scale raids that year did little further damage. To try and lessen the effects of such attack the *K* Site at West Wittering, some three miles south-east of Thorney, was adorned with very realistic dummy Blenheims and given an electric flare path making it into a *KQ* Site but whether it had any success in diverting the Luftwaffe is not known.

No 59 Squadron returned from Manston on March 15 1941 to continue Coastal's private war on French channel ports and a month later No 404 (RCAF) Squadron formed at Thorney with Blenheim IVs as a GR unit. They were followed by the similarly equipped No 407 (RCAF) Squadron on May 20, and No 415 (RCAF) Squadron on August 20 with Beauforts, but all three moved out before commencing operations.

No 22 Squadron were back on June 25 for fighter-supported torpedo strikes but sightings of enemy shipping in the Channel were rare and when attacks were made the results were depressingly poor. So much so that the Air Staff increasingly favoured bombing as the primary anti-shipping weapon and the Hudson/Blenheim squadrons paid frequent visits to Thorney Island whenever a target presented itself. Such a detachment produced one of the tragic accidents so common during the war. Taking off on an

Beaufort W6491/OA-R *of No 22 Squadron on 'stand-by' at Thorney Island. Other Beauforts can be seen dispersed around the airfield* (M.D. Howley via A.S. Thomas).

operational sortie on September 29, a No 59 Squadron Hudson III suffered under-carriage collapse, the aircraft swinging violently and catching fire. The crew escaped with minor injuries but the fire fighting party continued to play hoses on the aircraft, unaware that there was a full bomb load aboard. Group Captain H.S. Scroggs, the Station Commander, and Squadron Leader P.D. Dear, No 59 Squadron *B* Flight Commander, tried to get the fire-fighters away and when the aircraft exploded they were among the seven killed. Another 13 airmen/soldiers were injured in the blast.

No 217 Squadron swopped places with No 22 Squadron on October 28 1941, and at the end of the year No 280 Squadron formed with Ansons to extend the range of ASR work. Both units left in February 1942 by which time the first major changes to the appearance of the airfield were well advanced, with the construction of runways and extensive perimeter track. With rubble from bomb damaged Portsmouth providing plentiful hardcore the work progressed rapidly, and when completed mid-year the two landing grounds either side of the road were joined into one, the airfield presenting a fairly standard appearance, the longest runway 6,090 ft (1,856 m) SW/NE with subsidiary N/S and SE/NW ones. The original grass aerodrome had been very effectively camouflaged by painted hedges breaking it up into small fields, but the runways and later the extensive hardstandings to north and south made it very conspicuous. The two bomb-damaged *C* Type hangars were not rebuilt, but were replaced and supplemented by 17 Extra Oversize Blisters dispersed around the airfield.

Before No 217 Squadron left on February 16 1942, they had taken part in one of the biggest blunders of the war, one which allowed the escape from Brest of the German battleships *Scharnhorst* and *Gneisenau*. Engaged on night torpedo operations in the Channel the squadron had seven Beauforts at Thorney Island on February 12. Like the rest of the Beaufort force they were completely wrong-footed by the delays in detecting that the German ships had left harbour, and only four aircraft had torpedoes loaded when the squadron got the news that the ships were passing through the Straits of Dover. To make matters worse, the targets were given as three large merchantmen travelling at 8-10 knots.

The four torpedo Beauforts were already late for a rendezvous over Manston when they took off and updated information on the ships was not received because the aircraft had special R/T in place of their normal W/T sets. The fighters had received the revised position and proceeded direct to the target so when the Beauforts reached Manston there was no sign of them. After circling for some time, two crews set off for the briefed position, the other two landed to find out what was going on.

Meanwhile the remainder of the Thorney Island Beauforts had been hastily re-armed with torpedoes and set off for the updated position, followed belatedly by the two at Manston. The three aircraft of the second wave found the German force easily using their ASV radar and on sighting the *Gneisenau* the leader, Flight Lieutenant 'Ginger' Finch turned into the attack. The other two, harassed by Bf 109s, lost sight of him and made for the *Prinz Eugen* and both pressed home attacks but, under fire from both ships and escorting fighters, were unable to see the result. They were followed in by the two Beauforts from Manston who got inside the destroyer screen before they were seen, and before they saw the *Gneisenau*. They attacked together and both torpedoes were seen running well before they were lost in the mist.

The final two, who had set out abortively to search the wrong position landed at Manston, were rebriefed and 22 minutes later the leader, Pilot Officer T. Carson, set off again. He found the ships on radar in appalling weather and started a torpedo run, made hair-raising by the explosion of shells beneath the Beaufort, which at one stage was completely out of control. The final aircraft took off from Manston just as Carson set course for home. Again the crew were guided by radar and again it was the *Gneisenau* which attracted their attention. The pilot, Flight Sergeant M. Banning, had never dropped a torpedo before but he followed his briefing and was able to watch it converging with the ship. After it had travelled some two-thirds of the way, however, the *Gneisenau* went hard to port and the 'tinfish' ran harmlessly astern. Back at Thorney the surviving crews were both sad and angry as they prepared to leave for Skitten. They felt they hadn't been trusted with vital information, and had fought with one hand behind their backs.

Meanwhile, the 12 available Beauforts at St Eval, manned by a mixture of crews from Nos 22, 86 and 217 Squadrons, were flown to Thorney, arriving at about 14:30 hours. While the aircraft were refuelled the crews briefed, and took off in four flights of three shortly after 16:00 hours, to rendezvous over Coltishall. Setting course for the estimated position they saw nothing except four German minesweepers.

No 415 (RCAF) Squadron had exchanged their Beauforts for Hampdens during January-February 1942 and continued their work-up on these new torpedo bombers at Thorney until April, when they left for St Eval and No 489 (RNZAF) Squadron commenced conversion to the same aircraft. A string of Hudson, Blenheim and Hampden squad-

rons spent short periods at Thorney during the spring/summer of 1942, which was perhaps more noteworthy for the sudden appearance of the first fighter unit. Spitfire Vbs of No 129 Squadron arrived at the end of July, amongst the first to move into position for Operation *Jubilee*, the combined forces raid on Dieppe. Joined by No 130 Squadron on August 16, both units were briefed and ready by the evening of the 18th.

No 129 Squadron were up early next morning, their first duty an attack on the Point d'Ailly lighthouse which accommodated the observation post for the Hess gun battery, to the west of Dieppe. One of the two aircraft was hit by flak and crashed into the sea—the first Spitfire loss of *Jubilee*. The other strafed the lighthouse and its protecting flak tower and turned for home, on the way attacking two Fw 190s which had just shot down a Boston. An hour later 12 aircraft were attacking the Hess battery to give cover to Commandos as they went in to destroy the six 150 mm guns. No 129 Squadron was set upon by Fw 190s, and a brief dogfight resulted in some damaged Spitfires and a claim of a possible Fw 190.

No 130 Squadron took off at 08:00 hours to fly top cover for the ships. With them went Wing Commander M.V. Blake, DSO, DFC, who destroyed a Fw 190, but was then shot down himself and became a PoW.

Mid-morning No 129 Squadron were off again, escorting No 43 Squadron in an attack on the Bismarck battery to the east of Dieppe, strafing the beaches to divert fire from the Hurricanes. During the withdrawal they were put on top cover for the flotilla of ships mid-afternoon, and had the satisfaction of shooting down a Do 217 before being recalled as the weather closed in. Only four aircraft managed to

Amongst the many Coastal Command strike aircraft which operated from Thorney Island in 1942 were Hampdens of No 489 (RNZAF) Squadron (RAF Museum P7181).

squeeze into Thorney, one crashing into a hillside north of Tangmere, the rest landing anywhere they could. Whether the low cloud saved Thorney from a retaliatory raid like that suffered by Ford is surmise, but it was later in August that enemy bombers made their 17th, and last, attack on the airfield.

No 130 Squadron returned to Perranporth the next day, but No 129 Squadron stayed until relieved by No 131 Squadron on September 24. On the Coastal scene Thorney Island was now virtually a Liberator OTU, No 59 Squadron working-up on these four-engined aircraft, the first to be based on the airfield. Six crews were then transferred from No 120 Squadron for the re-birth of No 86 as a Liberator squadron, but their first task was to train crews for No 160 Squadron, a bomber unit intended for operations in the Middle East.

The gap in the operational anti-submarine cover of the Channel had been temporarily filled by the arrival of Whitley VIIs of No 612 Squadron late in August 1942, but they left for Wick on September 23 and it was a month before No 59 was ready to take their place in the front line. In December they suddenly received Fortress IIas as replacements and moved to Chivenor in February 1943. Meanwhile, No 86 Squadron had at last built up to its established nine Liberator IIIs, but left for Aldergrove on March 19 before becoming operational.

Channel cover was provided by 816 and 819 Squadrons which spent much of the autumn shore-based at Thorney Island, their Swordfish used for anti E-boat and shipping work. No 415 (RCAF) Squadron brought its Hampdens back in November 1942 for anti-shipping strikes and had the distinction of remaining for an almost unheard of length of time—a whole year. They gradually changed over to anti E-boat patrols at night using radar, and had some limited success against these elusive targets, though not without loss, both operational and accidental. Among the latter were a collision with a Fortress on the runway at the end of December and a Hampden fire whilst refuelling on February 26 1943. Two 500 lb (227 kg) bombs were being loaded and both exploded, damaging four more aircraft parked nearby. Fortunately the armourers and refuellers had time to get clear and there were no casualties. 816 Squadron left at the end of 1942 but was replaced by 833 and 836 Squadrons.

For anti-submarine work No 59 Squadron returned in March 1943 followed by No 53 Squadron in April, both re-equipping with Liberator Vs as these became available. No 59 Squadron moved to Aldergrove in May but No 53 stayed until September, commencing operations on May 25 with a *Musketry* patrol over the Bay of Biscay. These Bay operations were always at risk from Ju 88s and several crews were involved in running battles with them. On July 8 Liberator *B* flown by Flying Officer Handasyde was attacked by seven '88s for nearly 40 minutes, but despite one engine being put out of action early in the fight the aircraft got back to base, though with one gunner dead and another injured.

No 415 (RCAF) Squadron started to re-equip with Wellington GR XIIIs during September 1943 and the following month *A* Flight received six Albacores from 841 Squadron, FAA, both types intended for operations against German torpedo boats in the Channel and Dover Straits. On November 15 the squadron moved to Bircham Newton to provide room for No 547 Squadron, who started conversion to Liberators in November and resumed full scale operations from St Eval in January 1944.

This left Thorney Island empty except for a Warwick detachment from the ASR Training Unit at Thornaby, which had arrived in December 1943 but departed in March 1944. The reason became clear on the 15th when Typhoons of Nos 164 and 193 Squadrons moved in to form No 136 Airfield of No 84 Group, and Thorney joined the multitude of airfields taken over by 2nd TAF. No 164 Squadron, which had just converted from Hurricane IVs, was operational by the end of the month when the Airfield was joined by Nos 183 and 609 Squadrons, also with Typhoon Ibs.

It was not long before musical chairs commenced, No 193 Squadron going to the APC at Llanbedr on April 5 in place of No 198 which arrived at Thorney the next day to form No 123 Airfield with No 609 Squadron. A week later No 164 Squadron went on a ten-day APC but was back in time for an attack on a *Noball* site by Nos 136 and 146 Airfield (Needs Oar Point) on April 26, led by Wing Commander D.E. Gillam.

By the end of April Nos 123 and 136 Airfields were firmly established at Thorney, becoming Wings on May 15, and three days later Wing Commander

J.M. Bryan, DFC, led aircraft of Nos 164 and 183 Squadrons on an armed recce over the Gisen-Pontoise area, stumbling over two Bf 109s which were both summarily despatched in a short sharp dogfight. No 123 Wing made a very successful attack on a radar site on May 24 but, like *Noball* installations, these targets were heavily defended and No 198 Squadron lost two more aircraft, a total of three in two days. It was the turn of No 164 Squadron on May 28 when they lost their OC, Squadron Leader A.B. Russell, DFC, during a similar attack, but the Wing felt they had evened the score when the next day two Tiffies were scrambled and intercepted two Fw 190s, both of which were destroyed by Flying Officer A.R. Taylor using only 20 rounds from each cannon.

There was no let-up as D-Day approached, the two Wings concentrating on coastal radar stations. So effective were these operations that by D-Day all stations were out of action except one at Calais, deliberately spared so it could track the spoof radar returns made by Bomber Command to represent an invasion convoy.

On June 6 both Wings concentrated on German armour. No 198 Squadron claimed seven armoured fighting vehicles (AFVs) during their first sorties, but flak and the Luftwaffe took their toll No 183 Squadron losing three aircraft when bounced by 12 Bf 109s. No 164 Squadron also found itself involved in dogfights but claimed two Fw 190s during a day in which they completed three missions. On the 8th No 164 Squadron was again bounced by 12 Bf 109s, but it was the attackers who suffered, one being shot down and two damaged. Two days later however, when No 136 Wing was attacking troop columns Wing Commander J.M. Bryan was hit by flak and crashed in flames. Some Typhoons were now landing in Normandy to refuel and re-arm, occasionally operating from the beachhead all day. On June 17 No 164 Squadron moved to Funtington followed by Nos 183 and 198 the next day, when No 609 Squadron also left Thorney, but for B-2 (Bazenville) on the Continent.

They were immediately replaced by No 140 Wing (Nos 21, 464 and 487 Squadrons), No 2 Group, 2nd TAF. Flying Mosquito FB VIs, they continued both day and night operations without pause, each squadron despatching 15-20 sorties every flyable night. They roamed over German-held territory ensuring delays in supplies and reinforcements and keeping everyone awake. Big efforts were made to prevent the enemy redeploying, as on the night of July 3/4 when No 140 Wing shot up 13 trains and destroyed track, though flak could still be dangerous, No 487 (RNZAF) Squadron losing two Mosquitoes. On July 14 the Wing dropped nine tons of bombs on a Gestapo HQ at Bonneuil Matours in a classic daylight attack led by the redoubtable Group Captain P.G. Waykeham-Barnes, DFC and Bar. Six buildings occupied by the Gestapo were completely destroyed leaving the nearby village untouched. A similar attack followed on August 1 when ten Mosquitoes of No 21 and twelve from No 487 Squadron, escorted by Mustangs of No 122 Wing, went in low level on barracks at Poiters. Again the target was demolished with negligible damage to other buildings. Communications were also daylight targets, the Chagny marshalling yards at Dijon being successfully bombed by 12 aircraft of No 464 Squadron on August 22, though several Mosquitoes were damaged over Le Creusot and the leader, Wing Commander G. Panitz, DFC, failed to return.

A special effort was made by No 2 Group on September 17 1944 in support of the airborne assault on Arnhem and Nijmegen, Mosquitoes of Nos 138 and 140 Wings being heavily engaged. Seventeen aircraft from No 21 Squadron set out to attack barracks at Nijmegen, but the weather and sheer numbers of aircraft in the area made concentration difficult. The other two squadrons were held for night intruder work in the area, but the weather was so bad that the sorties had to be cancelled and two nights passed before rail communications around Arnhem could be attacked.

On October 31 Group Captain Wykeham-Barnes led 24 aircraft of No 140 Wing to the Gestapo's Jutland HQ, housed in two buildings of Aarhus University. They flew in four boxes, escorted by eight Mustangs. With the weather clearing just in time the usual No 2 Group precision attack was made, the flak being so late in opening up that only one Mosquito was lost, despite another flying so low it hit the ground, two being damaged by bomb blast and two by bird strikes. It was one of the longest flights made by the Wing, the round trip of 1,235 miles (1,988 km) taking 5½ hours.

Weather and ever increasing flak

defences continued to take their toll while fog at Thorney Island resulted in many cancelled sorties, though the Wing did manage to hammer away at Von Rundstedt's supply lines during his Ardennes offensive. During the night of January 1 1945 No 21 Squadron shot down two V-1 flying bombs, but operations during the month were difficult because of snow covered ground. With accommodation at last available on the Continent, No 140 Wing moved to Rosieres-en-Santerre (B-87) on February 5/6 to join No 138 Wing in France. Thorney Island was then left to Barracudas of 810 and 822 Squadrons, FAA, and the very mixed collection of aircraft flown by the Air Sea Warfare Development Unit which had arrived during January.

No 16 Group had retained a presence throughout nearly all of the 2nd TAF occupation of the airfield, mainly in the form of FAA squadrons operating under Coastal Command directives. Avengers of 848 Squadron had arrived on June 3 for *Channel Stop* operations, making one attack in June and four in July before departing for a carrier work-up. They were replaced by 854 and 855 Squadrons, who had been flying from Hawkinge as No 157 (GR) Wing but moved to Thorney on August 7 to continue anti-submarine patrols, shipping escorts and night *Rovers*. The latter were flown off the Dutch, Belgian and French coasts between the Hook of Holland and Fecamps. On August 14, Lieutenant Voak achieved the seemingly impossible by shooting down a V-1 flying bomb using the Avenger's front guns, but a fortnight later 854 Squadron was withdrawn prior to embarking in HMS *Indomitable*. 855 Squadron continued the patrols over the Channel until September 6 when the danger was considered over, but a sudden upsurge in activity resulted in 838 and 842 Squadron Swordfish operating from November,

replaced in January/February 1945 by Barracudas of 810 and 822 Squadrons for renewed anti-submarine patrols. These were uneventful except for spotting drifting mines, and in April both units moved to the east coast to help cope with midget submarines.

Meanwhile No 278 Squadron had been transferred from Fighter to Coastal Command, moving its HQ to Thorney Island in February and absorbing aircrews from the disbanded Nos 275 and 277 Squadrons. Surplus Warwick crews had been sorted out and despatched to Nos 279, 280, 281 and 282 Squadrons by the end of the month, and in March No 278 Squadron was operational on the amphibious Walrus, using Thorney Island and Beccles. During May Sea Otters were received and by August these were operational, though some Walrus were still in use over the English Channel.

No 703 Squadron, FAA, was re-formed on April 19 1945 as the naval component of ASWDU, flying Barracudas and Avengers, joined later by the odd Firebrand. The Mosquitoes of 704 Squadron arrived from Zeals in June but soon moved to Ford and when No 278 Squadron disbanded during October 1945 only ASWDU and its naval associates remained at Thorney.

More changes were afoot however, the final plan for Coastal Command leaving it with one Strike and a number of Anti-Submarine Wings, the former to be at Thorney Island. In May 1946 Nos 248 and 254 Squadrons, flying Mosquito VI and Beaufighter Xs respectively, moved in from Chivenor and Langham in readiness for conversion to the Brigand torpedo-fighter when it was declared fit for opera-

Spitfire LF XVIs of No 63 Squadron at Thorney Island in 1948 (H.M. Quinton via PSL).

tional service. On October 1 1946 the squadrons were re-numbered Nos 36 and 42 Squadrons and the following month No 1 Torpedo Training Unit arrived from Tain with Beaufighters, thus bringing all the available operational torpedo expertise together on one station. Training largely concerned dummy attacks on Fleet units whilst awaiting the Brigand, but the aircraft was continually delayed and in October 1947 another policy change resulted in abandonment of the Strike Wing concept. Disbandment of both squadrons and the TTU soon followed.

On December 15 1947 Thorney Island transferred to Fighter Command as a No 11 Group station, with ASWDU as a lodger until it moved to Ballykelly in May 1948. The first obvious sign of new ownership was the appearance of Spitfire LF XVIs of No 63 Squadron, these being joined by Meteor F 3/4s of No 56 Squadron early in February 1948. The Wing was completed by the arrival of No 222 Squadron on July 1 by which time all three squadrons were equipped with Meteor F 4s, No 63 Squadron having had the doubtful privilege of being the last front-line Spitfire squadron in Fighter Command when its 'XVIs departed in May 1948.

Meteors held sway at Thorney for just two years during which they took part in all the defence exercises held by No 11 Group, large and small. Changes on the airfield were few, in fact confined to a small extension of the N/S runway northwards when operational readiness platforms were constructed at each end. Early in May 1950 the Fighter Wing moved to Waterbeach and Thorney Island was transferred to No 21 Group, Flying Training Command, for use by No 2 ANS flying Anson T 21 and Wellington T 10 navigation trainers. The latter were already well past their prime and replacements soon appeared, Valetta T 3s in November 1951 and Varsity T 1s the following August. Less welcome were troublesome Marathon T 11s, foisted on an unwilling RAF by the Ministry of Supply. They replaced Ansons in April 1954 and remained three years before the survivors went to No 1 ANS. By this time Thorney was in No 25 Group, and Vampire NF 10s were on strength to give jet experience to embryo navigators. More policy changes resulted in the Vampires being withdrawn in July 1959, only the Valetta 'classrooms' and Varsities remaining in use.

With the change to No 25 Group a number of ex-ASWDU Sycamore helicopters arrived at Thorney, No 22 Squadron re-forming on February 15 1955 as an air-sea rescue unit. Whirlwind HAR.2s started arriving in June and as numbers built up B Flight moved to Martlesham Heath leaving the HQ and A Flight at Thorney as a Coastal Command lodger. Though much better than previous choppers, the HAR 2 Whirlwind was still horribly underpowered for ASR work and on warm summer days fuel had to be taken out to enable a useful load to be carried—a nicely judged balancing act was required. The HQ and A Flight moved to St Mawgan on June 4 1956 leaving a newly formed D Flight to hold the fort in the south-east until December 1959.

On the departure of No 2 ANS in January 1962, Thorney was transferred to No 38 Group, Transport Command, and No 242 OCU moved in from Dishforth. Initially Hastings and Beveleys were flown, joined by Argosy C 1s from Benson in April 1963. Early in the transport regime a new ATC tower was built near the main technical site on the western side, replacing the original watch office near the intersection between the N/S and NW/SE runways.

B Flight of No 22 Squadron returned on May 5 1964 with the much improved Whirlwind HAR 10 helicopter and for the next 8¾ years carried out the multitude of rescue tasks which come the way of all SAR units. The last Argosy OCU course was completed in December 1968, the unit then concentrating on the Hercules on which training had started in April 1967. This situation did not last long however, for during September 1970 the Andovers of No 46 Squadron and the Training Squadron moved in from Abingdon, the ATS merging with No 242 OCU on arrival. They remained at Thorney until more cuts decreed the withdrawal of the aircraft, the three OCU aircraft leaving during April 1975 followed by the disbandment of No 46 Squadron on August 31 that same year.

Local residents had long complained about the noise of training aircraft, resulting in much of the night flying being conducted at other airfields. This, allied with a further reduction in the overall size of the RAF, resulted in No 242 OCU officially moving to Lyneham on October 31 1975 though the last Hercules lingered into November before leaving the airfield to No 22 Squadron. They transferred to

Finningley in January 1976 to form a SAR Wing with No 202 Squadron and the airfield finally closed on March 31 1976. The met office, auto VHF triangulation and UHF Forward Relay transmitter remained under the care of RAF Odiham, but the remainder of the station was transferred to the Navy Department who were considering its use in place of Lee-on-Solent. This plan fell through, as did a proposal to use the northern half for light aircraft instead of Portsmouth. Covered storage was rented by Britten-Norman (Bembridge) Ltd for surplus Islander and Trislander production, with some 20 aircraft in the hangars by mid-1977, and in 1980 the Officers' Mess and adjacent buildings were renovated for use by Vietnamese boat-people refugees, their occupation lasting some two years.

That such a well-found permanent station should remain largely unused seemed criminal, and in August 1982 it was announced that Thorney Island was to be turned into an Army base for 580 officers and men of the Royal Artillery. Refurbishing and alteration took over two years and Thorney is now largely inaccessible. It is therefore extremely difficult to view the memorial plaque made by members of the Technical Wing and set up in May 1949 on the spot where the Fury piloted by Sergeant Hodge crashed in 1933 close to the present Officers' Mess.

Throwley, Kent

TQ991535. 5 miles S of Faversham off B2077

Set high in the wooded North Downs, the Home Defence aerodrome of Throwley was opened in October 1916 to house BE

A BE 12 of No 50 (HD) Squadron at Throwley complete with four Le Prieur rocket rails on the interplane struts (Crown Copyright H1949).

2Cs and BE 12s of C Flight, No 50 Squadron, which had its HQ at nearby Harrietsham. The aerodrome was roughly triangular in shape covering 87 acres, 1½ miles south-east of Throwley Forstal and between the village of Bells' Forstal and a large wood called Dodds Willows. At first accommodation was spartan, consisting of tents and requisitioned cottage property, but the site slowly increased in importance. No 112 Squadron was formed on July 30 1917 at Throwley by expanding *B* Flight of No 50 Squadron and three Bessoneaux hangars were erected close to Dodds Willows for the Sopwith Pups of the unit.

The purpose of the squadron was day and night defence of London against enemy airships and bombers, but despite strenuous efforts No 112 Sqaudron had no success during 1917, their morale receiving a much needed boost in the New Year when Pups were replaced by the much more effective Camel. They had been joined by No 188 (Training) Squadron when it formed on December 20 with Avro 504Ks, and by No 143 Squadron which assembled at Throwley on February 1 1918, also equipped with Camels. Space and accommodation were now very much at a premium but fortunately No 143 Squadron only stayed long enough to work up on their rather touchy steeds, moving to Detling in March. The building programme planned on the arrival of the training unit went ahead, trees being felled in Dodds Willows Wood and a large hutted camp for the 450 personnel erected. On the adjacent technical site was built workshops, three MT sheds and four substantial hangars, two of them 180 ft (54.8 m) long and 100 ft (30.5 m) wide.

Refreshed by a period free of operations and up to full strength, the German strategic bombing unit, Kagohl 3, was ready for another attack on London by mid-May. With favourable weather reports on the 19th the 40 Gothas of the unit, joined by the remaining three serviceable Giants, set off for the British capital during the evening. For more than two hours the raiders straggled in over Kent and Essex to be met by a tremendous gun barrage and some 84 defending fighters, all capable of giving a good account of themselves.

Amongst them was Captain C.J.Q. Brand, one of the original Camel night flyers. He took off from Throwley and during his patrol spotted a Gotha G IV illuminated by searchlights over Canterbury. Catching up with it at 8,700 ft (2,652 m) he gave the German aircraft a burst which put one of the bomber's engines out of action. The Gotha dived away but the Camel pilot held on, firing another long burst which caused it to burst into flames and crash at Harty Ferry on the Isle of Sheppey. Only 13 of the bombers penetrated as far as London, and six were shot down over England, shared equally by guns and fighters—a disaster for the German bombing force. It was the last such attack on Britain and for No 112 Squadron the first and only success of the 1914-18 War.

During July No 188 (NT) Squadron received some Camels to provide advanced training, while the strength of No 112 Squadron reached 24 Camels by September. Air defence gun belts were established with interceptors in free lanes between them, No 112 Squadron being allocated a north/south patrol line (Line H) from Throwley to Judd's Hill near Faversham and on to Warden Point on the north coast of the Isle of Sheppey.

With the Armistice came a considerable slowing of activity at Throwley and it is probable that the hangars were never completed though the remainder of the camp was finished. No 188 (NT) Squadron was disbanded on March 1 1919 but No 112 Squadron received a few Snipes postwar, and survived until June 13 of that year. In October 1919 the site was transferred to the Ministry of Munitions, presumably to store ammunition, but was subsequently cleared and returned to agriculture.

During July 1940 Detling was provided with a scatter ELG at Cadman's Farm, on which the 1914-18 Throwley had been sited. It was probably intended to include land to the south of the original aerodrome, but it is doubtful if any aircraft ever landed there despite the severe pounding suffered by Detling during that fateful summer.

Tipnor, Hampshire

SU638034. 2½ miles N of Portsmouth city centre off A3017

Built on 12 acres of land jutting out into Portsmouth harbour, Tipnor was opened in 1917 as an operational Kite Balloon station working under the control of the C-in-C Portsmouth. Close to Whale Island, it was an ideal spot to provide balloons for ships of the Portsmouth Command, used for spotting purposes whilst on convoy escort.

This kite balloon is typical of the type used at Tipnor (via D.G. Collyer).

A row of six balloon sheds and two MT sheds were built across the site together with a hydrogen gas production unit and accommodation for some of the 182 personnel.

With the formation of the RAF in April 1918 the unit became No 15 Kite Balloon Base and part of No 10 Group, Calshot, but remained under the operational control of the Portsmouth Command. In August 1919 the RAF handed over the base to the Admiralty and it was subsequently developed as a range. Part of the site is now crossed by the M27 motorway.

Walmer, Kent

TR375493. 2 miles S of Deal off B2057

A small 57-acre aerodrome on Hawkshill Down between Kingsdown and Walmer was established in May 1917 as a satellite of RNAS Dover, intended to provide cover for merchant ships anchored off Deal in The Downs. A variety of aircraft were used by a unit known as the Walmer Defence Flight, including BE 2Cs, Bristol Scouts and Sopwith Pups, some apparently fitted with flotation air bags. They were housed in Bessoneaux hangars ranged alongside the Firs, a narrow strip of woodland, NCOs and men being accommodated alongside in tents, soon to be replaced by wooden huts. Officers used Mayes Farm, later moving to Leelands in Grams Road.

Walmer-based aircraft also took part in Home Defence whenever the opportunity arose but with little success, until August 8 1917 when one of a formation of Gotha bombers from Kagohl 3 left the main formation and dropped its bombs on Margate before turning out to sea and was seen to crash-land on the beach near Zeebrugge. On the way home, Flight Lieutenant H.S. Kerby, a Canadian from Calgary, was attracted by anti-aircraft shell bursts over Southend and spotted the main Gotha formation 2,000 ft (610 m) above. He climbed his Pup to 18,000 ft (5,486 m) and fired on them without apparent result, then saw a straggler below and, diving into the attack, forced the Gotha down into the sea, where it turned over. Kerby threw his lifebelt to a man hanging on to the tail before flying back to Walmer.

A fortnight later the Germans returned, and again pilots from Walmer were prominent, Kerby claiming another victim though it was not confirmed. A total of nine twin-engined bombers were lost by Kagohl 3 in these two raids, convincing the Germans that daylight operations over England were no longer sustainable.

In November 1917 No 3 (Naval) Squadron arrived from France for a rest after the heavy fighting around Arras during the summer, and was joined by No 4 (Naval) in December. The Walmer Defence Flight became No 6 (Naval) Squadron at Dover in January 1918 and later that month No 3 (Naval) returned to France, these recuperation attachments continuing with the arrival of No 8 (Naval) on March 3 when they also exchanged their Clerget Camels for ones with 150 hp BR1 engines. Anticipation of the German Big Push resulted in a hasty return to France at the end of the month, accompanied by No 4 (Naval), and Walmer lay temporarily deserted. Not for long though, because with the formation of the RAF renewed efforts were made to improve reconnaissance and shipping cover, six Camels arriving as fighter escorts for Short 184 floatplanes and DH 9 landplane bombers. Three small aero-

A Walmer Defence Flight Pup with two Bristol Scout Ds, the nearest fitted with a Lewis gun on the top plane (Commander J.A. Shaw via D.G. Collyer).

plane sheds joined the one remaining Bessoneau on the western edge of the aerodrome and a charming country house was taken over at St Clare as accommodation for the 41 established personnel.

As 471 Flight, the Walmer unit became part of No 233 Squadron, Dover, in August 1918, operations continuing under No 5 Group control until the Armistice. In January 1919 No 491 (DH 9) Flight moved in from Guston Road, followed by No 233 Squadron HQ in March, but efforts to keep even a truncated coastal force were doomed to failure and the unit was finally disbanded on May 15 1919.

The aerodrome was soon abandoned but not forgotten, the Countess Beauchamp sponsoring a memorial. Dedicated on August 8 1920, it took the form of a thatched well head to which was attached a plate bearing the names of 15 airmen who had served at Walmer and subsequently lost their lives in action.

During World War 2 the site was used again by the RAF—as a motor transport base, while propaganda balloons were launched from a nearby field when winds were favourably inclined to take them over the Continent. By 1945 the World War 1 memorial had fallen into decay, but local interests resulted in it being refurbished and repositioned alongside the footpath crossing Hawkshill Down. Re-dedicated on July 7 1952 it is under the care of the local branch of the RAF Association. The Walmer site is now a holiday centre for deprived children, known as the South London Camp for Boys—certainly a more laudable use than that allowed many old airfields.

Wanborough, Wiltshire

SU220820. 5 miles SE of Swindon alongside Ermin Way

Some airfields have led a peculiarly shadowy life, never seemingly belonging to any recognised organisation. One of these was Wanborough, a small grass field just north of King Edwards Place and alongside the Ermin Way, a Roman road which once joined Cirencester with the fortified town of Silchester.

Developed during 1940 by Flying Training Command as an RLG, No 3 EFTS, Watchfield, requested its use but were turned down on the grounds that the surface was still not ready and that Wanborough was being reserved for a new unit at Lyneham. This finally

materialised as No 14 SFTS in August 1941 but by then Wanborough was already in use by the Oxfords of No 3 SFTS, South Cerney, and the Lyneham-based unit never actually used the North Wilts satellite.

Early in March 1942 No 3 SFTS became No 3 (P) AFU and handed over Wanborough to No 50 Group, thus enabling No 3 EFTS, now at Shellingford, to get their hands on it at last. It was soon humming with Tiger Moths on interminable circuits and bumps but passed to Watchfield on November 9 1942 prior to development work on the site—though it is probable that No 3 EFTS continued to use the landing area. Preparation for permanent occupation was concentrated on its eastern corner adjacent to the plantation dividing it from the King Edwards' Place estate. Here concrete bases were laid for a number of Laing wooden huts, some providing airmens' accommodation, others a combined Officers/SNCOs' Mess. Four Blister hangars were dispersed along the southern and western boundaries, connected by a vehicle access track.

The airfield was occupied by the School of Flying Control on June 14 1943, *A* and *B* Flights, totalling 40 pupil controllers, being in residence by August for preliminary training before moving to the main school at Watchfield. Lectures had to be given initially in marquees whilst the buildings were completed and the training programme was just getting properly established in December when No 3 GTS put out an SOS for an airfield because of severe waterlogging on both Stoke Orchard and their satellite of North Leach. Wanborough was selected and the S of FC moved out on December 18 to be replaced the same day by the advance party from No 3 GTS.

Flying at Wanborough commenced four days later with 12 Master II tugs, 15 Hotspur gliders, 23 staff pilots and 17 pupils on strength! Staff officers were billeted out but there was accommodation for 110 NCOs and airmen on the camp. A steady succession of accidents occurred, inevitable with the pressure to get courses out on time, the first incident being on December 28 when a landing Hotspur hit a hedge and then the ground so hard that a passenger was killed and the glider written off. Night flying accounted for more gliders, and on March 3 1944 a student crashed during his first solo—an extremely rare event.

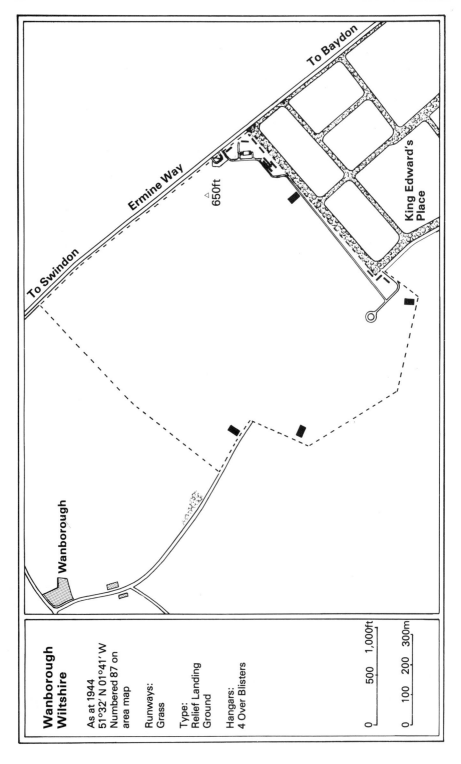

Wanborough
Wiltshire

As at 1944
51°32′ N 01°41′ W
Numbered 87 on
area map

Runways:
Grass

Type:
Relief Landing
Ground

Hangars:
4 Over Blisters

To Baydon

To Swindon

Ermine Way

King Edward's
Place

650ft

Wanborough

With North Leach back in operation the GTS detachment returned to Stoke Orchard during May 1944 and the S of FC regained their RLG, transferring their Airfield Controllers courses to Wanborough. In practice No 3 GTS also continued to use Wanborough until October, and for the best part of six months the small airfield was very busy. Airfield Controllers courses included American personnel during June and July, this work continuing into 1945, the RLG being vacated after the end of the war in Europe, and finally closed down by Flying Training Command on May 21 1946.

Very few signs of wartime use now remain. Some concrete bases are visible in the area used by the Ridgeway Riding School and Stables, and it is probable that one or two of their buildings are ex-RAF.

Welford, Berkshire

SU415745. 7 miles NW of Newbury

Yet another of the OTU airfields strung across the southern counties, Welford was situated on a flat plateau above the River Lambourne, a mile to the north-west of the village from which it took its name. It was intended for No 92 Group, Bomber Command, the plans revealing a standard three-runway layout with the main 2,000 ft (610 m) runway aligned NW/SE. When originally authorised in October 1941 as a second satellite for Membury the risk of Luftwaffe attack was still one of the major planning concerns, but as early as May 1942 a revised layout was agreed which brought the dispersed accommodation sites much closer to the airfield.

View north over Welford as it approached completion in May 1943. The technical and administrative sites were amongst the trees to the north of the airfield (RAF Museum W21/101/5).

Lower than forecast losses in Bomber Command and the need to find airfields for the promised flood of American units into the country led to Welford being earmarked for transfer, and on April 21 1943, with the site approaching completion, No 70 Group, RAF, assumed responsibility for its development. The opening-up party arrived on June 10 and used the intended WAAF site, situated in a copse to the north of the airfield, until the main accommodation was finished. Early in July USAAF ground units moved in, though work was still under way on the technical sites and only one of the 'T2' hangars was complete. As the Americans arrived the RAF strength was reduced and when the VIIIth Air Support Command officially took charge of USAAF Station 474 on September 6 1943 only the liaison officer and 'substitution party' remained.

With construction work complete the airfield had two 'T2' hangars on the north side and a total of 50 aircraft hardstandings, all but four of the loop type. It is believed that a technical sub-site planned in the south-west corner was not finished, and its two 'T2' hangars were not built.

Welford (which the USAAF usually referred to as Welford Park), was to be a Troop Carrier Wing base, but with the build-up of the airborne forces slower than anticipated no operational aircraft appeared until November 6, and then only the remnants of the 315th TCG from Aldermaston, the rest of the Group being in the Mediterranean area. A month later the 434th TCG (71st, 72nd, 73rd and 74th TCS) arrived from Fulbeck with C-47s and training started with airborne troops and gliders. More reshuffling resulted in the 434th returning to Fulbeck early in January 1944, replaced later in the month by the 435th TCG (75th, 76th, 77th and 78th TCS) from Langar. The 315th detachment left for Spanhoe in February

A Jeep trailer being loaded aboard a C-47A of the 74th TCS, 434th TCG at Welford in January 1944 (via D. Benfield).

but the 438th TCG (87th, 88th, 89th and 90th TCS) started flying in from the States, and the airfield was soon bulging at the seams with personnel and C-47 transport aircraft.

Welford was transferred to the IXth AF on February 22 1944 and things soon got sorted out. Fighter units were moved out of Greenham Common and the 438th TCG made the short ferry trip across Newbury on March 16, leaving Welford to the 435th which was able to get on with its heavy training commitment for the 101st Airborne Division at last. Carefully planned regimental combat exercises which had started in December 1943 now became larger and more complex. On March 23 a demonstration was laid on for Mr Churchill, General Eisenhower and many other VIPs, and later in the month 97 gliders were towed off and taken on a formation cross-country navigation exercise. Cast off near base, all landed back on the airfield at the planned ten-second intervals—a very spectacular demonstration of the rapidly increasing abilities of the Troop Carrier Command. Night towing of both Hadrian and Horsa gliders was introduced and many practice re-supply missions also flown as the invasion date approached.

On D-Day itself the 435th was in the first wave, dropping paratroops of the 501st PIR, 101st Airborne, near Cherbourg, the lead aircraft carrying General Taylor and members of his staff. Cloud cover over Normandy broke up the

formations and light flak picked off three stragglers. Seven more C-47s were damaged, but on return to Welford the serviceable aircraft were marshalled into position ready for tow ropes to be attached to 12 Hadrian and 38 Horsa gliders. They were taken to the same area that evening, accompanied by a lone paratroop aircraft which had failed to drop its load the previous night. More gliders were delivered to Normandy during the morning of June 7 before the squadrons started supply drops which, as landing strips became available, changed into freight deliveries of medical supplies, clothing, rations, fuel and ammunition. The C-47s returned with wounded on transfer to hospitals in the Newbury area. Surprisingly, they also found time for some snatch glider trials with CG-4A Hadrians during June.

On July 20 a 435th TCG detachment went to Tarquinia, Italy, to participate in Operation *Anvil*, the amphibious invasion of Southern France. 61 Hadrians and Horsas were towed to the LZs between Cannes and Toulon early in August 15 by units of the 53rd TCW including the Welford squadrons, to back up paratroops with support weapons. A re-supply was flown on the 16th, and the aircraft were retained in Italy until the end of August for freight humping.

On return to Welford training redoubled in preparation for Operation *Market Garden*, and just after 10:00 hours on September 17 the first of 36 C-47s started to roll down the runway carrying elements of the 101st Airborne to a DZ just north of the Wilhelmina Canal near Eindhoven. It was a good drop, followed by glider towing during the next two days, characterised by acts of bravery like that of 1st Lieutenant Jesse Harrison who carried on to the LZ in his blazing C-47 to accurately release his glider, before baling out with his co-pilot. Re-supply for the 82nd Airborne followed on the 20th and the 435th also took part in a lift of howitzer ammunition for the 101st on the 25th, just before *Garden* ran out of steam. Then it was back to freighting and casevac missions which continued after the 435th moved to Bretigny in France on February 13 1945, until the ground support units were withdrawn and the airfield returned to the British in June 1945.

Welford was taken over by Transport Command on June 30 and No 1336 (Transport Support) Conversion Unit was formed, despite much changing of plans as Air Staffs struggled with rapidly altering policy decisions. Delay was caused by the sudden surrender of the Japanese, but on August 20 flying commenced, and courses started six days later. Using Dakotas and Horsas as the main equipment, with a few Oxfords for instrument flying and navigation training, the unit managed to complete a number of courses before being closed on March 1 1946 when the glider towing commitment was savagely cut.

The station was reduced to C&M and then transferred to No 90 (Signals) Group in October 1946, which might have been expected to be the end of flying from the airfield. Not so, for the glider manufacturers, Elliotts of Newbury, had designed and built the Eon four-seat light aeroplane during 1946-47 and obtained Air Ministry permission to use Welford for initial flight trials, these commencing on August 7 1947. They coincided with the re-opening of at least part of the station as the HQ of Southern Signals Area, renamed HQ Radio Navigational Aids Wing three years later. This unit stayed for another two years despite the transfer of the airfield to Maintenance Command in December 1950, but was disbanded on August 1 1952 when Welford again reverted to C&M.

On September 1 1955, Welford re-opened as a logistics site for the 3rd Air Force, USAF and is still occupied by the Americans.

Westgate, Kent

TR328705. 1½ miles W of Margate off A28

During the spring of 1914, the Admiralty became increasingly concerned about the vulnerability of the Thames Estuary naval bases of Sheerness and Chatham to aerial or submarine attack. The Grain air station had already been established to protect these bases, but two additional sites were needed where seaplanes could be located in an emergency. One of these sub-stations was positioned at Clacton, the other in St Mildred's Bay near Westgate-on-Sea on the Isle of Thanet.

The latter, known as Westgate, was opened on August 1 1914 with Flight Commander J.T. Babington in command of a small party of officers and men who found themselves in competition for accommodation with the large number of holiday makers in the town. There was no permanent establishment of seaplanes during the early months, machines being seconded as available. Amongst early arrivals were Short Folders, the Short S 80 and a Sopwith 880 seaplane, all providing added interest for crowds who seemed more than satisfied watching the seaplanes being hauled up and down between the beach and their parking area on the grassy slopes above the cliff. This was fortunate because they could rarely be coaxed into the air even to provide anti-submarine cover for ships carrying the Expeditionary Force to France.

With the BEF safely in France, the sub-station was reduced to little more than a standby base, while work went ahead on the construction of slipways and a hangar on the seafront close to St Mildred's Hotel. The latter was taken over to

General view of Westgate before completion of the steel-framed hangar, the foundations of which can be seen on the right (G.S. Leslie/J.M. Bruce collection).

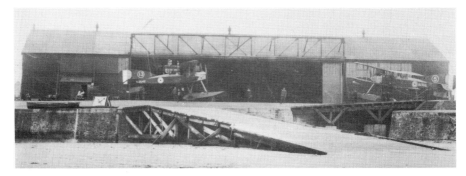

provide accomodation, a wireless station was built, and in December 1914 two seaplanes were permanently stationed to provide defence against German float-planes.

Early in 1915, land on the cliff top to the east of the seaplane base, was requisitioned from Mutrix Farm as an aerodrome (*TR335705*). The usual motley collection of wooden hangars and huts were erected and during April 1915 *A* Flight of No 2 Squadron, RNAS, commanded by Flight Commander A.B. Gaskell, arrived from Eastchurch with Avro 504s, Curtiss JN3s and the inevitable BE 2Cs, to provide air defence against Zeppelins. At this time German airship commanders were becoming over-confident and on May 17 Hauptmann Linnarz nearly paid the penalty by casually hovering at a mere 2,000 ft (610 m) over Ramsgate. He was intercepted by Flight Sub-Lieutenant R.H. Mulock up from Westgate in Avro 504B *1013* armed with two incendiary bombs and two grenades. Mulock attacked but the *LZ38*

escaped by hastily dropping its bombs and climbing rapidly out of the Avro's reach.

Another chance came on August 9 1915 when the German naval airship *L 12* appeared off Westgate and Flight Sub-Lieutenant R. Lord took off to intercept. Unfortunately he lost it in the darkness and was fatally injured while attempting to land in fog. Activities at Westgate increased during September under the enthusiastic leadership of Squadron Commander R.P. Ross, the landplanes of the War Flight carrying out defensive patrols whenever German airships or aeroplanes were expected and the seaplanes, now mainly Short 827s, extending their operations out into the North Sea.

Two more hangars were erected and the Ocean Hotel was acquired, extra accommodation being provided by tents on the lawns and ever increasing numbers of wooden huts spreading eastwards. On March 20 1916 Flight Commander R.J. Bone, on detachment from Detling, gained the first success for the Westgate station when he chased five seaplanes

attacking Dover and shot one down into a minefield near the Goodwin Sands. That same month, however, the previous doubts over the safety of the Westgate aerodrome came to a head. The prevailing wind meant that take-offs and landings had to be made towards the cliffs, which was also the shortest run. There had been several close shaves but in March the inevitable happened, Flight Sub-Lieutenant R.E. Bush going over the cliff in a Bristol Scout. This accident, coupled with gale damage resulting in several aircraft being destroyed, forced the authorities to find a new aerodrome and Manston, already in use as an ELG, was chosen. The War Flight moved there in July 1916 after which Westgate aerodrome was abandoned.

In contrast the marine base at St Mildred's Bay went from strength to strength. Sopwith Schneiders attempted to intercept nine airships which crossed the coast on September 23 1916 but it was another airship attack which provided the most newsworthy Westgate story. Among the aircraft which went up to intercept a raid on May 23/24 1917 were two Sopwith Baby seaplanes, the two pilots searching independently and without success. After three hours Flight Sub-Lieutenant H.M. Morris returned to base but there was no news of his comrade. Morris went off again with Air Mechanic G.O. Wright in a Short 827 to look for the missing Baby, which had actually been taken in tow by a hopper and was already in port when Morris started his search. Soon afterwards the Short's engine failed and, although the 827 alighted safely, choppy seas

smashed the starboard lower plane and the machine turned over and sank, leaving just the floats above the water. The two airmen clung to the wreckage, and with only a few malted milk tablets between them they survived five days and nights before they were sighted by the crew of a Felixstowe Curtiss H12 flying boat. They recovered, but never flew again after their terrible ordeal.

The introduction of the very reliable Short 184 seaplane produced a dramatic increase in utilisation and effectiveness and on April 1 the RNAS base became RAF Westgate, the personnel, aircraft and task remaining the same. During the summer the Short 184 patrols were intercepted 16 times in a six-week period by German aircraft, and had to be escorted by Camels, though not always effectively. On July 18 two Shorts on a special patrol between the Kentish Knock and the Sunk Light Vessel were under escort by two Camels when seven German seaplanes dived out of the sun, forcing one of the Shorts down on the water. A German two-seater alighted beside the Short 184 on the water and the fight continued, the Short eventually bursting into flames and sinking. The other Short was overtaken by the Camels as it made for home, and appeared undamaged so they continued on to Manston. Unfortunately the seaplane did not reach Westgate and the crew were presumed drowned.

In August 1918 No 219 Squadron took over the units at Westgate and Manston, Sopwith Babies and Short 184s operating as No 406 Flight while the Camels at Manston became No 470 Flight. Flying

Above left *Two Short 184s outside No 1 Shed at Westgate* (FAA Museum A/Stn 10).

Left *Typical operating conditions on a marine flying station. There are two WRNS amongst the ratings gathered around the nearer Short 184* (FAA Museum Short 32).

Right *The RNAS station at Westgate in its complete state, December 1918* (FAA Museum A/Stn 12).

did not cease with the Armistice, monotonous but essential anti-mine patrols continuing, some flown by Fairey IIIb floatplanes which formed No 442 Flight at Westgate.

On May 3 1919 the *Evening News* celebrated the rebirth of civil aviation by using a Fairey IIIc piloted by Sidney Pickles to pick up copies of the newspaper at Westminster and fly them to Westgate and Margate, but it was very much a publicity stunt, and not repeated. RAF operations ceased in the late summer and Westgate was closed on February 7 1920, its installations including the hangars, being dismantled and sold by auction.

Little evidence of either aerodrome or seaplane base remains. The former is largely covered by Westbrook housing while only the wide slipway, now used to launch pedal boats, survives at St Mildred's Bay. On the sides of the cutting which provides access to the sands for boats can be seen the cut off ends of joists which once supported a platform connecting the hangars to the slipway and over which the seaplane trolleys could be pushed. The hotel still stands, but the main No 1 hangar has been replaced by a corporation putting green and a wide road backed by a housing estate cuts a swathe through the ground on which the hutted camp once stood.

Westenhangar, Kent

TR120370. 3 miles NW of Hythe off B2068

A flying meeting held on the Folkestone Racecourse at the end of September 1910 was attended by three pilots and a very large crowd. It was rated successful but this early use of the racecourse, which is actually at Westenhangar some six miles west of Folkestone, was not continued nor, apparently, was it used for flying during World War 1.

During 1940-41, however, it was employed as a decoy airfield, probably for Lympne, and in April 1944 saw further flying when Auster AOP 4s of No 660 Squadron, No 84 Group, 2nd TAF moved in from East Grinstead for exercises with the Army units flooding into the area for the Normandy invasion. After detachment to Weston Zoyland in May for a practice crossing of the Bristol Channel, the unit returned to Westenhangar to wait impatiently for a move across the English Channel, which finally came on July 12 when the 12 Austers flew in line astern

behind an ASR Walrus doubling as rescue and navigation aircraft. The ground echelon then folded their tents and stole away leaving no permanent sign of this short military occupation.

Westhampnett (Goodwood), West Sussex

SU875075. 1½ miles NE of Chichester on minor road off A285

Hardly anyone in the Chichester area was unfamiliar with the shape and sound of a Spitfire by the middle of 1942, and few troubled to even glance up as a gaggle of them went in to land at Westhampnett on August 1. Those that did received a shock, for these Spitfire Vbs carried the star markings of the USAAF! The 309th FS of the 31st FG had come from Atcham to gain operational experience with the Tangmere Wing, just in time to take part in Operation *Jubilee*.

A lot had happened since December 7 1938 when acquisition of land on the Duke of Richmond's Goodwood Estate as an ELG for Tangmere was approved by the Air Ministry. Retained at first as open meadowland for use by aircraft in trouble, defeat in France during May 1940 resulted in Westhampnett being upgraded to satellite status to support operations by a fighter squadron.

It was officially re-opened on the last day of July 1940 when Hurricanes of No 145 Squadron moved over from Tangmere, though they had operated intermittently from the LG earlier in the month, and had already experienced the severe waterlogging resulting from heavy rain. In the thick of the action since moving to the south coast early in May, their 14 days at Westhampnett were the most strenuous of all, starting badly when the rear gunner of a Henschel Hs 126 (the German equivalent of the Lysander) sent a Hurricane and its FAA pilot, Sub-Lieutenant I.H. Keston, crashing into the sea on August 1.

Uneventful patrols followed until an attempt to pass Convoy *Peewit* through the Straits of Dover under the cover of darkness on the 8th. This provoked an attack by German E-boats, followed as daylight came by an assault by Luftflotte 3. Starting sporadically, this developed into a major attack during the early afternoon by nearly 60 Ju 87s from StG1, StG2 and StG77, escorted by 20 Bf 110s of V/LG1 and about 30 Bf 109s of JG27, when the convoy was off the Isle of Wight. Warned of the raid, 18 Hurricanes were in the vicinity as the Germans approached, but were intercepted by JG27 before they could close with the Stukas, except for three No 145 Squadron aircraft which slipped through and shot down two Ju 87s. A massive dogfight then developed and when the Germans finally departed they had lost three Ju 87s, a Bf 110 and three BF 109s, with more damaged. RAF losses amounted to two Hurricanes of No 238 Squadron, but four ships had been lost and seven more damaged.

As the scattered remnants of the convoy regrouped, Baron Von Richthofen was planning another attack, assembling 82 Ju 87s and 68 escorting Bf 109/110s. Led by their exuberant OC, Squadron Leader J.R.A. Peel, No 145 Squadron went out for the third time that day. Peel took his men to the south-west and attacked the dive bombers out of the sun. It was a complete success, the first pass being made before the German escorts could react, three Ju 87s going down. Including the early morning interceptions over a westbound convoy out of Weymouth, No 145 Squadron were credited with 11 German aircraft destroyed and six damaged for the loss of five Hurricanes and their pilots. Heaped with congratulations, the survivors were too tired to be elated, and found it hard to respond even when visited by HRH the Duke of Gloucester. Three days later they intercepted a large formation approaching the naval base at Portland, shooting down a Bf 109 and Bf 110, but lost four Hurricanes and two pilots. The next day No 145 Squadron were again in action over Portsmouth and again they came off worst, losing three Hurricanes and their pilots for the destruction of one Ju 88 of KG51. The strain was telling, they were tired out and knew it, ready for the well deserved rest they got at Drem when they changed places with 602 Squadron on August 14.

The new squadron arrived just as the Germans changed tactics and started attacking the RAF on the ground as well as in the air. For No 602 Squadron life at Westhampnett started quietly enough with the interception and destruction of a Do 17P of 3(F)/31 on reconnaissance near Portsmouth on the 15th, but the following day the Spitfires from Westhampnett were defending Tangmere against very aggressive and strongly escorted Ju 87s, taking on the Bf 109s of JG2 while Hurricanes of Nos 1, 43 and 601 Squadrons set about the Stukas. The resulting dogfight was inconclusive, but two days later they were amongst the squadrons scrambled to deal with a large formation seen crossing the Channel. The Germans confused the defenders by splitting into four groups and all four targets were successfully attacked. Ju 88s of KG54 bombed Gosport and withdrew without opposition but the 85 Ju 87s involved were not so lucky, the full fury of the RAF fighters falling upon them as they re-formed. Sixteen Stukas were shot down, of which four were credited to No 602 Squadron for the loss of one Spitfire, ditched off Middleton. It was the last time that the Ju 87 was used for main target attacks over Britain.

The next few weeks were hectic with almost constant standbys, scrambles, refuelling, re-arming and back to cockpit readiness. When the Germans started night raids on London No 602 Squadron, in common with other day fighter squadrons, tried their hand at night flying—disastrously. The pace slackened towards the end of September, though standing patrols had to be flown in an attempt to cope with low level raids on coastal targets by single aircraft, and the pilots became very jaded indeed. They were not sorry to see the Hurricanes of No 302 (Polish) Squadron arrive from Northolt on November 23, and even more grateful to leave for Prestwick in mid-December, when they handed over to 610 Squadron.

Waterlogging was still a problem, a start being made at the end of 1940 on a continuous perimeter track with circular hardstandings dispersed around it. Nissen huts replaced the original bell tents and seven Over-Blister and one Extra Over-Blister provided some shelter for technical work. A small corrugated iron-clad watch office was built in the north-eastern corner and Shopwyke Hall, a mile to the south-east was taken over as the officers' mess. Early in 1941 off-duty personnel moved out at night to Rusmans, a large house in Oving, to reduce the nuisance value of single Luftwaffe bombers making regular visits to the major RAF bases, in this case Tangmere.

No 302 Squadron found themselves doing south coast patrols, but soon tired of this and were more than happy to join No 610 Squadron on escort work for the hazardous No 2 Group *Circus* daylight raids over Belgium and France which started in January 1941. These highly planned operations were not frequent, however, and gradually more time was spent on pure fighter sweeps. The Poles left early in April and No 610 Squadron was alone for a month before No 616 Squadron arrived. Both ex-Auxiliaries now had Spitfire IIs, and with No 145 Squadron at Merston, formed the famous Wing led by Wing Commander Douglas Bader. Notching up fighter sweeps and bomber escorts they scored steadily whenever the Luftwaffe chose to respond.

Rhubarbs became more popular after the introduction of the Spitfire Vb and it was during one of these that Bader collided with a Bf 109 near Bethune and got one of his tin legs trapped while baling out. He was left dangling out of the cockpit in the full force of the slipstream but fortunately the retaining straps broke and he landed safely but injured. In hospital Bader arranged for his spare leg to be delivered, but when his damaged leg was found and repaired this indomitable character promptly escaped with the aid of French patriots. Betrayed and recaptured he was taken to St Omer, and even Bader was surprised when a long yellow box containing his leg was placed before him. It had been dropped on August 19 from one of six No 18 Squadron Blenheims which had swept across the airfield escorted by No 616 Squadron, as part of a standard *Circus* rejoicing in the name Operation *Leg*.

No 610 Squadron moved north, but was promptly replaced by the newly operational No 129 Squadron. While flying escort to No 139 Squadron Blenheims on September 21 they got involved in a dogfight with BF 109s, claiming three destroyed, three probables and four damaged—for the loss of three Spitfire Vbs and two pilots. A new sight at Westhampnett were two ASR Lysanders, but they only stayed until the end of November before moving to Shoreham—regretfully for they were a reassuring sight for fighter pilots who spent most of their airborne time over the cold waters of the Channel. No 616 Squadron exchanged places at Kirton-in-Lindsey with No 65 Squadron early in October and on November 1 No 129 Squadron went to Debden for short-lived convoy patrols. They were soon back in place of No 65 and with No 41 Squadron transferred from Merston, Westhampnett entered 1942 with two operational Spitfire Vb squadrons at readiness.

A varied round of *Circuses, Rhubarbs*, offensive sweeps and convoy patrols followed. No 41 Squadron returned to Merston at the beginning of April 1942 but was soon replaced by No 340 (Free French) Squadron which made its first offensive sweep three days after arrival, and was quickly in the thick of Hurribomber escorts, *Ramrods* and the much disliked convoy patrols. This pattern continued until the end of July when both squadrons left, No 129 Squadron to nearby Thorney Island and No 340 Squadron to Hornchurch.

Major H. Ruhe of the 31st FG arrived on July 30 with an advance party to take over Westhampnett as USAAF Station 352, though it remained under the operational control of Tangmere. American uniforms suddenly flooded Chichester, but personnel were soon hard at work, operations commencing on August 5 with convoy escorts, progressing to an offensive sweep in company with RAF Spitfires on August 18.

Jubilee, the combined operation at Dieppe, started the following day and the 309th were thrown in at the deep end. Called to readiness at 03:47 hours the first pilots, led by Major Harrison R. Thyng, and in company with Nos 130 and 131 Squadrons, RAF, were over the assault ships at 08:50 hours. They were immediately engaged by 25 Fw 190s of JG26 and in the mêlee three pilots from the 309th FS were shot down, one of them, Lieutenant S. Junkin, having just destroyed a Fw 190—the first confirmed victory by an VIIIth AF pilot. The squadron was off again with Nos 81 and 131 Squadrons just before midday escorting Boston light bombers, one 309th Spitfire going down, presumably a victim of flak. Finally they flew another top cover mission with No 41 Squadron, the Americans having a brief encounter with German bombers attacking the tail end of the ship flotilla—and claimed one damaged. It had been a long day and the survivors had much to think about.

On August 25 they were joined at Westhampnett by the 308th FS, while the 307th moved into Merston so that the 31st FG could work up as an autonomous unit. After a visit from the Commanding Officer of the VIIIth AF, General Carl Spaatz, on September 2 the Group was officially assigned to the XIIth AF on the 14th, but continued working with No 11 Group, RAF, until October 9 when they handed over their Spitfires to other USAAF units and packed for the long journey to North Africa and Operation *Torch*.

During October some P-38 Lightnings of the 14th FG, Atcham, used Westhampnett as a forward operating base to gain experience, flying practice sweeps with the RAF but without engaging the enemy. The next residents were old hands—No 616 Squadron who moved their pointed-wingtip Spitfire VI high-altitude fighters over from Tangmere at the end of the month. At Westhampnett they joined up with No 131 Squadron to carry out sweeps, *Ramrods, Rhubarbs* and *Jim Crows* though the specialised Mk VI was not the best aircraft for low level work.

From January to May 1943 Nos 485 (RNZAF) and 610 Squadrons were in residence, a Spitfire Vb of the former unit being involved in an accident on April 24 when it struck a visiting Hampden. One airman was killed and four injured—a result of the poor view forward from the Spitfire when on the ground. When Nos 167 and 501 Squadrons took over they added bomber escort to the activities of their 'clapped-out' mounts, but as the year wore on there was a lull in Luftwaffe fighter-bomber coastal raids and the two Spitfire XII squadrons which had been dealing with them also moved into Westhampnett at the end of June for bomber support duties. No 41 Squadron arrived first, supporting the withdrawal of 60 B-17s from Le Mans during the evening of June 26. Two days later No 91 Squadron flew in, and the Wing then started escorts for medium bombers of No 2 Group and No 83 Group Typhoon fighter-bombers.

Operation *Starkey*, an elaborate attempt to get the Luftwaffe into combat, followed early in September producing an increase in sortie rate for the Tangmere Wing and some *Rhubarbs* were involved in large scale dogfights, resulting in No 91 Squadron becoming the month's Fighter Command top scorer. The Spitfires moved to the main airfield during October and heavier metal arrived at Westhampnett in the form of Typhoons of Nos 174, 175 and 245 Squadrons, No 121 Airfield, No 83 Group. They used the airfield as winter quarters for which it was far from ideal, the surface becoming badly rutted in the wet conditions. The Typhoons operated as fighter-bombers, attacking shipping and targets in France, beginning a concentrated assault on the infamous *Noball* sites in January 1944. This involved dive bombing heavily defended pin-point targets, which resulted in many aircraft damaged and average monthly squadron losses of two or three from these sorties. It is likely that more dispersals and the 'T1' hangar at the north-eastern corner of the airfield were constructed at this time, for the servicing task was considerably increased with three squadrons on the airfield.

Long-range low-level sweeps were always exciting, a typical one on January 8 1944 seeing 'Tiffies' ranging over a wide area north of Paris, led by Wing Commander R.T.P. Davidson, DFC. A Luftwaffe transport was despatched by the leader and Pilot Officer Dickie of No 245 Squadron, but Flight Sergeant Waudby, last seen on the tail of a Ju 88, had obviously been hit for his aircraft was trailing white smoke—a tell-tale sign of a massive coolant leak. During February-March the aircraft were fitted for rockets and the squadrons went in turn to East-church APC. All back by the middle of March, they resumed Wing sweeps over northern France as the pre-invasion pressure started to build up.

On April 1, No 121 Airfield moved to Holmsley South in a general reshuffle of units which brought the Spitfire IXs of No 144 Airfield (Nos 441, 442 and 443 (RCAF) Squadrons) to Westhampnett. Their task was to complete their training which included a visit to an APC, but No 443 Squadron provided 12 Spitfires as top cover for Bostons and Mitchells bombing Dieppe on April 13, five of them then strafing Rouen on the way home. The OC, Squadron Leader H.W. McLeod, DSO, DFC and Bar, gained the unit's first victory on the 19th when he destroyed a Do 217 near Brussels while on close escort to Marauders of the IXth AF.

The Canadians left on April 22 and were immediately replaced by No 129 Airfield, No 83 Group. This unit was unusual in having only one squadron, No 184, which was equipped with Typhoons and trained for cab-rank operations over the Normandy beach-head under the command of a forward air controller. It went to Holmsley South for nine days mid-May, the Airfield having become No 129 Wing by the time it returned to join No 84 Group Communications Squadron at Westhampnett. All was ready for D-Day and when June 6 dawned No 184 Squadron was quick off the mark, attacking strongpoints and gun positions with rockets. Flak from German 88 mm guns was a menace, the squadron losing three aircraft on one cab-rank during June 7, but the pressure was maintained except when the weather interfered.

AVM Basil Embry, ACC No 2 Group, flew a Mosquito into Westhampnett on June 16 to see for himself if it was suitable as a desperately needed forward airfield. The idea was abandoned, officially because of lack of lighting, but it would have been a tight squeeze for Mosquitoes, especially on wet grass. The following day No 184 Squadron moved to Holmsley South and when Portsmouth and Southampton came under V-1 attack, Spitfire XIIs of No 41 Squadron returned, and No 610 Squadron brought in its Spitfire XIVs. They only stayed five days before moving to Friston, then it was back to mundane Merlin-powered Spitfires of Nos 130, 303 (Polish) and 402 (RCAF) Squadrons on beach-head patrols and No 2 Group bomber escorts. These were the first of a series of short stay Spitfire IX units all engaged on escort work, which ended on September 25 1944 with the

departure of Nos 118, 124 and 303 Squadrons.

Things were then very quiet at Westhampnett until No 83 Group Support Unit arrived from neighbouring Thorney Island on November 4. The GSU was concerned with providing replacement aircraft and pilots for the front-line Mustang and Spitfire squadrons and Westhampnett was not ideal for this task, particularly in the winter, a Spitfire skidding on the grass during delivery on January 4 1945 and colliding with two parked aircraft, while on the 8th a Mustang overshot an emergency landing and the pilot had to raise the undercarriage to stop. The unit completed its transfer to Dunsfold on February 22; indeed, the flying echelon had probably gone earlier for a minor puzzle is No 11 Group's assertion that Westhampnett reverted to C&M status on January 15! On March 1 the station was transferred to

Left *The 1941-style ATC tower at Westhampnett—seen in July 1981* (K.S. West).

Below right *The NDN Firecracker prototype at Westhampnett* (NDN Aircraft Ltd).

Below *Vertical of Westhampnett taken on April 19 1946. The south-easterly runway extension can be made out, while the 'T1' hangar looks strangely isolated by the road forming the northern boundary of the landing ground* (DoE/Crown Copyright).

the Air Staff SHAEF (Rear HQ) which used the accommodation for Air Disarmament Units waiting to move on to the Continent.

Westhampnett re-opened as an active airfield in July 1945, the Naval Air Fighting Development Unit moving in from Tangmere to relieve the pressure on that station. The NAFDU, which operated as part of the Central Fighter Establishment continued to fly a varied collection of aircraft, often supplemented by attachments from other units of the CFE. In the autumn CFE started to transfer all its departments to West Raynham, the NAFDU, the flying unit of which was 787 Squadron, being among the last to go. It moved out of Westhampnett on November 27 when the airfield again reverted to C&M, and it closed down completely on May 13 1946.

In pre-war days the Duke of Richmond & Gordon had been a renowned racing driver and he retained his enthusiasm for the sport. He recognised the potential of the somewhat convoluted 2½ miles of tarmac perimeter track at Westhampnett, and with the Blister hangars and other unsightly objects removed he opened the famous Goodwood Motor Racing Circuit in September 1948, the celebrated Reg Parnall winning the first race at an average of 80.56 mph. As speeds increased with advances in car technology, the track became dangerous. Some minor alterations were made in 1952 but Stirling Moss was involved in a nasty accident and it was appreciated that major changes to the corners and increased safety measures

such as crash barriers would have to be provided. The cost was prohibitive and reluctantly the Goodwood track, set in some of the most attractive surroundings enjoyed by any racing circuit, had to be closed in 1965.

The name did not disappear from the sporting calendar, however, for in 1958 planning permission had been granted for the centre of the track to be used as an airfield with three grass landing strips, the longest 4,320 ft (1,317 m) NW/SE. Aircraft movements grew steadily and the operators, Goodwood Terrana Ltd, erected a new hangar and flying club accommodation alongside ex-RAF buildings on the eastern side. In the mid-1970s Desmond Norman, co-designer of the Islander, formed NDN Aircraft Ltd and built a new basic trainer combining good performance with economy. The Firecracker made its first flight at Goodwood on May 26 1977 and the airfield was then used for development work on the prototype. More recently the design of a cropsprayer was undertaken and a mock-up built at Goodwood but the company has now moved to Sandown, Isle of Wight.

Officially renamed Chichester/Goodwood, this very pleasant and accessible little airfield remains active, with a thriving civilian club and a number of private owners based on it. Many of the wartime buildings are still in use, including the T1 hangar to the north of the Lavant-Woodcote road and the RAF control tower, the latter by a HGV driving school.

Wittersham, Kent

TQ886281. 3 miles S of Tenterden off B2082

Mispelt in various references as Withersham, West Hersham and West Mersham, the airship sub-station of Wittersham on the Isle of Oxney mid-way between Tenterden and Rye was established in 1918 for mooring out Capel-based airships.

As usual with such sites the moorings were camouflaged by trees, a clearing being made in Sheepwash Plantation at Wittersham for this purpose. One SS-Type coastal airship was usually located there to enable operations to continue when conditions were unsuitable at the parent station which was on high cliffs overlooking the English Channel and often affected by the weather.

The sub-station was closed immediately after the Armistice and no obvious evidence of its location exist, though there may be heavily overgrown remnants of concrete mooring bases in the woods.

Woodchurch, Kent

TQ945365. 5½ miles SW of Ashford off minor roads

In heavily wooded country on the Kentish Weald, the ALG at Woodchurch was one of only two selected in 1942 as 'round-up' light bomber bases, resulting in a bomb dump being established nearby.

Detailed planning in September 1942 resulted in an ALG fitted in between minor roads immediately to the west of Hengherst village and north of Shirkoak crossroads. The two landing strips were in the form of an upturned cross when looked at conventionally on a map, the main N/S strip being 4,800 ft (1,463 m) and the E/W subsidiary cutting the road between Shirkoak and Engeham Farm. The land gradient was considered acceptable and there was a good camp site near Hengherst House. Accommodation for 200 men was available in the house and adjacent army huts, and another 200 could live in nearby buildings.

With the dispersal layout added by Fighter Command staff the plans were approved early in December and work started, with the intention of completion by March 1 1943. Difficulty with the fall of the land reduced the length of the E/W strip to 4,090 ft (1,247 m) but most of the Sommerfeld tracking had been laid by March 1943, the plans for light bomber operations having been abandoned.

On completion the land was let for grazing but on July 28 the newly formed No 128 Airfield, No 39 (RCAF) Sector, No 83 Group, Tactical Air Force arrived from Dunsfold. The two operational squadrons, Nos 231 and 400 (RCAF), flew Mustang 1s and were quickly in action flying weather checks and Channel patrols. They commenced low level photo recce in September 1943 with a sortie over Dunkirk; and just before they left Woodchurch added *Rhubarbs* to their repertoire, concentrating on train busting. While at the ALG the squadrons maintained a high sortie rate despite the unaccustomed field conditions, at the same time checking the strip's suitability for operations. In general they, and the ALG, coped well though No 231 Squadron had two serious accidents during August, an engine failure on take-off producing an overrun, while an aircraft which cartwheeled on landing finished up on its back. The Airfield was joined on August 11 by No 39 (Recce) Wing HQ, also tasting life in the raw. It returned to Redhill on October 13, the squadrons following the next day.

In common with other ALGs in the south-east, Woodchurch then underwent a facelift. Extensive Sommerfeld taxitracking was laid together with many more hardstandings, these eventually numbering 70 after hand-over to the USAAF for fighter-bomber operations. A US Army unit arrived to regrade the E/W strip and extend it eastwards with PSP matting, increasing the total length to 5,000 ft (1,542 m) and cutting the road between Henherst and Woodchurch.

A ban on flying movements was placed on all ALGs until April 1 1944 so that preparation work could continue unhindered, but American ground parties assembled in March. All was ready when the 373rd FG, IXth TAC, under the command of Colonel William H. Schwartz, Jnr, arrived on April 4 and the squadrons (410th, 411th and 412th FS) started flying in their P-47 Thunderbolts. After a period of training and acclimatisation the Group flew its first combat mission on May 5 1944, a fighter sweep over Normandy. Their major pre-invasion task was the escort of IXth AF B-26 Marauders during attacks on bridges, rail communications and airfields in France, as part of the general softening up process. On D-Day itself they provided top cover for American beach-heads and once released from this duty became involved in strafing

Virginia Xs of No 58 Squadron—the unit was at Worthy Down with these stately craft for ten years (Real Photographs Ltd).

troops, tanks, roads, fuel and ammunition dumps in the close support role, these operations continuing at high intensity from Woodchurch until the FG moved across the Channel to a strip at Touen-Bassin on July 4 1944. The American rear party left Woodchurch a week later, so when a battle-damaged B-24 Liberator of 466 BG crashlanded on the strip on the 17th the crew found themselves very much on their own!

Verbal notification that the ALG was no longer required was issued by the Air Ministry on July 14, the USAAF being given permission to lift the PSP matting for use on the Continent, where it was desperately needed. Derequisition authority was given on September 18 but first the work of clearing the site had to be undertaken, two Flights of 5027 Works Squadron being engaged in this work throughout the autumn and into 1945.

There is now no obvious sign of the ALG, though a caravan site on the eastern edge of the site may use some concrete foundations dating back to wartime.

Worthy Down, Hampshire

SU470351. 3 miles N of Winchester on A34(T)

The old Winchester racecourse on Worthy Down was acquired in August 1917 for use by the Wireless & Observers School, forced out of Brooklands by the continual expansion of the aircraft manufacturers using that airfield.

A roughly rectangular aerodrome of 480 acres was carved out of the old racecourse, on grassland which sloped markedly down from the old grandstand and gave a maximum run of some 4,800 ft (1,463 m). The main technical buildings consisted of six large aeroplane sheds (built in two blocks of three) and an Aeroplane Repair and Salvage hangar, close to the railway line which formed the eastern boundary. The accommodation

huts and administrative sections were nearby and almost complete when the station finally opened in 1918, but only about half the hangars were usable. It was badly behind schedule, the Wireless & Observer School having already moved to nearby Hursley Park and been renamed the Artillery & Infantry Co-operation School.

Finally arriving at Worthy Down in August 1918, the unit became the RAF & Army Co-operation School a month later, and operated as a finishing school for Corps Recce pilots. They were given advanced instruction in artillery and infantry co-operation, contact patrolling and practical map-reading, while observers were also trained up to wings standard, the unit having 300 pupils in residence. A detached Flight of the Artillery Co-operation School, Lydd, also joined the main school at Worthy Down for work with seige artillery, bringing the aircraft strength up to 20 AW FK8s, 12 Bristol F 2Bs and 50 RE 8s, and the total personnel to 1,450.

With the Armistice came retrenchment and plans to build an aerodrome at Flowerdown for the recently arrived No 1 (T) Wireless School were abandoned, Worthy Down being used for the flying phases. The retitled RAF/Army Co-operation School continued to function on a reduced scale but moved to Old Sarum in December 1920, by which time No 1 (T) WS had become the Electrical & Wireless School and from March 1921 until May 1924 Worthy Down in practice was little more than Flowerdown's Flying Wing.

As the RAF emerged from near extinction in 1924 the situation changed dramatically. No 58 Squadron was reformed at Worthy Down on April 1 with Vimy aircraft, replacement by Virginia night bombers commencing before the end of the year. When new accommodation for the E&WS detachment was complete, No 7 Squadron moved down from Bircham Newton. They duly brought their dark green Virginias to Worthy Down early in April

1927 and friendly rivalry was soon established between the two squadrons, at its height during the annual Armament Practice Camp. These were held at Weston Zoyland, North Coates or Catfoss and from 1927 one or other of the Worthy Down squadrons held the Lawrence Minot Memorial Bombing Trophy until 1935.

Heavy snowfalls at the end of 1927 cut off the station except by rail, the CO, The Hon J.D. Boyle, CBE, DSO, getting about on skis. With improving weather in the New Year work started on the construction of permanent barrack blocks and a general clean-up of the station. A new church dedicated by the Bishop of Winchester on January 19 1930 was one of the last items on the eighteen month building programme.

During the summer of 1932 both squadrons spent nearly four weeks at Catfoss while efforts were made to drain and then level the airfield surface, the same procedure being repeated the following year with a little more success. In November a number of Victorias were ferried by the squadrons to the Middle East, the crews returning by boat just in time for Christmas! More long-distance flights followed in 1934, two Virginias of No 58 Squadron going to Marseilles on January 5 with urgent War Office stores, and on August 15 a special Valentia, piloted by Flight Lieutenant A. McKee, left to position in Iraq as a flight refuelling tanker for the projected non-stop flight to India by Sir Alan Cobham in an Airspeed Courier which was abandoned at Malta when a pin in the throttle control vibrated out.

No 7 Squadron started re-arming with the comparatively spritely Kestrel-powered Heyford II in April 1935. This impressive-looking machine had the fuselage attached to the underside of the top planes, dwarfing everything in sight and giving the pilot a very lofty view. Relief from Nivo camouflaged bombers was provided by the shiny silver Audax of No 2 Squadron which arrived in August for a month's Army co-operation exercises 'in the field', the personnel being under canvas and the aircraft dispersed around the aerodrome. Nos 4 and 13 Squadrons, similarly equipped with this neat little biplane also visited, but the big event was the formation of two new bomber squadrons on October 1 1935. *B* Flight of No 7 Squadron was renumbered No 102 Squadron, while *A* Flight of No 58 Squadron

became No 215 and initially flew that unit's few remaining Virginia Xs.

Nos 58 and 215 Squadrons went to Upper Heyford on January 14 1936, and with No 102 Squadron becoming completely independent in March, the stage was set for a major re-shuffle of units following the formation of Bomber Command on July 14. In August the Hinds of No 49 Squadron arrived from Bircham Newton and Nos 7 and 102 Squadrons left for Finningley, their advance parties departing on the 27th, the day before personnel of Nos 35 and 207 Squadrons arrived from the Sudan at the end of the Abyssinian crisis. They were sent on leave while their Gordons, off-loaded at Sealand in crates, were re-assembled and test flown.

With the move by Nos 7 and 102 Squadrons completed in September the station was transferred to No 2 Group, and the squadrons started the familiar round of exercises and armament camps, now at Aldergrove, West Freugh and Leuchars. Empire Air Day on May 29 1937 saw the number of visitors reach nearly 2,000 for the first time—a far cry from today's Battle of Britain displays, but there were many more stations open prewar and fewer people had transport.

The re-equipment of the Gordon units started on August 17 1937 when No 35 Squadron received the first of 12 Wellesleys. It was up to strength by mid-September when No 207 Squadron started conversion and both units were soon wrestling with the vagaries of retractable undercarriages, pneumatic brakes and variable pitch propellers. The enormous wingspan made taxiing a hazard but in practice they coped very well, the main problem being a weakness in the undercarriage which caused the legs to fold at inopportune moments. Armament training camps and tactical exercises took up most of the early months of 1938 —then No 49 Squadron took its Hinds to Scampton mid-March and the Wellesleys departed to Cottesmore on April 20 1938.

This exodus resulted from the transfer of Worthy Down to Coastal Command on April 15, the station being placed in No 17 (T) Group. Ansons of Nos 206 and 233 Squadrons arrived on attachment early in July for exercises with HMS *Centurion*, followed by No 220 Squadron later in the month, but the station was intended as a FAA shore base. The Nimrods and Ospreys of 800 Squadron were joined by trials Gladiators by the end of July, and

A Wellesley of No 35 Squadron is pulled out of a 'GS' hangar at Worthy Down during 1937 (Crown Copyright).

when the Munich Crisis erupted a sub-Flight of the Squadron, three Osprey and two Sea Gladiators, embarked in *Courageous*.

Lieutenant Commander B.M.H. Kendall, previously OC of 800 Squadron, started forming up 803 Squadron on November 21 1938 equipped with the much vaunted Skua. Early in January 1939 they had nine aircraft, 800 Squadron had nine Osprey IVs and in storage at Worthy Down were 14 Gladiators, three Saro Clouds, two Skuas, five Sharks and four Nimrods. Navy blue was the predominant colour of the uniforms, even after 800 Squadron embarked in *Ark Royal* for an early Spring Cruise. The Fleet Air Arm Pool arrived from Gosport on April 4 and the formal transfer of the station to the Admiralty was made on May 24 1939, when it was commissioned as HMS *Kestrel*, commanded by Commander R.St.A. Malleson, AFC, RN.

Soon afterwards No 1 Air Gunners School formed with three flying units, 755, 756 and 757 Squadrons, basically equipped with Shark and Osprey aircraft for TAG training, later supplemented by Walrus. The School and the Pool were still resident at the beginning of the war, soon joined by survivors from 811 and 822 Squadrons following the sinking of *Courageous*. 815 Squadron formed on October 15 1939 and started working up on Swordfish, while at the end of the year 763 Squadron assembled at Worthy Down as No 1 TSR Pool equipped with the same aircraft. Its main task was to keep newly qualified personnel in flying practice while awaiting berths aboard HMS *Ark Royal* and *Hermes*, but it was also responsible for training complete crews, and maintaining a small number of fully operational aircraft which could be used to strengthen front-line squadrons quickly if the need arose.

Fresh from Dunkirk, the Skuas of 806

Squadron made a brief appearance at Worthy Down at the end of May 1940 when pilots collected the first three Fulmars to enter front-line service. They went to Eastleigh for further training while 763 Squadron also departed in June. 808 Squadron, formed in July, was also equipped with Fulmars and was present on August 15 1940 when the airfield was attacked by Ju 88s. The raiders were part of a large force from LG1 escorted by Bf 110s of ZG2 which approached the south coast at 17:30 hours. Harried all the way, first by No 43 Squadron Hurricanes, then No 601 and finally by Spitfires of No 609 Squadron, the Luftwaffe pilots forced their way through taking heavy casualties, II/LG1 alone losing five Ju 88As to No 601 Squadron. Two Hurricanes were shot down and Worthy Down personnel got a nasty fright, but the station escaped lightly, little damage being done. 808 Squadron took its Fulmars to Castletown on September 5 and ten days later, 807 Squadron was formed with this two-seat naval fighter. Intended for service aboard HMS *Victorious*, this carrier was so delayed that they found themselves embarked in *Pegasus* at the end of the year, testing the catapult fighter scheme.

In the meantime, the devastating attack on Supermarines' Southampton factories on September 26 had caused a crisis in Spitfire production and fears for the test facilities at Eastleigh. Immediate dispersal of the production organisation was ordered and when two new Bellman hangars became available at Worthy Down in December 1940, Spitfire development flying was moved there with Jeffrey Quill in charge.

No 763 (FAA Pool) Squadron returned in February 1941 but was disbanded the following July, by which time a large dispersed storage facility had been constructed across the main A34 road to the west of the airfield. Accesssed by a single taxiway, it consisted of 48 Dutch barns, two Bessoneaux and a Fromson Blister hangar camouflaged by natural woodland, and to help protect this increasingly valuable airfield a decoy site was laid out at Micheldever, some three miles to the north-east.

The growing activity by Supermarine more than made up for the absence of the Pool, and with the arrival of many more Proctors for the TAG School during 1942 the airfield became very congested—to the detriment of test flying and resulting in a nasty accident when Quill was suddenly confronted by a Proctor as he breasted the notorious hump in the airfield. In the collision the Proctor was destroyed and the Spitfire badly damaged. The first Griffon-powered Spitfire was tested in November 1941 and much of the early Seafire development was done at Worthy Down, the first hooked Spitfire in January 1942 followed by the first AST conversion to Seafire standard in March. Flight trials which continued into 1943 included aileron and elevator modifications, redesigned tailplanes and undercarriages, stability and dive checks.

When the TAG School at Yarmouth, Nova Scotia, Canada, became fully operational the Worthy Down unit was run down, 756 and 757 Squadrons disbanding in 1943. 755 Squadron continued, but without its Lysanders which were converted into agent droppers, the squadron receiving the unpopular Curtiss Seamew which was used until April 1944.

Spitfire XIV trials started in November 1943 but, as facilities at High Post improved, Supermarine development flying was transferred from Worthy Down in March 1944. The station now became

the resting place for a series of unusual FAA units. 739 (Blind Approach Development Unit) Squadron moved in from Hinstock with Oxfords during September 1943, joined by 734 Squadron which formed during February 1944 equipped with Whitley GR VIIs. Large enough to perform the duty of flying classrooms, the Whitleys were converted by SS Cars to demonstrate correct engine handling to TBR aircrew converting from elderly biplanes to Merlin-powered Barracudas.

No 739 Squadron went to Donibristle in October 1944 and, despite the reforming of 700 (Maintenance Test Pilots' Training) Squadron in June 1945, activity slowly ran down. Both remaining units left later in the year, test pilot training going to Middle Wallop/Yeovilton and 734 Squadron to Hinstock. Southampton UAS operated two Tiger Moths until October 1946 when they moved to Eastleigh, and with inevitable economies biting deeper HMS *Kestrel* was paid off in November 1947.

The station re-opened during June 1952 as HMS *Ariel II* to house the Air Electrical School. No flying took place, the unit merely making use of the extensive accommodation. On November 1 1960 the AES moved to Lee-on-Solent and a month later the Admiralty again

The technical and domestic sites at Worthy Down in May 1943 with numerous aircraft outside the heavily camouflaged hangars. Attempts have been made to break up the airfield outline by painted 'hedges' (FAA Museum A/Stn 114).

Above Some of the 'Dutch barn' aircraft storage sheds at Worthy Down still survive—now in agricultural use!

paid off Worthy Down, this time handing it over to the Royal Army Pay Corps as their new HQ.

The hangars have been taken down and wind breaks, in the form of tree plantations, screen the HQ complex. Otherwise it has changed little since the war.

Wroughton, Wiltshire

SU140788. 4 miles S of Swindon off A361

On top of a north-west facing escarpment giving fine views across northern Wiltshire, the airfield at Wroughton has had a comparatively placid existence since opened over 40 years ago. The site was chosen at the height of the Expansion Scheme as the location for No 2 E&WS, but before much progress had been made this unit was switched to Yatesbury. The future of Wroughton was then under consideration and in 1938 it was announced that a storage unit would be built and that the airfield would be used for the proposed No 5 E&WS.

Levelling and draining of the site started in 1938 followed by the laying of foundations for the main technical area in the south-east corner, and six smaller sites dispersed around the perimeter. The latter had storage hangar clusters, mainly of the Lamella ('L') Type while the main site had the large 'C' and 'D' Types for servicing and preparation work. These hangars and the associated workshops on the technical sites were the only permanent buildings erected, the whole of the domestic and administration accommodation being in wooden huts later augmented by corrugated-iron Nissens.

Early in 1940 the proposed training unit became No 4 E&WS, but when RAF Wroughton opened on April 1 1940 it was as No 15 MU of No 41 Group, Maintenance Command, the school plans having been abandoned. In common with most airfields it was far from complete when the RAF moved in. Only one hangar was usable and a temporary landing field to the east had to be used when five factory-fresh Lysanders arrived on April 3. Equipment, personnel and accommodation shortages dominated the first weeks, not helped by waterlogging of the airfield and the temporary LG.

Blenheims started arriving in May, three of them becoming the first MU deliveries when they were speedily processed and went to No 107 Squadron on May 19. A week later Hurricanes were accepted for storage, three of them being used as a Battle Flight, flown by unit test pilots. Air raid sirens sounded on June 25 1940 but it was two months later that the airfield was attacked, two Blenheims being damaged on August 13. On the 19th four bombs were dropped on the airfield, one landing

Below A vertical of Wroughton showing the main technical site to the top (FAA Museum A/Stn 126).

close to an incomplete 'D' Type hangar, but causing little damage. Two Hurricanes took off but without proper control were unable to locate the raider, and it was similar story a week later when Station AA defences also fired unsuccessfully at the bomber.

During the Battle of Britain No 15 MU was heavily engaged preparing aircraft for Fighter Command, averaging 60 a month from September 1940 until well into the New Year. The number of aircraft far outstripped the available hangarage and in addition to the dispersal areas near Overton Hackpen, four outlying dispersal fields were brought into use near Barbury Castle, Burderop Park, Uffcott and Upper Salthorp Farm. The furthest was over two miles from the airfield, aircraft being towed to them on minor roads and access tracks.

With the storage sites approaching completion in April and waterlogging still causing delivery delays, plans for hard runways became a priority made even more urgent by the arrival on June 14 1941 of No 76 MU from Cosford. This unit was concerned with packing aircraft for shipment overseas and took up residence on No 2 Site which consisted of two 'D' Type hangars near Clouts Wood. Starting with Miles Masters for South Africa, the variety of types soon included Albacore, Defiant, Fulmar, Gladiator, Oxford, Roc, Sea Hurricane, Spitfire, Swordfish and Walrus, mainly for the Fleet Air Arm.

The construction of the runways proved a lengthy business and provided considerable disruption. The original LG was brought back into operation in 1943 for single-engined aircraft up to the size of the Walrus, and it was with great relief that all three concrete runways were finally declared ready for use on March 13 1944. The airfield then looked much the same as it does today except for the much larger number of aircraft visible, the strength peaking at 573 in May, many of them in open storage on outlying dispersals.

During August 1944 No 76 MU moved into the two 'L' Type hangars on No 3 Site in the north-west corner and continued their packing task, still predominantly for the FAA. At the end of the year it had some 220 RAF and 600 civilian personnel, but with the German capitulation in May 1945 the number of aircraft handled by No 76 MU dropped dramatically and its future was under review. On the other hand, No 15 MU was

just as busy though its role changed to long-term aircraft storage and a large scrapping programme started.

In September 1945 it was decided to retain No 76 MU at Wroughton and close No 222 MU High Ercall instead, but when even single-engined fighters started being flown out to their overseas destination the task faded away and the few remaining commitments were handed over to No 47 MU at Sealand in August 1946. No 76 MU was disbanded on September 30.

The rows of ex-operational wartime aircraft were gradually sold to scrap merchants and new production aircraft were stored. Initially these were Mosquitoes and Meteors, but the first of many Canberras arrived during 1953, this type becoming the unit's main preoccupation for several years. Helicopters made an appearance in August 1954 when two Whirlwinds were received, but fixed-wing aircraft remained the mainstay of the unit. A Station Flight was formed using Vampires and the Maintenance Command Communications Squadron moved in from Andover during 1956, the same year as the famous Nash Collection arrived for storage prior to the establishment of the RAF Museum. The Camel, Fokker Triplane and MF Shorthorn was refurbished whilst at Wroughton, their present condition a tribute to No 15 MU craftsmen.

In April 1958 No 41 Group Test Pilots' Pool was formed at Wroughton with Meteor T 7 aircraft, but the unit left for Lyneham just over a year later when the Station Flight was disbanded. By 1968 the main work was the modification and updating of Wessex, Sioux and Whirlwinds, but the last Canberras lingered until March 1972 when a 19-year association with Wroughton was ended.

The 1970 Templar Committee suggestion that helicopter maintenance should be centralised and responsibility given to the Admiralty was accepted, and on April 5 1972 the airfield was commissioned as Royal Naval Aircraft Yard, Wroughton, No 15 MU being disbanded at the same time. The first job tackled was the preparation of some 20 Scouts for Army units, followed by service modifications to Gazelles before issue as replacements for elderly Sioux, which came to Wroughton for storage and re-sale.

More defence cuts envisaged the closure of Wroughton on April 1 1979, the storage of Sea King and Lynx helicopters being diverted to Fleetlands and Culdrose. The run-down had begun before it was discovered that Fleetlands could not cope with the modification and issue of all helicopters in British military service. Late in 1978 Wroughton was reprieved.

Best of all from the enthusiast's viewpoint was the announcement in 1978 that the Science Museum was storing a number of their larger exhibits at Wroughton, including a civil transport aircraft collection. They took over six hangars on Nos 3 and 4 Sites near the western boundary of the airfield, the first arrival being a DC-3 on October 28, joined by an ex-Dan Air Comet 4B just over a year later. Other aircraft followed, the enterprising Museum staff successfully locating some rare speciments to illustrate airliner development. On Sunday, September 21 1980 the Science Museum area was opened to the public for the first time, and this has become a one-day annual event well worth attending.

Not part of the airfield, but associated with it, is the Princess Mary's Hospital which lies to the east and is one of the RAF's major medical units. The entrance is graced by Canberra B 2 *WJ676*, acting as gate guardian after a distinguished career with Bomber Command.

No operational flying has taken place from Wroughton throughout its career. Its task had been solely the receipt, storage, preparation and despatch of aircraft. Mundane, but essential.

Wye, Kent

TR044478. 4 miles NNE of Ashford on A28

Built early in 1916 on 86 acres of low lying grassland alongside the main Canterbury-Ashford road, Wye aerodrome was opened during May as a unit of No 6 Wing, RFC. No 20 Reserve Squadron moved in from Dover with BE 2C and RE 8 biplanes at the beginning of June to continue its pilot training task, and this remained the role of this small aerodrome for the rest of the war.

Wye was a delightful spot, easily located by the distinctive layout of roads, railway, river, and the shape of the Perry Court apple orchards immediately to the south, but the closeness of the heavily-wooded Downs meant that rapid changes of weather could occur, making flying difficult for students. For at least a year staff and pupils lived under canvas or in local billets. Protection for the aircraft was provided by Bessoneaux hangars, but

despite these rather primitive conditions No 51 RS arrived from Filton in January 1917 with BE 2C and BE 2E aircraft, to turn out more pilots for the British Expeditionary Force in France which needed every aviator it could get.

On May 1 1917 came further expansion, the two units spawning No 66 RS. Built for one training squadron, Wye was now very crowded, but this was put right very decisively by re-organisation of No 6 Wing, No 51 RS going to Waddington and No 66 leaving for Yatesbury, while the long-serving No 20 Training Squadron went to Wyton at the beginning of June.

Plans were then made for an Anglo-American Training Squadron to be based at Wye, three large metal-clad hangars, a storage shed and workshops being built during the summer alongside Maiden Wood, and accommodation huts erected in the south-east corner of the LG. Like most plans for American participation there were delays and No 86 Squadron, RFC, was transferred from Dover during the autumn to operate as an advanced training unit using Pups and Camels. It moved out in December 1917 to make room for the planned unit, No 42 TS, which arrived from Hounslow on the 16th, and was soon training pupils on Avro 504, Camel and RE 8 aircraft. Americans started moving into Wye during mid-1918 by which time live ammunition firing was taking place on the Crown, a memorial cut out of chalk on the steep hillside to the east of the town. The established strength of the unit was now 332 and the equipment standardised on 12 Avro 504Ks and 12 Sopwith Camels, though a 1½-Strutter and a Bristol M1C monoplane were also present, the latter for the amusement of the instructors.

After the Armistice flying decreased markedly and the Americans were soon posted away, leaving No 42 TS to grind to a halt and final disbandment on February 1 1919. That same month No 3 Squadron returned from the Continent without aircraft, and used the accommodation until moved to Dover in June 1919 when Wye was declared surplus. Disposal arrangements were made in October, the site quickly returning to agriculture.

Yapton (Ford), West Sussex
See Ford

Select index of units referred to in the text

Due to the sheer number of units involved in the region covered by this volume, the following is not a complete listing; this will be provided in *Action Stations 10* which will include a detailed index to all nine volumes in this series.

CAF/RCAF
1 (Fighter) Squadron, CAF—*255, 279*
2 (Bomber) Squadron, CAF—*255*
110 Squadron, RCAF—*230*
1 Wing, CAF—*255*

German Air Service/ Luftwaffe
ERPR GR210—*185, 203, 204*
JG2—*157, 268, 297;* JG26—*71, 207, 298;* JG27—*110, 279, 296;* JG53—*204*
3rd Bombing Sqn/ Kampfgeschwader 3/ Kagohl 3—*14, 47, 72, 90, 189, 199, 246, 287, 288*
KG1—*151;* KG2—*92, 151, 188, 203, 248;* KG3—*248, 265;* KG26 —*105;* KG51—*64, 130, 268, 297;* KG53—*248;* KG54—*105, 230, 297;* KG76—*151*
LG1—*42, 71, 151, 230, 296, 305;* LG2—*157*
SKG10—*208*
StG1—*192, 296;* StG2— *296;* StG3—*130;*

StG77—*110, 279, 296*
ZG2—*305;* ZG26—*64*
3(F)/31—*297*

Royal Air Force/Royal Flying Corps

FLIGHTS
406—*295;* 407—*8, 177;* 408—*224, 225;* 409—*224, 225*
412 & 413—*49*
420—*127;* 421—*127, 157, 158;* 422—*127, 256*
442—*128, 296;* 443 & 444—*177;* 449—*128*
460, 461 & 462—*127, 128;* 463 & 464—*127*
470—*200, 295;* 471—*289*
491—*80, 289*
511 & 512—*115;* 514—*275*
555 & 556— *200*
1310—*56*
1320—*180*
1401 (Met)—*208, 210;* 1407 (Met)— *130*
1419—*269*
1455—*269*
1488—*249, 250, 257*
1493—*93*
1511 (BAT)—*138;* 1516 (BAT)— *133*
1537 (BAT)—*237*
1622—*130, 131, 258;* 1624 —*75*
1631—*131, 258*
1903 (AOP)—*76*

GROUPS
1—*42, 191, 201;* 2—*23, 42, 50-52, 71, 83, 157, 159, 170, 171, 173, 191, 204, 221, 231, 271, 283, 297, 299, 304;* 3—*42, 212;* 4—*242;* 5—*15, 60,*

81, 165, 289; 6—*72;* 7—*41, 103;* 8—*63, 126;* 10—*15, 17, 49, 64, 65, 115, 127, 170, 176, 177, 238, 288*
11—*19, 21, 58, 62, 66, 83, 110, 113, 117, 121, 162, 171, 179, 188, 192, 203, 209-212, 220, 233, 249, 256, 259, 263, 270, 285, 298, 300;* 13—*267;* 15—*178;* 16—*19, 72, 92, 130, 160, 177, 209, 265, 266, 277, 278, 284;* 17—*19, 109, 128, 129, 177, 178, 278, 304;* 18—*177;* 19—*212*
21—*285;* 22—*42, 91, 103, 155, 160, 191, 201, 228, 230;* 23—*91, 201, 243;* 24—*103, 106, 191;* 25—*285;* 26—*256*
38—*234, 235, 273, 285;* 40—*42*
41—*42, 44, 307;* 42—*42, 47;* 46—*52, 211, 218, 233;* 47—*218;* 50—*248, 276, 289*
54—*93;* 60—*76*
62—*240;* 70—*65, 105, 130, 138, 170, 217, 230, 242, 291*
71—*105, 231;* 72—*93*
83—*23, 93, 112, 119, 120, 151, 170, 194, 232, 262, 299, 302;* 84—*23, 45, 56, 69, 71, 112, 120, 121, 150, 209, 252, 271, 272, 282, 301;* 85—*222;* 88—*83;* 90—*273, 293*
91—*216;* 92—*22, 36, 138, 241, 291*
Armament—*91*
'Z'—*93, 170*

Maintenance Units
3—*67*
15—*307, 308*
47—*308;* 49—*67, 131, 172*
71—*172, 250;* 76—*308*
86—*209*
222—*308*

MISCELLANEOUS
1 AACU—*103, 106, 129;* 2 AACU—*74, 75, 129, 130, 177, 178;* 6 AACU · —*251;* 7 AACU—*106*
7 AA Practice Camp— *258*
A&AEE—*67*
ADEE—*129, 202*
AFDU—*105*
3(P)AFU—*289;* 15(P)AFU—*43, 138, 242*
Air Defence Great Britain —*17, 19, 75, 117, 221, 223, 232*
Air Disarmament Unit— *76, 221*
17 APC—*250;* 18 APC— *93, 186, 258*
ATA—*147, 216*
ATDU—*129, 130, 131, 132*
CFE—*259, 272, 300*
1336 (Transport Support) Conversion Unit—*293*
Day Fighter Development Wing—*272*
7 Fighter Command Servicing Unit—*118*
1 Fighter Training Squadron—*230*
FIU—*110, 112, 223, 256, 257, 265, 268*
Fleet Requirements Unit —*178*
1 FPP—*64, 147;* 3 FPP—

147; 15 FPP—*64, 147, 148*
511 FRU—*232, 233*
GPEU—*65*
83 Group Communications Squadron—*56;* 84 Group Communications Squadron—*299*
41 Group Test Pilots Pool—*308*
1 GRU—*203;* 3 GRU—*203, 279*
83 GSU—*56, 83, 272, 299;* 84 GSU—*171, 172*
Maintenance Command Communications Squadron—*308*
Marine Aircraft Experimental Unit—*136*
NGTE—*106*
Night Fighter Development Wing—*112, 272*
1 Overseas Ferry Unit—*211*
Radio Navigational Aids Wing—*293*
RAE—*50, 102, 103, 105, 106*
RAF Airfield Construction Unit—*44*
403 R&SU—*82;* 405 R&SU—*162*
Short Range Conversion Unit—*234*
91 SP—*211;* 160 SP—*53*
Staff College Communications Squadron—*44*
Tactical Air Force—*27, 44, 82, 120, 170, 226*
2 Tactical Air Force—*75, 83, 169, 179, 194, 209, 210, 222, 232, 233, 252, 259, 271, 272, 283, 284*
Torpedo Development Unit—*129*
1 TTU—*285*
4 Works Squadron—*57;* 5 Works Squadron—*236;* 5027 Works Squadron—*45, 164, 169, 303*

Operational Conversion Units
240—*234, 235;* 242—*273, 285*

Operational Training Units
1—*97;* 6—*43*
24—*216*
41—*65, 66;* 42—*43;* 43—*43, 44*
61—*66*

Schools
Aerial Flying & Gunnery—*91*
Advanced Air Firing—*188*

1 Air Armament—*91;* 2 Air Armament—*91, 92*
Air Disarmament—*76*
Air Navigation—*42, 202*
Air Pilotage—*41, 42, 202*
1 ANS & 2 ANS—*285*
11 AONS—*147*
3 APS—*160*
Armament—*186*
Armament & Gunnery—*91*
Artillery & Infantry Co-operation—*303*
Artillery Co-operation—*303*
1 Basic Air Navigation—*149*
CFS—*126, 214, 236, 237*
Day & Night Bombing & Observation—*189*
ECFS—*236*
3 EFTS—*146, 147, 289;* 8 EFTS—*142, 275, 276;* 26 EFTS—*276*
E&W—*303;* 2, 4&5 E&W—*307*
3 E&RFTS—*146;* 16 E&RFTS—*256;* 34 E&RFTS—*248*
ETPS—*106*
Fighter Leaders—*272*
7 FIS—*237, 243*
4 FTS—*278;* 6 FTS—*200*
128 GS—*276*
141 GS—*76*
148 GS—*250*
161 GS—*113;* 163 GS—*240;* 166 GS—*160;* 168 GS—*76*
615 GS—*76, 212;* 617 GS—*214*
623 GS—*273*
3 GTS—*38, 289, 291*
Gunners & Observers—*90*
Machine Gun—*77, 85,188*
2 Marine Observers—*91*
Marine Operational Pilots—*79*
Navigation—*202*
1 Observers School—*91*
Pilots & Observers Aerial Gunnery & Aerial Fighting—*186*
RAF & Army Co-operation—*303*
RAF Artillery—*92, 93*
RAF & Naval Co-operation, RAF Seaplane & RAF Seaplane Training—*176*
1 RAS—*102;* 3 RAS—*254, 255;* 4 RAS—*124*
11 & 16 RAS—*124*
14 RFS—*148, 149*
1 RS—*102, 124, 125*
11 RS—*246;* 12 RS—*77;* 13 RS—*77, 78;* 20 RS—*78, 310*
21 RS—*255;* 27 RS—*124*

51 RS—*309*
64 RS—*78;* 66 RS—*309*
School of Aerial Gunnery—*85, 86, 164, 188, 226*
School of Air Navigation—*202, 278*
School of Air Traffic Control—*289, 291*
2 S of AC—*42, 43*
School of General Reconnaissance—*278*
School of Military Aeronautics—*245*
School of Naval Co-operation—*109, 177, 178*
School of Naval Co-operation & Air Navigation—*176*
2 School of Navigation & Bomb Dropping—*40, 41*
2 School of Observers—*200*
School of Wireless Operators—*102*
School of Wireless Telegraphy—*63*
3 & 14 SFTS—*289*
43 TDS—*63;* 50 TDS—*87*
53 TDS—*78, 79;* 55 TDS—*200*
61 TDS—*266*
203 TDS—*199, 200;* 204 TDS—*91;* 209 TDS—*176*
1 TS—*125;* 3 TS—*255;* 10 TS—*126*
13 TS—*78;* 20TS—*309*
25 TS—*125*
34 TS—*63*
42 TS—*309;* 43 TS—*63;* 50 TS—*109*
54 TS—*87;* 55 TS—*125*
61 TS—*266;* 62 TS—*78;* 65 TS—*78*
1 (T) Wireless—*102, 303*
Wireless & Observers—*303*

SQUADRONS
1—*75, 76, 100, 101, 153, 160, 193, 210, 266-270, 272, 273, 297;* 2—*41, 48, 77, 79, 100, 101, 115, 155, 180, 191, 201, 202, 232;* 3—*77, 79, 127, 155, 186, 201, 202, 204, 208, 209, 222, 223, 257, 258, 268, 270;* 4—*72, 75, 77, 79, 89, 96, 100, 101, 103, 109, 115, 120, 158, 204, 228, 229, 232, 304;* 5—*77, 79, 101, 122;* 6—*77, 101, 102;* 7—*101, 102, 153, 235, 303;* 8—*122, 153;* 9—*42, 77, 78, 201;* 10*

—*102, 109*
11—*41; 42, 92;* 13—*41, 48, 96, 109, 122, 124, 203, 227-229, 231, 304;* 14—*124, 255;* 15—*77, 78;* 16—*43, 50, 51, 83, 156, 191;* 17—*122, 124, 154, 156, 268;* 18—*191, 234, 235, 297;* 19—*56, 92, 112, 119, 168, 217, 221, 222, 250*
21—*44, 50, 92, 191, 283, 284;* 22—*96, 122, 124, 130, 212, 213, 273, 277-279, 281, 285;* 23—*107, 108, 110, 122, 124, 204-206, 269;* 24—*52;* 25—*154-156, 273;* 26—*27, 66, 75, 179, 180, 191, 234;* 28—*124;* 29—*111, 124, 211, 273;* 30—*221*
32—*115, 116, 151, 203, 205;* 33—*91, 121, 194, 235, 253, 272;* 34—*191, 273;* 35—*304;* 36—*285;* 37—*246, 247, 254;* 38—*153;* 40—*266*
41—*116-118, 124, 158, 159, 194, 219, 261, 266, 270, 271, 298, 299;* 42—*96, 129, 205, 278, 285;* 43—*230, 257, 258, 266-268, 270, 272, 273, 279, 281, 297, 305;* 45—*124;* 46—*211, 234, 285;* 48—*72, 92, 130, 202, 278;* 49—*78, 184, 304;* 50—*14, 15, 47, 72, 78, 189, 263, 286*
53—*74, 92, 102, 103, 191, 229, 230, 279, 282;* 54—*66, 151, 188, 203, 233, 234, 248, 249;* 56—*15, 47, 124, 154, 205, 208, 222, 223, 248, 285;* 58—*303;* 59—*42, 92, 191, 204, 230, 279, 280, 282;* 60—*124, 125*
61—*15, 246, 247;* 63—*179, 180, 285;* 64—*71, 249;* 65—*93, 112, 119, 120, 158, 168, 193, 203, 248, 250, 252, 269, 298;* 66—*56, 112, 121, 234, 250, 270, 272;* 70—*102*
71—*116;* 72—*191, 198, 213, 233, 234, 235, 266;* 74—*92, 194, 204, 248, 250, 253, 272;* 76—*50;* 78—*14, 15, 125, 274, 275;* 79—*156, 203, 248;* 80—*75, 210, 221*
81—*65, 298;* 82—*255;* 83—*153;* 85—*272;* 86—*78, 130, 255, 281, 282, 309;* 87—*266, 270;* 88—*50, 110, 111, 219*
91—*62, 63, 71, 158, 159,*

192, 193, 210, 271, 299;
92—62, 63, 204, 266,
267; 93—62; 94—255;
96—112, 233; 97—109;
98—82, 83, 189, 246,
273; 99—246; 100—102
101—42; 102, 204; 102
—189, 190, 304; 103—
42; 104, 105 & 106—40;
107—42, 50-52, 110,
171, 217, 219, 307; 108
—189, 190; 110—78,
204
111—92, 157; 112—15,
187, 286, 287; 115—
109, 273; 118—75, 76,
210, 220, 270, 299; 119
—210, 265; 120—153,
154, 189, 190, 282
121—250; 122—56, 57,
112, 119, 120, 168, 269;
124—76, 92, 210, 299;
127—112, 121, 194,
250, 272; 129—57, 69,
112, 281, 282, 298; 130
—164, 194, 211, 233,
281, 282, 298, 299

131—118, 219, 282, 298;
132—75, 93, 112, 160,
221; 133—193; 137—
194, 207-209, 211, 250;
139—298; 140—50, 51
141—72, 111, 151, 247;
142—42, 92; 143—72,
209, 210, 286; 144—
109; 145—219, 268,
269, 296, 297; 148—40,
108; 149—108
151—92; 152—247, 279;
158—50; 160—282
161—62; 162—52, 53;
164—120, 208, 282,
283; 165—75, 76, 93,
194; 167—52, 298; 168
—232; 170—43, 232
171—50, 231, 232; 174—
65, 93, 110, 111, 187,
188, 205, 207, 220, 232,
270, 299; 180—82, 83
181—44, 170, 220, 226,
227, 232; 182—44, 170,
187, 220, 226, 227; 183
—66, 120, 170, 271,
282, 283; 184—65, 75,
93, 168, 208, 220, 222,
232, 299; 186—127,
194; 187—218; 188
(T)—286, 287; 190
(Depot)—247
193—282; 196—50;
197—271; 198—120,
208, 209, 246, 247, 271,
282, 283
202—286; 206—202, 304;
207—40, 91, 304; 210—
127
213—179, 268; 214—42;
215—40, 109, 304; 217

—205, 266, 280, 281;
218—80; 219— 200,
269, 295; 220— 304
222—69, 121, 252, 253,
272, 285; 224—96, 202;
225—44, 230, 234, 256;
226—51, 83, 110; 229
—75, 210, 221; 230—
234, 235
231—302; 233—80, 81,
130, 233, 289, 304; 234
—71, 160; 235—73,
202, 203; 236—279;
238—64, 296; 239
—116, 204, 232
242—204-206, 224, 225,
275; 245—65, 156, 187,
193, 252, 257, 258, 270,
273, 299; 247—66, 220,
226, 227, 232-234; 248
—284; 249—130, 272
253—49, 108, 115, 116,
202, 203, 257, 275;
254—73, 130, 284; 254
—73, 130, 284; 256—
111; 257—271
264—51, 204, 233, 248,
249; 266—92, 97, 268,
271, 272; 268—120,
180, 232; 269—96
271—233; 274—75, 210,
221; 275—284; 276—
160; 277—158-160,
257-259, 270, 284; 278
—160, 284; 279—284;
280—74, 284
281—284; 282—284; 285
—106; 287—106, 250,
270; 290—106
291— 93; 296—43, 210;
297—210
301—52; 302—45, 62, 71,
112, 297; 303—221,
299; 305—52, 171, 206;
306— 57, 69, 112;
308—45, 62, 64, 112;
309—71; 310—45, 194,
211, 258, 272
311—52; 312—45, 194,
211, 258, 272; 313—45,
159, 194, 211, 249, 272;
315—57, 69, 112, 232;
316—118; 317—45, 62,
71, 112; 318—75;
320—83, 159, 163, 170,
171
322—51, 71, 159; 329—
120, 221, 253, 272
331—56, 112, 121, 206,
272; 332—56, 112, 121,
206, 272; 340—120,
221, 253, 272, 298
341—120, 221, 253, 272;
342—50, 259; 345—71,
258, 259; 349—69, 117,
121, 252, 253; 350—
117, 159, 160, 194, 250
400—82, 230-232, 302
401—93, 193, 205, 262,

271; 402—116, 160,
220, 221, 249, 299; 403
—162, 163, 173, 206,
249, 271; 404—279; 406
—210, 211; 407—279

411—249, 262, 271;
412—116, 170, 219,
262, 270, 271; 414—45,
82, 180, 232; 415—
208-210, 279, 281, 282;
416— 159, 220, 271;
418—52, 110, 111
421—162, 163, 173, 233,
271; 430—45, 50, 82,
232
436—233; 437—233;
438, 439 & 440—120
441, 442 & 443—112, 120,
299
451—198, 259; 453—75,
112, 194, 250; 456—
111, 112; 460—159
464—82, 283
485—69, 121, 220, 252,
253, 272, 298; 486—
222, 223, 271; 487—82,
283; 489—281
500—72, 73, 74, 109, 130,
201, 202, 278
501—64, 117, 151, 159,
201, 210, 267, 268, 270,
298; 503—201; 504—
64, 76, 155, 203, 210
520—130
525—218
543—212; 547—282
567—75, 76, 93, 160, 211
577—106
600—191, 201, 203, 204,
248
601—109, 191, 240, 267,
268, 279, 297, 305;
602—56, 75, 105, 110,
112, 116, 154, 168, 170,
193, 222, 247, 252, 279,
297; 603—204, 249;
604—111, 156, 203,
233; 605—52, 110, 111,
209, 210, 266, 267;
607—205, 248, 268; 608
—130; 609—120, 193,
194, 207, 208, 271, 282,
283, 305; 610—118,
151, 194, 217, 297-299
611—71, 249; 612—282;
613—52, 155, 156, 169,
171, 230; 614—116,
140, 230, 231; 615—
203, 205; 616—4, 159,
164, 202, 210, 248,
269-298
622—54
653—106, 184; 655—75,
184; 656—107; 657—
160; 659—151; 660—
43, 107, 150, 301
666—118; 667—83, 106,
131, 258

WINGS/TAF 'Airfields'
5—124; 6—78, 309; 7—
124
15 Fighter—75; 17 Fighter
162; 18 (HD)—78
21—153
34—50, 51, 63, 179; 35—
232; 38—65, 170;
39—82, 232, 302
50—228, 229, 247, 254
51—42; 53—106, 187,
189; 58—90
75 Signals—76; 76
Bomber—42
103—221; 110—52
120—233
121—168, 187, 188, 252,
299; 122—56, 57, 93,
112, 119, 120, 168, 250,
283; 123—120, 209,
232, 282, 283; 124—44,
170, 187, 221, 226, 227;
125—75, 112, 221, 222;
126—46, 162, 262, 271,
272; 127—162, 163,
173, 194, 271, 272; 128
—82, 232, 302;
129—45, 262, 299; 130
—120, 232
131—45, 62, 71, 112; 132
—56, 112, 121, 272;
133—57, 69, 112; 134—
45, 121, 272; 135—69,
70, 121, 252, 253, 272;
136— 52, 120, 282,
283; 137— 51, 52;
138—52, 169, 171, 283,
284; 139—52, 83;
140—171, 283, 284
141—51; 142—221; 143—
120; 144—112, 120,
299; 145—120, 221,
253, 272; 146—210,
271, 282; 147—233;
148—51; 149—71;
150—222
155 (GR)—209; 157 (GR)
—160, 265, 284

Royal Navy (FAA/
RNAS)
MISCELLANEOUS
Air Electrical School—
307
Air Engineering School—
183
1 Air Gunners School—
305, 306
Blind Approach Develop-
ment Unit—179
Channel Air Division—
114
Dover Defence Flight—80
Eastchurch Squadron—
89
FAA Maintenance Unit—
129, 130
816X Flight—74

Marine Experimental Air-
craft Depot—*134*
51 Miscellaneous Air
Group—*180*
3 Naval Fighter Wing—
179, 180; 4 Naval
Fighter Wing—*43*
Naval Air Fighting
Development
Unit—*272, 300*
Naval Air Trials Installa-
tion Unit—*183*
Naval Air Signals School
—*149*
Naval Flying School—
89, 90, 91, 185, 253
Naval Seaplane Training
School—*175*
Night Fighter School—
179
Observer School—*98*
2 Observer School—*178,
179*
Observer & Signals
School—*97*
RN Accident Investiga-
tion Unit—*183*
RN Operational Heli-
copter Flight—*132*
Seaplane Training Unit—
179
Service Trials Unit—*114*
'A' Squadron RNAS—
199
Strategic Bombing Wing
—*72*
1 TSR Pool—*305*
Walmer Defence Flight—
288
Westgate War Flight—
198, 295
1 Wing—*89;* 2 Wing—
89; 3 (Aeroplane)
Wing—*72, 198, 199;* 5
Wing—*80*

SQUADRONS
1—*79, 80, 122;* 2—*79, 89,
294;* 3—*288;* 4—*80, 89,
288;* 6—*80, 288;* 8—*288*
700—*114, 181, 306*
701—*182;* 702—*179, 182;*
703—*113, 180, 284;*
704—*284;* 705—*131,
132, 181, 182;* 706—
132; 707 & 708—*131;*
710—*178*
711—*131;* 716—*98;*
720—*113, 131, 180*
727—*131*
734—*306;* 739—*179, 306*
746—*112, 113*
750—*109*
751—*109, 110;* 752—*109;*
753—*109, 178, 179;* 754
—*178, 179;* 755, 756 &
757—
305, 306; 758, 759 &
760—*97*

763—*178, 179, 305;* 764—
131, 179; 765— *93,
178;* 770—*178*
771—*114, 179, 180;* 778
—*131, 178-180;* 779—
109; 780—*97, 179*
781—*178, 180-183;* 782
—*180;* 783—*148, 180;*
787—*113, 272, 300*
793—*110;* 799—*180;*
800—*96, 114, 180, 304*
801—*73, 74, 96;* 802—
96; 803—*114, 305;*
804—*113;* 806—*73, 97,
305;* 807—*180, 305;*
808—*43, 179, 180, 305;*
809—*43;* 810—*179, 284*
811—*97, 113, 179, 305;*
812—*74, 97, 113, 128,
279;* 813—*113, 128,
180, 181;* 814—*97;*
815—*305;* 816—*202,
282;* 818—*202, 278;*
819—*209, 265, 282;*
820—*181*
821—*74, 97, 128, 201;*
822—*96, 201, 211, 284,
305;* 823—*207, 208,
271;* 825—*72, 73, 196,
205;* 826—*72, 181;* 827
—*180;* 828—*110;* 829—
178
832—*207;* 833 & 836—
282; 838—*284*
841—*206-208, 282;* 842
—*284;* 845—*132, 181;*
848—*132, 284*
854 & 855—*160, 284*
879—*43*
885—*179, 180;* 886—
179
897—*179*
1791 & 1792—*180*
1840—*114*

**United States of
America/USAAF/
USAF/USAS**
DIVISIONS
3—*211;* 7—*140*

GROUPS
3 PRG—*216;* 4 FG—
173, 250
14 FG—*298*
31 FG—*216, 219, 271,
296, 298;* 36 FG—*168*
44 BG—*117, 168*
52 FG—*216;* 56 FG—
233; 60 TCG—*36, 38*
64 TCG—*241;* 67 Obs
—*216, 217*
92 BG—*75;* 93 BG—
168; 97 BG—*193;* 100
BG—*75, 93*
306 BG—*71*
315 TCG—*38, 291*
322 & 323 BG—*222*
354 FG—*139, 173, 174.*

217; 358 FG—*164, 173*
362 FG—*163, 173;* 363
FG—*173, 262, 263;* 366
FG—*217;* 368 FG—*65,
139;* 370 FG—*38, 43*
373 FG—*302*
386 & 387 BG—*222;*
388 BG—*160*
406 FBG—*47*
434 TCG—*39, 242, 291;*
435 TCG—*291-293;*
436 TCG—*217, 218;*
437 TCG—*242;* 438
TCG—*138-140, 292;*
439 TCG—*139*
442 TCG—*65, 239, 217,
242;* 446 BG—*75*
466 BG—*227, 303*

MISCELLANEOUS
American Engineer
Aviation Battalion—
27, 28
804 Engineer Aviation
Battalion—*140*
816 Engineer Aviation
Battalion—*168*
5 Tactical Air Depot—
65; 6 Tactical Air
Depot—*217*
755 Combat Support
Group—*141*
2911 Bombardment
Squadron (Light)—*217*
3909 Air Base Group—
140
7273 & 7512 Air Base
Group—*211*
7501 Air Base Squad-
ron—*140*

SQUADRONS
5 Photo—*216;* 9 ARS
—*211;* 10 TCS—*36*
11 TCS—*36;* 11 TMS—
142; 12 Photo—*217;* 12
TCS—*36;* 16, 17 & 18
TCS—*241*
22 & 23 FS—*168*
28 TCS—*36*
34 TCS—*38*
35 TCS—*241*
43 TCS—*38*
53 FS—*168*
71, 72, 73 & 74 TCS—*39,
291*
75, 76, 77 & 78 TCS—
291
79 & 80 TCS—*217*
81 & 82 TCS—*217*
83, 84, 85 & 86 TCS—*242*
87, 88, 89 & 90 TCS—
139, 292
92 FS—*211;* 97 Air
Refuelling—*140*
107 Photo—*217;* 109
Photo—*217*
140 Aero—*108*
153 Photo—*217*
303, 304 & 305 TCS—*65*

307 & 308 FS—*298;* 309
FS—*219, 270, 296, 298*
326 Aero—*108*
335 FS—*250*
353 FS—*173;* 355 FS—
173, 174; 356 FS—*173*
363, 366 & 367 FS—*164;*
368 FS—*139*
377, 378 & 379 FS—*163;*
380 FS—*262*
381 FS—*262, 263;* 382
FS—*262;* 389 & 390
FS—*217*
391 FS—*217;* 395, 396
& 397 FS—*65*
401 & 402 FS—*43*
410 FS—*302*
411 & 412 FS—*302*
485 FS—*43*
512 FBS—*211*
512 FS—*47, 211;* 513
FS—*47;* 513 & 514
FBS—*211;* 515 FS—
47

WINGS
1 BW—*206*
20FBW—*211;* 20
TFW—*141*
31 FEW—*211*
50 TCW—*139, 242*
51 TCW—*138, 217, 218,
242;* 53 TCW—*65, 139,
140, 217, 218, 292*
70 FW—*139*
71 FW—*38, 43, 139*
100 FW—*139, 163, 173*
123 FBW—211
303 BW—*140;* 303 FW
—*47, 169*
310 FW—*140*
406 FBW—*211*

Spitfire LF XVIs of 63 Squadron lined up at Thorney Island during May 1948.